D1305990

writing
PROSE

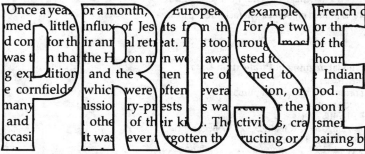

Techniques and Purposes

REVISED CANADIAN EDITION
Thomas S. Kane
Leonard J. Peters
David Jackel
Maurice R. Legris

Toronto
OXFORD UNIVERSITY PRESS

Oxford University Press, 70 Wynford Drive, Don
Mills, Ontario, M3C 1J9
Toronto Oxford New York Delhi Bombay
Calcutta Madras Karachi Kuala Lumpur
Singapore Hong King Tokyo Nairobi
Dar es Salaam Cape Town Melbourne
Auckland Madrid

and associated companies in
Berlin Ibadan

OXFORD is a trademark of Oxford University Press

This book is printed on permanent (acid-free) paper ∞.

Canadian Cataloguing in Publication Data
Main entry under title:
Writing prose : techniques and purposes
Rev. Canadian ed.
ISBN 0-19-540571-4
1. English language—Rhetoric. 2. College
readers. I. Kane, Thomas S.
PE1417.W74 1987   808'.0427   C87-093489-9

© Oxford University Press Canada 1987
Printed in Canada
by Webcom Ltd.
3 4 5 6—5 4 3 2

Preface to the Canadian Edition

The first edition of *Writing Prose: Technique and Purposes* was edited by Thomas S. Kane and Leonard J. Peters in 1959. The fifth edition of their deservedly-popular text appeared in 1980. The present volume, addressed to Canadian students, is based on the fifth edition, but approximately one-third of the material—by Canadian writers—is new.

In spite of this significant change in the contents of the book, its aim and structure remain essentially the same as those of previous editions. Students will closely analyze examples of good prose by both famous writers and others who are relatively unknown. They will consider the writer's purpose, insofar as it can be determined, and the sort of reader to whom the essay is addressed. They will then look carefully at the organization of the essay with regard to both its structural principles and, more specifically, to such matters as the use of topic sentences, transitions, organizing and concluding sentences, signposts, and so on. From there students will go on to analyze individual sentences—types of sentences, length and structure, punctuation, and logic. Finally, they will look at specific words: at definitions, etymologies, figures of speech, and connotations.

Having dealt with these elements of analysis, which are found in the critical apparatus accompanying each essay, students will find three final sections: a brief list of specific points to be learned from the study of the essay; some suggestions for writing assignments which are closely related to the analysis just finished; and some directions about specific points students are to include in the compositions they will write—points also related to the essay they have just analyzed. As Professors Kane and Peters remarked in the preface to their first edition, asking students to imitate good writers "does not mean a sterile conformity. But it does mean that any writer, if he is to be successful, must learn to use and to adapt to his own purposes the tools of others. It means that each writer must study the work of others if he is to learn to use the vast resources of the English language."

Since the intent of this book is to acquaint students with the various techniques of good prose, our primary criterion for selecting the works to be included has been high quality. Readers will notice, however, that there is a considerable diversity among the selections. Some are undoubtedly classics, such as Swift's "A Modest Proposal," which has been universally admired by generations of readers. Others are occasionally affected by weaknesses of one kind or another. This is merely to say, of course, that not all the writers included here are of the same genius as a Swift or a Thoreau. Yet they all worth reading and studying, and students will find that they can profit greatly from all of them.

The selections in this text range in length from short paragraphs (especially in the section devoted to exposition) to complete, full-length essays. Instructors may wish to begin with the shorter selections and have their students write only a paragraph or two before going on to read, and write, at greater length. The traditional categories have been used: exposition, argument, description, and narration. The section on exposition has been further divided into illustration, restatement, comparison, analogy, reasons, effects, and analysis. To description has been added a section on description of character; and a section on beginnings and closings deals with a problem too often given short shrift. There are, finally, sections on personal writing, in which the personality of the author emerges more strongly than in most of the other essays here; a chapter on writing about literature, for those classes in which the study of writing accompanies the reading of various forms of literature; and a section on style, in which the emphasis is on diversity of styles. It is made clear throughout that the various categories often intermingle, with exposition often involving description and narration, and persuasion including exposition.

Instructors may, of course, take up the selections in this text in any order they wish. They may want to start immediately with "Beginnings and Closings" in conjunction with exposition, and leave argument for later; as well, they may find that some of the questions following each selection are not appropriate for their classes and may wish to substitute their own. It should be noted that, since some technical terms have been used in the questions, these have been briefly explained in a glossary at the end of the book. These terms are marked with an asterisk the first time they are used in each set of questions. Because each selection and its questions are self-contained, some of the questions will prove repetitious; since we have assumed, however, that no class will read every selection, the repetition of some key points is justifiable.

However instructors wish to use this book—whether they change the order of the selections, or add or substitute questions of their own, or modify the suggestions for writing, or even have their students question the questions—they are urged, above all, to encourage their students to read more widely in the authors represented here and in many others. Instructors must, in short, constantly remind their students that the study of good writing is indispensable to the practice of good writing.

DAVID JACKEL

MAURICE LEGRIS

Preface to the Second Canadian Edition

This second Canadian edition of *Writing Prose* contains ten new selections by Canadian writers, all of them complete essays. Minor revisions have been made to the introductory material for some sections, to the headnotes, and to the critical apparatus. The Glossary has been revised to clarify some matters, and new material has been added. An author-title index has also been provided.

We are grateful to those who have used the first Canadian edition of *Writing Prose* and have offered suggestions for its improvement, in particular Jane Flick, of the University of British Columbia. We also thank our graduate assistant, Alison Coleman, for her valuable help in preparing this second edition. To Richard Teleky, our editor at Oxford University Press, we owe a special note of thanks; he made a number of valuable suggestions and saved us from a couple of serious blunders. Any remaining problems or deficiencies are, of course, our responsibility.

DAVID JACKEL

MAURICE LEGRIS

A Note to the Student

Unfortunately there is no quick and easy way of learning to write. Good writing is hard work, but when you bring it off—when you really succeed in saying what you set out to say—it is among the most rewarding of all activities. One way to acquire skill in composition is to look closely at what good writers do and to ask yourself questions about it. In this text we do just that—offer you examples of well-written prose and ask questions which we hope will lead you to discover some of its techniques and strategies.

We have tried to make the questions specific and clear and self-contained. As much as possible we have avoided technicalities of grammar and rhetoric. Occasionally, of course, it is necessary to use a word from those disciplines—"appositive" or "metaphor," for example. The first time such a term appears in any set of questions it is marked by an asterisk to indicate that it is briefly defined in the Glossary beginning on page 698. Generally, however, the questions will require only that you study the selection and think about it. What you learn you should apply to your own compositions, following the directions which are given after each selection for a writing assignment. That, finally, is the whole point: not simply to understand what another writer has done, but to do it yourself.

T.S.K./L.J.P.

Contents

*An asterisk means the selections are complete essays.

xi

DEFINITION, 138

PERSUASION, 180

DESCRIPTION, 327

PERSONAL WRITING, 522

WRITING ABOUT LITERATURE, 573

STYLE: A CLOSER LOOK, 647

WRITING PROSE

What does the mind enjoy in books? Either the style or nothing. But, someone says, what about the thought? The thought, that is the style, too.

CHARLES MAURRAS

If the cardinal virtue of poetry is love, the cardinal virtue of prose is justice; and, whereas love makes you act and speak on the spur of the moment, justice needs inquiry, patience, and a control even of the noblest passions . . . By justice here I do not mean justice only to particular people or ideas, but a habit of justice in all the processes of thought, a style tranquillized and a form moulded by that habit. ARTHUR CLUTTON-BROCK

Easy writing's vile hard reading. RICHARD SHERIDAN

Exposition

Different kinds of writing achieve different purposes. On the basis of controlling purpose we traditionally divide all prose into three kinds: narration, description, and exposition. Of these, exposition is especially important to the college student since much of what he reads, and most of what he writes, is expository prose. Exposition is writing that explains. In general, it answers the questions how? and why? If we go into any university library, most of the books we find on the shelves are examples of exposition. Philosophies, histories, literary essays, theories of economics, studies of government and law, the findings of sociology, the investigations of science—all these, however different, have for their purpose to explain. Although exposition often is formal and academic, it appears also in magazines and newspapers, in any place where people look for explanations. It is the most common kind of writing, the sort with which we conduct our workaday affairs—the business letter, the doctor's case study, the lawyer's brief, the engineer's report—and the writing with which we attempt to control our world, whether our means of doing so is a complicated system of philosophy or a cook book.

Exposition, then, is a wide net. What, we may ask, is not exposition? If the guiding purpose of the writer is to tell a story, to tell merely what happened, then we say the writing is narrative rather than exposition. If the writer intends to tell us how something looks, to re-create the thing in words, we may call it description. A narrative arranges its material in time. Description most often organizes in space. We might think of narrative as a stage play or motion picture in words, and of description as a verbal photograph or painting. Exposition organizes its subject not in time or space but by logic. The subject of the expository writer may be people, things, ideas, or some combination of these, but always he is a man thinking, interpreting, informing, and persuading. Although he may appeal to our emotions, he is more likely to appeal to our reason by using evidence and logic. In other words, exposition is less like a stage play or painting and more like a lecture, discussion, or debate.

Seldom is any piece of writing pure exposition. Just as the lecturer tells a story or uses maps, charts, or slides to interest his audience and clinch his point, so the expository writer may turn for aid to narration or

3

description. Often these kinds of writing become so fused as to be practically indistinguishable: the description of the structure of an atom is as much an explanation as it is a picture. The historical narrative is as much concerned with the why and how as with what happened. Even so, the traditional classification of prose into description, narration, and exposition is useful so long as we are aware of its limitations. The expository writer will do well to remember that his primary purpose—the purpose that guides and shapes his total organization—is to explain by logic and to show relationships.

The writing of exposition begins, therefore, in an understanding of the broad purpose to be achieved. It begins, like all composition, in the writer's head. Even before he sharpens his pencil, the expository writer must ask himself four questions: What specific point do I intend to make? Is it worth making? For whom am I writing? How can I best convey my point to my readers? Unless the writer has carefully answered each of these questions, no amount of good grammar and correct spelling will save him, and his composition is already worthless even before he begins to scribble. Deciding upon reader and purpose is easily half the task of writing. Once the writer has determined what point he intends to make, his composition is already half organized, if not completely planned. The writer has already saved himself time by eliminating several false starts, and he has already resisted the temptation to lose himself and his reader in the thickets and bypaths of his subject. With his reader in mind he has already solved many of his problems of diction and tone as well, and, however awkwardly he has expressed himself when he has done, he will know that he has fulfilled the first requirement of all writing—a definite point for definite readers.

On paper, the writing of exposition begins with paragraphs. Within each paragraph the writer shapes and develops a single unit of his thought. Every expository writer therefore must understand the nature and construction of paragraphs. To begin our definition we may say that paragraphs are like men. Each is an individual, unlike any other. Yet, as all men are alike in having a head, eyes, two arms, and two legs, every paragraph is like all the others, all possessing, so to speak, the same anatomy. Learning to write good paragraphs must begin with an understanding of the pattern common to all. We find that paragraphs of exposition contain two different kinds of statements. The first—a *general*, rather abstract statement—is called the topic sentence. Here, the writer says, "This is what I assert or believe in a general way; this is my opinion, my evaluation or conclusion about the subject of this paragraph." For instance, L. M.

Grayson and Michael Bliss, writing about the economic collapse of the 1930s, begin their first paragraph on page 21 with this topic sentence: "The Great Depression affected Canada more severely than any other industrial nation except the United States." Sometimes the general drift of a paragraph is so clear that the topic idea is only implied. To be sure, it is there, but the writer feels he will not lose his reader if he fails to state his topic idea in so many words. A second class of statements in every paragraph consists of *particular* facts, examples, illustrations, and supporting details that say, in effect, "This is why I believe or conclude what I do. You may not agree with what I say, but at least you understand now why I believe or conclude it. Here is my evidence."

Most often the topic sentence stands first in the paragraph, unless one or two sentences of transition go before. Less frequently, topic sentences appear last, or nearly so, when the paragraph is developed from particular to general, a pattern useful both for variation and, building as it does to a climax, for emphasis. Sometimes for the sake of clarity or emphasis the writer may restate his topic idea in a second or third sentence and again at the end of a paragraph. With or without restatement the expository writer usually moves from topic sentence to supporting details, from general to particular.

The particulars of exposition are patterns of logic and evidence, patterns that may shape individual paragraphs, a group of several paragraphs, or the composition in its entirety. Thus, Jay Scott begins his essay (page 23) with an anecdote, and, in the second paragraph, he shows how the problem summed up in the anecdote had both causes and effects. Again, the expository writer may throw new light upon two things by comparing and contrasting them, showing how they are alike and yet different, as Ruth Benedict does on page 65 when she explains how the Japanese method of bringing up children differs from the American. Or the writer may employ the logical pattern of cause and effect. "The Technological Revolution" (page 101) is organized by discussing the effects of machine production upon our society. The expository writer, in short, uses the common methods of logic and thinking: he develops his material by offering examples, by comparing and contrasting, by making analogies, by restating, by giving reasons, by classifying and analyzing his subject, by revealing cause and effect, by defining, by working from premise to conclusion. The selections that follow illustrate the common types of expository development. Every student of composition should learn to use them.

BARBARA W. TUCHMAN

Patterns

Historian and author, Barbara W. Tuchman is best known for *The Guns of August,* an account of the onset and early phases of World War I. Her other books include *The Zimmermann Telegram* (dealing with the causes of that war), *The Proud Tower* (a cultural and intellectual history of the period before the first World War), and *A Distant Mirror* (a history of Europe during the troubled fourteenth century).

This paragraph is taken from an essay, one of a collection by various authors on the problems of contemporary higher education. Tuchman's thesis is that educators must stand more firmly for the values they profess to believe and not be afraid of exercising discipline to maintain those values. The paragraph suggests that young people welcome a wise and responsible authority. It is a good instance of how to develop a topic by an illustration.

It is human nature to want patterns and standards and a structure of behavior. A pattern to conform to is a kind of shelter. You see it in kindergarten and primary school, at least in those schools where the children when leaving the classroom are required to fall into line. When the teacher gives the signal, they fall in with alacrity; they know where they belong 5 and they instinctively like to *be* where they belong. They like the feeling of being in line.

From "The Missing Element: Moral Courage" in *In Search of Leaders: Current Issues in Higher Education,* edited by G. Kerry Smith (1967). Reprinted by permission of the National Education Association.

Our Deteriorating Environment

Roger Revelle is an educator and scientist. He has directed the Scripps Institute of Oceanography and is a professor of science and public policy at the University of California at San Diego. Professor Revelle has written extensively about pollution and population control. This selection is taken from an essay, "Pollution and Cities" (1970), one of a collection of articles by various scholars dealing with the problems faced by modern cities. In his essay Professor Revelle surveys the various environmental dangers threatening cities and suggests possible solutions. Like the preceding paragraph by Barbara Tuchman, this one also reveals how to use illustrations effectively.

In many ways, the quality of our environment has deteriorated with each new advance of the gross national product. Increases in electric power production mean the burning of more coal and fuel oil, and hence the discharge of more sulphur dioxide into the air. The growth of the paper industry has brought a vast increase in trash. The production of new auto- 5 mobiles and the discard of old ones has resulted in unsightly piles of hulks. The growth of urban automobile transportation is choking both the mobility of the city and the lungs of city dwellers.

QUESTIONS

READER AND PURPOSE

1. Even if you knew nothing about Tuchman's larger purpose you might guess that she approves of a more patterned, disciplined mode of life that many people live today. What details in her paragraph suggest this?
2. Is Revelle trying to convince us of the truth of his assertion to the same degree that Tuchman is? If not, what is his purpose?

Reprinted by permission of the publishers from *The Metropolitan Enigma* edited by James Q. Wilson, Cambridge, Mass.: Harvard University Press, © 1967 by the Chamber of Commerce of the U.S.A.; © 1968 by the President and Fellows of Harvard College.

3. Beyond their larger aims, each writer has the immediate purpose of supporting a topic by examples, one of the easiest and most effective ways of generating an expository paragraph. Sometimes a paragraph is developed from only a single example; sometimes from several. Which of these selections uses only one illustration; which more than one?

4. Illustrations should be pertinent and specific—genuine and particular instances of the assertion stated in the topic sentence. Often specificity means translating an abstract * and general idea into an image, that is, something that we can see or hear (or grasp with any of our other senses). In Tuchman's paragraph the abstraction is "patterns and standards and a structure of behavior." What is the illustration? In what sense is it an image *? Why is it especially pertinent to the writer's point?

ORGANIZATION

5. Identify the topic sentence in each paragraph. At what point in the paragraph is it placed?

6. A good topic statement is clear and succinct. Often, too, its key term comes at the end. ("Key term" here means the word or phrase expressing what the rest of the paragraph will be chiefly concerned with.) In the light of these characteristics are the topic sentences of these two paragraphs well or poorly written?

7. A paragraph should have unity, its sentences hanging together. Do you notice anything about sentences 2-5 of Revelle's paragraph that makes them hang together? The final two sentences of Tuchman's paragraph contain four main clauses *. How are they unified?

SENTENCES

8. In prose that reads well sentences have enough similarity to sound alike, yet enough variety not to bore the reader. One way of achieving such a style is to vary a basic sentence pattern. For example, each of the five sentences in Revelle's paragraph is simple *, containing one subject-verb link. Study the final three sentences of his selection. How has Revelle made slight changes in the simple pattern of subject-verb-object so as to prevent monotony?

9. Do the final two sentences of Tuchman's paragraph show a similar variation of a basic pattern?

DICTION

10. Look up: (in Tuchman) *conform* (2), *alacrity* (5), *instinctively* (6); (in Revelle) *environment* (1), *deteriorated* (1), *hence* (3), *sulphur dioxide* (4).

11. Explain the meanings of these phrases as fully as you can: (in Tuchman) *a structure of behavior* (1); (in Revelle) *the gross national product* (2), *the mobility of the city* (7-8).

12. Tone * means roughly the feeling of a distinct personality which we intuit from a writer's words. It involves his attitudes toward his subject, his readers, and himself; and we sense it in sentence structure and especially in diction. One important aspect of tone is the degree of formality or informality in the relationship between writer and reader: whether he appears to be lecturing an audience, keeping a distance between them and himself; or seems more relaxed, as if he were talking to friends. How would Tuchman's tone be affected if we substituted *variety* for *kind* and *one* for *you* in line 2?

13. Why would these changes be less effective? (in Tuchman): an unitalicized *be* (6); (in Revelle): *ugly junk heaps* for *unsightly piles of hulks* (6), *decreasing* for *choking* (7), *breathing* for *lungs* (8).

POINTS TO LEARN

1. Good illustrations are pertinent and detailed. They support a generalization with a specific case, an abstraction with a concrete * instance.

2. A memorable sentence style has variety within similarity.

3. Read out loud what you write. Listen. Write to please your ears.

SUGGESTIONS FOR WRITING

Use one of the following assertions as a topic sentence and support it by illustration in a paragraph of five or six sentences (about 120 words). You may develop only a single example or several, but in either case be sure your examples are to the point and specific.

Young people do not want "patterns and standards and a structure of behavior"; they do not like the "feeling of being in line."

Some of my classmates are weird.

Some teachers have very little sense of what students really think.

Life in a big city is exciting and full of surprises.

IMPROVING YOUR STYLE

1. Somewhere in your paragraph compose three or four consecutive simple sentences with enough variation in each to keep them from sounding monotonous. As a way of testing the result, read your paragraph out loud. If the sentences seem too much alike vary their structure a little until they do not.

2. After you have finished the paragraph rewrite it twice, altering the diction where possible to make it sound (1) less formal and (2) more formal than your original version.

The London Poor

Literary critic and scholar, John Henry Raleigh is concerned in the essay from which this passage is taken with the social background of the English novel during the second half of the nineteenth century. He uses material from Henry Mayhew (1812–87), an English journalist and writer, best known for his graphic and detailed study of lower-class London, *London Labour and the London Poor* (1851–64), the work from which Professor Raleigh quotes. Raleigh's paragraphs show again the effective use of specific details to illustrate a topic idea.

1   The life of the London poor in the nineteenth century was, for the most part, miserable, and no one who has read Henry Mayhew, that great sociologist, can ever forget his grim and heartbreaking peoples and scenes. If man had set out consciously to fashion a hell for his fellow men, he could not have done better than nineteenth-century English culture did   5 with the poor who "lived" off the streets of London. Indeed Mayhew's descriptions in *London Labour and the London Poor* sometimes convey a kind of Pandemonium quality and one can almost sniff the sulphur in the air. His description of a crowd entering a "Penny Gaff"—a kind of temporary theater which put on salacious performances—suggests some of the horror.   10

> Forward they came, bringing an overpowering stench with them, laughing and yelling as they pushed their way through the waiting room. One woman carrying a sickly child with a bulging forehead, was reeling drunk, the saliva running down her mouth as she stared about with a heavy fixed eye. Two boys were pushing her from side to side,   15 while the poor infant slept, breathing heavily, as if stupified, through the din. Lads jumping on girls, and girls laughing hysterically from be-

From "Victorian Morals and the Victorian Novel," in *Time, Place, and Idea: Essays on the Novel* by John Henry Raleigh, Preface by Harry T. Moore. Copyright © 1968 by Southern Illinois University Press. Reprinted by permission of Southern Illinois University Press.

ing tickled by the youths behind them, every one shouting and jumping, presented a mad scene of frightful enjoyment.

2   But if anything, as over against this evil of stench and noise, the   20
lonely pathos of individual tragedies is even more frightful: the blind streetseller who had once been a tailor and had worked in a room seven feet
square, with six other people, from five in the morning until ten at night,
the room having no chimney or window or fire, though no fire was needed
even in the winter, and in the summer it was like an oven. This is what it   25
was like in the daytime, but "no mortal tongue," the man told Mayhew,
could describe what it was like at night when the two great gaslights went
on. Many times the men had to be carried out of the room fainting for air.
They told the master he was killing them, and they knew he had other
rooms, but to no avail. The gaslights burned into the man's eyes and into   30
his brain until, "at last, I was seized with rheumatics in the brain, and
obliged to go into St. Thomas's Hospital. I was there eleven months, and
came out stone blind"; or the crippled streetseller of nutmeg graters, who
crawled, literally, out into the streets where he stayed from ten to six eking
out his pitiful existence, six days a week. On wet days he would lie in bed,   35
often without food. "Ah," he told Mayhew, "It *is* very miserable indeed
lying in a bed all day, and in a lonely room, without perhaps a person to
come near one—helpless as I am—and hear the rain beat against your windows, all that with nothing to put to your lips." Thus, if in what follows
the life of the poor is shown to have some moments of joy, these are, it is   40
remembered, only oases in an illimitable desert of misery.

QUESTIONS

READER AND PURPOSE
1. This passage is preliminary to Professor Raleigh's discussion of the nineteenth-century novel. What fact does he wish to establish here?
2. A practical problem every writer faces is distinguishing between information
his readers may be expected to bring with them and special facts they probably
will not know and which therefore must be explained. To define for readers
what they already know is to risk insulting them; on the other hand, to fail to
explain what they do not know may annoy them. Where in his first paragraph
does Professor Raleigh presume his reader's ignorance? Are his explanations
necessary? Are they clear, sufficient to tell the reader what he needs to know?
Are they overelaborate?

ORGANIZATION

3. The topic sentence of paragraph 1 contains two broad ideas: express them in your own words. Does the second sentence add a new idea or merely repeat that of the first?

4. How does the extended quotation from Mayhew support Professor Raleigh's topics? That passage is not enclosed in quotation marks. Why not?

5. Why does the writer begin the second paragraph with *but?* Is there a logical contradiction here? If it is not logical, how might the "contradiction" be described? In the opening sentence of paragraph 2 what words other than *but* help to forge the link to the first paragraph?

6. What is the topic of paragraph 2? How does it differ from that of the opening paragraph? Paragraph 2 also develops by examples. How many are there?

7. The semicolon in line 33 marks a major dividing point in this paragraph. Explain why. Might it be argued that this semicolon is a bit confusing and that the organization would be clearer if a new sentence were begun at this point?

SENTENCES

8. How has the writer constructed his first sentence so as to throw great stress upon *miserable?* Why does the word merit such emphasis?

9. Professor Raleigh sets off the definition in lines 9-10 with dashes. What does this mark signal to the reader about how the enclosed material is related to the rest of the sentence? What other punctuation might have been used? Would commas have worked as well?

10. To an alert reader the colon in line 21 indicates something about how the material to follow relates to what has just been said. Explain.

11. The construction in line 24 ("the room having no chimney or fire") is called a nominative absolute *. Adapted into English from a syntactical pattern frequent in Latin prose, the nominative absolute is still useful (though generally restricted nowadays to rather formal writing). It often expresses a cause or necessary condition of an effect (which is then stated in the main clause): "Peace having been concluded, the troops returned to their homes." Sometimes it shows a looser relationship of thought described as "attendant circumstances": "They marched away, the people cheering and waving their hats." What does the nominative absolute show here: cause or attendant circumstance?

DICTION

12. Look up: *grim* (3), *salacious* (10), *stench* (11), *pathos* (21), *avail* (30), *eking* (34).

13. Which words or phrases in paragraph 1 repeat the idea expressed by *miserable* (2)? Which iterate the idea of *hell* (4)? What is the source of the term *Pandemonium* (8)?

14. *For the most part* (1-2) is a qualifier *. What purpose does it serve? What idea does the phrase *if anything* convey in line 20?

15. Sentences sometimes begin with connecting * words that alert the reader to how the ensuing idea is related to what has just been said. For instance, *however* indicates the new thought is somehow contradictory. What relationship is suggested by *indeed* (6) and by *thus* (39)?

16. Why are the following substitutes less effective in Professor Raleigh's context: *make* for *fashion* (4), *society* for *culture* (5), *smell* for *sniff* (8), *reveals* for *suggests* (10)?

17. Identify the figure of speech * found in "oases in an illimitable desert of misery" (41). Do you think it is effective?

18. The success of an illustration often depends upon its specificity. So judged, the example taken from Mayhew is successful. Examine its diction. What words are especially detailed? (A test is to consider the problem from the point of view of an artist trying to paint the scene from this description.) To how many senses does Mayhew appeal? What attitude toward the poor is implied by his diction?

POINTS TO LEARN

1. The value of an example often depends upon the detail with which it is presented.

2. When you write, think about what your reader may be presumed to know and what needs to be explained.

3. Important words may be stressed by being isolated within the sentence.

SUGGESTIONS FOR WRITING

Develop one of these topics in a short composition of one or two paragraphs, using detailed examples. If possible, include a quotation as one of your examples and try to incorporate the author and title smoothly into your text.

For the student, schoolwork is part boredom, part desperation.

For the poor, life is still miserable.

IMPROVING YOUR STYLE

1. Employ a colon to set up a specification of a general idea.

2. Expand or define an important point with a phrase set between dashes.

3. Compose a nominative absolute.

4. Use the connectives *however*, *indeed*, and *thus* to open sentences; be sure, of course, that the sentences are appropriately related in their logic to the preceding ideas.

JAMES McCOOK

Man's Best Friend?

A former associate editor of the *Ottawa Journal*, James McCook has for many years been interested in the history of western Canada. His numerous articles on this subject have appeared in such periodicals as *The Beaver* and *Canadian Geographic*. Now retired, he lives in Victoria but continues to write essays such as the one below, which illustrates, in a humorous but nonetheless realistic manner, one of the difficulties of life in the North—a difficulty implied in the question that serves as his title.

1   The snobbery of Indian and Eskimo sled dogs surprised and disappointed early fur traders on Hudson Bay. The newcomers admired the devoted service the animals gave, pulling sleds and carrying loads. They noted that the dogs were left to fend for themselves in periods of idleness and had to survive by ranging the countryside and eating everything from   5 birds' nests to scraps cast up by the sea. The traders naturally assumed that these undemanding beasts would be happy to serve them.

2   Nothing of the kind!

3   Andrew Graham, who served with the Hudson's Bay Company on the Bay from 1749 to 1775, observed that the dogs were as useful to the   10 natives as horses were to the Europeans. They assisted in the hunting of deer and their keen sense of smell enabled them to lead their masters to beaver lodges. James Isham, who was also with the Company on Hudson Bay in the eighteenth century, was impressed by the ability of a single dog to haul a fortnight's provisions for two men. This was a factor of growing   15 importance, as Hudson's Bay Company policy was encouraging the establishment of inland posts far from the sea.

From *The Beaver*, 310, 3 (Winter 1979). Reprinted by permission.

14

4   But the dogs would not serve the traders, not even when the white men took them into the forts as puppies and raised them kindly. They regarded the traders with fear and hostility, and amiable and co-operative 20 Newfoundland dogs had to be imported from England to perform work around the posts.

5   The Newfoundland dogs often mated with wolves and the traders waited confidently for their pups to show them goodwill. It was no use, Graham reported. The offspring retained the "moroseness" of the wolves. 25

6   In time, of course, the mixing of breeds and familiarity with the traders led to the development of dogs which deigned to take commands from Europeans. In the meantime, traders who used native dogs had to hire Indians or Eskimos to drive them.

7   The other complaint about native dogs concerned their skill and 30 audacity in thieving. Their way of life, which so often left them in a barren land where only the swift and venturesome could survive, made them reckless. A placid Newfoundland might be trusted alone with a piece of meat meant for its master's supper, but a sled dog could not even be trusted with meat in a tin. Robert J. Flaherty, prospector and filmmaker on Hudson 35 Bay, left a shocking account of the transformation of handsome, diligent sled dogs into wild creatures as they tore open cans of meat, heedless of the cuts they suffered from the metal.

8   The yarns about thieving dogs were endless. Whips, harness and gloves were carried off and chewed as a matter of course. A prairie guide 40 had a fine elk-skin coat and slept in it in cold weather. One morning he awoke to find that his dog had eaten his coat off his back, leaving only the collar and cuffs. A rancher slept under a buffalo robe and discovered in the morning that two dogs from his team had devoured it all except the hair.

9   A tobacco pipe was reduced to splinters by a dog who believed for a 45 moment that it had found a delicacy. One raider in a tent ate almost 20 pounds of lard and staggered off with the rest. Tins of molasses were spilled by disappointed dogs. Stewed fruit was hardly a dog's delight, but if there was nothing better, down it went.

10   The four-legged robbers were all over the country, but the parties 50 of surveyors and missionaries who made their way up James and Hudson Bay by boat, left some of the most vivid accounts of annoying experiences with marauding dogs, reinforced in that region by hordes of vicious mosquitoes.

11   It was customary to tie up on shore at night. There dogs from   55
Indian encampments would frequently pounce on the strangers. Tarpaulin
covers were ripped off anything left outside the tent. Wolfish dogs prowled
about in the dark, seeking a gap in the defenses. Unguarded kettles of food
were carried off—it was claimed that dogs would run off with kettles and
pans containing food and keep them upright without losing a mouthful.   60

12   The victory of the dogs and mosquitoes was complete when, in the
middle of the night, the weary travellers would leave their tents, board the
boats and move out into the bay seeking relief from their tormentors.

13   At other places where settlement was more advanced, dogs often
gave strangers an unfriendly welcome, although they did not rob them.   65
Reverend A. A. Boddy visited the Sarcee Indian Reserve near Calgary and
recalled that nearly 50 dogs rushed out, howling and showing their teeth.
"Then," he added, "they noticed that we carried stones in our hands for
their benefit and then suddenly they retired."

14   Having seen what could happen to any creature that got between a   70
northern dog and food, those who worked with dogs treated them with a
degree of caution. Still, the drivers usually came to feel affection for their
loyal servants and to boast about their achievements.

15   Governor George Simpson of the Hudson's Bay Company, who
seldom showed sympathy to man or beast, went so far as to comment that   75
sled dogs "had no sinecure." That, in a way, was a warm tribute. The final
service given by dogs, the Governor could have added, was to be killed and
eaten in hard times. And not necessarily in hard times only. In territories
where buffalo steaks were hard to come by the Indians feasted on dog meat
and taught the traders to share this practice.   80

16   Missionaries were among those who had to learn that sled dogs
were not placid pets. None of the missionaries had a more difficult experience with dogs than the Reverend E. J. Peck and his assistant, who lived in a
small mission hut on Blacklead Island in Cumberland Sound, Baffin Island.
To enable the Eskimos to attend church services under shelter the mission-   85
aries built a larger building near their hut, making use of light wood and,
because they had nothing else, nailing seal-skins to the wooden frame to
serve as a covering.

17   For some time over the winter, poor weather had prevented fishing, and by the end of January 1895 the Eskimos and their dogs were   90
suffering from near-starvation. At 3 a.m. one morning Reverend Peck and
his assistant were awakened by a pack of hungry dogs. "These creatures
had managed to climb up on the roof of our skin church, and to our dismay

were tearing the edifice to pieces . . . We were literally besieged by dogs, and they must in all have numbered over a hundred. Most of them were on 95 the roof, some had fallen through, others were devouring pieces of sealskin, and altogether such a confused mass of dogs—young, old, bruised and wounded—it would be hard to find anywhere else. After a sharp battle we managed to put these unwelcome visitors to flight . . ."

18   When the incident was later recounted to a class of girls in Scot- 100 land, one young woman remarked "Now that we have heard of a kirk being eaten by dogs, it is not hard to believe that a whale could have swallowed Jonah."

19   Some missionaries, such as the Methodist Reverend John McDougall and the Roman Catholic Father Lacombe, were expert dog drivers who 105 thought little of covering 50 miles a day. Other missionaries were as useless on the trail as bags of snow. The Anglican Canon William Newton described how in winter he was wrapped up in skins and placed in a carriole, a box shaped like a long cradle attached to the bottom board of the sled. There, warm but unable to move, he lay motionless while someone else drove the 110 dogs and ran with the sled. Newton wrote that "you are perfectly quiet, and have nothing to do, uphill, downhill or on level ground, except to observe the dogs, the drivers and the scenery."

20   One of McDougall's burdens was the much respected Methodist preacher, Reverend Thomas Woolsey, who was no help at all when travel- 115 ling. On one occasion McDougall undertook to drive two teams at once, breaking trail with one while the second, carrying Woolsey, followed. It was a disaster. Dogs in the Woolsey team soon realized he had no control over them. The lead dog took it easy. The quarrelsome snapped at each other. When the sled ran down a slope the dogs made no effort to keep ahead of it, 120 and the harness became tangled. Fights became more furious, and finally Woolsey, dogs and sled were a tangled mass at the bottom of the hill. McDougall had to leave his own team, unwrap Woolsey, sort out the harness, and drive the Woolsey team long enough to remind the dogs of their duty with his whip. 125

21   Widely distributed was the story of the driver who told a missionary that his dogs would not improve their slow pace because he could not swear at them in the presence of a reverend gentleman. It was said that the missionary told the driver to use whatever language was necessary to speed progress, and apparently, the bad language always worked! 130

22   Indeed, the dogs constantly found new ways of making their masters swear. A heavy overnight snowfall gave a team such an opportunity.

The drivers could not locate the dogs buried in snow, and not one animal made a move to betray its location until a man stumbled over it.

23   The bells attached to the harness gave dog teams a totally false   135
impression of Christmassy goodwill. The lead dog ruled because of superior intelligence and strength, and when necessary, reminded rebels of his authority. Lesser dogs grumbled and snapped at companions. Lazy dogs tried to avoid pulling their fair share of the load.

24   Strangers who saw Indians moving camp, with most of the burdens   140
carried by dogs directed by the women, were surprised at the noise—the growls and howls, the whines and whimpers, the sounds of general complaint made by as many as 500 dogs. The visitors also discovered that the silence of the night would be disturbed by one restless dog, and that the cry would be taken up by others of his kind and by the wolves and coyotes   145
running free.

25   The buffalo-hunters and the explorers from Britain who visited the prairies in the 1840s and later, left detailed accounts of experiences with dogs.

26   The Earl of Southesk, who travelled west to the Rocky Mountains   150
in 1859-60, had high hopes for a formidable-looking beast he thought would fight wolves. One night he had just snuggled down when the dog rushed into his tent and crouched beside the bed quivering. In hot pursuit came a large white wolf, which was later shot by a guide.

27   Between Carlton House and Fort Edmonton Southesk acquired   155
another dog which proved to be an amusing companion. This was a black Indian sleigh-dog named "Whisky," "as fat as a pig, and possessed of only four inches of tail." The fondness which Southesk developed for this comical animal is evident in his description: "Poor Whisky filled the place of the ancient domestic jester; One look at him dispelled melancholy; every move-   160
ment he made was a farce. With his cunningly timorous countenance and sleekly rounded plebeian body, he was a true Sancho Panza of dogs. He was a daily delight: I would not have exchanged him for the best dog in the Company's territories."

28   When Southesk travelled through mountainous country Whisky,   165
in spite of his bulk, developed a "mania" for climbing—although he squeaked with fear upon coming to the difficult places, and on one occasion narrowly escaped being crushed by a falling ram which Southesk had shot.

29   When the party reached Fort Edmonton, Whisky deserted, "pre-
ferring ignoble ease at the Fort to our good society." Southesk felt Whisky   170
would live to regret this choice once he was forced to resume the toilsome life of a sleigh-dog.

30   The hunter and explorer Captain John Palliser purchased a large white dog named "Ishmah" from an Indian couple. Ishmah was to be his sole companion on a nine-month excursion through the wilds of Montana 175 and North Dakota in 1847–48. At first the dog would not come within 250 yards of him or any other white man, but Palliser patiently tempted him with pieces of meat until Ishmah gave him his trust. Palliser later commented that "a more faithful, efficient, and devoted creature never breathed."

31   Ishmah struggled through deep snow from morning to night pull- 180 ing Palliser's heavily laden travois. "When supper was at last cooked and despatched (quickly enough on his part, poor fellow, for his share was sometimes very scanty), he sat up close beside me as I smoked my pipe and sipped my coffee; and when at last I got into bed he used to lie down at the edge of the robe with his back close up against my shoulders, and so we 185 slept till morning."

32   There were times, however, when even the admirable Ishmah fell from grace. On one occasion he ran off to gambol in the forest with a she-wolf. Unfortunately at the time he was harnessed to the travois containing all of Palliser's possessions, leaving his master in a serious predicament, 190 stranded 100 miles from the nearest known habitation. Then, after several anxious hours the "panting rascal" returned to his side. "I never felt so relieved, and laughed out loud from sheer joy, as I noticed the consciousness he showed by his various cringing movements of having behaved very badly. I was too well pleased, however, at his reappearance to beat him, 195 particularly when I found nothing of his harness and load either missing or injured in the slightest degree. Even the portion of meat which I had secured from the last deer I shot was untouched . . ."

33   Ishmah had less conscience about stealing food from strangers. On his way home from the prairies Palliser took Ishmah to his hotel in St. 200 Louis. The dog lay at his feet in the dining room, but "not content with beholding his master enjoying the good things of this life" crept up to the dishes on the side board and helped himself to a calf's head "with which savoury prize he decamped at racing speed, his bushy tail stretching out, like a fox's brush, behind him; the waiters merely pointing after him and 205 winking to one another, evidently enjoying the joke."

34   The story of one completely satisfactory partnership between man and dog comes from the Canadian West. Reverend Egerton Ryerson Young and a companion were travelling across the ice on Lake Winnipeg when they were caught in a severe blizzard, and became lost while many miles 210 from shore. The travellers were in danger of freezing to death. What to do?

35   The missionary "had a talk" with his sled dog "Jack," a 160-pound black St. Bernard described by his owner as "the noblest of them all." Young informed Jack that the chances were against the dog ever again having the opportunity to stretch out on the rug before the study fire unless 215 he could lead them to a place of shelter. Jack led the travellers through the raging storm and many hours later brought them safely to an Indian encampment on shore. Of course. *Noblesse oblige.*

QUESTIONS

READER AND PURPOSE

1. What attitude towards his subject—and towards his readers—does McCook express by his opening comment about "The snobbery of Indian and Eskimo sled dogs"?

2. What common assumptions about dogs is the author challenging by his opening comments about the sled dogs' hostility and thievery?

ORGANIZATION

3. Paragraph 2 has only four words. Can you justify such a short paragraph?

4. What shift in the introduction occurs in paragraph 7?

5. How does paragraph 10 both summarize and introduce?

6. How does the beginning of paragraph 13 effect a shift from paragraph 10?

7. What two functions does paragraph 14 have?

8. Does the lack of transition between paragraphs 18 and 19 seem to you a strength or a weakness? Justify your answer. Or is the transition skillfully concealed?

9. Consider the two concluding paragraphs in relation to introductory paragraphs 1 to 7. Is there any relationship between introduction and conclusion? If you think there is, explain it. If you think not, justify McCook's conclusion.

SENTENCES

10. In the second sentence of paragraph 11, should there be a comma after "there"? Is a misreading probable, or possible, without the comma? Compare this usage with the comma after "still" in paragraph 14.

11. Could the dash in paragraph 11 be replaced by a semi-colon? a period? parentheses? What different effects would result from such substitutions?

12. In the last sentence of paragraph 19, should there be a comma after "downhill"?

13. Sentences four to six in paragraph 20 could be rewritten this way: "Dogs in the Woolsey team soon realized he had no control over them, so the lead dog

took it easy and the quarrelsome snapped at each other." Keeping in mind the context, is the rewritten passage more effective than the original?
14. What is the inversion* in paragraph 21? Would the sentence be more effective with normal word order?
15. Point out the parallel elements in paragraph 23.
16. What does McCook mean by his last two brief sentences? How are they related to the rest of the essay?

DICTION

17. Look up: *fend* (4), *fortnight* (15), *moroseness* (25), *diligent* (27), *sinecure* (76), *placid* (82), *kirk* (101), *carriole* (108), *timorous* (161), *plebeian* (162), *travois* (181), *gambol* (188), *noblesse oblige* (218).
18. How do the following expressions affect the tone* of this essay: "these undemanding beasts" (7), "a dog's delight" (48), "four-legged robbers" (50), "the victory of the dogs" (61), "lesser dogs" (138), "lazy dogs" (138)?
19. Look up "alliteration" in the Glossary, and then comment upon the effectiveness, or lack of it, of the examples in paragraph 24.
20. At times McCook uses unusual and effective expressions, such as "stewed fruit was hardly a dog's delight" (48), "as useless on the trail as bags of snow" (106), "Christmassy goodwill" (136), "he squeaked with fear" (166). At other times, however, he is guilty of using cliches (expressions which, by being used frequently, have lost their original impact): "had high hopes" (151), "in hot pursuit" (153), "would live to regret" (171), "fell from grace" (187), "the raging storm" (217). List other examples of both kinds.

POINTS TO LEARN
1. Short paragraphs can be effective not only because of their brevity, in contrast to the rest of the paragraphs in an essay, but also because they can serve as contrasts, as transitions, and as introductions.
2. A paragraph can sometimes be effective even if there is no transition linking it to the previous paragraphs.
3. Even a serious topic can be dealt with in a drily comic manner, if an author chooses his tone carefully.

SUGGESTIONS FOR WRITING
In "Reluctant Villain," Roy Vontobel takes the wolverine seriously, with no attempt at humor. Choose an animal you are familiar with (the family dog or cat, for instance) and describe some of its activities, adopting either the serious tone of Vontobel or the serious-comic one of McCook.

IMPROVING YOUR STYLE

In your essay include:

1. A paragraph of no more than eight or ten words, which will serve as contrast, as transition, or as both.
2. At least three figures of speech which you have never before seen in print.
3. One sentence in which you deliberately use an inversion.

The Burnout Factory:
Canada's Hollywood

Jay Scott, a national-newspaper award winner, is movie critic for the Toronto *Globe and Mail*. His reviews of new films have been widely acclaimed for their wit and style, as well as for the extensive knowledge of films they display. A collection of his best pieces was published in 1985 under the title *Midnight Matinees*. This expository essay, from his book, could well serve as a history of the Canadian film industry, and of its strengths and weaknesses.

Prologue and Epilogue: December 15, 1980

1   Prime Minister Pierre Trudeau, in black tie, a blood-red rose ever so slightly wilted on his satin jacket collar, looked pensive. A journalist had gestured toward the ballroom at Toronto's Four Seasons Hotel, the scene of Canada's most elegant and expensive movie premiere party to date. As usual, the party was better than the movie to which it paid tribute, which   5 was *Tribute*. Taking in the furs, the diamonds, the hairdos, the journalist had commented, "Your government is in some sense responsible for all this." The prime minister smiled. "It's amazing what a few tax laws can do," he said. Then he added, with a shrug, "There are now many Canadian films. But there aren't too many good ones, are there?"   10

2   In fifteen words, Trudeau not only summed up the state of the Canadian film industry, he also implied that the Canadian Film Development Corporation, charged with creating a film industry in Canada, and the Film Festivals Bureau, charged with promoting that industry, were less than truthful. For months, they had been telling the world that Canada was   15 the Australia of North America. And now the man whose government had made an unprecedented movie-production boom possible—by allowing passage, in 1978, of a liberalized tax-shelter law for film investment—was

From *Midnight Matinees* (Toronto: Oxford University Press, 1985).

joining the critics. A year after the offhand comments at the *Tribute* party,
the Trudeau government would announce substantial revisions to the tax-   20
shelter law—revisions clearly designed to control what had become a flood
of con men, carpetbaggers, and some folks with real ability (such as Louis
Malle) to the "Hollywood of the North." From 1979 to 1981, a staggering one
hundred and thirty feature films were financed in Canada (compared with
fifteen a year in the mid-seventies); as 1981 drew to a close, almost half had   25
yet to see theatrical release.

3   The future of the industry in Canada remains uncertain. What is
beyond doubt is that the government is determined not to repeat the
wildest weeks of the past few years—weeks when movies were being made
from coast to coast, when second-rate American stars were being paid   30
fabulous sums to appear in disaster films shot "entirely on location in
Montreal," when inexperienced producers sent the negative and only print
of a $5-million picture through the luggage system of a commercial airline,
when to comply with government regulations Canadian personnel were
listed in movie credits while the real jobs went to Americans, when Dennis   35
Hopper would say, "Canada's a positive place, maybe I'll move there," and
when Canadian actress Colleen Dewhurst, disgusted by it all, would recall
her first day on the set of a thriller fittingly entitled *Final Assignment*. "It
was supposed to be in Russia," Dewhurst said in her inimitable growl. "I
walked up and fingered the set. It wiggled. I was to perform in front of a   40
cardboard Kremlin. Dear God, I knew then we were in trouble. It was
another Canadian film that was supposed to fool the audience into thinking it was an American film. We Canadians are *people*. Surely our stories are
as universal as French or German stories."

4   Dewhurst's complaint has been the most common criticism of the   45
New Canadian Cinema—that there *is* no New Canadian Cinema, that
there is instead a New American Cinema on Canadian soil. The Australians
make movies about and usually with Australians. The Canadians make
movies about and often with Americans. *Middle Age Crazy*, starring Bruce
Dern, was set in a Toronto disguised as Houston, and *The Changeling*,   50
starring George C. Scott, was set in a Vancouver disguised as Seattle. A
continual, cavalier disregard of their topography, not to mention their culture, infuriates many Canadians.

5   Outfitting New York as Paris on a movie set might not bother
Americans, but Americans, insecure about so much, are not insecure about   55
their identity. The very definition of Canadian identity, however, is that it is
too insecure to be defined. And Canadians have noticed that the quality

films of other countries do not go out of their way to grossly curry favor
with the Americans. The filmmakers of Italy do not seem terrified that a
film with an Italian locale will be dismissed out of hand by an American   60
audience merely for being *set* in Italy. But Canadian producers were convinced, for a time, that American audiences would bolt from the theater
should the words Winnipeg or Toronto or Ottawa fall from actor's lips, save
in jest; Canadian designations were permitted only when used as represen-
tations of the names of impossible, colorful, comic places.   65

Roots I: The Old New Wave

6   Canadian cinema—what there was of it—came into the seventies
carrying naught but goodwill. John Grierson had made the National Film
Board the toast of the civilized cinematic world, and animator Norman
McLaren was its in-house saint. It was true, as writer Robert Fulford remarked
to critic Martin Knelman, that "English-speaking Canadians grew up believ-   70
ing they would eventually *graduate* from Canada. Real things happened
elsewhere." But it was also true that Canadians were trying to understand
the reasons for that phenomenon and that in so doing they would soon
release a remarkable series of films. At the end of the sixties and in the early
seventies, there were, for example, Don Shebib's *Goin' Down the Road*,   75
about two hicks in the big city of Toronto, and Claude Jutra's *Mon oncle
Antoine*—widely thought to be the greatest Canadian film ever made, a
study of a mining town seen through the eyes of a child, a politicized
version of *The 400 Blows*.

7   *Goin' Down the Road* and *Mon oncle Antoine* were the strongest   80
examples of the new wave; strength to Canadians meant that the Jutra and
Shebib films opened in New York to good reviews. But there were others.
William Fruet's *Wedding in White*, with the then unknown Carol Kane as a
pathetic child-woman trapped in a Second World War prairie town, was one
of them. Today Fruet, who also wrote *Goin' Down the Road*, directs horror   85
movies of execrable quality (*Death Weekend*, *Cries in the Night*, the forth-
coming *Death Bite*). In 1972, Gilles Carle's *La vraie nature de Bernadette*
contained the dazzling debut of Micheline Lanctôt. Today, after embarrass-
ing himself with *Fantastica*, a self-indulgent ecological musical that merci-
fully vanished after opening the 1980 Cannes Film Festival, Carle has returned   90
to prominence with *Les Plouffe*. Derived from a popular novel of a French
Canadian family, it has been made into no fewer than three popular movie
editions (and Canadians are not an extravagant people)—one for Quebec,
one for English Canada, and one for an international audience.

8   Allan King's 1968 cinéma vérité record of A Married Couple, ninety-   95
seven minutes in the bickering lives of Billy and Antoinette Edwards, anticipated An American Family. Today King is the director of Ellen Burstyn's
Silence of the North, an inept paean to a pioneer woman, and a box-office
flop. Don Owen in 1964 directed Nobody Waved Goody-bye—"Marvelous,"
wrote Brendan Gill in The New Yorker. Today Owen has become a sadly   100
familiar fixture in Toronto, reduced to talking about projects he may never
be allowed to realize. In 1970 Paul Almond caused nationwide controversy
with Act of the Heart, in which Geneviève Bujold set herself aflame to
protest the way we were. Today Almond is famous as the director of Final
Assignment, which is famous for its cardboard Kremlin.   105
9   Most of the old new wave came to grief, on the beach. The reasons
are various, most traceable to money, the rest to bad timing. After the surge
in the early seventies, directors were left without outlets, unless they wished to
work for the National Film Board or the Canadian Broadcasting Corporation. The days of independent shoestring movies were all but over. By the   110
end of the decade, when tax-shelter productions were going strong, it had
been years since many of the old guard had worked. But their services were
frantically sought, and they were perplexed recipients of big stars and big
budgets from producers who often had no experience with either. There
were exceptions—Garth Drabinsky, producer of The Silent Partner, The   115
Changeling, and The Amateur; Denis Héroux and John Kemeny, producers
of Atlantic City and Quest for Fire—but they were of the rule-proving sort.
10   Worse, in conforming to the demands of "international production," directors who did work under the tax-shelter laws were wrenched
from subjects they knew, in order to direct ersatz American product. They 120
were asked to move comfortably in genres and styles hopelessly alien to
them. Paul Almond's cinema is personal and mystical—ergo, he is hired to
helm an international thriller. Jutra's greatest achievement is the stylized
celebration of a specific rural French Canadian milieu; he is therefore
restricted to other people's scripts in a language not his own (English). The 125
tax-shelter laws appeared on the surface to be great equalizers: everybody
got a chance. It was the exact nature of the chance that was the problem;
for some of the old new wave; being given a chance meant you never had
one.

Roots II: The New New Wave

11   In the mid-seventies, two Canadians were busy imitating Ameri-   130
can movies to commercial, if not esthetic, advantage. Ivan Reitman made

something called *Cannibal Girls*. David Cronenberg made *The Parasite Murders* (a.k.a. *Shivers* and *They Came From Within*), which Reitman produced. Then Reitman co-produced *National Lampoon's Animal House* and directed *Meatballs* (the most successful Canadian film of all time). Then 135
Cronenberg directed *Scanners*. Now Cronenberg is completing *Videodrome*, starring Deborah Harry, the ice queen of another kind of new wave.

12   Back in 1975, Bob Clark made an effectively nasty horror flick, *Black Christmas*—and went on to *Murder by Decree*, with Christopher Plummer as Sherlock Holmes and to that glossy $8-million Jack Lemmon 140
fan letter, *Tribute*. Daryl Duke made *Payday* in the early seventies and *The Silent Partner* in the late seventies.

13   Ted Kotcheff (*The Apprenticeship of Duddy Kravitz, North Dallas Forty*) and Norman Jewison (*In the Heat of the Night, Jesus Christ Superstar*), proud of being Canadian and prouder still, perhaps, of getting regular work 145
in the United States, became the elder statesman of Canadian film.

14   One of the upstarts unexpectedly fell short: Richard Benner, the American expatriate who directed *Outrageous!*, the $167,000 Craig Russell picture that in 1977 caused a sensation in both New York and Toronto with its robust profile of an outlandish female impersonator. Benner moved back 150
to New York and brought a version of the Albert Innaurato play *Gemini* to the screen. The result, *Happy Birthday, Gemini!*, was greeted in most quarters as a harbinger of herpes.

Where Were The Youngsters?
Where Were Their Elders?

15   1. Where one of the elders could be found: a demonstration of what could go wrong in Hollywood of the North.   155

16   Claude Jutra was hired by Toronto producer Beryl Fox (who did the Vietnam documentary *Mills of the Gods*) to direct *Surfacing*, based on a novel by Margaret Atwood. The book is in the we-are-the-Swedes-of-North-America tradition of Canadian literature; it is a bleak, allusive, metaphoric interior odyssey in which the unnamed heroine comes to terms (maybe) 160
with her dead father, with the Americans she nationalistically despises, with the land that begat her (the lake country of northern Quebec), and with the land to which she has repaired, the dank terrain of her own self-destructiveness. Imagine *The Bell Jar* in the bush.

17   Fox hired an American screen writer, Bernard Gordon, best known 165
for *55 Days at Peking*, of all things, to adapt the book. She hired the American actress Kathleen Beller as the Atwood alter ego, and the American

actors Timothy Bottoms and his younger brother, Joseph. Canadian actors, who in general respect Fox and the feminism she stands for, were furious— but privately. (When the elder Bottoms dropped out, though, the Canadian   170 R. H. Thomson took over.) Jutra, when it was all over, intimated he was enamored of neither novel nor screenplay; what he did not need to intimate was that he needed the work. When *Surfacing* finally emerged, an intransigently Canadian, intransigently anti-American novel had become an astonishing thing: a film *with* Americans, a film somewhat *by* Americans, and a   175 film almost *for* Americans—a film in which anything that might offend an American audience was carefully excised. (Canadians have yet to recognize a law to which the British have profitably adhered for years: Yanks will queue up for highbrow insults.)

18   2. Where one of the youngsters could be found: a demonstration of   180 what could go right in Hollywood of the North.

19   Francis Mankiewicz is a relative of Herman (*Citizen Kane*) Mankiewicz and Joseph (*All About Eve*) Mankiewicz. He is in his early thirties, he lives in Montreal, he is bilingual. He is the director of *Les bons débarras*, a film that won for Marie Tifo the best-actress award at the 1980 Chicago   185 Film Festival and that won virtually every Academy of Canadian Cinema award possible. And it did mighty fine in its New York release.

20   *Les bons débarras* is as Canadian as self-doubt. The film, set in a small Quebec town, was written by Réjean Ducharme in a poetic French Canadian patois impossible to translate adequately—consider a Gallic Ten-   190 nessee Williams by way of Flannery O'Connor. (Mankiewicz was anxious to see John Huston's adaptation of O'Connor's *Wise Blood* and said of Huston's *Fat City*, "It's a perfect Quebec movie.") *Les bons débarras*'s conflict is between a woman (Tifo) having an affair with a cop, and her preternaturally mature thirteen-year-old daughter (Charlotte Laurier). The daughter reads   195 *Wuthering Heights* and greets *mère*'s announcement she is pregnant with, "A baby cop? You make me sick!" The picture was made on a miniscule, $625,000 budget without taking advantage of the tax-shelter laws. Thanks to the expertise and artistry of Mankiewicz and Ducharme, and thanks to the genius of cameraman Michel Brault (director of the galvanizing 1975   200 documentary *Les ordres*), *Les bons débarras* has become one of the most honored Canadian movies in history.

Why Some Stories Have No Endings, Happy or Otherwise

21   Mankiewicz was lucky: *Les bons débarras* was distributed. Zale Dalen was not so lucky. He is a Vancouver filmmaker whose first picture, *Skip*

Tracer, a tough portrait of a bill collector, has been a staple on the festival 205
circuit. His second film was *The Hounds of Notre Dame*, based on the
renowned (in Canada) exploits of Père Athol Murray, who ran a school for
boys in the prairie during the Second World War. As stunningly brought to
larger-than-life in the film by actor Thomas Peacocke, Murray is a cross
between Jean Brodie and Mayor Daley. In accepting his Genie for best 210
actor, Peacocke thanked the cosmos and then noted ironically, "No one's
seen the movie." *The Hounds of Notre Dame* opened briefly in western
Canada; it has never played Vancouver, Montreal, or Toronto.

22   Most of those sixty-odd Canadian films that have failed to find
distribution are dreck. But as Margo Raport, editor of *Filmworld*, the Cana- 215
dian trade paper, observes, "They should be sold somewhere. There are all
kinds of markets." The federal government's Canadian Film Development
Corporation (CFDC), which invests in both commercial and arty films,
with an unfortunate emphasis on the former, has been supremely successful at getting movies made. But its mandate is sadly sketchy as to what it can 220
or cannot do once they are in the can; the CFDC refused, for example, to
assist in underwriting *Les bons débarras*'s New York opening.

Without Hands: The Post-Tax-Shelter Future

23   Jean Pierre Lefebvre is Canada's most accomplished filmmaker,
director of some twenty features, among them a sympathetic study of an
act of high-school vandalism, *Avoir 16 ans*; a look at the commercialization 225
of human emotion by late-night phone-in shows, *L'amour blessé*; and the
finest film extant on the subject of Canadian identity, *Le vieux pays où
Rimbaud est mort*. Conceptually indebted to Godard, Lefebvre has refined
his minimalist technique. *Avoir 16 ans*, his most recent feature, which critic
Peter Harcourt has described as combining "the human feeling of Renoir 230
with the formal austerity of Michael Snow," was shot in color in 35 mm. It
cost approximately $100,000. "You can make movies for ten people," com-
ments Lefebvre, whose visual essays are admittedly "difficult" and are
rarely distributed outside art galleries. "But if you make movies for ten
people, they better cost ten bucks." 235

24   There are and probably will continue to be funds for films per-
ceived as sure things: for Ralph Thomas's drama about Moonies, *Ticket to
Heaven*, which got greater critical and commercial acclaim in New York
than anywhere in Canada; for Charles Jarrott's *The Amateur*, a thriller with
John Savage filmed in Toronto and Vienna. Nothing else is predictable. 240
Lefebvre's economy works well for him, but the nurturing of a nascent

Francis Coppola in Canada is unthinkable right now.

25   "We are in a third era," Margo Raport says. "The first was pre-tax-shelter, the second was tax-shelter and now we have entered the post-tax-shelter era. That means that new ways of financing will have to be sought,   245 and I think you will see co-ventures with the major studios. The French will be less affected, because they never used the law much. Ironically, they were just getting ready to, but the revisions make it worthless for them. Pay television is going to determine to a large degree the direction of feature production. With Ottawa's Canadian content regulations, at least twenty-   250 five and up to forty new films have to be produced in this country every year for pay television. That's at minimum two a month, in a country of twenty-two million. How?"

26   There is no answer to Raport's question. The metaphor most often employed for Canada vis-à-vis the United States is of a mouse sleeping next   255 to an elephant: the elephant can move with impunity, but each twitch is for the mouse a potentially life-threatening situation. Many Canadians—French and English—think that the United States' cultural colonization of their nation may be, with the advent of pay television, a fait accompli. The tax-shelter law was seen as a last-ditch effort to create a film industry nearly   260 sixty years too late; for everyone but the producers, the result was a deluge of disappointment.

27   Shortly before the law was set in place, Pierre Berton looked at the development of Canada's image of itself at the movies. He entitled his witty book *Hollywood's Canada* in recognition of a bizarre paradox: from the   265 twenties on, Canadians bought at American movies an image of themselves that had nothing to do with their own reality. But given the opportunity to bring their disparate experiences to the screen, to engender their own dreams and to immortalize their own mythologies, they opted in most instances for a slavish imitation of American dreams, for a crude approxi-   270 mation of American mythology and its attendant iconography. The recent record of Canadian film industry might be called *Canada's Hollywood.*

(*March 1982*)

Without Minds: The Post-Tax-Shelter Past

28   Margo Raport was right, but not about pay TV—about television in general. They changed the name of the Canadian Film Development Corporation to Telefilm Canada and that said it all: the new "thrust" would   275 be toward hybrid productions, toward the creation of amphibious monster mutants meant to bask equally well in the lights of two environments, the television tube and the silver screen. The misunderstanding displayed by this policy toward the craft of television, let alone the art of film, was beneath contempt, if not comment. So the sequel to *Les Plouffe* showed up   280 in no less than four failed editions: as a two-hour feature in French and subtitled English, and as a six-hour mini-series in French and dubbed English. Denys Arcand directed the feature, which became the last two hours of the mini-series; the other four hours were directed by Gilles Carle. Said Arcand, "Now the trend is TV. If you don't have a story that will fit neatly into six   285 hours, forget it." Of his labors on two versions of *Joshua Then and Now*, Mordecai Richler said, "I had to write fat and thin at the same time. It's a contradiction. For the television series, I had to extend a scene beyond its natural length. I don't think it's going to work very well. It will be destructive to both TV and film. You will have ersatz versions of both."   290

29   There were surprisingly few films shot for pay TV, which turned out to have a more circumscribed future than anyone had predicted. One of the successes, the winner of the 1984 best-picture Genie (it beat *The Wars*), was *The Terry Fox Story*, produced by Robert Cooper for Home Box Office. Cooper affected shock and indignation when the film failed in   295 Canada, the country it was about and the only country in which it was theatrically released. How dumb did Cooper suppose Canadians to be? They knew the film had been made for TV and they knew where they could see it free in a few months. Besides: they knew how it came out. *The Terry Fox Story* opened in every second theater across Canada on Friday, May 27,   300 1983—it opened in *four times* as many theatres as did the other moderately well-known film that premiered the same day, an adventure flick called *The Return of the Jedi*. Directed by *Ticket to Heaven*'s Ralph Thomas, *The Terry Fox Story* was a gritty look at the reality behind the press clippings of the Marathon of Hope undertaken by the kid from Vancouver with the ath-   305 lete's muscles and the cupid's curls, the kid who lost his leg and then his life to cancer. In trying to explain Terry Fox, the media, the Great Explainers, had rendered him inexplicable: they had transformed an alternately angry and tranquil, frightened and courageous, self-centered and compassionate, manipulative and ingenuous kid—a dying boy—into a living doll. The film,   310 starring amputee Eric Fryer, reversed the process: in cutting the kid down to size, it returned the myth to the land of the living and paradoxically increased the boy's heroic stature. ("Terry's real heroism," Fryer, himself a cancer victim, confided to his director, "was not running across Canada, it was going back to take chemotherapy a second time.") But the marketing of   315 the movie was insane: treating it as a preordained blockbuster and opening it in every shopping mall guaranteed that it would look like a failure. Even if

every theater had attracted a substantial audience—*Jedi's* audience—the auditoriums would have remained half-full and the picture would have continued to carry the taint of failure. (*Gandhi* and *Chariots of Fire* origi-   320
nally opened in one theater each in Toronto, guaranteeing line-ups and the appearance of a hit.) Cooper complained one morning on the record about the mistakes, but when the story appeared in *The Globe and Mail* he telephoned angrily and announced, "You've killed the film." How? "You've made it look like a failure." Prime Minister Trudeau meanwhile snubbed   325
the opening of *The Terry Fox Story*; the ingrate was photographed taking his children to *The Return of the Jedi*.

30   Sandra Gathercole, the most consistent and intelligent critic the government's various film policies have had, wrote in 1984 that "pay television and the one-hundred-percent Capital Cost Allowance have come and   330
gone as the great white hopes for financing Canadian production." In English Canada there were no new hopes to replace them, but in the ever-irascible and -ingenious Quebec a new law, Bill 109, the Cinema Act, looked good. This law required that distributors invest a certain percentage of their revenue in Quebec films. It also attempted in various complicated   335
ways to beef up Canadian distributors by obtaining American films for them to distribute. (Canada is technically a foreign market for the United States, but the major American studios have long treated the nation as a fifty-first state; the Americans distribute their own movies in Canada, movies they are required by law to sell to local distributors in other countries.   340
Furthermore, every one of those other countries imposes taxes or quotas or both on American product. Good neighbor Canada imposes neither.) The lack of a secure distribution base, Gathercole said, meant "Canadian production will perpetually prostitute itself to the American market. There is no point in pouring public funds into production without corresponding   345
measures to open domestic distribution." The funds that would be used to finance production in Quebec as the result of Bill 109 were particularly important in that the population base was no longer substantial enough to support its own cinema—the cost of making movies had grown so excessive that even many minor independent features had to look to markets outside   350
the province to recoup their investment. The Academy of Canadian Cine-
ma's Maria Topalovich estimated in the spring of 1985 that the Americans took $500 million a year out of Canada—directly, through the box office. "They return," she charged angrily, "next to nothing." Bill 109 was a first step at containment, a beaver dam at the bottom of Niagara.   355

Where Were the Bureaucrats?
Where Were the Artists?

31   Over at the National Film Board, some good films were being made. Some. But the NFB was beleaguered as never before, and it was hard to care: *Not a Love story*, an inept and dishonest documentary that benefited from the pornography controversy, was instantly definitive of what happened to feminism when it became both bourgeois and fascist. The 360 men at the NFB, presumably distressed by the attention the women were receiving, emitted a movie about male consciousness-raising, *The Masculine Mystique*, that received favorable reviews from Americans who thought it was a put-on. Few of the documentaries produced between 1982 and 1985 by the NFB were distinguished (*Incident at Restigouche* was an exception) 365 and many were considerably less than that; the NFB had developed a house style at once pedantic, melodramatic, and patronizing, a way of seeing things that reduced the most complicated material to simplicities full of sound and fury. All too frequently, participating in a screening at the NFB was an experience in ghostliness that would leave spectators feeling they 370 had joined one of the ghastly card parties attended by the faded faces in *Sunset Boulevard*.

Why Some Stories Have a Happy Ending

32   The tax-shelter years gave a bad name to carpetbaggers and co-productions, but a few worked out after the fact. The French director Jean-Jacques Annaud (*Black and White in Color*) came to Canada to make his 375 lively caveman tragi-comedy, *Quest for Fire*, and the American director Richard Pearce (*Heartland*) came to Canada to make *Threshold* with Donald Sutherland as a heart surgeon in a film shot by Michel Brault, a film that captured exquisitely the politics and the egos in heart surgery, not to mention the unearthly submarine beauty of an act on the heart itself.   380

Roots III: The Tidal Wave

33   Jean Pierre Lefebvre made three movies in two years: *Wild Flowers* (1982), *To the Rhythm of My Heart* (1983), a black-and-white "film diary," and *Le jour S . . .* (also 1983), a quirkily self-indulgent comedy (this small delight, in which Marie Tifo plays all the women in Pierre Curzi's life, ironically became the first Lefebvre film to open commercially in English Canada). 385 The triumph of the trio is *Wild Flowers*, which is two hours and forty minutes long, won the International Critics' Prize at Cannes, was shot in fifteen days for $350,000, and covers a week in a Quebec summer when three generations—Simone, who is seventy, her daughter Michèle and Michèle's husband Pierre, and their two children Claudia and Eric—get to   390 know one another a bit better. "It was a short, simple week in our lives," one of them says, but *Wild Flowers* is a long, complex film—"difficult," said Lefebvre, "because it is so simple. I wanted it to be simple. I wanted everything in it to be true." It is a masterpiece. The editor, Marguerite Duparc, Lefebvre's wife, died of cancer in March 1982, and the movie is   395 very much about mortality and the immutability of personality. As the aged Simone, Marthe Nadeau gives flawlessly formed life to a woman who has come to complacent good terms with her own existence. "Like it or not," she mutters, "things never change." But they do change, a little, during her week with her family. "I don't believe in artificial transformations," Lefebvre   400 said. "But if it is impossible to transform some things, such as the gap between generations, it is possible to transform our way of looking at it. The premise for the movie was: for those who cannot talk to each other, a movie about what might have been said."

34   In less exalted forums, William Fruet was still making horror films: 405 his *Bedroom Eyes* was nominated for a minor Genie in 1985. Jean Beaudin, whose stately *J.A. Martin . . . photographe* had won a Cannes best-actress award for Monique Mercure in 1977, returned to the prize circuit in 1984 with *Mario*, a gorgeously photographed film that fostered a rather bewildering sentimentality toward autism and death, and that won a Genie for   410 cinematographer Pierre Mignot. Gilles Carle followed the first *Plouffe* with *Maria Chapdelaine*, which treated the 1914 Louis Hémon novel of unfulfilled love and everlasting fortitude in the north woods—Edna Ferber in the outback—as the libretto of a musical on the order of *Oklahoma!*, a kind of *Kay-Bec!*, in which the cast pops like toasters and perks like coffee pots but   415 never actually breaks out into song. The two leads, Carole Laure and Nick Mancuso, are blankly glossy beauties, but the love between them is never consummated and that's a blessing: watching them go at it would be like trying to make fire by rubbing a pair of magazine covers together. Don Shebib meanwhile directed *Running Brave*, a sensitive and convincing   420 story of the Indian Olympic runner Billy Mills and then demanded that his name be removed from the credits because he was dismayed by what the producers had done to the film. The director on record was a fictitious "D. S. Everett"; D. S. Everett was a man of considerable talents. Nothing was heard from Allan King, Claude Jutra, Paul Almond, Daryl Duke, Zale Dalen,   425 or Richard Benner. Don Owen at last was permitted to make a sequel to *Nobody Waved Good-bye*, but *Unfinished Business* was a disappointment, a Crunchy Granola irrelevancy about the sixties disguised as the eighties. Bob Clark (*Turk 182!*) joined Ted Kotcheff (*First Blood*) and Norman Jewison (*A Soldier's Story*) in the ranks of the fat cats, directors capable of making   430 Americans come to them—they are an affluent trinity cognizant of commercial success and artistic integrity (at least occasionally). Ivan Reitman surpassed all three in the former department by directing *Ghostbusters*, the most successful comedy ever made (Clark's *Porky's* meanwhile surpassed *Meatballs* as the most successful Canadian comedy ever made). In 1985   435 Reitman received a special lifetime-achievement Genie award; the buck talks here.

Look Back in Glory

35   In 1984, Toronto's festival polled Canadian and international critics on the subject of the best Canadian films of all time. The results, in order of preference:

1. *Mon oncle Antoine*, Jutra, 1971;
2. *Goin' Down the Road*, Shebib, 1970;   440
3. *Les bons débarras*, Mankiewicz, 1979;
4. *The Apprenticeship of Duddy Kravitz*, Kotcheff, 1974;
5. *Les ordres*, Michel Brault, 1974;
6. *The Grey Fox*, Borsos, 1982;
7.-8. (tie) *J.A. Martin . . . photographe*, Beaudin, 1976; *Pour la suite*   445 *du monde*, Pierre Perrault and Brault, 1963;
9.-10. (tie) *La vraie nature de Bernadette*, Carle, 1972; *Nobody Waved Good-bye*, Owen, 1964.

Roots IV: After the Deluge

36   As the years went on, the youngsters fared as their elders had, from great to gruesome. Francis Mankiewicz's follow-up to *Les bons débarras*, *Les*   450 *beaux souvenirs*, never opened in English Canada, a small mercy for Mankiewicz. Micheline Lanctôt's second film as a director, *Sonatine*, is divided into three parts: the first, in which a girl carries on an innocent flirtation with a bus driver, is charming; the second, in which another girl has a similar communication with a sailor, is dreary; and the third, in which   455 the two girls decide to kill themselves by taking downers on the Montreal Metro—they announce their intention with a placard and wait in vain (and vainly) for someone to notice—is a preposterous and vapid spasm of social criticism dramatized by a situation only an actress could have dreamed up: it's no coincidence the girls perish from receiving too little attention. They   460 go on stage, as it were, to better the world, and no one applauds. So they drop dead. The clever, dynamic Lanctôt, who had a history of winning weird awards—she was the recipient of the lifetime-achievement Genie on the occasion of the release of her sweet first film, *The Handyman*—received the best-director Genie for *Sonatine*. She said she was surprised.   465

37   There were debuts of promise. Léa Pool made a wonderfully assured, self-reflexive film about filmmaking, *La femme de l'hôtel*, that had the international jury at the 1984 Toronto film festival agog over her talent. *Une journée en taxi*, shot by the welcomely ubiquitous Pierre Mignot (*Maria Chapdelaine, Streamers, Come Back to the 5 & Dime Jimmy Dean, Jimmy*   470 *Dean*) was an amazingly confident study by Robert Ménard of the relation- ship a convict strikes up with the taxi driver who takes him away from prison. After years of wrangling, Robin Phillips's film of Timothy Findley's *The Wars* presented to Canadians for the first time an intelligent feature set in the hearts and minds of the English-speaking ruling class. And Philip   475 Borsos's *The Grey Fox*, the pre-eminent legend of Canadian film produc- tion in the eighties, proved again to those who required proof that Cana- dian stories *were* important and that Canadians *could* tell them beautifully, if given a chance. *The Grey Fox* and *The Wars* were long overdue, films hailing from the heart of Canada's Canada.   480

March 1985

QUESTIONS

READER AND PURPOSE

1. The selections by Tuchman, Revelle, and Raleigh are parts of larger works. Scott's essay is complete and shows how an extensive use of illustration can support a sustained argument. The essay may also, for some readers, present a problem: at what point does the amount of illustration become excessive rather than sufficient? In addition, some readers may judge the examples to be too specialized. Do you think Scott's essay would appeal mainly to readers with a good knowledge of contemporary films (particularly Canadian films)? Or is this essay concerned with larger issues that might extend its appeal to readers not well acquainted with all the films Scott refers to?
2. Scott's main purpose is never explicitly stated. What is it? In answering this question, consider his choice of title and his use of words and phrases such as

carpetbaggers (22), *curry favor* (58), *as Canadian as self-doubt* (188), *slavish imitation of American dreams* (270).

ORGANIZATION
3. Scott's essay was originally published as two articles (in 1982 and 1985). What devices are used to link the two parts as they appear here?
4. Does the rhetorical question* at the end of paragraph 1 receive an answer in the course of the essay?
5. What effects does Scott achieve by not adhering strictly to a year-by-year organization of his material?
6. Do all of Scott's sub-headings perform the usual functions of signposts* and organizing sentences*?
7. Are the short paragraphs 12 and 13 justifiable? Are paragraphs 15 and 18?
8. Why does Scott make no comment on the results of the poll described in paragraph 35?
9. Is Scott's argument strengthened by the many quotations from others involved in the film industry?
10. Is the conclusion (paragraph 37) weakened by the introduction of new material?
11. Does this conclusion deal with the whole of Scott's essay, or only the second part?

SENTENCES
12. Point out the parallel* elements in the second sentence of paragraph 3.
13. Is the dash in line 29 more effective than a colon would have been? Why is a dash used in line 77 instead of a comma as in line 76?
14. Would the sentence in lines 106-07 be improved if it were rewritten as: "The reasons are various; most are traceable to money and the rest to bad timing"?
15. Is the unusual use of a colon in line 299 defensible? Try rewriting the sentence without the colon. Does this change the tone* significantly?
16. Scott begins several sentences with "But." Would these sentences be improved by replacing "but" with a conjunctive adverb*? Deal with any three such sentences.
17. Scott often mixes formal and colloquial* diction in the same sentence: ". . . inept paean . . . box-office flop" (lines 98-99). Find other examples of this practice. What does it tell you about the author's attitude to his subject? Does the movement from formal to colloquial convey an unstated judgment?

DICTION
18. Look up: *tax-shelter* (18), *execrable* (86), *ersatz* (120), *ergo* (122), *queue up* (179), *dreck* (215), *fait accompli* (259), *bizarre* (265), *iconography* (271), *ingrate* (326), *pedantic* (367), *cognizant* (431), *vapid* (468).

19. Find the etymologies* of *intransigently* (173) and *preposterous* (468).
20. Scott refers to "exceptions . . . of the rule-proving sort" (115–17). This is a variation of the phrase "the exception that proves the rule," an expression often misunderstood and misused. Find the etymology of *prove* to learn what it rightly means in this expression.
21. Is Scott using *ironically* (211, 247, 384) in its formal or its colloquial sense?
22. Scott makes frequent use of figures of speech*. Identify those in lines 153, 188, 301–02, 355, 415, 429.
23. Does the author's use of adverbs in his brief judgments of films convey more than a personal and impressionistic view? Consider *effectively nasty* (138), *captured exquisitely* (379), *quirkily self-indulgent* (383), *flawlessly formed* (397), *amazingly confident* (471), and look for other examples of this practice.
24. Scott uses many allusions* to other arts and artists. See, for example, lines 173–74, 180–81, 195–96, 241, 368–69. Look up these and other allusions and decide whether they extend the essay's appeal to readers not as familiar with film as Scott obviously is.
25. Could it be argued that the image* in lines 1–2 both anticipates and sums up the main point Scott is making?

POINTS TO LEARN
1. Although illustration is necessary in an expository essay, the writer must carefully judge the amount required and the extent to which an audience can be assumed to have detailed and specific information about a subject.
2. Sub-headings can serve to guide the reader through the stages of an extended argument.
3. Style and tone may convey, indirectly, the writer's judgment of the issues being discussed.

SUGGESTIONS FOR WRITING
1. Write a short essay on a subject you know well, using as Scott does many specific examples. At the same time, attempt—through the use of allusion and careful control of your tone—to make your essay of interest to a reader less knowledgeable about the subject.
2. Write a short essay in which you describe ways in which the Canadian novelist, poet, painter, or musician is (or is not) affected by problems similar to those facing the Canadian film-maker.

IMPROVING YOUR STYLE

In your essay include:

1. Sentences in which you employ each of Scott's figures of speech.
2. A paragraph in which you mix formal and colloquial diction so as to suggest conclusions to your reader without stating them directly.

The Japanese-Canadian Dilemma

Joy Kogawa was born in Vancouver in 1935 and raised there. She has published three volumes of poetry and a novel, *Obasan* (1981), which won both the *Books in Canada* First Novel Award and the Book of the Year Award from the Canadian Authors Association. It is an autobiographical account of the hardships suffered by Japanese-Canadians soon after Pearl Harbor, when they were forced to leave their homes and spend the rest of the Second World War in internment camps. In this essay she describes the problems that must still be faced by a young member of a racial minority who is both intelligent and sensitive.

1   It's Wednesday night, downtown Toronto. Three of us are sitting in a basement room in the dark with our eyes closed. We're holding hands. This is a private hidden thing. We're praying together. Prayer is not something I talk about generally or write about except in my diary. It sounds too much like hocus-pocus. People think of Mackenzie King summoning up   5 ghosts or looking at the hands of a clock to give him direction. He sounds slightly nuts. So do those who pray.

2   Worship is a primitive impulse. People have always been trying to get to the big picture whether through telescopes and microscopes or the handier lens within. I believe in prayer with my primitive committed heart.   10 There's also doubt. Belief and doubt are both carried here to this basement room.

3   The three of us are each letting our "stuff" float up through the quiet spaces. I find myself talking about an article for *Toronto Life* that I've been asked to do. I'm blocked. I'm supposed to write about Japanese Cana-   15 dians and redress. Lord, I'm so tired of being a professional ethnic. There's no peeling off of the skin at 5 o'clock or getting weekends free.

4   I spoke earlier today with a fellow Japanese Canadian, a Nisei like myself, born in British Columbia. He said there were a lot of people working on redress and he was tired of the whole thing as well.   20

From *Toronto Life*, December 1985. Reprinted by permission of the author.

5   "You should do more important things," he said.

6   "You don't think the telling of our story is important?"

7   There are still many Canadians, politicians included, whose hearts and minds are uninformed about who we are or what was done to us. Surely that lack of information is our responsibility. Forty years ago we were treated as unwanted foreigners in this country. Today, we are still treated as foreigners—by strangers, at parties, in department stores. Bharati Mukherjee found it impossible to stay here in our bureaucratically fuelled grassroots racism and fled to the United States. She said if she'd stayed, she would have had to give up writing and become a political activist.

8   My friend raised his eyebrows. "Really!" he exclaimed. "I'm surprised. Do you personally experience racism here? You're obviously free to write and say anything you want."

9   I told him I thought our skin had grown thick in this jab-heavy environment. I asked him what he felt when former prime minister Trudeau went to Japan and apologized there for what was done to Japanese Canadians here. Would he have gone to France to apologize for the wrongs against French Canadians?

10   "Well," my friend said and shrugged. "Does it really matter? Is anyone suffering because of it?" He was suggesting it was a petty point.

11   "What do you think about the problems of the Native peoples?" he asked. I admitted there were more urgent issues in today's troubled world than Japanese-Canadian redress. "However every issue has its own legitimacy," I argued. "And more justice here doesn't mean less justice there. What's important to anyone is whatever they care about. Do you care about Japanese Canadians?"

12   "I don't find them a particularly imaginative group," he said.

13   "We're like everyone else," I said. His remark reminded me of a familiar old weight, one that I thought I'd put aside in recent months— a feeling something like irritation, or lethargy. I changed the topic. The conversation was beginning to have the texture of many warmed-over interviews—always about Japanese Canadians.

14   There in the basement room I tell my prayer group I'm confused about the article request and don't really know what I'm supposed to be doing. We hand it over. Our prayers keep on rambling. We pray for someone who's going in for a serious operation. Then somehow we're talking about Gandhi the man and *Gandhi* the movie and we get on to another area of confusion for me. The movie business. Some people are interested in making a movie of *Obasan*. Business is a world I don't much understand—a world of cactus plants, prickly to the touch, growing it seems to me, in a

desert of mistrust. Caesar reigns in the business desert, claiming what is
Caesar's due, for Caesar's short-lived glory. What's the difference between
Caesar and a thief? What's the difference between my mistrust of business
and the mistrust of Japanese Canadians in the past?

15   I've said I'm confused so often tonight that I feel embarrassed and   65
expect a certain censure. But censure is the opposite thing to expect from
an exercise in prayer. Everything is for handing over. I hand over the movie
concern along with the *Toronto Life* article. We pray about our kids. We
hand them over too. It feels like a great dumping ground.

16   Thursday morning and I wake up thinking vaguely that I'll call   70
Toronto Life to tell the editors I can't write the article. Every angle I think
up leads me to some fellow Japanese Canadian feeling hurt or enraged or
envious or fearful. I don't have the necessary freedom to write about us. Of
course some people in the community are always suggesting that an article
would straighten things out. It would take more than that.   75

17   I'm thinking of Earle Birney's poem about Vancouver—how the
city lights sparkle from the mountain. From far enough away, the Japanese-
Canadian community might look beautiful, but I've been in the back alleys
with the garbage pails recently. Horrible hurts happen in an environment of
fear. Kindest intentions seen through filters of mistrust are monstrously   80
transformed. It's a place to walk gingerly. Politics is the art of toe-watching
and what a tangle of toes and bunions leap about in the microcosm of
Japanese-Canadian politics. It's not the most elegant dancing. How much
more beautiful we would find ourselves if we could see one another from
the perspective of mountain tops. If we could break through our fears.   85

18   It's 10 o'clock, and I call up a friend—the one who first put the
article idea on to boil. I give her my reasons for not doing it. First, I'm tired.
I'm worn out by the push-pull in the Japanese-Canadian community. Some
people obviously fear a backlash, and having worked so hard to be as invisible as possible, can't bear the limelight. I've met a few whose energy is deep   90
and powerful and who battle "because of the principle of the thing." Some
are interested in legal perspectives and confine their involvement to the
pen. Some see justice in economic terms alone. Others see money as an
undignified and insulting measure of their suffering. One clergyman speaks of
forgiveness. Another replies that forgiveness applies to people, not to sys-   95
tems, and systems need overhauling. Yet another says that forgiveness is
meaningless without repentance and admission of wrong. Some say that
the door to these discussions should never have been opened. Others, that
the door should never be closed. Some community leaders are accused of
militancy and selfishness. Others are accused of selling out, or of using the   100

issue for purely personal political ambitions, or of having no social conscience. Some community members fear that greed or the appearance of
greed is the image being created and that our true stories will not receive a
sympathetic hearing. Some say there's been sympathy enough and we
should get on with all our tomorrows. Some want a full public inquiry of our   105
history in depth and in detail.

19   I tell my friend that the current tempest in the community teapot
will someday be past and that will be the time to write. I can hope that those
who now consider me to be their political enemy will change their minds.
Things are in such flux and I'm too close to it all. Witnesses are only as good   110
as their vision, I tell her, and I can't see. Besides, print is a solidifier and isn't
it wrong, I ask lamely, to solidify what is still flowing along? Isn't the pen
easily abused and thereby made an instrument of harm in times of turmoil?

20   She starts gunning me down. "You don't have to see a *Toronto Life*
article as your definitive statement to the Japanese-Canadian community,"   115
she says. "That's not who you're primarily speaking to." She tells me she
thinks I'm being a coward and that I'm really using all these arguments just
to cover up. "You're scared of what people will say," she says. That gets to
me.

21   I try one last shot. I tell her I believe the community needs support   120
and perspective from the outside and that non-Japanese Canadians should
take up the task. Someone else should write the article. It's the responsibility of others as much as ours. It's Canada's story.

22   She says bluntly that others already have and people who are obviously on the inside are obligated to speak up. "Write about the silence and   125
how awful it still is," she says.

23   I grit my teeth.

24   "You'll do it," she says.

25   I don't answer.

26   "Good," she says, and hangs up.   130

27   It's another bulldozing day. I stare out the window and think about
how much I hate writing and hate the subject. *The silence and how awful it
still is.* There's nothing to eat in the fridge. I should go and look for some
background material. Where did I put all those Muriel Kitagawa papers I
used for writing my novel? They're probably buried in the basement under   135
all the unpacked boxes of papers from the last move. Funny how Naomi,
the narrator in *Obasan*, went to the attic for these papers and I go to the
basement.

28   They're here under the steps in the box at the bottom. Good ol'
Muriel. All this stuff from—what was it—seven years ago? Hello again, dear   140

unrelenting ghost. The spirit of Muriel Fujiwara Kitagawa first haunted me through these papers in the Public Archives in Ottawa. She was an activist of the '40s, a young, married woman with a pen, a historian's guide. She wrote letters, poems, short stories, articles, passionate manuscripts, which her husband, Ed, sent to Ottawa's Public Archives. She died before I could meet her.   145

29   Some people didn't like her, they tell me. She was not known for diplomacy. In spite of all her trampled toes, Muriel's unpopular courage strides into tomorrow, more surely than the good and squeaky feet of some of her more diplomatic contemporaries.   150

30   When I first read her material, I was gripped. I carried her papers through the halls of the Archives, holding back the tears, facing the corners where no one could see me. Sometimes, around midnight, I would sit alone in the huge rooms of tables and let the floodgates loose.

31   Whatever else Muriel did or didn't do, she did not fail to love   155 Canada and Canadians. There was no other country for her. On page thirty-four of her manuscript titled "Go East," in which she describes some of the agonies of the time when we were being exiled, she writes ". . . even for the bitterest ones, there really was no choice at all, because whatever the provocation, we could not conceive of ourselves as anything but Cana-   160 dian." Her passionate loyalty, her rage, haven't been left to molder in the grave. A book by Muriel Kitagawa titled *This Is My Own*, edited by Roy Miki of Vancouver, is out this year. What a relief that is. What a cause for celebration.

32   I do so much wish she were here still, and I wish I'd met her. I wish   165 they could all come back—those passionate Niseis and Isseis who toiled and toiled and toiled till they dropped to prove and overprove that they were worthy of the love of their fellow Canadians. People such as George Tanaka, T. Buck Suzuki, Kunio Shimizu and all the other warriors who have died. What a cloud of unsung heroes surrounds us. Muriel says we "had to   170 choose our allegiance under such stress and strain, under duress." And she believed that "hardships, obstacles, persecutions tend to crystallize the instinctive loyalty. . ." It's interesting to think of loyalty as crystal—a jewel to cherish and to wear. But loyalty, whether to a person or a community or a country, can be destroyed. What seems marvellous to me about these politi-   175 cally active idealists in our community is that they remained loyal through-out their lives in spite of all the treachery. Such bright uncrushed diamonds.

33   But I don't know how Muriel and the other leaders coped with the bleatings of the critics in the community—those who are always complain-ing that the doers are doing too much or not enough, are going too fast or   180 too slow, are being too autocratic or indecisive etc. etc. Resentments, timidities, criticisms, envies are the plague of insects that anyone who tries to do anything has to face. Maybe Muriel became a fly swatter to survive the mosquito mob.

34   Addressing the security seekers of her day, she wrote: "Perhaps we want nothing better than to forget the raw wounds of yesterday, to cover the scars with delusions of security, but what was once taken away can be taken again. Who knows but that the next time will be made easier for the plunderers because we shrugged and said: 'Shikata-ga-nai' (it can't be helped)." 185

35   Her words still apply. We'd still like to cover our scars with delusions of security. It's so easy to forget that we do not live by bread alone and that the rumblings in our belly are not the best guide. We can become so malnourished, so hungry for spiritual bread that we barely wobble along, hardly knowing the difference between principles of justice and rationalizations for greed, between acts of generosity and acts based on fear. 190 195

36   Some people who remember the '40s say that our community today is reliving the same dynamics that were at work in the past. The terrors have by no means been forgotten. People remember the terrible helplessness, the confusion, the frustration, the conflicting reports, the need to be extra good, quiet and submissive and to pander to authorities. Many of us still believe that if we lie perfectly still and don't rock the boat, the storms will disappear and we'll be safe. The lessons of oppression can remain a lifetime. 200

37   At the official level, government taught us our lessons well, laboring to create disunity in the community, to disperse us, to destroy our will, and, toward the end, to provide a "final solution to the Japanese problem" by exiling us. 205

38   Cyril Powles, whom I see in church most Sundays, was writing back in the '40s, warning about the potential disaffection of Japanese Canadians unless policies changed. "A problem, sufficiently discouraging before the war, might be rendered practically insoluble," he wrote. It seems reasonable to suppose that if you treat loyal citizens as if they were spies and treacherous traitors, if you imprison them, steal their properties, deprive them of the means to earn their livelihoods, if you take away their rights of citizenship for seven years, if you exile them for no crime—if you do these despicable things, it seems reasonable to suppose that somewhere down the line problems will arise. 210 215

39   My tolerant friend who advised me to concern myself with more important matters agreed that it was all a terrible thing. "But," he said, "what do you think would have happened to us if we'd fought back?" He 220 shook his head as he answered himself. "We wouldn't be here. We just wouldn't be around. That's how bad it was."

40   It seems we were lucky that we had some friends. Although the White Canada Association argued that we were completely unassimilable, that each and every one of us was disloyal, that we would be happier out of the country, that we were a menace to working conditions and so on, we had powerful friends who knew better.

41   Thank God for friends. The Reverend James Finlay, the chairman of the Co-Operative Committee on Japanese Canadians, was a friend of Muriel. His was the home where Ed and Muriel and their family first stayed when they moved to Toronto. With Reverend Hugh MacMillan as executive secretary and Andrew Brewin as legal advisor, the Co-Operative Committee formed a powerful lobby team.

42   News Bulletin #5 of the Co-Operative Committee describes a conference of an hour and a half with Prime Minister Mackenzie King and Cabinet members on March 26, 1946. The deputation representing the Co-Operative Committee consisted of E.J. Tarr, KC, of Winnipeg; Charles Millard, national director, United Steelworkers of America and executive member of the Canadian Congress of Labour; Andrew Brewin, Hugh Mac-Millan, David Croll, Liberal MP, and M.J. Coldwell, national leader of the CCF. They were arguing against the deportation and exile of innocent Canadian citizens.

43   Two days later on March 28, 1946, Kunio Hidaka, executive secretary of the Citizenship Defence Commission, has a fulsome report of the meeting. He describes various reactions by Mr. King and Mr. St. Laurent, minister of justice. While sympathetic to the Co-Operative Committee, they are not willing to withdraw the deportation orders. The Honorable Ian Mackenzie, minister of veterans affairs from British Columbia, calls the efforts of the Co-Operative Committee, "frothy idealism" by persons unable to face "hard realities."

44   A full two years later, in March, 1948, Jack Scott writes a satirical piece in the *Vancouver Sun*—a dialogue between Goebbels and Hitler in Hell. They're gleefully discussing the good news from Canada that British Columbia Liberal Party members have become their men.

45   "What a splendid joke!" Hitler says, roaring with laughter.

46   Goebbels: "Good men. Good men all. And highly respected . . . Why, one of their leaders—now a senator—swore that he would leave public life if the Japs returned to that coastal strip."

47   Hitler: "Capital! A man after my own heart. Truly a real senator!"

48   Goebbels: "A Scotsman, by the way. Name of Mackenzie."   260
49   Hitler: "Hoot mon!"
50   Goebbels: "Ja, Mein Fuehrer, it is just as if you were there in
person. A helpless minority used beautifully for political and economic
purposes. A forthright stand against a race of a different color or creed. Just
as in our better days. And just think: a whole year ban on them!" [On March   265
8, 1948, the government announced we would be banned from the B.C.
coast for at least another year.]
51   Hitler: "Ach, Doctor. We are far from dead so long as we have our
friends up there."
52   Goebbels: "Hoot mon, Mein Fuehrer."   270
53   I find it not easy to believe, but I'm told that government bureaucrats are not so different today. They are as unimaginative as ever, caring
about their jobs, their families, their friends and little else. It's still who you
know that counts. And woe to those people who have no one to represent
them. I've heard that the same sentiments, the same arrogance and racial   275
contempt that raged upon us in the '40s are still present behind closed
doors among senators and Cabinet members. If that is true, we must seek
out our Desmond Tutus.
54   Kunio Hidaka, one of our lifelong warriors, died just this year, the
day after I saw him speaking to a public meeting of the National Associa-   280
tion of Japanese Canadians. I still mourn him. I hope his idealism never
stops frothing, never stops fighting against the terrible "hard realities" of
racism, political opportunism and the morally bankrupt merchants of
economic expedience. Thank heavens that some of Kunio's contemporaries
are still active and on the front lines of the continuing battle. People such as 285
Roger Obata, Canadian World War II veteran who fought for democracy in
the armed forces and still battles to set the record straight on the home
front. People such as Kay Shimizu, a politically astute social worker who
worked throughout the '40s and is one of the people at the helm providing
leadership.   290
55   There is no doubt that the NAJC has the support of Japanese-
Canadian scholars and leaders across the country. But it is by no means an
elitist organization. Nor, contrary to some mean-mouthed reports, is it a
bunch of young radicals. The average age of the National Council, the
governing body, is around 60.   295
56   There are still a great many Japanese Canadians who fled into the
woods as I did, to try to hide from our ethnicity. We learned to shun one
another and to view any Japanese-Canadian gathering as a gaggle of ghetto-

ized geese. One of my points of rediscovery came when I found that I could actually have Japanese-Canadian friends. It was something like my first women's liberation meetings in the '60s when I met articulate, challenging, stimulating women— some who terrified me with their intellectual shrapnel. Where had all the kitchen talk gone?

57   It was a surprise to meet and like and respect my fellow geese. I crept on board the Redress ship with all ten toes still intact, intending to set sail with them to slay the dragon of racism and save democracy. A ship of friends, unlike a ship of fools, is capable of quelling storms, and unsinkable friendships are the most formidable boats in the world. What an armada we are, I thought, and what a fool I was, I soon learned. Japanese-Canadian friends, no more nor less than women friends or friends joined for any cause, are just your regular people with sensitivities and easily wounded pride. And when political wizards are at work, storms are brewing. But the ship is by no means wrecked. There continue to be many heartwarming moments.

58   Speaking at a meeting at Harbord Collegiate attended by more than 500 Japanese Canadians, David Suzuki referred to the National Association of Japanese Canadians as the beginnings of a national community. We are a minority among minorities, hailing one another across huge distances as we go about the business of gathering our shipmates from their rafts and logs. Today we are becoming a community that is increasingly conscious of its responsibility to the wider society, to make sure that the Japanese-Canadian story is not repeated in any other Canadian community. We are a national community in a process of political maturation. Our strategies are not written in stone. Gradually we are becoming less frightened of the rocking boat as it rides through political storms.

59   Although the will to destroy our small ship has been made amply evident, we have more friends today than we had in the '40s. And more than anything else, I believe it's the love that comes through our friends in the media and elsewhere that will rescue us. We are drawn to life, Rollo May says, by love. Our new courage is evidence of love. And the Ian Mackenzies who talk their "hard realities" will not destroy the "frothy idealism" that keeps our compass pointed to a better world.

60   For me, the beginning, middle and end of redress has been reduced to a wish for community. During the last two years, although a new national Japanese-Canadian community has been coming into being, some old community members have been badly and needlessly hurt and confused in the political machinations. Redress, for me, has already been lost and won. The cup is half-empty and half-full.

61   My recent experiences in the political world have disabused me of

my more grandiose dreams. I used to think that a people who had been   340
persecuted were somehow made special by it and carried with them secrets,
tales of transformation, new dimensions of compassion. I dreamed that the
collective Japanese-Canadian voice could startle the country with its beauty,
with its stronghearted generosity, with its will to fight for the oppressed. I
dreamed that the moral hunger of people could be so filled by the nobility   345
of our vision that we would be released from our tyrannies of greed and
meanness of spirit. I dreamed that an unmistakable cry of love, for one
another, for Canada and for all who suffer, would transcend all our other
cries.

62   But one person's dream is another's nightmare. This has been a   350
time to drop my fantasies and to accept other promptings.

63   It's a hallmark of the oppressed that our energy turns against
ourselves. The challenge that faces us all is to discover the ways in which we
have been oppressors of our own. As a country, as a community and as
individuals we show maturity when we assume responsibility toward those   355
we harm. Only the most infantile can claim to be pure victim. Only the
mature concern themselves with their roles as victimizers. Japanese-Canadian
redress is an occasion for senators and members of Parliament, no less than
for Japanese Canadians, to discover the extent of our woundedness.

64   These days I do feel tired of the Japanese-Canadian focus, of the   360
victim/victimizer question and of political warfare. The place that is without question the closest spot to home, the safest place that I can imagine, is
that basement room where the three of us sit and wait—sometimes with
only a candle and the grey light from the windows as our sources of light.

QUESTIONS

READER AND PURPOSE

1. Several times early in this essay the author comments on the problems she
has in approaching her topic. That is, she describes the difficulties of writing
her account as she is actually writing it. Is this point of view* likely to gain
sympathy from the reader? or is the reader more likely to feel that, given the
problems the author is having, reading on would be a waste of time?

2. In the first part of this essay we see a number of rather surprising points:
"I'm supposed to write about Japanese Canadians and redress" (15); " 'You
don't think the telling of our story is important?' " (22); "I'm confused about
the article request and don't really know what I'm supposed to be doing" (53);
"I don't have the necessary freedom to write about us" (73); "someone else
should write the article" (122); "I stare out the window and think about how

much I hate writing and hate the subject" (131). In spite of her reluctance and confusion, however, Kogawa not only completes her essay but does a fine job of it. How is she able to get beyond her initial difficulties? What helps her to solve her problems about writing this article?

ORGANIZATION

3. How does the last sentence of paragraph 2 act as a summary of the first two paragraphs?
4. Could the one sentence of paragraph 6 be called the thesis statement of this essay? Whatever your answer, defend it by reference to the major points Kogawa makes throughout the essay.
5. Near the beginning of paragraph 18 Kogawa uses a signpost*: "First, . . ." She does not, however, go on to "second," "third," etc. Had she used these words, where would they go in the paragraph? Would the paragraph be more clearly organized had she used such words?
6. In the Old Testament, read chapter 8, verse 3 in the Book of Deuteronomy. Then discuss how Kogawa has used this verse to structure paragraph 35.
7. In paragraph 17 Kogawa writes that "Politics is the art of toe-watching. . . ," and in paragraph 57 that "I crept on board the Redress ship with all ten toes still intact." There are a number of such references to toes and toe-watching; point them out, and then discuss how Kogawa uses such references as one method of unifying her essay.
8. The double-spacing after paragraphs 13, 15, 17, and 26 would seem to indicate major divisions in the author's presentation of her subject. What are these major parts of her essay which she is dividing? Are there others which are not indicated by double-spacing? Should they have been?
9. How does paragraph 64 function as a closing by return*?

SENTENCES

10. How is the first sentence in paragraph 14 an organizing sentence*? If you think that it is not such a sentence, what other term would you give it?
11. In paragraph 14 we also find this passage: "Then somehow we're talking about Gandhi the man and *Gandhi* the movie and we get on to another area of confusion for me. The movie business." Is Kogawa's use here of a fragment* justifiable? Would there be a difference in effect if the fragment were joined to the previous sentence, with only a comma to separate them?
12. Paragraph 18 uses parallel* structure, based on the repetition of three words: "some," "others," "another." Look closely at the entry for parallelism in the Glossary, noting especially how sentences can be outlined to show their parallel structure. Then outline the sentences of paragraph 18 in the same manner.
13. The second sentence of paragraph 32 is somewhat unusual, with its repeti-

tion and variation. Do you think it is effective? Can you improve it by changing or adding punctuation, or by changing the word order?

DICTION

14. Look up: *committed* (10), *ethnic* (16), *redress* (20), *grassroots* (28), *censure* (66), *microcosm* (82), *turmoil* (113), *perspective* (121), *unrelenting* (141), *diplomacy* (150), *Niseis* (166), *Isseis* (166), *duress* (171), *autocratic* (181), *rationalizations* (194), *unassimilable* (224), *forthright* (264), *opportunism* (283), *astute* (288), *elitist* (293), *disabused* (339).

15. Why does the author place quotation marks around the word *stuff* in paragraph 3?

16. Do you think that the alliteration* at the end of paragraph 10 is effective? Or that in the second sentence of paragraph 56? Before answering, look closely at the entry for alliteration in the Glossary.

17. One of the most noticeable features of Kogawa's style is her frequent use of figures of speech, especially of metaphors*. Choose a paragraph (such as 17, 19, 29, 32, 35) and briefly explain all the metaphors. Then comment on what you see as their effectiveness, or lack of it. Do any of them strike you as especially powerful? or weak?

18. Kogawa uses colloquialisms* fairly often, as in, for example, the opening sentences of paragraphs 20, 21, and 27. How do such expressions affect the tone* of the essay? That is, are they appropriate to the context, or do they, in your opinion, strike a false note?

POINTS TO LEARN

1. A metaphor, repeated at strategic points, can be an effective unifying device, especially when each repetition involves a minor variation of the metaphor.

2. There is nothing to hinder a writer from using colloquialisms, but they must be appropriate to the context; they must, that is, be appropriate both to the subject and, especially, to the tone of the essay.

SUGGESTIONS FOR WRITING

Write an essay of some 1,000–1,5000 words in which you describe the problems faced by a minority group with which you are familiar. You need not restrict yourself to a group which is a minority solely because of race. Consider also, for instance, a religious minority, a cultural minority (a group trying to establish a chamber orchestra in a logging community), a philosophical minority (people wanting to live a life much different from the conventional), and so on.

IMPROVING YOUR STYLE

Include in your essay at least one metaphor which you will use as a unifying device, a metaphor which describes one of your central points. Introduce it fairly early; then refer to it several times later at points where it will serve to remind the reader of this key element of your presentation. These later references should not be merely repetitions of the central metaphor but variations on it.

L. M. GRAYSON and MICHAEL BLISS

Canada and the Depression

Linda Grayson and Michael Bliss are Canadian historians, and the selection that follows is from their introduction to *The Wretched of Canada: Letters to R. B. Bennett, 1930-1935*. The letters collected in the book present a moving account of the deprivation and despair endured by many Canadians during the Depression years, and these requests for help from Canada's millionaire Prime Minister give the collection a tone of combined pathos and irony. In their introduction Grayson and Bliss set the letters in the larger context of the causes and the development of the Great Depression, and, in this selection, compare its effects on Canada and the United States.

1   The Great Depression affected Canada more severely than any industrial nation except the United States. The causes of the collapse in the two countries, though, were not the same. The American economy ground to a halt because of the drying up of investment opportunities and investor confidence at home; the decline in international trade only made an already difficult situation worse. In Canada the virtual disappearance of markets for export staples—agricultural exports plummetted from $783 million in 1928 to $253 million in 1932, exports of wood products from $289 million to $131 million—triggered the economic decline. The stagnation of domestic investment, except in the mining industry (the hungry nations wanted our gold, not our food), only compounded and complicated the basic problem. In the farm belts of both countries the weather turned sour in keeping with the times.

2   There was a good chance that consistently expansionary government monetary and fiscal policies could have brought the United States back to reasonable prosperity, and Franklin Roosevelt almost understood this. In Canada the same policies would have helped, but by themselves

From *The Wretched of Canada* edited by L. M. Grayson and Michael Bliss. Copyright © University of Toronto Press 1971. Reprinted by permission.

could not have made up for the loss of income from exports. Because the United States was one of Canada's two most important trading partners, levels of American domestic recovery significantly influenced the volume 20 of Canadian trade. The 1930s were a lesson in the vulnerability of an open economy, particularly one specializing in a few staple products, to events outside its borders. There was no such thing as economic independence for the Canadian people.

QUESTIONS

READER AND PURPOSE

1. For whom are the authors writing? Look at the diction they use and the amount of detail they present. How much are they assuming about the reader's knowledge of the Depression?

2. Does this selection have any purpose other than to contrast the causes of the Depression in the United States with those in Canada?

ORGANIZATION

3. The material in this selection is organized in such a way as to lead up to the conclusion at the end of the second paragraph. How are the first two sentences of paragraph 1 used to begin this process?

4. Why do the authors qualify * their topic sentence in sentence 2?

5. How do the next three sentences of paragraph 1 develop the point made in the second sentence? Note that the writers use one sentence to describe the causes of the Depression in the United States and two to describe its causes in Canada. What other devices do they use to emphasize this contrast?

6. Where is the topic sentence of paragraph 2? Why do the authors continue their contrast between the United States and Canada in the first three sentences of this paragraph instead of stating their topic sentence at the outset? Compare sentences four and five of paragraph 2 with the first sentence of paragraph 1. Notice how sentence four serves both as a topic sentence and as a way of emphasizing the important qualification in the second sentence of paragraph 1. How does this help to strengthen the force of the authors' conclusion in the final sentence of paragraph 2?

SENTENCES

7. Compare the structure of the first three sentences of paragraph 1 with the structure of sentence four. What does the change in structure of the fourth sentence serve to emphasize?

8. In the third sentence of paragraph 1 the authors use such words and phrases as *ground to a halt, drying up,* and *decline* to describe what happened to the American economy. What is being emphasized by the use of the words and phrases *virtual disappearance, plummetted,* and *stagnation* in describing the Depression's effects in Canada?

9. Why do the authors use *could have* in the first sentence of paragraph 2 and *would have* in the second sentence?

10. Compare the length of the final sentence of paragraph 2 with the general length of most of the other sentences in the selection. Notice, too, that these other sentences are usually compound * or complex *. How do the length and form of this last sentence contribute to making it an effective conclusion? What would be lost if we rewrote it as follows: "For the Canadian people economic independence was impossible"? How does this change the emphasis of the sentence?

DICTION

11. Look up: *export staples* (7), *expansionary* (14), *monetary* (15), *fiscal* (15), *vulnerability* (21), *open economy* (21-22).

12. What would have been lost if *fell* had been used in place of *plummetted* (7), or *worsened* in place of *compounded and complicated* (11)? Can you think of a better short metaphor * than *turned sour* (12)?

POINTS TO LEARN

1. In developing an exposition that involves a comparison and contrast in which one side is to receive greater emphasis than the other, remember that this emphasis is not achieved merely by giving more space to the side being stressed. Paragraph organization, sentence structures, and diction, can all be used to reinforce your presentation.

2. The conclusion of an exposition of this kind should refer the reader back to its starting point; that is, closing by return *.

3. Strong verbs are preferable to colorless ones, such as *are, is, was, were*.

4. Specific examples should be used sparingly when the intention of the expository writer is to draw conclusions about an event or process rather than to describe the event itself.

SUGGESTIONS FOR WRITING

Develop a simple comparison-contrast paragraph on one of the topics below, emphasizing one side at the expense of the other. Having done this, rewrite the paragraph emphasizing the other side.

Living in western Canada is far better than living in the east.

I would rather study history (or sociology, or mathematics, or
any other subject) than literature.
Knowing one language well is preferable to bilingualism.

IMPROVING YOUR STYLE

1. Compose a brief simple sentence of less than ten words. Cluster stressed
syllables as if you were writing an emphatic conclusion.

2. Write three compound sentences, using different connectives *. Then rewrite each one as a complex sentence, varying the position of your dependent
clauses to produce different kinds of emphasis.

ROY VONTOBEL
Reluctant Villain

Roy Vontobel is an Ottawa-based freelance writer who has held editorial positions with such conservationist periodicals as *Natural History, Nature Canada,*
and the journal of the Canadian Conservation Institute. In his treatment of
the wolverine, the legendary villain of the Canadian north, he demonstrates
how restatement and contrast can be used for effective emphasis of a main
point.

1   From earliest times, the fertile imagination of man has populated
the world with a host of mythical and semi-mythical creatures. Most of
them have become quaint and interesting folklore, but others still haunt
and intrigue us. In curiosity and in fear, man has gazed with self-centred
eye upon the world in which he lives, giving to the beasts around him all 5
manner of human attributes. Unfortunately, this tendency remains with
us. Even today, in the minds of many, deep in the unknown reaches of the
trackless forest, the "good" animals frolic in a Walt Disney wonderland
while "evil" shadows lurk in the underbrush. Ancient prejudices run deep.
2   Perhaps no animal of the American or Eurasian wilderness has 10
been tagged with more negative human characteristics than the wolverine.
Today it is an animal of near mythological proportions. Yet Indian and
trappers' tales notwithstanding—very little is actually known about it.
Wildlife biologists have ventured estimates of its numbers, but studies of
its life and behavior have so far been impossible. As with most mythical 15
creatures, the tales are supported by a modicum of fact. The facts, however, have been gleaned for the most part from rare chance encounters
with the animal, usually when the wolverine is surprised while helping itself to a trapper's food cache or while fleeing into the bush. All in all, the
wolverine has been the prime candidate for the furtive and vicious villain 20

From "Reluctant Villain" by Roy Vontobel (*Nature Canada,* Vol. 8, No. 1, 1979),
reprinted by permission of the author.

of the North. The time could come when that legacy is all that is ever known about it.

QUESTIONS

1. Is Vontobel writing for an audience familiar with his subject? What aspects of the first paragraph would you use to support your opinion?
2. How does the tone * of the second paragraph differ from that of paragraph 1? In what other ways does the author emphasize his reasons for taking the wolverine seriously?

3. Vontobel develops paragraph 1 by restatement of the point made in the first sentence. He also uses this paragraph to pass judgment on anthropomorphic thinking (the giving of human attributes to animals). What other words or phrases, such as *self-centred eye*, indicate the kind of judgment he is making?
4. How does the last sentence summarize paragraph 1 while at the same time taking us back to the opening sentence?
5. Explain how the first sentence of paragraph 2 serves both as a topic sentence and as a link with the preceding paragraph. What specific words in paragarph 2 also provide such links?
6. Vontobel contrasts fantasy with fact in his second paragraph. How does he stress this contrast? Compare, for example, the fifth sentence of paragraph 1 with the fifth sentence of paragraph 2.
7. Note that the two paragraphs are also organized by references to "time." Point out these references, and trace the progression of Vontobel's exposition from the past (*earliest times*) to the future (*the time could come*).

8. Vontobel restates his point in three differently-constructed sentences to open the first paragraph. Describe the structure of each of these sentences; note the participial * construction in sentence three. If the three sentences had all been structured in the same way would they have been more effective? How would the rhythm of sentence three be affected if Vontobel had written "in curiosity and fear"?
9. What emphasis is achieved by the short fourth sentence of paragraph 1 and by the positioning of the adverb *unfortunately?*
10. What does the interrupted movement * of the fifth sentence of paragraph

1 serve to emphasize? What does the allusion * to Walt Disney contribute to the sentence?

11. Vontobel ends paragraph 1 with a short simple sentence. Explain why this serves well as a conclusion. What would be the result if the sentence were omitted?

12. Describe the ways in which Vontobel varies his sentence structures and sentence lengths in paragraph 2. Why do the sentences of this paragraph make more use of specific detail than those of paragraph 1?

DICTION

13. Look up: *mythical* (2), *quaint* (3), *folklore* (3), *frolic* (8), *prejudices* (9), *modicum* (16).

14. Why does the author put quotation marks around *good* (8) and *evil* (9)?

15. What would be lost if Vontobel had not paralleled *haunt and intrigue* (3-4) with *in curiosity and in fear* (4)?

16. What does *tagged* mean to you? Does it have another meaning for a zoologist?

17. Is Vontobel's use of *trackless forest* (8) ironic *?

POINTS TO LEARN

1. Restatement may involve repeating the same key words or repeating the same idea in different words.

2. Sentence structures and lengths can be varied for effective emphasis of main ideas.

3. Participial phrases are economic and allow you to subordinate ideas of secondary importance.

4. Interrupting phrases can be used both to vary sentence rhythms and to reinforce the main point of a sentence.

SUGGESTIONS FOR WRITING

Using restatement, compose two short paragraphs of six or seven sentences each (about 120 words) in which you develop one of the topics below. Contrast the main point of the second paragraph with that of the first—as Vontobel contrasts fantasy and fact—and be sure to provide a connecting link between the two paragraphs. (If none of the topics appeals to you, devise one of your own.)

Kittens seem naturally appealing.

Most people hate mathematics (or English, history, physics, whatever).

Automobiles are taken for granted as necessities in our way of life.

Canadians in other provinces generally view the people of Quebec as belonging to a totally different culture.

IMPROVING YOUR STYLE

1. Conclude one of the sentences in your essay with a participial phrase.
2. Write three sentences in which you vary the position of adverbs such as *unfortunately*.
3. Vary your sentence openings as follows:

> Begin two sentences directly with the subject-verb nucleus.
> Begin one with a prepositional phrase.
> Begin one with two interrupting phrases followed by the subject-verb nucleus.
> Begin one with a participial phrase.

4. Write two sentences in which you make use of allusions (one mythological or historical, and one drawn from current events).

A Report on the New Feminism

A journalist and free-lance writer, Ellen Willis is also rock critic for *The New Yorker* magazine. In the essay from which this selection comes she discusses the development of and justification for women's liberation. Here she offers a striking comparison between the situations of women and of black people. She confines herself to similarities, a reminder that it is important when developing a comparison to decide what you want to emphasize: likenesses, dissimilarities, or both.

1   Like the early feminist movement, which grew out of the campaign to end slavery, the present-day women's movement has been inspired and influenced by the black liberation struggle. The situation of women and blacks is similar in many ways. Just as blacks live in a world defined by whites, women live in a world defined by males. (The generic 5 term for human being is "man"; "woman" means "wife of man.") To be female or black is to be peculiar; whiteness and maleness are the norm. Newspapers do not have "men's pages," nor would anyone think of discussing the "man problem." Racial and sexual stereotypes also resemble each other: women, like blacks, are said to be childish, incapable of ab- 10 stract reasoning, innately submissive, biologically suited for menial tasks, emotional, close to nature.

2   Most important, both women and blacks have a history of slavery—only female slavery goes back much further. From the beginnings of civilization until very recently, women in most societies were literally the 15 property of their husbands and fathers. Even now, many vestiges of that chattel status persist in law and custom. Wives are still known by their husbands' names. In many states, a wife is legally required to perform domestic services, have sexual relations on demand if her health permits, and live with her husband wherever *he* chooses or be guilty of desertion. Res- 20

From *Mademoiselle*, September, 1969. Copyright © 1969 by Condé Nast Inc. Reprinted by permission of the author.

taurants, bars, and other public accommodations can legally refuse to admit a woman without a male escort or exclude her altogether. And vote or
no vote, politics has remained a male preserve. Women make up more
than half the population, but hold less than 1 per cent of elected offices.
They also get few political appointments, except for the inevitable "ad- 25
viser on consumer affairs" (women's place is in the supermarket).

3   In any case, the "emancipated" woman, like the freed slaves, has
merely substituted economic dependence for legal subjection. According
to Government statistics, white women workers earn even less than black
men. Most women, especially mothers, must depend on men to support 30
them, and that fact alone gives men power over their lives.

QUESTIONS

READER AND PURPOSE

1. Where is the focus of Willis' comparison—on blacks, on women, or equally
on both?
2. In her essay Willis is trying to convince her readers that women deserve true
equality but do not yet have it. How might this comparison between women
and blacks fit into her overall strategy? (Her next paragraph begins: "By now,
almost everyone recognizes racism as an evil. But in spite of all the parallels,
most people either defend sexism or deny its existence.")

ORGANIZATION

3. Which one sentence best serves as the topic of all three paragraphs?
4. Which serves as the topic of paragraph 1? Is the comparison in this paragraph organized by devoting one part to women and another part to blacks?
If not, how is it organized?
5. Where in paragraph 1 does the writer use illustrations?
6. How is the parenthetical statement in lines 5-6 related to the preceding
idea? Do the parentheses help to signal the relationship?
7. What is the topic sentence of paragraph 2? How does the focus of this
paragraph change from that of the first?
8. The second paragraph develops two points. Which sentence sets up the
first? The second? Such sentences might be called "sub-topic statements"; they
are useful for organizing portions of a paragraph.
9. Are there any illustrations in paragraph 2?
10. How is the parenthetical remark in line 26 related to what has just been
said? What is Willis implying here?
11. What is the topic of paragraph 3? How is it supported?

SENTENCES

12. The third sentence of paragraph 1 is balanced *, that is, split into roughly equal halves by a central pause. How many other sentences in this paragraph are balanced?

13. The longest sentences of paragraph 1 are the first and the last. How many words has each? How many words has each of the five sentences between them? Notice a pattern of sentence structure here: a series of shorter sentences of similar length enclosed within two longer statements.

14. Identify the parallel * elements in the sentence in lines 18-20. Point out one or two other instances of parallelism in this selection.

15. What does the colon in line 10 signal?

16. Suppose the two sentences in lines 5-7 used coordination * instead of semicolons:

> (The generic term for human being is "man," and "woman" means "wife of man.") To be female or black is to be peculiar, and whiteness and maleness are the norm.

Would the passage be as clear? If not, why? What rule might you suggest about when independent clauses are better separated by a semicolon than joined by *and?*

DICTION

17. Look up: *peculiar* (7), *norm* (7), *stereotype* (9), *menial* (11), *literally* (15), *vestiges* (16), *exclude* (22).

18. What is implied by the italicization of *he* in line 20? In what sense is *inevitable* (25) used ironically *? Why does Willis place quotation marks around *emancipate* (27)?

19. What relationships in thought do these connectives * signal: *nor* (8), *and* (22), *in any case* (27)?

POINTS TO LEARN

1. A broad topic statement, sometimes called a thesis statement, may introduce several paragraphs or even an entire essay.

2. Portions of a paragraph are sometimes set up by sub-topic statements.

3. A comparison may be developed within a single sentence, the total effect being built up by a series of such sentences.

4. Parentheses usually signal a special relationship between the enclosed remark and its context—for instance, that the remark is a definition, an illustration, an ironic comment.

5. A well-written paragraph often reveals some pattern in the structure and length of its sentences.

6. Semicolons are preferable to *and* between independent clauses when the second clause simply restates or particularizes what is expressed in the first.

SUGGESTIONS FOR WRITING

In two paragraphs (about 300 words total) develop the similarities between one of the following pairs of subjects:

> Husbands (or wives) and slavemasters
>
> Grade-school children and slaves (or composition students and slaves)
>
> Babies and pets

Give thought to focus—whether to concentrate upon one subject at the expense of the other or to deal evenly with both. Consider, too, whether you want to organize the comparison by devoting one paragraph to subject A, the other to B; by giving part of each paragraph to A, part to B; or by building the total comparison out of a series of specific similarities, each expressed within a single sentence.

IMPROVING YOUR STYLE

1. Compose several balanced sentences in your paragraphs.
2. Use parentheses to enclose an ironic comment, but let the reader see the irony for himself.
3. Introduce a clause or sentence by *nor*.

Bringing Up Children

Ruth Benedict (1887-1948) was an American anthropologist. Her most famous work is *Patterns of Culture*. *The Chrysanthemum and the Sword*, from which this excerpt comes, is a study of Japanese culture, a subject of much interest to Americans during and immediately after World War II. Here she contrasts the modes of child-rearing in Japan and the United States.

1   Japanese babies are not brought up in the fashion that a thoughtful Westerner might suppose. American parents, training their children for a life so much less circumspect and stoical than life in Japan, nevertheless begin immediately to prove to the baby that his own little wishes are not supreme in this world. We put him immediately on a feeding schedule 5 and a sleeping schedule, and no matter how he fusses before bottle time or bed time, he has to wait. A little later his mother strikes his hand to make him take his finger out of his mouth or away from other parts of his body. His mother is frequently out of sight and when she goes out he has to stay behind. He has to be weaned before he prefers other foods, or if he is bot- 10 tle fed, he has to give up his bottle. There are certain foods that are good for him and he must eat them. He is punished when he does not do what is right. What is more natural for an American to suppose than that these disciplines are redoubled for the little Japanese baby who, when he is a finished product, will have to subordinate his own wishes and be so care- 15 ful and punctilious an observer of such a demanding code?

2   The Japanese, however, do not follow this course. The arc of life in Japan is plotted in opposite fashion to that in the United States. It is a great shallow U-curve with maximum freedom and indulgence allowed to babies and to the old. Restrictions are slowly increased after babyhood till 20

From *The Chrysanthemum and the Sword* by Ruth Benedict. Copyright 1946 by Ruth Benedict. Copyright © renewed 1974 by Robert G. Freeman. Reprinted by permission of Houghton Mifflin Company.

having one's own way reaches a low just before and after marriage. This low line continues many years during the prime of life, but the arc gradually ascends again until after the age of sixty men and women are almost as unhampered by shame as little children are. In the United States we stand this curve upside down. Firm disciplines are directed toward the in- 25 fant and these are gradually relaxed as the child grows in strength until a man runs his own life when he gets a self-supporting job and when he sets up a household of his own. The prime of life is with us the high point of freedom and initiative. Restrictions begin to appear as men lose their grip or their energy or become dependent. It is difficult for Americans even to 30 fantasy a life arranged according to the Japanese pattern. It seems to us to fly in the face of reality.

3   Both the American and the Japanese arrangement of the arc of life, however, have in point of fact secured in each country the individual's energetic participation in his culture during the prime of life. To se- 35 cure this end in the United States, we rely on increasing his freedom of choice during this period. The Japanese rely on maximizing the restraints upon him. The fact that a man is at this time at the peak of his physical strength and at the peak of his earning powers does not make him master of his own life. They have great confidence that restraint is good mental 40 training (*shuyo*) and produces results not attained by freedom. But the Japanese increase of restraints upon the man or woman during their most active producing periods by no means indicates that these restraints cover the whole of life. Childhood and old age are "free areas."

QUESTIONS

READER AND PURPOSE

1. Interest in Japan had been thrust upon Americans by Pearl Harbor and the ensuing war. Usually the Japanese were presented in the garish colors of propaganda. Does Benedict's purpose seem propagandistic? If not, how would you describe it? What attitude toward the Japanese does she assume to exist in her readers?

ORGANIZATION

2. The opening sentence is not really the topic of paragraph 1. What does it set up? Which sentence does state the topic of the first paragraph? Where in that paragraph does the writer return to the idea expressed in the opening sentence?

3. Does the first paragraph focus equally upon both terms of the comparison?

4. How does the sentence in lines 13-16 prepare for paragraph 2?

5. Why is *however* used in the opening of the new paragraph? What words in this same sentence point back to the first paragraph? What phrase in the initial sentence of paragraph 3 has a similar linking function?

6. How does the focus of the comparison change in paragraph 2? This paragraph falls into two parts. Mark the dividing point. Here is a good example of one way of developing a contrast within a single paragraph.

7. Summarize how the focus of Benedict's comparison shifts from paragraph to paragraph. Where is it primarily concerned with America? Where with Japan? Where does it deal chiefly with a difference between the two cultures? Where with something they have in common?

SENTENCES

8. Benedict's writing avoids monotony by several means. For one thing, some sentences move straight through to their conclusions (the opening sentence, for example), while others employ interrupted movement * (the first sentence of paragraph 2). Find several other instances of each kind of sentence.

9. Another way she keeps her style interesting is by varying sentence length so that relatively long and complicated statements are relieved by shorter, simpler ones. Thus in paragraph 3 the final sentence is much shorter than the one that precedes it. Where else in this selection do you find such brief sentences? How, incidentally, is the idea expressed in the last sentence of paragraph 3 related to the preceding thought?

10. But while she skillfully varies her sentence style, Benedict also exploits similarity of pattern. In the first paragraph what other clauses repeat the syntactic pattern of "he has to wait"? Why is the repetition advantageous here?

11. The second sentence contains a participial phrase * ("training their children for a life so much less circumspect and stoical than life in Japan"). Would it blur the emphasis of the paragraph to express this as a separate sentence: "American parents train their children for a life so much less circumspect and stoical than life in Japan. Nevertheless they begin immediately . . ."?

12. The participial phrase is followed by a strong word of contradiction. What contradiction in thought is signalled by *nevertheless?*

DICTION

13. Look up: *thoughtful* (1), *unhampered* (24), *initiative* (29), *restraint* (40).

14. Check the etymologies * of the following words and explain how their present meanings evolve naturally out of their original senses: *schedule* (5), *punctilious* (16), *indulgence* (19).

15. Why are the following substitutions less effective in Benedict's context: *complains* for *fusses* (6), *adult* for *finished product* (15), *imagine* for *fantasy* (31)?

16. *Arc of life* (17) is a figure of speech *. What kind? Why is it effective here?

17. What relationship in thought is conveyed by the phrase *in point of fact* (34)? For example, if the sentence "We had a poor day of fishing" were followed by a sentence beginning "In point of fact," what would you expect the second sentence to say? What variations of this phrase can you think of? You should add these to your working list of connectives.

POINTS TO LEARN

1. The focus of a comparison need not remain fixed; it may be adjusted from time to time as suits the writer's needs.

2. A topic statement may set up more than a single paragraph.

3. Some variety in the length and complexity of sentences helps to sustain the reader's interest.

SUGGESTIONS FOR WRITING

You may know enough about two different ethnic groups to compose a short composition of two or three paragraphs contrasting how they rear their children. Or if not differences in child-rearing, perhaps in wedding customs, recreations, and so on. Should you have no knowledge of cultures other than your own, contrast how two friends or relatives handle their children. Do not be afraid to alter the focus of your comparison, but do it purposefully rather than haphazardly.

IMPROVING YOUR STYLE

1. In at least two places use short sentences for variety and emphasis.

2. Include a sentence with a participial phrase in an interrupting position between subject and verb.

3. Compose a metaphor *.

4. Begin one sentence with *in point of fact* (or simply *in fact*).

Tribal Gods

Robert Fulford is one of Canada's most respected journalists. His wide range of interests includes literature, the fine arts, popular culture, and Canadian social issues. Among his books are *Crisis at the Victory Burlesk: Culture, Politics and Other Diversions* (1968), and *An Introduction to the Arts in Canada* (1977). Fulford is the editor of *Saturday Night* and (under the pseudonym of Marshall Delaney) an influential reviewer of films. In his discussion of Marshall McLuhan and John Lennon, Fulford compares two vastly dissimilar persons—a brilliant Canadian intellectual, and a widely acclaimed rock musician.

1   The peaceful death in his sleep of Marshall McLuhan and the violent death by gunfire of John Lennon, coming within a few weeks of each other this winter, evoked poignant memories of the 1960s, the period when they were both at the peak of their reputations—when McLuhan's *mass-media* theories raced swiftly around the world, and when Lennon, as   5 the pivotal figure in the Beatles, could rightly claim to be better known than Jesus. But their lives were linked by much more than the accidental timing of their deaths. McLuhan, after all, was the prophet of a new age. Lennon was the embodiment of that age. And Lennon never embodied it more fully—more richly, suggestively, and eloquently—than in the week   10 after his death. The wave of grief that swept through the *mass media* and touched hundreds of millions of people now looks like a key moment in the history of the electronic revolution that McLuhan spent his career describing. It was the textbook example—one might almost say the fulfilment—of the theories of McLuhan.   15

2   McLuhan taught us to see the great event of our own time as the retribalizing of humanity. He pointed out that the invention of printing in the fifteenth century had made western humanity think in a linear way. It had shaped our minds to the logic of the printed word, and in the process had created everything from Protestantism to the assembly line. But now,   20

From *Saturday Night*, 96, 3 (March 1981). Reprinted by permission.

in the twentieth century, all this was changing. Radio and television were moving man back toward his pre-literate origins. The world was becoming one great tribe, with tribal emotions and tribal responses. Electronic culture was creating a global village—McLuhan's central metaphor—in which our separate intellectual identities would merge. Individualism was coming 25 to the end of its course. Now we would again, as in medieval times and before, experience life collectively—this time at the push of a button.

3   Moreover, we would experience it without the intrusion of logic. McLuhan became infamous in the academic world of the 1950s because he saw the end of the book culture that began with Johann Gutenberg in the 30 1430s. McLuhan didn't argue that books would soon cease to exist, as some thought he did. He argued that they had ceased to be the central means of communication in our culture, and that as they slipped from their place, the logic they embodied—one-word-after-another linear thinking—was also moving from the core to the periphery of human consciousness. Whether 35 McLuhan approved of this process is irrelevant (it was never easy to tell what he felt about something, and often he changed his mind). The technical details he described and invented—such as the transition from visual culture (books) to aural culture (post-books), or that whole baffling business about "hot" and "cool" media—had mostly lost their meaning by the end 40 of his career. What mattered, in all the confusion and contradiction of his work, was his persistent vision of a world returning to instinct, a world jerked out of five centuries of rule by logic. There were those who saw this vision as terrifying and those who saw it as impossible. There were also those who grasped it eagerly. In any case, most of the evidence I've noticed 45 has tended to support his encompassing idea.

4   The grief that followed John Lennon's death was phenomenal, and can be explained only in McLuhan's terms. Certainly it was entirely lacking in any quality related to logic. There was a powerful instinct at the core of it, an instinct for which McLuhan prepared us.   50

5   Lennon's followers had ruthlessly discarded him years before he died. They had rejected outright (by refusing to buy his records) his claim to be a performer on his own and a songwriter of independent stature. For ten years or so he had been, in mass-market terms, a failure. At his death he had recently completed a new record, yet one more attempt to overcome this 55 rejection and move into prominence again. He liked to say that, secure in his millions, he no longer cared about celebrity. In fact, at the end he was seeking it.

6   In those last seven or eight years he also abandoned the role of political spokesman for his generation. During the 1960s and early 1970s he 60

adopted a passionate anti-American stand on the Vietnam issue, and thereby established himself as a man of peace. But when that war ended and American youth retreated from the streets, he fell silent. Wars and massacres continued to appear all over the globe, and Lennon was not heard from. So far as the public was aware, he spent the 1970s mostly in silence, buying real 65 estate, emerging occasionally to make a record, occasionally to give a truculent interview. In his entire professional life there was only one important issue involving peace and reconciliation: his break with Paul McCartney, with whom he wrote the best songs of the 1960s. His failure (and McCartney's) to resolve that issue resulted in artistic decline for both of them. 70

7   None of this was touched on in the unprecedented media explosion that followed his murder. The media people, sensing what was appropriate, told the world in hundreds of ways that the loss of John Lennon was a terrible blow—even though most of the people who watched and listened to these eulogies hadn't cared to listen to Lennon's new music in years. The 75 media people also proclaimed Lennon a man of peace, a good man, a gentle man—things none of them would have bothered to say about him five minutes before he died. And the public immediately began to feed back the same messages, in TV man-in-the-street interviews, in letters to the editor, in phone calls to radio stations. Hundreds of thousands of people announced 80 themselves grief-stricken by the loss of a man from whom, effectively, they'd heard nothing in years. There was even a news story saying that a psychiatric institution in the United States had set up a group therapy program in which those who were stunned into severe depression by Lennon's death could learn how to deal with their sorrow. 85

8   McLuhan would have said that logical reservations about Lennon's career and his public posture were simply irrelevant at a moment like this; and he would have been right. Lennon's public life was lived electronically (though he did write two books of humour—both of them influenced by McLuhan's hero, James Joyce). 90

9   Electronic communications reach us at a level below, or beyond, logic. We were tuned to Lennon in the 1960s on a mythic, emotional wave-length, somewhere near the wave-length on which we receive impressions in childhood or the one on which we take in, without knowing it, the messages of the cleverest TV advertisers. In the 1960s the Beatles, their 95 careers charted by the genius of Brian Epstein, fitted themselves snugly into the new electronic format. They reached us simultaneously through records, radio, TV, movies, and still photos. The result of this sound-and-pictures bombardment was to demolish the distancing effect which is the main characteristic of print communication. 100

10   At this subliminal level, anything like logic—anything that goes under the term "thinking"—is no more than annoyance. We shut it out before it appears. To ask someone who has been put in this state by the electronic media to *think* even a little is like asking a Russian Orthodox peasant of the Middle Ages, praying before an icon, to analyze the way the   105 artist has depicted the virgin; or like asking a nineteenth-century Inuit, confronted by the terror of shamanism, to sign up for a course in comparative religion.

11   In the electronic world that McLuhan prophesied, assumptions are to be shared, not questioned—and the unexamined life (contrary to   110 Socrates' famous remark) is the *only* one that is worth living, the only one that provides a sense of wholeness and reassurance. That strange week when Lennon died, the people of the world went logically about their logical tasks—tasks inherited, McLuhan would say, from the pre-electronic era. They did their work, as thoughtfully or thoughtlessly as before, but   115 what mattered to them was something distant from work, from thought, from the logic that formed the society we all inherited from our parents. What mattered was their shared mourning for a tribal god.

QUESTIONS

READER AND PURPOSE

1. In this essay Fulford begins by showing McLuhan and Lennon as comparable in terms of their influence in the 1960s. Does he elaborate this point of comparison in the body of the essay?
2. Fulford emphasizes the effect of McLuhan's theories and the extent of the mourning for Lennon. Do we all live now in a global village, or is Fulford writing for an audience in only that part of the world (mainly the industrialized countries) most affected by new technologies?
3. Is it ironic* that Fulford is using print, and a logical structure, to describe events that are, he says, best understood in other terms? Do you think that Fulford himself, although he understands and describes the displacement of logic, approves of this change?

ORGANIZATION

4. Identify the topic sentence of paragraph 1.
5. In his essay Fulford argues that to understand the reaction to Lennon's death we must first understand McLuhan's theories. Where, in paragraph 1, is this strategy of organization indicated?
6. Identify the connectives* used in paragraphs 2 and 3.

7. What are the two key words from paragraphs 2 and 3 that Fulford uses in paragraph 4? How does this paragraph function to change the focus from McLuhan to Lennon? Why is it shorter than the preceding paragraphs?

8. In paragraphs 5 and 6 Fulford discusses Lennon's decline rather than his popularity during the 1960s. Explain how this leads effectively into paragraph 7.

9. What key word (or variants of it) is repeated in paragraphs 8 to 10? How is it used in paragraph 11 to establish the conclusion?

10. What references to the opening paragraph can be found in the conclusion?

11. How does the concluding paragraph make clear the main point of comparison between McLuhan and Lennon?

SENTENCES

12. Analyze the structure of the opening sentence and identify the use of antithesis*, interrupted movement*, and parallelism*.

13. Could commas or parentheses replace the dashes in paragraph 1 without weakening the effect of the sentences?

14. Would the first sentence of paragraph 4 be improved by eliminating the comma?

15. Fulford varies his use of personal pronouns. In some sentences we find "we," "us," and "our"; in others "those," "them," "they," "their." In paragraph 3 he makes his only use of the first-person singular: "I've." Locate all the personal pronouns in this essay and decide what they reveal about the author's point of view*.

16. Should the complete sentence in parentheses in paragraph 3 have been left to stand in the more usual form?

17. What would be the result if "effectively" (81) were removed from the sentence?

DICTION

18. Look up: *periphery* (35), *truculent* (66), *eulogies* (75), *subliminal* (101), *icon* (105), *shamanism* (107).

19. Find the etymology* of *phenomenal* (47). Is the word used correctly here?

20. Identify the controlling figure of speech* in paragraph 10.

21. What connotations* does the term *media people* (72) have as Fulford uses it?

22. Is the phrase *announced themselves grief-stricken* (80) an example of irony*?

POINTS TO LEARN

1. Comparison need not be only a listing of the aspects two subjects have in common.

2. Key words can be repeated to organize an argument and to establish its conclusion.

3. The writer's attitude to his subject and his audience may be indicated by careful choice of pronouns.

SUGGESTIONS FOR WRITING

Write a short essay of five or six paragraphs in which you compare two public figures, devoting one paragraph in the body of the paper to A and the next to B, and so on. Then rewrite the essay, this time dealing in the first part with A, in the second with B, and in the introduction and conclusion with both.

IMPROVING YOUR STYLE

In your essay include:

1. Three sentences, using antithesis in the first, interrupted movement in the second, and parallelism in the third.

2. A paragraph in which you use pronouns to indicate a group to which you belong ("we," "us"), one to which you do not belong ("they," "them"), and yourself.

3. Three sentences, setting material off with commas in one, parentheses in the second, and dashes in the third. Be prepared to defend your choice of punctuation in each case.

L. M. MYERS

The Parts of Speech

L. M. Myers is a professor of English, whose book *The Roots of Modern English* is a very readable history of the language. In this excerpt he is presenting the case for a change in the kind of grammar we use to analyze and talk about our language. His strategy is to employ an analogy, which is a special kind of comparison. Analogies compare two things, often of dissimilar natures, in order to suggest that what is true of one applies to the other.

1   It is quite easy for an American to see that our decimal system of coinage is better than the traditional (but soon to be changed) British system of pounds, shillings, and pence (not to mention half-crowns and guineas), because it is simpler in principle and very much more convenient to handle. But it is not nearly so easy for us to see that the metric system 5 of weights and measures has exactly the same advantage over our curious conglomeration of ounces and pounds, inches, feet, yards, and miles, pints, quarts, and gallons, and so forth. We may admit the advantage in theory, but we are likely to have a deep-seated feeling that our units are somehow real, and the metrical ones merely clever tricks. It is very hard indeed for 10 most of us to think of a hundred meters as simply a hundred meters, or as a tenth of a kilometer. We feel that it is really a hundred and nine-point-something yards, and wonder why the silly foreigners couldn't at least have made it come out an even hundred and ten. And of course the kilometer is too short to be a serious way of measuring long distances. How can any- 15 body be satisfied with anything that isn't quite five-eighths of a mile?

2   In a very similar way most of us have a strong feeling that the sort of grammar to which we were exposed when young is somehow real, and that any different analysis of our language is tampering with the truth. But there is no more reason to believe that all words fall naturally into eight 20

From L. M. Myers, *The Roots of Modern English*. Copyright © 1966 by Little, Brown and Company (Inc.). Reprinted by permission.

parts of speech than there is to think that silver comes naturally in either dollars or shillings, or butter in pounds or kilograms. We may have been taught that the sacred eight were permanent realities, no more open to question than the Ten Commandments or the multiplication table. Yet, since the second English grammar was written, there has never been a time 25 when "the authorities" agreed on what or how many the parts were (every number from zero to ten has been advocated), to say nothing of what words belonged in each part; and just now the disagreement is particularly acute.

QUESTIONS

READER AND PURPOSE

1. Professor Myers wishes to drive home an elusive idea: that it is nonsense to believe, as some people do, that there must be eight parts of speech and only eight. To make his point he employs an analogy, comparing the rather abstruse subject of parts of speech to something with which his readers are more familiar. Thus he draws a contrast between how Americans feel about their system of coinage (as compared with that then in use in Great Britain) and how they feel about the inch-pound system of measurements (as compared with the metric system). How do their attitudes differ in these two cases? Are their reactions consistent or illogical?

2. Explain how the analogy of coinage and of weights and measures supports Professor Myers' contention about the eight parts of speech.

ORGANIZATION

3. Does the writer begin with his main point or with his analogy?

4. In which sentence does he make it clear that he is developing his topic by analogy?

5. Which words in the first sentence of the opening paragraph are repeated in the second sentence? Where else in this paragraph do you find similar repetition of key terms? Note that these repetitions help to unify the paragraph. Unity is also aided by beginning some sentences with connectors *. Point these out.

6. How is the second paragraph tied to the first? Show how each sentence in this paragraph is linked to what precedes it.

SENTENCES

7. Suppose the word *that* were omitted in line 19: how would this affect the clarity of the sentence? To what earlier construction is the *that*-clause in line 19 parallel *?

8. Is Professor Myers asking a genuine question in lines 15-16?
9. Why is this revision inferior to the sentence in the text?

> *Revision:* We are likely to have a deep-seated feeling that our units are somehow real, and the metrical ones merely clever tricks, but we may admit the advantage in theory.

> *Myers:* "We may admit the advantage in theory, but we are likely to have a deep-seated feeling that our units are somehow real, and the metrical ones merely clever tricks." (8-10)

DICTION

10. Look up: *half-crowns* (3), *guineas* (4), *conglomeration* (7), *grammar* (18), *tampering* (19), *advocated* (27).
11. Why is *the authorities* (26) in quotation marks? Is there any irony * in Professor Myers' use of the term *sacred* in line 23? What is he mocking by his use of *silly* in the phrase *silly foreigners* (13)? And why, finally, does he preface *real* with *somehow*, both in line 9 and again in line 18?

POINTS TO LEARN

1. Analogy is a useful way of developing a subject.
2. Although analogy does not constitute logical proof (except under very special circumstances), it is an effective means of explaining a difficult or unfamiliar subject.

SUGGESTIONS FOR WRITING

Write a short essay developed by an analogy, choosing one of the subjects listed below or a comparable topic. Obviously there are differences between the things to be compared, but in developing your analogy do not waste time enumerating the differences, for that will only blur your focus and weaken your analogy. Work only with similarities.

> Learning the parts of a piece of machinery and learning grammar (of English or any other language). In either case one must learn new names, get to know how the various parts work, and so on.

> A cafeteria and college. Each offers a bewildering number of choices, and in each one may choose unwisely.

> Jugglers and good writers. Both must keep several things going at once.

> Algebra and abstract art. Both are concerned with patterns and relationships rather than with specific things, not with John who has three more apples than Mary, but with x + 3.

IMPROVING YOUR STYLE

1. Somewhere in your essay employ a rhetorical question *.
2. Be sure to provide an adequate link when you move from the first part of your analogy to the second.
3. Experiment with irony *, using one or two words in an ironic sense. Don't be heavy-handed; let the reader get the point for himself.

The Dissertation and the Mime

Nannette Vonnegut Mengel's essay appeared in an anthology by various women scholars, writers, and artists discussing the problems of work—especially professional and creative work—faced by women in our society. Mengel describes her experience in graduate school, in this excerpt the difficulties of writing her dissertation. She focuses her anxieties and frustrations by means of a compelling analogy.

1   The hardest part of graduate school was the dissertation. Yet, it was only here that the pieces of the work puzzle fell into place and that I gradually came to find myself in my work.

2   I remember many images of emotional hardship in dreams and fantasies during the three and a half years that I struggled to write my thesis, to find ways to "see" Dickens' novels whole and my own relationship to them clearly. The most persistent image—the one that best describes my fears as I worked—was of Svi Kanar, a student of Marcel Marceau, performing a pantomime called "The Ball."

3   It was May 1968; the thesis I was hatching on Dickens' comic technique in *Pickwick Papers*, a subject I had chosen because I thought I could live with it happily for months, was something I was not often proud of. It seemed a kind of comic luxury in a world that was everywhere in trouble. President Johnson had recently announced that he would not run for a second term and the black-student movement had just struck the campus with disturbing force. My Ph.D. orals were postponed because tear gas filled the English building. Who wouldn't have doubted, daily, the value of scholarship such as mine? But I always came back to my thesis. At the age of thirty-four I had gone too far in my graduate work to turn back.

From "Coming of Age the Long Way Around" in *Working It Out*, edited by Sara Ruddick and Pamela Daniels. Copyright © 1977 by Sara Ruddick and Pamela Daniels. Reprinted by permission of Pantheon Books, a Division of Random House, Inc.

4   It was 1968, and Kanar's mime gave symbolic shape to my anxi-   20
eties about myself as an academic. As his act began, Kanar, alone on the
stage, playfully bounced an imaginary basketball, tossed it in the air, and
dribbled rhythmically at varying speeds. Suddenly the imaginary ball asserted a life of its own; it began to expand at a frightening rate so that his
pleasure, and ours as well, turned to panic—it seemed unlikely that he   25
could regain control of the ball. It was a relief to see him stop the ball by
main force from expanding, and then to watch him, with enormous exer-
tion, force it back toward its original size until, finally, he had a basketball
again. True, he handled the ball more warily now, but it was once again
manageable. The game could go on.   30
5   The next time the ball asserted its mysterious growing-power,
Kanar was not so successful. He strained valiantly to contain it, but it became so large that his arms could barely support it. He ended the act in
the posture of Atlas, one knee on the floor, the ball weighing on his shoulders and the back of his neck. I remember that I clapped very hard for   35
Kanar's performance and that my hands were cold. There was something
familiar in it that frightened me. In retrospect, his act seems to have prefigured the life that lay ahead of me as I tried to control my thesis, to keep
it within bounds.
6   I do not remember that Kanar acted out the opposite problem—   40
shrinkage, the fear that the ball would diminish to the size of a jaw-
breaker and slip between the boards—but I retain that image of him as
clearly in my mind's eye as if he had. What if my ideas came to nothing?
What if my dissertation went the other way and vanished? These two fantasies of myself as Atlas and anti-Atlas were especially strong as my topic   45
slowly evolved. I was dismayed at the accumulation of my earlier drafts
and papers. Although it was painfully clear that I could not use most of
them, I was determined to do something with those excruciatingly hard-
won bits of work. Stubbornly, I filed them for later use, and at the same
time loaded my dissertation for a while with a pointless accumulation of   50
pages—until it reminded me of the children's book *Every Haystack Doesn't
Have a Needle.*
7   Weeding lines from draft after draft as my adviser returned them,
trying to glean whatever was salvageable, endlessly, gratefully, unquestion-
ingly, I retyped the phrases he liked. If he made the smallest positive sign   55
in the margin, I would not let that sentence go. Those phrases asserted a
claim to immortality even stronger than the mortification I felt each time
I redid them. On the one side, then, I was forever discarding, and on the

other, I was forever preserving, as I swung between the polar fears symbolized in Kanar's mime: the fear that my work was trivial and liable to   60
evaporate, and the fear that it was so enormous it would immobilize me.

QUESTIONS

READER AND PURPOSE

1. What advantages are there in explaining anxiety in terms of a pantomimist
struggling with an imaginary ball?
2. Do you think that Mengel is writing for people much like herself, or for
readers whose backgrounds and experience are very different? What kind of
knowledge does she expect her readers to have?

ORGANIZATION

3. How do paragraphs 1 and 2 relate to the rest of this selection? How does
paragraph 3? How do 4 and 5? 6 and 7? Make a rough outline of the passage,
giving a synoptic title to each major section and indicating which paragraphs
it includes.
4. What is the topic sentence of the third paragraph? How is it supported?
Do the final two sentences of this paragraph change the topic slightly?
5. The first sentence of paragraph 4 does not state the topic of this paragraph.
What does it do? Which is the topic sentence of paragraph 4? How is the
paragraph organized?
6. What is the topic sentence of the fifth paragraph? Where does the paragraph change direction?

SENTENCES

7. Most of Mengel's sentences are relatively long, containing at least two
clauses. Where does she use short simple * sentences effectively?
8. The rhetorical question * in lines 17-18 is a device of emphasis. What is
the writer asserting here? Are the two rhetorical questions in 43-44 also a form
of emphatic statement?
9. The phrase "to find ways to 'see' Dickens' novels" (6) is an appositive *.
To what? There is also an appositive in the very next line; identify it.
10. Notice that Mengel puts dashes around the appositive in lines 7-8. Would
commas have worked? Are dashes preferable here? Would the construction in
line 25 be clearer if the dashes were replaced by a comma plus *and*?
11. Suppose the semicolon in line 24 were similarly replaced by a comma plus
and: would it be an improvement?
12. Identify the parallel * elements in the sentence in lines 21-23. Why is
parallelism an especially good way of organizing this sentence?

13. Where is the nominative absolute * in the sentence in lines 33-35?

DICTION

14. Look up: *scholarship* (18), *asserted* (23), *warily* (29), *valiantly* (32), *prefigured* (37), *evolved* (46), *drafts* (46), *excruciatingly* (48), *trivial* (60), *immobilize* (61).
15. How do the etymologies * of these words help to clarify their modern meanings: *dissertation* (1), *pantomime* (9), *retrospect* (37), *mortification* (57)?
16. Explain the meanings of these phrases as fully as you can: *dreams and fantasies* (4), *comic luxury* (13), *symbolic shape* (20), *an academic* (21), *playfully bounced* (22), *pointless accumulation* (50).
17. *Hatching* (10), *weeding* (53), and *to glean* (54) are all metaphors *. Why are they better than more commonplace terms such as *working on, removing,* and *to keep*?
18. To whom is *Atlas* (34) an allusion *? Is the comparison apt? Where does the writer pick it up again?
19. *Yet* (1), *true* (29), and *then* (58) all signal the reader that the statements they introduce stand in particular logical relationships to what precedes them. Explain the relationship in each case.

POINTS TO LEARN

1. Analogies explain the unfamiliar in terms of the familiar, the abstract in an image the reader can see or hear.
2. Metaphors * and allusions * similarly express ideas in more familiar or concrete terms.
3. A topic sentence may set up several paragraphs rather than just one.
4. An occasional short simple sentence varies a style composed of relatively long ones.

SUGGESTIONS FOR WRITING

1. A famous bit of pantomime shows an actor trapped within four invisible walls trying vainly to escape, and finally accepting the reality of his absolute imprisonment. You may have seen Marcel Marceau or another mime act out this scene, but even if you haven't you can imagine what he would do. In a short essay of three or four paragraphs (totaling 400-600 words) describe the pantomime and apply it to one of your own frustrations. (If you are familiar with some other piece of pantomime, you may substitute this for the "invisible walls.")

2. In an essay of similar length use a scene or a plot from a movie or television show to explain a personal feeling or problem. First describe the scene or plot so that the reader understands its essentials, then apply it to your situation.

IMPROVING YOUR STYLE

Somewhere in your essay include the following:

1. Several short emphatic sentences.
2. A rhetorical question.
3. A parallel sentence describing the actions of the mime or the actor.
4. The word *true* to introduce a qualification *, and the word *then* to signal a conclusion.
5. One or two verbs like *hatching* or *to glean* to describe an abstract activity in a vivid image.

The Nineteenth Century

Bertrand Russell (1872-1970) was a British philosopher, one of the most important of this century, especially noted for his work in mathematics and symbolic logic. He was the author of many books, some of a technical nature, others directed at a general audience. Among the latter, A *History of Western Philosophy* (1945) was widely read and is the source of the following paragraph. The paragraph, taken from a chapter dealing with the nineteenth century, develops the topic by discussing why it is true, that is, by giving reasons.

The intellectual life of the nineteenth century was more complex than that of any previous age. This was due to several causes. First: the area concerned was larger than ever before; America and Russia made important contributions, and Europe became more aware than formerly of Indian philosophies, both ancient and modern. Second: science, which had been 5 a chief source of novelty since the seventeenth century, made new conquests, especially in geology, biology, and organic chemistry. Third: machine production profoundly altered the social structure, and gave men a new conception of their powers in relation to the physical environment. Fourth: a profound revolt, both philosophical and political, against tradi- 10 tional systems in thought, in politics, and in economics, gave rise to attacks upon many beliefs and institutions that had hitherto been regarded as unassailable. This revolt had two very different forms, one romantic, the other rationalistic. (I am using these words in a liberal sense.) The romantic revolt passes from Byron, Schopenhauer, and Nietzsche to Mus- 15 solini and Hitler; the rationalistic revolt begins with the French philosophers of the Revolution, passes on, somewhat softened, to the philosophical radicals in England, then acquires a deeper form in Marx and issues in Soviet Russia.

From A *History of Western Philosophy* by Bertrand Russell. Reprinted by permission of Allen & Unwin.

QUESTIONS

READER AND PURPOSE

1. Is Russell writing for a college freshman or for a reader with more general information than the freshman usually has? Explain what Russell assumes that his reader already knows.

ORGANIZATION

2. Russell organizes this paragraph by listing reasons. After a general statement at the beginning, he gives reasons intended to convince the reader of the truth of his statement. This is one of the most common and useful methods of paragraph development, and it may be used to organize the whole or a part of an essay. How many reasons does this paragraph contain? Are they arranged in any significant order? Which does Russell regard as the most important?

3. With what words does Russell clearly separate and organize his reasons? Explain the advantages and disadvantages of this device. Compare the first part of sentence 3 with the second part. What is the pattern of development? Is the same pattern apparent in any of the other reasons?

4. What sentence organizes the last part of the paragraph?

SENTENCES

5. Write down the subject, the verb, and the object (or complement) of the first sentence. Do the same for the third, fourth, and fifth sentences. In each case you have groups of three words (but several more for sentence 5). Do these words communicate the core of the meanings of their sentences? Do the same for this sentence from a student composition: "Barbaric ways became civilized ones." What is the difference? Improve the student sentence.

6. Examine each sentence of Russell's paragraph. Do you find many qualifications *, many maybe's, perhaps's, or would seem's? Does the absence of hedging really harm this passage? Does it have any positive value? When should the writer carefully qualify his generalizations? A good writer must avoid qualifying a statement out of existence, and he must also learn under what conditions a qualification makes his point all the more convincing.

7. Point out all the parallel * elements in the last sentence of the paragraph (14-19).

DICTION

8. Look up: intellectual (1), philosophical (10), hitherto (12), romantic (13), Byron (15), Schopenhauer (15), Nietzsche (15), radical (18).

9. Remove the adjectives from these expressions: intellectual life (1), social structure (8), new conception (8), traditional systems (10), and physical en-

vironment (9). Remove the adjectives from this sentence: *Upward progress characterizes this modern age.* What conclusions can you draw about the purpose of modifiers?

10. Notice the verbs in the clause beginning *the rationalistic revolt* (16-19). What is their voice? Are they important in themselves to the meaning of the clause, or do they merely link together the words that are important?

POINTS TO LEARN

1. Framing words *, like *First, Second, Third,* often help to organize a paragraph.
2. The writer often uses an organizing sentence *.
3. Words in the position of subject-verb-object should carry the heart of meaning in any sentence. These important positions should not be thrown away by being filled with unimportant words.
4. Of any qualifier always ask, "Is it necessary?" Don't be one of those who are afraid to say, "It is noon"—who say instead, "It would seem as if it were perhaps in the vicinity of noon." But do not be afraid to make honest qualifications in the interest of truth and accuracy.
5. Development by reasons will quickly organize many answers during your examinations.
6. Avoid verbs in the passive voice wherever possible. Active verbs generally improve the clarity and vigor of a sentence.

SUGGESTIONS FOR WRITING

Write a single paragraph about one of these topics, advancing three or four reasons to support the topic idea. Introduce each reason with a framing word.

I have chosen _____ as my profession for several reasons.

I should never have come to school this morning.

_____ lost the World Series for several reasons.

Modern painting reflects (or does not reflect) a sharp break with tradition.

Psychology ought to be a required subject for college students.

College students are becoming increasingly restless.

IMPROVING YOUR STYLE

1. Compose a sentence in which three or four predicates are made parallel to a single subject, as in the second clause of Russell's final sentence (16-18).
2. Be sure the verbs in that sentence, as well as throughout your paragraph, are precise, clear, and in the active voice.

The Evil of My Tale

T. E. Lawrence (1888-1935), popularly known as Lawrence of Arabia, was a British officer in the Near East during World War I. He organized and led Arab tribesmen in a revolt in the desert areas now part of Israel and Jordan, then belonging to the Turks, who were allied with Germany against England. The revolt played an important part in the British victory in the Near East, which led ultimately to the establishment of the modern Arab states. After the war Lawrence published a famous account of his exploits entitled *The Seven Pillars of Wisdom* (1926). These paragraphs open that book. They develop by giving reasons, though in a more complex manner than in the previous selection by Bertrand Russell.

1   Some of the evil of my tale may have been inherent in our circumstances. For years we lived anyhow with one another in the naked desert, under the indifferent heaven. By day the hot sun fermented us; and we were dizzied by the beating wind. At night we were stained by dew, and shamed into pettiness by the innumerable silences of stars. We were a 5 self-centered army without parade or gesture, devoted to freedom, the second of man's creeds, a purpose so ravenous that it devoured all our strength, a hope so transcendent that our earlier ambitions faded in its glare.

2   As time went by our need to fight for the ideal increased to an unquestioning possession, riding with spur and rein over our doubts. Willy- 10 nilly it became a faith. We had sold ourselves into its slavery, manacled ourselves together in its chain-gang, bowed ourselves to serve its holiness with all our good and ill content. The mentality of ordinary human slaves is terrible—they have lost the world—and we had surrendered, not body alone, but soul to the overmastering greed of victory. By our own act we 15

From *Seven Pillars of Wisdom* by T. E. Lawrence. Reprinted by permission of Seven Pillars Trust and Jonathan Cape Ltd.

were drained of morality, of volition, of responsibility, like dead leaves in the wind.

3   The everlasting battle stripped from us care of our own lives or of others'. We had ropes about our necks, and on our heads prices which showed that the enemy intended hideous tortures for us if we were caught. 20 Each day some of us passed; and the living knew themselves just sentient puppets on God's stage: indeed, our taskmaster was merciless, merciless, so long as our bruised feet could stagger forward on the road. The weak envied those tired enough to die; for success looked so remote, and failure a near and certain, if sharp, release from toil. We lived always in the stretch 25 or sag of nerves, either on the crest or in the trough of waves of feeling. This impotency was bitter to us, and made us live only for the seen horizon, reckless what spite we inflicted or endured, since physical sensation showed itself meanly transient. Gusts of cruelty, perversions, lusts ran lightly over the surface without troubling us; for the moral laws which had 30 seemed to hedge about these silly accidents must be yet fainter words. We had learned that there were pangs too sharp, griefs too deep, ecstasies too high for our finite selves to register. When emotion reached this pitch the mind choked; and memory went white till the circumstances were humdrum once more.   35

4   Such exaltation of thought, while it let adrift the spirit, and gave it licence in strange airs, lost it the old patient rule over the body. The body was too coarse to feel the utmost of our sorrows and of our joys. Therefore, we abandoned it as rubbish: we left it below us to march forward, a breathing simulacrum, on its own unaided level, subject to influences from which 40 in normal times our instincts would have shrunk. The men were young and sturdy; and hot flesh and blood unconsciously claimed a right in them and tormented their bellies with strange longings. Our privations and dangers fanned this virile heat, in a climate as racking as can be conceived. We had no shut places to be alone in, no thick clothes to hide our nature. Man 45 in all things lived candidly with man.

QUESTIONS

READER AND PURPOSE

1. In effect these paragraphs constitute a kind of apology. For what? What advantages do you see to beginning in this way?

2. Lawrence's prose is more difficult to read than that of Bertrand Russell in

the preceding selection. In part this is because he employs language for a somewhat different purpose. Russell is concerned chiefly with conveying information and ideas, and, since he is a master expositor, his style is transparent, allowing us immediate access to his thought. Lawrence's style, on the other hand, is denser, more opaque. He uses words not only to convey ideas but also to suggest a wide range of feeling, in short to re-create the experience of being in the desert, close by death. Point to words and phrases that are especially loaded with feeling. Would Russell's textbook on the history of philosophy have been so successful had it been written in Lawrence's style? Would *Seven Pillars of Wisdom* have been so impressive composed in the style of Russell?

ORGANIZATION

3. Make an analysis of this selection, outlining the relationships between the various causes and effects that Lawrence describes.

4. Why does Lawrence begin new paragraphs at lines 9, 18, and 36? How is paragraph 4 linked to the preceding one?

5. Study the internal coherence of paragraph 2, underlining in each sentence the word(s) linking it to what has gone before.

SENTENCES

6. In the sentence in lines 5-8 ("We were . . . in its glare") the word *second* (6) is an appositive *. To what? Is *purpose* (7) also an appositive? If so, to what? If not, what is it? What about *hope* (8)? The value of such words is that they enable a writer to predicate new ideas without the tiresome repetition of a subject already stated. For instance, one could break Lawrence's sentence into a series of briefer, self-contained propositions: "We were a self-centred army without parade or gesture. We were devoted to freedom. Freedom is the second of man's creeds. Our devotion to it constituted a purpose so ravenous that it devoured all our strength. It became a hope so transcendent that our earlier ambitions faded in its glare." This is plainly a very bad version of what Lawrence wrote. Why? Find one or two other sentences in these paragraphs that reveal such effective use of appositives.

7. In the sentence in lines 11-13 ("We had sold . . . ill content") what words parallel * *sold?*

8. The interrupting * construction in line 14 is set off by dashes. Why would it be confusing here to substitute commas? What other mark of punctuation might Lawrence have used? Why are dashes—given Lawrence's purpose—probably better than that other mark?

9. In the series in line 29 Lawrence does not write *and* between the two final items, which would have been conventional ("Gusts of cruelty, perversions, and lusts . . ."). He seems to prefer to handle series in this way; you should

easily be able to find several other examples. How does this treatment of a series subtly affect the tone * of Lawrence's prose?

DICTION

10. Look up: *pettiness* (5), *volition* (16), *sentient* (21), *ecstasies* (32), *exaltation* (36), *privations* (43), *candidly* (46).

11. Be able briefly to discuss the etymologies of these words: *willy-nilly* (10), *silly* (31), *simulacrum* (40).

12. Lawrence employs figurative * language more than is common in exposition; *like dead leaves in the wind* (16), for example, is a simile*, while *sentient puppets on God's stage* (21) is a metaphor *. Think about both these figures for a few minutes and write down all the implications you can see in them. Do the same for two or three other similes or metaphors in this selection. What advantages does figurative language offer the expository writer? Has it any dangers?

13. In line 22 Lawrence repeats *merciless* for emphasis. Could he have gotten the same effect by using an intensive (say, ". . . our taskmaster was exceedingly merciless, so long as our bruised feet . . ."), or by employing a synonym (". . . our taskmaster was merciless, without pity, so long as . . .")?

14. Why are these alternates less effective for Lawrence's purpose: *somehow* for *anyhow* (2), *empty* for *indifferent* (3), *cooked* for *fermented* (3), *ate* for *devoured* (7), *nervous agitation* for *stretch or sag of nerves* (25), *spells* for *gusts* (29), *blank* for *white* (34), *abdomens* for *bellies* (43), *manly* for *virile* (44)?

POINTS TO LEARN

1. Development by reasons and effects can become extremely subtle as the writer reveals the complex interplay of consequences and causes.

2. Appositives are an efficient, even elegant, way of introducing new ideas into a sentence.

3. Metaphors and similes are richly suggestive. For that reason they can enormously expand the writer's meaning in relatively few words. But for that reason, too, they must be carefully controlled.

SUGGESTIONS FOR WRITING

Lawrence is not an easy writer to model oneself upon. He possessed a sensitivity to experience and a sense of style most of us do not have. Still, try to analyze some deeply felt experience—a serious illness or accident (if you have been so unfortunate), a brush with danger, a severe disappointment in your personal life. Compose your short essay (about 500 words) in three or four paragraphs and concentrate upon why you felt or reacted as you did, that is, upon giving reasons.

IMPROVING YOUR STYLE

Somewhere in your paragraphs attempt the following:

1. An appositive.
2. A series of parallel verbs.
3. An interrupter set off by dashes.
4. At least one simile and one metaphor.

The Fall of Rome

Colin McEvedy is the editor of a three-volume historical atlas published by Penguin Books. These paragraphs come from his Introduction to the second volume, *The Penguin Atlas of Medieval History*. In them McEvedy offers his answer to the perennial question of why the Roman Empire came apart. The problem demands, of course, that he discuss reasons.

1   The final end of the classical world is a subject which for most people has a tragic aspect and this reaction is worth some analysis. Both the sheer size of the Empire, never equalled in the West before or since, and the many characteristics, absent in the Dark Ages, which our civilization shares with the Roman in the fields of culture, law, and administra- 5 tion, contribute to this feeling. But were the victories of the Germans really a disaster for mankind? Such a view is best examined by considering what would have happened if the Empire had survived—by considering China, for example, where, although individual Empires existed only for a span, it was fundamentally the same Empire that was recreated each 10 time. The result was a tendency to stagnation or at least the mere reshuffling of elements that had been created in the early days of Chinese history. The concept of a few eternal verities may be attractive, but there is a lot to be said for searching for new truths even at the expense of the old. Rome had given all it had to give, and, though considerable flexibility was 15 still exhibited in some ways, late Roman society lacked vitality. At the end, the talents were not multiplying, they were simply buried.

2   This brings us to a problem that can be considered in more concrete terms; why did the Western Empire fall when it did? The immediate answer is, of course, the advance of the Huns, which frightened the Ger- 20 mans into doing what they had long had the capacity to do, for both in

From *The Penguin Atlas of Medieval History*, p. 8. Copyright © 1961 by Colin McEvedy. Reprinted by permission of Penguin Books Ltd.

numbers and in arms they were by then superior to the legionaries who manned the frontiers. The decline in the Empire's total population may have been absolute or merely comparative to barbarian increase. It may have been due to the fact that a sizeable proportion of the masses were slaves (slaves had a notoriously low reproduction rate), or to a high death rate in the urban proletariat, which must have been decimated by endemic and epidemic diseases. But whatever the extent or the reason, the manpower situation of the Empire certainly deteriorated *vis-à-vis* the German, and this deterioration was exaggerated by the specialization of Roman society. While every adult male German was a seasonal soldier, each Roman legionary represented the defence effort of some tens or even hundreds of civilians. Though professional soldiery has advantages of discipline and experience and can usually be relied on to defeat several times their number of amateurs, their capacity for doing so is heavily dependent on their being well equipped, and it so happened that, at the moment when sheer numbers were beginning to tell against them, the legionaries found that their methods and equipment were hopelessly obsolete. The German soldier of the end of the fourth century had a better sword made of better steel, and the Goths had learnt the latest techniques of cavalry warfare from the nomads of the Russian steppe. The Romans were left dependent on discipline and generalship, and when these failed, as fail they must in the long run, on the hiring of Germans to fight Germans. This last could only be a stop-gap, for an indispensable soldier will set up on his own if even his most irresponsible demands are not met. In the end, the Western Empire was destroyed by the arms of the professional German soldiery that imperial necessity had created.

3   But if all this is true, why did not the East fall as well as the West? The answer here goes back to Julius Caesar, who, by conquering Gaul out of personal ambition, carried the Roman eagles into continental Europe. The Greeks and Carthaginians had colonized and economically unified the Mediterranean littoral, providing the basis for its political unification as achieved by Rome. Julius Caesar marched beyond the confines of this natural unit and introduced Mediterranean culture into France and England. There it flourished in an etiolated manner while the political climate was favourable. But when the Roman frontiers ceased to expand and defence costs began to rise, the slender trade of the north-west dried up in the hotter taxation, and the people left the cities, the foci of the tax man's attention. The West soon proved completely unable to pay its way. Once the division of the Empire became a reality and the West was deprived

of the support of the far wealthier, far more urbanized East, it collapsed almost spontaneously. The East was just rich enough to buy off invaders and hire guards. Thus it survived ingloriously for a century and by Justinian's time had rebuilt a native army on new lines.

QUESTIONS

READER AND PURPOSE

1. This selection is generally informative in purpose. The first paragraph, however, may be described as argumentative. Why?

2. Does McEvedy assume his reader to be an advanced student of Roman history, to be moderately informed, or to be completely ignorant of the ancient world?

ORGANIZATION

3. In three sentences (one devoted to each paragraph) totaling no more than one hundred words, summarize the main points of this selection.

4. What is the topic statement of paragraph 1? What phrase in the sentence suggests how the writer will develop the paragraph?

5. The rhetorical question * in lines 6-7 marks a turn of thought. Explain. Where else does the writer employ rhetorical questions to organize his material?

6. Which words at the beginning of paragraph 2 link it to paragraph 1? Which words provide a similar linkage at the beginning of paragraph 3?

7. How many reasons does McEvedy advance in the second paragraph to support his topic? List them. In paragraph 3 does he develop several reasons or only one?

SENTENCES

8. Explain how these revisions alter the emphasis of McEvedy's sentences and decide whether the change is for the better or the worse:

(a) *Revision:* This feeling is contributed to both by the sheer size of the Empire, never equalled in the West before or since, and the many characteristics, absent in the Dark Ages, which our civilization shares with the Romans in the fields of culture, law, and administration.

McEvedy: "Both the sheer size of the Empire, never equalled in the West before or since, and the many characteristics, absent in the Dark Ages, which our civilization shares with the Roman in the fields of culture, law, and administration, contribute to this feeling." (2-6)

(b) *Revision:* Rome had given all it had to give, and late Roman society lacked vitality, though considerable flexibility was still exhibited in some ways.

McEvedy: "Rome had given all it had to give, and, though considerable flexibility was still exhibited in some ways, late Roman society lacked vitality." (15-16)

(c) *Revision:* The West collapsed almost spontaneously once the division of the Empire became a reality and the West was deprived of the support of the far wealthier, far more urbanized East.

McEvedy: "Once the division of the Empire became a reality and the West was deprived of the support of the far wealthier, far more urbanized East, it collapsed almost spontaneously." (59-62)

9. What general conclusion may be drawn from question 8 about the importance of the closing position in a sentence?

10. The complex sentence * in lines 41-43 might be broken down into four shorter statements: "The Romans were left dependent on discipline and generalship. These failed. In the long run these must always fail. The Romans then had to hire Germans to fight Germans." Why would such a simplification be inferior to McEvedy's longer construction, with its much greater use of subordination *?

11. The compound sentence * in lines 16-17 is constructed so as to throw great weight on what two words?

12. Is the parenthetical remark in lines 25-26 integrated into the grammar of the sentence containing it, or is it simply a new and independent statement that has been intruded into the middle of the longer sentence? Could it be punctuated by dashes? By commas? What rule may be suggested about when such interrupting constructions have to be set off by dashes or parentheses and when they may be handled by commas?

13. What is the logical relationship between the idea expressed in the parenthetical statement and that conveyed by the larger sentence? What logical relationship is implicit between the participial construction * in lines 52-53 ("providing the basis for its political unification as achieved by Rome") and the main clause about the Greeks and Carthaginians?

14. In line 58 *foci* is an appositive *: to what?

DICTION

15. Look up: *tragic* (2), *stagnation* (11), *legionaries* (22), vis-à-vis (29), *deterioration* (30), *obsolete* (38), *steppe* (41), *littoral* (52).

16. Explain the meanings of these phrases: *classical world* (1), *eternal verities* (13), *urban proletariat* (27), *seasonal soldier* (31), *irresponsible demands* (45), *imperial necessity* (46), *Roman eagles* (50), *etiolated manner* (55).

17. How does a knowledge of the etymologies * of the following words help one to understand their meanings: *civilization* (4), *barbarian* (24), *decimated* (27), *sheer* (36), *nomads* (40)?

18. What precisely is the difference between a population decline that is *absolute* and one that is *merely comparative to barbarian increase* (24)? Between *endemic and epidemic diseases* (27-28)?

POINTS TO LEARN

1. Although they can be overused, rhetorical questions are an effective way of organizing paragraphs.

2. Dealing with complex intellectual problems requires a complex sentence style, in which several ideas are worked together, often with one or more subordinated to the main point.

3. When you look up a word, check its etymology; the information may help to explain how the word is used.

SUGGESTIONS FOR WRITING

You cannot tackle so grand a theme as the decline of Rome. However, try to explain in one or two paragraphs why a local business failed, or why one politician lost an election, or why a sports team was defeated.

IMPROVING YOUR STYLE

1. Someplace in your paragraph(s) construct a compound sentence like the one that closes McEvedy's first paragraph in which you emphasize an idea by negative-positive restatement *.

2. Compose an independent parenthetical sentence set between parentheses or dashes which explains something concerning the sentence within which it is enclosed without being grammatically a part of that sentence.

3. Include an appositive in one of your sentences.

The Courtroom

Boyce Richardson, a New Zealander by birth, has worked as a journalist in his native country, in Australia and Britain, and in Canada with the *Montreal Star*. He has published numerous articles and three books; he has also produced three documentary films about the Cree Indians. In this excerpt from his book *Strangers Devour the Land*, Richardson shows clearly that he is on the side of the Indians, that he is not trying to evaluate objectively the claims of the natives on the one hand and those of the Quebec authorities on the other. He is not, that is, merely reporting facts, but, in exposing the plight of the Indians, is giving his audience reason for supporting their cause. Thus, his writing is a combination of exposition and persuasion.

1   On a damp, cold December morning in 1972 a group of fifty or so rough-clad men marched along narrow, traffic-jammed Notre Dame Street in old Montreal, pushed open the swinging glass doors of the huge and impersonal Palais de Justice and stood uncertainly in the cavernous spaces of the lobby, an open space surrounded by balconies soaring four stories 5 above their heads. Even in this building, which every morning sees a procession of some of the stranger people in this large city—pimps and whores, petty thieves and con men, unhappy husbands and wives, debtors and drunks, shyster lawyers and pillars of society—even here their presence created a stir of interest.   10

2   They were a strange group, in their great, plain working boots, the laces tied with no concern for appearance, their wind jackets weather-beaten and torn, their shirts hanging below their jackets, their faces curiously open beneath their rude, home-fashioned haircuts. But they looked no stranger than they felt, for they were Cree and Inuit (Eskimo) hunters 15 from the huge Ungava Peninsula of northern Quebec, come to the city for

From *Strangers Devour the Land*, by Boyce Richardson. Copyright © 1975 by Boyce Richardson. Reprinted by permission of Alfred A. Knopf, Inc.

the first time to undertake the audacious and apparently hopeless task of asserting their rights as occupants of their hunting lands from time immemorial, and bringing to a halt a hydro-electric project on which the provincial government had staked the entire economic future of Quebec. The older men regarded the building with dignified incomprehension, for they had never seen such huge enclosed spaces before, and they waited patiently to be told what to do, whether to go into the strange room which moves up and down and which was causing them much trouble at their hotel, or whether to go to the other side of the lobby and try to mount that moving staircase as many other people were doing, and so be carried upstairs in the strange manner of the white man, without having to bother to walk a step. Not all of them were elderly men: the group included some younger men with fashionably long hair falling blackly to their shoulders, wearing purple jeans and the thin, high-heel boots fashionable in the city, and one or two girls with classic high-cheekboned faces, their eyes large and slanting, their noses straight, their foreheads high, their long black hair falling gloriously down their backs. The group was being ushered upstairs by some southern Indians, barely distinguishable from white men, members of the new Indian establishment that had arisen in the last decade, officials of the Indians of Quebec Association, cautious bureaucrats who after eighteen months of delay had agreed to help the Cree hunters go to court in their effort to stop the white man from damming the rivers around which they had lived for longer than anyone in North America could remember.

QUESTIONS

READER AND PURPOSE

1. The author is clearly sympathetic to the Cree and Inuit he is describing. How does his choice of concrete * details in the first two sentences of paragraph two reveal this sympathy?
2. What contrast does Richardson make in his first paragraph? How does this contrast help to introduce the second paragraph?
3. Does Richardson use irony in contrasting the natives and the whites? For example, are the expressions in lines 17-18 and 25-27 examples of exposition or subtle irony *?

ORGANIZATION

4. How does the author make the transition between his two paragraphs?

5. In which sentence does the author make his key point? Indicate how the introductory material leads up to this point, and how the material following the key point substantiates it.

SENTENCES

6. Comment on the repetition (*cavernous spaces . . . open space*) in lines 4-5. Does it seem effective to you?

7. The first sentence has a subject—*men*—that governs a series of three verbs: *marched, pushed,* and *stood.* Would you put a comma before the last item of the series (i.e., after the word *Justice*)? Explain your answer.

8. Although this selection is some forty lines long, it contains only seven sentences. Thus one might be led to think that the sentences are loosely constructed—numerous clauses linked by such coordinate conjunctions as *and, but,* and *or.* Is this the case?

9. How (if at all) would the second sentence in paragraph 1 be changed if parentheses were used in place of dashes?

DICTION

10. Look up: *cavernous* (4), *con men* (8), *shyster* (9), *audacious* (17), *immemorial* (18-19), *staked* (20), *bureaucrats* (36).

11. Richardson has occasionally combined two words to form an unusual compound adjective, such as *traffic-jammed* (2), *home-fashioned* (14), *high-cheekboned* (31). How effective are such words?

12. Compare the unusual compound adjectives mentioned above with the more common ones Richardson uses: *rough-clad* (2), *weather-beaten* (12-13). Which of these two kinds is more effective? Why?

13. Note how, in the first sentence, nearly every noun is modified by at least one adjective, and often two. Does this strike you as exaggerated striving for effect? In the second sentence it is the nouns that are multiplied. Is the effect here better? Worse?

14. Does Richardson's use of the phrases *strange room* (23) and *moving staircase* (25-26) help the reader see through native eyes things he takes for granted in white society?

15. *Time immemorial* (18-19) is usually considered a cliché (overworked expression). Is Richardson's use of this phrase effective? Look at the last sentence of this selection before answering.

POINTS TO LEARN

1. Contrast can be an effective method of introduction.
2. Multiplying nouns and adjectives effectively requires careful attention to the desired effects.

SUGGESTIONS FOR WRITING

Using as your subject some group that has a claim to public sympathy—abandoned mothers, underpaid nurses, orphans, unemployed college graduates—write a short essay (200-300 words) in which you contrast this group with an unsympathetic bureaucracy.

IMPROVING YOUR STYLE

1. For your essay write two sentences containing several compound adjectives of your own devising; then select only the most striking one for inclusion in the essay.

2. Experiment with your two sentences by substituting parentheses and dashes for commas; be prepared to explain which usage is the most effective.

The Technological Revolution

Carl Becker (1873-1945) was an American historian whose books include *Beginnings of the American People* (1915), *Progress and Power* (1936), and *The Declaration of Independence* (1942). These paragraphs are from *Modern Democracy* (1941) and discuss how the enormous increase in machine production has affected contemporary society. The paragraphs develop by treating the topic as a cause and tracing the consequences or effects that follow from it. Becker's prose is a model of the lucid exposition of subtle and complicated ideas.

1   . . . we are now living in the second great epoch of discovery and invention. Since the seventeenth century, the discovery of steam power, gas, electricity, and radiation have made possible those innumerable tools and appliances, those complicated and powerful machines, and those delicate instruments of precision which elicit our wonder and our admiration. The 5 result has been that the new technology, by giving men unprecedented control over material things, has transformed the relatively simple agricultural communities of the eighteenth century into societies far more complex and impersonal than anything the prophets of liberal-democracy could have imagined—mechanized Leviathans which Thomas Jefferson at least would 10 have regarded as unreal and fantastic and altogether unsuited to the principles of liberty and equality as he understood them.

2   I need not say that the influence of the technological revolution has not been confined to any particular aspect of social life. On the contrary, it has exerted and still exerts a decisive influence in modifying all the habitual 15 patterns of thought and conduct. But I am here concerned with the influence of the technological revolution in accelerating and intensifying that concentration of wealth and power in the hands of a few which the prin-

From *Modern Democracy*, copyright 1941. Reprinted by permission of the Yale University Press.

ciples of individual freedom in the economic realm would in any case have
tended to bring about.   20
3   The first and most obvious result of the technological revolution
has been to increase the amount of wealth in the form of material things
which can be produced in a given time by a given population. For example,
in 1913 there was produced in Great Britain seven billion yards of cotton
cloth for export alone. In 1750 the total population of Great Britain,   25
working with the mechanical appliances then available, could have produced only a small fraction of that amount. A second result of the technological revolution is that, as machines are perfected and become more
automatic, man power plays a relatively less important part in the production of a given amount of wealth in a given time. Fifty years ago, when 30
all type was set by hand, the labor of several men was required to print,
fold, and arrange in piles the signatures of a book. Today machines can
do it all, and far more rapidly; little man power is required, except that a
mechanic, who may pass the time sitting in a chair, must be present in
case anything goes wrong with the machine. And finally, a third result of 35
the technological revolution is that, under the system of private property
in the means of production and the price system as a method of dis-
tributing wealth, the greater part of the wealth produced, since it is
produced by the machines, goes to those who own or control the machines,
while those who work the machines receive that part only which can be   40
exacted by selling their services in a market where wages are impersonally
adjusted to the necessities of the machine process.

QUESTIONS

READER AND PURPOSE

1. Is Becker's tone * formal or informal? What is his point of view *? Suggest
several subjects that demand an impersonal, formal point of view. Suggest others
that must be treated informally and personally. Try to think of two or three subjects that may be handled either way. Describe Becker's reader and purpose.

ORGANIZATION

2. What does paragraph 1 contribute to our understanding of the subject? Does
it anticipate the remainder of the selection? Paragraph 2 divides into two parts.
Where? Why may the first part be called a qualification *? What does the
second part of paragraph 2 add to the development of the topic? Explain why
the last is obviously the most important of the three paragraphs.

3. Identify the parts of paragraph 3 and explain what device welds them together.

4. In this selection Becker develops his subject by listing the effects of a cause— here the technological revolution. Paragraph 3 is a very good example of development by effects. Show that the effects are arranged in a purposeful order, not simply put down haphazardly as they might have occurred to the writer. Along with his development by effects the writer has also used illustrations. Identify each one. Would the paragraph have been as clear and as effective without them? Observe that in addition to effects and illustration the third paragraph also involves comparison. Explain why comparisons are a necessary part of the writer's subject in this selection.

SENTENCES

5. A less experienced writer might have used a complete adjective clause in line 8, writing "societies *which are* far more complex and impersonal." Are the words omitted really necessary? What has the writer gained by omitting them? With what preceding word is *Leviathans* (10) in apposition *?

6. In his illustrations Becker's sentences become somewhat simpler. What is the reason for this easier style? The two sentences comprising the first illustration in paragraph 3 begin in much the same way. Why? Is this similarity of beginning also true of the sentences which develop the second illustration?

7. Becker's sentences are generally quite complicated, a style suited to the exposition of subtly related and highly abstract ideas. A good example is the final sentence (35-42). How many ideas does it contain? Rewrite this sentence in five or six shorter ones, keeping as much of the writer's phrasing as you can. Is the revision more, or less, clear than the original? Can you remove any words from the final sentence without damaging its meaning?

8. Label examples of interrupted movement *. In what way are these constructions useful to the writer of a rather formal, complex subject?

DICTION

9. Look up: *radiation* (3), *elicit* (5), *technology* (6), *unprecedented* (6), *exert* (15), *modifying* (15), *habitual* (15), *material* (22), *signatures* (32), *exacted* (41).

10. Becker uses *machine* and *instrument* (4-5) with a nice discrimination. How does *appliance* differ from both *machine* and *instrument*? Substitute *changed* for *transformed* (7) and *on the other hand* for *on the contrary* (14). Do these substitutions change the sense of either passage?

POINTS TO LEARN

1. In developing effects it is not enough simply to list them at random. They must be arranged according to a plan and held together in a unified whole.

2. Most exposition relies upon a number of developing techniques. Learn to use not effects alone, but effects assisted by other methods like illustration and comparison.

3. The writer must prune all words not absolutely necessary. To achieve this economy he may (1) use appositives * frequently; (2) abbreviate adjective clauses by omitting the relative pronoun, the auxiliary verb or the linking verb: "societies far more complex and impersonal" in place of "societies *which are* far more complex and impersonal."

SUGGESTIONS FOR WRITING
In several paragraphs explain three or four additional effects of the technological revolution: for example, the effect of the mass production of automobiles on the Canadian city; how the forty-hour week has changed Canadian recreation; the influence of television upon home life and habits. Choose one of these or a similar topic. Support your effects with brief but detailed illustrations. Make the reader see.

IMPROVING YOUR STYLE
1. Somewhere in your paragraphs construct two sentences that use interrupted movement.

2. Attempt a long, complex sentence *, something like Becker's in lines 35-42, bringing together five or six ideas in a subtle relationship of cause and effect.

Los Angeles Notebook

Joan Didion is an essayist and novelist. The paragraphs below come from the essay "Los Angeles Notebook," one of a collection published in the book *Slouching Towards Bethlehem* (1961). Like Becker in the preceding selection, Didion develops her topic primarily by effects. Her prose, however, is more personal and less formal than Becker's, a fact which suits her subject matter and which is also typical of the trend of modern exposition toward informality and the personal vision.

1   There is something uneasy in the Los Angeles air this afternoon, some unnatural stillness, some tension. What it means is that tonight a Santa Ana will begin to blow, a hot wind from the northeast whining down through the Cajon and San Gorgonio Passes, blowing up sandstorms out along Route 66, drying the hills and the nerves to the flash point. For a 5 few days now we will see smoke back in the canyons, and hear sirens in the night. I have neither heard nor read that a Santa Ana is due, but I know it, and almost everyone I have seen today knows it too. We know it because we feel it. The baby frets. The maid sulks. I rekindle a waning argument with the telephone company, then cut my losses and lie down, given over 10 to whatever it is in the air. To live with the Santa Ana is to accept, consciously or unconsciously, a deeply mechanistic view of human behavior.
2   I recall being told, when I first moved to Los Angeles and was living on an isolated beach, that the Indians would throw themselves into the sea when the bad wind blew. I could see why. The Pacific turned omi- 15 nously glossy during a Santa Ana period, and one woke in the night troubled not only by the peacocks screaming in the olive trees but by the eerie absence of surf. The heat was surreal. The sky had a yellow cast, the kind of light sometimes called "earthquake weather." My only neighbor would

Selection from *Slouching Towards Bethlehem* by Joan Didion. Copyright © 1967, 1968 by Joan Didion. Reprinted by permission of Farrar, Straus and Giroux, Inc.

not come out of her house for days, and there were no lights at night, and 20
her husband roamed the place with a machete. One day he would tell me
that he had heard a trespasser, the next a rattlesnake.

3   "On nights like that," Raymond Chandler once wrote about the
Santa Ana, "every booze party ends in a fight. Meek little wives feel the
edge of the carving knife and study their husbands' necks. Anything can 25
happen." That was the kind of wind it was. I did not know then that there
was any basis for the effect it had on all of us, but it turns out to be another of those cases in which science bears out folk wisdom. The Santa
Ana, which is named for one of the canyons it rushes through, is a *foehn*
wind, like the *foehn* of Austria and Switzerland and the *hamsin* of Israel. 30
There are a number of persistent malevolent winds, perhaps the best known
of which are the mistral of France and the Mediterranean sirocco, but a
foehn wind has distinct characteristics: it occurs on the leeward slope of a
mountain range and, although the air begins as a cold mass, it is warmed
as it comes down the mountain and appears finally as a hot dry wind. 35
Whenever and wherever a *foehn* blows, doctors hear about headaches and
nausea and allergies, about "nervousness," about "depression." In Los
Angeles some teachers do not attempt to conduct formal classes during a
Santa Ana, because the children become unmanageable. In Switzerland the
suicide rate goes up during the *foehn*, and in the courts of some Swiss can- 40
tons the wind is considered a mitigating circumstance for crime. Surgeons
are said to watch the wind, because blood does not clot normally during a
foehn. A few years ago an Israeli physicist discovered that not only during
such winds, but for the ten or twelve hours which precede them, the air
carries an unusually high ratio of positive to negative ions. No one seems 45
to know exactly why that should be; some talk about friction and others
suggest solar disturbances. In any case the positive ions are there, and what
an excess of positive ions does, in the simplest terms, is make people unhappy. One cannot get much more mechanistic than that.

4   Easterners commonly complain that there is no "weather" at all 50
in Southern California, that the days and the seasons slip by relentlessly,
numbingly bland. That is quite misleading. In fact the climate is characterized by infrequent but violent extremes: two periods of torrential sub-
tropical rains which continue for weeks and wash out the hills and send
subdivisions sliding toward the sea; about twenty scattered days a year of 55
the Santa Ana, which, with its incendiary dryness, invariably means fire. At
the first prediction of a Santa Ana, the Forest Service flies men and equipment from northern California into the southern forests, and the Los An-

geles Fire Department cancels its ordinary non-firefighting routines. The Santa Ana caused Malibu to burn the way it did in 1956, and Bel Air in 60 1961, and Santa Barbara in 1964. In the winter of 1966-67 eleven men were killed fighting a Santa Ana fire that spread through the San Gabriel Mountains.

5   Just to watch the front-page news out of Los Angeles during a Santa Ana is to get very close to what it is about the place. The longest 65 single Santa Ana period in recent years was in 1957, and it lasted not the usual three or four days but fourteen days, from November 21 until December 4. On the first day 25,000 acres of the San Gabriel Mountains were burning, with gusts reaching 100 miles an hour. In town, the wind reached Force 12, or hurricane force, on the Beaufort Scale; oil derricks were top- 70 pled and people ordered off the downtown streets to avoid injury from flying objects. On November 22 the fire in the San Gabriels was out of control. On November 24 six people were killed in automobile accidents, and by the end of the week the Los Angeles *Times* was keeping a box score of traffic deaths. On November 26 a prominent Pasadena attorney, depressed 75 about money, shot and killed his wife, their two sons, and himself. On November 27 a South Gate divorcée, twenty-two, was murdered and thrown from a moving car. On November 30 the San Gabriel fire was still out of control, and the wind in town was blowing eighty miles an hour. On the first day of December four people died violently, and on the third the wind 80 began to break.

6   It is hard for people who have not lived in Los Angeles to realize how radically the Santa Ana figures in the local imagination. The city burning is Los Angeles's deepest image of itself: Nathanael West perceived that, in *The Day of the Locust*; and at the time of the 1965 Watts 85 riots what struck the imagination most indelibly were the fires. For days one could drive the Harbor Freeway and see the city on fire, just as we had always known it would be in the end. Los Angeles weather is the weather of catastrophe, of apocalypse, and, just as the reliably long and bitter winters of New England determine the way life is lived there, so the violence 90 and the unpredictability of the Santa Ana affect the entire quality of life in Los Angeles, accentuate its impermanence, its unreliability. The wind shows us how close to the edge we are.

QUESTIONS

1. Didion's aim is not simply to communicate information, though she does tell us a great deal about what the Santa Ana is and about how it affects life in Los Angeles. More than reporting facts, however, she re-creates and comments upon experience. Accordingly her point of view * is personal, and in the first paragraph she uses verbs in a way calculated to suggest immediacy. How does she do this?

2. Ultimately her purpose includes even more than re-creating what it is to endure a Santa Ana. While Didion begins these paragraphs by putting us into the experience, she moves in the direction of philosophical speculation. Her final sentence is an example of such speculation. What does she mean by "close to the edge"? "Close to the edge" of what? Where earlier in the selection is this philosophical note sounded?

ORGANIZATION

3. Make a brief outline of this selection, giving an explanatory title to each paragraph. Is each new paragraph justified by a shift in topic?

4. Paragraph 3 is a bit longer and more complicated than the others. In terms of its development of thought divide it into its several parts and briefly describe the major idea in each part.

5. What single word toward the middle of paragraph 4 sets up the effects which Didion discusses?

6. Paragraph 5 describes a number of consequences of a particularly severe Santa Ana. How does the writer impose order upon these effects and thereby unify her paragraph?

SENTENCES

7. Why are the short, terse sentences in lines 8-9 particularly appropriate? There are individual short sentences elsewhere in this selection—in lines 15, 18, 25-26, and 92-93, for example. Consider what advantage each of these possesses.

8. In the sentence in lines 9-11 what verbs parallel * rekindle? Is given one of them? In the sentence in lines 18-19, to what is the phrase kind of light in apposition *?

9. The sentence in lines 19-21 is an example of what is sometimes called the "freight-train" style *. Why is that an appropriate name?

10. What is signaled by the colon in line 53?

11. Explain how the idea expressed in the participial * construction in lines 75-76 ("depressed about money") is related to the main thought of the sentence.

12. Slowly read aloud the sentence in lines 50-52. It is made interesting by— among other things—the repetition of sound. Point out several of these echoes,

and find one or two other sentences in the selection which show a similar repetition of sound.

DICTION

13. Look up: *surreal* (18), *cast* (18), *malevolent* (31), *leeward* (33), *ions* (45), *gusts* (69), *Beaufort Scale* (70), *radically* (83), *indelibly* (86), *apocalypse* (89), *accentuate* (92).

14. Explain the meanings of these phrases: *mechanistic view of human behavior* (12), *ominously glossy* (15-16), *eerie absence* (17-18), *folk wisdom* (28), *numbingly bland* (52), *incendiary dryness* (56).

15. Why is *weather* (50) in quotation marks?

16. What relationship in thought does *in fact* (52) signal?

17. In the sentence beginning *I rekindle* (9) what metaphors * can you find?

18. Each of these is a poor substitute for Didion's word. Why? *Whistling* for *whining* (3), *singing* for *screaming* (17), *falling into* for *sliding toward* (55).

POINTS TO LEARN

1. Exposition may involve more than "facts"; often it expresses a mind sensitively responding to facts.

2. Chronological sequence is one way of unifying a paragraph.

3. Learn to listen to your sentences; good prose pleases the ear.

SUGGESTIONS FOR WRITING

If you live in northern Ontario, or on the prairies, or in any other area with "long and bitter winters," discuss how the cold weather affects the quality of life. Alternatively, if you do not know winter as some other Canadians do, explain the effects of another aspect of climate—the humid summers of Ottawa or Toronto, for example, or the dry season of the interior of British Columbia, or a severe northeaster along the Atlantic coast.

IMPROVING YOUR STYLE

Somewhere in your composition include the following:

1. A series of three or four short emphatic sentences like Didion's in lines 8-9.

2. A sentence in which several verbs are paralleled to a single subject.

3. A freight-train * sentence.

4. An emphatic restatement introduced by *in fact*.

5. A metaphor *.

The Imperial Legion

The historian Edward Gibbon (1737-94) wrote *The Decline and Fall of the Roman Empire* (1776-88), one of the greatest works of history in English. In this selection he discusses the organization of the legion, a unit of the Roman army roughly equivalent in terms of relative strength and strategic function to a division in a modern army. Gibbon's method is to analyze his topic, that is, to break it into its parts and present each in turn. With something like a military unit, analysis is a natural way to proceed, since one need only follow principles of organization inherent in the subject. Gibbon's paragraphs are a lucid example of analysis in exposition, of explaining a complicated topic by saying, in effect: here are its parts and this is how they relate.

1 . . . The constitution of the Imperial legion may be described in a few words. The heavy armed infantry, which composed its principal strength, was divided into ten cohorts, and fifty-five companies, under the orders of a correspondent number of tribunes and centurions. The first cohort, which always claimed the post of honour and the custody of the eagle, 5 was formed of eleven hundred and five soldiers, the most approved for valour and fidelity. The remaining nine cohorts consisted each of five hundred and fifty-five; and the whole body of legionary infantry amounted to six thousand one hundred men. Their arms were uniform, and admirably adapted to the nature of their service: an open helmet, with a lofty crest; 10 a breast-plate, or coat of mail; greaves on their legs, and an ample buckler on their left arm. The buckler was of an oblong and concave figure, four feet in length, and two and a half in breadth, framed of a light wood, covered with a bull's hide, and strongly guarded with plates of brass. Besides a lighter spear, the legionary soldier grasped in his right hand the formidable 15 *pilum*, a ponderous javelin, whose utmost length was about six feet, and which was terminated by a massy triangular point of steel of eighteen inches. This instrument was indeed much inferior to our modern fire-arms;

From *The Decline and Fall of the Roman Empire*, 1788.

since it was exhausted by a single discharge, at the distance of only ten or
twelve paces. Yet when it was launched by a firm and skilfull hand, there   20
was not any cavalry that durst venture within its reach, nor any shield or
corslet that could sustain the impetuosity of its weight. As soon as the
Roman had darted his *pilum*, he drew his sword, and rushed forwards to
close with the enemy. His sword was a short well-tempered Spanish blade,
that carried a double edge, and was alike suited to the purpose of striking   25
or of pushing; but the soldier was always instructed to prefer the latter
use of his weapon, as his own body remained less exposed, whilst he inflicted a more dangerous wound on his adversary. The legion was usually
drawn up eight deep; and the regular distance of three feet was left between the files as well as ranks. A body of troops, habituated to preserve   30
this open order, in a long front and a rapid charge, found themselves prepared to execute every disposition which the circumstances of war, or the
skill of their leader, might suggest. The soldier possessed a free space for
his arms and motions, and sufficient intervals were allowed, through which
seasonable reinforcements might be introduced to the relief of the ex-   35
hausted combatants. The tactics of the Greeks and Macedonians were
formed on very different principles. The strength of the phalanx depended
on sixteen ranks of long pikes, wedged together in the closest array. But it
was soon discovered by reflection as well as by the event, that the strength
of the phalanx was unable to contend with the activity of the legion.   40
2   The cavalry, without which the force of the legion would have remained imperfect, was divided into ten troops or squadrons; the first, as the
companion of the first cohort, consisted of an hundred and thirty-two men;
whilst each of the other nine amounted only to sixty-six. The entire establishment formed a regiment, if we may use the modern expression, of seven   45
hundred and twenty-six horse, naturally connected with its respective legion, but occasionally separated to act in the line, and to compose a part of
the wings of the army. The cavalry of the emperors was no longer composed, like that of the ancient republic, of the noblest youths of Rome and
Italy, who by performing their military service on horseback, prepared   50
themselves for the offices of senator and consul; and solicited, by deeds of
valour, the future suffrages of their countrymen. Since the alteration of
manners and government, the most wealthy of the equestrian order were
engaged in the administration of justice, and of the revenue; and whenever
they embraced the profession of arms, they were immediately intrusted   55
with a troop of horse, or a cohort of foot. Trajan and Hadrian formed their
cavalry from the same provinces, and the same class of their subjects, which

recruited the ranks of the legion. The horses were bred, for the most part, in Spain or Cappadocia. The Roman troopers despised the complete armour with which the cavalry of the East was encumbered. Their more 60 useful arms consisted in a helmet, an oblong shield, light boots, and a coat of mail. A javelin, and a long broad sword, were their principal weapons of offense. The use of lances and of iron maces they seemed to have borrowed from the barbarians.

3   The safety and honour of the empire were principally intrusted to 65 the legions, but the policy of Rome condescended to adopt every useful instrument of war. Considerable levies were regularly made among the provincials, who had not yet deserved the honourable distinction of Romans. Many dependent princes and communities, dispersed round the frontiers, were permitted, for a while, to hold their freedom and security by 70 the tenure of military service. Even select troops of hostile barbarians were frequently compelled or persuaded to consume their dangerous valour in remote climates, and for the benefit of the state. All these were included under the general name of auxiliaries; and howsoever they might vary according to the difference of times and circumstances, their numbers were 75 seldom much inferior to those of the legions themselves. Among the auxiliaries, the bravest and most faithful bands were placed under the command of praefects and centurions, and severely trained in the arts of Roman discipline; but the far greater part retained those arms, to which the nature of their country, or their early habits of life, more peculiarly 80 adapted them. By this institution each legion, to whom a certain proportion of auxiliaries was alloted, contained within itself every species of lighter troops, and of missile weapons; and was capable of encountering every nation, with the advantages of its respective arms and discipline. Nor was the legion destitute of what, in modern language, would be styled 85 a train of artillery. It consisted in ten military engines of the largest, and fifty-five of a smaller size; but all of which, either in an oblique or horizontal manner, discharged stone and darts with irresistible violence.

4   The camp of a Roman legion presented the appearance of a fortified city. As soon as the space was marked out, the pioneers carefully 90 levelled the ground, and removed every impediment that might interrupt its perfect regularity. Its form was an exact quadrangle; and we may calculate, that a square of about seven hundred yards was sufficient for the encampment of twenty thousand Romans; though a similar number of our own troops would expose to the enemy a front of more than treble that 95 extent. In the midst of the camp, the praetorium, or general's quarters,

rose above the others; the cavalry, the infantry, and the auxiliaries, occupied their respective stations; the streets were broad, and perfectly straight, and a vacant space of two hundred feet was left on all sides, between the tents and the rampart. The rampart itself was usually twelve feet high, 100 armed with a line of strong and intricate palisades, and defended by a ditch of twelve feet in depth as well as in breadth. This important labour was performed by the hands of the legionaries themselves; to whom the use of the spade and the pick-axe was no less familiar than that of the sword or *pilum*. Active valour may often be the present of nature; but such 105 patient diligence can be the fruit only of habit and discipline.

QUESTIONS

READER AND PURPOSE

1. Gibbon's purpose is to make clear how a Roman legion was organized and equipped. Does he succeed?

2. Does he appear to be writing for mature, educated readers or for school-children?

ORGANIZATION

3. Gibbon develops his topic by analysis. First he divides it into primary parts. Do these correspond to the paragraph structure—that is, does each paragraph represent a major division of the subject?

4. One might entitle the first paragraph "The Infantry." Give similar titles to the remaining three paragraphs.

5. Make an outline showing how Gibbon analyzes the infantry. There are seventeen sentences in this first paragraph. Show that they correspond, roughly if not perfectly, to the way in which the writer has divided his material.

6. Why does Gibbon italicize *Their* (60)? Is this device clumsy? Can it be defended?

7. Gibbon occasionally develops his subject by comparison and contrast. Mark two or three examples in your book.

SENTENCES

8. Would you describe Gibbon's sentences as very long, moderately long, or quite short? Can you find examples of short, simple sentences?

9. In the sentence beginning "The buckler" (12), what words are parallel * to "framed" (13)? Find other examples of parallelism in Gibbon's writing. The last sentence contains both parallelism and balance *, two clauses of about the same length standing on either side of the semicolon. "Active valour" (105) balances what words in the second clause? What other words and phrases in

this sentence exactly balance one another? In normal speech is this construction common or rare? Is it more appropriate to a formal tone and subject or to informal writing?

10. Why in the list quoted in question 6 does Gibbon use semicolons between the separate items instead of commas, which are more usual?

DICTION

11. Look up: constitution (1), files (30), ranks (30), disposition (32), tactics (36), phalanx (37), pikes (38), equestrian order (53), maces (63), levies 67), peculiarly (80), pioneers (90), rampart (100).

12. Substitute simpler, less formal words for these: constitution (1), discharge (19), launched (20), durst (21), impetuosity (22), adversary (28), habituated (30), solicited (51), suffrages (52). Do you think any of these substitutions improve the vigor of the writing?

13. What does Gibbon mean by "dangerous valour" (72)? Why is it an accurate and forceful phrase?

14. Find the etymologies * of ponderous (16), equestrian (53), barbarians (64).

15. Describe Gibbon's tone *. Does he regard the Roman legion as a paltry affair in comparison with modern army units? Or does he greatly admire the legion? Underline words and phrases that support your answer.

POINTS TO LEARN

1. Broadly speaking, we say that Gibbon's purpose is description. Yet he has ordered his description by carefully dividing and subdividing the thing described into its parts. In developing these parts, Gibbon uses illustration and comparison. A single paragraph or essay is seldom developed by one technique. Yet one or two techniques usually stand out above the others and govern their use.

2. Two seemingly different subjects may appear in a single paragraph if their relationship is made clear in the topic sentence.

3. Parallelism varies the rhythm of the prose and permits an economy especially desirable when the subject is composed of many details. Parallelism appears in almost all kinds of writing, both formal and informal, being particularly useful in description. But the combination of parallelism and balance most often belongs to a formal style.

4. A knowledge of etymologies helps us to remember the meaning of a word and to use it accurately.

5. The careful reader will catch the tone * of whatever he reads. Through his sentence structure and diction, almost every writer will suggest how he feels toward his subject and his reader.

SUGGESTIONS FOR WRITING

Taking Gibbon's organization as a model, describe one of the following: a unit of the armed services, a sports team, an institution, a business, a club.

IMPROVING YOUR STYLE

1. In your composition write two parallel sentences. In one make three or four verbs parallel to a single subject; in the other make three or four subjects parallel to one verb.

2. Include as well a balanced sentence.

Out of the Shadow of the Bay

Charles K. Long is a frequent contributor to such nature magazines as *Harrowsmith* and *Equinox*. His avid interest in the self-sufficient life away from cities is reflected in his books, *How to Survive Without a Salary* and *The Stonebuilder's Primer*. He lives with his wife near Portland, Ontario, in a stone house that he built himself. His essay on the village of La Loche, Saskatchewan, is a fine example of expository analysis reinforced by striking descriptions.

1   When night approached, the woman crept into a cave to sleep. A dog-like creature followed her in and lay down beside her while she slept. In the night the woman dreamed that the creature turned into a handsome man. They performed an act of love. In the morning, when she awoke, she found that the creature beside her was still a dog. Then a giant appeared at 5 the mouth of the cave and tore the dog to shreds, scattering the pieces over the earth. The organs became the fish in the lakes. The flesh became the animals. And the bits of skin became birds. Before he disappeared forever, the giant told the woman that her children could kill these creatures and live from their abundance. That, for the Chipewyan people, is how the 10 world began.

2   The giant's undying mistake was in failing to register the title to that abundance with the government of Saskatchewan. Of course, the giant could hardly have known that the Hudson's Bay Company wanted the furs, that southern sportsmen cherished antlers, that fish could be 15 mounted on walls as well as eaten. He didn't say a word about the uranium under the ground and who had the rights to that. He didn't even warn the people that the Oblate fathers would come with an entirely different story of how the world began, and who would be in charge.

3   To find the offspring of Eve and the dog-like creature today, we 20 drive 547 miles northwest from Regina. The bank calendar view of Sask-

From *Equinox*, 1, 1 (January 1982). Reprinted by permission of Charles K. Long.

atchewan—the quilted sea of wheat—lasts for less than half that distance. Then the prairie begins to roll, and swathes of poplar and spruce creep up between farms, growing slowly wider and bolder until it seems that the farms are the timid interlopers. The pavement ends at Buffalo Narrows. It's another 62 miles of axle-bashing ruts to La Loche.

4   Getting to La Loche has never been easy. It has, however, been profitable. Peter Pond, the first white fur trader to reach Lac La Loche, arrived in the summer of 1778. At the northern end of the lake, Pond saw a small, winding creek. A mile up the creek was an already well-trodden path through the pines. At the end of that 12-mile trail, Pond and his voyageurs suddenly emerged from a thicket of trees on the crest of a bluff dropping 600 feet to the Clearwater Valley below them. For the next hundred years this would be the top of the voyageurs' world. Behind them, the narrow creek and Lac La Loche led all the way back to Hudson Bay. Before them, the waters flowed to the Arctic, through the fur-rich Athabasca and Mackenzie valleys. The La Loche portage did not just divide the waters, it also marked the outer limit of the fur monopoly held by the Hudson's Bay Company, from the even richer lands to the north and west where any British subject was free to trade.

5   Crossing the divide with a year's supply of trade goods and fur was a Herculean labour. Each man carried 180 pounds on his back, struggling across the divide, plagued with insects, heat and thirst. Sir George Simpson, HBC Governor, crossed the portage in 1828, using ten local Indians to carry the freight. The Chipewyan carriers were paid in notes for trade goods. They also received "a fathom of tobacco," and a lecture on the evils of drink and the perils of trading with anyone but the Honorable Company. He then gave them, "as a matter of great indulgence, a glass of weak rum."

6   Missionaries soon followed the trails opened by the Honorable Company's traders. By the mid-1800s the Oblate order, formed in France to renew the Church in the wake of the revolution, had dispatched priests to Canada and charged them with strengthening Catholicism among the rural poor. The first missionary reached the portage on June 4, 1845. The Reverend Mr. Thibault reported that the people of the area were "inexpressibly docile" and readily converted to Christianity.

7   The Chipewyans are a gentle, accommodating people. They trapped and hauled freight for the fur companies. They welcomed the missionaries, hauling lumber up the frozen Methye River to build the church at La Loche. They guided the first overland trip to Uranium City in 1955, blazing the trail at −50 degrees F. The trail is now a road, named for a Meadow Lake businessman and serving a uranium mine run by AMOK, a French

company. It remains to be seen whether uranium will do any more for the people of La Loche than The Company and the Oblate fathers have done. But, good or bad, the impact of the new money is already trickling down.

8   Modern La Loche is clustered at the rim of a low, sandy bank, 65 overlooking the lake. Some 10 miles to the northwest, across the grey, choppy water, is the beginning of the historic portage.

9   The church looms on the high point of land between the town and the shore. Clad in sombre grey insul-brick, and guarded by a rough stone grotto whose backside has fallen away, the mission seems a little down at 70 the heels, like a dowager queen whose senility is beginning to show.

10   The drabness, though, is not entirely the fault of the mission and its leader for the last thirty years, Father Matthew. In fairness, it is the town—not the mission—that has changed. There is a new hospital next to the church, and facing it, a bright new school, gymnasium and playground. 75 Across the street is a restaurant, and beside that a poolroom. Even the mission's historic partner, the HBC, has built a new store just across the narrow rectory lane. Mind you, The Bay has hunkered down for the '80s with a squat, windowless bunker whose every possible opening has been shuttered with steel mesh; but the colors are bright and the contents mod- 80 ern. High tech futurist, Alvin Toffler, is on the book rack. New TVs line the shelves, for $149 and up. There's fresh milk and large eggs for $1.53 a dozen. The IGA around the corner and a handful of smaller stores help to keep the prices down.

11   None of this is at all remarkable, though, unless it can be seen in 85 contrast to La Loche as it was just a short time ago.

12   Bob Luker arrived in La Loche in 1968. He was a shy, dishevelled redhead, a would-be community organizer for the Ottawa-based Company of Young Canadians. But the community, he learned, was already well-organized. Father Matthew was at the political—as well as the geographic— 90 centre of the town. There was the Department of Natural Resources, the RCMP and the Hudson's Bay manager. There were also a few transitory whites, mostly attached to the school. The rest of the town's 1,500 people were natives. Luker recalls that, for them, there was one half-ton truck for hauling firewood, and one paid job (helping in the DNR office). There was 95 lots of unpaid work to do—helping in the mission garden, for example—but the money economy for native people was one truck, one DNR job, fishing and trapping, welfare, child allowance and the old age pension.

13   When the Liberal government of Premier Ross Thatcher cut off all welfare for "employables," the economy of the town collapsed. There were 100 lots of "employables," but the only job in town was already filled.

14   Credit was tough. The post office was in the Hudson's Bay store. There was no bank. The only place to receive or cash cheques was at The Bay. The Bay made sure its own credit accounts were fully paid up as the cheques came in.   105

15   The Bay's only competition in La Loche had been the small Co-op store, run by Bobby Clarke. Clarke was too lenient with credit, however, and the Co-op failed. Bobby Clarke went back to trapping. Just before Christmas 1968, he and his partner died on the trapline. There was some debate in town as to whether the official search party had been organized   110 quickly enough to save the men.

16   Certainly Clarke had enemies. He was one of the few native activists in town. He had competed with The Bay and criticized the Mounties and the priest. He was involved with early attempts to organize a local chapter of the Métis Society. Father Matthew refused to let the Society use   115 the meeting hall. They met in private. Strong opposition kept many away. The organization failed.

17   After Clarke died, his widow and children had difficulty getting fuel for the winter. Stubbornly they stayed where they were, even at −50 degrees F. Then their home burned to the ground. They left town. Whis-   120 pers linked the persistent tragedies that followed the Clarkes with his refusal to bend where others had bowed.

18   That same year Luker and Susan Dann were pressured into leaving town. Dann, the other CYC volunteer in La Loche, was trying to organize a preschool program for children. "There wasn't much to do in the village   125 then," she recalls. "People drank a lot of tea. There was lots of sex. A lot of the girls and young women used to come to my cabin and we would just sit around talking and drinking tea. They wanted to talk about life mostly— and birth control. The priest was really against birth control. I had some of those pamphlets put out by McGill Planned Parenthood. The girls were   130 very covert in asking to see them. They told me that the priest didn't want them to have (the pamphlets) . . . . Later, when the priest organized the meeting to kick us out of town, giving out the pamphlets was one of the chief accusations against us."

19   La Loche, today, looks like a town reborn. A young town. Compact.   135 It hardly looks big enough to hold the 2,000 citizens advertised—and by all accounts there are even more people now. Most of them are young. Three-quarters of the population is under 21. They congregate in the dusty unpaved streets, where the wind plays shuffleboard with litter. The younger ones tumble happily over the stoops and unfenced yards.   140

20   In the fall, when fathers are looking for moose, little boys stalk the

forest of back yard sheds with slingshots, followed by their ubiquitous and much loved dogs. Dogs have strong spirits (shadows of the dream cave weave through the sanctioned Genesis) and bad things happen to anyone who mistreats a dog. During a rabies scare, all the dogs had to be destroyed. 145
No one would take on the task. The Mountie who finally volunteered soon died in a plane crash over Peter Pond Lake. The body was never found. The story ends with a knowing look.

21   Large, young families are bound to create some pressure in a town of small bungalows. More surprising is that the houses themselves are 150
closely bunched on 50-foot lots, dressed shoulder to shoulder in orderly ranks. Bob Long, economic development officer with the Local Community Authority (LCA), explains that the lots were surveyed and controlled under the rules of the Central Mortgage and Housing Corporation. Apart from bureaucratic tidiness, the reason for the close regimentation is utility 155
services. The services available are extensive by any standard. There is door-to-door garbage collection, a fire department, dial phones, day care, a liquor store, a health clinic, gas stations, a library, an airstrip—a wealth of services that would not be possible without a resource-rich provincial government to foot the bill. 160

22   It is not, however, a wealthy town. There are only 280 jobs in La Loche. Outsiders, mostly teachers and other public employees, hold 104 of them. The unemployment rate among locals is a staggering 80 per cent. Recent layoffs might take it closer to 90 per cent, says Alphonse Janvier. Janvier, an LCA employee and chairman of the local school board, looks 165
more like a student than the chairman of the board. "Social problems just won't be solved before real economic change takes place." He's talking about jobs, and about the regular failure of programs designed to create jobs. "The problem has been that the government was coming in with the ideas rather than the ideas coming from the people." Now the ideas are 170
starting to come from the local Economic Development Corporation, under the direction of an elected board.

23   The Development Corporation is beginning to show its mettle. In housing, for example. Nearly all of the old log cabins, scattered willy-nilly on common land, have been replaced by southern-style bungalows, lined 175
up side-by-side on a treeless grid. Hard to heat, dripping with condensation, doors and windows splintered from the effects of frost and too-light (i.e., cheap) hardware, the provincial houses quickly disintegrate. The Development Corporation is setting out to prove that it can build a better house for the same amount of money. The demonstration house is only half-built, but 180
it is already showing its distinctions. Set skew to the grid (and to every other

house on the street) it is aligned with the sun for maximum solar heat advantage. There is a full 12 inches of insulation in the double walls, and a wood/oil combination furnace in the basement. Inside air is vented through a heat exchanger. Heavy-duty hardware will keep the doors and windows straight. The native tradesmen building the house are rightfully proud of what is emerging. What is emerging may be very much more than a house.

24 Not everyone has the same kind of confidence in the community's future. Jonas Clark is 78. He has been trapping and fishing for seventy-one years. He speaks four languages, though he has never been to school. Clark is Métis. "My daddy came from Scotland," he explains. "He was Hudson's Bay man in Flin Flon. He make a girl friend there, and—you know what I mean 'make a girl friend?'—he make a girl friend there and have two babies. Then he come to La Loche to be Hudson's Bay man here. Then he make a girl friend with my mother. I was born here seventy-eight years ago. Then my daddy left again—somewhere else for Hudson's Bay Company."

25 Today, Clark sits in his kitchen, the remains of a duck on the table. "There's a lotta money now," he says, "but lotsa people got nothin'. In the old days everybody had gun, canoe, cabin, traps . . . . Now all they got is government money and too much liquor and poker. In ten years is gonna be hard times. Money goin' up and up and up."

26 Clark still hunts and traps and lives with a houseful of assorted grand- and great-grandchildren. Chipewyan families are extended and loving. Not all of them take his advice, however. Some younger charges are heard in a back room giggling over the Flintstones. Jonas is on his way to Thursday court for another errant grandson. "Drinking" is the only explanation offered.

27 Clark's neighbour, Dave O'Hara, has trapped and fished with the old man many times. "Jonas," he says, "has his past. And because he's a dreamer, he's got a future. The young people say, however, that 'the old have nothing to offer. They can tell what it was like in the past, but they can't tell us what the future will be like.' Three thousand people can't trap."

28 Just outside La Loche, a mile or so up a sandy trail that curves around the shore, is a tidy one-room cabin on a modest knoll of pine and birch. It looks across the northern water to the place where the creek still marks the old portage to the Athabasca country. The middle-aged couple who live in the cabin are busy with autumn chores. He is scraping fat from a fresh moose hide. He killed it himself. His moccasins are made from last year's moose. His wife will make a coat this year. He scrapes with a tool he has carved from the leg bone of a caribou. A loop braces the tool to his forearm in the ancient way. On the porch is a tub of water and ashes, and a

perfect deerskin is soaking. Smiling, he shows off his skill and abundance with a patient pantomime for visitors who speak neither Chipewyan nor Cree, his only languages. The cabin is solid, clean and spare. No water, sewers or telephone lines. The government pipes don't reach this far. Three   225
thousand people can't trap.

29   At night, the younger half of La Loche packs itself into the cavern-ous modern Robby Fontaine Memorial Arena. The name is important. Fontaine is described by former residents as an implacable opponent of the Bay, the priest and every vestige of the old establishment. Fontaine was   230
already an old man in the winter of 1969, when the first hockey team in La Loche was organized—from a donated pile of second-hand skates. Most of the kids had never skated before. They played a team from Buffalo Narrows and lost by something like 40 to 0. The game turned into a brawl.

30   Now hockey draws a quarter of the population to the arena. Before   235
the concrete floor is frozen over for the season, there are roller skates for rent. It is a beehive of exuberant youngsters jiving around on their vinyl wheels to the thunder of the Rolling Stones. A sprinkling of Mums and Dads supporting fawn-legged young, a swirl of flirting teens, and wave after wave of joyful kids, booming around in circles with white-dusted bums and   240
knees, shrieks, giggles and face bustin' ain't-the-circus-wonderful grins.

31   It is hard to reconcile this energetic joy with the sombre missionary past, with the quiet pride of the self-sufficient trapper's life, with the hope-less pit of alcoholism that looms through broken windows. They seem like parts of different lives. Jonas Clark isn't here tonight. He said he liked the   245
village life when he was a boy, "but now there's too much noise."

32   Parts of different lives—and yet it is folly to look for clear-cut factions within the town. Political activists belong to AMNSIS (the Associa-tion of Métis and Non-Status Indians of Saskatchewan); and yet Jonas Clark, who is widely known as "the priest's man," insists that the houses   250
being built by AMNSIS are the best in town. The priest campaigns against drinking; AMNSIS supports AA. Socialist Saskatchewan helps native capi-talists get started with development loans and consultants to show them the ropes. One white outsider keeps a dog sled in his living room, and enjoys teaching young Indians to trap. Stereotyped divisions get a little   255
blurry.

DECOLONIZATION

33   Rod Bishop is an AMNSIS field worker. He travelled regularly to La Loche in the shrill days of the '60s, when AMNSIS was the Métis

Society and Bishop was called the Minister of Housing and Guerrilla Warfare. Now Bishop sits in his living room, tired from a day of forking hay. A   260
small boy crawls onto his lap with a book. His wife Rose is in the adjoining
room, planning their daughter's wedding. It will be in the church, with a
white dress and all the trimmings. When asked about his memories of La
Loche, Bishop doesn't hesitate. "Father Matthew used to rule that place,"
he says, "but now the people are getting decolonialized."   265

34   Bishop and Jim Sinclair, AMNSIS President, recently travelled to
London to explain their position on the constitution. Sinclair told the
parliamentarians, "When the missionaries came to our land, they had the
Bible and we had the land. When they had finished, we ended up with the
Bible and they ended up with the land. Then the army followed and the rest   270
is history."

35   On a bright autumn day, we find Father Matthew directing a crew
of five strapping boys around the mission yard. The rectory is getting a new
wardrobe. The priest is driving the truck. The boys are doing the lifting.
The wardrobe goes on the second floor. Father Matthew gets things organ-   275
ized in fluent Chipewyan. The boys follow orders cheerfully.

36   Father Matthew refuses to be interviewed. Others tell us that he
opposed the building of the road to La Loche. He fought to keep out the
Métis Society. He stopped the reading of Planned Parenthood literature.
He kept out the Pentecostals. He fought the LCA to keep the hospital on   280
mission land. But he did it all in Chipewyan, and he still fills the church for
two services every Sunday. Tenacity is part of the Oblate code; the Oblates
vow to stay in their congregations until death. If the power of the mission
has not exactly withered away, the balance has nevertheless been tipped.
The power of the community, the state and a relentless southern culture is   285
unfolding all around. The twentieth century is coming to La Loche, and no
finger in the dike will be able to hold it back.

37   The reason, of course, is money. The old order has simply been
out-spent by the new. It's more than the relatively piddling sums spent in
La Loche itself. It's the whole web of connecting threads that breaks the old   290
pattern of isolation. It's the roads, airstrips and satellites—services that
were not designed to serve the people of La Loche, but which nevertheless
are bringing them pell-mell into the '80s.

38   Almost within the shadow of Father Matthew's spire is another
heavenly shaft. Down by the water's edge, incongruous beside the weath-   295
ered boats, is the slender mast of a satellite receiver. It brings in twenty-four
channels of mostly American sacraments—relentlessly. Sports and movies

are big, but anything will do. Sesame Street characters dance away behind
the counter of the gas station, the local news from Chicago, and a soap
opera version of the American Revolution fill the living rooms. The Bandit   300
is headed north, and Smokey can't stop him now. I asked Bob Long what
the town might do if the federal Department of Communications follows
through on its threats to close illegal stations like this one. "Move the
equipment onto the reserve and tell the DOC to go . . . ." he replies, in
deadly earnest.   305

39   For better or worse, the tide of change is sweeping over the dike.
Uranium money, government programs, roads and satellites make it inevitable. Still unanswered is the question of who will control those changes,
and what it will all mean for the progeny of Eve and the dog-like creature.

40   Behind the new arena, in a boxy office trailer that houses the   310
spillover of LCA offices, is a cramped reception bay and a half-open door.
The sign on the door says: "DANGER—RADIOACTIVITY." It is supposed to be a joke. Behind the rough-sawn lumber door is a tiny radio
station broadcasting Yoko Ono music on FM 89.9 to the people of La
Loche. That's the radio part.   315

41   The activity is in the effervescence of Mabel Park, disc jockey,
newscaster, producer, director, technician and everything else. The music
is modern. So is the lady. Her fingers flick over the controls with confidence.

42   If the radioactive sign is a joke, it is a superficial one. This kind of
activity, however mellow it may seem on the surface, is part of a more   320
promising future. There is nothing revolutionary in the music of Yoko Ono,
or even in the gentle Ms. Park. The promise of change comes from the
simple fact that the fingers on the controls are brown, the colour of smoke-
tanned doeskin.

43   Park admits she was nervous at first, but now she loves the job. She   325
flips through a pile of records and announcements, ordering the rest of the
program. "Who decides what goes on the air?" I ask her.

44   She leans back comfortably in the swivel chair. "I guess I do now,"
she says, letting the softest edge of a feline smile well up from somewhere
within.   330

QUESTIONS

1. Although this essay is mainly expository, it is also, to some extent, persuasive. Thus, when Long says that "Stereotyped divisions get a little blurry" (255–56), he seems to be discussing the subject in a neutral, objective manner. But paragraph 36, which discusses Father Matthew, concludes with this remark: "The twentieth century is coming to La Loche, and no finger in the dike will be able to hold it back." Does this comment lead you to believe that Long is not quite as objective as the earlier comment indicated? What other evidence can you find that shows Long to be generally on one side of the question rather than the other? Consider also, in this respect, the last two paragraphs of the essay.

ORGANIZATION

2. Long begins his essay by telling a brief story about the Chipewyan interpretation of creation. Did you think this is an effective introduction? Did it make you want to read more?

3. How are paragraphs 1, 2, 3 and 20 and 39 related?

4. After the introductory paragraphs 1 to 3, paragraphs 4 to 7 detail the history of the area. How does Long make this transition? Then how does he shift to his next topic?

5. How does paragraph 11 function as both summary and transition?

6. Explain how the following transitional expressions function: "Modern La Loche" (65), "Today, Clark sits" (197), "The reason, of course" (288), "For better or worse" (306).

7. Compare the structure of paragraphs 4, 5, and 6. Is the first sentence in each the topic sentence? or is the topic sentence elsewhere in the paragraph? or is it altogether missing? Could any one of the paragraphs be more tightly structured by the addition of a topic sentence? or the substitution of a better one?

8. How does the final paragraph make a fine contrast to paragraph 1 and, especially, to paragraph 2?

SENTENCES

9. Why does Long use dashes in paragraph 3 but parentheses in paragraph 20? Would there be much difference if the marks were interchanged?

10. Point out the parallel* elements in paragraph 7.

11. Comment on the effectiveness (or its lack) of the fragments* in paragraphs 19 and 23.

12. Compare the sentence structure of paragraph 12 with that of paragraph 23. How many simple,* compound,* and complex* sentences are there in each? Then do the same for paragraph 42. From this brief survey, what kinds of

generalizations can you make about Long's sentence structure?

13. Explain the irony* in the first sentence of paragraph 2.

DICTION

14. Look up: *swathes* (23), *interlopers* (25), *bluff* (32), *monopoly* (38), *indulgence* (48), *grotto* (70), *rectory* (78), *bunker* (79), *futurist* (81), *transitory* (92), *ubiquitous* (142), *feline* (329).

15. Does Long tend to use words which are abstract* and general, or concrete* and specific? Examine his diction in any four consecutive paragraphs.

16. Identify the images* in the first three paragraphs. Do any of these seem particularly effective? Explain your preferences.

POINTS TO LEARN

1. Exposition and persuasion are not mutually exclusive; they can be used together with considerable impact.

2. Sentence fragments* can be used effectively as appositives.*

SUGGESTIONS FOR WRITING

As the topic for an expository essay choose a location you know well where group activities often take place: a school-yard, the local hockey rink, a community league centre, the church basement or social hall, a gymnasium, an apartment recreation centre. Begin your exposition by focussing on one type of character: the bully, the quiet but efficient leader, the constant complainer, the arrogant loner, the trustworthy friend of all, the lonely braggart, etc. Although you will be describing the activities which take place in this centre, your focus will be on the people—particularly in their relationship to the one character you have chosen.

IMPROVING YOUR STYLE

Include in your essay the following:

1. At least two fragments,* used as appositives,* in the same paragraph.

2. Three sentences, using parallel structure,* in another paragraph.

3. At least one paragraph in which images* play an important part.

BHARATI MUKHERJEE

An Invisible Woman

Bharati Mukherjee was born in Calcutta and received her early education in India. Later she studied at Vassar and the University of Iowa, and taught at McGill. She is married to Clark Blaise, the Canadian novelist and short-story writer. She has been widely acclaimed for her novels, especially *Days and Nights in Calcutta* (1977) and *Darkness* (1985). Her essay is a precise and vivid analysis of the reasons that caused her to move from Canada to the United States.

1   This story begins in Calcutta and ends in a small town in New York State called Saratoga Springs. The very long, fifteen-year middle is set in Canada. In this story, no place or person fares well, but Canada comes off poorest of all.

2   I was born in Calcutta, that most Victorian and British of post-   5
independence Indian cities. It was not the Calcutta of documentary films—not a hell where beggars fought off dying cattle for still-warm garbage—but a gracious, green, sub-tropical city where Irish nuns instructed girls from better families on how to hold their heads high and how to drop their voices to a whisper and still be heard and obeyed above the screams of the city.   10

3   There was never a moment when we did not know that our city and our country were past their prime. We carried with us the terrible knowledge that while our lives were comfortable, they would be safer somewhere else. Ambition dictated emigration. In the 1950s everyone was waiting for the revolution. "The first thing the Communists do," my best friend   15
told me when we were fifteen, "is feel your hands. If your hands are soft, it's *kaput* for you." In our school every girl had soft hands. But when Stalin died, the nuns prayed for his soul: this was known as "fair play," an example for us pliant, colonial girls to follow.

4   In a city continually blistered with revolutionary fervour, we plod-   20
ded through our production of *The Mikado*. At least twice I was escorted by

From *Saturday Night*, 96, 3 (March 1981).

van loads of police past striking workers outside the gates of my father's factory so that I could go to school and dance a quadrille or play a walk-on part. "Our girls can take their places with the best anywhere in the world," Mother John-Baptist, the headmistress, had promised my father on my first 25 day of school. (And we have, all over India and the English-speaking, even German-speaking, world.) On a sticky August night in 1961, when my younger sister, who was going to Vassar College, and I, on my way to the University of Iowa, left by Air India for New York, I felt that I could.

5   Great privilege had been conferred upon me; my struggle was to 30 work hard enough to deserve it. And I did. This bred confidence, but not conceit. I never doubted that if I wanted something—a job, a scholarship—I could get it. And I did. I had built-in advantages: primarily those of education, secondarily those of poise and grooming. I knew that if I decided to return to India after my writing degree at Iowa was finished, my father would find 35 me a suitable husband. I would never work, never be without servants and comfort, and I could dabble in the arts until they bored me. My daughters would attend the same school as I had, my sons a similar school. It was unthinkable that they would not be class leaders, then national leaders, and that they would not perpetuate whatever values we wished to give them. 40 Such is the glory, and the horror, of a traditional society, even at its tattered edges.

6   I had no trouble at Iowa, and though I learned less about those Vietnam and assassination years than I might have, I liked the place well enough to stay on and arrange for extension of my scholarship. I married an 45 American, Clark Blaise, whose parents had come from Canada and then divorced, and whose mother had returned to Winnipeg. I stayed on for a Ph.D., thus cutting off forever the world of passive privilege I had come from. An M.A. in English is considered refined, but a doctorate is far too serious a business, indicative more of brains than beauty, and likely to lead 50 to a quarrelsome nature. We had a son, and when that son was almost two we moved to Canada. Clark had dreamed restless dreams of Canada, especially of Montreal. Still unformed at twenty-five, he felt it was the place that would let him be himself.

7   It is now the summer of 1966, and the three of us cross at Windsor 55 in a battered VW van. Our admission goes smoothly, for I have a lecturer's position at McGill. I say "smoothly," but I realize now there was one curious, even comic event that foreshadowed the difficulties faced by Indians in Canada. A middle-aged immigration officer, in filling out my applica-

tion, asked me the year of my birth. I told him, in that private-school accent   60
of which I was once so proud. Mishearing, he wrote down "1914" and
remarked, "Ah, we're the same age." He happened to be exactly twice my
age. He corrected his error without a fuss. Ten minutes inside Canada, and
I was already invisible.

8   The oldest paradox of prejudice is that it renders its victims simulta-   65
neously invisible and over-exposed. I have not met an Indian in Canada
who has not suffered the humiliations of being overlooked (in jobs, in
queues, in deserved recognition) and from being singled out (in hotels,
department stores, on the streets, and at customs). It happened to me so
regularly in Canada that I now feel relief, just entering Macy's in Albany,   70
New York, knowing that I won't be followed out by a security guard. In
America, I can stay in hotels and *not* be hauled out of elevators or stopped
as I enter my room. It's perhaps a small privilege in the life of a North
American housewife—not to be taken automatically for a shoplifter or a
whore—but it's one that my years in Canada, and especially my two years   75
in Toronto, have made me grateful for. I know objections will be raised; I
know Canadians all too well. Which of us has *not* been harassed at customs?
On a summer's night, which of us *can* walk down Yonge Street without
carloads of stoned youths shouting out insults? We have all stood patiently
in bakery lines, had people step in front of us, we've all waved our plastic   80
numbers and wailed, "But I was next—"

9   If we are interested in drawing minute distinctions, we can disregard or explain away nearly anything. ("Where did it happen? Oh, *Rosedale*.
Well, no *wonder* . . ." Or, "Were you wearing a sari? No? Well, no wonder . . ."
Or, "Oh, *we* wouldn't do such a thing. He must have been French or   85
something . . .") And I know the pious denials of hotel clerks. In a Toronto
hotel I was harassed by two house detectives who demanded to see my
room key before allowing me to go upstairs to join my family—harassed me
in front of an elevator-load of leering, elbow-nudging women. When I
complained, I extracted only a "Some of my best friends are Pakis" from   90
the night manager, as he fervently denied that what I had just experienced
was in fact a racial incident.

10   And I know the sanctimonious denials of customs officers, even as
they delight in making people like me dance on the head of a bureaucratic
pin. On a return from New York to Toronto I was told, after being forced to   95
declare a $1 valuation on a promotional leaflet handed out by a bookstore,
that even a book of matches had to be declared. ("I didn't ask if you *bought*
anything. Did you hear me ask about purchases? Did you? I'll ask you again

in very clear English. *Are you bringing anything into the country?"*).

11   Do not think that I enjoy writing this of Canada. I remain a Cana-   100
dian citizen. This is the testament of a woman who came, like most
immigrants, confident of her ability to do good work, in answer to a stated
need. After the unsophisticated, beer-swilling rednecks of Iowa, British-
commonwealth Canada, and Montréal in particular, promised a kind of
haven. At the road-stops in Iowa and Illinois, when I entered in a sari,   105
silverware would drop, conversations cease; it was not the kind of attention
I craved. It was never a hostile reaction (it might have been, in the Deep
South, but I avoided that region). It was innocent, dumbfounded stupefac-
tion, and I thought I would be happy enough to leave it behind. As we drove
past Toronto on the 401, we picked up the strains of sitar music on the   110
radio; Montréal had spice shops and was soon to have Indian restaurants. It
should have been a decent country, and we should have been happy in it.

12   I have been in America, this time, for only a few months, but in
that time I've been attacked by a streaker on Sixth Avenue in New York; my
purse has been snatched on Fifth Avenue; our car has been rammed and   115
our insurance defrauded in Saratoga Springs; a wallet has been stolen and
our children have complained of the drinking and dope-smoking even in
their classrooms. Yes, it's America: violent, mindlessly macho, conformist,
lawless. And certainly no dark-skinned person has the right to feel comfortable inside American history. Yet I do. If I am not exempt from victimiza-   120
tion here, neither are Clark or my sons, and neither am I exempt from
redress. I am less shocked, less outraged and shaken to my core, by a
purse-snatching in New York City in which I lost all of my dowry-gold—
everything I'd been given by my mother in marriage—than I was by a
simple question asked of me in the summer of 1978 by three high-school   125
boys on the Rosedale subway station platform in Toronto. Their question
was, "Why don't you go back to Africa?"

13   It hurt because of its calculation, its calm, ignorant satisfaction, its
bland assumption of the right to break into my privacy. In New York, I was
violated because of my suspected affluence (a Gucci purse) and my obvi-   130
ously foreign, heedless, non-defensiveness. Calcutta equipped me to survive theft or even assault; it did not equip me to accept proof of my
unworthiness. (Friends say, "Rosedale? Well . . ." or, "Teenagers, well . . ."
and I don't dispute them. But I owe it to my friends, and I have many
friends in Canada, to dig deeper.)   135

14   Thanks to Canadian rhetoric on the highest level, I have learned

several things about myself that I never suspected. The first is that I have no country of origin. In polite company, I am an "East Indian" (the opposite, presumably, of a "West Indian"). The East Indies, in my school days, were Dutch possessions, later to become Indonesia. In impolite company I'm a   140
"Paki," (a British slur unknown in America, I'm happy to say). For an Indian of my generation, to be called a "Paki" is about as appealing as it is for an Israeli to be called a Syrian. In an official Green Paper on Immigration and Population I learn that I'm something called a "visible minority" from a "non-traditional area of immigration" who calls into question the "absorptive   145
capacity" of Canada. And that big question (to which my contribution is really not invited) is, "What kind of society do we really want?"

15   A spectre is haunting Canada: the perfidious "new" (meaning "dark" and thus, self-fulfillingly, "non-assimilable") immigrant, coming to snatch up jobs, welfare cheques, subway space, cheap apartments, and blue-eyed   150
women.

16   The Green Paper in 1975—which seemed an admirable exercise in demographic planning, an open invitation to join in a "debate"—was really a premeditated move on the part of government to throw some bones (some immigrants) to the howling wolves. The "we" of that open question   155
was understood to mean the Anglo-Saxon or Québec-French "founding races"; it opened up the sewers of resentment that polite, British-style forbearance had kept a lid on. My kind of Canadian was assumed, once again, not to exist, not to have a legitimate opinion to offer. ("Well, you could have made an official deposition through the proper multi-cultural   160
channel whenever hearings were held in your community . . .")

17   Most Indians would date the new up-front violence, the physical assaults, the spitting, the name-calling, the bricks through the windows, the pushing and shoving on the subways—it would be, by this time, a very isolated Indian who has not experienced one or more of those reactions—   165
from the implied consent given to racism by that infamous document. I cannot describe the agony and the betrayal one feels, hearing oneself spoken of by one's own country as being somehow exotic to its nature—a burden, a cause for serious concern. It may have been rhetorically softened, it may have been academic in tone, but in feeling it was Nuremberg, and it   170
unleashed its own mild but continuing *Kristallnacht*. In that ill-tempered debate, the government itself appropriated the language, the reasoning, the motivation that had belonged—until then—to disreputable fringe groups. Suddenly it was all right, even patriotic, to blame these non-assimilable Asian hordes for urban crowding, unemployment, and welfare burdens.   175

And the uneducated, unemployed, welfare-dependent, native-born *lumpen* teenagers leaped at the bait.

18 It is not pleasant to realize your own government has betrayed you so coldly.

19 What about the "absorptive capacity" of the ambitious immigrant to take in all these new, startling descriptions of himself? It creates double-vision when self-perception is so utterly at odds with social standing. We are split from our most confident self-assumptions. We must be blind, stupid, or egomaniacal to maintain self-respect or dignity when society consistently undervalues our contribution. In Montréal, I was, simultaneously, a full professor at McGill, an author, a confident lecturer, and (I like to think) a charming and competent hostess and guest—*and* a house-bound, fearful, aggrieved, obsessive, and unforgiving queen of bitterness. Whenever I read articles about men going berserk, or women committing suicide, and read the neighbours' dazed pronouncements ("But he was always so friendly, so outgoing, never a problem in the world . . ."), I knew I was looking into a mirror. Knowing that the culture condescended toward me, I needed ways of bolstering my self-respect—but those ways, at least to politely raised, tightly disciplined women of my age and origin, can only be achieved in society, in the recognition of our contributions.

20 And there, of course, I am up against another Canadian dilemma. I have always been struck by an oddity, call it a gap, in the cultural consciousness of the Canadian literary establishment. For fifteen years I was a professor of English and of creative writing at McGill. I published novels, stories, essays, reviews. In a land that fills it airports with itinerant poets and story-tellers, I was invited only once to give a reading by myself (after *Days and Nights in Calcutta* appeared, Clark and I, who had written it together, were frequently invited together). On that one occasion, I learned, after arriving in a mining town at three in the morning, that I'd been invited from the jacket photo and was expected to "come across." ("The others did.") No provisions had been made for my stay, except in my host's bachelor house. ("Oh, you let him meet you at the airport at three a.m.? And you went back to his house thinking there was a wife?") Friends explained to me that really, since nothing happened (except a few shoves and pushes), I shouldn't mention it again. Until now, I haven't.

21 Of course, it is possible to interpret everything in a different light. While no one likes to be pawed, isn't it nice to be acknowledged, even this way? (Don't laugh, it was suggested.) My point is simply this: an Indian slips out of invisibility in this culture at considerable peril to body and soul. I've alluded briefly (in *Days and Nights*) to the fact that I was not invited to join the Writers' Union of Canada, back at its founding, even though at that particular moment I was a Canadian and Clark was not (my Indian citizenship conferred special dispensations that his American one did not). The first explanation for the oversight was that the invitation extended to Clark was "assumed" to include me. While even a low-grade feminist might react uncomfortably to such a concoction, another, and I think truthful explanation was offered. "We didn't know how to spell your name, and we were afraid of insulting you," a well-known writer later wrote me. She's right; I would have been insulted (just as I'm mildly insulted by Canada Council letters to "Mr. Bharati Blaise"). And then, with a tinge of self-justification, she continued: "Your book was published by an American publisher and we couldn't get hold of it, so . . ."

22   Well, it's an apology and an explanation and it's easy to forgive as an instance of the persistent amateurism in the Canadian soul. But if you scrutinize just a little harder, and if you've dipped into the well of forgiveness far too often, you see a very different interpretation. *If you don't have a family compact name, forget about joining us.* If you don't have Canadian content, forget about publishing here. "The only Canadian thing about the novel is that it was written by a woman who now lives in Montréal," said a reviewer for my second novel, *Wife*, in *Books in Canada* (she was herself a feminist and emerging ethnicist), not even recognizing a book aimed right at her. "How can you call yourself a Canadian writer if you didn't play in snow as a child?" asked a CBC television interviewer. And more severely: "How do you justify taking grants and then not writing about Canada?"

23   The answer to all that is that I do write about Canada, perhaps not as directly as I am writing now, but that I refuse to capitulate to the rawness of Canadian literature—and, more to the point, I refuse to set my work in Canada because to do so would be to reduce its content to the very subject of this essay: politics and paranoia and bitter disappointment. The condition of the Indian in Canada is a sociological and political subject. We've not yet achieved the ease that would permit us to write of the self and of the expanding consciousness. To set my work in Canada is necessarily to adopt an urgent and strident tone; I would find irony an ill-considered option in any such situation. I advocate, instead, fighting back.

24   In case anyone finds a copy of *Wife*, it should be read in the following way: the nominal setting is Calcutta and New York City. But in the mind of the heroine, it is always Toronto.

25   Fifteen years ago, the Indian was an exotic in America, except in university towns and maybe New York City. Now I doubt if there's a town in America without its Indian family—even Saratoga Springs has Indian   255 dentists and pediatricians. I am no longer an exotic butterfly (people used to stagger up to me, quite unconscious that there was a young woman inside the folds of brilliant cloth, just to feel the material, and then walk away). Nor am I a grubby, dishonest, smelly, ignorant, job-snatching, baby-breeding, unassimilable malcontent. For the first time in my adult life, I   260 am unemployed—the price I was obliged to pay for immigration to the United States. Clark this year is teaching in the local college. Our income is less than a third of what it has been, and dark times are coming. Next year, I can take the job Clark is filling now; the college has made us an interesting proposal, though it leaves many questions unanswered. Will Clark then stay   265 here or return? He doesn't know.

26   America trusts confrontation; its rough sense of justice derives from slugging it out. It tolerates contradictions that seem, in retrospect, monstrous. Perhaps it trusts to the constitution and the knowledge that somehow, someday, that document will resolve all difficulties. This is not   270 the British style, not the Canadian style, in which conflict is viewed as evidence of political failure. In Canada, Parliament's sacred duty is the preservation of order; its mandate, at least in recent years, is to anticipate disorder. I can appreciate that, and if I were a white mainstream Canadian I'd probably endorse it wholeheartedly. Toronto really is a marvellous, beau-   275 tiful city, as I tell all my American friends. Good God, if ever there was a city I should have been happy in, it was Toronto.

27   But when you are part of the Canadian and Toronto underbelly, invisible and nakedly obvious, you can't afford a white man's delusions. It's in Canada that a columnist can write a glib and condescending book, attack   280 the frail, ineffective civil liberties legislation in the country, and be called a brilliant and daring intellectual. It's Canada that struggles against a constitution of its own, and its premiers who downgrade the concept of a human rights charter.

28   While preparing to write this account, I interviewed dozens of   285 people, mostly of Indian or Pakistani origin, in many parts of Canada. I read until I grew sick—of the assaults, the recommendations, the testimonies. I attended meetings, I talked to grandparents, and I talked to high-schoolers. I walked with the police down the troubled streets of east-end Toronto; I pursued some of the more lurid stories of the past year in Toronto. I turned   290 down collaboration on some other stories; I did not feel Canadian enough to appear on a TV program celebrating the accomplishments of new

Canadians; nor did I wish to take part in a TV show that set out to ascribe suicides among Indo-Canadian women solely to community pressures to have male children. Friends who supported this research will probably not   295 find their observations in this piece; they will find, instead, that I turned it all inside out.

29   To a greater or lesser extent those friends and I share a common history. We came in the mid-1960s for professional reasons. We saw scope and promise, and we were slow to acknowledge the gathering clouds. Some   300 of us have reacted positively, working with the local or provincial governments, serving as consultants, as organizers, as impresarios of understanding. Others have taken hockey sticks on vigilante patrols to protect their people. Many, including myself, have left, unable to keep our twin halves together.

QUESTIONS

READER AND PURPOSE

1. Why do you think that Mukherjee states her purpose, in the opening paragraph, so precisely, briefly, and bluntly? In order to deal with this matter you must consider the entire essay, paying special attention to tone* and point of view*. Note also such remarks as the first sentence of paragraphs 11 and 23.

2. In the last sentence of paragraph 13, the author comments that she is attempting to "dig deeper" into the causes of the prejudice of which she has been the victim. Does she, in your opinion, succeed in this attempt? Is she more successful at uncovering root causes than, for example, Joy Kogawa (pp. 40–52)? You might also consider, in this regard, the essays by Margaret Atwood (pp. 251–55) and Anne Roiphe (pp. 256–64).

3. "We must be blind, stupid, or egomaniacal to maintain self-respect or dignity when society consistently undervalues our contribution" (183–85). "I refuse to set my work in Canada because to do so would be to reduce its content to the very subject of this essay: politics and paranoia and bitter disappointment" (242–44).
Which of these two statements best summarizes Mukherjee's thesis? Or are both insufficient?

ORGANIZATION

4. One of the unifying devices in this essay is the obvious chronological references: "In the 1950s everyone was waiting for the revolution" (14–15); "It is now the summer of 1966" (55); "I have been in America, this time, for only a few months" (113). Identify other references to time, both obvious and indirect. Is Mukherjee's chronology consistently clear, or are there sections of this essay in which the time of the events might have been more directly stated?

5. How does the first sentence of paragraph 7 function as both transition and summary? Does the last sentence of paragraph 11 have the same kinds of functions?

6. Paragraph 12 consists of two halves neatly balanced on the brief statement "Yet I do." What do these halves consist of, and how does that brief sentence balance them?

7. Is paragraph 18 a conclusion? a summary? a transition? all three? Was the author correct in making a separate paragraph out of this one sentence, or should it have been placed at the end of paragraph 17, as its conclusion?

8. In her final sentence Mukherjee states that she, and others, have been "unable to keep our twin halves together." Which "halves" is she referring to? Does such a reference make an effective conclusion to this essay?

SENTENCES

9. Parenthetical expressions are normally used to add incidental information which explains or illustrates. Mukherjee, however, gives her parenthetical expressions more important roles. Choose any three or four of them (as in, for example, paragraphs 9, 10, 13, 14, 16, 20, 25) and explain what role each plays and why these sentences are in parentheses.

10. Why does the author use dashes instead of parentheses in the second sentence of paragraph 2? Would a parenthetical expression have worked just as well, given the nature of parenthetical expressions throughout this essay? Could the same be said about the fourth sentence in paragraph 5?

11. In paragraphs 9 and 10 Mukherjee italicizes a number of words. Why? What difference would there be if these words were not italicized?

12. The first two sentences of paragraph 12 both consist of series. In the first the elements are separated by semi-colons, in the second by commas—that is, by asyndeton* or by a variation of it which uses semi-colons instead of commas. Rewrite both series using polysyndeton*. Which do you think is the more effective?

13. Is the first sentence of paragraph 19 a rhetorical question*? an organizing sentence*? both? neither?

DICTION

14. Look up: *fares* (3), *kaput* (17), *pliant* (19), *paradox* (65), *queues* (68), *sari* (84), *sitar* (110), *bland* (129), *absorptive* (145), *demographic* (153), *deposition* (160), *lumpen* (176), *alluded* (215), *ethnicist* (236), *mandate* (273).

15. In the last line of paragraph 3, why does a comma separate "pliant" and "colonial"? What would be the result if the comma were omitted?

16. Is the first word of paragraph 22 a colloquialism*? If so, is it appropriate to the tone* and the point of view* of the entire essay? If you think the word is not a colloquialism, how would you describe it?

17. Comment on the contrast between "blistered" and "plodded" in the first sentence of paragraph 4. Is this contrast reinforced to any extent in the rest of the paragraph? and if so, how?

18. Explain the following phrases as best you can: "pious denials" (86); "bureaucratic pin" (94–95); "beer-swilling rednecks" (103); "mindlessly macho" (118); "bland assumption" (129); "British-style forbearance" (157–58).

POINTS TO LEARN

1. An essay can begin with a short, blunt statement of purpose if it is in keeping with the tone of the rest of the essay.
2. Both direct and indirect references to time are useful means of unifying an essay.
3. A brief paragraph, even if it consists of only one sentence, can act effectively as both transition and summary.

SUGGESTIONS FOR WRITING

Bharati Mukherjee and Joy Kogawa (pp. 40–52) both deal with the same problem: the racial prejudice faced by a member of a minority group in Canada. Both authors deal with their own personal backgrounds as well as with the history of the racial problem concerning their own race. But there are marked differences in their approaches to the topic, differences not only with regard to facts but especially to tone and point of view.

The first third of your essay (of 1,000–1,200 words) will deal, in somewhat general terms, with the similarities between the two essays, with regard especially to their principal themes. The larger part of your essay will, however, treat the differences between the two, focussing especially on tone and point of view. You need not, however, limit your discussion to these two points.

IMPROVING YOUR STYLE

Your essay should include the following:

1. A brief, precise opening paragraph in which you state your purpose.
2. A one-sentence paragraph which serves as both transition and summary.

Definition

Although by placing it in a separate section we seem to be treating definition as something different from exposition, definition is in fact a form of expository writing. Indeed, it is a very important form, for to define something is certainly to explain it, and very often in order to explain one must first define. But because definition presents certain problems of its own, we have felt it convenient to treat it separately.

The Meaning of Definition

A definition is the effort to distinguish an entity from all other things for the purpose of being able to recognize it or in some way to understand it. To define "apple," for instance, is to find some means of isolating "apple" from all other things, especially from those things that superficially resemble it, like quinces or pomegranates. We must show that "apple" refers to a combination of features possessed by no other thing. But to find this combination of distinguishing features is not always easy; moreover, there are many ways to define and many complicated questions of psychology, philosophy, and logic concealed in the intellectual operation we call definition. One of the most significant concerns the thing-to-be-defined. In one sense, the term *apple* is merely a symbol—a combination of sounds made by the vocal apparatus or a certain combination of letters that stand for these sounds. In another sense *apple* signifies the physical object, the thing one can hold in one's hand and eat. We may reasonably ask, therefore, is definition concerned primarily with *apple* as word or with "apple" as thing? Although not all logicians would agree upon a single answer, most seem to admit that definition may deal either with words or with things. Some definitions focus our attention chiefly upon the thing, no matter whether we call it *apple, pomme,* or *Apfel.* This kind of definition attempts to give, as best it can, accurate, factual information about what an apple *is,* in some particular frame of reference. It is often concerned with the analysis of the thing, with its constituent parts, their nature, function, and purpose. It describes the thing in rela-

138

tion to other things. In contrast, other definitions stress the word or the word-thing relationship. Either they call our attention to how a word has been used in the past, or else they explain—by whatever the process—what words mean. Philosophers and logicians have called the former *real definition*, and the latter *nominal definition*. These terms designate the two most general purposes of definition, both of which are important intellectual goals, and it would be a mistake, no doubt, to regard one as, in itself, superior to the other. We must acknowledge, however, an understandable human tendency to regard real definition as the only kind that matters and to dismiss nominal definition as only juggling with words, as being "merely verbal." Yet real definition is probably the much rarer of the two. It is, most usually, the contribution of an original and creative thinker or of a pioneer in some form of research. More commonly, our definition of *atom* or *quantum* is likely to be an explanation of how original thinkers and research workers have used the term, a nominal rather than a real definition. But this fact need not humble us or dismay us, for surely one of man's greatest achievements is his ability to use words accurately and wisely both for learning and for communicating. Furthermore, concern with words always implies a concern for things. With words we are able to think clearly about things, to devise new concepts, and to gain increasing mastery over our world. Defining words is therefore among the most important of our intellectual activities.

Methods of Definition

How does one go about defining a word or thing? Since there is no one "correct" method, we must say that it all depends upon one's reader and purpose. Or put in a different way, the general principle is this: the writer may use any method or combination of methods known or devisable so long as he efficiently brings his reader to understand what something is or what a word means. The following is a list of some of the most common methods of definition, a list that does not claim to be either exhaustive or exclusive.

1. *Analysis.* The type of definition that is perhaps most familiar to the average reader consists of placing a word in a large class called the *genus* and then differentiating the word from other members of that class. This method, as old as Aristotle, results in the dictionary kind of definition, though it is by no means confined to dictionaries. A typical entry in *A Dictionary of Canadianisms*, for example, reads in part: "*pemmican* . . . beaten or pounded meat mixed with melted animal fat and, sometimes,

berries, the preparation being sewn in a skin bag to form a hard, compact mass that would keep for a long time under almost any conditions." This same kind of analysis appears in the first sentence of an essay defining *semantics* by Hugh R. Walpole: "Semantics, or semasiology, is the study of the meaning of words." But analysis does not always consist of this kind of classification into genus and differentia. Another form of analysis lists the most important characteristics of the thing-to-be-defined, as we see in Aldous Huxley's definition of *ectomorph*, one of three major body types:

> The extreme ectomorph is neither comfortably round nor compactly hard. His is a linear physique with slender bones, stringy, unemphatic muscles, a short and thin-walled gut. The ectomorph is a light-weight, has little muscular strength, needs to eat at frequent intervals, is often quick and highly sensitive. The ratio of skin surface to body mass is higher than in endomorphs or mesomorphs, and he is thus more vulnerable to outside influences, because more extensively in contact with them. His body is built, not around the endomorph's massively efficient intestine, not around the mesomorph's big bones and muscles, but around a relatively predominant and unprotected nervous system.

Both definition by genus and differentia, and definition by division into parts are common and extremely useful, but it would be a mistake to assume that all definitions must proceed by analysis.

2. *Synthesis.* Just as important is definition by synthesis. This form of definition relates the thing-to-be-defined to something already familiar to the reader or listener. It often reveals the thing-to-be-defined as part of some larger whole. Thus, it might also be called "relational definition." Consider the following definition of thirst:

> . . . the entire theory of the mechanism of thirst has been formulated on this basis: "When there is a diminution of the water content of the blood and tissues generally, the secretions of the body, including saliva, are diminished in volume. Because less saliva is secreted, the mouth and throat become dry. It is this sensation of dryness that has been called "thirst." (Anton J. Carlson and Victor Johnson, *The Machinery of the Body*)

It is possible to define *thirst* by analyzing it, by saying that it consists of unpleasant tension, burning, and tickling, instead of relating the sensation to the chemistry of the body. But some things cannot be analyzed in this way and must be defined by synthesis or by some other method. *Blue* is such a thing. To define *blue*, other than by pointing to some blue object, we shall have to say that *blue* is the color produced by light of a wavelength .000047 cm. Or we might define blue as the color of the sky on a cloudless day. Either is an example of definition by synthesis.

3. *Negative Definition*. Closely related to synthetic definition, indeed what may be a special form of it, is negative definition, which helps to define a thing by making clear what it is not. "Electricity," says Bertrand Russell, "is not a thing like St. Paul's Cathedral; it is a way in which things behave. When we have told how things behave when they are electrified, and under what circumstances they are electrified, we have told all there is to tell." Or again, when defining the modern cowboy, Donald Hough observes that "Cowboys do not know how to fire a six-shooter. Most of them have never seen one. They used to wear revolvers for much the same reason as those that prompted early-day farmers to carry a scythe over one shoulder and a blunderbuss over the other when they went to work in their fields. Their herds are now protected by the cops . . ." By itself, negative definition is of little value, but as an accessory method of development and definition it is a striking device. In connection with negative definition, we might add that definitions sometimes carefully distinguish the thing-to-be-defined from something resembling it and often confused with it. Thus, a definition of *stalactite* might very well distinguish that formation from *stalagmite*. As with negative definition, to make this kind of distinction is to define the thing by means of relationships, by synthesis.

4. *Exemplification*. Often appearing as an aid to definition by analysis or by synthesis is definition by example, for one of the best ways to define something is to give one or more examples of it. At times, however, the method of example by itself is sufficient. Lincoln Barnett, for instance, after discussing *relativity of place*, defines *relativity of motion* in this way: "Anyone who has ever ridden on a railroad train knows how rapidly another train flashes by when it is traveling in the opposite direction, and conversely how it may look almost motionless when it is moving in the same direction." The example is developed at greater length than is indicated here and is made to serve, quite properly, as the writer's definition. Sometimes, then, one example can define all by itself, but other methods of definition can seldom do without examples.

5. *Synonyms*. Almost as familiar as definition by example is definition by synonyms. Dictionaries often define words by listing synonyms of the word-to-be-defined. This method has the advantage of being brief, but

unless it is accompanied by some other method of definition, it runs the risk of misleading the reader, for no two words mean exactly the same thing, and, quite often, approximations are not good enough. For this reason, many small abridged dictionaries have a limited value. Still, this method is useful, if our purpose is simply to clarify the meaning of a word or term in passing, as in this sentence by Alfred North Whitehead: "It would therefore appear as if the idea of congruence, or metrical equality, of two portions of space (as empirically suggested by the motion of rigid bodies) must be considered as a fundamental idea incapable of definition in terms of those geometrical concepts which have already been enumerated."

Types of Definition

1. *Consensual Definition.* Whatever the method of definition, the purpose remains the same—to make clear what the word means. Usually the writer will mean by it what most others in his culture mean. Thus in defining *apple* he is trying to state the common public definition of the term, what it means by the consensus of its users. We may, in fact, call such a statement a consensual definition.

2. *Stipulative Definition.* On the other hand, a writer may occasionally want to assign to a word a meaning more precise or in some other way slightly different from that which it commonly has. H. W. Fowler, for example, stipulates a definition of *genteelism* in this way: "By *genteelism* is here to be understood the substituting, for the ordinary natural word that first suggests itself to the mind, of a synonym that is thought to be less soiled by the lips of the common herd, less familiar, less plebian, less vulgar, less improper, less apt to come unhandsomely between the wind & our nobility." What is the advantage of creating one's own definition? The answer is that one does so, first, for clarity, and second, for convenience. Words, often, have so many different meanings that they are potential sources of ambiguity. Whenever abstractions like *beauty, liberty, justice, Romanticism* are key words in an essay, it is wise to announce that, for this particular discourse, we intend to use the word in one sense only. *Genteelism,* for example, may refer to many kinds of affected behavior, but Fowler wishes, for his purpose, to restrict the term to affectation in one's choice of words. The result is concentration and clarity. In addition, making a stipulative definition is more convenient than each time dragging along a cumbersome phrase like "genteelism in one's choice of words." Stipulative definitions are closely related to the consensual meaning, being

essentially a precise denotation selected out of the several contained within the general definition. Of course, stipulative definitions do not have to be related to consensual definitions. A writer is free to stipulate any meaning he chooses for his words, as did Humpty Dumpty when he told Alice that when "I use a word . . . it means just what I choose it to mean—neither more nor less." Still, when stipulative meanings grow too idiosyncratic the writer ceases to communicate and thus ceases to be a writer. There must always be some good reason for making a stipulative definition, some kind of ambiguity in the writing situation that cannot otherwise be avoided, since a stipulative definition always places an extra burden of attention upon the reader. But a wise use of stipulation is one of the writer's sharpest tools in exposition and argument.

3. *Normative Definition.* Finally, a writer may make what is called a normative definition, which may or may not be more precise than the consensual one, but which is, in the writer's opinion, better. A political theorist, for example, might feel that most of us misuse the word *democracy.* We employ it, he complains, to mean X when it should mean Y. If he defines it to mean Y and says that it should never be used by anyone except to mean Y, he has framed a normative definition. This might seem to be a special kind of stipulative definition, but actually it is different. In a stipulative definition the writer says: "In this work I shall use *democracy* to mean Y"; he says nothing about how he may define it in other contexts, and he says nothing about how other people should use it. In a normative definition the writer says not only that "I shall define *democracy* here to mean Y"; he asserts, or implies, that he will always use it with that meaning and that so should everyone else, for it—and it alone—is the proper meaning. Both types, however, have in common the fact that they cannot depart too far from commonly accepted meanings.

In exposition and argument, as we have demonstrated, the writer is constantly defining. Sometimes his definition is a single word. Sometimes it is only a sentence or two. But almost as often it is a paragraph, a section, or even a chapter; and, at times, to make his definition clear the writer needs the space of an entire book, for a definition is not complete until a writer can be sure that his reader knows what his term means. Writing good definition thus depends upon a thorough knowledge of one's subject, a rudimentary acquaintance with logic, common sense, and good manners. The following selections illustrate these characteristics as they appear in the work of skillful writers.

Maps

In the following selection C. C. Wylie develops a simple analytical definition. First he classifies the definiendum (the word or thing being defined), and then he differentiates it from others in its class. Notice particularly how he uses paragraphing to organize his definition. Had all this been composed in a single paragraph—which could have been done—the phases of the definition would have been less clear.

1   A map is a conventional picture of an area of land, sea, or sky. Perhaps the maps most widely used are the road maps given away by the oil companies. They show the cultural features such as states, towns, parks, and roads, especially paved roads. They show also natural features, such as rivers and lakes, and sometimes mountains. As simple maps, most auto- 5 mobile drivers have on various occasions used sketches drawn by service station men, or by friends, to show the best automobile route from one town to another.

2   The distinction usually made between "maps" and "charts" is that a chart is a representation of an area consisting chiefly of water; a 10 map represents an area that is predominantly land. It is easy to see how this distinction arose in the days when there was no navigation over land, but a truer distinction is that charts are specially designed for use in navigation, whether at sea or in the air.

3   Maps have been used since the earliest civilizations, and explorers 15 find that they are used in rather simple civilizations at the present time by people who are accustomed to traveling. For example, Arctic explorers have obtained considerable help from maps of the coast lines showing settlements, drawn by Eskimo people. Occasionally maps show not only the roads, but pictures of other features. One of the earliest such maps 20

From *Astronomy, Maps and Weather* by C. C. Wylie. Copyright 1942 by Harper & Row, Publishers, Inc. Reprinted by permission of the publisher.

dates from about 1400 B.C. It shows not only roads, but also lakes with fish, and a canal with crocodiles and a bridge over the canal. This is somewhat similar to the modern maps of a state which show for each large town some feature of interest or the chief products of that town.

QUESTIONS

READER AND PURPOSE

1. Is Wylie's purpose to define *map* or map—that is, the word or the thing? How do you know?
2. What inferences can you draw about the kind of readers he is aiming at? Does he assume they are interested in the subject? Knowledgeable?

ORGANIZATION

3. This selection is a good example of definition by analysis. What words in the first sentence name the genus, or class, to which map belongs? Is the remainder of the paragraph (that is, after the first sentence) *essential* to the definition of map? If not, how does it contribute to our understanding?
4. Show that paragraph 1 is unified by the repetition of key words.
5. What important aspect of an analytical definition does the second paragraph fulfill? In drawing the distinction between map and chart what strategy does Wylie follow?
6. The third paragraph has two topics. Which sentence sets up the first? How is it supported? Which sentence introduces the second topic? What method of support is used here?

SENTENCES

7. Wylie's sentences are straightforward, without interrupting constructions * or numerous subordinated clauses * and phrases. Is this a good style for his purpose?
8. The opening sentence is simple *, having one subject-verb nucleus ("a map is"). Point out one or two other simple sentences. Are most of the sentences in this selection grammatically simple?
9. The sentence in lines 17-19 makes use of participial phrases * to convey ideas of secondary importance ("showing settlements, drawn by Eskimo people"). Where is another example of such a phrase? Incidentally, is that comma after "settlement" really necessary?

DICTION

10. Look up: *conventional* (1), *cultural* (3), *distinction* (9), *navigation* (12).
11. In line 22 does *this* refer to any specific word in the preceding sentence? If not, to what does it refer? Can you think of a way of opening the sentence with *this* without risk of puzzling the reader?

POINTS TO LEARN

1. The analytical definition first classifies, then differentiates.
2. A paragraph may have two topics, each introduced by its own sentence.
3. An uncomplicated, straightforward sentence style conveys information easily and clearly.
4. When using *this* as the subject of a sentence, be certain that the reader understands what it refers to. If there is any doubt, make *this* an adjective modifying a noun that clearly sums up the preceding idea.

SUGGESTIONS FOR WRITING

In two paragraphs (about 300 words total) compose an analytical definition of one of the following topics. The essential problem is to classify the definiendum and then to distinguish it from other members of the class. However, include whatever additional, non-essential information you think will help your reader's understanding.

book, desk, recipe, office, college, statue, boat, freeway

IMPROVING YOUR STYLE

In your paragraphs strive for a straightforward, uncomplicated sentence style. Include:

1. At least two grammatically simple sentences.
2. Two or three sentences using participial phrases.

Plot

E. M. Forster (1879-1970) was an English novelist, short story writer, and essayist. His best known novels include A *Passage to India, Howard's End*, and *A Room with a View*. This selection comes from *Aspects of the Novel*, the printed version of a series of lectures Forster delivered at Cambridge University in 1927. Like C. C. Wylie in the preceding selection Forster defines by genus and species. He spends, however, considerably more time on differentiation.

1   Let us define a plot. We have defined a story as a narrative of events arranged in their time-sequence. A plot is also a narrative of events, the emphasis falling on causality. "The king died and then the queen died," is a story. "The king died, and then the queen died of grief," is a plot. The time-sequence is preserved, but the sense of causality over- 5
shadows it. Or again: "The queen died, no one knew why, until it was discovered that it was through grief at the death of the king." This is a plot with a mystery in it, a form capable of high development. It suspends the time-sequence, it moves as far away from the story as its limitations will allow. Consider the death of the queen. If it is in a story we say "and 10
then?" If it is in a plot we ask "why?" That is the fundamental difference between these two aspects of the novel. A plot cannot be told to a gaping audience of cave men or to a tyrannical sultan or to their modern descendant the movie-public. They can only be kept awake by "and then—and then." They can only supply curiosity. But a plot demands intelligence and 15
memory also.

2   Curiosity is one of the lowest of the human faculties. You will have noticed in daily life that when people are inquisitive they nearly always have bad memories and are usually stupid at bottom. The man who begins by asking you how many brothers and sisters you have, is 20

From *Aspects of the Novel*. Copyright 1927 by Harcourt Brace Jovanovich, Inc.; renewed 1955 by E. M. Forster. Reprinted by permission of Harcourt Brace Jovanovich, Inc., and Edward Arnold Ltd.

never a sympathetic character, and if you meet him in a year's time he will probably ask you how many brothers and sisters you have, his mouth again sagging open, his eyes still bulging from his head. It is difficult to be friends with such a man, and for two inquisitive people to be friends must be impossible. Curiosity by itself takes us a very little way, nor does it take 25 us far into the novel—only as far as the story. If we would grasp the plot we must add intelligence and memory.

3   Intelligence first. The intelligent novel-reader, unlike the inquisitive one who just runs his eye over a new fact, mentally picks it up. He sees it from two points of view; isolated, and related to the other facts 30 that he has read on previous pages. Probably he does not understand it, but he does not expect to do so yet awhile. The facts in a highly organized novel (like *The Egoist*) are often of the nature of cross-correspondences and the ideal spectator cannot expect to view them properly until he is sitting up on a hill at the end. This element of surprise or mystery—the 35 detective element as it is sometimes rather emptily called—is of great importance in a plot. It occurs through a suspension of the time-sequence; a mystery is a pocket in time, and it occurs crudely, as in "Why did the queen die?" and more subtly in half-explained gestures and words, the true meaning of which only dawns pages ahead. Mystery is essential to a plot, 40 and cannot be appreciated without intelligence. To the curious it is just another "and then—" To appreciate a mystery, part of the mind must be left behind, brooding, while the other part goes marching on.

4   That brings us to our second qualification: memory.

5   Memory and intelligence are closely connected, for unless we re- 45 member we cannot understand. If by the time the queen dies we have forgotten the existence of the king we shall never make out what killed her. The plot-maker expects us to remember, we expect him to leave no loose ends. Every action or word ought to count; it ought to be economical and spare; even when complicated it should be organic and free from dead 50 matter. It may be difficult or easy, it may and should contain mysteries, but it ought not to mislead. And over it, as it unfolds, will hover the memory of the reader (that dull glow of the mind of which intelligence is the bright advancing edge) and will constantly rearrange and reconsider, seeing new clues, new chains of cause and effect, and the final sense (if the plot has 55 been a fine one) will not be of clues or chains, but of something aesthetically compact, something which might have been shown by the novelist straight away, only if he had shown it straight away it would never have become beautiful. We come up against beauty here—for the first time in

our enquiry: beauty at which a novelist should never aim, though he fails 60
if he does not achieve it. I will conduct beauty to her proper place later
on. Meanwhile please accept her as part of a completed plot. She looks a
little surprised at being there, but beauty ought to look a little surprised:
it is the emotion that best suits her face, as Botticelli knew when he painted
her risen from the waves, between the winds and the flowers. The beauty 65
who does not look surprised, who accepts her position as her due—she
reminds us too much of a prima donna.

QUESTIONS

READER AND PURPOSE

1. Does Forster assume that his readers know a great many novels and short
stories or that they have read very little fiction? Is his purpose anything more
than to make them understand clearly what *plot* means?

ORGANIZATION

2. What is the genus of *plot?* Name several other things that belong to the
same family. What characteristic of *plot* differentiates it from them? Does
Forster differentiate *plot* explicitly or implicitly?
3. How do the last two sentences of the first paragraph organize the rest of the
selection?
4. In Forster's sense, *plot* signifies a quality abstracted from narrative literature.
Curiosity, intelligence, and memory, however, belong to the reader of the story
rather than to any quality of the story itself. Can they be, then, part of a definition of *plot?* To put this another way, are these mental qualities essential
to Forster's definition, or are they accidental attributes of *plot?* Can you add
to Forster's third sentence so that curiosity, intelligence, and memory become
part of his formal definition: "A plot is . . . a narrative of events, the emphasis falling upon causality, which . . ."?
5. Why in line 44 does the writer set off his short sentence as a new paragraph?

SENTENCES

6. In his introductory note Forster says of the lectures he delivered at Cambridge that "they were informal, indeed talkative in their tone *, and it seemed
safer when presenting them in book form not to mitigate the talk, in case
nothing should be left at all. Words such as 'I,' 'you,' 'one,' 'we,' 'curiously
enough,' 'so to speak,' and 'of course,' will consequently occur on every page."
The fact that he was talking has also influenced Forster's sentence structure.
How?
7. Why does the writer begin by saying, "Let us define a plot"? Is that beginning more effective for his purpose than this opening: "If a story is a narra-

tive of events arranged in their time-sequence, a plot is also a narrative of events, the emphasis falling on causality"? Forster's sentences are relatively short and their effect is one of simplicity. Yet they are not monotonous or flat. How does he vary his sentence structure?

DICTION

8. Look up: *faculties* (16), *cross-correspondences* (33), *organic* (50), *Botticelli* (64), *prima donna* (67).

9. Describe the writer's tone and point of view *. What is the advantage of his point of view?

POINTS TO LEARN

1. Good definitions give several concrete examples of the thing defined.
2. A writer may define something by contrasting it with something similar, something with which it may be confused.
3. A writer may define by telling what a thing is not.
4. In defining, a writer may list the essential qualities or characteristics of a thing.
5. Writing intended to be read aloud must use short, emphatic sentences of transition and relatively simple constructions.

SUGGESTIONS FOR WRITING

Prepare a definition to be read aloud to your class. Make your purpose to inform without being dull or losing the attention of your audience. Pay careful attention to your sentence structure. Write down a number of things that one might define for an audience of college students. Choose one of these or define one of the following: theater in the round, surrealism, a stock car, culture (as used by the sociologist or anthropologist), the stock market, outer space.

IMPROVING YOUR STYLE

Your style should be that of someone talking, talking to a friendly and sophisticated audience. Avoid slang and street argot but work for a relaxed informal tone. Remember that a personality is inevitably revealed in your language and that your audience will respond to that personality. Seek therefore to be pleasing. Strive for modesty without appearing hesitant or wishy-washy, for confidence without seeming overbearing, for originality in idea and diction without sounding idiosyncratic. Use "I" and "me," and by an occasional judicious "we" or "us" suggest an identification between yourself and your listeners.

DWIGHT MACDONALD

Some Notes on Parody

Dwight Macdonald (1906–83) was a journalist and critic, whose books include: *Against the Grain: Essays on the Effects of Mass Culture* (1962), *Dwight Macdonald on Movies* (1969), and *Discriminations: Essays and Afterthoughts* (1974). These paragraphs are taken from the appendix to an anthology of parody edited by Macdonald. Parody is literature that mocks the style, sentiments, or ideas of other literature, a type of satire of which other species are travesty and burlesque. Macdonald attempts, successfully, to define all three of these varieties of literary satire. Such field definitions are not uncommon, for often entities, or words, derive much of their meanings from a close relationship to similar entities or terms. In such cases definition must involve not a single concept but a field—or linked series—of concepts, each being understood, in part, with reference to the others. So it is with parody, travesty, and burlesque.

1   The first question is: What *is* parody? The dictionaries are not helpful. Dr. Johnson defines parody as "a kind of writing in which the words of an author or his thoughts are taken and by a slight change adapted to some new purpose," which is imprecise and incomplete. The Oxford dictionary comes closer: "a composition . . . in which characteris- 5 tic turns of an author . . . are imitated in such a way as to make them appear ridiculous, especially by applying them to ludicrously inappropriate subjects." This at least brings in humor. But it does not distinguish parody from its poor relations, *travesty* ("a grotesque or debased imitation or likeness") and *burlesque* ("aims at exciting laughter by caricature of the man- 10 ner or spirit of serious works, or by ludicrous treatment of their subjects"). Such definitions tend to run together, which is just what a definition shouldn't do, since *definire* means "to set limits." I therefore propose the following hierarchy:

Reprinted from *Parodies: An Anthology from Chaucer to Beerbohm—and After*, edited by Dwight Macdonald (Random House, 1960). Reprinted by permission.

2   TRAVESTY (literally "changing clothes," as in "transvestite") is   15
the most primitive form. It raises laughs, from the belly rather than the
head, by putting high, classic characters into prosaic situations, with a corresponding stepping-down of the language. Achilles becomes a football
hero, Penelope a suburban housewife, Helen a beauty queen. Scarron did
it in the seventeenth century with his enormously popular *Virgile Travesti*,   20
John Erskine in the twentieth with his *The Private Life of Helen of Troy*.
Boileau was severe on Scarron:

> Au mépris du bon sens, le burlesque effronté
> Trompa les yeux d'abord, plut par sa nouveauté. . . .
> Cette contagion infecta les provinces,   25
> Du clerc et du bourgeois passa jusques aux princes.

It hardly bears thinking what his reaction would have been to Erskine's
book. Or to the contemporary imitation of Scarron by the English poetaster, Charles Cotton, which begins:

> I sing the man (read it who list)   30
> A Trojan true as ever pist,
> Who from Troy-Town by wind and weather
> To Italy (and God knows whither)
> Was pack'd and rack'd and lost and tost
> And bounced from pillar unto post.   35

3   BURLESQUE (from Italian *burla*, "ridicule") is a more advanced
form since it at least imitates the style of the original. It differs from parody
in that the writer is concerned with the original not in itself but merely as
a device for topical humor. Hawthorne's charming *The Celestial Railway*,
for example, is not a parody of Bunyan but a satire on materialistic progress   40
that is hung on the peg of *Pilgrim's Progress*. The instinct for filling a familiar form with a new content is old as history. The *Iliad* was burlesqued
a few generations after it was composed. Sacred themes were popular in the
Middle Ages, such as the Drunkards' Mass (*Missa de Potatoribus*), which
began: 45

> V*a*. Introibo ad altare Bachi
> R. Ad eum qui letificat cor homins.
>   Confiteor reo Bacho omnepotanti, et reo vino coloris rubei, et
> omnibus ciphis eius, et vobis potatoribus, me nimis gulose potasse per
> nimian nauseam rei Bachi dei mei potatione, sternutatione, ocitatione   50
> maxima, mea crupa, mea maxima crupa. . . . Potemus.

Twenty-five years ago, when the eleven-year-old Gloria Vanderbilt was the subject of a famous custody suit between her mother and her aunt, the court's decision awarding her to the aunt except for week ends was summarized by an anonymous newspaper wit: 55

> Rockabye baby
> Up on a writ,
> Monday to Friday, mother's unfit.
> As the week ends, she rises in virtue;
> Saturday, Sunday,   60
> Mother won't hurt you.

And last year, the London *Economist* printed a political carol:

> On the tenth day of Cwthmas,[1] the Commonwealth
>   brought to me
> Ten Sovereign Nations   65
> Nine Governors General
> Eight Federations
> Seven Disputed Areas
> Six Trust Territories
> Five Old Realms   70
> Four Present or Prospective Republics
> Three High Commission Territories
> Two Ghana-Guinea Fowl
>
> One Sterling Area
> One Dollar Dominion   75
> One Sun That Never Sets
> One Maltese Cross
> One Marylebone Cricket Club
> One Trans-Arctic Expedition
>
> And a Mother Country up a Gum Tree.   80

4   Finally and at last, PARODY, from the Greek *parodia* ("a beside- or against-song"), concentrates on the style and thought of the original.[2]

[1] Contraction of "Commonwealthmas." [Mr. Macdonald's note]
[2] Parody belongs to the family of para-words: parasite, parapsychology, paratyphoid, paranoia (against mind), paradox (against received opinion), paraphrase, paranymph (bridesmaid). It is not related to Paraguay, although that country is beside and against Uruguay. [Mr. Macdonald's note]

If burlesque is pouring new wine into old bottles, parody is making a new wine that tastes like the old but has a slightly lethal effect. At its best, it is a form of literary criticism. The beginning of Max Beerbohm's parody of 85 a Shaw preface may give the general idea:

A STRAIGHT TALK

When a public man lays his hand on his heart and declares that his conduct needs no apology, the audience hastens to put up its umbrellas against the particularly severe downpour of apologies in 90 store for it. I won't give the customary warning. My conduct shrieks aloud for apology, and you are in for a thorough drenching.

Flatly, I stole this play. The one valid excuse for the theft would be mental starvation. That excuse I shan't plead. I could have made a dozen better plays than this out of my own head. You don't 95 suppose Shakespeare was so vacant in the upper storey that there was nothing for it but to rummage through cinquecento romances, Towneley mysteries, and such-like insanitary rubbishheaps in order that he might fish out enough scraps for his artistic fangs to fasten on. Depend on it, there were plenty of decent original notions seething behind yon mar- 100 ble brow. Why didn't our William use *them?* He was too lazy. And so am I.

Shaw's polemical style is unerringly reproduced—the short, punchy sentences; the familiarity ("yon marble brow . . . our William"), the Anglo-Saxon vigor, the calculated irreverences ("and suchlike insanitary rubbish- 105 heaps"). But Beerbohm goes deeper, into the peculiar combination in Shaw of arrogance and self-depreciation, of aggressiveness and mateyness, so that the audience is at once bullied and flattered; shocking ideas are asserted but as if they were a matter of course between sensible people. Beerbohm's exposé of this strategy is true parody. 110

QUESTIONS

1. Sometimes a writer, in order to define one word, has perforce to define two. Macdonald deals with an even more extensive field of meaning involving three terms. Think of a phrase (as brief as possible) that would label the general type of writing of which travesty, burlesque, and parody are the species.
2. Is Macdonald making a nominal or a real definition? Much effort is given in scholarship to establishing the limits of closely related terms. You can easily

appreciate, for example, the confusion that would result in literary criticism from the careless interchange of the words with which Macdonald is concerned. Do you think he clearly differentiates travesty, burlesque, and parody? Explain. Look up these words in a good unabridged dictionary. Are Macdonald's definitions an improvement?

ORGANIZATION

3. The rhetorical question * that opens this selection is the topic sentence for all four paragraphs which follow. What other sentence in this paragraph helps to organize the rest of the selection? What is the topic sentence of paragraph 1?
4. Notice that at the beginnings of paragraphs 2 and 3 there are no explicit transitional words or phrases linking them with the preceding material. Why are such links unnecessary in these cases? What signpost * is set at the beginning of paragraph 4?
5. In paragraphs 2 and 3 Macdonald supports his topic by several illustrations. He does not literally announce these examples, writing, say, in line 18: "Achilles, for instance, becomes a football hero. . . ." Is the absence of such labels (for example, thus, say would be others) a virtue or a disadvantage here? Why? In the third paragraph what sentence sets up the last three illustrations? What principle governs the order in which they are presented?

SENTENCES

6. Point out two or three examples of effective short sentences in Macdonald's prose.
7. The sentence in line 28 beginning "Or to the contemporary imitation . . ." is a fragment *. Why? What words would have to be added to make it a complete sentence? What advantage is there to keeping it a fragment?

DICTION

8. Look up: Dr. Johnson (2), ludicrously (7), caricature (10), wit (55), writ (57), lethal (84), parapsychology (footnote on page 109), polemical (103).
9. Precisely what do these phrases mean: prosaic situations (17), topical humor (39), cinquecento romances (97), calculated irreverences (105), self-depreciation (107)?
10. Why are the following substitutions inferior to Macdonald's words: set of definitions for hierarchy (14), poet for poetaster (28), pithy for punchy (103), camaraderie for mateyness (107)?
11. In line 41 Macdonald writes that Hawthorne's story was "hung on the peg of Pilgrim's Progress." The metaphor * hung on the peg of is better than a phrase like based on because it is a fresher image *; it conveys the relationship between Hawthorne's story and Bunyan's allegory in sharper visual terms.

Where else in this selection does the writer employ an image to communicate an abstract idea visually?
12. Study the metaphors in the sentence in lines 95-99. What is Beerbohm making fun of here?
13. Are both *finally* and *at last* necessary in line 81? If they are not, can you think of any justification for using both?

POINTS TO LEARN

1. Often a set of closely related terms conveys a field of meaning. It is especially important that such terms be clearly differentiated, with as little overlapping as possible.
2. Fresh, sharp images often help a reader understand abstract conceptual relationships.

SUGGESTIONS FOR WRITING

Listed below are several three-term sets, each of which involves a field of related meanings. Select any one and in an essay of about four or five paragraphs define each term in the set. You may use examples; in fact you will probably find that you must use examples if you are successfully to distinguish each term in the set from the others.

> sport-game-hobby, opera-musical comedy-revue, panic-fear-dread, short story-novel-novella, magazine-journal-pamphlet, teacher-tutor-instructor, satire-irony-sarcasm, supper-dinner-meal, friend-acquaintance-pal, humor-wit-slapstick, sympathy-pity-compassion, happiness-joy-satisfaction, work-labor-toil, job-profession-career, love-lust-passion, chuckle-titter-snicker

IMPROVING YOUR STYLE

Somewhere in your composition attempt the following:
1. Three or four short emphatic sentences set against longer ones.
2. (With your instructor's approval) an effective fragment.
3. Several metaphors which convey an abstract idea or relationship in a sharp visual image.

Conservation Defined

Roderick Haig-Brown (1908-76) was born and educated in England. He emigrated to the state of Washington and then, in 1928, moved to British Columbia, where he worked as a logger, trapper, guide, and fisherman. Eventually he settled at Campbell River, on Vancouver Island, where he was appointed a local magistrate. Haig-Brown wrote extensively on the outdoors—especially on fishing, his seven books on this subject earning him the reputation of one of the best writers in North America on the topic. He also wrote several novels and children's books set in a sensitively-described natural world. Thus, his comments on conservation are those of a man who spent much of his life involved with the outdoors and thought deeply about nature.

1   An easy definition of the word conservation is "proper use of natural resources". But this still leaves a difficult and wide-open question: What is "proper use"?

2   This is as it should be because conservation is a dynamic, not a static, conception. It does not mean simply hanging on to things, like a 5 miser to his gold. It means putting them to use, seeking a valuable return from them and at the same time ensuring future yields of at least equal value. It means having enough faith in the future to respect the future and the needs of future people; it means accepting moral and practical restraints that limit immediate self-interest; it means finding a measure of 10 wisdom and understanding of natural things that few peoples have attained; ultimately, though we no longer see it in this way, it is a religious concept—the most universal and fundamental of all such concepts, the worship of fertility to which man has dedicated himself in every civilization since his race began. We may well believe now that an intellectual 15 and scientific approach is more likely to succeed than a mystical one. But

From 'Conservation Defined' in *The Living Land*, reprinted by permission of Ann Haig-Brown.

without moral concepts and without a sense of responsibility for the future of the human race, the idea of conservation could have little meaning. Since it deals for the future as well as for the present, it must always be as much an act of faith as an intellectual exercise.   20

3   The basic resources of any country are soil and water and, largely depending on these, climate. All three can be damaged by misuse, utterly destroyed by persistent misuse—and when they are so destroyed the civilizations that grew upon them, however great and powerful, are utterly destroyed with them. The Sahara Desert, the arid lands of the eastern Medi- 25 terranean and the Euphrates Valley all supported civilizations that were supreme in their time, wise in their time and secure in their time. But the wisdom of the time was not enough; the water failed, the soil eroded and blew away and desert sands blew in to bury the wonderful cities whose wealth the land had once supported.   30

4   Soil and water and climate are the permanent resources; together they make habitat, the set of conditions that favours the growth of timber, wildlife, fish, cattle and farm crops. Used within proper limits they are renewable and perpetual resources. Used without regard for those limits they deteriorate steadily and may quickly pass beyond the stage where the 35 knowledge and effort of man can restore them.

QUESTIONS

READER AND PURPOSE

1. Haig-Brown begins by asserting that the kind of definition of *conservation* we might find in a dictionary is inadequate. He is making, indirectly, an important point: that we define the meaning of a word by using other words, and that these other words may require their own definition and explanation. In this selection Haig-Brown explains the defining terms *proper use* and *natural resources*. Why does he begin with *proper use*? What does this way of beginning reveal about his purpose in writing?

2. How would you describe the tone * of this selection? How does it differ from the tone of a dictionary definition?

ORGANIZATION

3. The author's opening paragraph is very short. Paragraphs of this length are usually not advisable, but there are occasions on which they can be effective. What kind of effect does Haig-Brown achieve here? What would be lost if the paragraph were omitted?

4. A dictionary entry gives us information about the meaning of a word and also about its spelling, etymology *, grammatical function, pronunciation, and range of use. Consider the detailed way in which the concept of *proper use* is treated in paragraph 2. Do the last two sentences of the paragraph help you to see why Haig-Brown is "defining" the term in other than a dictionary fashion? Why does he make repeated use in this paragraph of words such as *faith, wisdom, religious, moral,* and *responsibility*? What connotations * do these words give to the term *conservation*?

5. Haig-Brown does not use transitional sentences between paragraphs 2 and 3, or between paragraphs 3 and 4. What other devices does he use to link these paragraphs? Try rearranging the paragraphs in a different order (1-3-4-2, for example) as a way of seeing why the selection is organized as it is.

6. The author stresses *time* (past and future) in paragraphs 2 and 3. How does the opening sentence of paragraph 2 serve to introduce this subject? Does this subject also appear in the concluding paragraph?

SENTENCES

7. Haig-Brown begins his second paragraph by stating briefly what *conservation* does not mean. He then moves from negative to positive statements, emphasizing the change of direction by contrasting the words *it means* with *it does not mean*. What effect is produced by the repetition of *it means*? Why does he end his statement in the third sentence with a period instead of joining it to the next sentence with a semi-colon, as he joins the clauses in sentence four?

8. Notice that the statements introduced by the repetition of *it means* in sentences three and four of paragraph 2 are deliberately arranged in ascending order of importance. This is particularly effective in a long sentence, such as sentence four, because it emphasizes for the reader the logical development of the author's ideas. Try rearranging the order of Haig-Brown's statements to see how their effect would be weakened.

9. The author introduces the final clause of sentence four in paragraph 2 with a conjunctive adverb *. What does this signal to the reader? Why does he set off the nominative absolute * at the end of sentence four with a dash? Would a colon have been more or less effective?

10. Repetition of key words is made use of again in paragraph 3. How would the rhythms of Haig-Brown's sentences be weakened if we were to use synonyms for *destroyed* (line 23) and for *time* (line 28)?

11. Explain the difference in tone between the sentences of paragraph 4 and those of paragraph 2 and 3. How does this change in tone affect the conclusion of this selection? Although Haig-Brown does not use the word, is he offering us a definition of *conservation* in this final paragraph? How have paragraphs 2 and 3 served to prepare us to understand not only the meaning of the term

but also its connotations? What additional force do they give to the three straight-forward sentences of paragraph 4?

DICTION

12. Look up: *dynamic* (4), *self-interest* (10), *fundamental* (13), *fertility* (14), *mystical* (16), *deteriorate* (35).
13. Why does Haig-Brown use *easy* (1) instead of "simple" or "elementary"? What connotations does *easy* have that the other two words lack?
14. Haig-Brown uses the word *proper* twice (1, 3). Look up the word and determine which of its meanings he is emphasizing.

POINTS TO LEARN

1. Definition may involve not only the denotative meaning of a word but also its moral connotations.
2. Words are defined by other words, and the reader should try to understand the meanings and implications of the words used in a definition.
3. Repetition of key words can be an effective way of organizing long sentences. Repetition can also produce effective sentence rhythms.
4. Statements within a paragraph can be arranged in ascending order of importance as one method of emphasizing the key point.

SUGGESTIONS FOR WRITING

Choose a word (such as *progress, socialism, welfare*) that has moral connotations for most people and compose a definition essay. Begin with a dictionary definition and then write two paragraphs in which you explain in more detail the implications of the definition. Conclude with a short paragraph defining your chosen word in light of these implications.

IMPROVING YOUR STYLE

Include the following in your essay:

1. A sentence in which the final phrase or clause is set off by a dash for emphasis.
2. A long sentence in which you begin several statements with a repeated word or phrase and join the statements with semi-colons. Introduce your final statement, for purposes of summing up, with a conjunctive adverb.
3. A sentence or two in which you try to achieve a pronounced rhythm by repeating a key word.

Love and Lust

Henry Fairlie is a British journalist and writer. This selection comes from one of a series of pieces he composed for *The New Republic* on the seven deadly sins (pride, anger, lust, envy, greed, gluttony, and sloth). In the essay which begins with the three paragraphs printed below Fairlie is concerned with more than defining love and lust. He attacks what he sees as our preoccupation with sex and our rejection of genuine love: "We have reduced love to sex, sex to the act, and the act to a mere quantitative measurement of it." He concludes by warning that permissive lust has become a dangerous social malaise working to the advantage of those who would manipulate us:

> The managers of our society much prefer that we are infatuated with our sexuality, than that we look long and steadily at what they contrive from day to day. . . . They have discovered that, now that religion has been displaced, sex can be made the opiate of the masses. When the entire society is at last tranquilly preoccupied in the morbid practices of onanism, they will know that there is nothing more for them to do but rule forever over the dead.

Thus Fairlie's broad purpose is that of social critic: to expose a vice in the hope that we shall be persuaded to lead better lives.

Here, however, his immediate concern is to define the vice he is attacking, and the selection is a good example of the fact that in composition defining is often not an end in itself but a required first step toward another goal.

1   Lust is not interested in its partners, but only in the gratification of its own craving: not even in the satisfaction of our whole natures, but in the appeasement merely of an appetite which we are unable to subdue. It is therefore a form of self-subjection; in fact of self-emptying. The sign

From "Lust or Luxuria" by Henry Fairlie (The New Republic, October 8, 1977). Reprinted by permission of *The New Republic*, © 1977 The New Republic, Inc.

it wears is: "This property is vacant." Anyone may take possession of it for 5
a while. Lustful people may think that they can choose a partner at will
for sexual gratification. But they do not really choose; they accept what is
available. Lust accepts any partner for a momentary service; anyone may
squat in its groin.

2   Love has meaning only insofar as it includes the idea of its con- 10
tinuance. Even what we rather glibly call a love affair, it if comes to an end,
may continue as a memory that is pleasing in our lives, and we can still
renew the sense of privilege and reward of having been allowed to know
someone with such intimacy and sharing. But Lust dies at the next dawn
and, when it returns in the evening, to search where it may, it is with its 15
own past erased. Love wants to enjoy in other ways the human being
whom it has enjoyed in bed. But in the morning Lust is always furtive. It
dresses as mechanically as it undressed, and heads straight for the door, to
return to its own solitude. Like all the sins, it makes us solitary. It is a self-
abdication at the very heart of one's own being, of our need and ability to 20
give and receive.

3   Love is involvement as well as continuance; but Lust will not get
involved. This is one of the forms in which we may see it today. If people
now engage in indiscriminate and short-lived relationships more than in
the past, it is not really for some exquisite sexual pleasure that is thus 25
gained, but because they refuse to become involved and to meet the demands that love makes. They are asking for little more than servicing, such
as they might get at a gas station. The fact that it may go to bed with a
lot of people is less its offense than the fact that it goes to bed with people for whom it does not care. The characteristic of the "singles" today is 30
not the sexual freedom they supposedly enjoy, but the fact that this freedom is a deception. They are free with only a fraction of their natures.
The full array of human emotions is hardly involved. The "singles bar"
does not have an obnoxious odor because its clients, before the night is
over, may hop into bed with someone whom they have just met, but be- 35
cause they do not even consider that, beyond the morning, either of them
may care for the other. As they have made deserts of themselves, so they
make deserts of their beds. This is the sin of Lust, just as it dries up human beings, so it dries up human relationships. The word that comes to
mind, when one thinks of it, is that it is parched. Everyone in a "singles 40
bar" seems to have lost moisture, and this is peculiarly the accomplishment
of Lust, to make the flesh seem parched, to deprive it of all real dewiness,
shrivelling it to no more than a husk.

QUESTIONS

READER AND PURPOSE

1. Actually this is a double definition, for love and lust are best understood with reference to one another. With which is Fairlie primarily concerned?
2. Is this an example of analytical definition? If not, how does the writer establish the essential natures of love and of lust? Is the definition logically complete at any specific point in these paragraphs? Could a definition like this ever be "logically complete"?
3. Love and lust both involve sexual gratification. In what way, according to Fairlie, do they differ with regard to this gratification?
4. Do you think Fairlie is writing directly for "swingers," those guilty of reducing "love to sex, [and] sex to the act"? Why or why not?

ORGANIZATION

5. The opening sentence of paragraph 1 makes an assertion. Does the second sentence illustrate that assertion, repeat it, compare it to something, or explain a reason for it? How is the third sentence related in thought to the second? The fourth to the third? Each of the remaining statements to the idea(s) preceding it?
6. Is the second paragraph justifiable: is there a good reason for beginning a new paragraph here?
7. Paragraph 2 contrasts love and lust with regard to what quality? Where is the emphasis in the contrast? (How many sentences are given to love, how many to lust?) Does the material from line 16 to the end of the paragraph (beginning "Love wants to enjoy") develop a second point of difference or simply repeat the first?
8. How does the second sentence of paragraph 2 relate to the idea of "continuance"—as a qualification * or as a kind of restatement?
9. What words link the third paragraph to the second?
10. Which term (or terms) in the opening sentence of paragraph 3 expresses the topic idea? How does the paragraph develop this topic—by restatement? examples? reasons? effects?

SENTENCES

11. In the statements in lines 7-9 and 22-23 how does the writer use sentence structure to reinforce the contrast?
12. Study the semicolons in lines 4, 7, 8, and 22. According to the conven-

tional rules of punctuation could any of these be replaced by a comma? Even if they could be, are the semicolons justified? What reason is there for the colons in lines 2 and 5?

13. Point out the parallel * elements in the sentence in lines 19-21.

14. Explain why each of the following revisions is less emphatic or clear than what Fairlie wrote:

> (a) *Revision:* Anyone may squat in its groin; lust accepts any partner for a momentary service.
> *Fairlie:* "Lust accepts any partner for a momentary service; anyone may squat in its groin." (8-9)
> (b) *Revision:* But Lust dies at the next dawn and returns with its own past erased in the evening, to search where it may.
> *Fairlie:* "But Lust dies at the next dawn and, when it returns in the evening, to search where it may, it is with its own past erased." (14-16)
> (c) *Revision:* But Lust is always furtive in the morning.
> *Fairlie:* "But in the morning Lust is always furtive." (17)

DICTION

15. Look up: *craving* (2), *glibly* (11), *intimacy* (14), *furtive* (17), *self-abdication* (19), *indiscriminate* (24), *"singles"* (30), *array* (33), *husk* (43).

16. How do the etymologies * of these words help to clarify their modern sense: *appeasement* (3), *exquisite* (25), *obnoxious* (34)?

17. Explain the metaphors * implicit in *sign* (4) and in *mechanically* (18). In the latter passage what other figure of speech * does Fairlie use to vivify lust?

18. Identify the simile * in line 27-28. Is it effective?

19. What relationships in thought are signalled by *therefore* and *in fact* in line 4?

20. Why would the following words be less effective in Fairlie's context: *appeasement of desire* for *appeasement of appetite* (3), *lonely* for *solitary* (19), *customers* for *clients* (34)?

21. *Squat* (9) and *hop* (35) are especially expressive verbs. What overtones of meaning do they have here? (There is a faint literary allusion * in Fairlie's use of *squat*. See John Milton's *Paradise Lost*, book IV, line 800.)

POINTS TO LEARN

1. Definition is often a necessary preliminary step to some other writing goal.

2. Qualities of mind and personality may perhaps be defined most easily in terms of observable behavior.

3. Strong expressive verbs are essential to strong expressive prose.

SUGGESTIONS FOR WRITING

In two or three paragraphs totaling 300-400 words, define one of the following pairs of qualities:

fear and courage, sympathy and callousness, open-mindedness and close-mindedness, initiative and lethargy, self-confidence and timidity, generosity and stinginess.

Decide where to place your emphasis and concentrate upon showing how the qualities reveal themselves in people's actions and relationships.

IMPROVING YOUR STYLE

Incorporate the following into your essay:

1. At least one metaphor and one simile.

2. Two or three verbs denoting vigorous action and implying strong feelings of approval or disapproval.

3. One sentence beginning with *therefore* and one beginning with *in fact*.

Anger

W. H. Auden (1907-73) was an English poet (he became an American citizen), one of the most important of this century. In addition to poetry he wrote plays and numerous essays. One of these—here reprinted in its entirety—is on anger. It appeared as a contribution to a collection of pieces on the seven deadly sins (pride, anger, lust, envy, greed, gluttony, and sloth), each by a different writer. Auden's essay is more personal and less moralistic than Fairlie's treatment of a similar theme (see pages 117-18). While he is not framing a definition in a narrow, logical sense, Auden is attempting to make clear what anger is. Thus his essay is an extended, if informal, definition.

1   Like all the sins except pride, anger is a perversion, caused by pride, of something in our nature which in itself is innocent, necessary to our existence and good. Thus, while everyone is proud in the same way, each of us is angry or lustful or envious in his own way.

2   Natural, or innocent, anger is the necessary reaction of a creature   5
when its survival is threatened by the attack of another creature and it cannot save itself (or its offspring) by flight. Such anger, accompanied by physiological changes, like increased secretion of adrenalin, inhibits fear so that the attacked creature is able to resist the threat to its extinction. In the case of young creatures that are not yet capable of looking after themselves,   10
anger is a necessary emotion when their needs are neglected: a hungry baby does right to scream. Natural anger is a reflex reaction, not a voluntary one; it is a response to a real situation of threat and danger, and as soon as the threat is removed, the anger subsides. No animal lets the sun go down upon its wrath. Moreover, Lorentz has shown that, in fights between the social   15
animals, when, by adopting a submissive posture, the weaker puts itself at the mercy of the stronger, this inhibits further aggression by the latter.

"Anger" from *The Seven Deadly Sins* by W. H. Auden. Reprinted by permission of *The Sunday Times*.

3   Anger, even when it is sinful, has one virtue; it overcomes sloth. Anybody, like a schoolmaster, a stage director or an orchestral conductor, whose business it is to teach others to do something, knows that, on occasions, the quickest—perhaps the only—way to get those under him to do their best is to make them angry.

4   Anger as a sin is either futile (the situation in which one finds oneself cannot or should not be changed, but must be accepted) or unnecessary (the situation could be mastered as well or better without it). Man is potentially capable of the sin of anger because he is endowed with memory—the experience of an event persists—and with the faculty of symbolization (to him, no object or event is simply itself). He becomes actually guilty of anger because he is first of all guilty of the sin of pride, of which anger is one of many possible manifestations.

5   Because every human being sees the world from a unique perspective, he can, and does, choose to regard himself as its centre. The sin of anger is one of our reactions to any threat, not to our existence, but to our fancy that our existence is more important than the existence of anybody or anything else. None of us wishes to be omnipotent, because the desires of each are limited. We are glad that other things and people exist with their own ways of behaving—life would be very dull if they didn't—so long as they do not thwart our own. Similarly, we do not want others to conform with our wishes because they must—life would be very lonely if they did— but because they choose to; we want DEVOTED slaves.

6   The British middle-class culture in which I grew up strongly discouraged overt physical expression of anger; it was far more permissive, for example, towards gluttony, lust and avarice. In consequence, I cannot now remember "losing" my temper so that I was beside myself and hardly knew what I was doing. Since childhood, at least, I have never physically assaulted anyone, thrown things or chewed the carpet. (I do, now and again, slam doors.) Nor have I often seen other people do these things. In considering anger, therefore, most of my facts are derived from introspection and may not be valid for others, or from literature, in which truth has to be subordinated to dramatic effect. No fits of temper in real life are quite as interesting as those of Lear, Coriolanus or Timon.

7   In my own case—I must leave the psychological explanation to professionals—my anger is more easily aroused by things and impersonal events than by other people. I don't, I believe, really expect others to do what I wish and am seldom angry when they don't; on the other hand I do expect God or Fate to oblige me. I do not mind losing at cards if the other players

are more skilful than I, but, if I cannot help losing because I have been dealt a poor hand, I get furious. If traffic lights fail to change obligingly to red when I wish to cross the road, I am angry; if I enter a restaurant and it is crowded, I am angry. My anger, that is to say, is most easily aroused by a 60 situation which is (a) not to my liking, (b) one I know I cannot change, and (c) one for which I can hold no human individual responsible.

Change of Nature

8   This last condition is the most decisive. I like others to be on time and hate to be kept waiting, but if someone deliberately keeps me waiting 65 because, say, he is annoyed with me or wishes to impress me with his importance, I am far less angry than I am if I know him to be unpunctual by nature. In the first case, I feel I must be partly responsible—if I had behaved otherwise in the past, he would not have kept me waiting; and I feel hopeful—perhaps I can act in the future in such a way that our relationship 70 will change and he will be punctual next time. In the second case, I know that it is in his nature to be late for others, irrespective of their relationship, so that, in order to be on time, he would have to become another person.

9   My fantastic expectation that fate will do as I wish goes so far that my immediate reaction to an unexpected event, even a pleasant surprise, is 75 anger.

10   Among the British middle class, repressed physical violence found its permitted substitute in verbal aggression, and the more physically pacific the cultural sub-group (academic and clerical circles, for instance), the more savage the tongue—one thinks of the families in Miss Compton- 80 Burnett's novels, or of Professor Housman jotting down deadly remarks for future use.

11   Compared with physical aggression, verbal aggression has one virtue; it does not require the presence of its victim. To say nasty things about someone behind his back is at least preferable to saying them to his 85 face. On the other hand, for intelligent and talented persons, it has two great moral dangers. First, verbal malice, if witty, wins the speaker social approval. (Why is it that kind remarks are very seldom as funny as unkind?) Secondly, since, in verbal malice, the ill-will of the heart is associated with the innocent play of the imagination, a malicious person can forget 90 that he feels ill-will in a way that a physically aggressive person cannot. His audience, however, is not so easily deceived. Two people may make almost the same remark; one, we feel immediately, is being only playful, the other has a compulsive wish to denigrate others.

Self-importance   95

12   Simone Weil has described how, when she was suffering from acute migraine, she felt a desire to strike others on the same spot where she felt the pain herself. Most acts of cruelty, surely, are of this kind. We wish to make others suffer because we are impotent to relieve our own sufferings (which need not, of course, be physical). Any threat to our self-importance   100 is enough to create a lifelong resentment, and most of us, probably, cherish a great deal more resentment than we are normally aware of. I like to fancy myself as a kindhearted person who hates cruelty. And why shouldn't I be kind? I was loved as a child, I have never suffered a serious injury either from another individual or from society, and I enjoy good health. Yet, now   105 and again, I meet a man or a woman who arouses in me the desire to ill-treat them. They are always perfectly harmless people, physically unattractive (I can detect no element of sexual sadism in my feelings) and helpless. It is, I realize with shame, their helplessness which excites my ill-will. Here is someone who, whatever I did to him or her, would not fight back, an   110 ideal victim, therefore, upon whom to vent all my resentments, real or imagined, against life.

13   If it were really possible for suffering to be transferred like a coin from one person to another, there might be circumstances in which it was morally permissible; and if, however mistakenly, we believed that it was   115 possible, acts of cruelty might occasionally be excusable. The proof that we do not believe such a transfer to be possible is that, when we attempt it, we are unsatisfied unless the suffering we inflict upon others is at least a little greater than the suffering that has been inflicted upon ourselves.

14   The transferability-of-suffering fallacy underlies the doctrine of re-   120 tributive punishment, and there is so little evidence that the threat of punishment—the threat of public exposure is another matter—is an effective deterrent to crime, or that its infliction—self-inflicted penance is again another matter—has a reformatory effect, that it is impossible to take any other theory of punishment seriously. By punishment, I mean, of course,   125 the deliberate infliction of physical or mental suffering beyond what the safety of others requires. There will probably always be persons who, whether they like it or not, have to be quarantined, some, perhaps, for the rest of their lives.

"Righteous Anger"

15   The anger felt by the authorities which makes them eager to punish is of the same discreditable kind which one can sometimes observe among parents and dog-owners, an anger at the lack of respect for his betters which the criminal has shown by daring to commit his crime. His real offence in the eyes of the authorities is not that he has done something wrong but that he has done something which THEY have forbidden.

16   "Righteous anger" is a dubious term. Does it mean anything more than that there are occasions when the sin of anger is a lesser evil than cowardice or sloth? I know that a certain state of affairs or the behaviour of a certain person is morally evil and I know what should be done to put an end to it; but, without getting angry, I cannot summon up the energy and the courage to take action.

17   Righteous anger can effectively resist and destroy evil, but the more one relies upon it as a source of energy, the less energy and attention one can give to the good which is to replace the evil once it has been removed. That is why, though there may have been some just wars, there has been no just peace. Nor is it only the vanquished who suffer; I have known more than one passionate anti-Nazi who went to pieces once Hitler had been destroyed. Without Hitler to hate, their lives had no *raison d'être*.

18   "One should hate the sin and love the sinner." Is this possible? The evil actions which I might be said to hate are those which I cannot imagine myself committing. When I read of the deeds of a Hoess or an Eichmann, from whom I have not personally suffered, though I certainly do not love them, their minds are too unintelligible to hate. On the other hand, when I do something of which I am ashamed, I hate myself, not what I have done; if I had hated it, I should not have done it.

19   I wish the clergy today—I am thinking of the Anglican Church because She is the one I know best—would not avoid, as they seem to, explaining to us what the Church means by Hell and the Wrath of God. The public is left with the impression, either that She no longer believes in them or that She holds a doctrine which is a moral monstrosity no decent person could believe.

20   Theological definitions are necessarily analogical, but it is singularly unfortunate that the analogies for Hell which the Church has used in the past should have been drawn from Criminal Law. Criminal laws are imposed laws—they come into being because some people are not what they should be, and the purpose of the law is to compel them by force and fear

to behave. A law can always be broken and it is ineffective unless the authorities have the power to detect and punish, and the resolution to act at once.   170

21   To think of God's laws as imposed leads to absurdities. Thus, the popular conception of what the Church means by Hell could not unfairly be described as follows. God is an omniscient policeman who is not only aware of every sin we have committed but also of every sin we are going to commit. But for seventy years or so He does nothing, but lets every human   175 being commit any sin he chooses. Then, suddenly, He makes an arrest and, in the majority of cases, the sinner is sentenced to eternal torture.

Souls in Hell

22   Such a picture is not without its appeal; none of us likes to see his enemies, righteous or unrighteous, flourishing on earth like a green bay tree.   180 But it cannot be called Christian. Some tender-minded souls have accepted the analogy but tried to give eternity a time limit: in the end, they say, the Devil and damned will be converted. But this is really no better. God created the world; He was not brought in later to make it a good one. If His love could ever be coercive and affect the human will without its co-   185 operation, then a failure to exercise it from the first moment would make Him directly responsible for all the evil and suffering in the world.

23   If God created the world, then the laws of the spiritual life are as much laws of our nature as the laws of physics and physiology, which we can defy but not break. If I jump out of the window or drink too much I   190 cannot be said to break the law of gravity or a biochemical law, nor can I speak of my broken leg or my hangover as a punishment inflicted by an angry Nature. As Wittgenstein said: "Ethics does not treat of the world. Ethics must be a condition of the world like logic." To speak of the Wrath of God cannot mean that God is Himself angry. It is the unpleasant ex-   195 perience of a creature, created to love and be happy, when he defies the laws of his spiritual nature. To believe in Hell as a possibility is to believe that God cannot or will not ever compel us to love and be happy. The analogy which occurs to me is with neurosis. (This, of course, is misleading too because, in these days, many people imagine that, if they can call their   200 behaviour neurotic, they have no moral responsibility for it.) A neurotic, an alcoholic, let us say, is not happy; on the contrary, he suffers terribly, yet no one can relieve his suffering without his consent and this he so often withholds. He insists on suffering because his ego cannot bear the pain of facing reality and the diminution of self-importance which a cure would involve.   205

24   If there are any souls in Hell, it is not because they have been sent there, but because Hell is where they insist upon being.

QUESTIONS

READER AND PURPOSE

1. The essays in the collection in which this piece first appeared varied in tone * from playful to serious. Which of those two words better describes Auden's tone? Does his purpose seem to be primarily to amuse his readers, to inform them, or to persuade them of something?

2. In a strict and formal sense Auden does not define anger. In fact, he uses the word in full confidence that his readers know what it means. In a broader sense, however, his essay may be said to define anger to the degree that it expands and explores what is involved in this state of mind. For one thing Auden distinguishes natural from sinful anger. What is the difference? What other aspects of anger does he throw light upon?

ORGANIZATION

3. What does paragraph 2 contribute to Auden's discussion of anger? Paragraph 3? Paragraphs 7 and 8? Indicate the topic sentence of paragraph 8. How is it supported?

4. Make a conceptual analysis of paragraph 11. This requires that you (a) state the topic idea and (b) show how the idea conveyd by each of the following sentences in the paragraph relates to the topic. Do the same thing for paragraph 12.

5. In paragraphs 19-24 Auden argues against the popular conception of hell. His argument is built upon a distinction between imposed law (which he defines in paragraph 20) and natural law (paragraph 23). Explain this distinction. Why does it lead to the conclusion that the usual conception of hell is absurd?

6. Is the closing of this essay effective? Why or why not?

7. Auden's organization is less schematic than that of many of the selections contained in this text. Rather than follow a plan rigorously laid out beforehand, Auden seems to spin his essay by a kind of association, one aspect of the subject suggesting another. Consider, for example, paragraphs 4, 5, and 6. Is there a necessary logical progression to the thought? Are the paragraphs carefully tied together by linking words and phrases? Would you conclude from your answers to these questions that Auden's essay is poorly organized, that it lacks coherence and shape?

Contrast the structure of "Anger" with Edward Gibbon's analysis of a Roman legion (page 79). Gibbon's method of organizing is schematic while Auden's is meditative. The first presents the subject thoroughly mastered—laid out in shaped and ordered blocks. A student reviewing for an examination would be grateful for Gibbon's clear analysis. Auden's essay, on the other hand, suggests less the finished product of thought than the actual process of thinking. Before he began his final draft one suspects that Gibbon knew exactly what he wanted to say; Auden—or so his essay suggests—creates his thought in the very process of writing. The two passages, in short, represent two kinds of prose, equally valuable but profoundly different. The one is a vehicle for ideas clearly formulated before the writer puts pen to paper; the other is a voyage of exploration and discovery.

SENTENCES

8. This difference is reflected in more than organization. For example, Auden's sentences contain more interrupted movement * than Gibbon's. Interrupted movement usually is closer to the actual process of thinking than is straightforward sentence structure. When we think, our ideas do not present themselves one by one like a file of obedient soldiers. They mix and interfere and clash. We begin one thought, but, before we finish, another intrudes, with which we play before returning, after a moment, to the first. Obviously a writer can ill afford literally to write as he thinks; he would keep the attention of very few readers. He must set his ideas down on paper in more orderly fashion than that in which he conceived them. But if he is the kind of writer willing even in his last draft to continue probing his subject, the chances are that interrupted movement—a sign of the mind at work—will be relatively frequent in his style. And so it is in Auden's sentences. Read closely, for instance, the final sentence of paragraph 12. Identify the interrupters it contains. Find six or seven other sentences in this selection notable for interrupted movement. If you can, discuss any particular advantages to the interruptions in these sentences, advantages in respect to emphasis, sentence rhythm, or subtlety of thought. On the other hand, Auden also employs the short, straightforward sentence effectively. Point out several.

9. Notice how the dash is used in this essay and list the functions it appears to have.

10. The first sentence of paragraph 3 is emphatic. Why is the term *announcement* a fair label for this kind of emphatic sentence structure? Can you find another of Auden's sentences that uses this technique?

11. Why in each of the following pairs of sentences is the revision inferior to what Auden wrote?

> (a) *Revision:* I am angry if traffic lights fail to change obligingly to red when I wish to cross the road or if I enter a restaurant and it is crowded.

Auden: "If traffic lights fail to change obligingly to red when I wish to cross the road, I am angry; if I enter a restaurant and it is crowded, I am angry." (58-60)

(b) Revision: Then He suddenly makes an arrest and the sinner is sentenced to eternal torture in the majority of cases.

Auden: "Then, suddenly, He makes an arrest and, in the majority of cases, the sinner is sentenced to eternal torture." (176-77)

12. Is the question in line 150 genuine or rhetorical *? Point to several other questions in this essay and be able to explain the purpose of each. Why is the question in lines 88-89 in parentheses?

13. Why is the first sentence of paragraph 8 a good example of a topic statement?

DICTION

14. Look up: adrenalin (8), inhibits (17), overt (42), introspection (48), malice (87), denigrate (94), migraine (97), vent (111), coercive (185), physiology (189), neurosis (199).

15. In paragraph 4 the words futile, unnecessary, and memory are all rather abstract. How does Auden clarify these terms? Actually what he does is an example of one of the kinds of definition referred to in the introduction to this section. Can you identify it?

16. Explain what relationship in thought the following connectors * prepare us for: thus (3), similarly (38), that is to say (60), say (66), nor (147), on the other hand (154). Does surely act as a kind of pointer in line 98?

POINTS TO LEARN

1. There is more than one way to organize an essay.

2. A writer may explore his subject in the very process of writing about it. If his exploration is directed and not merely haphazard, the essay that evolves will be organized; but it will be organized in a looser, more associative pattern than the essay composed according to a carefully wrought, pre-conceived plan or outline.

3. Extensive interrupted movement may make the syntax of a sentence more difficult to follow, but at the same time it creates the illusion of the thinking mind.

SUGGESTIONS FOR WRITING

There are six deadly sins besides anger. Select one of them—or, if you pre-fer, some other sin less deadly—and attempt an essay like Auden's. Do not begin by making an outline; instead simply sit for a while and think about your subject. Then compose a first draft. Probably it will be quite rambling. Work it over, adding and developing neglected points, pruning or even eradicating topics that on second reading seem insignificant. Go through this process several times until you feel you have clearly told your reader what you think and feel about envy or avarice or what have you. Support generalizations with specifics and do not be afraid to draw upon your own experience.

IMPROVING YOUR STYLE

In your essay include:

1. A rhetorical question.
2. A topic sentence of no more than six words.
3. Dashes to set off an explanation or qualification *.
4. The word *say* to identify an example.
5. The connectives *thus, similarly,* and *on the other hand* to introduce sen-tences.

Scouts

Allan Anderson was born in Calgary in 1915 and raised there; he later worked in Calgary as a broadcaster for the CBC. His interest in oral history—that is, history as recorded from the mouths of those who experienced it—has resulted in several books, including *Remembering the Farm* and *Salt Water, Fresh Water*. The latest book by this prolific speaker and lecturer, *Roughnecks and Wildcatters* (1981), from which "Scouts" is taken, is subtitled "an informal popular history of 'The Oil Patch.'"

1   Of all the many, varied, entertaining, or incredible stories told me by oilmen, in particular the old-timers, the ones that appealed to me as much as any were those about scouts. Scouts were simply company spies whose job it was to find out, in any devious or devilish or straightforward way they could, whether or not a rival company had struck oil. There was a 5 lot more to it than that, but that was what the game was all about.

2   The idea was very simple. If there was oil in that location, then the company for which the scout worked could be saved all the trouble and expense of drilling a well itself. If the scout could come up with evidence the other company had struck oil, then all that company had to do was lease 10 land around the producing well, and as fast as possible.

3   When a well was declared "a tight hole," it meant that the company drilling it was trying to bottle up all information about what was going on. Any number of scouts from other companies would arrive in the countryside around the well and use all the considerable ingenuity they pos- 15 sessed to ferret out what was really going on.

4   The obvious way was to buy beers for roughnecks from the well in a local beer parlor and pump them. Or scouts could fly over the well in helicopters. Or they could train high-powered binoculars on the well. They might even walk right up to the rig and claim they were working for a 20 service company. Any trick that would work.

From *Roughnecks & Wildcatters* (Macmillan, 1981). Used by permission of the author.

5   Scouts had an astounding zeal for their work. They would all but freeze to death in the bush scouting a well. They'd get lost. Their cars would break down on remote roads. They'd be chased by roughnecks from the rig under scrutiny. In the great days of scouting in the fifties and sixties, they lived on modest expense accounts and would get "Brownie points" from their companies if they came up with really valuable information. That meant they'd get a pat on the back and their salary at the end of the month and that was that. The company might make millions out of the information dug out by a scout.

6   Scouts had to be dedicated, they had to take pride in their work, and they had to be fiercely and frantically competitive. One can only applaud their zeal, while being astounded by the stunts they pulled to achieve their goal.

7   There are still commercial scouts who go out and spy on wells, but there's also a Canadian Oil Scouts Association. Members of the Association trade information each week at a "scout check," which is certainly a far cry from the old, individualistic days. A well can be treated as a tight hole for a year. Scout checks undoubtedly ferret out a certain amount of information valuable to company geologists and computers, but it seems to me it's about as interesting as a movie press conference.

QUESTIONS

READER AND PURPOSE

1. In the terms used in the introductory comments to the Definition section of this book, Anderson's essay is a *real definition*; its method is exemplification. Explain both points, referring to specific examples from the essay.
2. Setting aside your desire to know more about this subject (if, indeed, you do), does Anderson's definition satisfy you?
3. Obviously the author has some interest in his topic, since he has devoted a whole chapter of his book to it. But within the essay itself is there any evidence to show that he is interested? very interested? enthusiastic?

ORGANIZATION

4. How does paragraph 1 serve as introduction to the six paragraphs which follow?
5. How does the first sentence of paragraph 2 serve as transition?
6. Note how paragraph 4 is organized: the transitional phrase "the obvious way" refers to the scouts as they tried "to ferret out what was really going on." This transition is followed by four methods the scouts used: buying beer for roughnecks, flying over the well, using binoculars, and simply walking in to the

rig. The last sentence functions as both summary ("any trick") and conclusion. Analyze paragraph 5 in this same manner.

7. In paragraph 7 Anderson changes topic slightly, from scouts as extraordinary individuals to scouts as members of an association, and he ends his essay with a somewhat sarcastic comment upon "scout checks." How does this last paragraph affect the meaning of the whole? How does it cast light upon his perception of individual scouts? Since the book from which this essay is taken is a history of oil-field workers, does his conclusion seem appropriate?

SENTENCES

8. There are two series of parallel* adjectives in paragraph 1. Identify them and explain the nature of the parallelism. Where else does Anderson use parallel structure, either within sentences or among them?

9. This essay is quite simple and straightforward; no university student should have any difficulty in understanding it. Is this the result of Anderson's sentence structure, or is there some other reason? In order to answer this question, analyze the sentences of any two consecutive paragraphs. Are Anderson's sentences mainly simple*? compound*? complex*?

10. Does the author use any fragments*? If so, are they effective? or should he have used complete sentences?

DICTION

11. Look up: *devious* (4), *lease* (10), *ferret* (16), *roughnecks* (17), *zeal* (22), *scrutiny* (25), *individualistic* (38).

12. Why does the author use quotation marks around the phrase "Brownie points"? Could they just as well have been omitted? Would usage be the same for the expression "tight hole"?

13. Look up "colloquialism" in the Glossary. Is "stunts" in paragraph 6 such a word? Are there others?

14. Should the clause "the ones that appealed to me as much as any" (2–3) be rewritten "the ones that appealed to me as much as any others"? Why, or why not?

POINTS TO LEARN

1. Examples can be extremely usful in helping to define.
2. The difficult task of expressing the complex in a simple manner can be aided by carefully choosing both diction and sentence structure.

SUGGESTIONS FOR WRITING

Describe some task you are familiar with for an audience which could not be expected to know it. For a group of Inuit, for instance, living in the far North, describe your job bagging groceries in a supermarket, or delivering newspapers, or clerking in a clothing store, or stock-keeping in a warehouse. Don't go into great detail; deal with the main points, especially, and restrict your paper to just 6 or 7 fairly short paragraphs.

IMPROVING YOUR STYLE

In your essay pay special attention to these two points:
1. Brief but precise transitions between paragraphs.
2. Parallel series of adjectives; include at least two.

Persuasion

Thus far we have been concerned with problems of explaining and defining. Often, however, a writer desires to change his readers' beliefs or opinions, to persuade them to share his own values or conclusions. Of course, a clear-cut line is not easily drawn between exposition and persuasion. One, in fact, may imply the other. If you wish to convince someone that you are right about a controversial issue, you probably will have to define terms and explain facts and ideas. Contrarily, exposition—especially if it is effectively organized and expressed—is likely to have persuasive force, even though its composer had no persuasive intention. But however difficult it is to lay down in practice, there is a difference between writing to explain and writing to persuade.

Three modes of persuasion are common: argument, satire, and eloquence. Argument persuades by appealing to reason. To reason—the restriction is important, for it distinguishes argumentation from those other types of persuasion, which aim rather at our emotions than at our intellects. With emotion argument has little to do. Its essence is reason, and reason may work in two ways: by deduction and by induction. The first argues from general premise to particular conclusion, the second from particular fact to broad conclusion.

Deductive argumentation is usually cast in the form of a logical syllogism. At its simplest a syllogism contains two premises and an inference that necessarily follows from them. For example:

1. All hatters are mad.
2. X is a hatter.
3. Therefore X is mad.

If the major premise (1) and the minor premise (2) are true, the inference, or conclusion, (3) has got to be true, for the inference is logically valid. Logical validity, however, is not the same thing as empirical truth. Since all hatters are not mad, the factual truth of the conclusion about X is open to question. Syllogistic reasoning, in short, is no sounder than the premises upon which it rests. The writer arguing logically must begin from premises not easily denied by his opponents.

In working from these premises he must proceed carefully. It is not hard to make mistakes—called fallacies—in getting from premise to conclusion. Many arguments involve a chain of interlocked syllogisms, each more complicated than that about X the hatter. In most arguments the rigid form of the syllogism will be replaced by a more fluid prose, and here and there a premise or an inference may be omitted for economy. Under these conditions fallacies are especially easy to commit. There is no shortcut to learning sound logic. The student who wishes to argue well should consult a good textbook, master at least the rudiments of logic, and train himself to detect the common fallacies.

Exposing these fallacies is an effective way of attacking the arguments of others. One such flaw, quite frequent and quite easily demonstrated, is self-contradiction. It is a fundamental law of logic that if *a* is true, *a* cannot be non-true. For example, one cannot argue that the Romans were doomed to fall and then assert that they were fools because they failed to solve the problems that destroyed them. To argue the inevitability of their decline is to deny the Romans free will; to charge them with folly presupposes that they had the freedom to choose between acting wisely or not. All this seems very obvious; yet in more subtle matters a writer can easily contradict himself without realizing it. To be sure that he has not, he must examine, not only his argument itself, but all the assumptions which lie beneath it and all the implications which lie within.

About deductive argumentation, then, we may conclude: (1) that it must begin from true premises, and (2) that it must derive its conclusions from these premises according to the rules of inference. The writer who ignores either principle is himself open to attack. If his premises are untrue he may be answered factually; if his conclusions are invalid the fallacy can be revealed.

Inductive reasoning is somewhat more common in argumentation. The method of the scientist or the prosecutor, it begins with facts and builds from them to a general conclusion. In practice a writer will usually find it more convenient to indicate his conclusion first and then bring forward the evidence which supports it. This is only a matter of arrangement, however, and does not deny the essential order of particular to general. Like the syllogism, induction will be fallacious when it fails to observe certain rules, which may be called the laws of evidence.

The first, and most obvious, is that evidence must be accurate. The second, more easily forgotten, is that it must be relevant, relating meaningfully to the conclusion it is brought forward to support. To prove, for instance, that women have more accidents than men, a writer might cite figures which show that they bring more automobiles to body shops with damaged fenders. Granting the accuracy of the evidence, we may still question its relevancy. It may be that women are afraid of their husbands and hastily repair dents which men blithely ignore; it may be that most of the dents resulted from accidents with reckless males. Often relevancy is so obvious that it may be taken for granted, but sometimes, as in this example, the writer must show that his evidence connects with his conclusion.

The third rule is that evidence must be complete. One of the commonest mistakes in inductive reasoning is to ignore this rule, especially when dealing with what are called universal affirmative propositions. These are statements that assert a truth applicable to all members of a class; for example, All students love school. Such propositions can be proved only by testing each member to which they apply. Since so complete a demonstration is generally impossible, all that can be shown for most universal propositions is a strong probability. Usually probability will be all the argument requires, but honesty demands that the conclusion be stated as less than an absolute truth. In brief, a writer should never phrase his premise even one degree stronger than his evidence will support. Writers who scorn such qualifiers as *some* or *generally speaking*, expose themselves to easy counterattack. Their evidence may in itself be good, but they ride it too hard and are surprised when it collapses under the strain.

All evidence, then, must observe these rules; the evidence itself, however, may take different forms. Three are most frequent: common knowledge, specific examples, and statistical data. Evidence is often advanced in the form of common knowledge, which may be defined as what is so generally known that it can safely be asserted without the support of examples or statistical tables. No one can draw the line that separates common knowledge from particular assertion. It is common knowledge that school is sometimes dull. It is a particular assertion that crocodiles make fine household pets. Perhaps they do; still, most of us would require proof. Perhaps the best rule is this: if a writer is doubtful whether a statement is common knowledge or assertion, he had better support it with additional specific evidence.

Examples, especially when they are historical, often involve the problem of interpretation. For example, one might consider Louis Riel's refusal, during the Northwest Rebellion of 1885, to allow Gabriel Dumont and his Métis sharpshooters to ambush Colonel Irvine and his men on their way to Prince Albert. This example is often used to support the argument that Riel was a poor military strategist, but this argument itself rests on a prior assumption—that Riel should have sought a military victory. Such an interpretation ignores Riel's conception of himself as a religious visionary, a prophet who was obeying God's direct orders, however impractical they might seem to a modern historian.

Another type of specific evidence often misused is the rhetorical analogy. For clarification or emphasis an analogy is often excellent; for proof it is meaningless. No matter how similar two things may be, there must be some differences between them. However slight, these differences deny any possibility of proof. This does not mean that analogies have no place in argumentation, simply that they should be restricted to supporting more legitimate evidence. To do this they must be fair and not force similarities where none exist. A famous instance of an unfair, or false, analogy is Thomas Carlyle's comparison of a state to a ship in order to demonstrate the weakness of democracy. The analogy is used to argue that a state cannot survive danger unless its leader, like the captain of a ship, has power independent of majority consent. But ships and states are very different things, and what may hold at sea does not therefore hold on land. Analogies, then, are valuable in argument if they are fair and if they are not used for proof (see also pp. 75–83).

The third sort of evidence is statistical. Although subject to the same laws that govern all evidence, statistics are often employed less critically. Consider a very simple case. We wish to answer the charge based on the evidence of the dented fenders and to prove that, on the contrary, Canadian women are safer drivers than Canadian men. Selecting a small community, we show that in a single year 100 women had accidents as compared to 500 men. The figures seem strong evidence. Yet this town may contain 5000 male drivers and only 500 female drivers, and if so then only 10 per cent of the men had accidents as opposed to 20 per cent of the women. Or perhaps the community is not a typical sample of the Canadian population; or perhaps the police records included only some accidents, not all; or perhaps these figures cover a wide range of accidents, from mild bumps to head-on collisions.

Perhaps a great many things. As you see, statistics must be handled carefully. If it is too much to expect all writers to be trained in statistical method, it is not too much to ask them to subject any statistical data they use to the common-sense criteria of accuracy, relevancy, and completeness. So tested, statistics are good evidence.

Most of the faults of inductive reasoning follow from ignoring these criteria, or, even worse, from ignoring the spirit behind them. Induction begins with facts, and it stays with facts until it has established their truth. It does not select or distort facts to fit a preconceived notion. It is easy, for example, to blame juvenile delinquency on comic books by ignoring the complexity of forces that create juvenile crime. Such an argument may strike us for a moment, but only for a moment. It is neither true nor honest. And in argumentation, as in murder, truth will out.

We have stressed here the problems of reasoning well, for that is the essence of argumentation. Yet to be fully effective an argument must be not only well reasoned but well expressed. Its organization must be clear. The writer should make plain at the very beginning what he is arguing for or what he is contending against, and his paragraphs should march in perfect order from premise to inference or from evidence to conclusion. His syntax should be an easy yet a strong vehicle for the ideas it conveys, and his diction both honest and exact. In short, argumentation is reason finely phrased. Reason twisted in awkward prose is like a chisel of strong steel with a blunted edge. Beautiful writing that hides fallacy and misrepresentation is a shiny tool of cheap metal that soon cracks. To argue well the writer must begin with intelligence and with honesty, but he must hone them to the sharp edge of good prose.

There are times, however, when argument, no matter how beautifully expressed, is not as effective as those kinds of persuasion that appeal more directly to feeling. One way of making such an appeal is by satire. The satirist aims at our sense of the ridiculous and, latently at least, at our sense of shame. He mocks and exaggerates the faults and follies he would persuade us to disavow. His tone may range from light, witty humor to profound bitterness; but whether he be amused or enraged by human weakness, the satirist holds before us the disparity between what is and what ought to be, between the ideals we profess and the idiocies we practice.

To emphasize this disparity satirists often employ irony. Irony in its simplest form is using words so that their real significance is the reverse of their apparent meaning. If one were to say of a stingy man, "He's a generous person," the word "generous" would be ironic. (Heavy-handed and insulting irony of this sort is called sarcasm.) Irony, of course, must be clearly signaled so that the listener or reader will interpret it correctly. In speech this is often done by uttering the ironic word with a special emphasis or intonation ("He's a 'generous' person"), or by some non-verbal sign such as a raised eyebrow, a smile, a wink, a gesture, or a shrug. In writing, obviously, such cues are unavailable. While the writer can underline an ironic term or enclose it in quotation marks, these expedients are mechanical and not very effective. The skilful literary ironist depends upon the subtle use of context to make his intention clear, and usually, too, he counts upon the good sense of his readers to distinguish what he is really saying from what he appears to be saying.

Less subtly, the satirist may belabor his target with invective, hurling abuse at the faults he castigates. A famous example occurs in the second act of *King Lear*. When Oswald, a villainous steward to one of Lear's false daughters, encounters the Earl of Kent, he impudently asks, "What dost thou take me for?" Kent tells him in a classic instance of invective:

> A knave, a rascal, an eater of broken meats; a base, proud, shallow, beggarly, three-suited, hundred-pound, filthy worsted-stocking knave; a lily-livered, action-taking, whoreson, glass-gazing, superserviceable, finical rogue; one-trunk-inheriting slave; one that wouldst be a bawd in way of good service, and art nothing but the composition of a knave, beggar, coward, pander, and the son and heir of a mongrel bitch; one whom I will beat into clamorous whining if thou deny'st the least syllable of thy addition.

Such satire of insult, as we may call it, is less common than it was. Manners have softened in the modern world, and our sense of fair play is likely to be offended by invective. But it can still be wondrously effective, as H. L. Mencken's attack on William Jennings Bryan (on page 289) demonstrates.

Most of use enjoy clever, witty insult (if we are not the victims); the popularity of insult-comedians testifies to that. Still, it must be admitted that invective appeals to a base instinct: our enjoyment at seeing another person pilloried and made ridiculous. (Of course, we rationalize our pleasure by assuring ourselves that the fool had it coming.) The last type of persuasion sets its aim much higher. Eloquence evokes our noblest conceptions of humanity and elevates us to a plane of duty far above the petty preoccupation with self. It puts before us examples of great men and women, and urges, whether directly or by implication, that we imitate them. Thus the English poet Algernon Charles Swinburne—describing Lord Byron's death at Missolonghi, where he had gone to help the Greeks in their fight for independence from Turkey—concludes:

> His work was done at Missolonghi; all of his work for which the fates could spare him time. A little space was allowed him to show at least a heroic purpose, and attest a high design; then, with all things un-

finished before him and behind, he fell asleep after many troubles and triumphs. Few can ever have gone wearier to the grave; none with less fear. He had done enough to earn his rest. Forgetful now and set free for ever from all faults and foes, he passed through the doorway of no ignoble death out of reach of time, out of sight of love, out of hearing of hatred, beyond the blame of England and the praise of Greece. In the full strength of spirit and of body his destiny overtook him, and made an end of all his labours. He had seen and borne and achieved more than most men on record. "He was a great man, good at many things, and now he has attained this also, to be at rest."

Phrases such as "heroic purpose," "high design," "the full strength of spirit" express a level of being which few men attain but to which all worthy men should aspire. In a cynical age such expressions have a quaint, almost comic cast. But they possess a perennial truth: if we do not stretch toward stars, we fall back into mud.

Scotland's Fate: Canada's Lesson

Hugh MacLennan is one of Canada's most distinguished novelists. His works include *Barometer Rising* (1941), *Two Solitudes* (1945), *The Precipice* (1948), *Each Man's Son* (1951), and *The Watch That Ends the Night* (1959). In 1945, 1948, and 1959 his novels received the Governor General's Award for fiction. MacLennan is also a prolific and wide-ranging essayist, whose collections have twice won the Governor General's Award for non-fiction. His novels and essays display a continuing concern with the social, political, and cultural life of Canada. In the selection below, by means of an analogy, he argues that Canada faces the prospect of becoming merely a northern adjunct of the United States.

1   Ever since Washington announced its new economic policies two years ago, such parts of Canada as are political have been living in a trance. This is what often happens to people and nations when they are aware of something new they cannot bear to contemplate because, if they do, they will be confronted with unpleasant decisions they don't know how to 5 make.

2   It happened to millions of individuals immediately after the 1929 stock market crash. Over the centuries it has happened to many a nation— to the United States, for instance, in the decade before the Civil War when the Americans evaded the fact that their country could not endure 10 half-slave and half-free. And to Britain and France in the 1930s, when neither could endure the idea of another war fought to contain the Germans' ambitions. Ultimately, in such situations, the new reality strikes home. But first comes the national trance.

3   Canada today faces no Fort Sumter or *blitzkrieg*, but unless we 15 soon make up our minds about our future relations with the United States,

From "Scotland's Fate" by Hugh MacLennan (*Macleans*. 1973), reprinted by permission of the author.

we will drift or be pushed into such a position that our nation will become a mere territorial expression of American aspirations—as Scotland is a territorial expression of England.

4   When I was young I often heard people say, "Canada is the Scot- 20 land of North America." Only recently did it occur to me that it might be worthwhile considering the extent to which this is true. There are certainly some obvious parallels. As Scotland is the hard northern cap to the British island, with the rich farmlands and cities of England just below her, so is Canada to the United States. Both countries were gouged by the re- 25 treating glaciers, which left them on the subsistence level so far as good farmland was concerned. It also gave them a heritage of spectacular beauty uncrowded by cities and towns, and of this they were both inclined to boast. When one of Boswell's friends told Dr. Johnson that Scotland had "many wild, noble prospects," Johnson retorted that Lapland also had wild 30 noble prospects, but that "the noblest prospect which a Scotchman ever sees is the high-road that leads him to England!"

5   A good many high-roads for a good many years led Canadians into the United States, where most of them maintained a pawky pride in the country they had abandoned. So did the Scotch who went to England. A 35 well-known story has it that when an Edinburgh man returned from a week of business in London and was asked how he liked the English, his reply was, "I don't rightly ken: I was only meeting the heads of companies and they were all Scots." (He should have added that these company heads were permanently lost to Scotland, for invariably they sent their sons to 40 English schools and universities.) Still another resemblance is the belief held by Scotsmen and Canadians that they are more moral than their rich southern neighbors. But the most interesting parallels, of course, are political and economic, and here the resemblances are balanced by many important differences.   45

QUESTIONS

READER AND PURPOSE
1. MacLennan is presenting an argument by analogy. What form does his analogy take?
2. What dangers should the reader be alert to in an argument of this kind? What tends to make analogy less persuasive than reasoned argument?

3. At any point in this selection does MacLennan show that he is aware of the limits of argument by analogy?

4. MacLennan also draws on personal experience in this selection. How does this affect his relationship with the reader?

5. He also mentions Boswell and Dr. Johnson as if they were familiar to his audience. Are they to you? If not, look them up (in the *Oxford Companion to English Literature* or, for longer entries, in the *Dictionary of National Biography*) and try to decide whether they are appropriate to MacLennan's analogy.

ORGANIZATION

6. What purpose is served by the first two paragraphs? Could they have been omitted, or do they have some bearing on the analogy when it is presented for the first time in paragraph 3? What relevance, if any, do MacLennan's historical examples have for his analogy?

7. In view of the changing relationship between Canada and the United States, is the reference to one incident "two years ago" (1-2) sufficient to persuade the reader that Canada is in a national "trance" (2)?

8. MacLennan develops his analogy in paragraphs 3, 4, and 5, and states that there are "some obvious parallels" (23) in the Scotland-Britain, Canada-United States relationships. How many parallels does he mention? Could you think of others? Do you find all of those cited by MacLennan convincing? For example, in paragraph 4 he states that the farmland of Scotland and Canada is similar. What would a student on the Canadian prairies think of this claim?

9. Does the final sentence of paragraph 5 leave the reader convinced that MacLennan's analogy has been a useful persuasive device?

SENTENCES

10. MacLennan uses a dash to set off the final clause of the second sentence of paragraph 2. What would be lost if the sentence were rewritten with a comma in place of the dash?

11. Sentence three of paragraph 2 is a fragment *. Fragments should be used sparingly, but in certain cases they can be effective. How would the effect be changed here if the fragment were rewritten as a complete sentence?

12. What key word links the last sentence of paragraph 2 with the opening sentence of paragraph 1?

13. Paragraph 3 is a one-sentence paragraph. It does not conform to the usual pattern of topic sentence and supporting evidence, yet its short length makes it all the more striking. What strong effect is MacLennan trying to achieve here?

14. Why does MacLennan put the fourth sentence of paragraph 5 in parentheses?

DICTION
15. Look up: *trance* (2), *Fort Sumter* (15), *blitzkreig* (15), *aspirations* (18), *subsistence* (26), *spectacular* (27), *prospects* (30), *pawky* (34).
16. What does MacLennan mean by the phrase *territorial expression* (18-19)?
17. Explain the meaning of *I don't rightly ken* (38).

POINTS TO LEARN
1. Analogies are not, by themselves, persuasive.
2. Analogies can be effectively used in argument, but only when they are supported by more tangible evidence.
3. Personal opinion or experience may also be used, provided that the writer has more objective means of supporting his case.

SUGGESTIONS FOR WRITING
Use one of the following analogies or invent one of your own: Alberta is the Texas of Canada; British Columbia is the California of Canada; or something along these lines. Write a paragraph in which you present as many parallels as you can think of to support your analogy. Then write another paragraph in which you use specific evidence, statistics, or common knowledge to show the limits of your analogy.

IMPROVING YOUR STYLE
1. Include in your paragraphs one aspect of your analogy that you present in the first person and draw from your own experience.
2. Write three sentences in which you present three different parallels in three different sentence forms: simple, compound *, complex *.
3. Write one sentence in which you make use of allusion * to historical events.

Of Marriage and Single Life

Francis Bacon (1561-1626) was an English statesman, philosopher, and writer. First under Elizabeth I (who reigned from 1558 until 1603), then under James I (1603-25), Bacon rose to high political office. He published important works on philosophy, history, and law, and he is the first English essayist. Bacon's essays (1591-ff., first collectively printed in 1625) are short, moralistic, and written in a terse, pointed prose. In the one printed below he considers the relative merits of marriage and the single life. While Bacon's diction and sentence style are old-fashioned, the issue he discusses is still alive (more alive in some ways than ever), and his approach to it can still provide a model for contemporary writers.

He that hath wife and children hath given hostages to fortune, for they are impediments to great enterprises, either of virtue or mischief. Certainly the best works, and of greatest merit for the public have proceeded from the unmarried or childless men, which both in affection and means have married and endowed the public. Yet it were great reason that those that have 5 children should have greatest care of future times, unto which they know they must transmit their dearest pledges. Some there are who though they lead a single life, yet their thoughts do end with themselves, and account future times impertinences.[1] Nay, there are some other that account wife and children but as bills of charges. Nay more, there are some foolish, rich, 10 covetous men that take a pride in having no children, because they may be thought so much the richer. For perhaps they have heard some talk, *Such an one is a great rich man,* and another except to it, *Yea, but he hath a great charge of children,* as if it were an abatement to his riches. But the most ordinary cause of a single life is liberty, especially in certain self-pleas- 15

From *Essays or Counsels, Civil and Moral,* edited by Richard Foster Jones (New York: Odyssey Press, 1937).

[1] Matters of no importance.

ing and humorous[2] minds, which are so sensible of every restraint, as they
will go near to think their girdles and garters to be bonds and shackles. Unmarried men are best friends, best masters, best servants, but not always
best subjects, for they are light to run away; and almost all fugitives are of
that condition. A single life doth well with churchmen, for charity will   20
hardly water the ground where it must first fill a pool. It is indifferent for
judges and magistrates, for if they be facile and corrupt, you shall have a
servant five times worse than a wife. For soldiers, I find the generals commonly in their hortatives put men in mind of their wives and children; and
I think the despising of marriage amongst the Turks maketh the vulgar   25
soldier more base. Certainly wife and children are a kind of discipline of
humanity; and single men, though they may be many times more chari-
table, because their means are less exhaust,[3] yet, on the other side, they are
more cruel and hardhearted (good to make severe inquisitors), because
their tenderness is not so oft called upon. Grave natures, led by custom and   30
therefore constant, are commonly loving husbands, as was said of Ulysses,
vetulam suam prætulit immortalitati.[4] Chaste women are often proud and
froward, as presuming upon the merit of their chastity. It is one of the
best bonds both of chastity and obedience in the wife, if she think her
husband wise, which she will never do if she find him jealous. Wives are   35
young men's mistresses, companions for middle age, and old men's nurses.
So as a man may have a quarrel[5] to marry when he will. But yet he was
reputed one of the wise men, that made answer to the question, when a
man should marry?—*A young man not yet, an elder man not at all*. It is
often seen that bad husbands have very good wives; whether it be that it   40
raiseth the price of their husband's kindness when it comes, or that the
wives take a pride in their patience. But this never fails if the bad husbands
were of their own choosing, against their friends' consent, for then they
will be sure to make good their own folly.

QUESTIONS

READER AND PURPOSE

1. What advantages does Bacon find in the single life? What disadvantages in
marriage? Does he admit any vices in the former or virtues in the latter?

[2] Eccentric, odd.
[3] Exhausted, used up.
[4] "He preferred his old wife to immortality."
[5] A reason, an excuse.

2. Do you think Bacon is trying to persuade men either to marry or to remain single? Or is he examining both sides of a controversial issue?

3. What assumptions does Bacon appear to have made about his readers? Is he, for example, aiming at adults or at young people? At the educated or the ignorant? The worldly or the naïve?

ORGANIZATION

4. In Bacon's "Essays" the term *essay* retains something of its early sense of a tentative attempt to discuss a topic and does not signify what it means today: a careful and polished composition. Even so, it would be a mistake to think of a Bacon essay as no more than the hasty jotting down of random thoughts. This paragraph is organized in the sense that it is a reasoned analysis of a topic. The analysis is revealed by considering how the sentences relate and group together. Thus sentences 1, 2, and 3 compose a unit. The first asserts that a disadvantage of married life is that it keeps men from great enterprises; the second repeats this point negatively by noting that the best and most valuable achievements have come from unmarried men; and the third reinforces the initial idea by noting the paradox that married men, having children, ought in theory to be more concerned with the public welfare than single men without offspring. What thread of thought similarly unites sentences 4 through 8? Sentences 9 through 12?

5. Try to analyze the remaining nine sentences of the paragraph (beginning with "Certainly a wife and children . . ." in line 26). Is there any place where you find it difficult to establish continuity of thought?

6. *Nay* (9), *Nay more* (10), *For* (12), and *So as* (37) are all pointers *. For what turn of thought does each prepare us?

7. How does Bacon unify the three sentences in lines 20-23?

SENTENCES

8. Point out the parallel * words in the sentences in lines 1-5.

9. The sentence in lines 30-32 contains three ideas: (a) that grave natures make good husbands, (b) that grave natures are led by custom and are therefore constant, and (c) that Ulysses was a loving husband. Which of these is the main point of the sentence? How are the other two ideas logically related to it?

DICTION

10. Look up: *hostages* (1), *impediments* (2), *endowed* (5), *covetous* (11), *abatement* (14), *facile* (22), *vulgar* (25), *froward* (33), *reputed* (38), *folly* (44).

11. When studying writers who flourished several centuries in the past it is necessary to remember that some of their words have meanings very different

from what the words possess for us. In Bacon's essay this fact is true of *mischief* (2), *impertinences* (9), *except* (13), *charge* (14), *humorous* (16), and *girdles* (17). How does the sense in which Bacon employs these words differ from their meaning today? (You may have to consult an unabridged dictionary such as *The Oxford English Dictionary* or *Webster's Third New International Dictionary*.)

12. Render these phrases into modern English idiom: *bills of charge* (10), *light to run away* (19), *generals in their hortatives* (24), *make good their own folly* (44).

13. What metaphor * is contained in Bacon's remark in line 17 that some men think their "girdles and garters to be bonds and shackles"? Explain the metaphor involved in the assertion that a wife and children are "hostages to fortune." In lines 20-21 Bacon says that it is better for clergymen to remain single because "charity will hardly water the ground where it must first fill a pool." Here too is a metaphor. What does *ground* stand for? *Pool?* Express in your own words why Bacon considers clergymen are better off unmarried. What advantage is there to expressing the idea metaphorically?

14. To what does *this* (42) refer?

POINTS TO LEARN

1. In most controversies there is something to be said on either side. A writer's task is sometimes to consider both sides without prejudice.

2. When reading older prose do not take the meanings of words for granted; they may in fact be quite different from what you suppose.

3. A metaphor may not be as immediately clear as the direct expression of an idea, but it stimulates the willing reader, forcing him to think.

SUGGESTIONS FOR WRITING

The problem Bacon discusses is still with us. Examine it from your own point of view; is it better to marry or to remain single? If the topic of marriage versus the single life does not appeal, attempt a judgment essay on one of these subjects:

Going to college or learning a skilled trade

Owning a television set or living without one

Life in the city versus life in the country

Strict discipline at home or school compared with a liberal, permissive atmosphere

IMPROVING YOUR STYLE

In your essay include:

1. Two or three examples of parallelism.
2. A sentence in which three explanatory or illustrative ideas are subordinated to a fourth, controlling idea.
3. Several metaphors.

From Our Sexist Language

In her essay "Our Sexist Language" feminist Ethel Strainchamps attacks the bias against women latent in everyday words—the use of *man*, for instance, as a generic term for human beings, or of *him* as the third-person pronoun referring to such sexually undifferentiated words as *person, student, anyone*, and so on. These paragraphs, however, are concerned less with the specific issue of biased words than with a preliminary question. Ask yourselves how the passage fits into the writer's larger purpose of exposing sexism in language, and what kind of evidence she calls upon to support her argument.

1   Few people would care to take the negative side of the proposition that the women of the world are oppressed and scorned. Statistics are against them. What has not been made so clear, however, is that the women of America, the world's most highly advanced (that is, technological) society, may be among the most oppressed and scorned of all.   5

2   Various data suggest the conclusion. Compared to other advanced nations, we have had fewer women in high government offices and fewer women in the professions. American men are more attracted by the primal aggressive activities of hunting and fishing than are men of other nations. More of them are seduced by the atavistic appeal of all-male organiza-   10
tions—reminiscent of the male-bonding propensities of the apes—from the Knights of Columbus to the Rotary Club. Our culture heroes are not benevolent rulers or noble wise men, in spite of the schools' efforts on behalf of Washington, Jefferson, and Lincoln, but aggressive men of action: cowboys, aviators, baseball players, outlaws, military men. All *muy macho*.   15

From "Our Sexist Language" in *Women in Sexist Society: Studies in Power and Powerlessness*, edited by Vivian Gornick and Barbara K. Moran. © 1971 by Basic Books, Inc., Publishers, New York. Reprinted by permission.

QUESTIONS

1. An argument may be positive in the sense that it contends something *is* the case, or negative in the sense that something is *not*. (A negative argument is sometimes called a refutation.) What is Strainchamps' contention? Is her strategy * negative or positive?

2. Is the argument deductive or inductive—that is, does the author derive her conclusion from some broad, self-evident principle, or rather support it by specific evidence?

3. Strainchamps does not quote statistics, but is her argument ultimately based upon them? Does she suggest anywhere that it is? Do you think her argument is sound even though she does not cite figures and percentages? If it is not statistical, how would you describe her evidence?

4. Describe the tone of this selection. Is it angry, amused, objective?

ORGANIZATION

5. Suppose that in paragraph 1 Strainchamps spelled out the logical relationship between the first and second sentences, writing, for instance, in line 3: "This is because statistics are against them." Would this be more, or less, effective? What word ties these sentences together?

6. Which is the topic sentence of the second paragraph? Is it a good topic statement? Outline this paragraph, showing how each sentence relates logically to what precedes it.

SENTENCES

7. Could the enclosed remark in lines 4-5 be punctuated with commas or dashes instead of parentheses?

8. Where does Strainchamps use short sentences effectively for emphasis? Besides its brevity, for what other quality is her final sentence notable?

9. The construction beginning in line 4—"the world's most highly advanced (that is, technological) society"—is an appositive *. What preceding word or idea does it repeat? Presumably, Strainchamps' readers are Americans and know that theirs is the world's most technologically advanced society: why, then, does she stress the point? Is there any irony * in Strainchamps' parenthetical explanation that by "advanced" she means "technological"?

10. What does the colon signal in line 14?

11. The final sentence of this selection is a fragment *. Is it effective, or would it have sounded better joined to the preceding idea? Something like this, perhaps:

Our culture heroes are not benevolent rulers or noble wise men, in spite of the schools' efforts on behalf of Washington, Jefferson, and Lincoln, but aggressive men of action: cowboys, aviators, baseball players, outlaws, military men, who are all *muy macho*.

DICTION

12. Look up: *oppressed* (2), *technological* (4), *professions* (8), *reminiscent* (11), *benevolent* (13).

13. Explain the meanings of these phrases: *the negative side of the proposition* (1), *primal aggressive activities* (9), *atavistic appeal* (10), *male-bonding propensities* (11), *culture heroes* (12), muy macho (15).

14. What does the phrase *that is* (4) prepare the reader to expect?

15. Why are these substitutes less effective than the words the writer chose: *prove* for *suggest* (6), *attracted* for *seduced* (10), *higher primates* for *apes* (11)?

16. What are the implications of the Spanish phrase *muy macho* (15)?

POINTS TO LEARN

1. The strategy of an argument may be positive (that is, to prove) or negative (to disprove).

2. An inductive argument rests upon specific evidence.

3. In developing an argument begin by making clear what you are for or against.

4. Short sentences are emphatic.

SUGGESTIONS FOR WRITING

Compose a short argument (three paragraphs, 400-500 words) on one of the topics below. You may argue either side, but make your position clear at the very beginning. Work inductively and cite evidence—statistics (if you can find them), examples, general knowledge.

Men are actually more oppressed than women.

The value—both economic and social—of a college degree has declined.

The typical high-school graduate today is better educated than were those of a generation ago.

IMPROVING YOUR STYLE

In your essay use:

1. Two or three short sentences for emphasis.

2. A parenthetical remark explaining or commenting upon the preceding statement.

3. The phrase *that is* to introduce an explanation.

Of Love in Infants

Harry Harlow is a scientist specializing in animal behavior. The following piece, which is complete, is his report on an experiment. It is a model of how to write up an experiment—beginning with the problem to be investigated, explaining the procedure and results in detail, and clearly stating the conclusion. In a narrow sense the essay is not avowedly persuasive. Yet viewed more broadly it has great persuasive force, convincing us by the careful application of reason and gathering of evidence.

1   The use of infant monkeys in many laboratory experiments is perhaps dictated by necessity, but few scientists would deny that it is also remarkably convenient. Monkeys are far better coordinated at birth than human infants; their reactions can be evaluated with confidence at an age of ten days or earlier, yet their development follows the same general line   5 as that of humans.

2   The monkeys' well-being and even survival pose a number of problems, however—particularly if they must, in the course of experimentation, be separated from their mothers only a few hours after birth. Nonetheless, at the University of Wisconsin's Primate Laboratory we were able, using   10 techniques developed by Dr. Gertrude van Wagenen of Yale, to rear infant monkeys on the bottle with a far lower mortality than is found among monkeys nursed by their mothers. Now one of the components of our technique involved the use of a gauze diaper folded on the floor of the infant monkeys' cages, following Dr. van Wagenen's observations that monkeys   15 would maintain contact with soft, pliant surfaces during nursing. We were struck by the deep attachment our monkeys formed for these diaper pads and by the distress they showed when, once a day, the pads were removed for reasons of sanitation. This observation led us into quite a new series of

"Of Love in Infants" by Harry F. Harlow from *Ants, Indians and Little Dinosaurs* edited by Alan P. Ternes is used by permission of Charles Scribner's Sons. Copyright © 1975 by The American Museum of Natural History.

experiments—research into the importance of bodily contact in infant love.   20

3   Love of infants for their mothers is often regarded as a sacred or mystical force, and perhaps this is why it has received so little objective study. But if facts are lacking, theory on this subject is abundant. Psychologists, sociologists, and anthropologists usually hold that the infant's love is learned through the association of the mother's face and body with the   25
alleviation of such physical tensions as hunger and thirst. Psychoanalysts specially emphasize the importance to emotional development of attaining and sucking at the breast. Our experiments suggest something else is involved.

4   We contrived two substitute "mothers." One was a bare cylinder   30
made of welded wire and surmounted by a wooden head. In the other, the wire framework was covered by a layer of terry cloth. We put eight new-born monkeys in individual cages, each with equal access to a cloth and to a wire mother. Four received their milk from one type of mother, four from the other—the milk being obtained from nursing bottles fixed in the   35
mothers' "breasts."

5   Physiologically, the two mothers proved to be equivalent—the monkeys in both groups drank as much milk and gained weight at the same rate. But psychologically, the two mothers were not at all equivalent. Both groups of monkeys spent far more time climbing over and embracing their   40
cloth mothers than they did their plain wire ones; they even left their electric heating pads to climb on the unheated cloth mother. Those that suckled from the wire mother spent no more time than feeding required.

6   The theory that infant love is related to satisfaction of hunger or thirst was thus contradicted, and the importance of bodily contact in form-   45
ing affection underscored. This finding was supported by the next phase of our investigation. The time the monkey infants spent cuddling their surrogate mothers was a strong indication of emotional attachment, but it was perhaps not conclusive. Would they also turn to their inanimate mothers for comfort when they were subjected to emotional stress?   50

7   With this question in mind, we exposed our infant monkeys to strange objects likely to frighten them, such as a mechanical teddy bear that moved forward, beating a drum. It was found that, whether the infants had nursed on the wire mother or the cloth one, they overwhelmingly sought comfort in stress from the cloth one. The infant would cling to it,   55
rubbing its body against the toweling. With its fears thus assuaged, it would turn to look at the previously terrifying bear without the slightest

sign of alarm. It might even leave the comfort of its substitute mother to approach the object that had frightened it only a minute before.

8   It is obvious that such behavior is analogous to that of human infants, and we found that the analogy held in situations that less obviously involved stress. If a human child is taken to an unfamiliar place, for example, he will usually remain calm and happy so long as his mother is nearby, but if she leaves him, fear and panic may result. Our experiments showed a similar effect in infant monkeys. We put the monkeys in a room that was much larger than their usual cages, and in the room we placed a number of unfamiliar objects—a crumpled piece of newspaper, blocks of wood, a metal plate, and a doorknob mounted on a box. If a cloth mother was present, the monkey, at the sight of these objects, would rush wildly to her and, rubbing against the toweling, cling to her tightly. Its fear would then diminish greatly or else vanish altogether, as in the previous experiment. Soon the monkey would leave its mother to explore its new world. It now regarded the objects as playthings. Returning from time to time to the mother for reassurance, it followed an outgoing pattern of behavior.

9   If, on the other hand, the cloth mother were absent, the infant would rush across the room and throw itself head down on the floor, clutching its head and body and screaming in distress. The bare wire mother afforded no more reassurance than no mother at all—even monkeys that had known only the wire mother from birth showed no affection for her and got no comfort from her presence. Indeed, this group of monkeys showed the greatest distress of all.

10   In a final comparison of cloth and wire mothers, we adapted an experiment originally devised by Robert A. Butler in this laboratory. Butler had found that monkeys enclosed in a dimly lighted box would press a lever to open and reopen a window for hours on end, with no other reward than the chance to look out. The rate of this action depended on what the monkeys saw: a glimpse of another monkey elicited far more activity than that of an empty room.

11   When we tested our infant monkeys in such a box, we found that those raised with both cloth and wire mothers showed as great an interest in the cloth mother as in another monkey but responded no more to a wire mother than to an empty room. In this test, as in all others, the monkeys that had been fed on a wire mother behaved in the same way as those that had been fed on a cloth-covered mother surrogate.

12   Thus, all objective tests we have been able to devise indicate that

the infant monkey's relationship to its substitute mother is a full one. There are, of course, factors other than bodily contact involved. For example, the simple act of clinging, in itself, seems important: a newborn monkey has difficulty surviving in a bare wire cage unless provided with a cone to which it can cling.   100

13   Yet our experiments have clearly shown the importance of the comfort derived from bodily contact in the formation of an infant's love for its mother and revealed the role of breast-feeding to be negligible or nonexistent. They have also established an experimental approach to subtle and dramatic relationships.   105

QUESTIONS

READER AND PURPOSE

1. What question is Harlow attempting to answer? Does he?

2. Harlow's argument appeals to reason, and its method is inductive, depending upon evidence. Yet its evidence differs from that of Strainchamps (page 148), who asserts generalizations based upon statistics from everyday life. Harlow devises an experiment. What essential features distinguish the experimental method of gathering data?

3. Does Harlow appear to be writing for people who share his scientific interests and knowledge or for a more general audience: would you be more likely to find this article in a scientific journal or in *The Reader's Digest?*

ORGANIZATION

4. Which paragraphs constitute the beginning of this essay? Within that beginning what one sentence most clearly sets up the problem? Which paragraphs compose the closing?

5. The middle of the essay has three major sections. Give a title to each and indicate the paragraphs it includes.

6. In paragraph 1 how is the second sentence related in idea to the first?

7. In paragraph 6, the second sentence performs an important transitional function. Which words point backward to what has just been said? Which point forward, directing the reader to the next topic?

8. What is the topic of paragraph 8? How is the second sentence related to the topic? The third? How are the remaining sentences of the paragraph related to the third?

9. What phrase at the beginning of paragraph 9 prepares the reader for a shift in idea?

SENTENCES

10. What relationship in thought does the dash in line 20 help to signal? The colon in line 87?

11. Point out the nominative absolute * in the final sentence of paragraph 4.

12. The first two sentences of paragraph 5 open in the same way. What does the similarity serve to emphasize?

13. Identify the participial * phrase in the sentence in lines 55-56. Find three or four other effective participial phrases in this selection. What advantages do such constructions offer a writer?

DICTION

14. Look up: *coordinated* (3), *pose* (7), *components* (13), *hold* (24), *access* (33), *conclusive* (49), *analogous* (60), *reassurance* (74), *devise* (95), *negligible* (103).

15. How do the etymologies * of these words help to clarify their sense: *primate* (10), *pliant* (16), *alleviation* (26), *assuaged* (56)?

16. What is the difference between the interests or functions of *psychologists, sociologists, anthropologists* (23-24), *psychoanalysts* (26)?

17. What relationships in thought are signaled by these connecting * words: *nonetheless* (9), *now* (13), *thus* (45, 95), *of course* (97), *yet* (101)?

18. Why does Harlow put quotation marks around *mothers* in line 30?

POINTS TO LEARN

1. Effective arguments begin by making clear what is to be proved or disproved.

2. A good essay has a well-defined beginning, middle, and end.

3. Transitional sentences direct readers from one section of an essay to the next.

4. Participial phrases are an economic and efficient way of conveying subordinate information.

SUGGESTIONS FOR WRITING

1. Compose a report of 500-600 words on an experiment done in one of your lab courses. Begin by stating what you sought to determine, devote the bulk of your essay to describing the procedure, and end by drawing the appropriate conclusion.

2. If you have not had any experience in an actual laboratory, imagine an experimental situation in everyday life—for example, trying several methods of study to decide which works best, or using various approaches to impress someone you wish to please. Follow the general organization suggested in the first exercise.

IMPROVING YOUR STYLE

1. Include participial phrases in at least six of your sentences. Vary their position—according to the logical progression of your ideas or the demands of emphasis—so that some open the sentence, others close it, and one or two occur in interrupting positions.

2. Use each of the following connective * words or phrases at least once somewhere in your essay: *of course, for example, nonetheless, thus, yet.*

PLATO
(trans. by Benjamin Jowett)

The Banishment of Dramatists

Plato (the name signifies his broad shoulders) lived from 427? to 347 B.C. He was an Athenian philosopher, a disciple of Socrates, and the teacher of Aristotle. In 387 Plato founded the Academy, which evolved into the first university of the western world. Plato's philosophy is revealed in a series of *Dialogues*, discussions in dramatic, question-and-answer form between Socrates and various of his followers and opponents—the so-called Socratic method or dialectic. It is difficult to judge in the *Dialogues* when Plato is reporting what Socrates actually said or believed and when he is spreading his own ideas by putting them in the mouth of the older philosopher. In either case the *Dialogues* develop the Platonic philosophy—a set of beliefs concerning the real, the good, and the beautiful.

This selection comes from the *Republic*, one of the longest and most important of the *Dialogues*. In the *Republic* Socrates (or Plato) is concerned with the nature of justice and with how a state ought ideally to be constituted so as to serve justice. He arrives at an intellectual autocracy: sovereignty is to be exercised by a small elite circle of philosopher-kings; laws enforced by a larger, though still select, group of warrior-policemen; work provided by the masses. It all sounds suspiciously like the totalitarian state we have seen too often in the twentieth century. It is only fair to add, however, that Plato's philosopher-kings were to be chosen (never mind by whom) for their wisdom and goodness.

In this passage from the Tenth Book of the *Republic* Socrates ("I" in the dialogue) is discussing with a young man named Glaucon ("he") how poets and dramatists would fit into his ideal state. He concludes that they would not fit in at all. The conclusion must strike modern readers as peculiar, for we are accustomed to thinking of writers as ornaments and safeguards of society, not as dangers. Even so, set aside your own beliefs for a moment and try to understand the logic that leads Socrates to banish dramatists from his Utopia.

From Plato's *Republic* from *The Dialogues of Plato* trans. by Benjamin Jowett. Reprinted by permission of Oxford University Press.

1   But we have not yet brought forward the heaviest count in our accusation:—the power which poetry has of harming even the good (and there are very few who are not harmed), is surely an awful thing?

2   Yes, certainly, if the effect is what you say.

3   Hear and judge: The best of us, as I conceive, when we listen to a   5
passage of Homer, or one of the tragedians, in which he represents some pitiful hero who is drawling out his sorrows in a long oration, or weeping, and smiting his breast—the best of us, you know, delight in giving way to sympathy, and are in raptures at the excellence of the poet who stirs our feelings most.   10

4   Yes, of course I know.

5   But when any sorrow of our own happens to us, then you may observe that we pride ourselves on the opposite quality—we would fain be quiet and patient; this is the manly part, and the other which delighted us in the recitation is now deemed to be the part of a woman.   15

6   Very true, he said.

7   Now can we be right in praising and admiring another who is doing that which any one of us would abominate and be ashamed of in his own person?

8   No, he said, that is certainly not reasonable.   20

9   Nay, I said, quite reasonable from one point of view.

10   What point of view?

11   If you consider, I said, that when in misfortune we feel a natural hunger and desire to relieve our sorrow by weeping and lamentation, and that this feeling which is kept under control in our own calamities is satis-   25
fied and delighted by the poets;—the better nature in each of us, not having been sufficiently trained by reason or habit, allows the sympathetic element to break loose because the sorrow is another's; and the spectator fancies that there can be no disgrace to himself in praising and pitying any one who comes telling him what a good man he is, and making a fuss   30
about his troubles; he thinks that the pleasure is a gain, and why should he be supercilious and lose this and the poem too? Few persons ever reflect, as I should imagine, that from the evil of other men something of evil is communicated to themselves. And so the feeling of sorrow which has gathered strength at the sight of the misfortunes of others is with difficulty repressed   35
in our own.

12   How very true!

13   And does not the same hold also of the ridiculous? There are jests which you would be ashamed to make yourself, and yet on the comic stage,

or indeed in private, when you hear them, you are greatly amused by them, 40
and are not at all disgusted at their unseemliness;—the case of pity is repeated;—there is a principle in human nature which is disposed to raise a
laugh, and this which you once restrained by reason, because you were
afraid of being thought a buffoon, is now let out again; and having stimulated the risible faculty at the theatre, you are betrayed unconsciously to 45
yourself into playing the comic poet at home.

14   Quite true, he said.

15   And the same may be said of lust and anger and all the other af-
fections, of desire and pain and pleasure, which are held to be inseparable
from every action—in all of them poetry feeds and waters the passions in- 50
stead of drying them up; she lets them rule, although they ought to be controlled, if mankind are ever to increase in happiness and virtue.

16   I can not deny it.

17   Therefore, Glaucon, I said, whenever you meet with any of the
eulogists of Homer declaring that he has been the educator of Hellas, and 55
that he is profitable for education and for the ordering of human things,
and that you should take him up again and again and get to know him and
regulate your whole life according to him, we may love and honor those
who say these things—they are excellent people, as far as their lights extend; and we are ready to acknowledge that Homer is the greatest of poets 60
and first of tragedy writers; but we must remain firm in our conviction that
hymns to the gods and praises of famous men are the only poetry which
ought to be admitted into our State. For if you go beyond this and allow
the honeyed muse to enter, either in epic or lyric verse, not law and the
reason of mankind, which by common consent have ever been deemed best, 65
but pleasure and pain will be the rulers in our State.

18   That is most true, he said.

QUESTIONS

READER AND PURPOSE

1. In paragraph 15 Socrates clearly implies what the relationship between reason and emotion ought to be in a virtuous man. Express that relationship in
your own words. This is the fundamental premise upon which Socrates grounds
his argument against poetry. Where else in these paragraphs does he state or
imply that premise?

2. Essentially, what is his complaint against poetry? Does he offer evidence to
support his charge?

3. If his initial premise be granted, is Socrates' argument sound? If you wished to attack it, would it be easier to do so by disputing his evidence or by denying his premise?

4. Does Glaucon here contribute any ideas to the argument? Does he seriously oppose Socrates? What exactly is his function? Describe Socrates' attitude toward Glaucon: is he courteous, overbearing, condescending?

ORGANIZATION

5. How do paragraphs 3 and 5 contribute to the argument? Which of these two paragraphs establishes the basic ethical premise and which offers evidence that poets violate that ethical ideal?

6. In paragraph 9 Socrates appears to contradict himself: he has just gotten Glaucon to agree that it is not reasonable to admire emotionalism in drama when men repress it in their own lives; but here he tells Glaucon that it is reasonable. Actually Socrates is correcting Glaucon, who in his answer confuses "right" and "reasonable." Socrates is suggesting that while a spectator's approval of theatrical emotionalism is not right, it is reasonable, or as we might say, "natural." How in the philosopher's view does the theater encourage emotional excess? Where does he argue that this excess is bad? Does Socrates' argument in paragraph 11 suggest that he believes that men are naturally virtuous, or rather that virtue must be acquired as the result of rational effort and discipline?

7. Paragraph 13 marks a minor turn of thought. Explain. Where in this paragraph does Socrates allude to a dangerous natural tendency of man which reason must correct, but which the theater indulges?

SENTENCES

8. In line 8 Socrates repeats "the best of us," the same phrase with which he began the sentence. Partly the repetition is emphatic, but it also has a more important function. Can you explain what it is?

9. The long and complicated sentence in lines 54-63 contains a good deal of parallelism *: point out all the parallel constructions you can find.

10. In the sentence in lines 63-66 what words are set antithetically * against "law and reason"?

DICTION

11. Look up: smiting (8), fain (13), deemed (15), calamities (25), fancies (29), risible (45), lust (48), eulogists (55).

12. What are the etymologies * of oration (7), raptures (9), supercilious (32), buffoon (44), virtue (52)?

13. Socrates, a good logician, clearly establishes the connection between his ideas. Indicate the pointers * by which he does this.

14. The word *now* in line 17 is not, strictly speaking, a logical pointer. What exactly does it do here?

POINTS TO LEARN

1. The strategy in the type of argument Socrates employs is to get your opponent to accept your premise and then to demonstrate that your position logically follows from that premise.

2. Where the subject of a sentence is followed by extensive modification, it may help the reader if you repeat the subject just before the verb.

SUGGESTIONS FOR WRITING

1. Literary figures have not accepted Socrates' banishment of poets, and there have been many counterclaims of the value of poetry, among which the essays by Sir Philip Sidney and Percy Bysshe Shelley are well known in English literature. How would you answer Socrates? You might develop your reply by expanding the role of Glaucon, putting into his mouth objections to Socrates' premise or his evidence.

2. If there is a particular amusement or social activity which you feel is harmful to social order, work out a Socratic argument on the question-and-answer pattern to prove that it should be outlawed. Possibilities—which you may accept or reject as a matter of preference—include: television, pornographic films or books, football, comic cartoons for children, grand opera, rock (or disco, or country and western) music, Wayne and Shuster, hunting, literature classes, marriage.

IMPROVING YOUR STYLE

In your composition include:

1. Several examples of parallelism.

2. Several of antithesis.

3. Connectives * which mark the flow of your logic (words like *therefore, and so, consequently, thus, now, however*).

The Third Knight's Speech

T. S. Eliot (1888-1965) was one of the most important and influential poets and critics of the twentieth century. Born an American, he lived most of his life in England and adopted British citizenship. Eliot's political and moral views were generally conservative and Christian. They are expressed in *Murder in the Cathedral* (1935), a blank-verse drama about the assassination in 1170 in the Canterbury cathedral of Archbishop Thomas à Becket.

Becket had been appointed to the archbishopric through the influence of the powerful English king, Henry II. Henry hoped that Becket, who had been his political right hand as chancellor, would, in his new post, subvert the interests of the church to those of the state. Events proved very different. When Becket vigorously upheld the authority of the church, Henry discovered that he had lost the ablest man of his kingdom to his enemies. After a series of confrontations and maneuverings Becket was hacked to death by four Norman knights, followers of King Henry. Nobody then or since has proved that the King ordered the murder or conspired in it. But as someone has said, kings do not have to issue such orders: their wishes are known.

Eliot's play, roughly modeled on a Greek tragedy, has two parts separated by a brief interlude. The first dramatizes Becket's return to Canterbury (he had sought refuge from Henry in France) and his gradual understanding and acceptance of his role as God's martyr. The martyrdom itself occurs near the beginning of part II. The thematically climactic scene of that part, however, is the Knights' efforts to justify their deed. They address the audience directly, speaking not in blank verse but in modern idiomatic prose. By having them step, as it were, from the twelfth century into the twentieth, Eliot implies the essential modernity of the Knights: in their avowal of the preeminence of the state and their rejection of God they are men of our time.

The First Knight acts as master of ceremonies, introducing the other three, each of whom argues a different justification. The initial claim (that of the Second Knight) is that they really admired Becket and did not enjoy kill-

From *Murder in the Cathedral* by T. S. Eliot. Reprinted by permission of Faber and Faber Ltd.

ing him. The last (by the Fourth Knight) is that they did not really kill Becket at all: in effect he committed suicide by refusing to listen to reason. Both arguments are silly and logically pointless. But between them Eliot places the Third Knight's speech. It is a masterpiece of logic and rhetoric, thoroughly reasoned and skillfully presented by an adroit, calculating speaker who understands his audience and plays subtly upon their beliefs and prejudices. Eliot, of course, does not accept what the Third Knight says: it rests upon assumptions which the play denies. But Eliot was an artist sufficiently mature and honest to allow the other side to state its case. It could not have been stated better than it is in the speech by the Third Knight.

1   I should like first to recur to a point that was very well put by our leader, Reginald Fitz Urse: that you are Englishmen, and therefore your sympathies are always with the under dog. It is the English spirit of fair play. Now the worthy Archbishop, whose good qualities I very much admired, has throughout been presented as the under dog. But is this really the case? I am 5 going to appeal not to your emotions but to your reason. You are hardheaded sensible people, as I can see, and not to be taken in by emotional clap-trap. I therefore ask you to consider soberly: what were the Archbishop's aims? and what are King Henry's aims? In the answer to these questions lies the key to the problem. 10
2   The King's aim has been perfectly consistent. During the reign of the late Queen Matilda and the irruption of the unhappy usurper Stephen, the kingdom was very much divided. Our King saw that the one thing needful was to restore order: to curb the excessive powers of local government, which were usually exercised for selfish and often for seditious ends, and to 15 systematise the judiciary. There was utter chaos: there were three kinds of justice and three kinds of court: that of the King, that of the Bishops, and that of the baronage. I must repeat one point that the last speaker has made. While the late Archbishop was Chancellor, he whole-heartedly supported the King's designs: this is an important point, which, if necessary, I can sub- 20 stantiate. Now the King intended that Becket, who had proved himself an extremely able administrator—no one denies that—should unite the offices of Chancellor and Archbishop. No one would have grudged him that; no one than he was better qualified to fill at once these two most important posts. Had Becket concurred with the King's wishes, we should have had an 25 almost ideal State: a union of spiritual and temporal administration, under the central government. I knew Becket well, in various official relations; and I may say that I have never known a man so well qualified for the highest

rank of the Civil Service. And what happened? The moment that Becket, at the King's instance, had been made Archbishop, he resigned the office of   30 Chancellor, he became more priestly than the priests, he ostentatiously and offensively adopted an ascetic manner of life, he openly abandoned every policy that he had heretofore supported; he affirmed immediately that there was a higher order than that which our King, and he as the King's servant, had for so many years striven to establish; and that—God knows why—the   35 two orders were incompatible.

3   You will agree with me that such interference by an Archbishop offends the instincts of a people like ours. So far, I know that I have your approval: I read it in your faces. It is only with the measures we have had to adopt, in order to set matters to rights, that you take issue. No one regrets   40 the necessity for violence more than we do. Unhappily, there are times when violence is the only way in which social justice can be secured. At another time, you would condemn an Archbishop by vote of Parliament and execute him formally as a traitor, and no one would have to bear the burden of being called murderer. And at a later time still, even such temperate measures as   45 these would become unnecessary. But, if you have now arrived at a just subordination of the pretensions of the Church to the welfare of the State, remember that it is we who took the first step. We have been instrumental in bringing about the state of affairs that you approve. We have served your interests; we merit your applause; and if there is any guilt whatever in the mat-   50 ter, you must share it with us.

QUESTIONS

READER AND PURPOSE

1. Most arguments, in the modern world at least, tend to be inductive, proceeding from particular to general. This selection, however, is different: the Third Knight argues deductively. Beginning from certain general principles, he infers from them a conclusion which, in his own mind if not in everyone's, justifies the murder of Becket. Of course, he adduces facts here and there to support some of the premises of his logic, but his method is one of deductive rather than of inductive reasoning. Read as part of Eliot's play the Third Knight's defense is less imposing; we are better able to see what is wrong with it. Considered apart from the play, however, does the argument seem to achieve its purpose? Does it convince you that Becket's assassination was necessary and just? Why or why not?

2. In one or two sentences sketch the sort of people at whom the Knight is

aiming his logic, considering such matters as their social position and income, their education, their political and religious beliefs, and their general values.

ORGANIZATION

3. In paragraph 1 the Knight very skillfully does three things: he flatters his audience, sets the tone of his argument, and establishes the lines along which he will proceed. Show where he does each of these. Why is the Knight wise to begin with flattery and to end with setting up his argument, rather than the other way round?

4. Although the bones of its logic are well hidden in the enthymemes * in which it develops, the argument in paragraphs 2 and 3 is essentially a syllogism, or rather linked syllogisms, which the paragraphing is used to separate. Paragraph 2 develops the first, the major premise of which is this: the Church must be subordinated to the State. Does the Knight offer any evidence to justify this principle? What is the minor premise of this syllogism? (Do not waste your time looking for something labeled "minor premise"; the Knight is more subtle, and you will have to read carefully and think.) What conclusion follows from these two premises?

5. Fill in the missing term in this syllogism, which is, in essence, the burden of paragraph 3:

> major premise: *Becket must be removed.*
> minor premise: _____.
> conclusion: *Therefore Becket must be executed.*

6. How is the syllogism of paragraph 3 linked to that of 2?

7. Now outline the logic of the total argument. Eliot does not intend that we accept this as justifying Becket's murder. Is its logic, then, faulty? If not, what is wrong with the argument?

SENTENCES

8. The Third Knight is as able a speaker as he is a logician. Read paragraph 1 aloud. Its sentences are short and straightforward, and therefore easy for listeners to follow. Besides lucidity, such a style has here another value. What does his sentence structure suggest about the kind of man the Knight is—or at least the kind he wishes the audience to think he is?

9. At places in paragraphs 2 and 3 the sentences grow more complicated. (E.g. those in 13-16, 16-18, 29-36.) Yet how are even these kept simple to follow?

10. Read the final three sentences (46-51) out loud. The deliberate repetitions of *we have* bind the passage into unity, but they have another purpose as well. What idea do these repetitions convey?

11. Suppose the final clause were written: "and you must share with us whatever guilt there is in this matter." Why is this less effective?

12. Look up: *clap-trap* (8), *usurper* (12), *seditious* (15), *substantiate* (20), *concur* (25), *ostentatiously* (31), *temperate* (45), *pretension* (47).

13. As logician and as political speaker, the Knight is equally adept. These make, indeed, a peculiar combination for, however well logic may serve the philosopher, it is a weaker instrument for the needs of the politician, who must often persuade audiences immune to logic. This fact, too, the Knight realizes. He seeks to move men by appealing to their self-esteem and to their prejudices as well as to their minds, the so-called *ad populum* fallacy. Thus in paragraph 1 the Knight flatters his audience. What words in paragraph 3 are similarly flattering?

14. In paragraph 2 what words descriptive of Becket are calculated to prejudice an English audience against him? This is an example of *argumentum ad hominem*. Define this phrase.

15. As his syntax suggests, the Knight is trying to play a role designed to catch the audience's sympathy and admiration. His diction reveals the role more clearly. What does *Unhappily* (41) tell us about the kind of man the Knight wishes to seem? And why does he not simply begin in line 1: *I shall first* instead of *I should like first*?

16. Notice that at the very end of his speech the Knight tells his listeners that "if there is any guilt whatever in this matter, you must share it with us." This is known as the *tu quoque* fallacy. What is it, and why is it a fallacy?

17. Although the Third Knight is not above flattery and the other fallacies we have mentioned, he does avoid more obvious excesses. What, for example, might a more impassioned speaker have done with the "chaos" to which the Knight refers in line 16? All in all, do you think the Knight's plea is dishonest? Be prepared to defend your answer.

POINTS TO LEARN

1. Logic may be more effective in persuasion when it is hidden.

2. No logical argument, however subtle, is better than the premises upon which it rests.

3. While flattery, prejudice, and the *argumentum ad hominem* are not proper to logical reasoning, they often accompany it. It is wise, both as a writer and as a reader, to learn to recognize them.

4. The *tu quoque* argument may be a clever diversion, but it is rarely to the point.

SUGGESTIONS FOR WRITING

1. Accused of one of the "crimes" listed below, you must defend your action as logical and just. Use deductive logic to build your defense, but bear in mind the values and prejudices of the particular audience that judges you.

> Refusing to obey a policeman
> Falling asleep during class
> Knocking down a man who insulted you
> Disobeying your parents or school authorities

2. Addressing yourself to the same audience, answer the Third Knight. Keep your argument essentially logical, but do not ignore the values and prejudices of your audience.

IMPROVING YOUR STYLE

In your argument observe these conditions:

1. Keep your sentence style uncomplicated and straightforward. You are writing for people's ears, not their eyes; they cannot read back over your sentences. Therefore your syntax must not become too complex. At the same time remember that you are writing for adults; do not insult them with a "Jane-sees-Jack" primer style.

2. At one place begin three or four sentences with "I" + an appropriate verb and try to establish a bond of value or interest between yourself and your audience.

3. Use specific words or phrases that will subtly please and flatter your listeners, others that will enlist their sympathy by appealing to their beliefs or biases.

Speech in the Legislative Assembly, February 6, 1865

Sir John Alexander Macdonald (1815-91) was Canada's first Prime Minister (1867-73, 1878-91) and the chief architect of the principles of confederation that created the Dominion of Canada in 1867. Macdonald entered provincial politics in 1844, and, in the pre-Confederation period, displayed his remarkable talent for forging political combinations while at the same time demonstrating his grasp of parliamentary and constitutional ideas. These abilities, and his confidence of success, contributed much to the later achievement of Confederation. In the years after 1878 the National Policy of Macdonald's Conservative government was to lead eventually to Canada's economic development and westward expansion—the latter made secure in 1885 with the completion of the transcontinental Canadian Pacific Railway. Westward expansion also contributed, in the same year, to the Northwest Rebellion of the Métis, led by Louis Riel and Gabriel Dumont (see p. 507).

Because of his long tenure as Prime Minister, his political shrewdness, and his leadership in achieving Confederation, Macdonald is widely regarded as the most notable politician in Canada's history. His speech of February 6, 1865, exhibits both his talent and his ideas. It is a skillful piece of argumentation, soundly based on political realities combined with an eloquent presentation of political ideas. Many readers will recognize that in his defense of federalism Macdonald is taking up an issue that is, after more than a century, still one of concern in Canada.

1   The whole scheme of Confederation, as propounded by the Conference, as agreed to and sanctioned by the Canadian Government, and as now presented for the consideration of the people, and the Legislature, bears upon its face the marks of compromise.

From Sir John A. Macdonald's "Speech in the Legislative Assembly, February 6, 1865" in *Parliamentary Debates on the Subject of the Confederation of the British North American Provinces*, 3rd Session, 8th Provincial Parliament of Canada.

2   Of necessity there must have been a great deal of mutual conces- 5
sion. When we think of the representatives of five colonies, all supposed
to have different interests, meeting together, charged with the duty of protecting those interests and of pressing the views of their own localities and
sections, it must be admitted that had we not met in a spirit of conciliation, and with an anxious desire to promote this union; if we had not been 10
impressed with the idea contained in the words of the resolution—"That
the best interests and present and future prosperity of British North America would be promoted by a Federal Union under the Crown of Great Britain,"—all our efforts might have proved to be of no avail. If we had not
felt that, after coming to this conclusion, we were bound to set aside our 15
private opinions on matters of detail, if we had not felt ourselves bound to
look at what was practicable, not obstinately rejecting the opinions of
others nor adhering to our own; if we had not met, I say, in a spirit of
conciliation, and with an anxious, overruling desire to form one people
under one government, we never would have succeeded. With these views, 20
we press the question on this House and the country.
3   I say to this House, if you do not believe that the union of the
colonies is for the advantage of the country, that the joining of these five
peoples into one nation, under one sovereign, is for the benefit of all, then
reject the scheme. Reject it if you do not believe it to be for the 25
present advantage and future prosperity of yourselves and your children.
But if, after a calm and full consideration of this scheme, it is believed, as
a whole, to be for the advantage of this province—if the House and country believe this union to be one which will ensure for us British laws,
British connection, and British freedom—and increase and develop the so- 30
cial, political and material prosperity of the country, then I implore this
House and the country to lay aside all prejudices, and accept the scheme
which we offer. I ask this House to meet the question in the same spirit in
which the delegates met it. I ask each member of this House to lay aside
his own opinions as to particular details, and to accept the scheme as a 35
whole if he think it beneficial as a whole.
4   As I stated in the preliminary discussion, we must consider this
scheme in the light of a treaty. By a happy coincidence of circumstances,
just when an Administration had been formed in Canada for the purpose
of attempting a solution of the difficulties under which we laboured, at the 40
same time the Lower Provinces, actuated by a similar feeling, appointed a
Conference with a view to a union among themselves, without being cognizant of the position the government was taking in Canada. If it had not

been for this fortunate coincidence of events, never, perhaps, for a long series of years would we have been able to bring this scheme to a practical 45 conclusion.

5   But we did succeed. We made the arrangement, agreed upon the scheme, and the deputations from the several governments represented at the Conference went back pledged to lay it before their governments, and to ask the legislatures and people of their respective provinces to assent to 50 it. I trust the scheme will be assented to as a whole. I am sure this House will not seek to alter it in its unimportant details; and, if altered in any important provisions, the result must be that the whole will be set aside, and we must begin *de novo*. If any important changes are made, every one of the colonies will feel itself absolved from the implied obligation to deal 55 with it as a Treaty, each province will feel itself at liberty to amend it *ad libitum* so as to suit its own views and interests; in fact, the whole of our labours will have been for nought, and we will have to renew our negotiations with all the colonies for the purpose of establishing some new scheme.

6   I hope the House will not adopt any such a course as will post- 60 pone, perhaps for ever, or at all events for a long period, all chances of union. All the statesmen and the public men who have written or spoken on the subject admit the advantages of a union, if it were practicable: and now when it is proved to be practicable, if we do not embrace this opportunity the present favorable time will pass away, and we may never have 65 it again. Because, just so surely as this scheme is defeated, will be revived the original proposition for a union of the Maritime Provinces, irrespective of Canada; they will not remain as they are now, powerless, scattered, helpless communities; they will form themselves into a power, which, though not so strong as if united with Canada, will, nevertheless, be a powerful 70 and considerable community, and it will be then too late for us to attempt to strengthen ourselves by this scheme, which, in the words of the resolution, "is for the best interests, and present and future prosperity of British North America."

7   If we are not blind to our present position, we must see the haz- 75 ardous situation in which all the great interests of Canada stand in respect to the United States. I am no alarmist. I do not believe in the prospect of immediate war. I believe that the common sense of the two nations will prevent a war; still we cannot trust to probabilities. The Government and Legislature would be wanting in their duty to the people if they ran any 80 risk. We know that the United States at this moment are engaged in a war of enormous dimensions—that the occasion of a war with Great Britain

has again and again arisen, and may at any time in the future again arise. We cannot foresee what may be the result; we cannot say but that the two nations may drift into a war as other nations have done before. It would 85 then be too late when war had commenced to think of measures for strengthening ourselves, or to begin negotiations for a union with the sister provinces.

8   At this moment, in consequence of the ill-feeling which has arisen between England and the United States—a feeling of which Canada was 90 not the cause—in consequence of the irritation which now exists, owing to the unhappy state of affairs on this continent, the Reciprocity Treaty, it seems probable, is about to be brought to an end—our trade is hampered by the passport system, and at any moment we may be deprived of permission to carry our goods through United States channels—the bonded goods 95 system may be done away with, and the winter trade through the United States put an end to. Our merchants may be obliged to return to the old system of bringing in during the summer months the supplies for the whole year. Ourselves already threatened, our trade interrupted, our intercourse, political and commercial, destroyed, if we do not take warning now when 100 we have the opportunity, and while one avenue is threatened to be closed, open another by taking advantage of the present arrangement and the desire of the Lower Provinces to draw closer the alliance between us, we may suffer commercial and political disadvantages it may take long for us to overcome.   105

9   The Conference having come to the conclusion that a legislative union, pure and simple, was impracticable, our next attempt was to form a government upon federal principles, which would give to the General Government the strength of a legislative and administrative union, while at the same time it preserved that liberty of action for the different sections 110 which is allowed by a Federal Union. And I am strong in the belief—that we have hit upon the happy medium in these resolutions, and that we have formed a scheme of government which unites the advantages of both, giving us the strength of a legislative union and the sectional freedom of a federal union, with protection to local interests.   115

10   In doing so we had the advantage of the experience of the United States. It is the fashion now to enlarge on the defects of the Constitution of the United States, but I am not one of those who look upon it as a failure. (Hear, hear.) I think and believe that it is one of the most skillful works which human intelligence ever created; is one of the most perfect 120 organizations that ever governed a free people. To say that it has some de-

fects is but to say that it is not the work of Omniscience, but of human intellects. We are happily situated in having had the opportunity of watching its operation, seeing its working from its infancy till now. It was in the main formed on the model of the Constitution of Great Britain, adapted to 125 the circumstances of a new country, and was perhaps the only practicable system that could have been adopted under the circumstances existing at the time of its formation. We can now take advantage of the experience of the last seventy-eight years, during which that Constitution has existed, and I am strongly of the belief that we have, in a great measure, avoided 130 in this system which we propose for the adoption of the people of Canada, the defects which time and events have shown to exist in the American Constitution.

11   In the first place, by a resolution which meets with the universal approval of the people of this country, we have provided that for all time 135 to come, so far as we can legislate for the future, we shall have as the head of the executive power, the Sovereign of Great Britain. (Hear, hear.) No one can look into futurity and say what will be the destiny of this country. Changes come over nations and peoples in the course of ages. But, so far as we can legislate, we provide that, for all time to come, the Sovereign of 140 Great Britain shall be the Sovereign of British North America.

12   By adhering to the monarchical principle, we avoid one defect inherent in the Constitution of the United States. By the election of the President by a majority and for a short period, he never is the sovereign and chief of the nation. He is never looked up to by the whole people as 145 the head and front of the nation. He is at best but the successful leader of a party. This defect is all the greater on account of the practice of re-election. During his first term of office, he is employed in taking steps to secure his own re-election, and for his party a continuance of power. We avoid this by adhering to the monarchical principle—the Sovereign whom 150 you respect and love. I believe that it is of the utmost importance to have that principle recognized, so that we shall have a Sovereign who is placed above the region of party—to whom all parties look up—who is not elevated by the action of one party nor depressed by the action of another, who is the common head and sovereign of all. (Hear, hear and cheers.)   155

13   In the Constitution we propose to continue the system of Responsible Government, which has existed in this province since 1841, and which has long obtained in the Mother Country. This is a feature of our Constitution as we have it now, and as we shall have it in the Federation, in which, I think, we avoid one of the great defects in the Constitution of the 160

United States. There the President, during his term of office, is in a great measure a despot, a one-man power, with the command of the naval and military forces—with an immense amount of patronage as head of the Executive, and with the veto power as a branch of the legislature, perfectly uncontrolled by responsible advisers, his cabinet being departmental offi- 165 cers merely, whom he is not obliged by the Constitution to consult with, unless he chooses to do so. With us the Sovereign, or in this country the Representative of the Sovereign, can act only on the advice of his ministers, those ministers being responsible to the people through Parliament.

14   Prior to the formation of the American Union, as we all know, the 170 different states which entered into it were separate colonies. They had no connection with each other further than that of having a common sovereign, just as with us at present. Their constitutions and their laws were different. They might and did legislate against each other, and when they revolted against the Mother Country they acted as separate sovereignties, 175 and carried on the war by a kind of treaty of alliance against the common enemy. Ever since the union was formed the difficulty of what is called "State Rights" has existed, and this had much to do in bringing on the present unhappy war in the United States.

15   They commenced, in fact, at the wrong end. They declared by 180 their Constitution that each state was a sovereignty in itself, and that all the powers incident to a sovereignty belonged to each state, except those powers which, by the Constitution, were conferred upon the General Government and Congress. Here we have adopted a different system. We have strengthened the General Government. We have given the General Legis- 185 lature all the great subjects of legislation. We have conferred on them, not only specifically and in detail, all the powers which are incident to sovereignty, but we have expressly declared that all subjects of general interest not distinctly and exclusively conferred upon the local governments and local legislatures, shall be conferred upon the General Government and 190 Legislature.

16   We have thus avoided that great source of weakness which has been the cause of the disruption of the United States. We have avoided all conflict of jurisdiction and authority, and if this Constitution is carried out, as it will be in full detail in the Imperial Act to be passed if the colo- 195 nies adopt the scheme, we will have in fact, as I said before, all the advantages of a legislative union under one administration, with, at the same time the guarantees for local institutions and for local laws, which are insisted upon by so many in the provinces now, I hope, to be united.

QUESTIONS

1. Sir John A. Macdonald's original audience was composed of his colleagues in the provincial parliament, and his appeal to them was delivered orally. Note that Macdonald makes extensive use of repetition and restatement for the purpose of emphasizing his main points. Can you see any other devices that characterize this extract as an example of oral-persuasion discourse rather than written?

2. Describe the tone * of Macdonald's speech, taking into account his subject, his diction, and his sentence structures.

3. This speech treats subjects and issues of great concern to the British North American provinces in the 1860s. If you are not familiar with these questions learn all that you can about them by visiting your library and reading the relevant section of a good, recently-published, general history of Canada.

4. Compile a list of the main points Macdonald makes in each of his paragraphs, and then consider the order in which these points are presented. Is he arguing inductively (that is, reasoning from particulars to general conclusions)? Is he drawing the same conclusion repeatedly, but using evidence arranged in order of increasing importance to make his conclusion seem—as he proceeds—to be the only correct one?

5. Note that the transitions between most of the paragraphs are fairly simple, involving the repetition of a single word or the use of two words of similar meaning. For example, *compromise* in paragraph 1 leads to *mutual concession* in paragraph 2; *scheme* at the end of paragraph 3 is repeated at the beginning of paragraph 4. Are transitions of this kind as effective in written discourse as they can be in oral persuasion? Is Macdonald's argument weakened by his failure, in some places, to provide any transitions whatever?

6. Macdonald makes several different kinds of appeals to his audience—to their intelligence, to their self-interest, to their higher sense of the national good. Identify the places where these appeals are made. Are they related to Macdonald's ordering of his material? For example, in the first six paragraphs he makes extensive use of the logical pointers * *if* and *then*. Does he continue to do so in the following paragraphs?

7. How much use of specific evidence or detail does Macdonald make? List as many examples as you can.

8. Macdonald's first sentence is periodic * in structure. Does he use this kind of sentence elsewhere?

9. Like most writers and orators of his time, Macdonald frequently uses long, balanced * sentences containing several qualifications * or interrupting * phrases set off by commas or dashes. But these sentences can be structured in different ways to avoid monotony. Analyze closely the structures of sentence one, paragraph 3; sentence two, paragraph 4; sentence eight, paragraph 12. Explain the differences that you find.

10. Can you find in Macdonald's speech any examples of parallel * construction?

11. Macdonald also uses short sentences for emphasis. Make a list of these and describe the kinds of emphasis they achieve and how this emphasis is related to Macdonald's argument.

DICTION

12. Look up: *scheme* (1), *compromise* (4), *conciliation* (9-10), *anxious* (10), *implore* (32), *happy* (39). What meanings and connotations * did these words have in the mid-nineteenth century? Do any of them have different meanings and connotations today? Consult the *Oxford English Dictionary* (OED), which gives examples of how words have shifted their meanings over time.

13. How do the etymologies * of the following words help to explain their meanings? *Concession* (5-6), *cognizant* (43-44), *despot* (163), *patronage* (164), *jurisdiction* (195).

14. What do the Latin phrases *de novo* (55) and *ad libitum* (57-58) mean?

POINTS TO LEARN

1. Repetition and restatement can be effective in emphasizing the main points of an argument, especially in oral persuasion.

2. Persuasive argument can successfully combine appeals to both the intellect and the emotions.

3. Complex sentence structures and formal diction can combine effectively to produce a consistently serious tone when the subject of an argument is of great importance.

SUGGESTIONS FOR WRITING

Professor Morton's essay, "Canadian Nationhood and American World Power" (p. 265) makes a number of points about Canadian political organization similar to those we find in Macdonald's argument. Rewrite Morton's essay, in three paragraphs, trying to copy Macdonald's style, method, and tone.

IMPROVING YOUR STYLE

Include in your essay the following:

1. Two periodic sentences.
2. Two sentences employing parallel constructions.
3. Three sentences in which you use qualifying or interrupting phrases or clauses, set off by commas.
4. Three sentences using logical pointers (*if* this is so, and *if* this is so, . . . *then* the conclusion follows).
5. Three short direct sentences to emphasize main points, or to stress the seriousness of your argument.

Liberalism and Censorship

Ralph Heintzman is a teacher of history and was for several years the editor of the *Journal of Canadian Studies*, a quarterly published at Trent University in Peterborough, Ontario. His editorials, of which the following selection is an example, were consistently thought-provoking and well-argued discussions of a wide range of contemporary political, social, economic, and cultural issues. Heintzman's examination of censorship is a persuasive attempt to deal rationally with a subject usually clouded by emotion and inflated or misleading rhetoric.

1   After a period of more than a decade in which it had seemed to fade from view, the issue of censorship has emerged again in the last year as a matter of public debate in Canada. The reemergence of the issue suggests that certain questions many had thought settled were in fact only temporarily set aside. The assumption of a portion of the community—that 5 the state has no right to restrict public expression—has proven to be less widely accepted than seemed for a time to be the case. The attempted reassertion of the state's right to control certain kinds of public expression— apparently with the support of a wide segment of opinion—has alarmed those who assumed such a right was already extinct, or on the point of be- 10 coming so.

2   The reaction of many within the intellectual and artistic community has been commendably energetic. The Book and Periodical Development Council has formed a special task force on censorship chaired by Timothy Findley. A recent broadcast of *Cross-Country Check-Up* was 15 mobilized against censorship. Among many others, the editor of *Saturday Night* and the book columnist of the *Globe and Mail* have strongly deplored the reassertion of a right to censorship, the latter repeatedly and in sensational terms.

From *Journal of Canadian Studies*, Vol. 13, No. 4. Reprinted by permission.

3   All of these voices are perfectly correct in diagnosing a problem of   20
censorship, but the real problem is a rather different one than most of
them seem to think: it is a failure to think clearly about the issue. The bulk
of recent commentary on censorship in Canada has been a crude mixture
of knee-jerk reactions, unexamined premises, and the wielding of bogeys.
This is as true of those who oppose censorship as of those who favour it,   25
but it is perhaps more surprising and regrettable in the case of the former.
The censorship debate has not been characterized by the careful thought
and distinctions one would hope to find on such a sensitive and divisive
issue, especially from the "intellectuals" whose special care it ought to be
to make just such distinctions.   30

4   The result is a state of high confusion in which a number of separate issues have been mixed together and the real issue has been almost entirely obscured. One is scarcely justified, for example, in mixing up the
right of parents and school boards to decide what the children in their
care shall be required to read with the issue of censorship properly so-called.   35
The exercise of this right does not interfere with what may be published
and sold, or even with what young people may read, but only with what
they may be *required* to read, which is a different matter altogether. Like
all other rights, this one may be exercised with good judgement or bad—
and, more often than not, with the latter—but the existence of the right   40
itself cannot be questioned. Indeed, parents who failed to exercise it would
probably be more open to censure than those who did.

5   Similarly, it is an abuse of common sense to confuse the well-
meaning efforts of a city council to license and supervise—not ban—the
sale of pornographic literature with a limitation, even a potential one, on   45
political expression, as William French has done. The lack of proportion
involved in this kind of judgement goes to the heart of the confusion surrounding the discussion of censorship and the refusal of those engaged in
it to make the necessary distinctions.

6   It is essential to distinguish, for example, between the maintenance   50
of a minimum level of public decorum and the censorship of political debate. Those who refuse to acknowledge this distinction and who argue, as
Robert Fulford has, that any form of censorship leads inevitably to totalitarianism are just as guilty as if they were to attack liberals as communists
or conservatives as fascists: they are indulging in a form of intellectual Mc-   55
Carthyism. It cannot be seriously maintained that insistence on a certain
standard of public decorum is a threat to political life, any more than con-

cern for a decent level of manners is a threat to social life. In fact the reverse is more probable in both cases: a high standard of public manners
may well be the condition for a high standard of political and social life. 60
In any event, the increasing license of our own time does not seem to
have raised the level of political discourse noticeably, to say the least, above
the standard achieved in another age by a Burke, a Marx, or a Mill.

7   One ought also to make a more careful distinction than is usually
the case today between the practice of censorship and the level of artistic 65
expression. It is by no means self-evident, as many today assume without
adequate reflection, that the existence of censorship inevitably entails a loss
of artistic power. As everyone knows, nineteenth-century Russia was subject to a high degree of political censorship (though not nearly as high as
in the Soviet Union today), yet it also witnessed one of the greatest flower- 70
ings of literary creativity in the history of the world, thus perhaps confirm-
ing Northrop Frye's suggestion that literature actually flourishes in difficult
circumstances. The facts are so striking that one is almost tempted to suggest that a measure of censorship might be a reasonable price to pay for a
Pushkin, a Turgenev, or a Chekhov, let alone a Dostoevsky or a Tolstoy! 75
Though utterly facetious, such a thought does underline the fact that those
who oppose any form of censorship cannot do so on the ground that it inevitably means a lowering of artistic standards. Once again the reverse
could be just as easily maintained. In fact, the celebrated critic George
Steiner has done precisely that in his most recent book, *On Difficulty*.   80

8   That certainly does not mean, of course, that the case against censorship is without merit, but it suggests that those who argue it must give
more sustained attention than they have yet done to their premises. All too
often these remain unexplored, while the weight of their argument rests
on a number of bogeys exploited to intimidate and silence their opponents. 85
Since these bogeys will not withstand serious criticism, the opponents of
censorship must strengthen and refine their case. In doing so, they will
have to take a harder look at their own presuppositions.

9   One of the curious things is the inconsistency these presuppositions often involve. In my own experience—and it is worth emphasizing 90
that the views expressed here are those of the editor alone and do not
necessarily reflect those of any other persons or institutions associated with
the *Journal*—virtually all those who oppose censorship on principle are
equally strongly in favour of legislation against hate literature and various
forms of racial abuse. Yet this too is a form of censorship. Thus the opposi- 95

tion is not really to censorship at all but only to certain forms of it. The right of the state to enact controls on public expression is admitted: only the objects of censorship remain in dispute.

10   This concession alters the nature of the debate fundamentally. It is no longer a question of whether censorship should exist—this being now admitted—but of what should be censored, and how. Answers to these questions presuppose answers to others. Most of the recent controversy about censorship in Canada has been about censorship of pornography or of explicitly sexual material. If, as I have suggested, one cannot successfully argue that censorship in any form is necessarily a threat to political life or to artistic integrity, then in order to decide whether the state ought to exercise its right to censorship in relation to these matters one requires a coherent view of the place of sexuality in the human spirit and of the implications of this view for the development or preservation of a civil society.

11   Supplying answers to *these* questions is enormously complicated in our time by the role of liberalism as the prevailing ideology of the intellectually influential. In fact, the intellectual confusion surrounding the issue of censorship—the *real* problem of censorship defined above—is largely the consequence of both the strengths and weaknesses of the liberal mind.

12   As Lionel Trilling remarked in his suggestive review of the Kinsey report, later reprinted in *The Liberal Imagination*, the good side of liberalism in sexual matters is "its impulse toward acceptance and liberation, its broad and generous desire for others that they be not harshly judged." This generous side of liberalism is greatly to be cherished and admired, but when it has been given due credit "as a sign of something good and enlarging," Trilling wrote,

> we cannot help observing that it is often associated with an almost intentional intellectual weakness. It goes with a nearly conscious aversion from making intellectual distinctions, almost as if out of the belief that an intellectual distinction must lead to a social discrimination or exclusion. We might say that those who most explicitly assert and wish to practice the democratic virtues have taken it as their assumption that all social facts—with the exception of exclusion and economic hardship—must be *accepted*, not merely in the scientific sense but also in the social sense, in the sense, that is, that no judgement must be passed on them, that any conclusion drawn from them which perceives values and consequences will turn out to be 'undemocratic.'

13   The prevailing liberal view of sexuality is shaped by the behaviourist assumption that human acts can only be judged—if indeed they can

be judged at all—according to generalizations drawn from the observation ¹³⁵
of what people actually do. The liberal mind shrinks, therefore, from judging sexual behaviour

> except, presumably, in so far as it causes pain to others . . . the pre-
> ponderant weight of its argument is that a fact is a physical fact, to be
> considered only in its physical aspect and apart from any idea or ideal ¹⁴⁰
> that might make it a social fact, as having no ascertainable personal or
> cultural meaning and no possible consequences—as being, indeed, not
> available to social interpretation at all. In short, [liberalism] . . . by
> its primitive conception of the nature of fact quite negates the im-
> portance and even the existence of sexuality as a social fact. ¹⁴⁵

14   Yet it is precisely the meaning of sexuality as a social fact with
which one must grapple before the question of censorship can be satisfactorily resolved. This is a very large matter and no approach to it can be
suggested here, but it is obvious that much will depend on one's notion of
the human mind or spirit. It is not common nowadays to think of the ¹⁵⁰
mind in Platonic terms, that is, as requiring mental "guardians" to keep
in order the potentially unruly energies and forces of which it is in large
part composed. But since this view of mind has been held even longer than
our modern one, perhaps it deserves more attention than it now receives.

15   In this view, the passions are conceived as being a vitally impor- ¹⁵⁵
tant element of mind, perhaps even its centre, but, by their very power,
being also capable of great destruction and therefore in need of careful
direction and control. The individual citizen's control over his own passions
is, in fact, the foundation of social discipline and social order. The sexual
passions in particular have almost always been regarded as forces of tre- ¹⁶⁰
mendous power for good or evil. An intuition of their awesome power explains why so many religions incorporate elements of sexuality into their
own mythology and worship, yet also encircle them with a great variety of
prohibitions and taboos. The purpose and origin of such prohibitions vary
greatly but their fundamental source is the intuition that this power can- ¹⁶⁵
not safely be trifled with, that it should not be taken in hand lightly or
frivolously, but reverently, discreetly. . . . They are warning signs posted
around the passions to caution the unwary: "Handle with care." Chastity,
as Benedict Domdaniel remarks in A *Mixture of Frailties*, is having the
body in the soul's keeping: just that and nothing more. ¹⁷⁰

16   The modern or liberal frame of mind regards the passions in a very
different light. For one thing, it approaches them with far less awe. In its
classical mood, it is more sanguine about the power of naked rationality to

control and direct them for good. In its romantic mood, it is inclined to look on every impulse of the human spirit as potentially creative and there- 175 fore not to be checked or disciplined without loss: the romantic hero is often one who by giving in to his passions and violating the taboos achieves a level of knowledge or experience denied to others. The view that almost every impulse is potentially creative is not wrong, of course. But it over- looks the complementary Platonic or Augustinian insight that there is a 180 hierarchy in the realm of the good and that evil enters the world not through the triumph of bad over good, but through our own preference for a lesser good to the exclusion of a greater. Thus it gravely minimizes the potential for evil implicit in acts or impulses which may be, in their own terms, good. 185

17   For another thing, the liberal mind interprets sexuality in terms of certain analogies drawn from modern technology. The Freudian or twen- tieth-century notion of sexuality was shaped by the analogy of the steam engine. As pressure builds up within the steam boiler or the human psyche, it must be let off in some form if an explosion is to be avoided. Thus the 190 liberal mind concludes that the basic sexual "drives" demand "release" if damage is not to be done to the personality. However, as Tom Wolfe has pointed out, the usefulness of this analogy appears increasingly doubtful. As both electronic technology and neurological research advance, we have learned that the mind is far more comparable to a computer than to a 195 steam engine. If so, the conclusion to be drawn about human behaviour is exactly reversed. Far from providing a healthful "release" each successive act or thought actually "programmes" the mind for continued activity of the same kind, until, if the programming is sufficiently complete, the mind can dwell on little else. Obviously a theory of mind which took this con- 200 temporary analogy seriously would adopt a very different attitude to censor- ship than the prevailing one, especially censorship of material which might become available to children and so "programme" their imaginations.

18   If the assumptions of the liberal mind about human nature and sexuality are shown to be flawed or incomplete, then it may be wise to give 205 correspondingly greater attention to that other tradition of thought which approaches the powers of the spirit with greater awe, which conceives the mind as requiring "guardians" and as having to be kept in order, with no little difficulty. If the need is admitted, then influences which increase the difficulty can be rightfully considered anti-social, since tending to break 210 down that inner self-control on which social order depends. In this view, the process of civilization, the process of establishing an ever-increasing de-

gree of civility in social and political life, depends upon each member of
the community establishing greater dominion over his or her own psyche
and emotions. To the degree that self-control is inhibited by the deliberate 215
arousal of passion or desire, to that degree a civil society becomes a more
distant and elusive goal and society moves closer to a state of barbarism.

19   If so, the recent reassertion of the public's right to establish minimum standards of decorum may not be necessarily unwelcome. Now that
we have enjoyed the fruits of forty years or so of liberalism in sexual mat- 220
ters as in political, there is perhaps room for the reassertion of another
range of values and for a reexamination of the claims of excellence, in human behaviour and social conduct as in other things. The liberal impulse
to tolerance and acceptance is wholly admirable, but it needs to be balanced and complemented by something else. If it leads to a paralysis of the 225
faculty of judgement, it becomes one of those good things by which so
much evil can be done. We need to transcend what Trilling called liberalism's "primitive conception of the nature of fact" and to learn again to
make balanced judgements about the ultimate meaning and consequence of
human behaviour.   230

20   If the apparent public concern with censorship expresses a confused groping toward a revival of critical judgement in sexual and social
matters, then it may deserve more than contempt, however misguided or
badly motivated some of the noisiest advocates of censorship may be. The
role of the intellectual community should not be to thwart or deny the 235
right to censorship—a denial which would not be sincere in any case—but
rather to guide it and help it avoid the crude and harmful purposes to
which it might be put. If certain works, films, or publications do not under-
mine civility as alleged but contribute instead to the process of civilization,
then it should not be beyond the power of the intellectual community to 240
say why. But it will have to do so with greater intellectual and moral rigour
than in the recent past. The public is not as foolish as the cognoscenti
often believe. It may sometimes fall into the error of thinking that a truly
moral work of art cannot contain what it considers to be "immoral" scenes
or characters, but it rarely makes the opposite mistake, to which so many 245
artists and intellectuals are vulnerable, of thinking that art is beyond good
and evil, and should not be judged, in the final analysis, by moral standards
as well as aesthetic ones.

21   The intellectual, artistic, and journalistic communities would perhaps do well to embrace the claims of civility and excellence and to work 250
out their implications for the public depiction of sexuality in more satisfy-

ing terms than they have yet done, rather than fighting the principle of censorship itself. Above all, they should avoid basing opposition to censorship on the defence of civil liberties. For one thing, there is no opposition between them. In fact, the first may be a prerequisite for the second, since 255 it is improbable that civil liberty would long survive in a society threatened by social decadence and disorder. For another thing, there can be little doubt which of the two the public would ultimately choose if forced to do so. That is why the choice should not be forced upon it. To suggest that civil liberties and censorship are not compatible is to call into question, in 260 the long run, not censorship, as many assume, but liberty itself.

QUESTIONS

READER AND PURPOSE

1. Which of the following kinds of people do you think this article is intended for: a) high school student? b) lawyer? c) any professional person? d) university professor? e) minister? f) any university graduate? Prove your point by quoting any three sentences (each from a different paragraph). For example, if your answer is "a," you might refer to the sentence beginning in line 20; if "d," to the sentence beginning in l. 68.

2. Now discuss the validity of both the question above and your answers to it. Consider such matters as context, quoting out of context, and the relationship between context and overall purpose.

3. Summarize briefly (no more than 100 words) the main point Heintzman is persuading his reader to accept.

ORGANIZATION

4. How does the expression *the reaction* (11) serve as transition between paragraphs 1 and 2? In commenting on the effectiveness (or lack of it) of this expression, try substituting three or four of your own transitional words or expressions. Are they as effective? Why or why not?

5. Consider the following transitions: *in this view* (155), *for another thing* (186), *if so* (218). Are these transitions too obvious? Does Heintzman's subject matter require some fairly obvious signposts *?

6. How do you explain that, in spite of the title of this essay, the word *liberalism* occurs for the first time only in paragraph 11? What does this tell you about the probable structure of the essay?

7. Which of the first four paragraphs most clearly states the topic of the

essay? How is paragraph 8 related to any of these four? And to paragraph 11?

8. In order to deal adequately with questions 6 and 7, you will probably have to outline the argument of Heintzman's article. Once you have done this, describe briefly the major steps in the argument, paying particular attention to paragraphs 11, 14, and 19.

9. To what extent do paragraphs 20 and 21 constitute a closing by return *? Which paragraphs (or sentences) are recalled?

10. *In this view* (155) and *in a very different light* (171-172) are the two parts of a contrast. What points is the author contrasting?

SENTENCES

11. In paragraph 1, the first sentence begins with a subordinate clause *, while the next three sentences begin with independent clauses *. In paragraph 2, the pattern is reversed, with only the last sentence beginning with something other than an independent clause (in this case, a prepositional phrase). Compare the sentence structures in paragraphs 5 and 6, and 18 and 19, to see if there is any pattern.

12. To which of the following classes of sentences does each sentence in paragraph 18 belong: antithetical *, balanced *, cumulative *, freight-train *, organizing *, periodic *?

13. Substitute both parentheses and commas for the dashes in paragraph 1, and then explain which is the more effective of the three. Do the same for paragraphs 4 and 5, and then see what conclusions you can come to about the author's use of dashes.

14. In paragraph 11 the author has emphasized two words by italicizing them. Rewrite these sentences, trying to achieve the same emphasis by placing the important words at the beginning or end of each sentence.

15. Outline the parallel * elements of the sentences in paragraph 15.

DICTION

16. Look up: *assumption* (5), *reassertion* (7-8), *commendably* (13), *knee-jerk* (24), *premises* (24), *bogeys* (24), *decorum* (51), *totalitarianism* (53-54), *discourse* (62), *facetious* (76), *intimidate* (85), *presuppositions* (88), *concession* (99), *aversion* (123-124), *behaviourist* (133-134), *negates* (144), *Platonic* (151), *taboos* (164), *sanguine* (173), *hierarchy* (181), *analogy* (188), *psyche* (214), *transcend* (227), *aesthetic* (248), *decadence* (257).

17. Look up *liberalism* (111); then compare the dictionary definition with the explanations of this word given in paragraphs 12, 13, and 16. What conclusions can you draw about the differences between defining a word and explaining it?

18. Consider the expression *not be . . . unwelcome* (219). Is this double

negative effective? Or clumsy? Would rephrasing the sentence as a positive statement be an improvement?

19. Explain the metaphor * *all of these voices* (20). Is the expression *a state of high confusion* (31) also a metaphor? What about *heart of the confusion* (47)?

POINTS TO LEARN

1. In dealing with a complex topic, the writer will assist the reader by using clear, even obvious, transitions and signposts.

2. The steps of a complicated argument need not all be revealed at the beginning but may be clarified gradually throughout most of the essay.

3. A writer may contrast not only successive sentences but successive paragraphs.

SUGGESTIONS FOR WRITING

In a fairly well-developed essay (800-1,000 words), try to persuade your reader of your point of view about a complex topic, such as one of these: the most successful political party on campus; the necessity of proper dress in class; the real inequality of the sexes; the place of religion in the classroom; plagiarism and the demand for high grades; the morality of the single life.

IMPROVING YOUR STYLE

Somewhere in your essay include the following:

1. An explanation—which goes beyond a mere definition—of any key words you use about which there might be either uncertainty or confusion.

2. Two pairs of contrasting paragraphs.

3. At least three balanced and three periodic sentences.

GEORGE F. WILL

Mayhem of the Week

George F. Will is a newspaper columnist. Usually he writes about politics. Occasionally, however, he turns to other aspects of American life, as he does here in an indictment of the violence of football. In football Will is tackling a sacred cow of American culture—not an easy task, metaphorically or actually. As you read his argument, think about the evidence he offers and judge whether or not it supports his case.

1   The desecration of autumn by football has begun. By Christmas, 1.5 million players will have been injured seriously enough to miss practices or games. And coaches and fans will have said, 1.5 million times, that injuries are "part of the game." How big that part is has been demonstrated by Sports Illustrated's John Underwood in a three-part series on football 5 violence.

2   In 1905, President Theodore Roosevelt, who enjoyed war and other forms of the strenuous life, demanded civilizing rules changes for football, which had killed 18 players that year. In 1973, an Indiana high school team suffered four broken backs and four broken legs. Oklahoma 10 State's physician was called onto the field 13 times in one game. The Detroit Lions had 21 knee operations.

3   The NFL argues that only one percent of injuries result from acts against the rules. Underwood responds that, if 99 percent of injuries (like the broken neck that paralyzed Darryl Stingley of the New England Patriots 15 last month) result from play within the rules, the rules should be changed.

4   Helmets have virtually eliminated skull fractures, but blows by helmets cause about 30 percent of the worst injuries—spinal damage, ruptured spleens, bruised kidneys. Underwood believes helmets should be padded, and that rules should prohibit a player from using his helmet to 20 make the first contact in a block or tackle.

© 1978, the Washington Post Company. Reprinted with permission.

5   "Any injuries are the result of playing styles taught by coaches"—
techniques like the "chop block," where a player blocks down onto an
opponent's knees; "spearing," where a player plunges his helmet into an
opponent; and "rake-blocking," where a blocker rakes his facemask into an   25
opponent's chin. Although "clubbing" with forearms has been prohibited
in college football since 1949, Coach Fred Akers of Texas cringes when he
sees rival teams "with their arms taped to the elbows."

6   Ara Parseghian, former Notre Dame coach, favors banning all
below-the-waist blocks away from the line of scrimmage. John Madden,   30
coach of the Oakland Raiders, suggests something like a "grab" rule requiring defenders to use only hands and arms against a quarterback who is
vulnerable because he is in the act of passing. And there almost certainly
should be a rule against hitting backs or receivers (like Stingley) who do not
have the ball and who often are hit when in a vulnerable position and from   35
a blind side. But there are limits to what rules changes—even 30-yard penalties for unnecessary roughness—can do for a game that is fundamentally
unsafe.

7   Football is more than a "contact sport." As a coach has said: Dancing is a contact sport, football is a collision sport. Football is physics: Force   40
equals Mass times Acceleration. It is especially dangerous for youngsters,
whose neck muscles have not developed, but it is always dangerous to all
spines and knees. They are not built for the kinds of collisions inevitable in
football, collisions that are becoming worse as the weight differential between linemen and backs increases.   45

8   Quarterbacks suffer one-seventh of all serious injuries. On the last
weekend of this year's exhibition games, four NFL quarterbacks were injured. Last season, 20 quarterbacks on the 28 NFL teams were incapacitated.
On the first Saturday of last season, half the Big Eight teams lost their first-
string quarterbacks. By midseason, eight Southwest Conference first-string   50
quarterbacks were out, and Texas was using its fourth quarterback. Georgia
lost its fourth and fifth in the final game. Such injuries are not always
unintentional: "Taking out" quarterbacks is a tactic.

9   As Underwood says, the insecurity of coaches, the short careers of
players who are competing for high stakes, and the inherent violence, not   55
to say frenzy, of the game produce a "war ethic." And often there is chemical
warfare as players, and especially defensive linemen, use amphetamines in
order to achieve (in the decorous words of Fran Tarkenton, Minnesota
Vikings quarterback) "a final plateau of endurance and competitive zeal."

10   Most coaches want "gang tackling" in which most tackles are, as   60

Underwood says, "vicious exclamation points." Sportscasters burble praise of those who play with "complete abandon" in an atmosphere of rule-bending.

11   Football involves large squads of players who are increasingly specialized according to an elaborate division of labor ("special teams" and   65 linemen who play only on "third and short yardage"). This is why football is primarily a coaches' game. If the mayhem continues to increase, some coaches may find themselves defendants in lawsuits, and the web of liability may ensnare schools and officials.

12   It is only a matter of time before a national television audience sees   70 a player killed as "part of the game."

QUESTIONS

READER AND PURPOSE

1. What is Will arguing exactly: that football needs to be made safer, or that it should be banned altogether?

2. Is his argument deductive or inductive? If the latter, what sort of evidence does he advance?

3. Will frequently cites the remarks of coaches. Why are their comments particularly effective for his purpose?

4. Do you think that Will is writing primarily for football fans? If not, for what kind of reader? Be able to support your answer by details from the text.

5. Considering Will's purpose, is his title a good one? Is it fair? (Think carefully about what "fair" means in such a case.)

ORGANIZATION

6. This selection was written for newspapers. Compared to more formal essays it uses briefer paragraphs and looser organization. For instance, paragraphs 3, 4, 5, 9, 10, and 11 each consist of only two sentences; the final paragraph of only one. There are no explicit links between paragraphs 2 and 1, 4 and 3, 10 and 9, 11 and 10; and elsewhere the linkage is light. Such features are characteristic of journalistic prose and certainly not to be construed as flaws. What advantages do you find in the shorter paragraphing and looser structure? What disadvantages?

7. Paragraph 1 is the beginning of the article. Is it skillful—identifying the subject, establishing a point of view, attracting the reader's interest?

8. Is the final paragraph a good closing? Would it have been more effective, or less, if it had been joined to paragraph 11 instead of being paragraphed separately? Notice that it repeats a phrase used at the beginning: what phrase?

This technique of repeating at the close of an essay a word, phrase, or image used at the beginning is a way of signaling readers that you are coming to the end. It is called cyclic return.

9. Study the sentences in paragraph 2. By their similar openings the first two statements draw our attention to dates. Why does Will do this—what is he implying? Except for the phrase "In 1973" the final three sentences of this paragraph also open in the same way. What is the advantage of the similarity?

10. Paragraph 3 is a good example of "anticipation and refutation," a device of argument in which you think ahead to the kind of evidence or assertion that may be used against you and counter it in advance. What opposing argument does Will anticipate? How does he neutralize it?

11. What is the topic of the eighth paragraph? How is it supported?

SENTENCES

12. The first sentence of paragraph 2 contains three ideas: President Theodore Roosevelt demanded in 1905 that football be made safer, Roosevelt enjoyed war and the strenuous life, and in 1905 eighteen football players were killed. Which of these is the main clause *? Which two are expressed in subordinate clauses *? Why is the information conveyed by the subordinate constructions important to the writer's point? But if it is important, why doesn't he express it in independent clauses or in separate sentences, perhaps as in the following revision?

> President Theodore Roosevelt enjoyed war and other forms of the strenuous life. In 1905 he demanded civilizing rules changes for football. The game had killed 18 players that year.

13. What does the dash in line 18 signal? Suppose the series in that sentence had read "spinal damage, ruptured spleens, and bruised kidneys," instead of "spinal damage, ruptured spleens, bruised kidneys": would the sense have been subtly altered?

14. Identify the appositive * in the sentence in lines 29-30. Why is the information it conveys necessary? In line 44 there is another appositive: the repetition of "collision." Imagine the sentence without that repetition: would the point be as clear? What purpose does the appositive serve here?

15. In lines 64-66 which word(s) in the main clause does the parenthetical remark expand? Is there any advantage to placing it within parentheses?

DICTION

16. Look up: strenuous (8), virtually (17), vulnerable (33), fundamentally (37), tactic (53), mayhem (67), liability (68).

17. What precisely does each of these phrases mean: blind side (36), weight differential (44), inherent violence (55), war ethic (56)?

18. In paragraph 5 indicate the verbs that convey vigorous action.

19. In line 30 why does the writer use hyphens in *below-the-waist?*

20. Explain why each of these revisions is poorer than Will's diction: *marring* for *desecrating* (1), *late December* for *Christmas* (1), *praise* for *burble praise of* (61), *engulf* for *ensnare* (69).

21. In what sense is the phrase *decorous words* (58) ironic *? What is Will implying?

POINTS TO LEARN

1. Evidence is particularly compelling when it derives from those who sympathize with the other side.

2. Anticipate and neutralize the arguments of your opponents.

3. One way of signaling "the end" is to repeat a phrase or word made prominent in the beginning.

4. Subordinate ideas which are necessary to your main point but are of lesser significance.

5. In describing physical action use strong, vigorous verbs.

SUGGESTIONS FOR WRITING

Compose an essay of about 500 words on one of the topics listed below. Do not merely voice your opinion: give substance to your argument by citing specific evidence. You may use only three or four paragraphs, adequately linked, or you may imitate the short paragraphs and loose structure of Will's piece.

An answer to Will's complaints against football

An argument for (or against) the abolition or tighter control of automobile racing, hunting, ice hockey

An argument that our culture's wide-spread involvement in sports is (or is not) healthy

IMPROVING YOUR STYLE

In your essay include:

1. An eye-catching title.

2. At least one place where you anticipate and refute a possible objection.

3. A brief closing paragraph using a cyclic return.

4. Several appositives.

5. Two or three ironic * words or phrases like Will's *burble the praises of* or *decorous words.*

The Iks

Lewis Thomas is a physician and scientist, president of the Memorial Sloan-Kettering Cancer Center in New York. In addition to scientific research he writes on a variety of subjects—personal, sensitive, meditative essays about the conditions of modern life. "The Iks" appears in a collection of such essays, *The Lives of a Cell* (1974). It is a response to a book by the anthropologist Colin Trumbull, who spent several years living with a primitive African tribe whose society had degenerated into a kind of demented individualism—a war of each against all. While Thomas does not quarrel with Trumbull's assessment of the Iks themselves, he does take issue with the philosophical conclusion the anthropologist draws from his experience with the tribe. As you read, consider the basis of Thomas's disagreement and what alternative meaning he sees in the Iks.

1   The small tribe of Iks, formerly nomadic hunters and gatherers in the mountain valleys of northern Uganda, have become celebrities, literary symbols for the ultimate fate of disheartened, heartless mankind at large. Two disastrously conclusive things happened to them: the government decided to have a national park, so they were compelled by law to give   5 up hunting in the valleys and become farmers on poor hillside soil, and then they were visited for two years by an anthropologist who detested them and wrote a book about them.

2   The message of the book is that the Iks have transformed themselves into an irreversibly disagreeable collection of unattached, brutish   10 creatures, totally selfish and loveless, in response to the dismantling of their traditional culture. Moreover, this is what the rest of us are like in our inner selves, and we will all turn into Iks when the structure of our society comes all unhinged.

"The Iks" from *The Lives of a Cell* by Lewis Thomas. Copyright © 1973 by the Massachusetts Medical Society. Originally appeared in the *New England Journal of Medicine*. Reprinted by permission of Viking Penguin Inc.

3   The argument rests, of course, on certain assumptions about the 15
core of human beings, and is necessarily speculative. You have to agree in
advance that man is fundamentally a bad lot, out for himself alone, dis-
playing such graces as affection and compassion only as learned habits. If
you take this view, the story of the Iks can be used to confirm it. These
people seem to be living together, clustered in small, dense villages, but they 20
are really solitary, unrelated individuals with no evident use for each other.
They talk, but only to make ill-tempered demands and cold refusals. They
share nothing. They never sing. They turn the children out to forage as soon
as they can walk, and desert the elders to starve whenever they can, and the
foraging children snatch food from the mouths of the helpless elders. It 25
is a mean society.

4   They breed without love or even casual regard. They defecate on
each other's doorsteps. They watch their neighbors for signs of misfortune,
and only then do they laugh. In the book they do a lot of laughing, having
so much bad luck. Several times they even laughed at the anthropologist, 30
who found this especially repellent (one senses, between the lines, that the
scholar is not himself the world's luckiest man). Worse, they took him
into the family, snatched his food, defecated on his doorstep, and hooted
dislike at him. They gave him two bad years.

5   It is a depressing book. If, as he suggests, there is only Ikness at the 35
center of each of us, our sole hope for hanging on to the name of humanity
will be in endlessly mending the structure of our society, and it is changing
so quickly and completely that we may never find the threads in time.
Meanwhile, left to ourselves alone, solitary, we will become the same
joyless, zestless, untouching lone animals. 40

6   But this may be too narrow a view. For one thing, the Iks are
extraordinary. They are absolutely astonishing, in fact. The anthropologist
has never seen people like them anywhere, nor have I. You'd think, if they
were simply examples of the common essence of mankind, they'd seem
more recognizable. Instead, they are bizarre, anomalous. I have known my 45
share of peculiar, difficult, nervous, grabby people, but I've never encountered any genuinely, consistently detestable human beings in all my life.
The Iks sound more like abnormalities, maladies.

7   I cannot accept it. I do not believe that the Iks are representative of
isolated, revealed man, unobscured by social habits. I believe their behavior 50
is something extra, something laid on. This unremitting, compulsive re-
pellence is a kind of complicated ritual. They must have learned to act this
way; they copied it, somehow.

8   I have a theory, then. The Iks have gone crazy.

9   The solitary Ik, isolated in the ruins of an exploded culture, has 55
built a new defense for himself. If you live in an unworkable society you
can make up one of your own, and this is what the Iks have done. Each Ik
has become a group, a one-man tribe on its own, a constituency.

10   Now everything falls into place. This is why they do seem, after all,
vaguely familiar to all of us. We've seen them before. This is precisely the 60
way groups of one size or another, ranging from committees to nations,
behave. It is, of course, this aspect of humanity that has lagged behind the
rest of evolution, and this is why the Ik seems so primitive. In his absolute
selfishness, his incapacity to give anything away, no matter what, he is a
successful committee. When he stands at the door of his hut, shouting 65
insults at his neighbors in a loud harangue, he is city addressing another
city.

11   Cities have all the Ik characteristics. They defecate on doorsteps,
in rivers and lakes, their own or anyone else's. They leave rubbish. They
detest all neighboring cities, give nothing away. They even build institutions 70
for deserting elders out of sight.

12   Nations are the most Iklike of all. No wonder the Iks seem familiar.
For total greed, rapacity, heartlessness, and irresponsibility there is nothing
to match a nation. Nations, by law, are solitary, self-centered, withdrawn
into themselves. There is no such thing as affection between nations, and 75
certainly no nation ever loved another. They bawl insults from their doorsteps, defecate into whole oceans, snatch all the food, survive by detestation,
take joy in the bad luck of others, celebrate the death of others, live for the
death of others.

13   That's it, and I shall stop worrying about the book. It does not 80
signify that man is a sparse, inhuman thing at his center. He's all right. It
only says what we've always known and never had enough time to worry
about, that we haven't yet learned how to stay human when assembled in
masses. The Ik, in his despair, is acting out this failure, and perhaps we
should pay closer attention. Nations have themselves become too frighten- 85
ing to think about, but we might learn some things by watching these
people.

QUESTIONS

READER AND PURPOSE

1. How does Thomas's conclusion about the Iks differ from Trumbull's?

2. What sort of evidence does he call upon: statistics, examples, his own beliefs, common knowledge?

3. Would you describe his tone * as formal and "lecturish," or as relaxed and conversational? Is his point of view * personal or impersonal? Which word (or words) best describes his attitude toward his subject—angry, amused, bitter, calm, contemptuous, pessimistic, optimistic?

4. Does Thomas suppose that his readers are familiar with Trumbull's book? What does he assume they know?

ORGANIZATION

5. This essay has two major sections. Which sentence swings us from the first to the second? What does Thomas do in part 1? In 2? Can you discern subdivisions within each of these parts?

6. How does the brief eighth paragraph function in the organization of the essay?

7. What words provide the linkage between paragraphs 2 and 1? Between 6 and 5? 11 and 10?

8. Study paragraphs 9-13 and show that there is a change of topic to justify each new paragraph.

9. What is the topic of paragraph 11? How is it supported?

10. Analyze the internal linkage of paragraph 3, explaining how each sentence is tied to what precedes it, whether by the repetition of key terms, by sentence pattern, or by connective words.

11. In line 32 how does *worse* help to link the last sentence of the paragraph to the one before it?

SENTENCES

12. Thomas is very readable, in part because he varies sentence length and structure. Study paragraph 4 in this regard and be able to discuss how it avoids the monotony of this revision:

> They breed without love or even casual regard. They defecate on each other's doorsteps. They watch their neighbors for signs of misfortune. Only then do they laugh. In the book they do a lot of laughing. They have had so much bad luck. Several times they even laughed at the anthropologist. He found this especially repellent. (One senses, between the lines, that the scholar himself is not the world's luckiest

man.) Worse, they took him into the family. They snatched his food. They defecated on his doorstep. They hooted dislike at him. They gave him a bad two years.

13. This essay contains a number of short sentences. Do they serve purposes other than variety?

14. Identify the appositives * in the sentences in lines 1-4 and 57-58. The parallelism * in the sentence in lines 76-79.

15. What does the colon signal in line 4?

DICTION

16. Look up: *dismantling* (11), *unhinged* (14), *assumptions* (15), *graces* (18), *forage* (23), *repellent* (31), *zestless* (40), *bizarre* (45), *compulsive* (51), *constituency* (58), *harangue* (66), *rapacity* (73), *detestation* (77), *sparse* (81).

17. What is meant by each of the following phrases: *nomadic hunters and gatherers* (1), *ultimate fate* (3), *brutish courage* (10), *traditional culture* (12), *an exploded culture* (55)?

18. How do the etymologies * of these words help to clarify their use: *anthropologist* (7), *speculative* (16), *compassion* (18), *scholar* (32), *essence* (44), *anomalous* (45), *maladies* (48), *primitive* (63).

19. Thomas frequently employs *you* (line 16, for example) in the generic sense of "anyone," "people in general," rather than in the specific sense of the individual(s) he is addressing. Does this usage make his tone more formal, or less? Some teachers object to the generic *you* (it does get out of hand easily). Do you think the objection is sound? What alternatives to the generic *you* can you think of? What rule might writers follow with regard to this use of the pronoun?

20. In the sentence in lines 35-38 what later word picks up the image suggested by *mending*? Would *fabric* be a better choice than *structure* in line 37?

21. Explain the relationship in thought signaled by these connectives *: *moreover* (12), *of course* (15), *instead* (45), *then* (54).

22. The parenthetical remark in lines 31-32 is an example of the figure of speech called "litotes." Look up this term.

POINTS TO LEARN

1. Personal beliefs and opinions are a legitimate kind of evidence, provided they are not outrageous and not disguised as something else.

2. The major sections of an essay should be clearly indicated, and transitions provided between them.

3. Varying sentence length and structure while retaining some similarity helps make prose readable.

4. Short sentences make good topic statements.

5. The generic *you* ought to be employed sparingly and only with an informal tone.

SUGGESTIONS FOR WRITING

In 500-600 words (4-5 paragraphs) compose an argument on one of the topics below. Support your contention by examples and by your own beliefs and opinions. Write from a personal point of view and try for a relaxed, conversational tone.

> Young people today are (are not) less aggressive and more tolerant than were previous generations.

> Human beings really are "Iks"; their "Ikness" simply does not show itself when things are going well.

IMPROVING YOUR STYLE

1. Begin at least two paragraphs of your essay with short simple sentences of no more than eight words.

2. In one paragraph unify a series of three or four sentences by keeping them all short and simple and beginning them with the same word.

3. Use *moreover, of course,* and *then* once each to introduce sentences.

4. Try an example of litotes.

The Implications of a Free Society

Lester Bowles Pearson (1897-1972) was, successively, a teacher of history at the University of Toronto, a brilliant civil servant in Canada's Department of External Affairs (twice President of the United Nations Assembly, he received the Nobel Prize for Peace because of his role in bringing about a resolution of the Suez crisis in 1956), and Liberal Prime Minister of Canada (1963-68). In the following selection, which offers a summary of Pearson's political philosophy, he uses description and metaphor to persuade his audience of the importance for Canada of the values of tolerance and cooperation.

1   The essential lubricant for a free society is tolerance. This, however, does not necessarily apply to *all* societies. There are obvious examples of states which are held together without the least regard for tolerance. It does apply, however, to all states where there is government by consent. Canada, where various groups live and work together within the boundaries 5 of a national state, is a good example of this principle in operation. This country exists on the assumption that, as far as is humanly possible, the interests of no group—racial, geographic, economic, religious, or political— will prevail at the expense of any other group. We have committed ourselves to the principle that by compromise and adjustment we can work 10 out some sort of balance of interests which will make it possible for the members of all groups to live side by side without any one of them arbitrarily imposing its will on any other. It is my belief that this is the only basis upon which Canada can possibly exist as a nation, and that any attempt to govern the country on any other basis would destroy it. In these 15 circumstances, the basic quality of tolerance in our national character is of the first importance.

2   Of almost equal importance for our national welfare, and indeed

From *Words and Occasions* by Lester Pearson. Copyright © University of Toronto Press 1970. Reprinted by permission.

246

arising out of the practice of tolerance, is the avoidance of extreme policies. This is often called walking in the middle of the road. This of course is 20 not so easy as people usually think. It imposes both self-restraint and discipline, even when we assume that the traffic is all going in the one direction. Anyone who chooses to travel in the middle of the road must not deny the use of either side of it to persons who prefer to walk there. He condemns himself, therefore, to accept during the journey the constant 25 jostling of companions on either side. This middle ground is, I think, becoming more and more difficult to maintain, and the temptation to abandon it is constantly increasing, especially in the face of the road blocks thrown up by unfriendly fellow travellers. I do not wish here to criticize those who choose other ground upon which to walk, or to question the 30 basis of their choice. I wish only to make a strong plea for the preservation of this middle position in our national life. Paradoxically, it is only in this way that the existence of many of those on each side can also be preserved. If the middle group is eliminated, less tolerant elements fall under the irresistible temptation to try to capture the whole roadway. When the middle 35 of the road is no longer occupied firmly by stable and progressive groups in the community, it is turned into a parade ground for those extremist forces who would substitute goose-stepping for walking. All others are driven to hide, disconsolate and powerless, in the hedges, ditches, and culverts.

3   How can the meaning of the middle way in our free society be de- 40 scribed in a few words? What principle does it stand for? Where does it lead in practice? Is it merely the political line of least resistance along which drift those without the courage of their convictions, or simply without convictions? It is, or should be, far more than that. The central quality of this approach is the stress which it always lays on human values, the 45 integrity and worth of the individual in society. It stands for the emancipation of the mind as well as for personal freedom and well-being. It is irrevocably opposed to the shackling limitations of rigid political dogma, to political oppression of, and to economic exploitation by, any part of the community. It detests the abuse of power either by the state or by private 50 individuals and groups. It respects first of all a person for what he is, not who he is. It stands for his right to manage his own affairs, when they *are* his own; to hold his own convictions and speak his own mind. It aims at equality of opportunity. It maintains that effort and reward should not be separated and it values highly initiative and originality. It does not believe 55 in lopping off the tallest ears of corn in the interests of comfortable conformity.

4   The middle way presents no panacea for the easy attainment of general welfare, but it accepts the responsibility of government to assist in protecting and raising the living standards of all, and, if necessary, to take 60 bold and well-planned action to help maintain economic activity for that purpose.

5   The middle way, unlike extremism in political doctrine, has positive faith in the good will and common sense of most people in most circumstances. It relies on their intelligence, their will to co-operate, and their 65 sense of justice. From its practitioners, it requires determination and patience, tolerance and restraint, the discipline of the mind rather than the jackboot, and the underlying belief that human problems, vast and complicated though they may be, are capable of solution.

QUESTIONS

READER AND PURPOSE

1. Because Mr. Pearson (later Prime Minister of Canada, 1963-1968) was, at the time of this speech, one of the more honored statesmen in the Western world, his views were likely to be accorded close attention. To whom do you think his remarks were addressed?
2. Is Pearson trying to persuade us that the issue he is treating is a contentious one? That is, are the points he is making likely to be the subject of discussion, or of argument?
3. To what extent is this as much a descriptive essay as a persuasive one?

ORGANIZATION

4. Pearson begins with a sweeping statement to which he immediately adds a qualification *. Then, in the third sentence, he makes another generalization. Do the beginnings of paragraphs 2 and 3 have this same sort of structure? If not, how do they begin?
5. In paragraph 1 Pearson describes tolerance as both a *principle* (10) and *a basic quality* (16). Is there a contradiction here? What is his justification? Does he make any further use of this distinction?
6. What two transitional expressions does Pearson use at the beginning of paragraph 2? Why does he use two, instead of the more common one?
7. In paragraph 2 Pearson introduces the metaphor * *walking in the middle of the road* (20). Describe how this metaphor affects the construction of the rest of the paragraph.
8. Pearson continues to refer to *the middle way* in paragraphs 3, 4, and 5. Is

he still using a metaphor? Or has this metaphor become an abstraction *? Or is it both?

9. Is there a transition between paragraphs 2 and 3? If so, describe how it functions. If not, show how Pearson was justified in omitting it.

10. How is paragraph 4 a logical conclusion to paragraph 3? Should it not, rather, be a part of 3?

11. What is the principal device Pearson uses to maintain the flow * of paragraph 3?

12. What does the phrase *in these circumstances* (15-16) refer to? Why does it occur in the last sentence of the paragraph?

13. What is the function of the four questions which begin paragraph 3? Are they rhetorical questions *?

SENTENCES

14. Pearson's essay contains a number of balanced sentences * (such as the one beginning in l. 13) and antitheses * (such as lines 51-52). Are there any other examples? Justify your choices.

15. Is the sentence beginning in l. oo a tricolon *? Why is there no comma after *integrity* (46)?

16. Which sentence of paragraph 1 comes closest to being a definition, or explanation, of tolerance?

17. What is the function of the phrase *the meaning of the middle way* (40)?

18. In the first sentence of paragraph 5 we can see interrupted movement *, parallelism *, and balanced construction *. Point out the example of each, and then analyze the other sentences in this paragraph in the same manner.

DICTION

19. Look up: *consent* (4), *assumption* (7), *prevail* (9), *compromise* (10), *arbitrarily* (12-13), *assume* (22), *paradoxically* (32), *goose-stepping* (38), *disconsolate* (39), *emancipation* (46-47), *irrevocably* (47-48), *conformity* (56-57), *panacea* (58), *extremism* (63), *jackboot* (68).

20. Explain the metaphor in the first sentence.

21. In the sentence beginning in l. 35, we have an example of what can be called a metaphor within a metaphor. Explain.

22. Why does Pearson write *values highly* (55) instead of *highly values?* Would there be any difference in emphasis between these two expressions?

23. Pearson uses expressions which either are, or are close to being, clichés (outworn or over-used figures of speech—such tired expressions as "white as snow," "strong as a bull," "as quick as a cat," "as pretty as a picture"), such as *shackling limitations* (48) and *the jackboot* (68). Can you find any others? What does the use of such expressions reveal about an author? Does Mac-

donald (p. 216) also use clichés in his political speech on the question of Canadian unity?

POINTS TO LEARN
1. A persuasive essay can include much that is descriptive.
2. A controlling metaphor is a very useful device for unifying a paragraph.
3. A paragraph may be effectively introduced by a series of questions that are answered in the main part of the paragraph.

SUGGESTIONS FOR WRITING
1. In a paragraph of about 100 words write a précis of Pearson's argument.
2. Write an essay of 600 to 800 words in which you argue that Pearson's *middle way* is the way of the compromiser, of the political and social coward.

IMPROVING YOUR STYLE
In your essay include:

1. One paragraph based on a controlling metaphor.
2. Two balanced sentences.
3. Two sentences using parallelism.
4. A closing sentence like Pearson's, in which you try to create a rhythm based on the balancing of pairs.

Paradoxes and Dilemmas: The Woman as Writer

Margaret Atwood's international reputation is based on more than twenty books—poetry, novels, and literary criticism. Born in 1939, she studied at the University of Toronto, Radcliffe, and Harvard, and has taught at several Canadian universities. Among her better-known works are *The Circle Game* (1966), for which she won the Governor General's Award for poetry; *The Journals of Susanna Moodie* (1970), *Power Politics* (1973), and *Two-Headed Poems* (1970); novels such as *Surfacing* (1972), *Life Before Man* (1979), and *Bodily Harm* (1981); and *Survival: A Thematic Guide to Canadian Literature* (1972), a controversial work of literary criticism. She has also edited *The New Oxford Book of Canadian Verse in English* (1982) and co-edited with Robert Weaver *The Oxford Book of Canadian Short Stories in English* (1986). The essay here perceptively summarizes the difficulties of being a woman writer while at the same time it employs a variety of persuasive techniques.

"I knew . . . what a writer can be at his best . . . an interpreter, a revealer of secrets. . . ."

1   I approach this article with a good deal of reluctance. Since promising to do it, in fact, I've been procrastinating to such an extent that my own aversion is probably the first subject I should attempt to deal with. Some of my reservations have to do with the questionable value of writers, male or female, becoming directly involved in political movements 5 of any sort: their involvement may be good for the movement, but it has yet to be demonstrated that it's good for the writer. The rest concern my sense of the enormous complexity not only of the relationships between Man and Woman, but also of those between such other abstract intangibles as Art and Life, Form and Content, Writer and Critic, and so forth. 10

Reprinted from "Paradoxes and Dilemmas: The Woman as Writer" by Margaret Atwood, in *Women in the Canadian Mosaic*, ed. Gwen Matheson, by permission of PMA Books.

251

2   Judging from conversations I've had with many other women poets
and novelists in this country, my qualms are not unique. I can think of
only one fiction or poetry writer I know who has formal connection with
any of the diverse organizations usually lumped together under the titles
of women's liberation or the women's movement. There are even several 15
who have gone out of their way to disavow even fellow-feeling. But the
usual attitude is one of grudging admiration, tempered with envy: the
younger generation, they feel, has it a hell of a lot better than they did.
Most writers old enough to have a career of any length behind them grew
up when it was still assumed that a woman's place was in the home and 20
nowhere else, and that anyone who took time off for an individual selfish
activity like writing was either neurotic or wicked or both, derelict in her
duties to some man, child or aged relative. I've heard stories of writers so
consumed by guilt over what they had been taught to feel was their ab-
normality that they did their writing at night, secretly, so no one would 25
accuse them of failing as housewives, as "women". These writers accomplished what they did by themselves, often at great personal expense. In
order to write at all, they had to defy other women's as well as men's ideas
of what was proper, and it's not finally all that comforting to have a phalanx of women—some younger and relatively unscathed, others from their 30
own generation, the bunch that was collecting china, changing diapers and
sneering at any female with intellectual pretensions twenty or even ten
years ago—come breezing up now to tell them they were right all along. It's
like being judged innocent after you've been hanged: the satisfaction, if
any, is grim. There's a great temptation to say to feminists, "Where were 35
you when I really needed you?" or "It's too late for me now." And you can
see, too, that it would be fairly galling for these writers, if they have any
respect for historical accuracy, which most do, to be hailed as products,
spokeswomen, or advocates of the women's movement. When they were
undergoing their often drastic formative years there *was* no women's move- 40
ment. No matter that a lot of what they say can be taken by the theorists
of the movement as supporting evidence, useful analysis, and so forth.
Their own inspiration was not theoretical; it came from wherever all writing comes from. Call it experience and imagination. These writers, if they
are honest, don't want to be wrongly identified as the children of a move- 45
ment that did not give birth to them. Being adopted is not the same as
being born.

QUESTIONS

1. How is the title of this essay effective? In order to answer this question you should consider a further one: what sorts of problems does the title warn us we are going to be dealing with?

2. The first paragraph is not only the introduction but is, as well, an *apologia*: that is, a justification, or defense, of the points the writer is about to make and of her attitude towards her subject. Why does Atwood feel that an *apologia* is necessary?

3. How does the epigraph serve to reveal the author's purpose?

4. What is the author's attitude towards the reader: sarcastic? condescending? confidential? sympathetic? antagonistic? friendly? Choose the two words you think best describe her attitude, and be prepared to defend them.

5. Consider Atwood's tone * as the result of her attitude towards both her subject and her reader.

6. Summarize, in one or two sentences, what Atwood is trying to persuade the reader to think.

7. In what sense could one say that Atwood's introduction is "disarming"? Consider, for example, the connotations of such words as *reluctance* (1), *promising* (2), *procrastinating* (2), *reservations* (4). Do such words, placed at the beginning, tend to make the reader sympathize with the writer? Feel indifferent? Antagonistic?

8. Do you find the first paragraph effective as the introduction to this persuasive essay? Why or why not?

9. Since the second paragraph is quite long, you might think that the argument would be clearer if there were another paragraph. Where might such a division occur: l. 26? l. 36? l. 39? none of these?

10. In view of your answer to the previous question, do you conclude that Atwood's paragraph is tightly organized, with sentences following logically from each other? Or is it loosely organized—that is, could some points be interchanged without seriously affecting the argument?

11. How is the last sentence an effective conclusion? Is it a closing by return *?

12. Since the selection in this book is only part of Atwood's essay, the last sentence should prepare for the first sentence of the next paragraph (which is not included here). What point might that next sentence logically introduce?

13. What does *the rest* (7) refer to? Would the sentence (and the unity of the

paragraph) be improved by replacing *the rest* with the expression to which it refers?

14. Is the first sentence an organizing sentence *? Why, or why not?

15. Why is the modifying phrase *in fact* (2) placed where it is? To answer this question, try placing this phrase in different positions in the sentence, such as at the beginning or the end. Do these different positions affect the meaning of the sentence? Its emphasis? Its rhythm?

16. The sentence beginning in line 23 includes "so no one would accuse them"; would it be preferable to change this to "so that no one would accuse them"? Should "that" be excluded from the previous line?

17. Is the expression "women's as well as men's ideas" rather clumsy? Try to improve on this sentence by rewriting it in two or three ways.

DICTION

18. Look up: *paradoxes* (title), *dilemmas* (title), *procrastinating* (2), *aversion* (3), *intangibles* (9-10), *qualms* (12), *disavow* (16), *neurotic* (22), *derelict* (22), *phalanx* (29-30), *galling* (37), *advocates* (39).

19. Atwood uses expressions such as *lumped together* (14), *a hell of a lot* (18), *the bunch* (31), and *come breezing up* (33). How do such expressions affect the tone of the essay?

20. The writer also frequently uses contractions—*I've, it's, there's, don't*. How (if at all) do such contractions affect the tone?

21. Cross out the contractions in this essay and pencil in the full constructions (for example, *do not* instead of *don't*). Then reread the essay. Replacing the contractions results in what gain? Or loss?

22. Why has the author capitalized a number of words at the end of paragraph 1? What difference would there be had these words not been capitalized?

POINTS TO LEARN

1. An introductory paragraph can also serve as a justification, or defense, of one's ideas.

2. The disarming introduction is one strategy * that can be effectively used in a persuasive essay.

3. Unusual diction can help a writer establish the tone of an essay.

SUGGESTIONS FOR WRITING

Compose a two- or three-paragraph essay in which you attempt to persuade your reader of the difficulties you face concerning a specific dilemma: you drink but you also drive; you believe strongly in giving a good example to children but you swear often; you are a religious person but you also plagiarize; you believe in the extreme importance of charity towards one's fellow man but you are very selfish.

IMPROVING YOUR STYLE

In your essay include:
1. A disarming introduction that is also an *apologia*.
2. A number of slang expressions and contractions.
3. A title that briefly points to the nature of the dilemma.

ANNE ROIPHE

Confessions of a Female Chauvinist Sow

Anne Roiphe is an author and journalist whose works include *Digging Out* (1967), *Up the Sandbox* (1970), and *Long Division* (1972). In the following essay she works against the grain of feminism. Her argument, however, is not a defense of the traditional view of women. Consider as you read, exactly what Roiphe is arguing and what kind of evidence she calls upon.

1   I once married a man I thought was totally unlike my father and I imagined a whole new world of freedom emerging. Five years later it was clear even to me—floating face down in a wash of despair—that I had simply chosen a replica of my handsome daddy-true. The updated version spoke English like an angel but—good God!—underneath he was my father 5 exactly: wonderful, but not the right man for me.

2   Most people I know have at one time or another been fouled up by their childhood experiences. Patterns tend to sink into the unconscious only to reappear, disguised, unseen, like marionette strings, pulling us this way or that. Whatever ails people—keeps them up at night, tossing 10 and turning—also ails movements no matter how historically huge or politically important. The women's movement cannot remake consciousness, or reshape the future, without acknowledging and shedding all the unnecessary and ugly baggage of the past. It's easy enough now to see where men have kept us out of clubs, baseball games, graduate schools; it's easy enough 15 to recognize the hidden directions that limit Sis to cake-baking and Junior to bridge-building; it's now possible for even Miss America herself to identify what *they* have done to us, and, of course, *they* have and *they* did and *they* are. . . . But along the way we also developed our own hidden prejudices, class assumptions and an anti-male humor and collection of expecta- 20 tions that gave us, like all oppressed groups, a secret sense of superiority

Confessions of a Female Chauvanist Sow by Anne Roiphe from: *New York Magazine.* Copyright ©, 1972 by Anne Roiphe. Reprinted by permission of Brandt & Brandt Literary Agents, Inc.

(co-existing with a poor self-image—it's not news that people can believe two contradictory things at once).

3   Listen to any group that suffers materially and socially. They have a lexicon with which they tease the enemy: ofay, goy, honky, gringo. "Poor 25 pale devils," said Malcolm X loud enough for us to hear, although blacks had joked about that to each other for years. Behind some of the women's liberation thinking lurk the rumors, the prejudices, the defense systems of generations of oppressed women whispering in the kitchen together, presenting one face to their menfolk and another to their card clubs, their 30 mothers and sisters. All this is natural enough but potentially dangerous in a revolutionary situation in which you hope to create a future that does not mirror the past. The hidden anti-male feelings, a result of the old system, will foul us up if they are allowed to persist.

4   During my teen years I never left the house on my Saturday night 35 dates without my mother slipping me a few extra dollars—mad money, it was called. I'll explain what it was for the benefit of the new generation in which people just sleep with each other: the fellow was supposed to bring me home, lead me safely through the asphalt jungle, protect me from slithering snakes, rapists and the like. But my mother and I knew young 40 men were apt to drink too much, to slosh down so many rye-and-gingers that some hero might well lead me in front of an oncoming bus, smash his daddy's car into Tiffany's window or, less gallantly, throw up on my new dress. Mad money was for getting home on your own, no matter what form of insanity your date happened to evidence. Mad money was also a 45 wallflower's rope ladder; if the guy you came with suddenly fancied someone else, well, you didn't have to stay there and suffer, you could go home. Boys were fickle and likely to be unkind; my mother and I knew that, as surely as we knew they tried to make you do things in the dark they wouldn't respect you for afterwards, and in fact would spread the word and 50 spoil your rep. Boys liked to be flattered; if you made them feel important they would eat out of your hand. So talk to them about their interests, don't alarm them with displays of intelligence—we all knew that, we groups of girls talking into the wee hours of the night in a kind of easy companionship we thought impossible with boys. Boys were prone to have a good 55 time, get you pregnant, and then pretend they didn't know your name when you came knocking on their door for finances or comfort. In short, we believed boys were less moral than we were. They appeared to be hypocritical, self-seeking, exploitative, untrustworthy and very likely to be show-

ing off their precious masculinity. I never had a girl friend I thought would   60
be unkind or embarrass me in public. I never expected a girl to lie to me
about her marks or sports skill or how good she was in bed. Altogether—
without anyone's directly coming out and saying so—I gathered that men
were sexy, powerful, very interesting, but not very nice, not very moral, humane and tender, like us. Girls played fairly while men, unfortunately, re-   65
served their honor for the battlefield.

5   Why are there laws insisting on alimony and child support? Well,
everyone knows that men don't have an instinct to protect their young and,
given half a chance, with the moon in the right phase, they will run off and
disappear. Everyone assumes a mother will not let her child starve, yet it   70
is necessary to legislate that a father must not do so. We are taught to accept the idea that men are less than decent; their charms may be manifold
but their characters are riddled with faults. To this day I never blink if I
hear that a man has gone to find his fortune in South America, having left
his pregnant wife, his blind mother and taken the family car. I still gasp   75
in horror when I hear of a woman leaving her asthmatic infant for a rock
group in Taos because I can't seem to avoid the assumption that men are
naturally heels and women the ordained carriers of what little is moral in
our dubious civilization.

6   My mother never gave me mad money thinking I would ditch a   80
fellow for some other guy or that I would pass out drunk on the floor. She
knew I would be considerate of my companion because, after all, I was
more mature than the boys that gathered about. Why was I more mature?
Women just are people-oriented; they learn to be empathetic at an early
age. Most English students (students interested in humanity, not artifacts)   85
are women. Men and boys—so the myth goes—conceal their feelings and
lose interest in anybody else's. Everyone knows that even little boys can
tell the difference between one kind of a car and another—proof that their
souls are mechanical, their attention directed to the nonhuman.

7   I remember shivering in the cold vestibule of a famous men's ath-   90
letic club. Women and girls are not permitted inside the club's door. What
are they doing in there, I asked? They're naked, said my mother, they're
sweating, jumping up and down a lot, telling each other dirty jokes and
bragging about their stock market exploits. Why can't we go in? I asked.
Well, my mother told me, they're afraid we'd laugh at them.   95

8   The prejudices of childhood are hard to outgrow. I confess that
every time my business takes me past that club, I shudder. Images of large

bellies resting on massage tables and flaccid penises rising and falling with the Dow Jones average flash through my head. There it is, chauvinism waving its cancerous tentacles from the depths of my psyche.   100

9   Minorities automatically feel superior to the oppressor because, after all, they are not hurting anybody. In fact, they feel they are morally better. The old canard that women need love, men need sex—believed too long by both sexes—attributes moral and spiritual superiority to women and makes of men beasts whose urges send them prowling into the night.   105 This false division of good and bad, placing deforming pressures on everyone, doesn't have to contaminate the future. We know that the assumptions we make about each other become a part of the cultural air we breathe and, in fact, become social truths. Women who want equality must be prepared to give it and to believe in it, and in order to do that it is not   110 enough to state that you are as good as any man, but also it must be stated that he is as good as you and both will be humans together. If we want men to share in the care of the family in a new way, we must assume them as capable of consistent loving tenderness as we.

10   I rummage about and find in my thinking all kinds of anti-male   115 prejudices. Some are just jokes and others I will have a hard time abandoning. First, I share an emotional conviction with many sisters that women given power would not create wars. Intellectually I know that's ridiculous; great queens have waged war before; the likes of Lurleen Wallace, Pat Nixon and Mrs. General Lavelle can be depended upon in the   120 future to guiltlessly condemn to death other people's children in the name of some ideal of their own. Little girls, of course, don't take toy guns out of their hip pockets and say "Pow, pow" to all their neighbors and friends like the average well-adjusted little boy. However, if we gave little girls the six-shooters, we would soon have double the pretend body count.   125

11   Aggression is not, as I secretly think, a male-sex-linked characteristic: brutality is masculine only by virtue of opportunity. True, there are 1,000 Jack the Rippers for every Lizzie Borden, but that surely is the result of social forms. Women as a group are indeed more masochistic than men. The practical result of this division is that women seem nicer and kinder,   130 but when the world changes, women will have a fuller opportunity to be just as rotten as men and there will be fewer claims of female moral superiority.

12   Now that I am entering early middle age, I hear many women complaining of husbands and ex-husbands who are attracted to younger fe-   135

males. This strikes the older woman as unfair, of course. But I remember a time when I thought all boys around my age and grade were creeps and bores. I wanted to go out with an older man: a senior or, miraculously, a college man. I had a certain contempt for my coevals, not realizing that the freshman in college I thought so desirable, was some older girl's creep. Some women never lose that contempt for men of their own age. That isn't fair either and may be one reason why some sensible men of middle years find solace in young women.

13   I remember coming home from school one day to find my mother's card game dissolved in hysterical laughter. The cards were floating in black rivers of running mascara. What was so funny? A woman named Helen was lying on a couch pretending to be her husband with a cold. She was issuing demands for orange juice, aspirin, suggesting a call to a specialist, complaining of neglect, of fate's cruel finger, of heat, of cold, of sharp pains on the bridge of the nose that might indicate brain involvement. What was so funny? The ladies explained to me that all men behave just like that with colds, they are reduced to temper tantrums by simple nasal congestion, men cannot stand any little physical discomfort—on and on the laughter went.

14   The point of this vignette is the nature of the laughter—us laughing at them, us feeling superior to them, us ridiculing them behind their backs. If they were doing it to us we'd call it male chauvinist pigness; if we do it to them, it is inescapably female chauvinist sowness and, whatever its roots, it leads to the same isolation. Boys are messy, boys are mean, boys are rough, boys are stupid and have sloppy handwriting. A cacophony of childhood memories rushes through my head, balanced, of course, by all the well-documented feelings of inferiority and envy. But the important thing, the hard thing, is to wipe the slate clean, to start again without the meanness of the past. That's why it's so important that the women's movement not become antimale and allow its most prejudiced spokesmen total leadership. The much-chewed-over abortion issue illustrates this. The women's-liberation position, insisting on a woman's right to determine her own body's destiny, leads in fanatical extreme to a kind of emotional immaculate conception in which the father is not judged even half-responsible—he has no rights, and no consideration is to be given to his concern for either the woman or the fetus.

15   Woman, who once was abandoned and disgraced by an unwanted pregnancy, has recently arrived at a new pride of ownership or disposal.

She has traveled in a straight line that still excludes her sexual partner from an equal share in the wanted or unwanted pregnancy. A better style of life 175 may develop from an assumption that men are as human as we. Why not ask the child's father if he would like to bring up the child? Why not share decisions, when possible, with the male? If we cut them out, assuming an old-style indifference on their part, we perpetuate the ugly divisiveness that has characterized relations between the sexes so far.   180

16   Hard as it is for many of us to believe, women are not really superior to men in intelligence or humanity—they are only equal.

QUESTIONS

READER AND PURPOSE

1. Roiphe's argument has two sides, one negative—something she is against —and the other positive—something she is for. In your own words summarize both aspects of her argument. Which single sentence of this selection best expresses her essential point?

2. How does Roiphe support her argument: logically, by deriving her conclusions from self-evident premises; or empirically, by offering evidence from experience?

3. Which of these adjectives best describes Roiphe's tone *, "angry," "amused," "frivolous"? If none seems adequate, how would you characterize the tone of this selection? Is she writing primarily for men or for women? Or equally for both?

ORGANIZATION

4. Which paragraph(s) constitute the beginning? Which the closing?

5. How does paragraph 1 contribute to the writer's argument? Paragraphs 2, 3, 4, and 5?

6. Is the sixth paragraph ironic * or are we intended to take it literally? How does it develop the argument?

7. Does the ninth paragraph mark a turn in thought?

8. How is paragraph 14 tied to 13? Show that in paragraph 14 Roiphe's concern becomes more positive—less with what is presently wrong and more with what ideally ought to be. How does she support the point she makes in this paragraph?

9. What is the function of the rhetorical question * in line 67?

10. Notice that in paragraph 10 Roiphe uses the organizing word *first*. Does she continue this scheme with *second, third*, and so on?

11. The ellipsis * in line 19 has a kind of organizational function. Explain.

SENTENCES

12. The sentence in lines 4-6 is colloquial * not only in its diction, but also in the way it is put together. What about its structure suggests speech?

13. *Keeps* in line 10 is an appositive *. To what? Why are the dashes more helpful here to a reader than commas would be?

14. Point out the parallelism * in the sentence in lines 27-31; that in the sentence in 55-57.

15. Suppose that in line 38 a semicolon had been used instead of a colon. Would it help or hinder clarity?

16. Consider the following pairs of sentences and discuss why in each case the revision is poorer than the sentence in the text:

   (a) *Revision:* To this day I never blink if I hear that a man has gone to find his fortune in South America, having taken the family car and left his pregnant wife and blind mother.
   Roiphe: "To this day I never blink if I hear that a man has gone to find his fortune in South America, having left his pregnant wife, his blind mother and taken the family car." (73-75)

   (b) *Revision:* This false division of good and bad doesn't have to contaminate the future, placing deforming pressures on everyone.
   Roiphe: "This false division of good and bad, placing deforming pressures on everyone, doesn't have to contaminate the future." (106-7)

   (c) *Revision:* Hard as it is for many of us to believe, women are only equal and not really superior to men in intelligence and humanity.
   Roiphe: "Hard as it is for many of us to believe, women are not really superior to men in intelligence or humanity—they are only equal." (181-82)

DICTION

17. Look up: *replica* (4), *lexicon* (25), *ofay* (25), *goy* (25), *exploitative* (59), *manifold* (72), *contaminate* (107), *Jack the Ripper* (128), *Lizzie Borden* (128), *coevals* (139), *vignette* (155), *perpetuate* (179).

18. What do these phrases mean: *wallflower's rope ladder* (46), *dubious civilization* (79), *cultural air we breathe* (108-109), *fanatical extreme* (168), *emotional immaculate conception* (168-69)?

19. How do the etymologies * of the following words help one understand their present meanings? *Prejudices* (19), *hypocritical* (58), *alimony* (67), *artifacts* (85), *chauvinism* (99), *psyche* (100), *canard* (103), *masochistic* (129), *cacophony* (160).

20. Point out several examples of colloquial diction; several of learned, literary

words. Such multi-level diction is typical of much contemporary prose. Success-fully used, as it is here, it suggests a wide-ranging sensitivity, attuned both to books and to life, able to be serious without being pompous and learned with-out being pedantic.

21. Why is *they* italicized in the clause in lines 18-19? In that clause what is Roiphe implying by her use of the intensives *even* and *herself* in the expression "for even Miss America herself"?

22. Now and again Roiphe employs alliteration * effectively. Point out several examples.

23. Explain how these pointers * prepare us for the idea they introduce: *in short* (57), *altogether* (62), *well* (67), *in fact* (102), *true* (127). How does *either* (142) help to unify paragraph 12?

24. What is the reason for hyphenating *much-chewed-over* (166) and *women's-liberation* (166-67)?

25. Why are the following alternatives less effective for Roiphe's purpose than the word she employed? *Father* for *handsome daddy-true* (4), *crawling* for *slithering* (40), *realized* for *gathered* (63), *belief* for *myth* (86), *examine* for *rummage about and find in* (115)?

26. Do you think the metaphor * in line 3 and the simile * in line 9 are effective devices of communication?

POINTS TO LEARN

1. Sometimes the best and the easiest way to develop an empirical argument is to look to your own experience.

2. A modern style, especially one that leans toward informality, plucks words from various levels of use—formal and colloquial, learned and slang. The essential consideration is that the word be the best expression of what one wants to say.

SUGGESTIONS FOR WRITING

Examine your own preconceptions about the opposite sex, or about the older generation, or about a different ethnic, social, or occupational group than your own. Organize your essay by distinguishing specific prejudices and support your discussion with detailed illustrations drawn from your own experience.

IMPROVING YOUR STYLE

1. In your composition strive for a wide spectrum of diction, ranging from the slang and colloquial to the more literary. Do not throw words in just to fulfill the assignment. Remember that any word, slang or learned, is justified only if it conveys exactly what your context suggests it should convey.

2. Use at least one metaphor and one simile.

3. Compose a colloquial, interrupted sentence like Roiphe's in lines 4-6.

4. In other sentences include:

An appositive.

Parallel constructions.

At least one case of two independent * clauses joined paratactically (that is, without a conjunction and punctuated with a semicolon).

Canadian Nationhood and American World Power

William Lewis Morton (1908-1980) was born in Gladstone, Manitoba. He is generally regarded as the most prominent historian of the Canadian West. Among his books are the Governor General's Award-winning *The Progressive Party in Canada* (1950), *Manitoba: A History* (1957), *The Canadian Identity* (1961), and *The Kingdom of Canada* (1964). Morton's interests were not, however, restricted to western-Canadian subjects. In the selection below he offers a logically-developed argument that distinguishes between the bases of American and Canadian nationhood in order to explain why the former might be seen as a threat (even if an unintentional one) by many Canadians.

1   If then Canada's destiny is in its own hands, why is it disturbed by fear and resentment of America? The answer is plain. What Canada really fears is not the old America, but America in its new role of world power. It fears that America in seeking to maintain its world power will make demand after demand on Canada, each reasonable in itself, until the 5 substance of independence is modified out of existence. More than that, it fears that the United States, in some sudden convulsion of the world balance, will simply occupy Canada. Circumstances may easily arise in which the United States would have no more choice than Canada. It fears also, out of its knowledge of the American temperament in action, that such an 10 occupation could be made needlessly, or that once made, would not be unmade. For, the government and people of the United States, while they have come to accept Canadian nationhood, do not understand it and therefore do not value it. Canadian concern with this fact arises from a mature awareness that while Americans in their friendly way accept Canada as a 15 neighbour, they are not in their heart of hearts convinced that Canadian

From W. L. Morton, *The Canadian Identity*, 2nd edition, (University of Toronto Press), © 1961 The Board of Regents of the University of Wisconsin System, reprinted by permission.

nationhood is possessed of a moral significance comparable with that of their own great nation.

2   If a great simplification may be attempted, in order to cut to the root of the matter, this is so because Americans, by being Americans, are 20 in a measure precluded from understanding Canada. Americans are a people of the covenant, as Clinton Rossiter has so brilliantly demonstrated. That may be taken to mean three things. The first is a need for a measure of uniformity; the covenant is among the like-minded. The second is that the covenant to a degree cuts the covenanted off from the uncovenanted. 25 Third, the covenant implies not only uniformity and isolation, but also a mission. America is a messianic country periodically inspired to carry the republic into other lands for the liberation of the Gentiles, the lesser breeds without the covenant.

3   Nor is this the whole of the fundamental character of America. If 30 the mission is denied, as by present-day China, if the messianic complex is thwarted, then occurs that search for the domestic traitor, the uncovenanted, which today is called McCarthyism, from which America has suffered so much, and from which Canada too suffered in the death of Herbert Norman.   35

4   This fundamental American character, a barrier to understanding any nation, is particularly an obstacle to understanding Canada, for Canada is not the creation of a covenant, or a social compact embodied in a Declaration of Independence and written constitution. It is the product of treaty and statute, the dry legal instruments of the diplomat and the legis- 40 lator. It is the pragmatic achievement of the little-regarded labours of clerks in the Colonial Office and obscure provincial politicians, still unknown to the world. Beneath their work the moral core of Canadian nationhood is found in the fact that Canada is a monarchy and in the nature of monarchical allegiance. As America is united at bottom by the covenant, 45 Canada is united at the top by allegiance. Because Canada is a nation founded on allegiance and not on compact, there is no process in becoming Canadian akin to conversion, there is no pressure for uniformity, there is no Canadian way of life. Any one, French, Irish, Ukrainian or Eskimo, can be a subject of the Queen and a citizen of Canada without in any way 50 changing or ceasing to be himself. This is a truth so fundamental that it is little realized and many, if not most, Canadians would deny its truth, but it is central to any explanation or understanding of Canadian nationhood.

QUESTIONS

READER AND PURPOSE

1. The purpose of Professor Morton's argument is to answer the question that he poses in his first sentence. Do you think that he does so?

2. Summarize the stages of the argument. Is the author proceeding deductively or inductively?

3. What kind of reader is Morton addressing ? Are the names Clinton Rossiter and Herbert Norman familiar to you? If not, look them up in, respectively, *The Directory of American Scholars* and *The Macmillan Dictionary of Canadian Biography.*

4. What effect is produced on the reader by the second sentence of paragraph 1? Do you consider this statement to be a useful tactic of argument, or do you think it merely a rhetorical flourish? Explain your answer.

ORGANIZATION

5. In paragraph 1 locate all the instances in which Morton uses logical pointers *: words such as *if, then, for, because, therefore.* What is the relationship between these words and the development of his argument? Does he use these words in subsequent paragraphs?

6. Does the first sentence of paragraph 2 function effectively as both a topic sentence and a transitional sentence? What new topic is being introduced? How is it related to the topic of paragraph 1?

7. Does the author's admission that he is simplifying his argument weaken its effectiveness? Is enough evidence offered to support the claim "this is so" (20)? Is this evidence organized in the same fashion as in paragraph 1?

8. Explain Professor Morton's purpose for continuing the subject of paragraph 2 in paragraph 3.

9. What methods of organization are used in paragraph 4 but not in the preceding three paragraphs? In answering this question pay special attention to Morton's use of the verb "is."

10. Can you see any ways in which Morton's final sentence is related to the rest of his argument?

11. Compare this selection with MacLennan's (p. 139), giving primary attention to the differences between them. For example, what place do the two writers give to the "moral" character of Canada?

SENTENCES

12. Morton repeats the key word *fear* in the first part of paragraph 1. Is he making use of restatement or of logical progression? Explain your answer.

13. The author begins nearly all his subordinate clauses * in paragraph 1 with the conjunction *that.* Do you find this repetitious? Or is Morton deliberately

using parallelism *? Does he continue this sentence format in the following paragraphs?

14. What effect is achieved by the placing of the two metaphors *—*liberation of the Gentiles* and *lesser breeds* (28, 29)—side by side? Find the sources of the two metaphors before answering.

15. What repeated word in sentence two of paragraph 3 indicates that Professor Morton is appealing to the emotions of Canadians as well as to their understanding?

16. What verb is used most frequently in paragraph 4? Is it appropriate here in the conclusion of an argument? Would more forceful verbs have been more effective, or would they weaken the assertive tone * that Morton adopts?

DICTION

17. Look up: *convulsion* (7), *covenant* (22), *messianic* (27), *McCarthyism* (33), *compact* (38), *treaty* (40), *statute* (40), *pragmatic* (41), *allegiance* (46).

18. Is Professor Morton employing the same connotations * of *messianic* as Barbara Ward did (p. 32)?

18. Consider the diction of paragraph 2, such words as *covenant, covenanted, uncovenanted, mission, messianic, inspired, liberation, Gentiles*. What religious connotations* do these words have? What is their function in Morton's argument?

POINTS TO LEARN

1. The evidence offered in support of an argument can be arranged in different ways (such as the order of increasing importance, or the order of logical enumeration).

2. Pointers such as *if, then, so, because,* and *therefore* are effective in directing the reader's attention to the logical development of an argument.

3. Repetition of key words and phrases can be used to create the style and tone desired by an author.

4. Appeals to emotion, if used sparingly, and with reference to a widely-shared feeling, have a part to play in effective persuasion.

SUGGESTIONS FOR WRITING

1. Write two paragraphs in which you argue that most Canadians do not fear the United States.

2. Write two paragraphs arguing that most Canadians cannot understand the United States because they are unable to grasp the significance of Professor Morton's distinction between *covenant* and *allegiance*.

3. Write four paragraphs in which you argue that grade-school education does not prepare students to understand the essential differences between Canada and its neighbor.

IMPROVING YOUR STYLE

In your composition include:

1. Evidence, in the form of common knowledge and specific examples, to persuade your reader that your conclusions are soundly based.
2. Repetition of a different sentence structure in each paragraph.
3. Logical pointers indicating the development of your argument.
4. A brief and judiciously-chosen appeal to the emotions of your readers.

Hemlock at 65

Russell Baker writes a daily newspaper column which appears in *The New York Times*. Baker's pieces are usually humorous or satiric treatments of current political and social questions. Below the humor, however, there is serious intent. This selection, published in January 1971, concerns the attempt by some of the younger newly-elected representatives to the ninety-second Congress (1971-72) to upset the seniority system. According to seniority, House and Senate members with the longest terms of service are awarded the most prestigious and powerful committee assignments. In the view of young liberals the system results in an overly conservative Congress. Their effort was thus in part an attack of liberals upon conservatives. But in part, too, it was a denial by youth of the privileges of age. In dealing with the issue Baker's strategy is satiric. He persuades us less by logic and evidence than by irony and comic exaggeration. Yet the satire expresses a serious view of the problem— not a simple view, for Baker is not a knee-jerk defender of liberalism or conservatism, of youth or age. He sees the problem more subtly and reveals the faults both of seniority and of those who attack it without thinking through what they are doing.

Baker's title refers to the execution in 399 B.C. of the Athenian philosopher Socrates, who was made to drink hemlock after being convicted of impiety and of misleading the youth of the city. The charges were the response of reactionaries to the liberal open-mindedness of the aging philosopher, a fact not without irony in the context of Baker's essay.

1   It has been a bad week for old people. Another bad week. Bad weeks for old people seem to occur with increasing frequency. If it isn't "Where's Poppa?"[1] at the movie house it's another rise in the real-estate tax, the kind that must make you say "Oof!" if you are over 65 and, there-

From *The New York Times*, January 21, 1971. © 1971 by The New York Times Company. Reprinted by permission.
[1] A comic film about a young lawyer's efforts to get out of taking care of his aged and widowed mother. [Editors' note]

fore, automatically ineligible for those 17.4 per cent salary increases that 5
make it easier for the rest of us to roll with the punch.

2   This week there has been a sustained battery by insult on the very
fact of being old. Old people have been able to hear and see oldness
abused, ridiculed, denounced and scorned in a barrage of speeches, editorials, columns and broadcasts, most of them arguing the liberal political 10
position that the Congressional seniority system must be abolished because
old committee chairmen are mentally and socially inferior.

3   Some will dismiss the churlishness of the argument against the old
men on grounds that in any political struggle language is merely a blunt instrument, and should not be listened to seriously. In this case that argu- 15
ment is unpersuasive.

4   The attack on the seniority system is, in fact, merely a late-
in-the-day part of the same general assault upon the aged that has pretty
well cleaned them out of both corporate and public life.

5   The most effective weapon in the attack has been the policy of 20
forced retirement, usually at 65. It is, of course, job discrimination of the
most blatant sort, yet governments and companies, which wouldn't dream
of putting a person out of work on account of race, sex, religion or hair
style, blindly chop you off for the offense of becoming 65 years old.

6   Psychological warfare makes it easy to keep the old people sub- 25
dued. For one thing we have successfully promoted the idea that getting
old is an act in very bad taste. The smart people in America are the young
people, or so it must seem to anyone who keeps his eyes and ears open.

7   A person who lets himself become unyoung. . . .

8   Well! Shouldn't he be grateful that we don't put him out of work 30
without enough income to pay his way into the movies to see "Where's
Poppa?"

9   Provided the real-estate tax doesn't go up?

10   The reason the seniority system has failed in Congress is not because it concentrates power in the hands of the old. That isn't the vice at 35
all. The problem is that it concentrates power in the hands of old men who
have never had experience of democracy.

11   The prizes are awarded, not for great age, but for long service in
Congress. Long service in Congress almost invariably requires a one-party
district or state—a rotten borough, if you will, in which a Senator or Repre- 40
sentative never becomes acquainted with the democratic process.

12   The rotten borough tends to breed tyrants, and from this tendency

rises the real problem with the seniority system, which is not that it raises up old men, but that it exalts old tyrants.

13   Reforming the Congressional power structure needn't involve any 45 attack on age. The seniority rule, in fact, can be safely left as the guiding principle, with the exception that members would be unqualified for power positions if they were returned from districts where the democratic process is not in use.

14   This amended rule would still permit members in their 70's and 50 80's to rule over committees. And why not? Any man of advanced years who has been re-elected twenty times against opposition will surely have qualities that can only do the country great service at the top of its government.

15   The attack should be upon old tyrants, not old age. Old age gives 55 the country great strengths. Bob Dylan, to take a case, is fine, as are Senator Kennedy and Senator Dole. But even with all that youthful splendor, Socrates helps a lot. He was 70 when he took the hemlock, "at the peak of his powers," the obituary writers might say today.

16   Socrates would have been treated more cruelly in America. He 60 would have been forcibly retired to shuffleboard at Sunville at 65. There wouldn't have been all that disturbing thought at Athens.

17   The Athenian youth, instead of sitting around using their heads, would have been running great corporations, getting out those dynamic press releases, announcing new mergers, and there would have been a lot 65 more bankruptcy, as well as alienation, in Athens.

QUESTIONS

READER AND PURPOSE

1. Baker is arguing two related issues, one a specific instance of the other. What are these issues? Does his argument consist simply of assertions, or does he offer evidence from experience?

2. His tone is ironic *. How, for example, are we supposed to read the last sentence of paragraph 16? What is ironic in the final paragraph? Point out other instances of irony.

3. Is Baker writing for a relatively sophisticated audience? What does he expect them to know?

ORGANIZATION

4. Do you think the opening of this selection is effective? What about its closing?

5. Paragraph 10 marks a major turn of thought. What has the writer been concentrating upon up to this point? How does his focus change in paragraph 10?

6. Explain how the third paragraph contributes to Baker's argument; the fourth and fifth. Paragraphs 6, 7, and 8 make up a conceptual unit. What is their point?

7. What answer does Baker make to those who claim that old age should disqualify legislators from occupying positions of power?

8. The paragraphing in this selection is typical of journalism: numerous brief paragraphs. Some, in fact, consist of only a single short sentence. Would it be an improvement to combine such paragraphs (7 and 9 for example) with the preceding material?

9. How is the twelfth paragraph linked to the eleventh? The fourteenth to the thirteenth?

10. In the opening sentences of this selection Baker achieves a high degree of coherence by repeating the phrase *bad week(s)*. In fact, he ends the second sentence with these words and immediately picks them up to begin the third sentence, a pattern of repetition that in ancient rhetoric was called *anadiplosis* (accent on *plo*). Where else in these paragraphs do you find *anadiplosis*?

SENTENCES

11. Comment upon these revisions of Baker's sentences:

(a) *Revision:* It has been another bad week for old people.
Baker: "It has been a bad week for old people. Another bad week." (1)

(b) *Revision:* Well, shouldn't he be grateful that we don't put him out of work without enough income to pay his way into the movies to see "Where's Poppa?" provided the real-estate tax doesn't go up?
Baker: "Well! Shouldn't he be grateful that we don't put him out of work without enough income to pay his way into the movies to see 'Where's Poppa?'
"Provided the real-estate tax doesn't go up?" (30-33)

12. "And why not?" (51) is a fragment *. Why? What other fragments can you find in this essay? Are they effective, or would Baker's points be more effectively expressed in grammatically complete sentences?

13. The ellipsis * in line 29 is an example of a thought deliberately left incom-

plete, a trick in Greek rhetoric called *aposiopesis* (accent on *pe*). What is the thought being implied here? What is the advantage of leaving it implicit?

14. What does Baker mean by the clause "if you will" in line 40?

15. The statement in lines 42-44 is a good example of how a well-constructed sentence thrusts ideas forward. The sentence consists of five clauses. How does the second derive from the first? The third, fourth, and fifth from the second? Why are the final two clauses parallel *?

DICTION

16. Look up: *barrage* (9), *liberal* (10), *abolished* (11), *assault* (18), *blatant* (22), *vice* (35), *tyrants* (42), *amended* (50), *mergers* (65), *alienation* (66).

17. What do these phrases mean: *corporate and public life* (19), *psychological warfare* (25), *guiding principle* (46-7)?

18. Explain the etymologies of these words: *salary* (5), *battery* (7), *churlishness* (13), *obituary* (59), *dynamic* (64), *bankruptcy* (66).

19. How do the following pointers * prepare us for the idea each introduces: *in fact* (17 and 46), *of course* (21), *yet* (22), *to take a case* (56)?

20. Comment upon how these suggested substitutions would alter the tone or the sense of Baker's text: *cut* for *chop* (24), *old* for *unyoung* (29), *cinema* for *movies* (31), *old man* for *man of advanced years* (51), *tennis at Phoenix* for *shuffleboard at Sunville* (61).

21. In lines 14-15 *blunt instrument* is a fine metaphor *. Applied to language, it has two senses. Explain.

22. Baker usually contracts a verb and a negative term. How would his tone change if he wrote these out in full—*is not* for *isn't* in line 2, for instance, or *need not* for *needn't* in line 45?

POINTS TO LEARN

1. Irony, while no substitute for logical proof or for empirical evidence, can prove effective strategy in argumentation.

2. Fragments and brief, single-sentence paragraphs, if not over-used, are valuable means of emphasis.

3. Sometimes it is better to let the reader complete a thought for himself.

SUGGESTIONS FOR WRITING

1. Compose a one- or two-paragraph argument against compulsory class attendance, dormitory regulations, or any aspect of life where you feel the young are discriminated against. Support your points by appealing to common knowledge and by offering examples, but try also to achieve a tone of irony.

2. Baker proposes in paragraphs 12-14 a way of reforming the American Con-

gressional power structure without necessarily discriminating against old men. Examine the implications of his proposal and construct an argument against it.

IMPROVING YOUR STYLE
In your composition include:

1. An example of anadiplosis.
2. An example of aposiopesis.
3. (With your instructor's approval) one or two effective fragments.
4. These connectives * introducing sentences—*in fact, of course, yet, to take a case.*
5. A brief metaphor like *blunt instrument* (lines 14-15).

A Modest Proposal

Jonathan Swift (1667-1745) is the greatest writer of satire in English literature and one of the greatest in the world. He is best known for *Gulliver's Travels* (1726), popularly thought of as a fantasy for children, but actually a biting attack upon a variety of targets—politicians, courtiers, travel books, scientists, humanity in general. A *Tale of a Tub* (1704) is a funny and scandalous treatment of religious follies. The essay reprinted here satirizes England's policy toward Ireland. (Swift, though English, was born and educated in Dublin and served for many years as Dean of the Anglican St. Patrick's Cathedral in that city.)

During the eighteenth century Ireland suffered under an English rule that was repressive and exploitative. Religious intolerance was strong and Protestant England imposed harsh religious, political, and economic restrictions upon the native Irish, who were virtually all Catholic. Even the Anglo-Irish, Swift's class, who descended from English settlers and were themselves Protestant, suffered under unjust laws forbidding Ireland to trade with nations other than England. Swift had proposed solutions to some of these inequities, solutions that seemed to him workable and fair. No one listened. In "A Modest Proposal" (1729) he suggested a more horrendous scheme, saying to England, in effect: Since you are determined to destroy the Irish for profit, let me show you how to conduct your slaughter-house policy more systematically and efficiently. Although the "Irish Question" is still unsettled, Swift's "A Modest Proposal" remains the finest example of sustained irony ever written.
ever written.

A Modest Proposal

for
Preventing the Children of Poor People in Ireland from Being a

The text and notes are taken from *The Restoration and the Eighteenth Century,* ed. Martin Price. Copyright © 1973 by Oxford University Press, Inc. Reprinted by permission of the publisher.

Burden to Their Parents or Country, and for Making Them Beneficial to the Public

1   It is a melancholy object to those who walk through this great town, or travel in the country, when they see the streets, the roads, and cabin-doors crowded with beggars of the female sex, followed by three, four, or six children, all in rags, and importuning every passenger for an alms. These mothers, instead of being able to work for their honest liveli-   5
hood, are forced to employ all their time in strolling to beg sustenance for their helpless infants: who, as they grow up, either turn thieves for want of work, or leave their dear native country to fight for the Pretender* in Spain, or sell themselves to the Barbadoes.[1]

2   I think it is agreed by all parties, that this prodigious number of   10
children in the arms, or on the backs, or at the heels of their mothers, and frequently of their fathers, is, in the present deplorable state of the kingdom, a very great additional grievance; and, therefore, whoever could find out a fair, cheap, and easy method of making these children sound and useful members of the commonwealth, would deserve so well of the public,   15
as to have his statue set up for a preserver of the nation.[2]

3   But my intention is very far from being confined to provide only for the children of professed beggars; it is of a much greater extent, and shall take in the whole number of infants at a certain age, who are born of parents in effect as little able to support them as those who demand our   20
charity in the streets.

4   As to my own part, having turned my thoughts for many years upon this important subject, and maturely weighed the several schemes of other projectors, I have always found them grossly mistaken in their computation. It is true, a child, just dropped from its dam,[3] may be supported   25
by her milk for a solar year with little other nourishment; at most, not above the value of two shillings, which the mother may certainly get, or the value in scraps, by her lawful occupation of begging; and it is exactly at one

* The Old Pretender, James Edward, son of James II (last Catholic king of England, deposed in 1688) and Mary of Modena. The Pretender was a Catholic and, possessing a claim to the English throne, posed a threat to Protestant England. [Editors' note]
[1] Many Irish Catholics enlisted in French and Spanish forces, the latter employed in the effort to restore the Stuart Pretender to the English throne in 1718; emigration to the West Indies from Ireland had reached the rate of almost fifteen hundred a year (and often led to desperate servitude).
[2] The idiom of the "projector," the enthusiastic proponent of public remedies (often suspected of having an eye on his own glory).
[3] The idiom now of the cattle breeder.

year old that I propose to provide for them in such a manner, as, instead of being a charge upon their parents or the parish, or wanting food and raiment for the rest of their lives, they shall, on the contrary, contribute to the feeding, and partly to the clothing, of many thousands.

5   There is likewise another great advantage in my scheme, that it will prevent those voluntary abortions, and that horrid practice of women murdering their bastard children, alas, too frequent among us, sacrificing the poor innocent babes, I doubt more to avoid the expense than the shame, which would move tears and pity in the most savage and inhuman breast.

6   The number of souls in this kingdom being usually reckoned one million and a half, of these I calculate there may be about two hundred thousand couple whose wives are breeders; from which number I subtract thirty thousand couple, who are able to maintain their own children (although I apprehend there cannot be so many, under the present distresses of the kingdom); but this being granted, there will remain an hundred and seventy thousand breeders. I again subtract fifty thousand for those women who miscarry, or whose children die by accident or disease within the year. There only remain a hundred and twenty thousand children of poor parents annually born. The question therefore is how this number shall be reared and provided for? which, as I have already said, under the present situation of affairs, is utterly impossible by all the methods hitherto proposed. For we can neither employ them in handicraft or agriculture; we neither build houses (I mean in the country) nor cultivate land: they can very seldom pick up a livelihood by stealing until they arrive at six years old, except where they are of towardly parts; although I confess they learn the rudiments much earlier; during which time they can, however, be properly looked upon only as probationers; as I have been informed by a principal gentleman in the county of Cavan,[4] who protested to me, that he never knew above one or two instances under the age of six, even in a part of the kingdom so renowned for the quickest proficiency in that art.

7   I am assured by our merchants that a boy or a girl before twelve years old is no saleable commodity; and even when they come to this age they will not yield above three pounds or three pounds and half-a-crown at most, on the exchange; which cannot turn to account either to the parents or kingdom, the charge of nutriment and rags having been at least four times that value.

[4] One of the poorest districts of Ireland.

8   I shall now, therefore, humbly propose my own thoughts, which I hope will not be liable to the least objection.

9   I have been assured by a very knowing American[5] of my acquaintance in London, that a young healthy child, well nursed, is, at a year old, a most delicious, nourishing, and wholesome food, whether stewed, roasted, 70 baked, or boiled; and I make no doubt that it will equally serve in a fricassee or a ragout.[6]

10   I do therefore humbly offer it to public consideration, that of the hundred and twenty thousand children already computed, twenty thousand may be reserved for breed, whereof only one-fourth part to be males; which 75 is more than we allow to sheep, black cattle, or swine; and my reason is, that these children are seldom the fruits of marriage, a circumstance not much regarded by our savages, therefore one male will be sufficient to serve four females. That the remaining hundred thousand may, at a year old, be offered in sale to the persons of quality and fortune through the kingdom; 80 always advising the mother to let them suck plentifully in the last month, so as to render them plump and fat for a good table. A child will make two dishes at an entertainment for friends; and when the family dines alone, the fore or hind quarter will make a reasonable dish, and, seasoned with a little pepper or salt, will be very good boiled on the fourth day, especially 85 in winter.

11   I have reckoned, upon a medium, that a child just born will weigh twelve pounds, and in a solar year, if tolerably nursed, increaseth to twenty-eight pounds.

12   I grant this food will be somewhat dear, and therefore very proper 90 for landlords, who, as they have already devoured most of the parents, seem to have the best title to the children.

13   Infants' flesh will be in season throughout the year, but more plentifully in March, and a a little before and after: for we are told by a grave author, an eminent French physician,[7] that fish being a prolific[8] diet, 95 there are more children born in Roman Catholic countries about nine months after Lent than at any other season; therefore, reckoning a year after Lent, the markets will be more glutted than usual, because the num-

[5] Presumably American Indian, many of whom were believed by the English to enjoy cannibalism.

[6] A French stew, one of the foreign dishes ("olios and ragouts") Swift mocks elsewhere as affectations.

[7] François Rabelais (c. 1494-1553), Gargantua and Pantagruel V.29.

[8] Generative.

ber of popish infants is at least threee to one in this kingdom; and therefore
it will have one other collateral advantage, by lessening the number of   100
papists among us.

14   I have already computed the charge of nursing a beggar's child (in
which list I reckon all cottagers, labourers, and four-fifths of the farmers)
to be about two shillings per annum, rags included; and I believe no gentleman would repine to give ten shillings for the carcass of a good fat child,   105
which, as I have said, will make four dishes of excellent nutritive meat,
when he has only some particular friend, or his own family, to dine with
him. Thus the squire will learn to be a good landlord, and grow popular
among his tenants; the mother will have eight shillings net profit, and be
fit for work till she produces another child.   110

15   Those who are more thrifty (as I must confess the times require)
may flay the carcass; the skin of which, artificially dressed, will make admirable gloves for ladies, and summer-boots for fine gentlemen.

16   As to our city of Dublin, shambles[9] may be appointed for this purpose in the most convenient parts of it, and butchers we may be assured   115
will not be wanting; although I rather recommend buying the children
alive, and dressing them hot from the knife, as we do roasting pigs.

17   A very worthy person, a true lover of his country, and whose virtues
I highly esteem, was lately pleased, in discoursing on this matter, to offer a
refinement upon my scheme. He said, that many gentlemen of this king-   120
dom, having of late destroyed their deer, he conceived that the want of
venison might be well supplied by the bodies of young lads and maidens,
not exceeding fourteen years of age, nor under twelve; so great a number of
both sexes in every country being now ready to starve for want of work and
service; and these to be disposed of by their parents, if alive, or otherwise   125
by their nearest relations. But, with due deference to so excellent a friend,
and so deserving a patriot, I cannot be altogether in his sentiments; for as
to the males, my American acquaintance assured me from frequent experience, that their flesh was generally tough and lean, like that of our school-
boys, by continual exercise, and their taste disagreeable; and to fatten them   130
would not answer the charge. Then as to the females, it would, I think,
with humble submission, be a loss to the public, because they soon would
become breeders themselves: and besides, it is not improbable that some
scrupulous people might be apt to censure such a practice (although indeed

9 Slaughterhouses.

very unjustly) as a little bordering upon cruelty; which, I confess hath al- 135
ways been with me the strongest objection against any project, how well
soever intended.

18   But in order to justify my friend, he confessed that this expedient
was put into his head by the famous Psalmanazar,[10] a native of the island
Formosa, who came from thence to London above twenty years ago; and 140
in conversation told my friend, that in his country, when any young person
happened to be put to death, the executioner sold the carcass to persons of
quality as a prime dainty; and that in his time the body of a plump girl of
fifteen, who was crucified for an attempt to poison the emperor, was sold to
his Imperial Majesty's prime minister of state,[11] and other great mandarins 145
of the court, in joints from the gibbet, at four hundred crowns. Neither indeed can I deny, that if the same use were made of several plump young
girls in this town, who, without one single groat to their fortunes, cannot
stir abroad without a chair, and appear at playhouse and assemblies[12] in
foreign fineries which they never will pay for, the kingdom would not be 150
the worse.

19   Some persons of a desponding spirit are in great concern about that
vast number of poor people who are aged, diseased, or maimed; and I have
been desired to employ my thoughts what course may be taken to ease the
nation of so grievous an encumbrance. But I am not in the least pain upon 155
that matter, because it is very well known, that they are every day dying,
and rotting, by cold and famine, and filth and vermin, as fast as can be
reasonably expected. And as to the younger labourers, they are now in almost as hopeful a condition: they cannot get work, and consequently pine
away for want of nourishment, to a degree, that if at any time they are ac- 160
cidentally hired to common labour, they have not strength to perform it;
and thus the country and themselves are happily delivered from the evils to
come.

20   I have too long digressed, and therefore shall return to my subject.
I think the advantages by the proposal which I have made are obvious and 165
many, as well as of the highest importance.

21   For first, as I have already observed, it would greatly lessen the
number of papists, with whom we are yearly overrun, being the principal

---

[10] George Psalmanazar (1679-1763), a Frenchman who pretended to be a Formosan
and wrote (in English) a fraudulent book about his "native" land.
[11] Probably a reference to Walpole.
[12] Social gatherings (Swift had sought an Irish boycott of all such foreign luxuries of
dress or diet).

breeders of the nation as well as our most dangerous enemies; and who stay at home on purpose with a design to deliver the kingdom to the Pretender, hoping to take their advantage by the absence of so many good Protestants, who have chosen rather to leave their country than stay at home and pay tithes against their conscience to an idolatrous Episcopal curate.[13]

22   Secondly, the poorer tenants will have something valuable of their own, which by law may be made liable to distress, and help to pay their landlord's rent; their corn and cattle being already seized, and money a thing unknown.

23   Thirdly, whereas the maintenance of an hundred thousand children, from two years old and upwards, cannot be computed at less than ten shillings a piece per annum, the nation's stock will be thereby increased fifty thousand pounds per annum; besides the profit of a new dish introduced to the tables of all gentlemen of fortune in the kingdom who have any refinement in taste. And the money will circulate among ourselves, the goods being entirely of our own growth and manufacture.

24   Fourthly, the constant breeders, besides the gain of eight shillings sterling per annum by the sale of their children, will be rid of the charge of maintaining them after the first year.

25   Fifthly, this food would likewise bring great custom to taverns; where the vintners will certainly be so prudent as to procure the best receipts for dressing it to perfection, and, consequently, have their houses frequented by all the fine gentlemen, who justly value themselves upon their knowledge in good eating: and a skilful cook, who understands how to oblige his guests, will contrive to make it as expensive as they please.

26   Sixthly, this would be a great inducement to marriage, which all wise nations have either encouraged by rewards, or enforced by laws and penalties. It would increase the care and tenderness of mothers towards their children, when they were sure of a settlement for life to the poor babes, provided in some sort by the public, to their annual profit instead of expense. We should soon see an honest emulation among the married women, which of them could bring the fattest child to the market. Men would become as fond of their wives during the time of their pregnancy,

---

[13] Swift is mocking the castigation of the Catholics, for he regarded it as a typical propaganda device of the Whigs and Protestants; his own experience as a clergyman in northern Ireland had given him reason to fear and distrust the energies of the dissenting Protestants, and he questions their motives (money or conscience) for leaving Ireland. The word "idolatrous" was added in 1735 after renewed agitation to remove the Sacramental Test, with the implication that Anglican forms and doctrines were intolerable to other Protestants.

as they are now of their mares in foal, their cows in calf, or sows when they are ready to farrow; nor offer to beat or kick them (as is too frequent a practice) for fear of a miscarriage.

27   Many other advantages might be enumerated. For instance, the 205 addition of some thousand carcasses in our exportation of barrelled beef; the propagation of swine's flesh, and improvement in the art of making good bacon, so much wanted among us by the great destruction of pigs, too frequent at our tables, which are no way comparable in taste or magnificence to a well-grown, fat yearling child, which, roasted whole, will make 210 a considerable figure at a Lord Mayor's feast, or any other public entertainment. But this, and many others, I omit, being studious of brevity.

28   Supposing that one thousand families in this city would be constant customers for infants' flesh, besides others who might have it at merry meetings, particularly weddings and christenings, I compute that Dublin 215 would take off annually about twenty thousand carcasses; and the rest of the kingdom (where probably they will be sold somewhat cheaper) the remaining eighty thousand.

29   I can think of no one objection that will possibly be raised against this proposal, unless it should be urged, that the number of people will be 220 thereby much lessened in the kingdom. This I freely own, and it was indeed one principal design in offering it to the world. I desire the reader will observe that I calculate my remedy for this one individual kingdom of Ireland, and for no other that ever was, is, or I think ever can be, upon earth. Therefore let no man talk to me of other expedients:[14] of taxing our ab- 225 sentees at five shillings a pound: of using neither clothes nor household-furniture except what is of our own growth and manufacture: of utterly rejecting the materials and instruments that promote foreign luxury: of curing the expensiveness of pride, vanity, idleness, and gaming in our women; of introducing a vein of parsimony, prudence, and temperance: of learning 230 to love our country, wherein we differ even from Laplanders, and the inhabitants of Topinamboo:[15] of quitting our animosities and factions, nor act any longer like the Jews, who were murdering one another at the very moment their city was taken:[16] of being a little cautious not to sell our country and consciences for nothing: of teaching landlords to have at least 235 one degree of mercy towards their tenants: lastly, of putting a spirit of hon-

---

[14] The following are, of course, Swift's own genuine proposals for Ireland.
[15] A region of Brazil known for wildness and barbarous stupidity.
[16] When Jerusalem fell to Nebuchadnezzar (II Kings 24, 25; II Chronicles 36), with the suggestion that English domination is Ireland's Babylonian captivity.

esty, industry, and skill into our shopkeepers; who, if a resolution could now be taken to buy only our native goods, would immediately unite to cheat and exact upon us in the price, the measure, and the goodness, nor could ever yet be brought to make one fair proposal of just dealing, though often 240 and earnestly invited to it.

30   Therefore I repeat, let no man talk to me of these and the like expedients, till he hath at least some glimpse of hope that there will ever be some hearty and sincere attempt to put them in practice.

31   But, as to myself, having been wearied out for many years with 245 offering vain, idle, visionary thoughts, and at length utterly despairing of success, I fortunately fell upon this proposal; which, as it is wholly new, so it hath something solid and real, of no expense and little trouble, full in our own power, and whereby we can incur no danger in disobliging England. For this kind of commodity will not bear exportation, the flesh being of too 250 tender a consistence to admit a long continuance in salt, although perhaps I could name a country which would be glad to eat up our whole nation without it.

32   After all, I am not so violently bent upon my own opinion as to reject any offer proposed by wise men which shall be found equally inno- 255 cent, cheap, easy, and effectual. But before something of that kind shall be advanced in contradiction to my scheme, and offering a better, I desire the author, or authors, will be pleased maturely to consider two points. First, as things now stand, how they will be able to find food and raiment for a hundred thousand useless mouths and backs? And, secondly, there being 260 a round million of creatures in human figure throughout this kingdom, whose whole subsistence put into a common stock would leave them in debt two millions of pounds sterling, adding those who are beggars by profession, to the bulk of farmers, cottagers, and labourers, with the wives and children who are beggars in effect; I desire those politicians who dislike my 265 overture, and may perhaps be so bold as to attempt an answer, that they will first ask the parents of these mortals, whether they would not at this day think it a great happiness to have been sold for food at a year old, in the manner I prescribe, and thereby have avoided such a perpetual scene of misfortunes as they have since gone through, by the oppression of land- 270 lords, the impossibility of paying rent without money or trade, the want of common sustenance, with neither house nor clothes to cover them from the inclemencies of weather, and the most inevitable prospect of entailing the like, or greater miseries, upon their breed for ever.

33   I profess, in the sincerity of my heart, that I have not the least per- 275

sonal interest in endeavouring to promote this necessary work, having no other motive than the public good of my country, by advancing our trade, providing for infants, relieving the poor, and giving some pleasure to the rich. I have no children by which I can propose to get a single penny; the youngest being nine years old, and my wife past child-bearing.   280

QUESTIONS

1. Swift's purpose, of course, is to attack English policy toward Ireland, but not so much any specific act as the fundamental attitude toward the Irish which determined policy in general. To do this he pretends to accept that attitude. In your own words express what Swift implies is the way in which the English regard the Irish.

2. In reading "A Modest Proposal" one must distinguish Swift from the "I," the pious projector ("do-gooder," we might call him today), who puts forward this cannibalistic scheme. On occasion Swift does speak almost directly through the "I"; but sometimes the "I" is part of the satire, expressing the moral platitudes typical of many Englishmen, who could see no contradiction between the Christianity they avowed and the harsh policy toward Ireland they preached and practiced. An example of this kind of shallow piety is the sympathy the speaker expresses for the Irish poor in the very opening sentence. Again, in paragraph 17 he speaks warmly of the virtues of his friend who suggests that Irish boys and girls might take the place of venison. Point out one or two other passages in which Swift, by giving pious sentiments to his speaker, reveals the disparity between Christian pretensions and political realities. Several times the "I" refers to himself as "humble." Is he?

3. On the surface the tone * of "A Modest Proposal" is sober and objective, carefully avoiding any direct expression of emotion. The Irish problem is approached simply as a matter of economics, calculable solely in terms of cost and profit. Now and then, however, the emotionless objectivity slips and we see a flash of anger. The very end of paragraph 18 is an example, where Swift lashes out at the vanity and idleness of society girls. Where else do you detect anger?

4. But such passages are exceptional. Generally the surface discipline holds, and emotion is kept in check. Below the surface, it is another story. Describe this deeper tone—"undertone," as it might be called. How does it differ from the tone of the irony * in the selection by Baker?

ORGANIZATION

5. Roughly, "A Modest Proposal" divides into these sections: (1) the introduction, in which the problem is identified and laid out; (2) the solution to the problem; (3) the advantages of that solution; (4) answers to possible objec-

tions; and (5) conclusion. Indicate in terms of paragraph numbers where each of these parts begins and ends.

6. The organizational scheme is not absolutely rigid. For instance, Swift touches upon the advantages of his proposal in places other than the third section. Where?

7. Paragraphs 8 and 20 do not really contribute to the proposal Swift is elaborating. What is their function?

8. Swift organizes the sixth paragraph by analyzing the problem in arithmetic terms. Explain why his use of arithmetic is a device of irony. Toward the end of this paragraph Swift gets involved in a discussion of whether or not children can support themselves by stealing. Is he wandering away from his point here, or does this apparent digression contribute to the general irony?

9. Paraphrase the point Swift makes in paragraph 12.

10. How are paragraphs 21-26 unified?

11. In paragraph 29 how does Swift answer the objection that his scheme would depopulate Ireland?

12. The final paragraph of "A Modest Proposal" is frequently praised as an excellent ending to the satire. Do you agree?

SENTENCES

13. Point out the parallel * constructions in these sentences:

    (a) ". . . who, as they grow up, either turn thieves for want of work, or leave their dear native country to fight for the Pretender in Spain, or sell themselves to the Barbadoes." (7-9)

    (b) "For we can neither employ them in handicraft or agriculture; we neither build houses (I mean in the country) nor cultivate land. . . ." (51-52)

14. Why are these revisions poorer than Swift's sentences?

    (a) *Revision:* I grant this food will be somewhat dear, and therefore very proper for landlords who seem to have the best title to the children since they have already devoured most of the parents. *Swift:* "I grant this food will be somewhat dear, and therefore very proper for landlords, who, as they have already devoured most of the parents, seem to have the best title to the children." (90-92)

    (b) *Revision:* Fifthly, this food would likewise bring great custom to taverns. Vintners will certainly be so prudent as to procure the best receipts for dressing it to perfection. Consequently they will have their houses frequented by all the fine gentlemen. Such gentlemen justly value themselves upon their knowledge in good eating. Therefore a skilful cook, who understands how to oblige his guests, will contrive to make it as expensive as they please.

Swift: "Fifthly, this food would likewise bring great custom to taverns; where the vintners will certainly be so prudent as to procure the best receipts for dressing it to perfection, and, consequently, have their houses frequented by all the fine gentlemen, who justly value themselves upon their knowledge in good eating: and a skilful cook, who understands how to oblige his guests, will contrive to make it as expensive as they please." (188-93)

15. Study the following sentence, which is a fine example of the kind of long, complex statement Swift was master of:

"But, as to myself, having been wearied out for many years with offering vain, idle, visionary thoughts, and at length utterly despairing of success, I fortunately fell upon this proposal; which, as it is wholly new, so it hath something solid and real, of no expense and little trouble, full in our own power, and whereby we can incur no danger in disobliging England." (245-49)

What is the main clause? What do "having been wearied" and "utterly despairing of success" modify? What does the long "which" clause modify? Point out all the parallel constructions. This sentence tells us three things: (1) what the speaker did, (2) the conditions under which he did it, and (3) why he considers it worthwhile. In what sequence are these elements placed in Swift's sentence? Why are they in that particular order?

DICTION

16. Look up: *raiment* (31), *fricassee* (71), *glutted* (98), *computed* (102), *repine* (105), *flay* (112), *discoursing* (119), *deference* (126), *expedient* (138), *gibbet* (146), *groat* (148), *idolatrous* (173), *emulation* (199), *absentees* (short for *absentee landlords*) (225), *parsimony* (230), *incur* (249).

17. Explain the etymologies * of these words: *melancholy* (1), *importuning* (4), *alms* (5), *vermin* (157), *digressed* (164), *curate* (173), *overture* (266).

18. What is the difference between *beggars by profession* (263) and *beggars in effect* (265)?

19. As the second footnote makes clear, the word *projector* meant for Swift something very different than it means for us. Similarly, the following words, still in use today, have different meanings than they had in Swift's time; explain the difference: *passenger* (4), *artificially* (112), *vintners* (189), *politicians* (265), *prudent* (189), *receipts* (189). Suggest in each case a modern word that would be the equivalent of what Swift meant.

20. Explain the irony in the following expressions: "so deserving a patriot" (127), "to fatten them would not answer the charge" (130-31), "some scrupu-

lous people might be apt to censure such a practice (although indeed very unjustly) as a little bordering upon cruelty" (133-35), "refinement in taste"
(183), "vain, idle, visionary thoughts" (230), "although perhaps I could name
a country which would be glad to eat up our whole nation without it" (251-53).

21. *Dam* (25) is normally applied to animals, not to human beings. Why does
Swift use it as he does here? Point out other instances of his applying to humans words commonly restricted to animals.

22. One of the tricks Swift uses in "A Modest Proposal" is the inclusion of
little details, seemingly irrelevant, but which have the effect of increasing our
sense of horror. For instance, in arguing that the forequarter of a child will
make a tasty leftover dish, he adds (85-86) "especially in winter." Or in line
117 he suggests that it might be better to buy the children alive and dress
them "hot from the knife." Find several other such horrific details. If you
agree that these do intensify our repulsion, can you explain why they do?

POINTS TO LEARN

1. Often an essayist who uses "I" is creating a persona, a mask through which
he speaks, but which is not identical to him.

2. Moral outrage may be strengthened by being suppressed.

SUGGESTIONS FOR WRITING

1. Taking him at face value compose a character sketch in several paragraphs
of the speaker of "A Modest Proposal."

2. Complete the following topic sentence and then support it in a paragraph
or two by evidence from Swift's text: "The speaker of 'A Modest Proposal'
considers the Irish to be _____."

3. In a paragraph or two answer this criticism of "A Modest Proposal": "The
essay is too revolting to be effective; it exaggerates English policy in so disgusting a manner that it defeats its own purpose."

IMPROVING YOUR STYLE

In your composition include:

1. Two or three sentences using parallelism.

2. A complex * sentence with a main clause and three or four subordinate *
constructions arranged so that their order reflects the actual sequence of events
or the logic of ideas (the arrangement must still be within the patterns
allowed by English grammar).

3. A series of three or four sentences tied together by *First, Second, Third,*
(*Fourth*).

4. Several examples of irony.

In Memoriam: W. J. B.

H. L. Mencken (1880-1956) was many things: reporter, editor, critic, essayist, scholar (his *The American Language*, 1918, remains one of the classics of language history). But he is best remembered as a satirist, a master of invective, who delighted in kicking sacred cows. Here he kicks William Jennings Bryan.

Bryan (1860-1925) was a Democratic politician and orator, a member of The House of Representatives for two terms, three times the unsuccessful Democratic candidate for President, and Secretary of State from 1912 to 1915 under Woodrow Wilson: In his final years he became a crusader for Christian fundamentalism and served as special prosecutor for the state of Tennessee in the 1925 trial of a Dayton, Tennessee, high school English teacher named John T. Scopes. Scopes was accused of teaching Darwinian evolutionary theory in violation of a state law which forbade any account of creation contradicting that of the Bible. Scopes was defended by the famous liberal lawyer Clarence Darrow and, while convicted, was later freed on a technicality. The trial attracted wide attention as a battleground between liberals and reactionaries; its outcome was generally regarded as a victory of at least a moral sort for Darwinism and for intellectual freedom. Bryan, exhausted by his efforts, died in Dayton five days after the trial ended. Mencken reported the events in Dayton for the Baltimore *Evening Sun* from a point of view sympathetic to Scopes and Darrow. His memorial essay to Bryan, while hardly a monument to the spirit of charity, is a classic example of satiric invective.

1   Has it been duly marked by historians that William Jennings Bryan's last secular act on this globe of sin was to catch flies? A curious detail, and not without its sardonic overtones. He was the most sedulous flycatcher in American history, and in many ways the most successful. His quarry, of course, was not *Musca domestica* but *Homo neandertalensis*. 5 For forty years he tracked it with coo and bellow, up and down the rustic

Copyright 1926 by Alfred A. Knopf, Inc. and renewed 1954 by H. L. Mencken. Reprinted from *The Vintage Mencken*, by H. L. Mencken, edited by Alistair Cooke, by permission of Alfred A. Knopf, Inc.

backways of the Republic. Wherever the flambeaux of Chautauqua[1] smoked and guttered, and the bilge of idealism ran in the veins, and Baptist pastors dammed the brooks with the sanctified, and men gathered who were weary and heavy laden, and their wives who were full of Peruna[2] and as fecund as the shad (*Alosa sapidissima*), there the indefatigable Jennings set up his traps and spread his bait. He knew every country town in the South and West, and he could crowd the most remote of them to suffocation by simply winding his horn. The city proletariat, transiently flustered by him in 1896, quickly penetrated his buncombe and would have no more of him; the cockney gallery jeered him at every Democratic national convention for twenty-five years. But out where the grass grows high, and the horned cattle dream away the lazy afternoons, and men still fear the powers and principalities of the air—out there between the corn-rows he held his old puissance to the end. There was no need of beaters to drive in his game. The news that he was coming was enough. For miles the flivver dust would choke the roads. And when he rose at the end of the day to discharge his Message there would be such breathless attention, such a rapt and enchanted ecstasy, such a sweet rustle of amens as the world had not known since Johann fell to Herod's ax.

2   There was something peculiarly fitting in the fact that his last days were spent in a one-horse Tennessee village, beating off the flies and gnats, and that death found him there. The man felt at home in such simple and Christian scenes. He liked people who sweated freely, and were not debauched by the refinements of the toilet. Making his progress up and down the Main street of little Dayton, surrounded by gaping primates from the upland valleys of the Cumberland Range, his coat laid aside, his bare arms and hairy chest shining damply, his bald head sprinkled with dust—so accoutred and on display, he was obviously happy. He liked getting up early in the morning, to the tune of cocks crowing on the dunghill. He liked the heavy, greasy victuals of the farmhouse kitchen. He liked country lawyers, country pastors, all country people. He liked country sounds and country smells.

3   I believe that this liking was sincere—perhaps the only sincere thing in the man. His nose showed no uneasiness when a hillman in faded over-

---

[1] A kind of adult education program, named for Chautauqua, New York, where it began in 1874 as a Methodist Episcopal camp-meeting offering lectures in the sciences and humanities. For about fifty years numerous traveling Chautauquas brought enlightenment of a sort to all sections of the country. [Editors' note]

[2] A patent medicine famous as a tonic; Mencken is punning on the old expression "full of prunes." [Editors' note]

alls and hickory shirt accosted him on the street, and besought him for light upon some mystery of Holy Writ. The simian gabble of the crossroads was not gabble to him, but wisdom of an occult and superior sort. In the presence of city folks he was palpably uneasy. Their clothes, I suspect, annoyed him, and he was suspicious of their too delicate manners. He knew   45 all the while that they were laughing at him—if not at his baroque theology, then at least at his alpaca pantaloons. But the yokels never laughed at him. To them he was not the huntsman but the prophet, and toward the end, as he gradually forsook mundane politics for more ghostly concerns, they began to elevate him in their hierarchy. When he died he was the peer   50 of Abraham. His old enemy, Wilson, aspiring to the same white and shining robe, came down with a thump. But Bryan made the grade. His place in Tennessee hagiography is secure. If the village barber saved any of his hair, then it is curing gall-stones down there today.

4   But what label will he bear in more urbane regions? One, I fear,   55 of a far less flattering kind. Bryan lived too long, and descended too deeply into the mud, to be taken seriously hereafter by fully literate men, even of the kind who write schoolbooks. There was a scattering of sweet words in his funeral notices, but it was no more than a response to conventional sentimentality. The best verdict the most romantic editorial writer could   60 dredge up, save in the humorless South, was to the general effect that his imbecilities were excused by his earnestness—that under his clowning, as under that of the juggler of Notre Dame, there was the zeal of a steadfast soul. But this was apology, not praise; precisely the same thing might be said of Mary Baker G. Eddy.[3] The truth is that even Bryan's sincerity will   65 probably yield to what is called, in other fields, definitive criticism. Was he sincere when he opposed imperialism in the Philippines, or when he fed it with deserving Democrats in Santo Domingo? Was he sincere when he tried to shove the Prohibitionists under the table, or when he seized their banner and began to lead them with loud whoops? Was he sincere when   70 he bellowed against war, or when he dreamed of himself as a tin-soldier in uniform, with a grave reserved at Arlington among the generals? Was he sincere when he fawned over Champ Clark, or when he betrayed Clark?[4]

[3] Founder of the Christian Science Movement. [Editors' note]
[4] At the Democratic Convention of 1912 Bryan deserted Champ Clark, Speaker of The House of Representatives and presidential favorite. Throwing his support to Woodrow Wilson, Bryan was rewarded by being appointed Secretary of State when Wilson was elected President. [Editors' note]

Was he sincere when he pleaded for tolerance in New York, or when he
bawled for the faggot and the stake in Tennessee?   75
5   This talk of sincerity, I confess, fatigues me. If the fellow was sincere, then so was P. T. Barnum. The word is disgraced and degraded by
such uses. He was, in fact, a charlatan, a mountebank, a zany without sense
or dignity. His career brought him into contact with the first men of his
time; he preferred the company of rustic ignoramuses. It was hard to be- 80
lieve, watching him at Dayton, that he had traveled, that he had been received in civilized societies, that he had been a high officer of state. He
seemed only a poor clod like those around him, deluded by a childish
theology, full of an almost pathological hatred of all learning, all human
dignity, all beauty, all fine and noble things. He was a peasant come home 85
to the barnyard. Imagine a gentleman, and you have imagined everything
that he was not. What animated him from end to end of his grotesque
career was simply ambition—the ambition of a common man to get his
hand upon the collar of his superiors, or, failing that, to get his thumb into
their eyes. He was born with a roaring voice, and it had the trick of in- 90
flaming half-wits. His whole career was devoted to raising those half-wits
against their betters, that he himself might shine.
6   His last battle will be grossly misunderstood if it is thought of as a
mere exercise in fanaticism—that is, if Bryan the Fundamentalist Pope is
mistaken for one of the bucolic Fundamentalists. There was much more in 95
it than that, as everyone knows who saw him on the field. What moved
him, at bottom, was simply hatred of the city men who had laughed at him
so long, and brought him at last to so tatterdemalion an estate. He lusted
for revenge upon them. He yearned to lead the anthropoid rabble against
them, to punish them for their execution upon him by attacking the very 100
vitals of their civilization. He went far beyond the bounds of any merely
religious frenzy, however inordinate. When he began denouncing the notion that man is a mammal even some of the hinds at Dayton were agape.
And when, brought upon Clarence Darrow's cruel hook, he writhed and
tossed in a very fury of malignancy, bawling against the veriest elements of 105
sense and decency like a man frantic—when he came to that tragic climax
of his striving there were snickers among the hinds as well as hosannas.
7   Upon that hook, in truth, Bryan committed suicide, as a legend as
well as in the body. He staggered from the rustic court ready to die, and
he staggered from it ready to be forgotten, save as a character in a third- 110
rate farce, witless and in poor taste. It was plain to everyone who knew him,

when he came to Dayton, that his great days were behind him—that, for all the fury of his hatred, he was now definitely an old man, and headed at last for silence. There was a vague, unpleasant manginess about his appearance; he somehow seemed dirty, though a close glance showed him as carefully shaven as an actor, and clad in immaculate linen. All the hair was gone from the dome of his head, and it had begun to fall out, too, behind his ears, in the obscene manner of Samuel Gompers.[5] The resonance had departed from his voice; what was once a bugle blast had become reedy and quavering. Who knows that, like Demosthenes, he had a lisp? In the old days, under the magic of his eloquence, no one noticed it. But when he spoke at Dayton it was always audible.

8   When I first encountered him, on the sidewalk in front of the office of the rustic lawyers who were his associates in the Scopes case, the trial was yet to begin, and so he was still expansive and amiable. I had printed in the *Nation*, a week or so before, an article arguing that the Tennessee anti-evolution law, whatever its wisdom, was at least constitutional—that the yahoos of the State had a clear right to have their progeny taught whatever they chose, and kept secure from whatever knowledge violated their superstitions. The old boy professed to be delighted with the argument, and gave the gaping bystanders to understand that I was a publicist of parts. Not to be outdone, I admired the preposterous country shirt that he wore—sleeveless and with the neck cut very low. We parted in the manner of two ambassadors.

9   But that was the last touch of amiability that I was destined to see in Bryan. The next day the battle joined and his face became hard. By the end of the week he was simply a walking fever. Hour by hour he grew more bitter. What the Christian Scientists call malicious animal magnetism seemed to radiate from him like heat from a stove. From my place in the courtroom, standing upon a table, I looked directly down upon him, sweating horribly and pumping his palm-leaf fan. His eyes fascinated me; I watched them all day long. They were blazing points of hatred. They glittered like occult and sinister gems. Now and then they wandered to me, and I got my share, for my reports of the trial had come back to Dayton, and he had read them. It was like coming under fire.

10   Thus he fought his last fight, thirsting savagely for blood. All sense departed from him. He bit right and left, like a dog with rabies. He descended to demagogy so dreadful that his very associates at the trial table

[5] Samuel Gompers (1850-1924), a labor leader, one of the founders and first president of The American Federation of Labor. [Editors' note]

blushed. His one yearning was to keep his yokels heated up—to lead his forlorn mob of imbeciles against the foe. That foe, alas, refused to be 150 alarmed. It insisted upon seeing the whole battle as a comedy. Even Darrow, who knew better, occasionally yielded to the prevailing spirit. One day he lured poor Bryan into the folly I have mentioned: his astounding argument against the notion that man is a mammal. I am glad I heard it, for otherwise I'd never believe it. There stood the man who had been thrice a 155 candidate for the Presidency of the Republic—there he stood in the glare of the world, uttering stuff that a boy of eight would laugh at. The artful Darrow led him on: he repeated it, ranted for it, bellowed it in his cracked voice. So he was prepared for the final slaughter. He came into life a hero, a Galahad, in bright and shining armor. He was passing out a poor 160 mountebank.

QUESTIONS

READER AND PURPOSE

1. How might the title of this essay mislead a reader who knew nothing about H. L. Mencken or William Jennings Bryan? What are the conventions that usually govern an "in memoriam" for a dead public figure? Is the title really misleading, or is the essay genuinely a "memorial"?

2. Mencken's satire includes more than Bryan. What else is he attacking?

3. Do you think Mencken was writing for a highly sophisticated, literate audience, or for more general, less "hip" readers? For urbanites or for small-town Americans? How would you describe his tone *, especially his attitude toward Bryan?

ORGANIZATION

4. Does the rhetorical question * work as a way of opening the essay? What does Mencken mean by his remark that Bryan's final action on earth has "sardonic overtones"?

5. Mencken achieves considerable unity in his paragraphs by ringing variations on key ideas. What later terms in paragraph 1 echo the words "catch flies" (or are suggested by association with that phrase)? Which repeat "rustic backways"? Point out echoes of these expressions in later paragraphs.

6. Paragraph 2 consists of seven sentences. The first states the topic. How does the second support that topic? How does Mencken unify the remainder of the paragraph?

7. What words link the third paragraph to the second? Does paragraph 3 introduce a new idea or merely refine the topic of paragraph 2?

8. What change in thought occurs in paragraph 4? Identify the topic statement of this paragraph. In the second and third sentences Mencken answers the rhetorical question he poses in line 55. In what sense are his next two statements (58-64) a qualification * upon the answer? Where does Mencken disarm the qualification and reassert his own conclusion? How, finally, do the series of rhetorical questions support the conclusion?

9. How is paragraph 5 linked to 4? Paragraph 6 to 5? Paragraph 7 to 6?

SENTENCES

10. Something of the vitality of Mencken's prose derives from his skill in varying sentence structure. The final portion of paragraph 1 (from lines 17 to 25) offers an example. The first sentence ("But out where the grass grows high . . .") is long and leisurely, reflecting the bucolic life it ironically describes. Point out the parallel * constructions in this sentence. How does the style change in the next three sentences? Does the last sentence of the paragraph continue the pattern of the preceding three, or is it more like the one with which this passage begins? Might it be said that the very pattern and movement of these five sentences suggest Bryan's effect upon a rural community? Explain.

11. Find one or two other places where Mencken varies long and short sentences with similar skill.

DICTION

12. Look up: secular (2), sedulous (3), fecund (11), debauched (29), accoutred (34), palpably (44), alpaca (47), hierarchy (50), tatterdemalion (98), frenzy (102), inordinate (102), manginess (114), progeny (128).

13. What are the etymologies * of flambeaux (7), buncombe (often shortened to bunk) (15), occult (43), grotesque (87), bucolic (95), demagogy (148)?

14. As fully as you can explain what Mencken conveys by the following phrases: bilge of idealism (8), winding his horn (14), city proletariat (14), powers and principalities of the air (18-19), baroque theology (46), mundane politics (49), Tennessee hagiography (53), faggot and stake (75), pathological hatred (84), bucolic Fundamentalists (95).

15. What irony * is concealed in these expressions: sweet rustle of amens (24) and debauched by the refinements of the toilet (29-30)?

16. Here are some of the nouns Mencken applies to Bryan: charlatan (78), zany (78), clod (83), peasant (85), the Fundamentalist Pope (94), a dog with rabies (147). What range of faults and follies is implied by those words?

17. Mencken also effectively characterizes Bryan's speech and actions: coo and bellow (6), writhe (104), and bawling (105) are examples. Find other words which throw a satiric light upon Bryan in speech and action, and be able to comment upon what they imply.

18. Similarly Mencken uses invective to mock Bryan's natural constituency, the *yahoos*, as he calls them in line 128. What is a yahoo? Where did the word originate? List other insulting expressions the writer applies to the country people who idolized Bryan.

19. Why are these alternates poorer than Mencken's words for his particular purpose? *Blazed and shone* for *smoked and guttered* (8), *fence* for *dunghill* (35), *poorly cooked* for *heavy, greasy* (36), *trousers* for *pantaloons* (47), *especially* for *even* (57), *shone* for *glittered* (142), *clever* for *artful* (157).

20. Who is *Galahad* (160)? Is Mencken applying the allusion ironically or seriously? What is a *mountebank* (161)? The two words sum up Mencken's estimate of Bryan. Would his closing have been better arranged like this: "He was passing out a poor mountebank who had begun life a hero, a Galahad, in shining armor"?

POINTS TO LEARN

1. Invective is the simplest, most direct form of satire. It is a pick-handle where irony is a rapier. Its effectiveness depends upon the variety and the originality of the insults of which it consists.

2. Long sentences need short ones. Variety is vital to a good sentence style.

SUGGESTIONS FOR WRITING

1. Mencken does not explain exactly why he despises William Jennings Bryan and the kind of people who support him. Still, it is possible to deduce his reasons. Write a short essay of two or three paragraphs explaining the grounds of Mencken's contempt and support your account with citations from Mencken's prose.

2. How would you answer the complaint that satire of this sort is unfair because it is exaggerated and one-sided?

3. A more ambitious project: consult a biography of William Jennings Bryan or a scholarly history of his times which discusses him in detail and then argue whether Mencken's account (even after we have discounted the exaggeration allowed a satirist) is fair.

4. Picking a target that engages your imagination, attempt a paragraph of invective satire. Keep it clean and avoid the clichés of name-calling. Invective works to the degree that the insults are witty and reveal genuine follies and faults.

IMPROVING YOUR STYLE

1. Whatever topic you choose work for a mix in sentence style—longer, more complicated sentences varied by shorter more direct ones.

2. Use several examples of irony.

3. Use four or five verbs which graphically express in terms of physical action how you feel about your subject.

4. Think of an allusion *, literary or historical, which, like Mencken's reference to Galahad, conveys a complex set of ideas and attitudes.

The Funeral Oration of Pericles

In 431 B.C. the Peloponnesian War broke out between Athens, along with her allies, and a rival league of Greek city-states led by Sparta. The war dragged on until 404 B.C., when it ended disastrously for Athens. At the close of the first year's campaigning, however, Athenian hopes were high, and the city's pride and faith are reflected in the famous oration of Pericles, a great war leader and statesman. He spoke at the funeral for the Athenians killed in that first year of the war, who were being buried at public expense, then as now a customary honor for soldiers killed fighting for the state. The occasion was recorded by Thucydides, himself a general on the Athenian side, who, after being dismissed from command, wrote an unfinished history of the war, one of the great works of ancient historiography.

Pericles's speech is a fine example of ancient oratory, an art carefully studied by ambitious Athenians in schools of rhetoric. More specifically this oration is of a type known as epideictic—speeches delivered on public ceremonial occasions, as distinguished from those given in courts of law (forensic oratory) and political assemblies (deliberative oratory). The epideictic oration depended upon eloquence more than logic. It persuaded by appealing to the ideals and aspirations of its audience.

While we no longer use the terms of Greek rhetoric to describe and classify the various modes and techniques of speaking, the value of eloquence is still real. A great political leader—a Lincoln, a Churchill, a Franklin Roosevelt—is marked by the capacity to lift our vision above the concerns of daily life, to inspire us to be better than we are. This can be done only by language, eloquent language that rings in our ears long after its moment has passed, memorable because it expresses in finely tuned words what men and women can be. Words like these:

> With malice toward none; with charity for all; with firmness in the right as God gives us to see the right, let us strive to finish the work we are in. . . .

From Thucydides, *The History of the Peloponnesian War*, edited in translation by Sir R. W. Livingstone. Reprinted by permission of Oxford University Press, Inc.

298

Let us therefore brace ourselves to our duties, and so bear ourselves that, if the British Empire and its Commonwealth last for a thousand years, men will still say: "This was their finest hour."

The only thing we have to fear is fear itself.

Eloquence involves more than noble sentiments. It requires a mastery of language—the ability to select the precise word and to control the structure and rhythm of sentences. Eloquence is noble feeling focused and intensified by words.

1   Most of those who have stood in this place before me have commended the institution of this closing address. It is good, they have felt, that solemn words should be spoken over our fallen soldiers. I do not share this feeling. Acts deserve acts, not words, in their honor, and to me a burial at the State's charges, such as you see before you, would have appeared suf- 5 ficient. Our sense of the deserts of a number of our fellow-citizens should not depend upon the felicity of one man's speech. Moreover, it is very hard for a speaker to be appropriate when many of his hearers will scarce believe that he is truthful. For those who have known and loved the dead may think his words scant justice to the memories they would hear honored: 10 while those who do not know will occasionally, from jealousy, suspect me of overstatement when they hear of any feat beyond their own powers. For it is only human for men not to bear praise of others beyond the point at which they still feel that they can rival their exploits. Transgress that boundary and they are jealous and distrustful. But since the wisdom of our 15 ancestors enacted this law I too must submit and try to suit as best I can the wishes and feelings of every member of this gathering.

2   My first words shall be for our ancestors; for it is both just to them and seemly that on an occasion such as this our tribute of memory should be paid them. For, dwelling always in this country, generation after gener- 20 ation in unchanging and unbroken succession, they have handed it down to us free by their exertions. So they are worthy of our praises; and still more so are our fathers. For they enlarged the ancestral patrimony by the Empire which we hold to-day and delivered it, not without labor, into the hands of our own generation; while it is we ourselves, those of us who are 25 now in middle life, who consolidated our power throughout the greater part of the Empire and secured the city's complete independence both in war and peace. Of the battles which we and our fathers fought, whether in the winning of our power abroad or in bravely withstanding the warfare

of foreigner or Greek at home, I do not wish to say more: they are too fa- 30
miliar to you all. I wish rather to set forth the spirit in which we faced
them, and the constitution and manners with which we rose to greatness,
and to pass from them to the dead; for I think it not unfitting that these
things should be called to mind in to-day's solemnity, and expedient too
that the whole gathering of citizens and strangers should listen to them. 35
3   For our government is not copied from those of our neighbors: we
are an example to them rather than they to us. Our constitution is named
a democracy, because it is in the hands not of the few but of the many.
But our laws secure equal justice for all in their private disputes, and our
public opinion welcomes and honors talent in every branch of achievement, 40
not for any sectional reason but on grounds of excellence alone. And as we
give free play to all in our public life, so we carry the same spirit into our
daily relations with one another. We have no black looks or angry words
for our neighbor if he enjoys himself in his own way, and we abstain from
the little acts of churlishness which, though they leave no mark, yet cause 45
annoyance to who so notes them. Open and friendly in our private intercourse, in our public acts we keep strictly within the control of law. We
acknowledge the restraint of reverence; we are obedient to whomsoever is
set in authority, and to the laws, more especially to those which offer protection to the oppressed and those unwritten ordinances whose transgres- 50
sion brings admitted shame.
4   Yet ours is no work-a-day city only. No other provides so many
recreations for the spirit—contests and sacrifices all the year round, and
beauty in our public buildings to cheer the heart and delight the eye day
by day. Moreover, the city is so large and powerful that all the wealth of 55
all the world flows in to her, so that our own Attic products seem no more
homelike to us than the fruits of the labors of other nations.
5   Our military training too is different from our opponents'. The
gates of our city are flung open to the world. We practice no periodical de-
portations, nor do we prevent our visitors from observing or discovering 60
what an enemy might usefully apply to his own purposes. For our trust is
not in the devices of material equipment, but in our own good spirits for
battle.
6   So too with education. They toil from early boyhood in a laborious
pursuit after courage, while we, free to live and wander as we please, march 65
out none the less to face the self-same dangers. Here is the proof of my
words. When the Spartans advance into our country, they do not come
alone but with all their allies; but when we invade our neighbors we have

little difficulty as a rule, even on foreign soil, in defeating men who are
fighting for their own homes. Moreover, no enemy has ever met us in full   70
strength, for we have our navy to attend to, and our soldiers are sent on
service to many scattered possessions; but if they chance to encounter some
portion of our forces and defeat a few of us, they boast that they have
driven back our whole army, or, if they are defeated, that the victors were
in full strength. Indeed, if we choose to face danger with an easy mind   75
rather than after a rigorous training, and to trust rather in native manliness
than in state-made courage, the advantage lies with us; for we are spared all
the weariness of practicing for future hardships, and when we find ourselves amongst them we are as brave as our plodding rivals. Here as elsewhere, then, the city sets an example which is deserving of admiration.   80

7   We are lovers of beauty without extravagance, and lovers of wisdom
without unmanliness. Wealth to us is not mere material for vainglory but
an opportunity for achievement; and poverty we think it no disgrace to acknowledge but a real degradation to make no effort to overcome. Our citizens attend both to public and private duties, and do not allow absorption   85
in their own various affairs to interfere with their knowledge of the city's.
We differ from other states in regarding the man who holds aloof from
public life not as "quiet" but as useless; we decide or debate, carefully and
in person, all matters of policy, holding, not that words and deeds go ill together, but that acts are foredoomed to failure when undertaken undis-   90
cussed. For we are noted for being at once most adventurous in action and
most reflective beforehand. Other men are bold in ignorance, while reflection will stop their onset. But the bravest are surely those who have the
clearest vision of what is before them, glory and danger alike, and yet notwithstanding go out to meet it. In doing good, too, we are the exact op-   95
posite of the rest of mankind. We secure our friends not by accepting
favors but by doing them. And so we are naturally more firm in our attach-
ments: for we are anxious, as creditors, to cement by kind offices our relation towards our friends. If they do not respond with the same warmness it
is because they feel that their services will not be given spontaneously but   100
only as the repayment of a debt. We are alone among mankind in doing
men benefits, not on calculations of self-interest, but in the fearless confidence of freedom.

8   In a word I claim that our city as a whole is an education to
Greece, and that her members yield to none, man by man, for independ-   105
ence of spirit, many-sidedness of attainment, and complete self-reliance in
limbs and brain.

9   That this is no vainglorious phrase but actual fact the supremacy
which our manners have won us itself bears testimony. No other city of the
present day goes out to her ordeal greater than ever men dreamed; no other   110
is so powerful that the invader feels no bitterness when he suffers at her
hands, and her subjects no shame at the indignity of their dependence.
Great indeed are the symbols and witnesses of our supremacy, at which pos-
terity, as all mankind to-day, will be astonished. We need no Homer or
other man of words to praise us, for such give pleasure for a moment, but   115
the truth will put to shame their imaginings of our deeds. For our pioneers
have forced a way into every sea and every land, establishing among all
mankind, in punishment or beneficence, eternal memorials of their
settlement.

10   Such then is the city for whom, lest they should lose her, the men   120
whom we celebrate died a soldier's death: and it is but natural that all of
us, who survive them, should wish to spend ourselves in her service. That,
indeed, is why I have spent many words upon the city. I wished to show
that we have more at stake than men who have no such inheritance, and
to support my praise of the dead by making clear to you what they have   125
done. For if I have chanted the glories of the city it was these men and
their like who set hand to array her. With them, as with few among
Greeks, words cannot magnify the deeds that they have done. Such an end
as we have here seems indeed to show us what a good life is, from its first
signs of power to its final consummation. For even where life's previous   130
record showed faults and failures it is just to weigh the last brave hour of
devotion against them all. There they wiped out evil with good and did
the city more service as soldiers than they did her harm in private life.
There no hearts grew faint because they loved riches more than honor;
none shirked the issue in the poor man's dreams of wealth. All these they   135
put aside to strike a blow for the city. Counting the quest to avenge her
honor as the most glorious of all ventures, and leaving Hope, the uncertain
goddess, to send them what she would, they faced the foe as they drew near
him in the strength of their own manhood; and when the shock of battle
came, they chose rather to suffer the uttermost than to win life by weak-   140
ness. So their memory has escaped the reproaches of men's lips, but they
bore instead on their bodies the marks of men's hands, and in a moment of
time, at the climax of their lives, were rapt away from a world filled, for
their dying eyes, not with terror but with glory.

11   Such were the men who lie here and such the city that inspired   145
them. We survivors may pray to be spared their bitter hour, but must dis-

dain to meet the foe with a spirit less triumphant. Fix your eyes on the greatness of Athens as you have it before you day by day, fall in love with her, and when you feel her great, remember that this greatness was won by men with courage, with knowledge of their duty, and with a sense of honor in action, who, if they failed in any ordeal, disdained to deprive the city of their services, but sacrificed their lives as the best offerings on her behalf. So they gave their bodies to the commonwealth and received, each for his own memory, praise that will never die, and with it the grandest of all sepulchres, not that in which their mortal bones are laid, but a home in the minds of men, where their glory remains fresh to stir to speech or action as the occasion comes by. For the whole earth is the sepulchre of famous men; and their story is not graven only on stone over their native earth, but lives on far away, without visible symbol, woven into the stuff of other men's lives. For you now it remains to rival what they have done and, knowing the secret of happiness to be freedom and the secret of freedom a brave heart, not idly to stand aside from the enemy's onset. For it is not the poor and luckless, as having no hope of prosperity, who have most cause to reckon death as little loss, but those for whom fortune may yet keep reversal in store and who would feel the change most if trouble befell them. Moreover, weakly to decline the trial is more painful to a man of spirit than death coming sudden and unperceived in the hour of strength and enthusiasm.

12   Therefore I do not mourn with the parents of the dead who are here with us. I will rather comfort them. For they know that they have been born into a world of manifold chances and that he is to be accounted happy to whom the best lot falls—the best sorrow, such as is yours today, or the best death, such as fell to these, for whom life and happiness were cut to the self-same measure. I know it is not easy to give you comfort. I know how often in the joy of others you will have reminders of what was once your own, and how men feel sorrow, not for the loss of what they have never tasted, but when something that has grown dear to them has been snatched away. But you must keep a brave heart in the hope of other children, those who are still of age to bear them. For the newcomers will help you to forget the gap in your own circle, and will help the city to fill up the ranks of its workers and its soldiers. For no man is fitted to give fair and honest advice in council if he has not, like his fellows, a family at stake in the hour of the city's danger. To you who are past the age of vigor I would say: count the long years of happiness so much to set off against the brief

space that yet remains, and let your burden be lightened by the glory of the 185
dead. For the love of honor alone is not staled by age, and it is by honor,
not, as some say, by gold, that the helpless end of life is cheered.

13   I turn to those amongst you who are children or brothers of the
fallen, for whom I foresee a mighty contest with the memory of the dead.
Their praise is in all men's mouths, and hardly, even for supremest heroism, 190
you will be adjudged to have achieved, not the same but a little less than
they. For the living have the jealousy of rivals to contend with, but the dead
are honored with unchallenged admiration.

14   If I must also speak a word to those who are now in widowhood on
the powers and duties of women, I will cast all my advice into one brief 195
sentence. Great will be your glory if you do not lower the nature that is
within you—hers greatest of all whose praise or blame is least bruited on
the lips of men.

15   I have spoken such words as I had to say according as the law pre-
scribes, and the graveside offerings to the dead have been duly made. Hence- 200
forward the city will take charge of their children till manhood: such is the
crown and benefit she holds out to the dead and to their kin for the trials
they have undergone for her. For where the prize is highest, there, too, are
the best citizens to contend for it.

16   And now, when you have finished your lamentation, let each of you 205
depart.

QUESTIONS

READER AND PURPOSE

1. Certainly Pericles' primary aim is to praise the dead. But remembering the
occasion, do you detect any other purpose in his words? Might his oration be
described as persuasive as well as laudatory?

2. In paragraph 14 he addresses the widows of the dead soldiers, urging that
they do not lower "the nature that is within" them and that they bear their
grief in dignified silence, for the greatest credit belongs to those "whose praise
or blame is least bruited on the lips of men." The passage reveals the attitude
Pericles assumes toward his fellow-citizens. Describe that attitude.

ORGANIZATION

3. Pericles arrests his audience's attention by surprising them at the very beginning of his speech. How? What reason does he offer in paragraph 1 to support his surprising position?

4. How does the opening paragraph serve to establish an appropriate relationship between the speaker and his audience?

5. The organization of Pericles' speech reveals the close communion of spirit the ancient Greeks felt to exist between the state and the individual. The state, moreover, was conceived as extending through time, encompassing the past and the future as well as the present. Accordingly, with what subject does Pericles begin his oration proper?

6. Paragraphs 3 through 9 make up a section. What is Pericles doing here? Give a brief descriptive title to this part of the oration. Give one- or two-word titles to paragraphs 3, 4, 5, 6, and 7, and show how each of these paragraphs is linked to what precedes it.

7. To whom is Pericles contrasting the Athenians in paragraphs 5 and 6?

8. How might one answer the objection that in this portion of his oration Pericles appears to have forgotten the dead he was supposed to praise?

9. Why may we regard paragraphs 10 and 11 as making up the second major section of the speech?

10. The third section begins in paragraph 12. What has the speaker turned to here? Where does this section end?

11. Which paragraphs compose the conclusion? Does Pericles manage a skillful ending, neatly rounding off his oration? Or is his closing too abrupt, letting things down with a bump? Might it be said that, below its matter-of-fact surface, his final sentence implies a profound moral truth?

SENTENCES

12. Pericles is fond of the balanced sentence *, which divides into two roughly equal parts, as in: "For our government is not copied from those of our neighbors: we are an example to them rather than they to us" (36-37). Point out five or six other such sentences.

13. This type of structure permits the emphasis of similar, and the antithesis * of contrasting, ideas. Study the following sentences and decide what contrasts or similarities are made prominent by the sentence structure:

   (a) "For our trust is not in the devices of material equipment, but in our own good spirits for battle." (61-63)

   (b) "We are lovers of beauty without extravagance, and lovers of wisdom without unmanliness." (81-82)

   (c) "Wealth to us is not mere material for vainglory but an opportunity for achievement; and poverty we think it no disgrace to acknowledge but a real degradation to make no effort to overcome." (82-84)

14. Look again at the sentence in lines 36-37 and identify the chiasmus * in the second clause.

DICTION

15. Look up: *felicity* (7), *transgress* (14), *patrimony* (23), *consolidated* (26), *churlishness* (45), *vainglory* (82), *array* (127), *rapt* (143), *sepulchres* (155), *vigor* (183), *bruited* (197).

16. Pericles is careful to establish the logical flow of his thought. Identify in paragraph 1 those connectives * which signal the structure of his ideas.

17. Does Pericles play upon the emotions of his audience, using words which are likely to intensify their grief? Or does his diction have an emotionally dampening effect?

18. Which of his words are especially chosen to appeal to a high sense of duty? What does Pericles imply is the proper manner for Athenians to deal with the facts before them—the bones of their dead, fallen in battle?

POINTS TO LEARN

Eloquence appeals to our nobler sentiments, seeking to move us from narrow self-interest to the contemplation of wider, less egocentric values.

SUGGESTIONS FOR WRITING

1. Write a paragraph or two describing the Athenian conception of the ideal citizen.

2. How do you think a modern audience would respond to Pericles' speech? Develop your conclusions in one or two paragraphs.

IMPROVING YOUR STYLE

In your composition attempt:

1. Four or five balanced sentences in which you place key terms in the same positions in the two parts of the sentence so as to emphasize their similarity or difference.

2. An example of chiasmus.

On Receiving the Nobel Prize

William Faulkner (1897-1962) was one of the best American novelists of the twentieth century. Born and educated in Mississippi, he wrote primarily about his native region. In 1949 he was awarded the Nobel Prize for literature. This selection is the speech he delivered on that occasion. Like the oration of Pericles in the preceding selection, this is also a fine example of eloquence. It is less formally constructed, less rhetorical in the technical sense of that term. But Faulkner's speech passes the test of true eloquence: a high-minded sense of human destiny expressed in moving and memorable language.

1   I feel that this award was not made to me as a man but to my work— a life's work in the agony and sweat of the human spirit, not for glory and least of all for profit, but to create out of the materials of the human spirit something which did not exist there before. So this award is only mine in trust. It will not be difficult to find a dedication for the money part of it 5 commensurate with the purpose and significance of its origin. But I would like to do the same with the acclaim, too, by using this moment as a pinnacle from which I might be listened to by the young men and women already dedicated to the same anguish and travail, among whom is already that one who will some day stand here where I am standing.   10

2   Our tragedy today is a general and a universal physical fear so long sustained by now that we can even bear it. There are no longer problems of the spirit. There is only the question: When will I be blown up? Because of this, the young man or woman writing today has forgotten the problems of the human heart in conflict with itself which alone can make good writ- 15 ing because only that is worth writing about, worth the agony and the sweat.

3   He must learn them again. He must teach himself that the basest of all things is to be afraid; and, teaching himself that, forget it forever,

From *The Faulkner Reader*. Copyright 1954 by William Faulkner. Reprinted by permission of Random House, Inc.

leaving no room in his workshop for anything but the old verities and truths   20
of the heart, the old universal truths lacking which any story is ephemeral
and doomed—love and honor and pity and pride and compassion and sacrifice. Until he does so he labors under a curse. He writes not of love, but of
lust, of defeats in which nobody loses anything of value, of victories without hope and worst of all without pity or compassion. His griefs grieve on   25
no universal bones, leaving no scars. He writes not of the heart but of the
glands.

4   Until he relearns these things he will write as though he stood
among and watched the end of man. I decline to accept the end of man. It
is easy enough to say that man is immortal simply because he will endure;   30
that when the last ding-dong of doom has clanged and faded from the last
worthless rock hanging tideless in the last red and dying evening, that even
then there will still be one more sound: that of his puny inexhaustible voice
still talking. I refuse to accept this. I believe that man will not merely endure: he will prevail. He is immortal, not because he alone among creatures   35
has an inexhaustible voice, but because he has a soul, a spirit capable of
compassion and sacrifice and endurance. The poet's, the writer's, duty is to
write about these things. It is his privilege to help man endure by lifting his
heart, by reminding him of the courage and honor and hope and pride and
compassion and pity and sacrifice which have been the glory of his past.   40
The poet's voice need not merely be the record of man, it can be one of
the props, the pillars to help him endure and prevail.

QUESTIONS

READER AND PURPOSE

1. Faulkner clearly defines his purpose in the first paragraph. In which sentence?
2. To whom does he imagine himself to be talking? Of what does he wish to
persuade these listeners?

ORGANIZATION

3. If the first paragraph establishes the writer's intention, how does the second
fit into his strategy? What does it contribute to his thesis? Give it a brief descriptive title.
4. What words tie the beginning of the third paragraph to the second? How
are the topics of these two paragraphs related?
5. Make a conceptual analysis of paragraph 3, showing how the writer's thought
progresses from sentence to sentence. Explain why the passage beginning in

line 23 ("Until he does so he labors under a curse") marks a major turn of thought within the paragraph. How does Faulkner use sentence structure to unify paragraph 3?

6. What words connect the fourth paragraph to the third? Which sentence marks a major turn in this paragraph?

7. Compare the following revisions with Faulkner's sentences and comment upon the differences in meaning, emphasis, or rhythm:

   (a) *Revision:* The only question is when I'll be blown up.
       Faulkner: "There is only the question: When will I be blown up?" (13)
   (b) *Revision:* He will write as though he stood among and watched the end of man until he relearns these things.
       Faulkner: "Until he relearns these things he will write as though he stood among and watched the end of man." (28-29)
   (c) *Revision:* I believe that man will prevail and not merely endure.
       Faulkner: "I believe that man will not merely endure: he will prevail." (34-35)

8. Point out one or two places where Faulkner employs short sentences very effectively.

9. In the sentence in lines 18-23 to what are "love and honor and pity and pride and compassion and sacrifice" in apposition *? Suppose a comma rather than a dash had preceded these words—would the clarity of the sentence have been helped or hindered?

10. In that list Faulkner joins all the items with *ands* instead of following the more commonplace formula: "love, honor, pity, pride, compassion, and sacrifice." Where else does he handle a list or series with multiple conjunctions * (a technique called polysyndeton *)? Can you see any reason why he does it this way?

11. Look up: *acclaim* (7), *anguish* (9), *travail* (9), *basest* (18), *prevail* (42).

12. Explain the etymologies * of *commensurate* (6), *verities* (20), *ephemeral* (21), *doom* (31), *endurance* (37).

13. Several times Faulkner couples *compassion* and *pity*. What is the difference?

14. Would it be an improvement in lines 25-26 to write something like "his griefs sadden no universal bones," avoiding the repetition of "griefs grieve"? What, incidentally, does Faulkner mean by "universal bones"?

15. In line 31 Faulkner uses the striking phrase "the last ding-dong of doom." *Ding-dong* and *doom* arouse quite different associations in one's mind. Explain.

Do you think this clash of associations makes the image awkward and ineffective? Why in this same passage does Faulkner specify the rock as being "tideless"?

16. Identify the alliteration * in the final sentence. What values does it have? Where else does Faulkner employ alliteration?

POINTS TO LEARN
1. Faulkner's speech is a notable testament to the human spirit. This faith in man is the foundation of all eloquence.
2. Like all effective persuasion, eloquence requires a clear sense of purpose and a strategy efficacious in achieving that purpose.

SUGGESTIONS FOR WRITING
Write a paragraph or two describing your reaction to Faulkner's words. Did they move you or not? Do you agree with what he says about man and about the moral responsibilities of the writer? Do you think he is unduly pessimistic, guilty of an unjustifiable optimism, or expresses a balanced view of human possibilities?

IMPROVING YOUR STYLE
Include in your composition:
1. A portion of the paragraph unified by several sentences beginning in the same way.
2. An appositive.
3. An instance of polysyndeton (see question 10).
4. A passage using alliteration.

JOHN McPHEE

The Search for Marvin Gardens

John McPhee is among the best of the so-called new journalists, who add a dimension of personal judgment and sensitivity to the reporter's traditional job of reporting the facts. His essays, often appearing in *The New Yorker* magazine, deal with people and places—Alaska, a canoe trip in northern Maine, the Jersey pine barrens, the basketball star—now Senator—Bill Bradley. In the following essay McPhee writes about Atlantic City, the once-fashionable resort on the coast of New Jersey whose fortunes declined in the 1950's and '60's. (Since McPhee wrote—1972—the city has been revived, financially at least, by the introduction of legalized casino gambling.)

McPhee organizes his essay in an unusual way, using the game of "Monopoly" to counterpoint his account of the city. The relationship between "Monopoly" and Atlantic City is not fortuitous; in its layout the game borrows street names from the resort. Probably, like most of us, you have played "Monopoly"; if so you may skip to the last paragraph of this headnote. But if you are unfamiliar with the game, a word about how it is played will help you to understand what McPhee is doing.

"Monopoly" is a board game for two, three, four, or more players. Each player is represented by a small token (a top hat, a satchel, a flat iron, a racing car) which he moves around a board nineteen inches square according to the number shown by the roll of a pair of dice. The edge of the board is divided into forty spaces. The four corner ones are labeled "Go" (the starting point), "Jail," "Free Parking," and "Go to Jail." Of the thirty-six remaining spaces, two force players landing upon them to pay a tax, three are designated "Chance" and three "Community Chest" (these six require a player to pick the top card from one of two piles and to do whatever it says—go to jail and lose his turn, pay a fine, or even by a lucky chance to receive an unexpected stock dividend). The other twenty-eight spaces represent pieces of property: four "Railroads," an "Electric Company," a "Waterworks," and twenty-two streets.

The streets are grouped in units of two or three, each street in the

From *Pieces of the Frame.* Copyright © 1972, 1975 by John McPhee. Reprinted by permission of Farrar, Straus & Giroux, Inc.

group being of the same color ("Atlantic Avenue," "Ventnor Avenue," and "Marvin Gardens," for example, are yellow; "Pacific," "North Carolina," and "Pennsylvania" Avenues are green). The streets increase in value as one moves around the board: "Mediterranean" and "Baltic" Avenues, immediately after "Go," are the cheapest, while "Park Place" and the "Boardwalk," farthest along, are the most expensive. These values correspond roughly with the economic realities of Atlantic City: Baltic Avenue really is a poor neighborhood while the Boardwalk is prime property.

At the beginning of the game the players are given equal sums of play money. The remaining cash, along with small cardboard "Deeds" to the properties, is placed in a "Bank," tended by one of the players (hopefully the most honest). As players move in turn round and round the board (which they continue to do until the game is over) they may buy from the bank the deed to any property they land upon, if they have the cash and if it is not already owned. Should it be owned the player landing upon it must pay a stipulated rent, keyed to the value of the property.

A player's immediate object is to acquire a monopoly—all four railroads, for instance, or all three avenues in the green group. When he has done so he may charge a higher rent and, on the street properties, build houses and hotels (purchased from the bank), which dramatically increase the charges unlucky visitors must pay. Property may be mortgaged for ready cash and, according to the ground rules adopted by the players, "deals" may be negotiated in the form of exchanging or selling properties, accepting deeds in lieu of rent, and so on. The ultimate object is to form a sufficient number of monopolies to force one's opponents into bankruptcy, at which point they must surrender to the bank whatever deeds and cash they retain and leave the game. The final player is the winner, owning, in effect, all the property and all the money.

"Monopoly" was invented in the 1930's during the great depression and was an immediate, and phenomenal, success. More than forty years later, while no longer a phenomenon, the game remains popular. It obviously appeals to a society based upon economic individualism and competition, giving us the chance to play a role real life denies: the "Grand Monopolist," financially omnipotent, owner of all he surveys.

On the surface "The Search for Marvin Gardens" is not persuasion. It mounts no formal argument; it is not a satire. Yet below the surface it implies, with considerable persuasive force, feelings and judgments about the values of our society.

1   Go. I roll the dice—a six and a two. Through the air I move my token, the flatiron, to Vermont Avenue, where dog packs range.

2   The dogs are moving (some are limping) through ruins, rubble,

fire damage, open garbage. Doorways are gone. Lath is visible in the
crumbling walls of the buildings. The street sparkles with shattered glass. 5
I have never seen, anywhere, so many broken windows. A sign—"Slow,
Children at Play"—has been bent backward by an automobile. At the
lighthouse, the dogs turn up Pacific and disappear. George Meade, Army
engineer, built the lighthouse—brick upon brick, six hundred thousand
bricks, to reach up high enough to throw a beam twenty miles over the 10
sea. Meade, seven years later, saved the Union at Gettysburg.

3   I buy Vermont Avenue for $100. My opponent is a tall, shadowy
figure, across from me, but I know him well, and I know his game like a
favorite tune. If he can, he will always go for the quick kill. And when it
is foolish to go for the quick kill he will be foolish. On the whole, though, 15
he is a master assessor of percentages. It is a mistake to underestimate
him. His eleven carries his top hat to St. Charles Place, which he buys
for $140.

4   The sidewalks of St. Charles Place have been cracked to shards by
through-growing weeds. There are no buildings. Mansions, hotels once 20
stood here. A few street lamps now drop cones of light on broken glass
and vacant space behind a chain-link fence that some great machine has in
places bent to the ground. Five plane trees—in full summer leaf, flecking
the light—are all that live on St. Charles Place.

5   Block upon block, gradually, we are cancelling each other out—in 25
the blues, the lavenders, the oranges, the greens. My opponent follows a
plan of his own devising. I use the Hornblower & Weeks opening and the
Zuricher defense. The first game draws tight, will soon finish. In 1971, a
group of people in Racine, Wisconsin, played for seven hundred and sixty-
eight hours. A game begun a month later in Danville, California, lasted 30
eight hundred and twenty hours. These are official records, and they stun
us. We have been playing for eight minutes. It amazes us that Monopoly
is thought of as a long game. It is possible to play to a complete, absolute,
and final conclusion in less than fifteen minutes, all within the rules as
written. My opponent and I have done so thousands of times. No wonder 35
we are sitting across from each other now in this best-of-seven series for the
international singles championship of the world.

6   On Illinois Avenue, three men lean out from second-story windows. A girl is coming down the street. She wears dungarees and a bright-
red shirt, has ample breasts and a Hadendoan Afro, a black halo, two feet 40
in diameter. Ice rattles in the glasses in the hands of the men.

7   "Hey, sister!"

8   "Come on up!"

9   She looks up, looks from one to another to the other, looks them
flat in the eye.   45

10   "What for?" she says, and she walks on.

11   I buy Illinois for $240. It solidifies my chances, for I already own
Kentucky and Indiana. My opponent pales. If he had landed first on Illinois, the game would have been over then and there, for he has houses
built on Boardwalk and Park Place, we share the railroads equally, and we   50
have cancelled each other everywhere else. We never trade.

12   In 1852, R. B. Osborne, an immigrant Englishman, civil engineer,
surveyed the route of a railroad line that would run from Camden to
Absecon Island, in New Jersey, traversing the state from the Delaware
River to the barrier beaches of the sea. He then sketched in the plan of   55
a "bathing village" that would surround the eastern terminus of the line.
His pen flew glibly, framing and naming spacious avenues parallel to the
shore—Mediterranean, Baltic, Oriental, Ventnor—and narrower transsect-
ing avenues: North Carolina, Pennsylvania, Vermont, Connecticut, States,
Virginia, Tennessee, New York, Kentucky, Indiana, Illinois. The place as   60
a whole had no name, so when he had completed the plan Osborne wrote
in large letters over the ocean, "Atlantic City." No one ever challenged
the name, or the names of Osborne's streets. Monopoly was invented in
the early nineteen-thirties by Charles B. Darrow, but Darrow was only
transliterating what Osborne had created. The railroads, crucial to any   65
player, were the making of Atlantic City. After the rails were down, houses
and hotels burgeoned from Mediterranean and Baltic to New York and
Kentucky. Properties—building lots—sold for as little as six dollars apiece
and as much as a thousand dollars. The original investors in the railroads
and the real estate called themselves the Camden & Atlantic Land Com-   70
pany. Reverently, I repeat their names: Dwight Bell, William Coffin, John
DaCosta, Daniel Deal, William Fleming, Andrew Hay, Joseph Porter,
Jonathan Pitney, Samuel Richards—founders, fathers, forerunners, archetypical masters of the quick kill.

13   My opponent and I are now in a deep situation of classical Mo-   75
nopoly. The torsion is almost perfect—Boardwalk and Park Place versus
the brilliant reds. His cash position is weak, though, and if I escape him
now he may fade. I land on Luxury Tax, contiguous to but in sanctuary
from his power. I have four houses on Indiana. He lands there. He
concedes.   80

14   Indiana Avenue was the address of the Brighton Hotel, gone now.

The Brighton was exclusive—a word that no longer has retail value in the city. If you arrived by automobile and tried to register at the Brighton, you were sent away. Brighton-class people came in private railroad cars. Brighton-class people had other private railroad cars for their horses— dawn rides on the firm sand at water's edge, skirts flying. Colonel Anthony J. Drexel Biddle—the sort of name that would constrict throats in Philadelphia—lived, much of the year, in the Brighton.

15   Colonel Sanders' fried chicken is on Kentucky Avenue. So is Clifton's Club Harlem, with the Sepia Revue and the Sepia Follies, featuring the Honey Bees, the Fashions, and the Lords.

16   My opponent and I, many years ago, played 2,428 games of Monopoly in a single season. He was then a recent graduate of the Harvard Law School, and he was working for a downtown firm, looking up law. Two people we knew—one from Chase Manhattan, the other from Morgan, Stanley—tried to get into the game, but after a few rounds we found that they were not in the conversation and we sent them home. Monopoly should always be *mano a mano* anyway. My opponent won 1,199 games, and so did I. Thirty were ties. He was called into the Army, and we stopped just there. Now, in Game 2 of the series, I go immediately to jail, and again to jail while my opponent seines property. He is dumbfoundingly lucky. He wins in twelve minutes.

17   Visiting hours are daily, eleven to two; Sunday, eleven to one; evenings, six to nine. "NO MINORS, NO FOOD. Immediate Family Only Allowed in Jail." All this above a blue steel door in a blue cement wall in the windowless interior of the basement of the city hall. The desk sergeant sits opposite the door to the jail. In a cigar box in front of him are pills in every color, a banquet of fruit salad an inch and a half deep— leapers, co-pilots, footballs, truck drivers, peanuts, blue angels, yellow jackets, redbirds, rainbows. Near the desk are two soldiers, waiting to go through the blue door. They are about eighteen years old. One of them is trying hard to light a cigarette. His wrists are in steel cuffs. A military policeman waits, too. He is a year or so older than the soldiers, taller, studious in appearance, gentle, fat. On a bench against a wall sits a good-looking girl in slacks. The blue door rattles, swings heavily open. A turnkey stands in the doorway. "Don't you guys kill yourselves back there now," says the sergeant to the soldiers.

18   "One kid, he overdosed himself about ten and a half hours ago," says the M.P.

19   The M.P., the soldiers, the turnkey, and the girl on the bench are

white. The sergeant is black. "If you take off the handcuffs, take off the belts," says the sergeant to the M.P. "I don't want them hanging themselves back there." The door shuts and its tumblers move. When it opens again, five minutes later, a young white man in sandals and dungarees and a blue polo shirt emerges. His hair is in a ponytail. He has no beard. 125 He grins at the good-looking girl. She rises, joins him. The sergeant hands him a manila envelope. From it he removes his belt and a small notebook. He borrows a pencil, makes an entry in the notebook. He is out of jail, free. What did he do? He offended Atlantic City in some way. He spent a night in the jail. In the nineteen-thirties, men visiting Atlantic 130 City went to jail, directly to jail, did not pass Go, for appearing in topless bathing suits on the beach. A city statute requiring all men to wear full-length bathing suits was not seriously challenged until 1937, and the first year in which a man could legally go bare-chested on the beach was 1940.   135

20   Game 3. After seventeen minutes, I am ready to begin construction on overpriced and sluggish Pacific, North Carolina, and Pennsylvania. Nothing else being open, opponent concedes.

21   The physical profile of streets perpendicular to the shore is something like a playground slide. It begins in the high skyline of Boardwalk 140 hotels, plummets into warrens of "side-avenue" motels, crosses Pacific, slopes through church missions, convalescent homes, burlesque houses, rooming houses, and liquor stores, crosses Atlantic, and runs level through the bombed-out ghetto as far—Baltic, Mediterranean—as the eye can see. North Carolina Avenue, for example, is flanked at its beach end by the 145 Chalfonte and the Haddon Hall (908 rooms, air-conditioned), where, according to one biographer, John Philip Sousa (1854-1932) first played when he was twenty-two, insisting, even then, that everyone call him by his entire name. Behind these big hotels, motels—Barbizon, Catalina—crouch. Between Pacific and Atlantic is an occasional house from 1910— 150 wooden porch, wooden mullions, old yellow paint—and two churches, a package store, a strip show, a dealer in fruits and vegetables. Then, beyond Atlantic Avenue, North Carolina moves on into the vast ghetto, the bulk of the city, and it looks like Metz in 1919, Cologne in 1944. Nothing has actually exploded. It is not bomb damage. It is deep and 155 complex decay. Roofs are off. Bricks are scattered in the street. People sit on porches, six deep, at nine on a Monday morning. When they go off to wait in unemployment lines, they wait sometimes two hours. Between Mediterranean and Baltic runs a chain-link fence, enclosing rubble. A pa-

trol car sits idling by the curb. In the back seat is a German shepherd. A   160
sign on the fence says, "Beware of Bad Dogs."
22   Mediterranean and Baltic are the principal avenues of the ghetto.
Dogs are everywhere. A pack of seven passes me. Block after block, there
are three-story brick row houses. Whole segments of them are abandoned,
a thousand broken windows. Some parts are intact, occupied. A mattress   165
lies in the street, soaking in a pool of water. Wet stuffing is coming out
of the mattress. A postman is having a rye and a beer in the Plantation
Bar at nine-fifteen in the morning. I ask him idly if he knows where Marvin Gardens is. He does not. "HOOKED AND NEED HELP? CONTACT N.A.R.C.O."
"REVIVAL NOW GOING ON, CONDUCTED BY REVEREND H. HENDERSON OF TEXAS."   170
These are signboards on Mediterranean and Baltic. The second one is upside down and leans against a boarded-up window of the Faith Temple
Church of God in Christ. There is an old peeling poster on a warehouse
wall showing a figure in an electric chair. "The Black Panther Manifesto"
is the title of the poster, and its message is, or was, that "the fascists have   175
already decided in advance to murder Chairman Bobby Seale in the electric chair." I pass an old woman who carries a bucket. She wears blue
sneakers, worn through. Her feet spill out. She wears red socks, rolled at
the knees. A white handkerchief, spread over her head, is knotted at the
corners. Does she know where Marvin Gardens is? "I sure don't know,"   180
she says, setting down the bucket. "I sure don't know. I've heard of it
somewhere, but I just can't say where." I walk on, through a block of shattered glass. The glass crunches underfoot like coarse sand. I remember
when I first came here—a long train ride from Trenton, long ago, games
of poker in the train—to play basketball against Atlantic City. We were   185
half black, they were all black. We scored forty points, they scored eighty,
or something like it. What I remember most is that they had glass backboards—glittering, pendent, expensive glass backboards, a rarity then in
high schools, even in colleges, the only ones we played on all year.
23   I turn on Pennsylvania, and start back toward the sea. The win-   190
dows of the Hotel Astoria, on Pennsylvania near Baltic, are boarded up. A
sheet of unpainted plywood is the door, and in it is a triangular peephole
that now frames an eye. The plywood door opens. A man answers my
question. Rooms there are six, seven, and ten dollars a week. I thank him
for the information and move on, emerging from the ghetto at the Catho-   195
lic Daughters of America Women's Guest House, between Atlantic and
Pacific. Between Pacific and the Boardwalk are the blinking vacancy signs
of the Aristocrat and Colton Manor motels. Pennsylvania terminates at

the Sheraton-Seaside—thirty-two dollars a day, ocean corner. I take a walk on the Boardwalk and into the Holiday Inn (twenty-three stories). A 200 guest is registering. "You reserved for Wednesday, and this is Monday," the clerk tells him. "But that's all right. We have *plenty* of rooms." The clerk is very young, female, and has soft brown hair that hangs below her waist. Her superior kicks her.

24   He is a middle-aged man with red spiderwebs in his face. He is 205 jacketed and tied. He takes her aside. "Don't say 'plenty,' " he says. "Say 'You are fortunate, sir. We have rooms available.' "

25   The face of the young woman turns sour. "We have all the rooms you need," she says to the customer, and, to her superior, "How's that?"

26   Game 4. My opponent's luck has become abrasive. He has Board- 210 walk and Park Place, and has sealed the board.

27   Darrow was a plumber. He was, specifically, a radiator repairman who lived in Germantown, Pennsylvania. His first Monopoly board was a sheet of linoleum. On it he placed houses and hotels that he had carved from blocks of wood. The game he thus invented was brilliantly con- 215 ceived, for it was an uncannily exact reflection of the business milieu at large. In its depth, range, and subtlety, in its luck-skill ratio, in its sense of infrastructure and socio-economic parameters, in its philosophical char- acteristics, it reached to the profundity of the financial community. It was as scientific as the stock market. It suggested the manner and means 220 through which an underdeveloped world had been developed. It was chess at Wall Street level. "Advance token to the nearest Railroad and pay owner twice the rental to which he is otherwise entitled. If Railroad is unowned, you may buy it from the Bank. Get out of Jail, free. Advance token to nearest Utility. If unowned, you may buy it from Bank. If owned, 225 throw dice and pay owner a total ten times the amount thrown. You are assessed for street repairs: $40 per house, $115 per hotel. Pay poor tax of $15. Go to Jail. Go directly to Jail. Do not pass Go. Do not collect $200."

28   The turnkey opens the blue door. The turnkey is known to the in- mates as Sidney K. Above his desk are ten closed-circuit-TV screens—as- 230 sorted viewpoints of the jail. There are three cellblocks—men, women, ju- venile boys. Six days is the average stay. Showers twice a week. The steel doors and the equipment that operates them were made in San Antonio. The prisoners sleep on bunks of butcher block. There are no mattresses. There are three prisoners to a cell. In winter, it is cold in here. Prisoners 235 burn newspapers to keep warm. Cell corners are black with smudge. The jail is three years old. The men's block echoes with chatter. The man in

the cell nearest Sidney K. is pacing. His shirt is covered with broad stains of blood. The block for juvenile boys is, by contrast, utterly silent—empty corridor, empty cells. There is only one prisoner. He is small and black 240 and appears to be thirteen. He says he is sixteen and that he has been alone in here for three days.

29   "Why are you here? What did you do?"

30   "I hit a jitney driver."

31   The series stands at three all. We have split the fifth and sixth 245 games. We are scrambling for property. Around the board we fairly fly. We move so fast because we do our own banking and search our own deeds. My opponent grows tense.

32   Ventnor Avenue, a street of delicatessens and doctors' offices, is leafy with plane trees and hydrangeas, the city flower. Water Works is 250 on the mainland. The water comes over in submarine pipes. Electric Company gets power from across the state, on the Delaware River, in Deepwater. States Avenue, now a wasteland like St. Charles, once had gardens running down the middle of the street, a horse-drawn trolley, private homes. States Avenue was as exclusive as the Brighton. Only an apartment 255 house, a small motel, and the All Wars Memorial Building—monadnocks spaced widely apart—stand along States Avenue now. Pawnshops, convalescent homes, and the Paradise Soul Saving Station are on Virginia Avenue. The soul-saving station is pink, orange, and yellow. In the windows flanking the door of the Virginia Money Loan Office are Nikons, Pola- 260 roids, Yashicas, Sony TVs, Underwood typewriters, Singer sewing machines, and pictures of Christ. On the far side of town, beside a single track and locked up most of the time, is the new railroad station, a small hut made of glazed firebrick, all that is left of the lines that built the city. An authentic phrenologist works on New York Avenue close to Frank's 265 Extra Dry Bar and a church where the sermon today is "Death in the Pot." The church is of pink brick, has blue and amber windows and two red doors. St. James Place, narrow and twisting, is lined with boarding houses that have wooden porches on each of three stories, suggesting a New Orleans made of salt-bleached pine. In a vacant lot on Tennessee is a 270 white Ford station wagon stripped to the chassis. The windows are smashed. A plastic Clorox bottle sits on the driver's seat. The wind has pressed newspaper against the chain-link fence around the lot. Atlantic Avenue, the city's principal thoroughfare, could be seventeen American Main Streets placed end to end—discount vitamins and Vienna Corset 275 shops, movie theatres, shoe stores, and funeral homes. The Boardwalk is

made of yellow pine and Douglas fir, soaked in pentachlorophenol. Down-beach, it reaches far beyond the city. Signs everywhere—on windows, lamp-posts, trash baskets—proclaim "Bienvenue Canadiens!" The salt air is full of Canadian French. In the Claridge Hotel, on Park Place, I ask a clerk 280
if she knows where Marvin Gardens is. She says, "Is it a floral shop?" I ask a cabdriver, parked outside. He says, "Never heard of it." Park Place is one block long, Pacific to Boardwalk. On the roof of the Claridge is the So-larium, the highest point in town—panoramic view of the ocean, the bay, the salt-water ghetto. I look down at the rooftops of the side-avenue mo- 285
tels and into swimming pools. There are hundreds of people around the rooftop pools, sunbathing, reading—many more people than are on the beach. Walls, windows, and a block of sky are all that is visible from these pools—no sand, no sea. The pools are craters, and with the people around them they are countersunk into the motels. 290

33   The seventh, and final, game is ten minutes old and I have hotels on Oriental, Vermont, and Connecticut. I have Tennessee and St. James. I have North Carolina and Pacific. I have Boardwalk, Atlantic, Ventnor, Illinois, Indiana. My fingers are forming a "V." I have mortgaged most of these properties in order to pay for others, and I have mortgaged the 295
others to pay for the hotels. I have seven dollars. I will pay off the mort-gages and build my reserves with income from the three hotels. My cash position may be low, but I feel like a rocket in an underground silo. Mean-while, if I could just go to jail for a time I could pause there, wait there, until my opponent, in his inescapable rounds, pays the rates of my ho- 300
tels. Jail, at times, is the strategic place to be. I roll boxcars from the Reading and move the flatiron to Community Chest. "Go to Jail. Go directly to Jail."

34   The prisoners, of course, have no pens and no pencils. They take paper napkins, roll them tight as crayons, char the ends with matches, 305
and write on the walls. The things they write are not entirely idiomatic; for example, "In God We Trust." All is in carbon. Time is required in the writing. "Only humanity could know of such pain." "God So Loved the World." "There is no greater pain than life itself." In the women's block now, there are six blacks, giggling, and a white asleep in red shoes. 310
She is drunk. The others are pushers, prostitutes, an auto thief, a burglar caught with pistol in purse. A sixteen-year-old accused of murder was in here last week. These words are written on the wall of a now empty cell: "Laying here I see two bunks about six inches thick, not counting the one I'm laying on, which is hard as brick. No cushion for my back. No 315

pillow for my head. Just a couple scratchy blankets which is best to use it's said. I wake up in the morning so shivery and cold, waiting and waiting till I am told the food is coming. It's on its way. It's not worth waiting for, but I eat it anyway. I know one thing when they set me free I'm gonna be good if it kills me."   320

35   How many years must a game be played to produce an Anthony J. Drexel Biddle and chestnut geldings on the beach? About half a century was the original answer, from the first railroad to Biddle at his peak. Biddle, at his peak, hit an Atlantic City streetcar conductor with his fist, laid him out with one punch. This increased Biddle's legend. He did not   325 go to jail. While John Philip Sousa led his band along the Boardwalk playing "The Stars and Stripes Forever" and Jack Dempsey ran up and down in training for his fight with Gene Tunney, the city crossed the high curve of its parabola. Al Capone held conventions here—upstairs with his sleeves rolled, apportioning among his lieutenant governors the states   330 of the Eastern seaboard. The natural history of an American resort proceeds from Indians to French Canadians via Biddles and Capones. French Canadians, whatever they may be at home, are Visigoths here. Bienvenue Visigoths!

36   My opponent plods along incredibly well. He has got his fourth   335 railroad, and patiently, unbelievably, he has picked up my potential winners until he has blocked me everywhere but Marvin Gardens. He has avoided, in the fifty-dollar zoning, my increasingly petty hotels. His cash flow swells. His railroads are costing me two hundred dollars a minute. He is building hotels on States, Virginia, and St. Charles. He has tempo-   340 rarily reversed the current. With the yellow monopolies and my blue monopolies, I could probably defeat his lavenders and his railroads. I have Atlantic and Ventnor. I need Marvin Gardens. My only hope is Marvin Gardens.

37   There is a plaque at Boardwalk and Park Place, and on it in relief   345 is the leonine profile of a man who looks like an officer in a metropolitan bank—"Charles B. Darrow, 1889-1967, inventor of the game of Monopoly." "Darrow," I address him, aloud. "Where is Marvin Gardens?" There is, of course, no answer. Bronze, impassive, Darrow looks south down the Boardwalk. "Mr. Darrow, please, where is Marvin Gardens?" Nothing.   350 Not a sign. He just looks south down the Boardwalk.

38   My opponent accepts the trophy with his natural ease, and I make, from notes, remarks that are even less graceful than his.

39   Marvin Gardens is the one color-block Monopoly property that is

not in Atlantic City. It is a suburb within a suburb, secluded. It is a   355
planned compound of seventy-two handsome houses set on curvilinear
private streets under yews and cedars, poplars and willows. The compound
was built around 1920, in Margate, New Jersey, and consists of solid buildings of stucco, brick, and wood, with slate roofs, tile roofs, multimullioned
porches, Giraldic towers, and Spanish grilles. Marvin Gardens, the ulti-   360
mate outwash of Monopoly, is a citadel and sanctuary of the middle class.
"We're heavily patrolled by police here. We don't take no chances. Me?
I'm living here nine years. I paid seventeen thousand dollars and I've been
offered thirty. Number one, I don't want to move. Number two, I don't
need the money. I have four bedrooms, two and a half baths, front den,   365
back den. No basement. The Atlantic is down there. Six feet down and
you float. A lot of people have a hard time finding this place. People that
lived in Atlantic City all their life don't know how to find it. They don't
know where the hell they're going. They just know it's south, down the
Boardwalk."   370

QUESTIONS

READER AND PURPOSE

1. McPhee uses a personal point of view * rather than striving for the appearance of objectivity. And his essay is richly implicative. Both of these characteristics are typical of the new journalism. The meaning of the essay does not lie
on top; it must be dug for like the theme of a short story or a poem. His piece
is not simply an account of "Monopoly," nor is it merely a report upon the
decline of Atlantic City, though it includes both these topics. But if neither
is his essential subject—what is?
2. The essay is not argument in any technical sense. Indeed, it is not even
persuasion, as we normally understand that term. Yet McPhee is trying to
convince us of something. What?

ORGANIZATION

3. McPhee does not develop his essay in a series of topics, each leading logically into the next. He organizes by moving back and forth between two related themes. Which paragraphs are concerned primarily with "Monopoly"
and which with Atlantic City?
4. The structure of the essay is almost musical in its use of alternating themes,
and we might adapt the terms *counterpoint* and *contrapuntal* to describe it.
The counterpointed themes are linked by details common to both, such as the
various streets and the jail. These details act as bridges, shifting us from one

theme to the other. Thus at the end of the opening paragraph the phrase "where the dog packs range" transposes us from the blue space on the "Monopoly" board to the actual street. Point out other details which swing us from game to city or from city to game.

5. In some cases there are no links, simply abrupt jumps from theme to theme—between paragraphs 26 and 27, for example. Where else do you find such discontinuities? Are they faults, or do they serve a purpose?

6. Is McPhee's first paragraph a good beginning? Why, or why not?

7. Which paragraph (or paragraphs) constitutes the closing of this essay? Is the closing effective?

8. Which is the topic sentence of paragraph 21? Of 22? How is each supported?

9. Does paragraph 4 have a topic statement? If not, is its absence a fault? Can you supply one easily? Try it.

SENTENCES

10. McPhee often uses a series of short simple * sentences—in lines 4-6, for instance. Point out three or four similar passages. Does he employ such sentences for particular topics?

11. The sentences in paragraph 12 are longer and more complicated. Is the subject different here than in lines 4-6?

12. McPhee sometimes omits *and* between paired constructions where normally the conjunction would appear: for example in line 28 "The first game draws tight, will soon finish" (instead of "and will soon finish"). Find other instances of this kind of ellipsis *. Why do you suppose he does it?

13. Identify the fragments * in paragraph 37. Where else in this selection do you find fragments? Would they be improved by being made grammatically complete?

14. Could commas be used instead of dashes in lines 6-7, 23-24, 87-88, 108, and 289? If they could be, is there any justification for the dashes?

15. How do these revisions alter the emphasis of McPhee's sentences?

(a) *Revision:* We are gradually cancelling each other out, block upon block . . .
    McPhee: "Block upon block, gradually, we are cancelling each other out . . ." (25)

(b) *Revision:* Motels such as the Barbizon and the Catalina crouch behind these big hotels.
    McPhee: "Behind these big hotels, motels—Barbizon, Catalina—crouch." (149-50)

(c) *Revision:* It is a secluded suburb within a suburb.
    McPhee: "It is a suburb within a suburb, secluded." (355)

DICTION

16. Look up: *shards* (19), *traversing* (54), *glibly* (57), *transliterating* (65), *burgeoned* (67), *constrict* (87), *plummets* (141), *ghetto* (144), *mullions* (151), *rubble* (159), *pendent* (188), *abrasive* (210), *infrastructure* (218), *jitney* (244), *trolley* (254), *monadnocks* (256), *phrenologist* (265), *curvilinear* (356).

17. Explain as fully as you can the meanings of the following phrases: *master assessor of percentages* (16), *immigrant Englishmen* (52), *barrier beaches* (55), *archetypical masters of the quick kill* (74), *mano a mano* (98), *city statute* (132), *burlesque houses* (142), *business milieu* (216), *socio-economic parameters* (218), *chestnut geldings* (332), *leonine profile* (346), *ultimate outwash* (360-61).

18. McPhee uses the present tense when writing about both the game and Atlantic City. He could as easily have made the past his primary tense. What advantage does the present have for his purpose? Suppose that he had used the past throughout:

> Go. I rolled the dice—a six and a two. Through the air I moved my token, the flatiron, to Vermont Avenue, where dog packs ranged.
>
> The dogs were moving (some were limping) . . .

Would the change in tense affect the tone * of his essay in any way?

19. In the opening passage just quoted McPhee might have written simply: "I move my token to Vermont Avenue, where dog packs range," omitting the phrase *through the air* and any reference to the flatiron. It doesn't really matter if he picks up his token or shoves it, and the flatiron has no symbolic value. Why, then, do you suppose he adds these apparently trivial details?

20. Who were the Visigoths (333)? Is the allusion * apt?

21. Explain the metaphors * implicit in *seines* (101), *warrens* (141), and *the city crossed the high curve of its parabola* (328-29).

22. Certain images * are repeated throughout the essay so that they become motifs. The dog packs referred to in paragraph 1 and again in paragraphs 2 and 22 is an example. While the dogs do not symbolize anything, they are a laden image—that is, a visual detail that implies more than it literally states. What is suggested by the dog packs? Point out one or two other motifs and explain their significance.

23. What ambiguity * is contained in the word *game* as it is used in line 321?

24. All these devices—allusions, metaphors, laden images, ambiguity *—are ways of enriching meaning by adding overtones of feeling and thought. An even more important way of creating such overtones is the symbol *, a detail which functions both on the literal level of meaning and on a second level where it conveys a more abstract * idea—often moral, political, or philosophi-

cal. The culminating symbol of McPhee's essay is, of course, "Marvin Gardens." Actually Marvin Gardens is a double symbol, for it exists both in the game and in the city, and in each it has a literal and a symbolic value. Within the context of the game the author and his friend are playing, what does Marvin Gardens signify literally and what does it represent symbolically?

25. With reference to Atlantic City, what does Marvin Gardens literally designate? What does it symbolize? Is there a connection between its symbolic values in the game and in the city?

26. As a symbol Marvin Gardens operates, perhaps, on multiple levels, possessing economic, social, and political values, and, on the most abstract level of all, a philosophical significance. Can you sort out these various levels of meaning?

27. Finally, we return to the first question: What is "The Search for Marvin Gardens" about?

POINTS TO LEARN

1. Do not be afraid of the first person. You are the chief observer of what you see and do; your thoughts and feelings have value, even in reporting.

2. An essay may be organized contrapuntally by moving back and forth from one theme to another.

3. Short, strong sentences are good for rendering scene and action.

4. Think about the advantages and limitations of the tense you select as primary.

5. Laden images, metaphors, and symbols enrich—and complicate—meaning.

SUGGESTIONS FOR WRITING

1. In about 500 words describe a board game (but not "Monopoly") or an athletic sport such as baseball. Assume that your reader is intelligent but ignorant about the activity and that your job is to acquaint him with its basics (explaining baseball to an Englishman would be an example). This is not an easy assignment; in fact, describing a game clearly and succinctly is one of the most difficult of all writing tasks. It tests your ability to distinguish essentials from non-essentials and to organize the former without getting bogged down in the latter. You may be able to play baseball or chess, but are you able to lay out the fundamental facts of such games?

2. A more ambitious assignment: Compose an essay of about 1000 words using a game as a controlling metaphor to report upon some aspect of your experience, moving back and forth between the two themes as McPhee does with "Monopoly" and Atlantic City. There should be an inherent connection

between the topics, as, for example, a varsity football game counterpointed against a report on one of the colleges or a description of the spectators.

IMPROVING YOUR STYLE

1. In two or three places in your essay use a series (four or five) of short simple sentences to set a scene or render dramatic action.

2. If your teacher agrees, experiment with fragments in several places, and with the kind of elliptical construction McPhee uses in line 28.

3. (This applies only to the second assignment.) Work one or two motifs into your composition, and try to develop a culminating symbol comparable to Marvin Gardens in McPhee's essay.

Description

Description is the art of translating perceptions into words. All description thus involves two elements: the object—that which is seen or heard—and the observer—he who sees or hears it. According to which predominates, description is of two basic types: objective and impressionistic.

Objective description attempts to report accurately the appearance of the object as a thing in itself, independent of the observer's perception of it or feelings about it. It is a factual account, the purpose of which is to inform a reader who has not been able to see with his own eyes. The writer regards himself as a kind of camera, recording and reproducing, though in words, a true picture. In his detachment he becomes much like the scientist, rigorously excluding from his work his opinions and emotions.

Objective description often begins with a brief general picture comprehending the object in its entirety. This it then develops analytically, using paragraphs—or, in a short description, sentences—to divide the object into its parts, handling each in turn with as much detail as the purpose requires. These parts are placed in an order that reflects the arrangement in space of the object. Thus a writer depicting the interior of a house would likely organize his description by floors, and in describing the rooms on each floor he would probably move from left to right or from front to rear.

Usually objective description is written impersonally, and the writer wanders freely about the object or scene without bothering to record his own movements. When, for example, he has finished the first floor, he need not report, "I am now going upstairs"; he merely writes, "On the second floor . . ." Similarly the tone must be kept factual, and the writer should avoid words that connote a personal reaction. "A large elm," for example, states a fact; "a magnificent elm" suggests a feeling. This is not to say that such feelings are always a fault in composition—in much writing they are a virtue. But in objective description they are immaterial to the writer's purpose.

Given these restrictions, objective description often appears prosaic,

327

even dull; and too often the appearance is real. It is not, however, inherently dull—it is only difficult to do well. Even though his impressions are excluded, the writer can create interest by the fidelity and the skill with which he translates into words the thing he sees. A dying goldfish is hardly an intriguing topic; yet consider this passage from *The Natural History of Selborne* by Gilbert White: "As soon as the creature sickens, the head sinks lower and lower, and it stands as it were on its head; till, getting weaker, and losing all poise, the tail turns over, and at last it floats on the surface of the water with its belly uppermost." This is interesting because it is accurate, precise, economical; because it reproduces exactly what White saw. To see accurately is, as any painter knows, far from easy; to reproduce accurately, whether in prose or paint, what one sees is even more difficult. But when it has been achieved, such description is one of the most satisfying kinds of writing.

Impressionistic description is very different. Focusing upon the mood or feeling the object evokes in the observer, rather than upon the object as it exists in itself, impressionism does not seek to inform but to arouse emotion. It attempts to make us feel more than to make us see. Thus the communication of feeling is the primary purpose of impressionistic description. The process begins in the writer, and it must originate in genuine feeling. But if he is to succeed, the writer must do more than feel deeply; he must in his own mind define that feeling. Impressionistic descriptions often fail because the writers have not really defined in their own minds what their responses are. Only when the writer has understood his own mood can he communicate that mood to his readers.

The actual communication may be achieved in two ways: directly and indirectly. The direct method, the simpler, is merely to describe the feeling itself. The indirect is to project the emotion back into the object and, by the careful selection and treatment of its details, so to infuse the object with feeling that it will arouse in the reader a response similar to the writer's. Both methods are illustrated in this brief description of a clipper ship from John Masefield's *A Tarpaulin Muster: A Memory*: "She bowed and curveted, the light caught the skylights on the poop; she gleamed and sparkled; she shook the sea from her as she rose. There was no man aboard of us but was filled with the beauty of that ship." The second sentence is direct impressionism; it tells us that in the men who watched her the clipper stirred feelings of beauty. The first is indirect. Masefield judiciously selects only those details that suggest grace, power, beauty. If there were facts about the ship inimical to his impression—stained and weathered sails, a shabby figurehead—these he has excluded.

Of the two methods, the indirect is more effective. If the writer's purpose is to communicate a mood, he succeeds better by re-creating the object as he sees it. A writer who tells us he is afraid does not necessarily frighten us; but if he can throw before us the fearsome thing in all its horror, he probably will. In practice, however, impressionistic description uses both methods, often employing direct statement of mood as a center about which to organize the more precise details of indirect description.

In his treatment of these details the writer frequently follows a technique that in art is called expressionism. Broadly, expressionism is the distortion of objective reality in order to communicate the inner reality of emotion. At its simplest, expressionism is the blurring of a film image to suggest dizziness or shock. Similarly the writer may blur or intensify the details he selects, and, by the clever use of figures of speech, he may compare them to things calculated to evoke the appropriate emotion. To impress us with the dreary ugliness of a house, he may exaggerate the drabness of its paint or metaphorically describe the flaking as *leprous*. In such exaggeration the writer is like the caricaturist, but like the caricaturist he is allowed to distort only within limits. Distortion becomes illegitimate when it passes belief and leads us, not toward, but away from the truth the writer seeks to express. It may be objected that impressionism has little to do with truth, if the writer is free to exaggerate some facts and to ignore others. Certainly it is true that impressionistic description draws no very accurate picture. But objective accuracy is not its concern; it tells the truth of feeling. Impressionism tells us not what the clipper ship is, but what it is to the man who sees it.

Thus the objective and the impressionistic are the broad categories of description. Neither ever exists purely. The most detached and scientific observer cannot totally repress his own feelings; and the most impressionistic writer suggests something about the objective reality of what he describes. Most actual description makes use of both. The two techniques are the ends of a continuum, between which, partaking of each, all descriptive writing falls. Yet if no fine line can be drawn between the objective and the impressionistic, they are essentially different in purpose and method. The competent writer must realize when to use the one, when the other. But he must know how to write both.

W. SOMERSET MAUGHAM

The Opium Den

W. Somerset Maugham (1874-1965) was an English novelist, short story writer, and playwright. His best known novels include *Of Human Bondage* (1915), *The Moon and Sixpence* (1919), and *Cakes and Ale* (1930); and his plays, *A Man of Honour* (1903), *East of Suez* (1922), and *The Constant Wife* (1927). In addition to stories and plays Maugham composed essays, travel books, and a notable autobiography. This selection comes from a book of sketches Maugham wrote about a trip to China, specifically from a piece describing a visit to an opium den. It is a particularly revealing example of how impressionistic description works. To emphasize the contrast between what he expected and what he found, Maugham carefully selects details and presents them in diction calculated to arouse appropriate responses.

On the stage it makes a very effective set. It is dimly lit. The room is low and squalid. In one corner a lamp burns mysteriously before a hideous image and incense fills the theatre with its exotic scent. A pig-tailed Chinaman wanders to and fro, aloof and saturnine, while on wretched pallets lie stupe- fied the victims of the drug. Now and then one of them breaks into frantic 5 raving. There is a highly dramatic scene where some poor creature, unable to pay for the satisfaction of his craving, with prayers and curses begs the villainous proprietor for a pipe to still his anguish. I have read also in novels descriptions which made my blood run cold. And when I was taken to an opium den by a smooth-spoken Eurasian, the narrow, winding stairway up 10 which he led me prepared me sufficiently to receive the thrill I expected. I was introduced into a neat enough room, brightly lit, divided into cubicles, the raised floor of which, covered with clean matting, formed a convenient couch. In one an elderly gentleman, with a grey head and very beautiful hands, was quietly reading a newspaper, with his long pipe by his side. In 15

From "Opium Den" in *On a Chinese Screen*. Copyright 1922 by W. Somerset Maugham. Reprinted by permission of A. P. Watt & Son Ltd.

another two coolies were lying, with a pipe between them, which they alternately prepared and smoked. They were young men, of a hearty appearance, and they smiled at me in a friendly way. One of them offered me a smoke. In a third, four men squatted over a chess-board, and a little further on a man was dandling a baby (the inscrutable Oriental has a passion for chil- 20 dren) while the baby's mother, whom I took to be the landlord's wife, a plump, pleasant-faced woman, watched him with a broad smile on her lips. It was a cheerful spot, comfortable, home-like, and cosy. It reminded me somewhat of the little intimate beer-houses of Berlin, where the tired working-man could go in the evening and spend a peaceful hour. Fiction is 25 stranger than fact.

QUESTIONS

READER AND PURPOSE

1. The parenthetical remark in lines 20-21 cleverly questions our conventional notions of the Chinese. What does their passion for children suggest about their inscrutability? At whom is Maugham poking fun here—the "inscrutable Oriental" or the average Westerner?

ORGANIZATION

2. Indicate the two parts of this paragraph. Which sentence makes the transition between them?

3. Study how the description in lines 1-9 is organized. What do we see first? What does the writer show us next? Then what? Explain why this pattern of development reflects the way in which we actually see things.

4. Show that the second section develops in much the same manner. What advantage is there to organizing both parts of this description according to the same pattern?

5. What function does the final sentence serve? Would its omission have improved the selection?

SENTENCES

6. Why is the style of the first few sentences well suited to the impression the writer is trying to convey?

7. In lines 9 ff. the sentences become longer and their rhythms smoother. Why does Maugham's purpose require such a change? Even here, however, he occasionally employs a shorter sentence for variety. Point out one or two examples.

DICTION

8. Look up: *squalid* (2), *exotic* (3), *aloof* (4), *saturnine* (4), *pallet* (4), *dramatic* (6), *craving* (7), *Eurasian* (10), *cubicle* (12), *inscrutable* (20).

9. In the first ten lines Maugham uses his diction, especially modifiers, to satirize the clichés of melodrama. The incense, for example, is *exotic*, an overworked adjective that suggests similarly trite stage properties. Point out three or four other modifiers that are deliberately trite. Is the very title of this selection ironic? Explain.

10. What words in the first eleven lines suggest the kind of melodramatic action which the writer is mocking?

11. Like the syntax, the diction also changes in the second part. It becomes less dramatic and more matter-of-fact. Maugham now uses words to re-create what he really saw. Notice, for instance, the details that characterize the "elderly gentleman" (14-15). What kind of man do they suggest he is? What details characterize the "landlord's wife"? What kind of woman is she?

12. The comparison of an opium den to a beer-house in line 24 is slightly shocking to a Western mind. What is Maugham implying here?

13. Comment upon these changes in diction, explaining why each substitute is a better or a poorer choice: *ugly* for *hideous* (2), *man* for *creature* (6), *holding* for *dandling* (20), *heavy* for *plump* (22).

POINTS TO LEARN

1. Good description usually develops in the natural order of general to particular.

2. Sentence rhythm can enter into and become a part of the descriptive process.

SUGGESTIONS FOR WRITING

The difference between naïve preconception and reality is a common experience, often humorous, sometimes bitterly disappointing. Choose one of the topics listed below and write a description in two parts; in the first develop what you anticipated, in the second what you found.

a night club, a pool room, college (or high school), a blind date, your first cigar, a museum, a cocktail party, a fraternity (or sorority) house, any famous tourist attraction for which the publicity outruns the truth

IMPROVING YOUR STYLE

In your composition:

1. Use sentence structure to reinforce the contrast—short, staccato sentences to enhance drama contrasted with longer ones, more relaxed in movement.

2. Select your diction carefully to direct the readers' responses, and be able to defend your choice of particular words by explaining what emotion you wished to evoke.

Stagecoach Station

At the beginning of the Civil War in 1861, Mark Twain (1835-1910) gave up his profession of steamboat pilot on the Mississippi and traveled by stagecoach to the Nevada Territory. During 1861-66 he remained in the West as a prospector in Nevada and then as a journalist for several newspapers. Some six years later—newly married and living in Buffalo, New York—Twain began to record his western experiences in a book called *Roughing It* (1872). Twain's purpose was to tell the truth about frontier life, a truth, in Twain's opinion, not found in the idealizing novels of James Fenimore Cooper or in the sentimental tales of Bret Harte. Throughout *Roughing It*, as in others of his books, a part of Twain's theme is the difference between romantic imaginings and grotesque realities. In the following excerpt Twain describes the buildings where stagecoach passengers stopped for breakfast about a day's drive away from Kearney, Nebraska, enroute from St. Joseph, Missouri, to Carson City, capital of the Nevada Territory.

1   The station buildings were long, low huts, made of sun-dried, mud-colored bricks, laid up without mortar (*adobes*, the Spaniards call these bricks, and Americans shorten it to *'dobies*). The roofs, which had no slant to them worth speaking of, were thatched and then sodded or covered with a thick layer of earth, and from this sprung a pretty rank growth of weeds 5 and grass. It was the first time we had ever seen a man's front yard on top of his house. The buildings consisted of barns, stable-room for twelve or fifteen horses, and a hut for an eating-room for passengers. This latter had bunks in it for the station-keeper and a hostler or two. You could rest your elbow on its eaves, and you had to bend in order to get in at the door. In 10 place of a window there was a square hole about large enough for a man to crawl through, but this had no glass in it. There was no flooring, but the ground was packed hard. There was no stove, but the fireplace served all needful purposes. There were no shelves, no cupboards, no closets. In a

From Chapter Four of *Roughing It*, originally published by Harper & Row.

corner stood an open sack of flour, and nestling against its base were a couple 15
of black and venerable tin coffee-pots, a tin teapot, a little bag of salt, and a
side of bacon.

2   By the door of the station-keeper's den, outside, was a tin wash-
basin, on the ground. Near it was a pail of water and a piece of yellow bar-
soap, and from the eaves hung a hoary blue woolen shirt, significantly—but 20
this latter was the station-keeper's private towel, and only two persons in all
the party might venture to use it—the stage-driver and the conductor. The
latter would not, from a sense of decency; the former would not, because he
did not choose to encourage the advances of a station-keeper. We had towels—in the valise; they might as well have been in Sodom and Gomorrah. 25
We (and the conductor) used our handkerchiefs, and the driver his pantaloons and sleeves. By the door, inside, was fastened a small old-fashioned
looking-glass frame, with two little fragments of the original mirror lodged
down in one corner of it. This arrangement afforded a pleasant double-
barreled portrait of you when you looked into it, with one half of your head 30
set up a couple of inches above the other half. From the glass frame hung
the half of a comb by a string—but if I had to describe that patriarch or die,
I believe I would order some sample coffins. It had come down from Esau
and Samson, and had been accumulating hair ever since—along with certain
impurities. In one corner of the room stood three or four rifles and muskets, 35
together with horns and pouches of ammunition. The station-men wore
pantaloons of coarse, country-woven stuff, and into the seat and the inside of
the legs were sewed ample additions of buckskin, to do duty in place of leg-
gings, when the man rode horseback—so the pants were half dull blue and
half yellow, and unspeakably picturesque. The pants were stuffed into the 40
tops of high boots, the heels whereof were armed with great Spanish spurs,
whose little iron clogs and chains jingled with every step. The man wore a
huge beard and mustachios, an old slouch hat, a blue woolen shirt, no sus-
penders, no vest, no coat—in a leathern sheath in his belt, a great long
"navy" revolver (slung on right side, hammer to the front), and projecting 45
from his boot a horn-handled bowie-knife. The furniture of the hut was
neither gorgeous nor much in the way. The rocking-chairs and sofas were
not present, and never had been, but they were represented by two three-
legged stools, a pine-board bench four feet long, and two empty candle-
boxes. The table was a greasy board on stilts, and the table-cloth and nap- 50
kins had not come—and they were not looking for them, either. A battered
tin platter, a knife and fork, and a tin pint cup, were at each man's place,
and the driver had a queens-ware saucer that had seen better days. Of course,

this duke sat at the head of the table. There was one isolated piece of table furniture that bore about it a touching air of grandeur in misfortune. This 55 was the caster. It was German silver, and crippled and rusty, but it was so preposterously out of place there that it was suggestive of a tattered exiled king among barbarians, and the majesty of its native position compelled respect even in its degradation. There was only one cruet left, and that was a stopperless, fly-specked, broken-necked thing, with two inches of vinegar in 60 it, and a dozen preserved flies with their heels up and looking sorry they had invested there.

QUESTIONS

READER AND PURPOSE

1. Like many descriptions, "Stagecoach Station" contains both objective and impressionistic elements. List several examples of each. Overall, which predominates—impressionism or objectivity?

2. Explain how the descriptions of things—buildings, furniture, utensils, clothing—serve to characterize the stationmen and frontier life.

3. If this scene were to be shown as part of a television western, in what ways might the visual details differ from Twain's description? Would the eating room, for example, be so low "you had to bend in order to get in at the door"? What do these probable differences reveal about Twain's purpose? About the legend of the Old West then and now?

4. Is Twain writing primarily for Easterners or Westerners? Give several reasons for your conclusion.

ORGANIZATION

5. Show that Twain's first paragraph is organized by the pattern of general to particular.

6. Demonstrate that the second paragraph is organized spatially, that it falls into two parts, and that the beginning of the second part is signaled by verbal repetition.

7. The second paragraph might be said to lack unity. It can easily be divided into four shorter paragraphs without making any verbal changes. Where can these divisions occur? How might Twain's paragraph be defended against the charge that it is not unified?

SENTENCES

8. In each of the following cases, what is the significant difference between Twain's sentences and the revision?

(a) *Revision:* The latter contained bunks for the station-keeper and a hostler.
Twain: "This latter had bunks in it for the station-keeper and a hostler or two." (8-9)

(b) *Revision:* There was no flooring, but the ground was packed hard. The room was without a stove; however, the fireplace served all needful purposes. Nowhere were to be found shelves, cupboards, or closets.
Twain: "There was no flooring, but the ground was packed hard. There was no stove, but the fireplace served all needful purposes. There were no shelves, no cupboards, no closets." (12-14)

(c) *Revision:* We had towels in the valise but they might as well have been in Sodom and Gomorrah.
Twain: "We had towels—in the valise; they might as well have been in Sodom and Gomorrah." (24-25)

9. What variety of purposes do the dashes serve in lines 20, 22, 32, 44, and 51?

10. In the sentence beginning "Near it was a pail of water" (19) what word is given great emphasis by isolation?

DICTION

11. Look up: *hostler* (9), *venerable* (16), *hoary* (20), *pantaloons* (26), *horns* (36), *bowie-knife* (46), *queens-ware* (53), *caster* (56), *cruet* (59).

12. Citing specific words and phrases, show how Twain's diction reveals his attitude toward the stagecoach station and the men who tend it.

13. How does Twain's diction distance him from his subject and ally him with his Eastern readers?

14. Is *mustachios* (43) a better word here than *mustache?* Why or why not?

15. Like many nineteenth-century writers Twain is fond of biblical allusions *. The Bible was widely read and provided a common coin of exchange by which complex sets of feelings and attitudes and judgments could be easily conveyed. Who or what were Esau and Samson (33-34), Sodom and Gomorrah (25)? What is Twain implying by these allusions?

POINTS TO LEARN

1. Most good descriptions are a mixture of objective facts and the writer's feelings about those facts.

2. How the writer feels about his or her subject guides the selection of details and helps to give the description unity and purpose.

3. A bad description often seems pointless—a mere laundry list with no theme.

4. Descriptive details of the things people use or own may serve to characterize them.

5. Description characterizes the writer as well as the places or people he or she is describing. Obviously, if the description is to prove effective, the reader should be made to like the writer.

SUGGESTIONS FOR WRITING

1. Describe the buildings and equipment of a summer camp for young people, or those of a farm or small factory. If possible use details of places and things to characterize those who live or work at the camp, farm, factory. Be conscious of tone *, and work for one appropriate to what you feel and how you want the reader to respond.

2. Describe some work area not generally seen by the public—a warehouse, the kitchen of a restaurant, an upholsterer's shop, a lumber mill. Try for a distinct tone, while at the same time making yourself agreeable to the reader.

IMPROVING YOUR STYLE

1. In your description imitate Twain's anaphora * in lines 12-14, beginning three successive sentences (kept fairly short) with "There was (were)." Mark the anaphora in the margin of your paper.

2. Use diction that implies your feelings about what you are describing, your response to it. Don't be afraid to exaggerate, even to be outrageous. Exaggera-. tion is one way in which Twain gets his comic effect, as in the description of the dirty comb.

Tourists

Nancy Mitford (1904–73) was an English writer of novels, biographies, and essays. This passage is from an essay called "The Tourist," part of a collection published under the title of *The Water Beetle* (1962). Mitford has acknowledged about herself that "when I take up my pen my thoughts are wicked." "Wicked" is a bit much, but certainly she is not given to pious platitudes. Her vision is satiric. She looks through appearances, through the phony surfaces most of us show the world, and reveals what people are in clever, mocking phrases. Notice in this selection how she uses her diction to ridicule both the tourists and the natives who make a living bamboozling them.

1   The most intensive study I ever made of tourists was at Torcello, where it is impossible to avoid them. Torcello is a minute island in the Venetian lagoon: here, among vineyards and wild flowers, some thirty cottages surround a great cathedral which was being built when William the Conqueror came to England. A canal and a path lead from the lagoon to 5 the village; the vineyards are intersected by canals; red and yellow sails glide slowly through the vines. Bells from the campanile ring out reproaches three times a day (*"cloches, cloches, divins reproches"*) joined by a chorus from the surrounding islands. There is an inn where I lived one summer, writing my book and observing the tourists. Torcello which used to be 10 lonely as a cloud has recently become an outing from Venice. Many more visitors than it can comfortably hold pour into it, off the regular steamers, off chartered motor-boats, and off yachts; all day they amble up the towpath, looking for what? The cathedral is decorated with early mosaics— scenes from hell, much restored, and a great sad, austere Madonna; Byzan- 15 tine art is an acquired taste and probably not one in ten of the visitors has acquired it. They wander into the church and look round aimlessly. They come out on to the village green and photograph each other in a stone arm-

From *The Water Beetle* by Nancy Mitford. Copyright © 1962 by Nancy Mitford. Reprinted by permission of A. D. Peters & Co., Ltd.

chair, said to be the throne of Attila. They relentlessly tear at the wild roses
which one has seen in bud and longed to see in bloom and which, for a day   20
have scented the whole island. As soon as they are picked the roses fade
and are thrown into the canal. The Americans visit the inn to eat or drink
something. The English declare that they can't afford to do this. They take
food which they have brought with them into the vineyard and I am
sorry to say leave the devil of a mess behind them. Every Thursday Ger-   25
mans come up the tow-path, marching as to war, with a Leader. There is a
standing order for fifty luncheons at the inn; while they eat the Leader lectures them through a megaphone. After luncheon they march into the
cathedral and undergo another lecture. They, at least, know what they are
seeing. Then they march back to their boat. They are tidy; they leave no   30
litter.

2   More interesting, however, than the behaviour of the tourists is
that of the islanders. As they are obliged, whether they like it or not, to live
in public during the whole summer, they very naturally try to extract some
financial benefit from this state of affairs. The Italian is a born actor; be-   35
tween the first boat from Venice, at 11 a.m. and the last on which the ordinary tourist leaves at 6 p.m., the island is turned into a stage with all the
natives playing a part. Young men from Burano, the next island, dress up
as gondoliers and ferry tourists from the steamer to the village in sandolos.
One of them brings a dreadful little brother called Eric who pesters every-   40
body to buy the dead bodies of sea-horses, painted gold. "Buona fortuna",
he chants. I got very frond of Eric. Sweet-faced old women sit at the cottage
doors selling postcards and trinkets and apparently making *point de Venise*
lace. They have really got it, on sale or return, from relations in Burano,
where it is made by young girls. Old women, with toil-worn hands, cannot   45
do such fine work. It is supposed that the tourists are more likely to buy if
they think they see the lace being made, but hardly any of them seem to
appreciate its marvellous quality. Babies toddle about offering four-leafed
clovers and hoping for a tip. More cries of "Buona fortuna". The priest organizes holy processions to coincide with the arrival of the steamer. And so   50
the play goes on. The tourists are almost incredibly mean, they hardly leave
anything on the island except empty cigarette boxes and flapping *Daily
Mails*. The lace is expensive, but they might buy a few postcards or shell
necklaces and give the children some pennies; they seem to have hearts of
stone.   55

3   As soon as the last boat has gone, down comes the curtain. The
"gondoliers" shed their white linen jackets and silly straw hats and go back

to Burano, taking Eric, highly dissatisfied with his earnings and saying if this goes on he will die of hunger. The sweet old women let the smiles fade from their faces, put away their lace-making pillows, and turn to ordinary 60 activities of village life such as drowning kittens. The father of the clover babies creeps about on his knees finding four-leafed clovers for the next day. The evening reproaches ring out, the moon comes up, the flapping *Daily Mails* blow into the lagoon. Torcello is itself again.

QUESTIONS

READER AND PURPOSE

1. Is Mitford a willing student of that strange animal—the modern tourist? (Perhaps her opening sentence, especially its final clause, will give you a clue.)
2. Whether or not she studies them willingly, Mitford is obviously critical of tourists. (Tourists seem to be disliked by everyone, even by other tourists.) Generally, however, she leaves her complaints implicit, contenting herself with simply describing what the visitors to Torcello do and allowing the facts to speak for themselves. Compose one or two sentences which summarize her criticisms of tourists. Do you think that Mitford's charges against sightseers would have been clearer and more effective if she had expressed them openly? Why or why not?
3. Does Mitford dislike the German tourists more than any of the others, or does she consider them the least objectionable?
4. Although she ridicules the typical tourist, Mitford resists the temptation to sentimentalize the natives of the island, to render them better than life so as to make the visitors seem worse. What details do we learn about the inhabitants of Torcello that keep them human and not impossibly idealized?

ORGANIZATION

5. Make an outline of this selection, indicating its major parts and at least the primary subdivisions under each of those.
6. What is the topic sentence of paragraph 1? Of paragraph 2? Of 3? How has the writer linked the beginning of the second paragraph to the first? The beginning of the third to the second?
7. What does the first part of paragraph 1 ("Torcello is . . . from the surrounding islands," lines 2-9) contribute to Mitford's discussion of tourists?
8. Paragraphs 2 and 3 are unified in part by the running metaphor * which compares the island to a stage set and its inhabitants to actors. What sentence sets up this comparison? Indicate all subsequent words or constructions that continue the metaphor.

9. While it is not actually the end of the essay from which this passage is taken, the third paragraph does bring the selection nicely to a close. Try to explain why it does.

SENTENCES

10. Mitford's sentences are effectively varied. She uses short, direct statements, longer sentences with several subordinate constructions, interrupted * movement, balanced * sentences, and parallelism *. Point out one or two examples of each of these sentence styles and be able to discuss why each is effective in its context. The writer even employs one fragment *. Where?

11. To what is *scenes* (15) in apposition *?

12. How does Mitford use sentence structure to help unify the portion of her first paragraph from line 17 to line 31?

13. Each of the following revisions is less effective, for Mitford's purpose, than the sentence she wrote. Why?

> (a) *Revision:* They wander into the church and aimlessly look around.
> *Mitford:* "They wander into the church and look round aimlessly." (17)
>
> (b) *Revision:* They know what they are seeing at least.
> *Mitford:* "They, at least, know what they are seeing." (29-30)
>
> (c) *Revision:* The curtain comes down as soon as the last boat has gone.
> *Mitford:* "As soon as the last boat has gone, down comes the curtain." (56)

DICTION

14. Look up: *lagoon* (3), *campanile* (7), *mosaic* (14), *austere* (15), *Byzantine* (15), *Attila* (19), *coincide* (50), *mean* (51).

15. What words in the first paragraph indicate the tourists' lack of purpose?

16. The phrase *lonely as a cloud* (11) is an echo from a famous poem. Do you recognize it? Mitford embeds another well known quotation in her prose. See if you can spot it. What advantages do such literary allusions * offer a writer? The absence of quotation marks around these phrases is deliberate. Why do you suppose Mitford did not use quotes? (She is not trying to pass these expressions off as her own; she expects her readers to recognize them.)

17. Is there possibly a double meaning in the phrase *much restored* in line 15?

18. Why is *Leader* capitalized in line 26?

19. Comment upon these proposed changes in Mitford's diction: *listen to* for *undergo* (29), *go* for *march* (30), *wander* for *toddle* (48), *discarded* for *flapping* (52).

POINTS TO LEARN

1. In description, facts often speak louder than opinions.
2. A metaphor can effectively organize and unify a paragraph or even a group of paragraphs.
3. A varied sentence style is more apt to be interesting.

SUGGESTIONS FOR WRITING

1. Think of tourists you have known. Write an essay in which you classify them by type, describing each in detail and trying to convey a distinct impression by the details you select.
2. Instead of tourists, you might prefer to describe the kinds of spectators one sees at an athletic contest—a football game, say—perhaps contrasting their actions with those of the players or officials.

IMPROVING YOUR STYLE

1. In your composition use (and label in the margin) at least one of each of these kinds of sentences: short and straightforward, balanced, parallel, a sentence showing interrupted movement, a sentence containing an appositive.
2. Try to embed a literary quotation somewhere in your prose. Do not explicitly identify it either by quotation marks or by acknowledging the source. It should be something sufficiently well-known that your reader will immediately recognize it.

PIERRE BERTON

Nitro-Glycerine

Pierre Berton is one of Canada's most popular and distinguished men of letters. He has, for many years, been a widely-read newspaper columnist and a radio and television personality. The range of his books includes *Klondike* (1958), a history of the Yukon gold rush; *The Secret World of Og* (1963), a children's book; *The Comfortable Pew* (1965), a critical treatment of apathetic church-goers; and a bestselling and critically-acclaimed two-volume history of the Canadian Pacific Railway: *The Great Railway* (1970) and *The Last Spike* (1971), which won the Governor General's Award for non-fiction, one of three such awards Berton has won. His extraordinary account of the laborers who transported nitro-glycerine is taken from *The Great Railway*.

1   In the dismal land west of Lake Superior, nature seemed to have gone to extremes to thwart the railway builders. When they were not lay-ing track across the soft porridge of the muskegs they were blasting it through some of the hardest rock in the world—rock that rolled endlessly on, ridge after spiky ridge, like waves in a sullen ocean.   5

2   Dynamite, patented in the year of Confederation, was as new as the steam shovel and, though the papers were full of stories of "dyna-miters" using Alfred Nobel's new invention for revolutionary purposes, the major explosive was dynamite's parent, nitro-glycerine. This awesomely un-stable liquid had been developed almost thirty years before the first sod 10 was turned on the CPR but was only now beginning to replace the weaker blasting powder, being ten times more expensive not to mention more dan-gerous. It had been in regular use as a railway-building explosive only since George M. Mowbray in 1866 demonstrated its efficiency in the building of the Hoosac Tunnel—the successful results there having sprung largely from 15 the development of a new kind of detonator, electrically fired. It had never

From *The National Dream: The Great Railway 1871-1881* by Pierre Berton, reprinted by permission of The Canadian Publishers, McClelland and Stewart Limited, Toronto.

before been used as extensively as it was west of the lakehead in the late seventies.

3   Here the technique was to pour the explosive into holes drilled often by hand but sometimes with the newly developed Burleigh rock drill, worked by compressed air. The liquid was then poured into the holes, each about seven feet deep, and set off by a fuse. In less than two years some three hundred thousand dollars was spent on nitro-glycerine on Section Fifteen, often with disastrous results. There was among the workmen an almost cavalier attitude to the explosive. Cans of nitro-glycerine with fuses attached were strewn carelessly along the roadbed in contravention of all safety regulations, or carried about with such recklessness that the fluid splashed upon the rocks. Whole gangs were sometimes blown to bits in the resultant explosions, especially in the cold weather, because the chemical was notoriously dangerous when frozen; the slightest jar could touch it off. Under such conditions it was kept under hot water and at as uniform a temperature as possible.

4   It could not be transported by wagon; the jarring along those corrugated trails would have made short work of the first drover foolhardy enough to risk it. It had to be carried in ten-gallon tins on men's backs. The half-breed packers and the Irish navvies remained contemptuous of it. Armstrong, the engineer, saw one packer casually repairing a leak in a tin by scraping mud over it with his knife, oblivious of the fact that the tiniest bit of grit or the smallest amount of friction would blast him heavenwards. Sometimes the packers would lay their tins down on a smooth rock and a few drops would be left behind from a leak. The engineers travelling up and down the line watched the portage trails with hawk's eyes seeking to avoid those telltale black specks which could easily blow a man's leg off. On one occasion a teamster took his horse to water at just such a spot. The horse's iron shoe touched a pool of nitro-glycerine and the resulting blast tore the shoe from his foot and drove it through his belly, killing him and stunning the teamster.

5   In drilling holes for the explosive, it was the practice to fill them first with water and then pour in the heavier liquid; the water then floated to the top and acted as tamping. Often, however, some of the explosive ran out, causing secondary explosions later on when the cut was trimmed. The number of men killed or maimed by accidental explosions was truly staggering. In one fifty-mile stretch of Section B, Sandford Fleming counted thirty graves, all the result of the careless handling of nitro-glycerine. Mary Fitzgibbon, on her way to homestead in Manitoba, watched in awe as a

long train of Irish packers tripped gaily down a hill, each with a can of
liquid explosive on his back, making wry, funereal comments all the while:

6   "It's a warm day."

7   "That's so but maybe ye'll be warmer before ye camp tonight."

8   "That's so, d'ye want any work taken to the Divil?"   60

9   "Where are ye bound for, Jack?"

10   "To hell, I guess."

11   "Take the other train and keep a berth for me, man!"

12   "Is it ye're coffin ye're carrying, Pat?"

13   "Faith ye're right; and the coroner's inquest to the bargain, Jim."   65

14   Mrs. Fitzgibbon wrote that in spite of the banter "the wretched
expression of these very men proved that they felt the bitterness of death
to be in their chests."

15   There were, indeed, some terrible accidents. A youth climbing a
hill with a can of explosive stumbled and fell; all that was ever found of 70
him was his foot in a tree, one hundred yards away. A workman in a rock
cut handed a can to one of the drillers and as he did so his foot slipped:
four men died, three more were maimed. One workman brushed past a
rock where some explosive had been spilled; he lost his arm and his sight
in an instant. At Prince Arthur's Landing, an entire nitro-glycerine factory 75
blew up in the night, hurling chunks of frozen earth for a quarter of a mile
and leaving a gaping hole twenty feet deep and fifty feet across. And then
there was the case of Patrick Crowley, an over-moral Irishman, who objected so strenuously to Josie Brush's bawdy-house at Hawk Lake that he
blew it up, and himself into the bargain.   80

QUESTIONS

READER AND PURPOSE

1. Which of the two types of description—objective and impressionistic—mentioned on pages 327-9 is Berton using? Or is he using a combination of both?
If so, why? What reasons could you give for his using just one type (if that is
what he does)?

2. What was your reaction to Berton's description? Did it stimulate any specific
feelings in you? If so, what purpose do you believe Berton had in mind?

ORGANIZATION

3. Which two words in the first paragraph most clearly reveal what the rest of
this selection is about? Be prepared to justify your choice.

4. Now show how the whole of paragraph 1 is centered on these two words.

5. In paragraph 2, show how the last sentence is the logical result of the first sentence. Are there any gaps in the development of this paragraph?

6. Paragraph 3 is a good example of a paragraph in which the topic is expressed not in the first sentence but in a later one—here, in the fourth sentence. Analyze the structure of paragraph 3 to see why this is true.

7. What transition (if any) is there between paragraphs 3 and 4? If there is a transition, comment upon its effectiveness. If not, discuss whether Berton is justified in omitting it.

8. Analyze the nature of the relationship between sentence 4 of paragraph 3 and paragraphs 3, 4, and 5.

9. Why does Berton make paragraph 6 a separate one instead of making it part of paragraph 5?

10. Is the last sentence an effective conclusion to this selection? Why or why not?

11. Is there a closing by return * at the end of this selection?

SENTENCES

13. Discuss how sentences 2, 3, and 4 of paragraph 7 are balanced * sentences.

14. Of the three sentences mentioned above, two use semi-colons and one uses a colon. Why the difference?

15. Is the first sentence of this selection an effective introductory sentence? Justify your answer by examining each paragraph in relation to this first sentence.

16. In sentence 1 of paragraph 3, Berton refers to *the explosive;* in sentence 2 to *the liquid;* in sentence 3 to *nitro-glycerine;* in sentence 4 to *the explosive.* What other words finish this pattern in the paragraph? What variation does he use in the next paragraph?

17. What is the appositive * in sentence 4 of paragraph 4? Does Berton use any other appositives in this selection?

DICTION

18. Look up: *thwart* (2), *muskegs* (3), *sullen* (5), *extensively* (17), *cavalier* (25), *contravention* (26), *uniform* (31), *drover* (34), *navvies* (36), *oblivious* (38), *funereal* (57), *banter* (66).

19. Like Boyce Richardson, Berton uses a number of hyphenated expressions, such as *nitro-glycerine* (9), *railway-building* (13), *ten-gallon* (35), *half-breed* (36), *fifty-mile* (53), *over-moral* (78), *bawdy-house* (79). Read the comments on hyphenated expressions (p. 67), and then, using these remarks as a rough guide, make your own comments on Berton's use of the hyphen.

20. Why does Berton put the word *dynamiters* (7-8) in quotation marks?

21. In his introductory paragraph Berton uses the adjectives *dismal, soft, hardest, spiky, sullen.* Comment on the appropriateness of these adjectives to the rest of the selection.

POINTS TO LEARN
1. The first sentence of a description is not necessarily the topic sentence.
2. An essay may be effectively concluded without using a closing by return.
3. A subject may be frequently recalled to the reader's attention by the use of synonyms and pronouns.

SUGGESTIONS FOR WRITING
Write an essay of five or six paragraphs in which you describe a dangerous process or experience you deliberately took part in, such as climbing a high cliff, killing a dangerous animal or poisonous snake, taking a canoe over some bad rapids, facing up (physically or psychologically) to a bully, hiking in severe weather, making an unpopular point at a public meeting, criticizing the student-union president, etc.

IMPROVING YOUR STYLE
In your essay:
1. Use an introductory paragraph that does not include the topic sentence.
2. Include both objective and impressionistic details.
3. Use synonyms in one paragraph to replace the subject, and, in another paragraph, a repeated pronoun.

Bubbles in the Ice

Henry David Thoreau (1817-62) is best known for *Walden* (1854) and *Civil Disobedience* (1849), inspired by his opposition to the Mexican War. Thoreau is often thought of as a writer about nature, and indeed there is much observation of the natural world in *Walden*, as in such books as *Cape Cod* and *A Week on the Concord and Merrimack Rivers*. But Thoreau's primary subject is not really trees and rivers and ponds. It is the world within man—the world of mind and spirit. He is, finally, a moralist, not in the narrow brush-your-teeth-and-say-your-prayers sense, but in the larger meaning of a person for whom moral commitment is the essence of life. The following selection (from *Walden*) may not seem to be moralism. In its literal content it is not. Yet in a more subtle way "Bubbles in the Ice" illustrates one of Thoreau's most fundamental commitments: to see things whole, to see them as they are, and to be precise and honest about what he sees.

The pond had in the mean while skimmed over in the shadiest and shallowest coves, some days or even weeks before the general freezing. The first ice is especially interesting and perfect, being hard, dark, and transparent, and affords the best opportunity that ever offers for examining the bottom where it is shallow; for you can lie at your length on ice only an inch thick, 5 like a skater insect on the surface of the water, and study the bottom at your leisure, only two or three inches distant, like a picture behind a glass, and the water is necessarily always smooth then. There are many furrows in the sand where some creature has travelled about and doubled on its tracks; and, for wrecks, it is strewn with the cases of caddis worms made of minute 10 grains of white quartz. Perhaps these have creased it, for you find some of their cases in the furrows, though they are deep and broad for them to make. But the ice itself is the object of most interest, though you must improve the earliest opportunity to study it. If you examine it closely the morning after it freezes, you find that the greater part of the bubbles, which 15

From *Walden*, edited by Owen Thomas (New York: W. W. Norton & Co., 1966).

at first appeared to be within it, are against its under surface, and that more are continually rising from the bottom; while the ice is as yet comparatively solid and dark, that is, you see the water through it. These bubbles are from an eightieth to an eighth of an inch in diameter, very clear and beautiful, and you see your face reflected in them through the ice. There may be thirty or forty of them to a square inch. There are also already within the ice narrow oblong perpendicular bubbles about half an inch long, sharp cones with the apex upward; or oftener, if the ice is quite fresh, minute spherical bubbles one directly above another, like a string of beads. But these within the ice are not so numerous nor obvious as those beneath. I sometimes used to cast on stones to try the strength of the ice, and those which broke through carried in air with them, which formed very large and conspicuous white bubbles beneath. One day when I came to the same place forty-eight hours afterward, I found that those large bubbles were still perfect, though an inch more of ice had formed, as I could see distinctly by the seam in the edge of a cake. But as the last two days had been very warm, like an Indian summer, the ice was not now transparent, showing the dark green color of the water, and the bottom, but opaque and whitish or gray, and though twice as thick was hardly stronger than before, for the air bubbles had greatly expanded under this heat and run together, and lost their regularity; they were no longer one directly over another, but often like silvery coins poured from a bag, one overlapping another, or in thin flakes, as if occupying slight cleavages. The beauty of the ice was gone, and it was too late to study the bottom. Being curious to know what position my great bubbles occupied with regard to the new ice, I broke out a cake containing a middling sized one, and turned it bottom upward. The new ice had formed around and under the bubble, so that it was included between the two ices. It was wholly in the lower ice, but close against the upper, and was flattish, or perhaps slightly lenticular, with a rounded edge, a quarter of an inch deep by four inches in diameter; and I was surprised to find that directly under the bubble the ice was melted with great regularity in the form of a saucer reversed, to the height of five eighths of an inch in the middle, leaving a thin partition there between the water and the bubble, hardly an eighth of an inch thick; and in many places the small bubbles in this partition had burst out downward, and probably there was no ice at all under the largest bubbles, which were a foot in diameter. I inferred that the infinite number of minute bubbles which I had first seen against the under surface of the ice were now frozen in likewise, and that each, in its degree, had operated like a burning glass on the ice beneath to melt and rot it.

These are the little air-guns which contribute to make the ice crack and whoop.

QUESTIONS

READER AND PURPOSE

1. Is Thoreau observing the ice with an objective, scientific detachment; or is he viewing it impressionistically, projecting his values and emotions into what he sees? Does he do more than passively observe—conduct experiments, say, or take specimens?

2. What assumptions does Thoreau appear to have made concerning his reader's attitude toward nature? What effect do you believe Thoreau wishes to have upon his reader? Does he succeed?

ORGANIZATION

3. Which clause near the beginning of the paragraph serves as a topic statement?

4. Thoreau's paragraph is quite long (though this is not unusual; paragraphs tended to be longer in the literary prose of the nineteenth century). What is Thoreau primarily concerned with up to line 13? What shift in topic occurs at that point? There are at least two other places where similar minor turns of thought occur. Identify them.

5. Study the passage from lines 14 to 24 and be able to discuss how Thoreau organizes his discussion of the bubbles.

SENTENCES

6. Read the two following sentences carefully and decide what principle Thoreau has observed in arranging the sequence of their phrases and clauses:

   (a) "I sometimes used to cast on stones to try the strength of the ice, and those which broke through carried in air with them, which formed very large and conspicuous white bubbles beneath." (25-28)

   (b) "Being curious to know what position my great bubbles occupied with regard to the new ice, I broke out a cake containing a middle sized one, and turned it bottom upward." (39-41)

7. Why is this revision less effective than Thoreau's sentence?

   Revision: You find that the greater part of the bubbles are against the under surface of the ice (though at first they appeared to be within it),

if you examine the ice closely the morning after it freezes, and that
more are continually rising from the bottom. . . .

Thoreau: "If you examine it closely the morning after it freezes, you
find that the greater part of the bubbles, which at first appeared to be
within it, are against its under surface, and that more are continually
rising from the bottom. . . ." (14-17)

8. In the clause in lines 21-23, to what is *cones* in apposition *?

DICTION

9. Look up: *coves* (2), *quartz* (11), *Indian summer* (31), *opaque* (33), *cleavages* (38), *middling* (41), *lenticular* (44), *inferred* (51).
10. Find specimens of Thoreau's diction which suggest the exact, scientific eye. Find others which suggest a more impressionistic, emotionally colored vision.
11. In several places Thoreau uses similes * and metaphors *. Point these out and consider what purpose he probably intended them to serve and whether or not they succeed.

POINTS TO LEARN
1. Exactness of detail is vital to objective description.
2. When possible organize sentences to reflect the order of perception or of thought.

SUGGESTIONS FOR WRITING
Look closely at some commonplace natural object and describe it as exactly as you can: a stalk of grass or of grain, a mackerel, a pumpkin, an ear of corn, a gladiola.

IMPROVING YOUR STYLE
In your description include:
1. A sentence containing an appositive.
2. A long sentence (25-30 words minimum) in which the sequence of elements (that is, the words, phrases, clauses) exactly follows the order of events.
3. Two metaphors and two similes.

The Subway

Tom Wolfe (not to be confused with the novelist Thomas Wolfe of an earlier generation) is one of the new journalists. The new journalism, more an idea than a movement, loosely designates a group of younger authors who write, like journalists, about the people, the places, the events of the contemporary world, but who write with the imagination, the personal vision, and the rhetorical flair we usually associate with the creative writer. Indeed, in the new journalism the distinction between reporting and literature fades, and the term *story* includes in full measure of ambiguity both its newspaper and literary senses.

Wolfe's stories appear in magazines such as *Confidential* and *Harper's Bazaar*. The subjects of a few of those that were collected in his book *The Kandy-Kolored Tangerine-Flake Streamline Baby* (1965) will indicate his range: Las Vegas, Muhammad Ali, The Museum of Modern Art in New York City, the business of customizing cars (the subject of the title essay), and the penchant of New Yorkers for self-aggrandizement ("The Big League Complex," source of the following paragraphs about the subway). Wolfe, like any good reporter, observes closely, but far from striving for objectivity he observes from a particular angle of vision—often satiric—and he projects what he feels and thinks into his description by the details he selects to show us and the words he chooses to describe them.

1   In a way, of course, the subway is the living symbol of all that adds up to lack of status in New York. There is a sense of madness and disorientation at almost every express stop. The ceilings are low, the vistas are long, there are no landmarks, the lighting is an eerie blend of fluorescent tubing, electric light bulbs and neon advertising. The whole place is a gross assault 5 on the senses. The noise of the trains stopping or rounding curves has a high-pitched harshness that is difficult to describe. People feel no qualms

Excerpt from "The Big League Complex" from *The Kandy Kolored Tangerine Flake Streamline Baby* by Tom Wolfe. Copyright © 1964 by the New York *Herald Tribune*. Reprinted by permission of Farrar, Straus & Giroux, Inc.

about pushing whenever it becomes crowded. Your tactile sense takes a crucifying you never dreamed possible. The odors become unbearable when the weather is warm. Between platforms, record shops broadcast 45 r.p.m.   10
records with metallic tones and lunch counters serve the kind of hot dogs in which you bite through a tensile, rubbery surface and then hit a soft, oleaginous center like cottonseed meal, and the customers sit there with pastry and bread flakes caked around their mouths, belching to themselves so that their cheeks pop out flatulently now and then.   15

2   The underground spaces seem to attract every eccentric passion. A small and ancient man with a Bible, an American flag and a megaphone haunts the subways of Manhattan. He opens the Bible and quotes from it in a strong but old and monotonous voice. He uses the megaphone at express stops, where the noise is too great for his voice to be heard ordinarily,   20
and calls for redemption.

3   Also beggars. And among the beggars New York's status competition is renewed, there in the much-despised subway. On the Seventh Avenue IRT line the competition is maniacal. Some evenings the beggars ricochet off one another between stops, calling one another ———s and   25
———s and telling each other to go find their own ——— car. A mere blind man with a cane and a cup is mediocre business. What is demanded is entertainment. Two boys, one of them with a bongo drum, get on and the big boy, with the drum, starts beating on it as soon as the train starts up, and the little boy goes into what passes for a native dance. Then, if   30
there is room, he goes into a tumbling act. He runs from one end of the car, first in the direction the train is going, and does a complete somersault in the air, landing on his feet. Then he runs back the other way and does a somersault in the air, only this time against the motion of the train. He does this several times both ways, doing some native dancing in between.   35
This act takes so long that it can be done properly only over a long stretch, such as the run between 42nd Street and 72nd Street. After the act is over, the boys pass along the car with Dixie cups, asking for contributions.

4   The Dixie cup is the conventional container. There is one young Negro on the Seventh Avenue line who used to get on at 42nd Street and   40
start singing a song, "I Wish That I Were Married." He was young and looked perfectly healthy. But he would get on and sing this song, "I Wish That I Were Married," at the top of his lungs and then pull a Dixie cup out from under the windbreaker he always wore and walk up and down the car waiting for contributions. I never saw him get a cent. Lately, however,   45
life has improved for him because he has begun to understand status com-

petition. Now he gets on and sings "I Wish That I Were Married," only when he opens up his windbreaker, he not only takes out a Dixie cup but reveals a cardboard sign, on which is written: "MY MOTHER HAS MULTIPLE SCHLERROSSIS AND I AM BLIND IN ONE EYE." His best touch is sclerosis, which   50 he has added every conceivable consonant to, creating a good, intimidating German physiology-textbook solidity. So today he does much better. He seems to make a living. He is no idler, lollygagger or bum. He can look with condescension upon the states to which men fall.

5   On the East Side IRT subway line, for example, at 86th Street, the   55 train stops and everyone comes squeezing out of the cars in clots and there on a bench in the gray-green gloom, under the girders and 1905 tiles, is an old man slouched back fast asleep, wearing a cotton windbreaker with the sleeves pulled off. That is all he is wearing. His skin is the color of con-gealed Wheatena laced with pocket lint. His legs are crossed in a gentle-   60 manly fashion and his kindly juice-head face is slopped over on the back of the bench. Apparently, other winos, who are notorious thieves among one another, had stripped him of all his clothes except his windbreaker, which they had tried to pull off him, but only managed to rip the sleeves off, and left him there passed out on the bench and naked, but in a gentlemanly   65 posture. Everyone stares at him briefly, at his congealed Wheatena-and-lint carcass, but no one breaks stride; and who knows how long it will be before finally two policemen have to come in and hold their breath and scrape him up out of the gloom and into the bosom of the law, from which he will emerge with a set of green fatigues, at least, and an honorable seat at night   70 on the subway bench.

QUESTIONS

READER AND PURPOSE

1. In the essay from which these paragraphs are excerpted Wolfe is writing about the New Yorker's preoccupation with being "big league," with his never-ending struggle for status. As an example he points out that certain New Yorkers take a snobbish pride in never riding the subway, which they consider, not merely literally, to be beneath them. The example leads Wolfe into a descrip-tion of the subway. What general impression of it does he convey?

2. Do you think that Wolfe is primarily concerned with affecting his readers in some particular way or with expressing clearly what he perceives and how he feels about it?

ORGANIZATION

3. Which sentence controls the entire selection? Which states the topic of paragraph 1?

4. In paragraph 1 how is the third sentence related to the second? Does it merely repeat the preceding idea in more specific terms, explain why that idea is true, or compare it with something else?

5. Which is the topic statement of paragraph 2? Does it set up only this paragraph? How is it supported in the second paragraph? By what technique are the sentences in lines 18-21 unified?

6. Explain how the third paragraph is linked to the second. What short sentence sets up most of the third paragraph? Study the seven sentences from lines 28 to 38 and be able to show how each is tied to what precedes it.

7. What effects the link between paragraphs 4 and 3? Paragraph 4 has two parts: where is the dividing point? How is flow * maintained in its final four sentences?

8. At the beginning of paragraph 5 Wolfe uses the phrase "for example": what is he illustrating? Is there a topic statement in this paragraph? If not, what words at the end of the preceding paragraph serve that purpose?

SENTENCES

9. The sentence in lines 3-5 consists of four asyndetic * clauses (independent clauses butted together without conjunctions). Such constructions are usually separated by semicolons. Wolfe, however, uses what is called the comma link. Do you think commas are sufficient here? Why or why not? What would be the effect upon the movement of this sentence if the clauses were punctuated in the conventional manner with semicolons?

10. Do you think the fragment * that opens the third paragraph is effective? Would anything be gained by turning it into a complete sentence, such as: "There are also beggars"? Would anything be lost?

11. How do the following alter the emphasis of Wolfe's sentences?

(a) *Revision:* The competition is maniacal on the Seventh Avenue IRT line.
Wolfe: "On the Seventh Avenue IRT line the competition is maniacal." (23-24)

(b) *Revision:* Then he goes into a tumbling act if there is room.
Wolfe: "Then, if there is room, he goes into a tumbling act." (30-31)

(c) *Revision:* But he would get on and sing this song, "I Wish That I Were Married," at the top of his lungs and then pull a Dixie cup out from under the windbreaker he always wore and walk up and down the car waiting for contributions, though I never saw him get a cent.

Wolfe: "But he would get on and sing this song, 'I Wish That I Were Married,' at the top of his lungs and then pull a Dixie cup out from under the windbreaker he always wore and walk up and down the car waiting for contributions. I never saw him get a cent." (42-45)

DICTION

12. Look up: *symbol* (1), *disorientation* (2), *vistas* (3), *eerie* (4), *redemption* (21), *intimidating* (51), *physiology* (52), *lollygagger* (53), *notorious* (62), *congealed* (66).

13. Explain the meanings of these phrases: *gross assault* (5), *metallic tones* (11), *eccentric passion* (16), *mediocre business* (27), *kindly juice-head face* (61).

14. Why are these substitutions less effective than the words Wolfe uses? *Mushy* for *oleaginous* (13), *patrols* for *haunts* (18), *crazy* for *maniacal* (24), *bump* for *ricochet* (25), *pouring* for *squeezing* (56), *groups* for *clots* (56), *old* for *1905* (57), *remove him from* for *scrape him up out of* (68-69)

15. In the description of the hot dog in lines 11-13, what words arouse unpleasant associations? What do you think Wolfe's purpose is in this description? Does he succeed? How does he wish us to respond to the customers eating "pastry and bread" (13-15)?

16. How does the phrase *of course* (1) affect Wolfe's tone *? What does it say to his reader?

POINTS TO LEARN

1. In writing description it is good practice to set up and control details with short introductory sentences.

2. Sometimes (though not usually) a topic statement may be placed outside the paragraph in which it is developed.

SUGGESTIONS FOR WRITING

1. Describe something which, like the subway, assaults the senses with multifarious sights and sounds and smells—an amusement park, a holiday crowd at a bus station or airport, a supermarket on a busy shopping day. The impression you communicate may be pleasant or unpleasant, but in either case decide beforehand what it is and select and arrange your details accordingly.

2. In a paragraph or two discuss what range of impressions (they are varied and complicated) Wolfe conveys about the naked drunkard he describes in paragraph 5. Support your discussion by specific examples of the writer's diction and by analyzing how individual words aroused particular responses in you.

IMPROVING YOUR STYLE

Include the following in your description:

1. A sentence consisting of 3 or 4 short clauses closely related in idea but grammatically independent. Punctuate them, as Wolfe does the sentence in lines 3-5, with commas.

2. (With your instructor's permission) two fragments (*effective* fragments).

3. The phrase *of course* to introduce a sentence.

4. (If it fits with your topic) a description of an item of junk food made to seem unappetizing, even sickening.

ROBERT MOON

The Regina Riot

Robert Moon was born and raised in Moose Jaw, Saskatchewan. A graduate of the University of Saskatchewan, he spent his working life as a journalist in that province. His account of the rioting men who were on relief because they could not find work during the Great Depression exemplifies some of the qualities of good journalistic writing: clear presentation of the relevant facts, simplicity, precision, and vividness.

1   One of the most sombre episodes in Regina's history came in the middle of this decade. Relief camp strikers began a trek from British Columbia to Ottawa in early June, 1935. They had simply wanted to place their complaints about camp conditions and about receiving relief rather than a work and wages programme before the federal government at Ot- 5 tawa. On June 14th the long freight train bearing the 1,600 rolled into Regina from the west. The men formed fours and marched to the Stadium where they were to stay during the stop. Their leaders warned them there was to be: "No hooliganism in Regina."

2   Meanwhile the federal government ordered the R.C.M.P. to stop 10 the march in the Queen City. In spite of this, it became evident the marchers did not intend submitting to the ultimatum to return to the B.C. relief camps. A mass meeting of 5,000 Reginans approved a resolution urging the then Prime Minister R. B. Bennett to remove all obstacles imped- ing the eastward trek. Regina service clubs offered to organize a voluntary 15 motor cavalcade to carry the men toward the Manitoba border. Two fed- eral cabinet ministers, Railways Minister R. J. Manion and Agriculture Minister Robert Weir, came west to negotiate with the strike leaders.

From *This is Saskatchewan*, reprinted by permission of the author.

With 10,000 milling about on downtown streets, a truce was arranged. Out of the discussions came a decision to send eight leaders to Ottawa to pre- 20 sent demands. Nothing came out of the talks and they returned.

3   There was no doubt a move by rail would be blocked by police— four hundred of them were now mobilized in the city. The strikers decided to use trucks. Two truckloads started east on the night of June 28th. They were stopped on the outskirts by steel-helmeted mounted policemen and 25 five strikers were arrested. A tense week-end followed.

4   The R.C.M.P. then decided to arrest the strike leaders. They planned to go to a mass meeting of strikers and citizens on Market Square behind the police station. At dusk on July 1st, with speakers on the plat- form addressing the crowd a police whistle sounded and R.C.M.P. and city 30 policemen swept onto the open ground where travelling carnivals occa- sionally pitch their tents today, where a weigh scale sits on one side, and where no one would suspect one of the worst street battles in Canadian history began.

5   When the police drove in, the crowd was thrown into a panic and 35 surged back. The strikers, armed with clubs and pieces of cement and brick as if expecting a fight, then moved forward toward the police, who used tear gas bombs, quirts and the occasional pot shot. For the next three hours, lasting until eleven o'clock, the battle raged in chaos, wild confu- sion, bloodshed, and at times curious *bathos.* Mounted police on horseback 40 rode through the streets. Automobiles were overturned. Downtown store windows were smashed—children sat in one, eating displayed candy while strikers and police fought hand to hand outside.

6   As the riot went on and before it finally subsided, there was a strange lull and in its midst there came a grim note of humour, as there 45 is humour at some time in most tragedies. An old Englishman, a retired military man, cane in hand, walked stiffly across Market Square toward the fire hall where strikers were hurling rocks through windows.

7   "Chief," he shouted, raising his cane. "Get your revolver. Shoot those men."   50

8   The men stopped their throwing to gaze in awe at the audacity of this unarmed old gentleman. The fire chief's mouth fell open. Had he owned a revolver, he would have obeyed the command.

9   During the riot thousands of dollars' damage was done. One hun- dred and twenty were arrested. More than one hundred strikers, citizens 55 and police were injured, half requiring hospitalization. One city detective was killed by a blow on the head from a club as he attempted to prevent

marchers taking some wooden stakes piled on Market Square. No one was ever brought to justice for the killing.

10   The events leading up to the riot were tense enough. The method chosen by the police to arrest the leaders was ill-advised. The men themselves were ill-led, some leaders were Communist inspired. The combination had had all the elements of conflict. Five days later the strikers, appalled like everyone else by what had happened, swung aboard two westbound freights and headed home.

11   The day had been one of the most tragic in recent Canadian times. Yet no one could have witnessed this combat, no one could have seen these men as they marched through the streets of cities they stopped at on their way east until riot stopped them at Regina without recognizing that here in this ill-dressed, ill-fed band was a dramatic witness to the depression times.

12   "Are we downhearted," one would cry.

13   "No," they all shouted back, not in carefully rehearsed, synchronized mass chorus as were uniformed young men in the military states of Europe of that era but with the voices of individuals. These were hard times in a democracy, but even in adversity there was hope.

14   There are some who say there is a direct connection between that sad July day of 1935 and the 1944 election of the Co-operative Commonwealth Federation—more commonly, C.C.F.—government of Saskatchewan, the first Socialist administration in North America. There is not quite that but in the political factors of Saskatchewan today the depression is still a haunting spectre.

QUESTIONS

READER AND PURPOSE

1. Since this essay is taken from a history of Saskatchewan, one might expect that it would be written entirely as objective description, as simply a factual account of what occurred. Is this correct?

2. Would you, as reader, want a purely factual description of the Regina riot? Or would you prefer that the writer interpret the event for you as he himself feels about it?

3. Would the use of expressionism in this description have been valid?

4. What sort of reaction from his reader do you think Moon is trying to achieve in the last sentence of paragraph 4 and in paragraph 10?

ORGANIZATION

5. What are the two elements of the contrast Moon is establishing in the first two paragraphs?
6. What is the function of paragraph 3 in relation to paragraphs 1 and 2?
7. Paragraph 5 tells of the fighting, paragraph 6 tells of a comic incident, and paragraph 9 summarizes the damage and the injuries. What order (if any) is being followed here?
8. What is the function of paragraphs 9 and 10 with regard to the causes and nature of all that has preceded?
9. Rearrange, in several combinations, the order of paragraphs 5 through 10. For example, could paragraph 10 come after 4? Why or why not? Could paragraphs 8 and 9 be interchanged? 9 and 6?
10. Why does paragraph 9—"the events leading up to the riot"—come where it does instead of following, or even being incorporated into, paragraph 1? Do they not both deal with the causes of the riot?
11. Is there a transition between paragraphs 2 and 3? Explain why or why not.
12. Why does Moon bother with the incident he relates in paragraph 6? How does it affect the rest of the essay?

SENTENCES

13. The third sentence of paragraph 1 begins "They had simply wanted to place . . . ." Could it also be written "They had wanted simply to place . . ."? Or "They had wanted to simply place . . ."? Defend your choice of one of these three as preferable.
14. Why is there a colon in the last sentence of paragraph 1? Would a comma be as effective? A semi-colon?
15. Should there be a comma in l. 30? Two commas? None?
16. Why is there a comma after *bloodshed* (40) but none after *quirts* (38)? Is Moon's usage here consistent?
17. Compare the sentence structure of paragraph 8 with that of paragraph 9. Is there a pattern? If not, are there any similarities at all?
18. How effective is the last sentence as a sentence (not as a conclusion)? Does the metaphor function logically with the expression *political factors*?

DICTION

19. Look up: *sombre* (1), *trek* (2), *hooliganism* (9), *ultimatum* (12), *impeding* (14-15), *mobilized* (23), *dusk* (29), *quirts* (38), *bathos* (40), *subsided* (44), *appalled* (64), *synchronized* (73-74), *adversity* (76), *spectre* (82).
20. The expression *relief camp strikers* (2) is a shortened form of "strikers from relief camps." In the shortened form a noun, *strikers*, is modified by a combination of a noun, *camp*, and its modifying adjective, *relief*—although now

both *relief* and *camp* become adjectives. Some grammarians object to such a piling up of adjectives before a noun, especially when some of these words are not normally used as adjectives.

Find some other expressions of this sort, and defend, or condemn, Moon's use of them.

21. What does Moon mean by the expression "curious *bathos*" (40)? Does he give an example? Can you think of an example of bathos that would not be curious?

POINTS TO LEARN

1. The use of impressionistic details can lend feeling and strength to an objective description.

2. The cause-effect relationship of an event can be made at places other than the introduction.

SUGGESTIONS FOR WRITING

Describe, in five to seven short paragraphs, a turbulent public gathering at which you have been present, such as an election rally (university, civic, federal), a strike meeting, a protest rally (against corruption in government, nuclear arms, abortion, the legal drinking age, contraception), a march against city hall, a protest meeting against fluoridation or pornography or the legal driving age or the use of pesticides—etc.

IMPROVING YOUR STYLE

1. At the beginning of your essay describe clearly the two sides involved and the immediate context of the events.

2. In describing the actual confrontation use three or four specific incidents and further details.

3. End your essay with a paragraph that briefly summarizes the lessons to be learned from the confrontation.

A Paris Plongeur

George Orwell (1903-50) was born in India of middle-class English parents. His real name was Eric Blair; Orwell being a pen name. After being sent to England to be educated, he earned a scholarship to Eton. Upon leaving school, he worked for five years as a member of the British Imperial Police in Burma, but in 1927 he left his job and returned to England, utterly disillusioned with the injustice and oppression of colonial rule. Determined to become a writer, he went to Paris, hoping to support himself by giving English lessons. When his efforts to live by teaching failed, he became almost destitute. His life among the nearly starving poor of Paris and later as a tramp in England was the subject of his first book, *Down and Out in Paris and London* (1933). Today he is best remembered for his political satires *1984* (1949) and *Animal Farm* (1945). In the following excerpt from *Down and Out in Paris and London* he describes working as a dishwasher (*plongeur*) in a luxury hotel in Paris.

1   Our cafeterie was a murky cellar measuring twenty feet by seven by eight high, and so crowded with coffee-urns, breadcutters and the like that one could hardly move without banging against something. It was lighted by one dim electric bulb, and four or five gas-fires that sent out a fierce red breath. There was a thermometer there, and the temperature never 5 fell below 110 degrees Fahrenheit—it neared 130 at some times of the day. At one end were five service lifts, and at the other an ice cupboard where we stored milk and butter. When you went into the ice cupboard you dropped a hundred degrees of temperature at a single step; it used to remind me of the hymn about Greenland's icy mountains and India's coral 10 strand. Two men worked in the cafeterie besides Boris and myself. One was Mario, a huge, excitable Italian—he was like a city policeman with operatic gestures—and the other, a hairy, uncouth animal whom we called the

From *Down and Out in Paris and London*. Copyright 1933 by George Orwell; renewed 1961 by Sonia Pitt-Rivers. Reprinted by permission of A. M. Heath & Company Ltd, Mrs Sonia Brownell Orwell, and Martin Secker & Warburg.

Magyar; I think he was a Transylvanian, or something even more remote. Except the Magyar we were all big men, and at the rush hours we collided 15 incessantly.

2   The work in the cafeterie was spasmodic. We were never idle, but the real work only came in bursts of two hours at a time—we called each burst *"un coup de feu."* The first *coup de feu* came at eight, when the guests upstairs began to wake up and demand breakfast. At eight a sudden bang- 20 ing and yelling would break out all through the basement; bells rang on all sides, blue-aproned men rushed through the passages, our service lifts came down with a simultaneous crash, and the waiters on all five floors be- gan shouting Italian oaths down the shafts. I don't remember all our duties, but they included making tea, coffee and chocolate, fetching meals from 25 the kitchen, wines from the cellar and fruit and so forth from the dining- room, slicing bread, making toast, rolling pats of butter, measuring jam, opening milk-cans, counting lumps of sugar, boiling eggs, cooking porridge, pounding ice, grinding coffee—all this for from a hundred to two hundred customers. The kitchen was thirty yards away, and the dining-room sixty 30 or seventy yards. Everything we sent up in the service lifts had to be cov- ered by a voucher, and the vouchers had to be carefully filed, and there was trouble if even a lump of sugar was lost. Besides this, we had to supply the staff with bread and coffee, and fetch the meals for the waiters upstairs. All in all, it was a complicated job. 35

3   I calculated that one had to walk and run about fifteen miles dur- ing the day, and yet the strain of the work was more mental than physical. Nothing could be easier, on the face of it, than this stupid scullion work, but it is astonishingly hard when one is in a hurry. One has to leap to and fro between a multitude of jobs—it is like sorting a pack of cards against 40 the clock. You are, for example, making toast, when bang! down comes a service lift with an order for tea, rolls and three different kinds of jam, and simultaneously bang! down comes another demanding scrambled eggs, coffee and grapefruit; you run to the kitchen for the eggs and to the dining- room for the fruit, going like lightning so as to be back before your toast 45 burns, and having to remember about the tea and coffee, besides half a dozen other orders that are still pending; and at the same time some waiter is following you and making trouble about a lost bottle of soda-water, and you are arguing with him. It needs more brains than one might think. Mario said, no doubt truly, that it took a year to make a reliable cafetier. 50

4   The time between eight and half-past ten was a sort of delirium. Sometimes we were going as though we had only five minutes to live; some-

times there were sudden lulls when the orders stopped and everything seemed quiet for a moment. Then we swept up the litter from the floor, threw down fresh sawdust, and swallowed gallipots of wine or coffee or 55 water—anything, so long as it was wet. Very often we used to break off chunks of ice and suck them while we worked. The heat among the gas-fires was nauseating; we swallowed quarts of drink during the day, and after a few hours even our aprons were drenched with sweat. At times we were hopelessly behind with the work, and some of the customers would have 60 gone without their breakfast, but Mario always pulled us through. He had worked fourteen years in the cafeterie, and he had the skill that never wastes a second between jobs. The Magyar was very stupid and I was inexperi-enced, and Boris was inclined to shirk, partly because of his lame leg, partly because he was ashamed of working in the cafeterie after being a waiter; 65 but Mario was wonderful. The way he would stretch his great arms right across the cafeterie to fill a coffee-pot with one hand and boil an egg with the other, at the same time watching toast and shouting directions to the Magyar, and between whiles singing snatches from *Rigoletto*, was beyond all praise. The *patron* knew his value, and he was paid a thousand francs a 70 month, instead of five hundred like the rest of us.

5   The breakfast pandemonium stopped at half-past ten. Then we scrubbed the cafeterie tables, swept the floor and polished the brasswork, and, on good mornings, went one at a time to the lavatory for a smoke. This was our slack time—only relatively slack, however, for we had only ten min- 75 utes for lunch, and we never got through it uninterrupted. The customers' luncheon hour, between twelve and two, was another period of turmoil like the breakfast hour. Most of our work was fetching meals from the kitchen, which meant constant *engueulades* from the cooks. By this time the cooks had sweated in front of their furnaces for four or five hours, and their tem- 80 pers were all warmed up.

6   At two we were suddenly free men. We threw off our aprons and put on our coats, hurried out of doors, and, when we had money, dived into the nearest *bistro*. It was strange, coming up into the street from those firelit cellars. The air seemed blindingly clear and cold, like arctic summer; 85 and how sweet the petrol did smell, after the stenches of sweat and food! Sometimes we met some of our cooks and waiters in the *bistros*, and they were friendly and stood us drinks. Indoors we were their slaves, but it is an etiquette in hotel life that between hours everyone is equal, and the *engueu-lades* do not count. 90

7   At a quarter to five we went back to the hotel. Till half-past six

there were no orders, and we used this time to polish silver, clean out the coffee-urns, and do other odd jobs. Then the grand turmoil of the day started—the dinner hour. I wish I could be Zola for a little while, just to describe that dinner hour. The essence of the situation was that a hundred or two hundred people were demanding individually different meals of five or six courses, and that fifty or sixty people had to cook and serve them and clean up the mess afterwards; anyone with experience of catering will know what that means. And at this time when the work was doubled, the whole staff was tired out, and a number of them were drunk. I could write pages about the scene without giving a true idea of it. The chargings to and fro in the narrow passages, the collisions, the yells, the struggling with crates and trays and blocks of ice, the heat, the darkness, the furious festering quarrels which there was no time to fight out—they pass description. Anyone coming into the basement for the first time would have thought himself in a den of maniacs. It was only later, when I understood the working of a hotel, that I saw order in all this chaos.

8   At half-past eight the work stopped very suddenly. We were not free till nine, but we used to throw ourselves full length on the floor, and lie there resting our legs, too lazy even to go to the ice cupboard for a drink. Sometimes the *chef du personnel* would come in with bottles of beer, for the hotel stood us an extra beer when we had had a hard day. The food we were given was no more than eatable, but the *patron* was not mean about drink; he allowed us two litres of wine a day each, knowing that if a *plongeur* is not given two litres he will steal three. We had the heeltaps of bottles as well, so that we often drank too much—a good thing, for one seemed to work faster when partially drunk.

9   Four days of the week passed like this; of the other two working days, one was better and one worse. After a week of this life I felt in need of a holiday. It was Saturday night, so the people in our *bistro* were busy getting drunk, and with a free day ahead of me I was ready to join them. We all went to bed, drunk, at two in the morning, meaning to sleep till noon. At half-past five I was suddenly awakened. A night-watchman, sent from the hotel, was standing at my bedside. He stripped the clothes back and shook me roughly.

10   "Get up!" he said. "*Tu t'es bien saoulé la gueule, eh?* Well, never mind that, the hotel's a man short. You've got to work to-day."

11   "Why should I work?" I protested. "This is my day off."

12   "Day off, nothing! The work's got to be done. Get up!"

13   I got up and went out, feeling as though my back were broken and

my skull filled with hot cinders. I did not think that I could possibly do a day's work. And yet, after only an hour in the basement, I found that I was perfectly well. It seemed that in the heat of those cellars, as in a turkish bath, one could sweat out almost any quantity of drink. *Plongeurs* know this, and count on it. The power of swallowing quarts of wine, and then sweating it   135 out before it can do much damage, is one of the compensations of their life.

QUESTIONS

READER AND PURPOSE

1. Orwell is not writing for the down-and-out in Paris and London. At what kind of reader is he aiming? What does he assume the reader to know and not to know?

2. Is Orwell's purpose best described as accurate, detailed reporting of a personal experience, as social criticism, as some combination of these, or as something else altogether? Give reasons for your answer, citing passages in the text.

ORGANIZATION

3. The first paragraph sets the stage and lists the cast of characters. The second and third paragraphs describe the narrator's job. What organizing principle is at work in paragraphs 4-8?

4. Give a title to paragraphs 9-13, indicating the essential topic of that section.

SENTENCES

5. In line 6 a semicolon in place of the dash would be more conventional. Why? What is the advantage of the dash, if any? Find another example of this usage in paragraph 3.

6. In lines 12 and 13 the dashes might be replaced with two commas or with parentheses. Yet dashes, commas, and parentheses would each create a slightly different effect. Explain.

7. What is the difference in the emphasis upon *drunk* in this sentence by Orwell and its revision?

> *Revision:* We all went to bed drunk at two in the morning, meaning to sleep till noon.

> *Orwell:* "We all went to bed, drunk, at two in the morning, meaning to sleep till noon." (122-23)

8. In paragraph 6 identify an example of emphasis by inversion *.

9. What three ways of achieving emphasis are at work in the sentence beginning "The Magyar was very stupid" in line 63?

DICTION

10. Look up: *Magyar* (14), *spasmodic* (17), *porridge* (28), *voucher* (32), *scullion* (38), *gallipots* (55), *Rigoletto* (69), *heeltaps* (115).

11. Throughout this passage Orwell uses French words and phrases. In one case he quotes what the nightwatchman said, using part English and part French (126-27). Should Orwell have avoided French altogether? Why or why not? What rule of thumb can you formulate about using foreign words in your own writing?

12. Does Orwell's diction tend to be abstract * and general or concrete * and particular? List examples of both types.

13. Does Orwell rely more heavily upon adjectives or upon nouns and verbs? Underline the adjectives in the first two paragraphs.

14. List Orwell's similes * and metaphors *.

15. Using examples, demonstrate the relationship between Orwell's diction and tone *. Describe his attitudes toward his job, the "Magyar," Mario, and toward himself.

SUGGESTIONS FOR WRITING

Loosely following Orwell's organization and employing the first-person point of view *, describe your job in a supermarket, restaurant, factory, hospital, department store, or elsewhere. Convey a distinct tone toward your work and your fellow employees. Your problem is to interest your reader by making clear exactly what you do and how you feel about it.

IMPROVING YOUR STYLE

1. In your composition write a sentence similar to that in lines 101-04. Use a long series of parallel * nouns (or gerunds and nouns) concluded by a dash and short clause, the subject of which refers to all the nouns in the series. A similar but slightly different pattern occurs in lines 24-30. Either model is suitable. Notice the occurrence of this kind of sentence in other descriptions or narrations. It is very useful to convey multiplicity and complexity.

2. Use a dash as Orwell employs it in line 6.

3. Include two or three metaphors and two or three similes.

4. In one sentence achieve emphasis by inversion.

From The Great Lone Land

William Francis Butler (1838-1910) was born in Ireland; he first came to Canada in the year of Confederation as an officer in the British Army. He subsequently returned to Ireland where, in 1869, he learned of the Red River resistance led by Louis Riel. Butler was never a man to pass up a chance for action and adventure, and, hastily returning to Canada, he served as an intelligence officer for Colonel Wolseley, the commander of the force sent to put down the resistance. In 1870 he was dispatched by the Lieutenant-Governor of Manitoba to report on the conditions at the Hudson Bay Company's posts on the Saskatchewan River, and to carry medicines to the Indians in the region, who were suffering the ravages of a smallpox epidemic. Butler was by nature an enthusiastic traveller and explorer, and gladly took up this assignment. In 1872, he published an account of his six-month journey of 1870-71, which took him 2,700 miles up the Saskatchewan as far as the Rocky Mountains. This book, *The Great Lone Land*, was widely read in Butler's time, and it remains a vivid and perceptive narrative by a writer acutely aware of details and able to record them in clear, vigorous prose.

1   About midway between Fort Ellice and Carlton a sudden and well-defined change occurs in the character of the country; the light soil disappears, and its place is succeeded by a rich dark loam covered deep in grass and vetches. Beautiful hills swell in slopes more or less abrupt on all sides, while lakes fringed with thickets and clumps of good-sized poplar balsam 5 lie lapped in their fertile hollows.

2   This region bears the name of the Touchwood Hills. Around it, far into endless space, stretch immense plains of bare and scanty vegetation, plains seared with the tracks of countless buffalo which, until a few years ago, were wont to roam in vast herds between the Assineboine and 10 the Saskatchewan. Upon whatever side the eye turns when crossing these

From William Francis Butler, *The Great Lone Land*, 4th ed. (London: Sampson Low, Marston, Low & Searle, 1873).

WILLIAM FRANCIS BUTLER   371

great expanses, the same wrecks of the monarch of the prairie lie thickly strewn over the surface. Hundreds of thousands of skeletons dot the short scant grass; and when fire has laid barer still the level surface, the bleached ribs and skulls of long-killed bison whiten far and near the dark burnt 15 prairie. There is something unspeakably melancholy in the aspect of this portion of the North-west. From one of the westward jutting spurs of the Touchwood Hills the eye sees far away over an immense plain; the sun goes down, and as he sinks upon the earth the straight line of the horizon becomes visible for a moment across his blood-red disc, but so distant, so 20 far away, that it seems dream-like in its immensity. There is not a sound in the air or on the earth; on every side lie spread the relics of the great fight waged by man against the brute creation; all is silent and deserted— the Indian and the buffalo gone, the settler not yet come. You turn quickly to the right or left; over a hill-top, close by, a solitary wolf steals away. 25 Quickly the vast prairie begins to grow dim, and darkness forsakes the skies because they light their stars, coming down to seek in the utter solitude of the blackened plains a kindred spirit for the night.

QUESTIONS

READER AND PURPOSE

1. Butler begins by describing the Touchwood Hills (located in what is now southern Alberta). Would you agree that his description is, for the most part, objective rather than impressionistic? Explain the basis of your answer.

2. Why do the Touchwood Hills serve as an appropriate vantage point from which Butler can describe the surrounding prairie in paragraph 2?

3. List some of the more striking words and phrases from paragraph 2 that Butler uses to make us share his feelings about the prairie. How would you briefly summarize those feelings?

ORGANIZATION

4. Does the first sentence of paragraph 2 logically belong at the end of paragraph 1? Explain why.

5. The topic sentence of paragraph 2 is sentence five. Is this an effective place for it? Would Butler's feeling of melancholy have been more or less convincing to the reader if it had been stated in the first sentence of the paragraph in place of the sentence now there? Could it have been omitted altogether?

6. In sentences two, three, and four of paragraph 2, Butler makes use of repetition to emphasize what particular aspects of the prairie. Give some examples of

words and phrases that are either repeated directly or with slight variation. Are these effective in making the reader share Butler's general impression as stated in sentence five? Why?

7. Before reaching sentence five Butler tells us what he "sees." Does he do the same in sentences six to nine? Does he appeal to other senses as well?

8. What colors does Butler associate with the prairie? Is his image * of "the blood-red disc" (20) meant to contrast with these colors? Before answering look at the image in the final sentence of this selection.

9. Butler's focus is on the emotions evoked in him by the prairie. Does the second paragraph provide enough concrete * detail to produce similar emotions in the reader?

SENTENCES

10. Although most of Butler's sentences are long and complicated, they are nevertheless varied in structure. How many sentences does he begin with prepositional phrases? With the subject-verb nucleus? How often does he use interrupting * phrases? Coordinate clauses *? Differently positioned subordinate clauses *?

11. Suppose that the second sentence of paragraph 2 were broken down into shorter, more direct sentences:

> Immense plains of bare and scanty vegetation stretch around it, far into endless space. The plains are seared with the tracks of countless buffalo. These animals were wont to roam, until a few years ago, in vast herds between the Assineboine and the Saskatchewan.

How has our perception of the scene been altered by changing the emphasis and the flow * of Butler's sentence?

12. Explain why the author uses semi-colons, rather than periods, in the seventh sentence of paragraph 2.

13. Compile a list of the verbs Butler uses. Could these be described as strong verbs, capable of stimulating emotion? If not, explain what kinds of words Butler does use to create his impression, giving as many examples as possible.

DICTION

14. Look up: *loam* (3), *vetches* (4), *immense* (8), *wont* (10), *melancholy* (16), *brute creation* (23), *kindred* (28).

15. How do their etymologies * help you to understand the following words: *scanty* (8), *seared* (9), *relics* (22)?

16. What cumulative effect does Butler produce through the connotations * of words and phrases such as *bare* (8), *wrecks* (12), *bleached* (14), *utter solitude* (27)? List some other words and phrases in this selection that have similar connotations.

17. What kind of figure of speech * is *the monarch of the prairie* (12)?

POINTS TO LEARN

1. Good description usually appeals to more than one of the senses.
2. The impression that a writer wishes to convey need not be stated at the outset, nor at length. It can even be omitted if the descriptive details can be made to speak for themselves.
3. Impressionistic description should contain sufficient concrete detail to enable the reader to see what has stimulated particular feelings in the writer.

SUGGESTIONS FOR WRITING

1. Write an impressionistic description of the students in one of your classes. Then rewrite the same description objectively.
2. Describe the crowd at a hockey game (or a student rally, or some other public event familiar to you). Write your description with a clear sense of the impression you want your reader to receive, but do not state this impression directly.

IMPROVING YOUR STYLE

In your description include:
1. A cumulative * sentence (like the second sentence of Butler's second paragraph).
2. Three sentences in which you make use of repetition of a key word or its synonyms.
3. Examples of precise visual and aural images.
4. Vivid nouns, adjectives, and adverbs.
5. One or two metaphors.

ADRIAN FORSYTH

Flights of Fancy

One of the most prominent natural-science writers in North America, Adrian Forsyth has received a number of distinguished awards. His work has been published frequently in such periodicals as *Equinox, Saturday Night, Horticulture,* and *Natural History.* His books include *Tropical Nature,* an introduction to tropical biology; *Mammals of the Canadian Wild* (1985); and *A Natural History of Sex* (1986). He now divides his time between Canada and Costa Rica, doing research on animal behaviour and rain-forest ecology.

1   Fledgling common swifts, perched on the edge of their nest in preparation for their first flight, are about to embark on the natural world's greatest odyssey. Common swifts are so completely at home in the air that biologists believe they spend two years in continuous flight, feeding, mating and even sleeping in the air. A young swift will fly nonstop for 300,000   5 miles—a distance equal to six flights around the world—from the time it leaves its parental nest until it settles to build its own nest.

2   Among birds, swifts are but one of many species capable of outstanding aerial exploits. Peregrine falcons can descend on prey at 175 miles per hour. Hummingbirds manoeuvre with more finesse than any bee. Arc-   10 tic terns fly an 18,000-mile annual migration from the Arctic to the Antarctic. Dippers plunge into mountain torrents in pursuit of underwater insects and emerge from the water flying.

3   All of these athletic feats of flight depend on a single evolutionary development: feathers. Insects, fish, bats, squirrels and lemurs can fly or   15 glide. But it is feathers that allow birds to fly for thousands of miles, to dive at speeds greater than any land or marine animal can achieve and to move with unsurpassed agility and grace.

4   The usefulness of feathers is a product of both the construction of

From *Equinox,* 25 (January/February 1986).

individual feathers and the way they are arranged on a bird's body. True to   20
the cliché, feathers are light, but their design makes them strong and flexi-
ble as well. Flight feathers have a hollow central shaft. Hundreds of hairlike
barbs run out from the shaft to form the flat surface of the feather. Barbs
are connected to each other by hooked, overlapping barbules. A single
pigeon feather may have more than one million barbs, barbules and hooks.   25
The resulting complex, tightly knit surface is light, sheds water and presents
little friction against air.

5   Large flight feathers can provide sophisticated aerodynamics. Feathers increase the surface area and curvature of a bird's wing, giving it more
lift and control than the fixed membrane of a bat or insect wing. Flight   30
feathers have muscles around their base, allowing them to move like the
flaps on the tail of an airplane. By spreading the feathers on the rear edge of
its wings, a bird can create slots that reduce air resistance when it lifts it
wings between down beats. Many bird species also have small secondary
wings called alula. Located near the centre of the front edge of the wing,   35
the alula feathers capture air currents and can increase the lift of a wing by
up to 20 percent. Many birds are unable to get off the ground if their alula
feathers are damaged.

6 Although flight and feathers seem inseparable, flying is only one of
many functions that feathers perform for birds. Like a mammal's hair or a   40
reptile's scales, feathers insulate and protect a bird's body. Down, which is
composed of small feathers that lack the hooks which bind the barbules of
flight feathers, has a puff of fine barbs that create millions of pockets of
dead air. Anyone who has snuggled into a down parka at 20 below zero can
attest to the insulating properties of down.   45

7   Feathers around the ears of birds such as owls act as sound amplifiers.
Other nocturnal raptors have feathers that resemble bristles around their
faces and feet. Like the whiskers of a cat, the bristles provide the night fliers
with information about the location of prey. Hairlike feathers called filo-
plumes have a large number of nerve endings at their base and are believed   50
to act as sensory devices to help the bird adjust its other feathers to pressure
changes.

8   Most birds have excellent color vision, which is in keeping with
their multihued plumage. One nineteenth-century ornithologist catalogued
1,115 shades in bird feathers. The great range of color is due to the diverse   55
roles played by feathers. Bright colors are important for courtship and
species identification. The bright red epaulets of the red-winged blackbird,
for example, signal other blackbirds that the bearer is a mature breeding
male. Immature males have only a faint red patch, and females have no red.

Such signalling enables a bird to escape harassment by members of the 60
wrong sex or by competitors that are larger, older and stronger. Researchers
have found that if the feathers of a young red-winged blackbird are red-
dened, it is subject to fierce challenges by bona fide adult territorial males.

9   Bright colors and elaborate feathers are also used by males in courtship displays directed at females. The most colorful feathers of all are those 65
worn by courting pheasants, peacocks and quetzals. In some cases the tail
feathers are six feet long, and many of these birds feature spectacular
iridescent eyespots complete with countershading. Humans have, at various times, become enamoured of these ornamental feathers and have sought
to adorn themselves in comparable fashion. At the turn of the century, the 70
thirst of Western women for feathers was so great that egret plumes sold for
$80 an ounce, more than the price of gold. The trade involved about one
milllion pounds of feathers a year, resulting in the estimated destruction of
200 million birds.

10   Because nine-tenths of a feather is pure protein, producing plum- 75
age requires substantial amounts of nutrients and energy, especially in view
of the large number of feathers a bird grows: roughly 1,500 by the ruby-
throated hummingbird and 25,000 by the whistling swan. In species such as
frigate birds and tropic seabirds, which spend most of their lives soaring
above the ocean, the feathers weigh more than the bird's skeleton. It is 80
somewhat surprising, then, that birds moult and grow new feathers at
regular intervals.

11   Flying, brooding, fighting and feeding, along with exposure to wind,
sunlight and other elements, such as seawater, cause feathers to fray and
tear and, in time, to become less efficient. To compensate, most birds shed 85
their feathers once a year, although some tropic birds have a longer period
between moults. The moulting cycle is a complex process that reflects the
ecological pressures on a species. Aquatic birds like loons or dippers, which
can escape underwater from danger and are not particularly vulnerable
even when they cannot fly, shed all their feathers at once. Birds which must 90
be able to fly to escape predators or which have to keep hunting often have
a prolonged moult so that old feathers are lost gradually as new ones grow
in. This ensures that the bird is never grounded. Some species fit all their
feather changing into a brief period of food abundance at the peak of
summer, when the cost of growing a new set of feathers is low. 95

12   Moulting is an adaptation that not only eliminates worn feathers
but also enables a bird to match its appearance to changing seasons and
social necessities. Many birds use the moult for camouflage. Willow ptarmi-

gan and other northern birds moult from their white winter coat to an
inconspicuous dirty summer plumage that blends with the tundra. Male 100
ducks, such as the blue-winged teal, moult from a colourful courtship coat
to a drab summer coat known as "eclipse" plumage, which conceals them
from predators.

13 The moult may also be a means of shedding parasites. The intricate spaces within and among feathers harbour a rich array of fleas, flies, 105
lice and mites, many of which feed directly on the feathers and skin. As
many as 1,000 lice have been found on the feathers of a single curlew, and
there are an estimated 25,000 species of feather lice. The presence of these
vermin accounts for the enthusiasm that many birds display for bathing in
water and dust. 110

14 Like all evolutionary adpatations, feathers are not perfect. They
lack the flexibility of hair and are ill suited to tasks that involve getting
rubbed the wrong way. That is why vultures have lost the feathers on their
heads and necks. Sticking a feathered head inside a rotting carcass would
result in a formidable mess when the head was withdrawn. Nevertheless, 115
feathers have been successfully modified, shortened and compacted enough
to enable many species of birds to nest in underground burrows and to
swim well underwater. As a result, there is virtually no habitat on Earth,
except for the ocean depths, unexploited by feathered species.

15 When observing a bird in flight, it is hard to imagine that the 120
origins of this freedom can be traced to a scaly reptile sleeping in the sun.
Yet most evolutionary biologists believe that birds had such an ancestor.
The best explanation for the evolution of feathers has nothing to do with
flying. Instead, feathers appear to have originated from long, pointed scales
that were used as heat shields by the basking reptiles. The ancestors of birds 125
were probably small upright reptiles that pursued prey and hopped around
the shrubbery and treetops. Wings developed as gliding structures. Feathers,
meanwhile, had already evolved because they were useful in shedding and
capturing heat. As the prototype birds began to rely on gliding and wing
flapping, their feathers became aerodynamic structures. Thus feathers were 130
present before birds became full-fledged fliers. In fact, feathers may have
existed before birds became truly birdlike and could have been the device
necessary to launch the group forward into true sustained flight.

16 There is a biological moral in this aspect of feathers: one cannot
predict the evolutionary future of a characteristic or behaviour. As we look 135
into the fossilized past, we discover that some small change in the scales of
reptiles, an alteration that may have seemed trivial at the time of its origin,

eventually produced profound adaptations. Just as we owe much of our evolutionary success to a few minor changes—the shifting of the thumb, perhaps, or a propensity to forage on the ground instead of in the trees— 140 birds owe much of their success to a reptile scale that gradually grew longer and more elaborate and finally became a feather.

17   The success of birds—both evolutionarily and in the eyes of humanity—is inextricably based on feathers and flight. Birds are the most mobile of organisms and some would say the most beautiful and inspiring. 145 A plucked bird looks ignominious and pathetic, but a bird possessed of feathers and flight is a symbol of freedom and peace, of escape and independence.

QUESTIONS

READER AND PURPOSE

1. The author's subject is one that most people will have given little thought to. What does his essay offer that could not be found in a dictionary definition?
2. Is this essay simply an example of objective description? Are there also places where the author draws conclusions from his material which suggest that the study of feathers can lead us to think about larger and more controversial issues?

ORGANIZATION

3. How many paragraphs constitute the introduction? In what paragraph is the main subject of the essay introduced? What would be lost if Forsyth's essay had begun with paragraph 4?
4. Between the introductory paragraphs and the concluding paragraph the essay exhibits a clearly-defined four-part structure. Indicate which paragraphs belong to each part. Identify the connectives* between each part.
5. What are the main topics of each of the four parts? What effect is achieved by putting the parts in the order Forsyth gives them? How does this order serve the purpose of his essay?
6. How does Forsyth prepare the reader for the evolutionary theory introduced in paragraph 15?
7. What relationship is established between the bird as symbol* of independence (paragraph 17) and the "biological moral" of paragraph 16? Is the concept of independence anticipated in other parts of the essay?

SENTENCES

8. Identify some of the places where Forsyth uses a series of sentences to introduce a generalization and then follows it with particularizing detail, as in paragraphs 2 and 3.

9. Examine Forsyth's sentences in paragraphs 4 and 5 and state how many of them are compound*, complex*, or simple*. What does the proportion of each kind reveal about Forsyth's descriptive method? How does this proportioning serve the purpose of his essay?

10. Nearly all of Forsyth's sentences present straightforward statements of fact. What significant change in this method is evident in paragraph 15? Why is the change appropriate?

DICTION

11. Look up: *odyssey* (3), *barbules* (24), *epaulets* (57), *quetzals* (66), *iridescent* (68), *ecological* (88), *ignominious* (146).

12. Find the etymologies* of: *camouflage* (98), *aerodynamic* (130).

13. Explain the meaning of these phrases: *fixed membrane* (30), *nocturnal raptors* (47), *bona fide* (63).

14. Identify the figure of speech* in paragraph 7. Is the same device being employed in paragraph 6?

15. Examine Forsyth's choice of nouns in paragraphs 10 to 14, and then indicate the proportion of abstract* terms to concrete* ones. How does his preference for one or the other suit the purpose of his essay?

POINTS TO LEARN

1. Description of apparently insignificant objects can be used to draw or suggest conclusions of wider importance.

2. Abstract terms need particular supporting detail to make them clear to an unspecialized reader.

3. An introduction may require more than one paragraph in order to focus the topic.

SUGGESTIONS FOR WRITING

1. Copy out a dictionary definition of some general term (such as hand, foot, eye, claw, or fur). Then write three paragraphs in which you lead your reader to an understanding of how this general term has a particular and important interest.

2. Write three paragraphs in which you begin with a general topic (such as living with your parents, wanting to meet a famous person, trying to get along with a friend) and then provide specific examples which make it particular.

IMPROVING YOUR STYLE

1. Write three paragraphs of description (an awkward animal, unusual cloud formations, an odd-looking tree or plant, a particularly ugly insect), the first in simple sentences, the second in compound sentences, and the third in complex. Then rewrite the three paragraphs using all three types of sentences in each one.

2. Write two or three paragraphs in which you use similes to explain, or clarify, the subject you chose from the previous topic in terms of its resemblance to something quite unlike itself.

HUGH DEMPSEY

The Snake Man

Hugh Dempsey is chief curator of the Glenbow-Alberta Institute in Calgary, and he has for many years edited the quarterly magazine *Alberta History*. As a result of his long interest in the history of western Canada, and particularly of the Blackfoot tribes, he has published a large number of articles and books, including *Crowfoot, Chief of the Blackfeet* (1972), and *Charcoal's World* (1978). His wife, Pauline, is a daughter of the famous Blackfoot chief James Gladstone, once a member of the Canadian Senate. Dempsey's latest book is *James Gladstone—Canada's First Indian Senator* (1986).

1   On a lonely hill near the Belly Buttes lies the unmarked grave of a Blood chief who, upon his death in 1901, carried with him one of the strangest secrets of the Canadian West. The man was Calf Shirt, or *Onistahsi-sokasim*; his secret was a strange power which permitted him to talk to rattlesnakes.   5

2   Calf Shirt was a paradox, for in 57 years of life he played with equal dexterity the roles of informer and tribal leader, police scout and criminal. But his power over rattlesnakes was his strangest trait, a gift of his own religion. This power came to him when he was 36 years old, just before the Bloods and their Blackfoot allies began to experience the bitterness of life   10 on a reserve and to hunger for the vanished buffalo.

3   Calf Shirt's career was filled with adventure. Even in the years before his strange control over rattlesnakes, he had had an eventful life. Born in 1844, the son of The Shoulder, he was a member of the Many Tumors band and earned a favorable reputation as a warrior. After one   15 particular experience, he took the name of Calf Shirt which had belonged to an uncle killed by whiskey traders during the winter of 1873–74. Names were considered to be family possessions which could be claimed after some particular achievement or event.

From *Alberta History*, 29, 4 (Autumn 1981). Reprinted by permission of the author.

4   Calf Shirt did his best to live up to his name. He joined several war 20
parties, mostly against the Crows in Montana, and became so highly regarded
that he was a leader of revenge war parties. These were formed whenever
the Bloods suffered humiliating defeat at the hands of the enemy. He took
part in a great battle between the Crees and Blackfoot near the present city
of Lethbridge in the fall of 1870. He had been out hunting and, upon his 25
return, was told by his father that the battle was in progress. The young
warrior let his father daub bright war paint on his face and, as a gesture of
scorn, promised that should he be struck by an enemy arrow, he would
leave it in his body for his father to remove.

5   Grasping a double bladed knife from his religious Bear medicine 30
bundle, Calf Shirt arrived while the battle was in progress in time to see the
Crees being trapped in a long shallow coulee. Among those making a stand
were two warriors, one tall and the other wearing a calfskin robe. Armed
only with his Bear knife and singing his war song, Calf Shirt rushed the
men, but took an arrow in the wrist before he reached them. Heedless of 35
the shaft protruding from his arm, the warrior grabbed the bow with his
wounded hand and struck the tall Cree a mortal blow with his knife. The
calf-skinned comrade, waiting for a clear shot, was stabbed to death in a
similar manner.

6   After the fight, people offered to remove the enemy arrow, but 40
Calf Shirt reminded them of his promise and accompanied the victorious
Bloods back to their camp. On the way, his arm became greatly swollen
until he could not travel unaided but when he still refused to remove the
arrow, he was lashed onto a travois and dragged into camp where his father
was waiting to take out the shaft.   45

7   According to elderly Bloods, Calf Shirt received his special rattlesnake powers through a vision in the late 1870s. The event occurred shortly
after Calf Shirt's father had died and the young warrior had wandered away
by himself to mourn. The Bloods were camped in a rattlesnake-infested
area east of the present Medicine Hat, at a place called "Where We Drowned." 50
Calf Shirt walked aimlessly in his sorrow until, at last, he laid down exhausted
on a sand hill and fell asleep. While there, he had a dream in which a person
appeared before him. "I've heard you mourning the loss of your father and
have taken pity on you," said the stranger. "My father has sent me to you to
say that you'll be his son and we'll be brothers. All of our people who live 55
here are his children and you're now one of us. You'll become a leader of
your people and we'll watch over you. Always carry some sagebrush with
you so that we'll know you and so you can use it to treat those who are sick."

8   In his dream, Calf Shirt could see the person but still did not recognize him. Realizing this, the figure explained, "I'm from the Big 60 Snake tribe; our people are rattlesnakes. When you die, you'll become one of us."[1]

9   Returning to his home camp, Calf Shirt soon demonstrated his newly-gained powers. Grasping a rattlesnake, he wrapped it around his waist, carried it before a shocked group of Bloods, and played with it as 65 though it were a child. At first his friends shunned him, for they feared the rattling serpents, but in time they learned that they had nothing to fear as the snakes were his brothers and did his bidding. If he whistled, they slithered through the grass to his feet; if he made a sign, they quietly slipped away.   70

10   By the time the Bloods settled on their reserve in 1881, Calf Shirt had become a prominent member of the tribe. He was not a chief, for the Many Tumors were then under the leadership of the aged Medicine Calf and a younger brother, Strangling Wolf. But Calf Shirt was an ambitious man and to gain the coveted role of chief, he chose to turn his back on his 75 people and become an informer for the Indian agent. He saw that enough support for a chieftainship would not likely come from his band, but was astute enough to realize the Indian agent needed chiefs who would co-operate in matters of farming and rationing, even if these wishes were not always in the best interest of the tribe.   80

11   Calf Shirt also knew that Medicine Calf could not live many more years and if outside influence was not used, Strangling Wolf would become sole leader of the band.

12   The warrior's first move took place at the autumn treaty payments in 1884, at a time when Medicine Calf was on his death bed. The agent later 85 explained to his superiors that "Calf Shirt sat at the pay table with me and through his honesty I was in a position to refuse paying a number of South Peigans representing themselves to be Bloods. Through services rendered, this Indian has got the ill will of all the Blood tribe . . . I may state that of his own free will he reduced his family three souls."[2]   90

13   This statement was based on the government's belief that Indians resorted to the wholesale padding of ration lists, claiming to have more persons in their families than was the fact. This, believed the Indian agent, often was accomplished by borrowing friends' children and dressing them so they would not be recognized during treaty and ration payments.   95

14   After the death of Medicine Calf in October, 1884, Calf Shirt vigorously pursued his plan of action. Three months later, he reported to the

agent that white men were selling alcohol to the Bloods in the form of Jamaica ginger, essence and Pain Killer. Then, during the 1885 Riel rebellion, he kept the agent informed of all activities, rumours and gossip among the Bloods, as well as intelligence of any runners or visitors from other tribes. This concentrated program of helping the Indian agent had the desired effect for, in the summer of 1885, Calf Shirt was made a minor chief to replace the deceased Medicine Calf.

15 Once appointed, Calf Shirt knew the agent would have a hard time deposing him, so the astute Blood promptly abandoned his policy of co-operation. He had used the Indian agent for his own advantage and now was prepared to resume a position of prestige among his people.

16 His first opportunity came late in 1886, when the Bloods learned that six of their men had been killed and scalped by Assiniboine Indians in Montana. These included three of Calf Shirt's close relatives. As a ripple of excitement swept through the camps, the once-peaceful Calf Shirt stirred the young people into action. He organized a revenge party of some two hundred warriors, just as he had in the buffalo days, and was prepared to lead them out against their enemy when an autumn snowstorm cut short his plan. Continued cold weather made the raid impractical and before the snows had melted in the spring, the Blood elders had made a peace treaty with their old enemies.

17 In the following winter of 1887–88, Calf Shirt displayed his disregard for the white man's law when he smuggled a supply of whiskey onto the reserve from Montana. Then sitting placidly in his tepee, he bragged that the Mounted Police were afraid to arrest him. However, he was wrong and was sentenced to one month in Fort Macleod guardhouse.

18 During these years, Calf Shirt continued to live with his snakes and to turn his remarkable gift into a profitable enterprise. As early as 1881, he was a visitor to Fort Macleod where he collected money for performing tricks with a large snake. On one such visit a local newspaper man wrote that "Calf Shirt is the snake charmer of the Blood branch and the great Blackfoot nation, and he handles the deadly rattlesnake with the most consummate indifference to the awful absolute death that is contained in it slender fangs. He keeps it coiled round his body next to the skin, inside the shirt, where it lovingly nestles, and anyone who is willing to pay for his curiosity can see him put his hand in and drag the living, writhing death out.

19 "Calf Shirt claims," continued the writer, "to have some subtle power over snakes and to see him take his present specimen up, she measuring about three feet long, catch it by the neck and cram about eight inches of it, the deadliest reptile in America, head downwards down his throat, is calculated to make the marrow in any man's bones shiver. He also puts it out on the ground and playfully pats it on the back of the head with his fingers, till the snake rattles as if it was performing for the benefit of all the babies in Canada. It is not a pleasant sight for one with weak nerves and who understands what a rattlesnake is."[3]

20   In 1888, Calf Shirt broke away from the Many Tumors band and, retaining his chieftainship, formed a new band called the Crooked Backs. He and about 40 followers left the main Blood camps on the Belly River and settled on the northern tip of the reserve, just across the river from Lethbridge. The location had two good features for the snake-loving chief, for it was close to the only supply of rattlers on the reserve and was almost on the outskirts of the coal mining town. Calf Shirt soon became friends of the shopkeepers and regularly earned money by performing with his venomous pets.

21   But the chief also had problems, for his camp, being so near the town, was a convenient focal point for prostitution. To discourage this demoralizing practise, the government had forbidden the Indians from entering any white settlements unless they had passes. However, the location of Calf Shirt's camp made it easy for female members of the tribe to slip into town in the evening, or for whites to come out. The situation was observed by the Indian agent who said that "the authorities in Lethbridge will not allow Indians to stay in the town, consequently these Indians having good-looking squaws want to get as near Lethbridge as possible so that they can run back and forth . . ."[4]

22   To combat the problem, Calf Shirt was appointed a scout for the North-West Mounted Police. During the time he held this position, he fought to keep the undesirables out of his camp and succeeded to some extent in stamping out prostitution. As a scout he also mixed with white people more than any other Blood chief and his facility for handling snakes was enough to grant him respectful attention from his non-Indian audience.

23   One day, when a circus featuring a lady snake charmer came to Lethbridge, Calf Shirt was urged by residents of the town to see the show. He watched the entertainer pick up her de-fanged reptiles then twist them around her body and over her head. Calf Shirt was unimpressed. The townspeople, who crowded the tent to see the Indian's reaction, did not have long to wait, for as soon as the show was over, he nonchalantly pulled a venomous rattler, one of his biggest, out of his shirt and offered it to the

charmer. The woman took one look at the beady-eyed reptile, screamed, and fled. Calf Shirt snickered, returned his pet to its resting place, and commented in broken English, "I gave that pretty white woman something to wear around her neck, but she nearly jumped out of her nice dress to get away from it."[5]   180

24   On another occasion, a rancher brought a live rattler into Lethbridge to show the townspeople. The clerk at the Hudson's Bay Company store saw it as a unique attraction, so he bought the reptile and put it on display. But no sooner had the snake been placed in the rudely-constructed cage than it escaped and disappeared into a stock of dry goods.   185

25   Frightened, everyone fled from the store and the clerk did not know what to do until someone suggested Calf Shirt. The scout was summoned and, agreeing on a price for his services, he went into the store, poked around the counters, and finally found the missing reptile curled up in some cotton goods. He picked up the frightened creature and played   190 with it while carpenters hurriedly built a sturdier cage.

26   Calf Shirt's exploits became well known in western Canada, so when plans were made to hold a large Territorial Exhibition in Regina in 1895, the chief received an invitation to attend. Not only was he happy to make the long journey with his pets, but he confided to his friends that the   195 capital city was close to the Sand Hills, so he might have a chance to pick up some new snakes.

27   The exhibition was the biggest ever held in the West. There were two circus tents, agricultural exhibits, rodeo events, and examples of Indian life, past and present. Calf Shirt was depicted as part of the "pagan" past   200 and delightedly demonstrated his great gift over his snakes.

28   Some people did not believe the performance was genuine and claimed that Calf Shirt's snakes had been defanged. They were convinced of this when they saw the Blood chief put a snake's head in his mouth.

29   "Calf Shirt told one white man that, if he would give him a dollar   205 he would allow a snake to bite a dog which was standing near," commented the *Regina Progress*. "The white man put up the dollar and the Indian immediately made one of the snakes bite the dog, which died in a few minutes."[6]

30   Another experience with his snakes occurred at Calf Shirt's home   210 camp when his sister, the wife of Coming Singing, had a fight with her husband. He had collected their treaty money but being an inveterate gambler, he had lost it and came home with nothing. In anger, his wife deserted him and when she moved in with Calf Shirt, her husband asked

for her to be sent back. Calf Shirt commented that the woman was not   215
being forced to stay with him but added, "if you really want your wife back,
you do as I say."[7]

31   Calf Shirt pointed to a coulee and told the man to ride in that
direction until he found two rattlesnakes together, then to pick the biggest
of them and bring it back. Coming Singing went as directed and soon found   220
the two snakes coiled and ready to strike.

32   "Don't do that," he told the reptiles. "Calf Shirt has sent me to get
you." Coming Singing chewed some sage brush, as he had been instructed,
rubbed it on his hands and as he walked close to the biggest snake he spat
some of the mixture on its head. The creature immediately uncoiled, allow-   225
ing Coming Singing to pick it up and put it inside his shirt. There the snake
coiled tightly around the body of the frightened Blood. Riding back to the
camp, Coming Singing tried to trot but the jogging made the snake tighten
its grip, so he slowed to a walk. By the time he reached the camp, he was
shaking with fear and sweat was trickling down his brow.   230

33   The chief, gathered with others in front of his tepee, took the
snake and praised his brother-in-law for proving that he truly wanted his
wife back. "You gambled away your $5.00 treaty money," he said, "but I'm a
chief and get $15.00. I'll give you $5.00 for this deed and tell my sister to go
back home with you."[8]   235

34   During the latter years of his life, Calf Shirt lived in a small log
cabin with his wives Double Killer and Many Stars. Visitors observed,
sometimes with anxiety, the numerous snake holes under the cabin's log
walls and the dusty trails across the earthen floor. Sometimes, if he felt in a
good mood, the chief might whistle to bring one of the reptiles slithering   240
across the room to be with his human brother.

35   After his death in 1901, Calf Shirt was buried on a lonely hill near
his camp not far from Snake Coulee. Soon after, travellers swore that a
huge rattler had joined the pack and liked to lie in the sun near Calf Shirt's
grave, just as though he belonged there. And perhaps he did.   245

NOTES

1. Interview with Jim White Bull, Blood Reserve, Dec. 29, 1955. In author's
possession.
2. Letter, Indian Agent William Pocklington to the Indian Commissioner,
Sept. 30, 1884. Letter-book, RG-10, 1552:56, Public Archives of Canada.
3. *The Macleod Gazette*, Nov. 2, 1894.
4. Indian Agent William Pocklington, monthly report for March, April 8,

1888. Letter-book, RG-10, vol. 1555, Public Archives of Canada.

5. "Byegone Days of the Blackfeet Nation,' by Joe Beebe. Manuscript in author's possession.

6. Cited in *The Macleod Gazette*, Aug. 23, 1895.

7. Interview with Jim White Bull, *op. cit.*

8. *Ibid.*

QUESTIONS

READER AND PURPOSE

1. Although Dempsey mentions Calf Shirt's strange power over rattlesnakes in the first paragraph, he doesn't explain the reasons for this power until paragraph 7. Why not?

2. In dealing at length with Calf Shirt as Indian warrior and leader, Dempsey is attempting to show that Calf Shirt was not a wild, eccentric, romantic young man given to passionate extravagances, but that he was, rather, a sensible and level-headed person who claimed to have had, only once, a vision, a vision that affected the rest of his life. But does Dempsey, in your opinion, provide too much background of this sort? Does it get in the way of the subject of his essay? On the other hand, would it be correct to say that Dempsey's topic is not just Calf Shirt's prowess at handling snakes, but, rather, the Indian's life as a whole, of which the snakes are just a small part?

3. What tone* does Dempsey adopt towards his extraordinary subject? Is there any evidence to show that Dempsey believes in Calf Shirt's vision? that he disbelieves? or does he simply retell the tale as it was told to him, without in any way indicating his attitude towards it?

4. Some of the sources Dempsey refers to in his end-notes (not reprinted here) are an interview with a Blood Indian, official government documents, and newspaper reports which appeared in *The Macleod Gazette*. How do references to such sources affect the reader's attitude towards this essay?

ORGANIZATION

5. In the first paragraph the author briefly answers several questions: where? who? when? what? Do the next two paragraphs provide further answers to these questions, or do they answer other questions?

6. Paragraphs 7 and 8 recount Calf Shirt's vision, and paragraph 9 gives some examples of his power over snakes. However, neither the snakes nor his power over them are mentioned again until paragraph 18. Why not? What is Dempsey doing in paragraphs 10 to 17?

7. For the most part, this essay follows Calf Shirt's life chronologically, beginning, in the third paragraph, with his birth. However, there are places where the

chronological order is either not followed, as in the opening paragraph, or where there is no clear indication of time. Find three or four occasions of this sort, and explain why references to time are unnecessary, or why the time sequence has been rearranged.

8. Could paragraphs 24 and 25 be joined into one paragraph? If they were joined, what would the effect be on the immediate context? on the entire essay?

9. How are the opening and closing paragraphs related? Is a closing by return* involved here? If not, what would you call this sort of closing?

SENTENCES

10. Identify the absolute* in paragraph 2 and briefly explain its function.

11. Should there be a comma after "essence" and after "rumours" in paragraph 14? Or is the comma here optional? Should commas be placed around "but" in the last sentence of paragraph 6?

12. Is the first sentence in paragraph 4 an organizing sentence*? Why, or why not? What about the first sentence in paragraph 7? in paragraph 18?

13. In the 4th sentence of paragraph 16, should the comma after "days" be replaced by a semi-colon? Would either mark be correct?

14. Are the first two sentences in paragraph 17 examples of inversion*? Do you think they are effective sentences? Try to explain your answer.

15. Should the quotation in paragraph 18 be introduced by a colon?

16. "But" usually functions as a coordinate conjunction, a form of connective.* Is that its function at the beginning of paragraph 21? If not, what other functions does it have?

17. Why is there a comma after "however" in paragraph 21?

DICTION

18. Look up: *paradox* (6), *trait* (8), *daub* (27), *scorn* (28), *coulee* (32), *travois* (44), *sagebrush* (57), *bidding* (68), *coveted* (75), *astute* (78), *consummate* (130), *inveterate* (212).

19. Why is the word "pagan" enclosed by quotation marks in paragraph 27? What does this say about the author's attitude towards his subject?

20. Identify the figure of speech* in paragraph 10. Can you find any other places where Dempsey uses figurative language?

21. Phrases such as "mortal blow" (37), "ripple of excitement" (111–12), and "shaking with fear" (230) have, through over-use, become clichés. Can you find any others? Do they weaken Dempsey's essay?

POINTS TO LEARN

1. One effective way of introducing a topic is to answer briefly some, or all, of the questions who? what? where? when? why?

2. The chronological ordering of an event may be interrupted in order to provide background, to establish reasons, to clarify motives.

SUGGESTIONS FOR WRITING

It is not likely that you have ever known a person as unusual as Calf Shirt. Nevertheless, you undoubtedly have encountered two or three person who, because of some character trait, struck you as extraordinary, or at least quite unusual. In an essay of two or three pages (or even more, if you wish), describe this person. Your emphasis should be on what makes this person stand out, but you should not neglect such matters as family history, education, travels, unusual experiences, and so on.

IMPROVING YOUR STYLE

In your essay include:

1. An introductory paragraph which briefly supplies some information about the character you have chosen.

2. At least 3 paragraphs which begin with organizing sentences.*

Description of Character

Essentially the description of character is no different from the description of things. The same general principles and techniques govern both. Yet, character drawing has special problems of its own. There are different ways of approaching the description of character, and many kinds of characters for the writer to create, each serving different purposes. In the broad we can divide all characters into either types or individuals. Types, or flat characters as they are sometimes called, possess only a single trait. Individuals, or round characters, have a number of traits, a complexity that is closer to real life than the single dimension of the type.

All types fall into one of four classes, depending upon the kind of trait the writer depicts: there are (1) national types—the typical Australian, Englishman, or American; (2) the occupational type—the typical farmer, policeman, professor, movie actress, disc jockey, barber, or business executive; (3) the social type—the typical bachelor uncle, the distant cousin, the blind date, the hostess, the week-end guest; (4) the personality type—The Tactful Man, The Tactless Man, The Nervous Man, The Steady Man, The Worry-Wart, The Happy-Go-Lucky Man. The types of all four categories have one thing in common—they have only a single characteristic. Actually, they are not real people at all, but only the single characteristic abstracted from an observation of many people. The type is a single trait personified.

In describing a type, therefore, the writer chooses only those details that bear directly upon the one characteristic of nationality, occupation, social role, or personality. The writer may know a Vancouver taxi driver who spends all his leisure time reading Shakespeare; but in so far as the driver does, he is an individual, not a type. The writer rigorously excludes all details of physical description, clothing, interests, and personality that do not help to define the typical taxi driver.

What is the point behind the description of types? Besides appealing to our delight in the vivid description of the familiar and commonplace, the type may serve either of two purposes. The less common is to inform. A social historian, for example, may wish to describe the typical medieval peasant, showing how he looked, how he worked, what pleasure he had, if any, and how he felt about his station in life. More often the description of a type intends to instruct the reader in manners or behavior. If we describe The Braggart, we are saying in so many words, "Don't be like this." We may, of course, serve the same purpose in a different, more positive way by describing The Modest Man. Usually the negative, satiric approach is more effective and is more fun both to write and to read.

As the character acquires more than one trait, he becomes an individual. He is more than a walking occupation or trait of personality: he is a Vancouver cab driver *and* a reader of Shakespeare. But the fact that the individual has many dimensions poses a problem. What traits shall the writer include and what traits shall he ignore? The answer depends upon the writer's impression of the individual, for almost all description of round characters is impressionistic. It is well-nigh impossible for any but a highly trained psychologist to write objectively about something so complex as the total personality of a human being. Character drawing of the individual must be both partial and interpretive. It may be more or less shrewd and accurate, but it remains an impression nevertheless. The impression may be simple or complex, and it may require qualification, but the impression guides the writer's selection of details. Our impression of an individual may range anywhere between love and admiration to hatred and loathing. We may see him as mysterious, a bundle of contradictions, or we may see beneath the variety of his traits a pattern that reveals some truth about human behavior or human values. In any case, we always begin with some reaction to the round character we are describing.

To convey this reaction, we may use many different kinds of details. Among the most useful are details of physical appearance, clothing, and personal belongings. These make the reader see, but they also suggest both the writer's impression and the character's personality. Whether it be sound psychology or not, the reader responds in one way to a tall, thin-lipped, steely-eyed man carrying a tightly furled umbrella, and in a totally different way to a robust, smiling, sloppily-dressed man carrying a fishing rod. In prose, a character's appearance, clothing, and possessions are, by convention, clues to his personality.

In addition to these, a writer may describe the "stage" or the setting within which the character moves about and lives—his room, his home, his place of work. For these, too, are extensions of the character's personality.

The shrewd observer can write pages about a man he has never seen—about his income, his social position, his tastes, his interests, even his values—if only he can study for a bit the room or the house in which he lives.

Viewing the individual in a wider perspective, we may describe his relation to society by making clear what he says and does, what he likes and dislikes, what goals he is seeking, what he values most. We may show him in action, in conflict with others, how they react to him, what they say about him. In short, our portrait may be static or dynamic or in part both.

How much vivid detail the writer will use and what he selects will depend both upon his purpose and the space at his disposal. A very short description may evoke the writer's impression with only two or three striking details, having the force or suggestiveness of an unfinished pencil sketch. If the writer has the space of a novel, he may use all kinds of details and dramatic situations to create his character over hundreds of pages. Ample space alone will not insure good characterization. It is the telling, the representative detail, the vividness that count. It is more effective to make the reader see a character's modesty in action, for example, than to say merely that he is modest.

Round characters in prose have the purpose of informing, instructing, entertaining, or doing all these at once. The historian who writes the character of a great man may have as his guiding intention to explain the impact of a personality upon the course of history. His character, without being obviously moralistic, may contain a lesson for the reader. Any character that is vivid can scarcely fail to entertain the reader. All of us are interested in people—in their motivations, their eccentricities, in the fascinating variety and complexity that make up the human comedy. For that reason any character of any individual, no matter how great or how obscure, is likely to be a pleasant task for the writer and a pleasure to the reader.

The Penurious Man and The Coward

Theophrastus (c. 371-c. 287 B.C.) was a Greek rhetorician and philosopher. Today he is best remembered for what he considered a minor work, his *Characters*, a series of sketches originally intended as models for students of rhetoric. The *Characters* (the word in Greek meant "distinctive marks") consists of satires of comic, foolish, or cloddish types. The sketches follow a formula: first a definition of the trait to be illustrated, then a number of situations and responses that dramatically reveal the trait in terms of behavior. For example: "After dinner, the waiter brings the check; the stingy man drops his napkin and hides beneath the table until someone else has paid."

The *Characters* was translated into Latin and widely imitated by French and English writers in the seventeenth and eighteenth centuries. Today the Theophrastian "Character" is no longer a literary genre. But one doesn't have to look far to find the same people—the bores and cheapskates, the know-it-alls and B.M.O.C.'s. Satirizing them is still a pleasant diversion, and the best way to do it is, as Theophrastus shows, to describe them in action.

1   Penuriousness is too strict attention to profit and loss.
2   The Penurious man is one who, while the month is current, will come to one's house and ask for a half-obol. When he is at table with others he will count how many cups each of them has drunk; and will pour a smaller libation to Artemis than any of the company. Whenever a person   5
has made a good bargain for him and charges him with it, he will say that it is too dear. When a servant has broken a jug or a plate he will take the value out of his rations; or, if his wife has dropped a three-farthing piece, he is capable of moving the furniture and the sofas and the wardrobes, and of rummaging in the curtains. If he has anything to sell he will dispose of it   10
at such a price that the buyer shall have no profit. He is not likely to let one eat a fig from his garden, or walk through his land, or pick up one of the

From *The Characters of Theophrastus*, ed. and trans. R. C. Jebb, London, Macmillan and Company, 1870.

olives or dates that lie on the ground; and he will inspect his boundaries day by day to see if they remain the same. He is apt, also, to enforce the right of distraining, and to exact compound interest. When he feasts the men of his parish, the cutlets set before them will be small: when he markets, he will come in having bought nothing. And he will forbid his wife to lend salt, or a lamp-wick, or cummin, or verjuice, or meal for sacrifice, or garlands, or cakes; saying that these trifles come to much in the year. Then in general it may be noticed that the moneyboxes of the penurious are mouldy, and the keys rusty; that they themselves wear their cloaks scarcely reaching to the thigh; that they anoint themselves from very small oil-flasks; that they have their hair cut close; that they take off their shoes in the middle of the day; and that they are urgent with the fuller to let their cloak have plenty of earth, in order that it may not soon be soiled.

1   Cowardice would seem to be, in fact, a shrinking of the soul through fear.

2   The Coward is one who, on a voyage, will protest that the promontories are privateers; and, if a high sea gets up, will ask if there is any one on board who has not been initiated. He will put up his head and ask the steersman if he is halfway, and what he thinks of the face of the heavens; remarking to the person sitting next him that a certain dream makes him feel uneasy; and he will take off his tunic and give it to his slave; or he will beg them to put him ashore.

3   On land also, when he is campaigning, he will call to him those who are going out to the rescue, and bid them come and stand by him and look about them first; saying that it is hard to make out which is the enemy. Hearing shouts and seeing men falling, he will remark to those who stand by him that he has forgotten in his haste to bring his sword, and will run to the tent; where, having sent his slave out to reconnoitre the position of the enemy, he will hide the sword under his pillow, and then spend a long time in pretending to look for it. And seeing from the tent a wounded comrade being carried in, he will run towards him and cry "Cheer up!"; he will take him into his arms and carry him; he will tend and sponge him; he will sit by him and keep the flies off his wound—in short he will do anything rather than fight with the enemy. Again, when the trumpeter has sounded the signal for battle, he will cry, as he sits in the tent, "Bother! you will not allow the man to get a wink of sleep with your perpetual bugling!" Then, covered with blood from the other's wound, he will meet those who are returning from the fight, and announce to them, "I have run some risk to save one of

our fellows"; and he will bring in the men of his parish and of his tribe to see his patient, at the same time explaining to each of them that he carried him with his own hands to the tent.

QUESTIONS

READER AND PURPOSE

1. By what standard of behavior does Theophrastus judge his characters? Is Theophrastus writing, if unintentionally, for all men in all times?

ORGANIZATION

2. Theophrastus begins with a short definition of the folly, foible, or disagreeable trait being depicted and then writes, "The _____ man is one who . . ." After this beginning he follows with several sharp images of the type in action, stopping when he feels like it. Is there any plan or organization in the examples of penuriousness and cowardice? Which of the two characters is the better organized? How might one improve the character less well organized?

SENTENCES

3. The sentences of Theophrastus have two characteristic patterns. One of these is balance *. In the first half of his balanced sentence he describes briefly a setting or situation, and in the second half, the character's typical reaction in that setting or situation. For example, in "The Penurious Man" (3), we read: "When he is at table with others [situation], he will count how many cups each of them has drunk [reaction]." The first half of the balanced sentence is usually a dependent adverbial clause * or a participial * phrase. Find other examples of balanced sentences and identify the grammatical construction with which each begins. Why is it better to place the situation first rather than last, as in this revision: "He will count how many cups each of them has drunk, when he is at table with others"?

4. A second common pattern groups several illustrations of typical behavior in one sentence, making them parallel * in structure. The last sentence of "The Penurious Man" is a good example. Find others.

DICTION

5. Look up: (in "The Penurious Man") half-obol (3), libation (5), Artemis (5), distraining (15), cummin (18), verjuice (18), fuller (24) (see also the verb to full and fuller's earth); (in "The Coward") promontories (3), privateers (4), reconnoitre (15). In line 5 of "The Coward" initiated refers to initiation

into the Eleusinian Mysteries, one of the religious cults of ancient Greece. Anyone not so initiated was believed to bring bad luck to a ship. If he had lived much later, the Theophrastian coward might have asked, "Is there anyone on board who isn't a good Christian?"

POINTS TO LEARN

1. In the *Characters*, Theophrastus combines definition, description, and narration. Although a writer must learn the various techniques of development, he must also learn that a single technique seldom appears by itself. Yet one technique usually organizes his use of the others.

2. Examples within a paragraph should be grouped according to some plan. Often the various groups are introduced by framing words *. In "The Coward" we find the phrases "on a voyage" (3) and "On land" (10).

3. Balance and parallelism are very common and very useful sentence patterns. Balance allows the writer to make a sharp contrast. Theophrastus often implies a contrast between what the situation calls for and the behavior of his character. For example, the image * of men at table suggests geniality and relaxation; but we find the penurious man scowling and counting cups. If the writer uses balance frequently, he must take care to vary the grammatical construction of the first half of the sentence.

Parallelism allows the writer to vary his sentence rhythm and sentence structure. It has the advantage of variety, economy, and conviction by sheer bulk.

SUGGESTIONS FOR WRITING

Ever since the third century B.C. men have delighted in the creating of characters, and Theophrastus has had many imitators—among them Joseph Hall, John Earle, Sir Thomas Overbury, Nicholas Breton, Jean de La Bruyère, Joseph Addison—some of whom wrote much better characters than the originator of this literary form. Try your hand at one or two characters in the manner of Theophrastus.

Here is the beginning of a long list of possible subjects—The Braggart, The Inside Dopester, The Tactless Man, The Snob, The Joiner, The Gossip, The Name Dropper, The Big Man on Campus, The Busybody. Add ten or fifteen titles to this list and then select one or two types you especially dislike. Be sure to describe types, not individuals, though you may construct your type from several individuals you have known. Begin with a short definition of the trait. If possible, be brilliantly acidic here, but keep your definition short. Then follow with "The _____ is one who . . ." Then group several well-chosen examples of the type in action.

IMPROVING YOUR STYLE

1. In your sketch vary the situation-response pattern in some of these ways:

> Two balanced independent clauses separated by a semicolon.
> An adverbial clause followed by a main clause.
> A participial phrase followed by a main clause.
> Two short sentences in sequence.

2. Include at least one sentence using a series of parallel constructions to describe four or five typical actions or qualities of the subject.

The Medieval Gentleman

Morris Bishop (1893–1973) was a teacher, poet, scholar. This selection is from his popular and eminently readable history, *The Middle Ages* (1970). Bishop's "gentleman" is a type, embodying qualities and behavior found in many aristocrats from the twelfth to the fifteenth centuries. No single specimen of the breed ever possessed all the characteristics of Bishop's gentleman or behaved in exactly the same way. Bishop's subject represents that range of possible attributes and behavior which define the aristocrat of the middle ages. The advantage of describing types is that it enables an historian or social scientist, a satirist or psychologist to depict a great many persons in a single figure. But it requires, of course, that the writer know such persons well enough to select the common attributes which make them members of the same group.

1   The proper medieval gentleman had many virtues. He was generally loyal to his feudal obligations and conscientious in the administration of justice. He was generous, particularly in bequeathing land and money to the church. He was sincerely religious, respectful of church authority, and faithful to his duties. He took his knightly vows seriously and seldom vio- 5 lated an oath or solemn promise, knowing that these are recorded in heaven and that the breach of an oath may be divinely punished as perjury. He could be sympathetic to lesser humans. "Courtesy to the poor is of a humble heart," said the thirteenth-century writer the Knight of La Tour-Landry, telling how a great lady bowed to a tailor. (Some reproached her; others 10 praised her meekness.)

2   However, the gentleman's faults loom larger in retrospect than do his virtues. Pride of birth and class turned readily into arrogance; bravery, into foolhardiness. Many great battles were lost by the knights' disregard of orders, their refusal to wait for the command to charge. The story of the 15 crusades is full of such splendid folly. The Templars especially were so eager

From *The Horizon Book of the Middle Ages.* © 1968 by American Heritage Publishing Company, Inc. Reprinted by permission of the publisher.

to be always in the van that they got themselves killed for nothing but honor, and not much of that.

3   Generosity, much extolled by the minstrels who profited by it, became absurd display. When Thomas à Becket visited Paris in 1157, his train was like a circus parade. It included a traveling chapel, wagons with vestments, carpets, and bedcoverings, twelve horses carrying table plate, grooms and hawkers with hounds and gerfalcons, and on the back of each lead horse a long-tailed ape. The whole was guarded by armed men with fierce dogs on leashes. Display developed conspicuous waste, rivalry in destruction as in an Indian potlatch. One knight had a plot of ground plowed and sown with small pieces of silver. Another used precious wax candles for his cooking; another, "through boastfulness," had thirty of his horses burned alive. The result of such rivalry was that many or most nobles were perpetually in debt to usurers. If worse came to worst, they were sometimes forced to murder their creditors.

4   They were a rapacious crew, often merely out of economic necessity. The noble troubadour Bertrand de Born speaks for his class, rejoicing in the approach of war with its breakdown of law and order: "We'll soon seize the usurer's gold; there won't be a packhorse on the roads; no burgher will go without fear, nor any merchant heading for France. If you want to be rich you have only to take!"

5   Whereas the king's authority often protected the merchant, the family feuds of the nobles were beyond control. Revenge was regarded rather as an act of private justice than as a crime. The remotest members of a clan were bound by the obligations of the vendetta, which had its special home in Italy. Its history in the Middle Ages is largely one of family feuds that turned into wars. These ended either by the extermination of one party or by the intervention of the emperor or the church, imposing reconciliation and indemnities.

6   Our courteous, chivalric knights could readily become demons of brutality. The *chansons de geste* are filled with rolling heads, strewn brains, gushing bowels, baby spearing, and nun raping. Some part of this joy in deeds of blood must be literary, an appeal to the perverse spirit, as in the sadistic fiction recrudescent today. But much of the brutality was unquestionable fact. I shall give none of the abundant examples, not to abet what I would condemn.

7   Another contrariety in noble behavior was in the matter of sex. The adept of courtly love, fresh from sighing at his unapproachable lady's feet,

could pause on his homeward journey to tumble a shepherdess in her 55
meadow, a fresh-faced village girl under a hedge. The Moslems in Spain and
Syria were shocked by the licentiousness of the French. The famous *jus
primae noctis* (the lord's right to spend the first night with a peasant bride)
may well be a fable. Nevertheless, the noble regarded his female serf as his
chattel, to do with as he would. Often, no doubt, what he would was what 60
she would; but if she defended her rustic honor and was then undone, neither she nor her family had any means of redress.

8   Such were some of the traits of the noble. He was a bundle of
paradoxes—a romantic lover and a libertine, a gallant knight and a blood-
thirsty brute, a devout Christian and a flouter of the elements of morality. 65
But he shared his paradoxes with the rest of humanity.

QUESTIONS

READER AND PURPOSE

1. Describe Bishop's reader. Is he another historian? Someone who reads for
vicarious adventure and thrills? A student? What does Bishop assume his reader
knows and does not know?

2. If Bishop's purpose is to describe the Middle Ages for a twentieth-century
reader, would he have been wiser to depict in detail an actual individual like
the Knight of La Tour-Landry or Thomas à Becket? Why or why not?

ORGANIZATION

3. By omitting *however* (12) the writer might have begun with the second
paragraph and placed paragraph 1 near the end, between 7 and 8. But while it
is possible, this organization would be less effective than the plan Bishop followed. Why?

4. Paragraph development by "specification" lists all (or most) of the particular forms of the topic. In paragraph development by example, on the other
hand, only a few representative cases of the topic are treated. In paragraph 1
the topic is "virtues." Is it developed by specification or by examples?

5. Each sentence after the topic sentence of the first paragraph begins with *he*.
Is that repetition effective or awkward? Give reasons for your answer.

6. How are the following pairs of paragraphs linked: 1 and 2, 3 and 4, 6 and 7?

7. It might be argued that the coherence between paragraphs 2 and 3 is weak.
But notice that the relationship involving all the paragraphs from 2 through 7 has
been clearly established in paragraph 2. By what sentence?

8. Why are the following revisions inferior to Bishop's sentences?

(a) *Revision:* Pride of birth and class turned readily into arrogance. Bravery often became foolishness.

Bishop: "Pride of birth and class turned readily into arrogance; bravery, into foolishness." (13-14)

(b) *Revision:* It included a traveling chapel, wagons with vestments, carpets, and bedcoverings, twelve horses carrying table plate, grooms and hawkers with hounds and gerfalcons, and on the back of each lead horse, a long-tailed ape, the whole being guarded by armed men with fierce dogs on leashes—display developing conspicuous waste, rivalry in destruction as in an Indian potlatch.

Bishop: "It included a traveling chapel, wagons with vestments, carpets, and bedcoverings, twelve horses carrying table plate, grooms and hawkers, with hounds and gerfalcons, and on the back of each lead horse a long-tailed ape. The whole was guarded by armed men with fierce dogs on leashes. Display developed conspicuous waste, rivalry in destruction as in an Indian potlatch." (21-26)

(c) *Revision:* The family feuds of the nobles were beyond control, whereas the king's authority often protected the merchant.

Bishop: "Whereas the king's authority often protected the merchant, the family feuds of the nobles were beyond control." (38-39)

9. Look up: *Templars* (16), *minstrels* (19), *Thomas à Becket* (20), *gerfalcons* (23), *usurers* (30), *troubadour* (33), *burgher* (35), *vendetta* (41), *chansons de geste* (47), *adept* (54), *courtly love* (54), *paradoxes* (64), *libertine* (64).

10. How does *foolhardiness* (14) differ from *foolishness?*

11. Are there any cases in the following list where you can substitute a single simpler (or more familiar) word and still say the same thing? *Arrogance* (13), *van* (17), *gerfalcons* (23), *potlatch* (26), *rapacious* (32), *sadistic* (50), *recrudescent* (50), *licentiousness* (57).

12. If Bishop's final sentence were omitted how would the tone * be modified?

POINTS TO LEARN

1. Well-done, the description of a type conveys the general truth about a large number of individuals.

2. Some types embody a social or moral ideal. Other types, usually depicted by satirists such as Theophrastus, represent negative modes of behavior. Still oth-

ers, like Morris Bishop's "medieval gentleman," exhibit in one portrait the features of an historical, social, professional, or national group.

SUGGESTIONS FOR WRITING

Showing both faults and virtues, describe one of the following types: the cowboy hero of the grade-B movie, the male chauvinist, the feminist, the college teacher, the freshman or sophomore, the politician, the member of a rock group. Whatever type you select, it should involve contrarieties or paradoxes, as does Bishop's "medieval gentleman."

IMPROVING YOUR STYLE

In your composition:

1. Use an example of balance * and ellipsis *, modeling your sentence upon Bishop's in lines 13-14 beginning "Pride of birth."

2. Use three or four rare and unusual words; use them because they say precisely what you want to say and could not be replaced by simpler terms.

HELEN BEVINGTON

The *Festivitas* of Sir Thomas More

Helen Bevington is a teacher and writer whose books include *Doctor Johnson's Waterfall* (1946), *When Found, Make a Verse Of* (1961), *Charley Smith's Girl* (1965), *A Book and a Love Affair* (1968), *The House Was Quiet and the World Was Calm* (1971), and *Beautiful Lofty People* (1973). The last is a collection of essays about literary figures and topics. The hero of the first essay is Sir Thomas More (1478-1535), an English statesman and author whose most famous work is *Utopia*, a fictional account of an ideal state. More became lord chancellor of England under Henry VIII but resigned rather than take an oath denying the pope's authority and upholding the legitimacy of Henry's divorce from Catherine of Aragon. More was subsequently tried for treason and beheaded.

1   The word for him is *festivitas*. Yet his life, had someone else lived it, would seem calamitous, unbearably tragic.

2   He lived for fifty-seven years and then was put to death. Through his refusal to support Henry VIII in his claim to be Supreme Head of the Church of England or to sign the Oath of Supremacy which went, More 5 said, against his conscience and would imperil his soul, More was found guilty of high treason and beheaded at the Tower of London, July 5, 1535. Afterward his head was exposed on London Bridge till his daughter Margaret took it down and carried it home to preserve in spices till she died. Perhaps it was buried with her. He was a peaceable and loving man, a just 10 and equable man, but for putting God before his king, Henry had him murdered.

3   Only Margaret knew of his punishing his body with whips to subdue it, the cords knotted to tame his flesh till the blood came. It was she who washed the hair shirt he wore next to his skin. In his youth More had 15 longed for the monastic life and for four years lived with the monks of

From *Beautiful Lofty People*. © 1974 by Helen Bevington. Reprinted by permission of Harcourt Brace Jovanovich, Inc.

Charterhouse in London, tempted to take the final vows. He longed for that peace. Instead he returned to the world, went courting at the house of John Colt who had three daughters, and, though most attracted to the middle girl, married the eldest, Jane, lest she be hurt if rejected for her sister. Jane became the "little wife" he so faithfully loved, the mother of his children, Margaret, Elizabeth, Cecily, and a son John. Then Jane Colt died. More's second wife, Mistress Alice Middleton, was a widow and a scold, a dull-hearted woman older than he with whom he lived content, often adjuring her to be merry.

4   Merry. The word stayed ever on More's tongue and in his heart. To Dame Alice he said, "I pray you with my children be merry in God." From the Tower during the last fifteen months of his life, he wrote to Margaret, "I beseech Him make you all merry in the hope of Heaven." The day before his execution he sent her the hair shirt and a letter written with a piece of coal: "Tomorrow I long to go to God; it were a day very meet and convenient for me."

5   On the morrow as he climbed the scaffold, which was weak and ready to fall, More said, "I pray you, Master Lieutenant, see me safe up, and for my coming down let me shift for myself." By light words he took his leave. Without solemnity, with courtesy and compassion for others, with a cheerful serene face and three jests on the scaffold he went to die, speaking to the executioner, "Pluck up thy spirits, man, and be not afraid to do thine office. My neck is very short." He removed his beard from the block, "for it at least hath not offended the king."

6   The test of a man in the Utopia[1] is the way he dies. Those who die "merrily and full of good hope, for them no man mourneth." They are praised for their merry death and monuments are erected to them. More showed how it was done. He died as he had lived.

7   William Roper, More's son-in-law and husband to Margaret, attempted to measure his shining worth. In the sixteen years of living in More's genial house and being daily conversant with him, said Roper, "I could never perceive him as much as once in a fume."

8   He was never angry. His character was marked by kindness. As described by Erasmus (who loved that tranquillity he himself couldn't find and loved More, who had enough for both), he was of medium height, fair

[1] Utopia (the term translates as "Nowhere Land") is More's major literary work. Written in Latin and published in 1516, it describes an ideal society. It was early translated into English and other European languages and soon became popular and influential. [Editors' note]

complexion, auburn hair, thin beard, blue-gray eyes, his face alight forever
breaking into a smile, merry of word and manner. Quarrels were unknown
in his hospitable house. He loved gaiety and wit (but not at another's expense), and in fits of laughter ruled his household. His gift for friendship   55
was immense. He had an easiness that made him forget even the gravest
injuries.

9   John Aubrey in *Brief Lives* calls More "extraordinary facetious."
One night when More was riding with friends, suddenly he crossed himself
and cried out, "Jesu Maria! doe not you see that prodigious Dragon in the   60
skye?" They all looked but nobody could see it. Then one did spy it, and
the rest promptly saw it too. Everybody saw it. "Whereas there was no such
phantome," says Aubrey. He tells of a time when Roper came to More's
house with a proposal to marry one of his daughters. More led the young
man into the bedchamber where, since it was morning, two of them lay   65
still asleep. Taking the sheet by the corner and whipping it off, More revealed the girls lying on their backs, their smocks up to their armpits. Thus
awakened, they stirred and turned on their bellies. "Quoth Roper, 'I have
seen both sides,' and so gave a patt on the buttock he made choice of,
sayeing, 'Thou art mine.' " You can still hear the laughter at that wooing.   70
10   More's favorite jest, told him by his father, he would repeat to
tease the females in his house: "A good Woman (as the old Philosopher
observeth) is but like one Ele[2] put in a bagge amongst 500 Snakes, and if a
man should have the luck to grope out that one Ele from all the snakes, yet
he hath at best a wet Ele by the Taile."   75
11   In a letter to his children More wrote, "If ever I flogged you, it was
but with a peacock's tail." By giving them the greatest praise in the world,
which is approval, he taught them and made them love learning—the son
and the three daughters, who studied with their father Greek and Latin,
logic, philosophy, theology, astronomy. (They learned the Greek alphabet   80
by shooting bows and arrows at the letters.) As one would expect, he believed in the equality of the sexes. "Both are reasonable beings," he said,
"suited equally for those studies by which reason is cultivated."
12   Incredulous and amazed, Erasmus viewed More's happy family life
that grew to contain some twenty members: "There is not any man living   85
so affectionate to his children as he, and he loveth his old wife as if she
were a girl of fifteen." In this commodious house in Chelsea, Holbein is

---

[2] Eel. [Editors' note]

said to have stayed three years. Erasmus, a difficult guest who spoke no English, loathed the smell of fish and the taste of English beer, wrote *The Praise of Folly* while laid up with lumbago and dedicated it to his beloved   90
friend: "I chose to amuse myself with a praise of folly (*moria*) because of your name of More, which comes as close to the word for folly as you are far from the thing itself." Erasmus said, "We had but one soul between us." His praise of More became a litany.

13   Besides this huge family, More kept a noisy collection of birds and   95
animals inside the house and in the garden—a monkey, rabbits, a fox, a ferret, a weasel. On all of life he lavished love; he found joy in everything; his *festivitas* never forsook him. And since his fate was to die a martyr and be made a saint, thank God he was a merry one.

QUESTIONS

READER AND PURPOSE

1. Would this essay be useful to a student trying to bone up on Sir Thomas More before a test? Why or why not?

2. Does Bevington assume that her reader already knows the essential facts about More? If she does, what is her purpose in writing about him?

3. The writer has a definite conception of the essential temperament of More. Summarize her conception in a sentence.

ORGANIZATION

4. Bevington's essay in not organized in a tight analytical manner. This does not mean, however, that her essay lacks organization. Rather it has a kind of solar structure, in which one dominant theme or idea acts as a central mass holding everything together. What is that central idea?

5. What is the topic of paragraph 4? Why may paragraphs 4, 5, and 6 be said to constitute a unit? How do these paragraphs support the central thesis? Do the first three paragraphs illustrate the thesis directly? If not, how do they relate to it?

6. There is a slight change of focus in paragraph 7. Describe it. Give a title to paragraphs 7-13 suggesting the aspect of More's life the writer concentrates upon here. Be able to show how each of these paragraphs supports the central thesis.

7. How is paragraph 4 linked to paragraph 3? Paragraph 5 to 4?

SENTENCES

8. How do the following revisions alter the emphasis of Bevington's sentences?

(a) *Revision:* Henry had him murdered for putting God before his king, even though he was a peaceable and loving man, a just and equable man.

Bevington: "He was a peaceable and loving man, a just and equable man, but for putting God before his king, Henry had him murdered." (10-12)

(b) *Revision:* She washed the hair shirt he wore next to his skin.

Bevington: "It was she who washed the hair shirt he wore next to his skin." (14-15)

(c) *Revision:* He said, "Both are reasonable beings, suited equally for those studies by which reason is cultivated."

Bevington: " 'Both are reasonable beings,' he said, 'suited equally for those studies by which reason is cultivated.' " (82-83)

(d) *Revision:* He lavished love on all of life. . . .

Bevington: "On all of life he lavished love. . . ." (97)

9. Study the following sentence:

"Without solemnity, with courtesy and compassion for others, with a cheerful serene face and three jests on the scaffold he went to die, speaking to the executioner, 'Pluck up thy spirits man, and be not afraid to do thine office.' " (36-39)

Underline all the parallel * elements. Is the main clause * at the beginning, in the middle, or at the end of the sentence? What principle has the writer followed in arranging the ideas of the sentence?

10. What is the grammatical name of the construction in line 14: "the cords knotted to tame his flesh till the blood came"?

11. To what is "dull-hearted woman" (24) in apposition *?

DICTION

12. Look up: *calamitous* (2), *equable* (11), *hair shirt* (15), *scold* (23), *adjuring* (24), *beseech* (29), *meet* (31), *scaffold* (33), *shift* (35), *tranquillity* (50), *wit* (54), *gravest* (56), *facetious* (58), *theology* (80), *commodious* (87), *loathed* (89), *lumbago* (90), *litany* (94), *lavished* (97).

13. Who were Erasmus (50), John Aubrey (58), Holbein (87)?

14. If you have access to a good Latin dictionary, look up *festivitas* and learn its full range of meaning.

15. Why are these alternates not as good as the words in the text: *executed* for *murdered* (12), *gags* for *jests* (37), *incredible* for *incredulous* (84), *happy* for *merry* (99)?

POINTS TO LEARN

1. Rather than proceeding in step-by-step analysis, an essay may be organized by centering everything on a core idea whose weight and importance holds the paragraphs together.

2. A character sketch may be less concerned with laying out the facts of someone's life than with revealing the essence of personality.

SUGGESTIONS FOR WRITING

Compare Bevington's account of Sir Thomas More with the entry in a good encyclopedia or in a handbook of history or of religion. Discuss differences in purpose and show how they influence organization, the inclusion or omission of details, and diction and sentence style.

IMPROVING YOUR STYLE

Include in your composition:

1. Two parallel sentences.
2. An appositive.
3. An elliptical nominative absolute * like Bevington's construction in line 14.

From Memoirs of Montparnasse

John Glassco (1909–1981) was a highly regarded poet (his *Selected Poems* received the Governor General's Award in 1971), a novelist (under several pseudonyms), and a superb translator—as shown in *The Poetry of French Canada in Translation* (1970) and in his brilliant rendering into English of *The Journal of Saint-Denys-Garneau* (1962). The first chapter of *Memoirs of Montparnasse* was published in *This Quarter* in 1929; the remainder is now thought to have been written in 1964, although Glassco claimed in his preface when the book was published in 1970 that he had completed it during 1932–33. Glassco arrived in Paris in 1928, at the age of eighteen. His three-year stay is recorded in perceptive detail and written in a style that is elegant, precise, and witty. *Memoirs of Montparnasse* provides today's reader with an unsurpassed account of the life and the personalities (Hemingway, Callaghan, Joyce, Gertrude Stein, and dozens of others, famous or unknown) of a memorable, and now vanished, literary milieu. Glassco's narrative ability and descriptive skill make *Memoirs of Montparnasse* one of the classics of Canadian prose. Even in the following brief description of an anonymous Parisian eating crayfish, the author shows how seemingly trivial events can be given vividness and significance when presented with descriptive artistry.

1   Coming back into the glare of the Place Saint-Lazare I felt immensely alone, and the heat was so stifling I almost fainted. I could not face the prospect of going back alone to the rue Daguerre and wandered around the Right Bank, ending up by walking across the Pont des Arts and up the rue de Seine to the boulevard Saint-Germain. My feet and head 5 both seemed on fire. I remembered hearing that the Brasserie Lipp served the best gin fizz in town and I went inside and ordered one.

2   The people here were quite different from the Montparnasse types— older, better dressed, with an air of affluence and raffishness. The men were florid, distinguished looking and vaguely rapacious; the women had the air 10

From *Memoirs of Montparnasse* by John Glassco, reprinted by permission of the publisher, Oxford University Press.

of being kept. But no one looked happy or carefree. I found the atmosphere curiously refreshing and watched a stout iron-grey-haired gentleman with the rosette of the Legion of Honour, who was sitting with a chic, haggard-looking woman, as he guzzled a plateful of langoustines and a bottle of white wine in an ice-bucket. His hands, between cracking the shells, 15 dabbling the bodies in mayonnaise, stuffing them into his mouth, splitting and sucking the claws, wiping his lips, breaking bread, and pouring and drinking wine, were never still—yet the economy of their motion was marvellously organized: there was not a single wasted movement. The performance was underlined by the fact that he never stopped talking to his 20 companion for a moment—and, as far as I could gather, with ease and wit, for she smiled with an amusement that was clearly not assumed.

3   How wonderful, I thought, to be so distinguished looking, so deft, so self-satisfied, to have such a fine appetite and so smart a mistress; this man is obviously the product of at least three generations of polish, sagacity 25 and indulgence. I watched him as he finished his crayfish and raised his napkin to his lips to smother a slight belch.

QUESTIONS

READER AND PURPOSE
1. The reader should be aware that Glassco emphasizes his feeling of being "alone" in the first paragraph because his best friend has just left to return to Canada. Does he continue to dwell for very long on his own emotional state?
2. Note that he finds the unfamiliar atmosphere of the Brasserie "curiously refreshing" (12). Does this suggest to the reader that Glassco enjoys observing other people?
3. Would you define Glassco's observation of the "stout iron-grey-haired gentleman" (12) as objective or subjective? Or a combination of both?

ORGANIZATION
4. Glassco's strategy in paragraph 2 is to begin with a general description of the people in the restaurant. What individual words in the first three sentences lead us to conclude that his observation is combined with judgment about what he sees?
5. When he turns to observation of a particular individual what aspects of this character's behavior does he draw attention to? What specific words make it clear that Glassco is once again passing judgment? Why does he refer to the man's way of eating as a "performance" (19-20)?

6. Does Glassco change his tone * in paragraph 3? Is the phrase "how wonderful" (23) an instance of irony *? What else in the paragraph would lead the reader to suspect that Glassco is being ironic? How would you describe the qualities he terms "wonderful"? As moral qualities? Or as superficial aspects of behavior?

7. How does the final sentence of paragraph 3, especially the last word of the sentence, sum up the impression Glassco has tried to give us?

SENTENCES

8. Glassco begins the first four sentences of paragraph 2 with the subject-verb nucleus. Yet the structure of the fourth sentence differs considerably from that of the other three. Describe its structure and explain what purpose it serves in shifting the focus of Glassco's description.

9. What descriptive effect is produced by the series of participial * phrases in sentence five of paragraph 2? Is this an example of an author trying to match the rhythms of his sentence to what is being described? What other purposes does the sentence serve?

10. The first sentence of paragraph 3 gives us Glassco's ironic commentary on the "gentleman" (12). Look closely at the qualities Glassco purports to admire: "distinguished looking" (not "distinguished") (23), "so deft" (23), "so self-satisfied" (24). Do these qualities truly evoke our admiration? Explain why not.

11. Observe Glassco's arrangement of the words "polish, sagacity and indulgence" (25-26). What does this reveal about his feelings that would be lost if we rearranged the words?

DICTION

12. Look up: *Brasserie* (6), *raffishness* (9), *florid* (10), *rapacious* (10), *Legion of Honour* (13), *chic* (13), *haggard* (14), *polish* (25), *sagacity* (25).

13. What are the etymologies * of *marvellously* (18-19) and *wonderful* (23)? Does an understanding of the etymologies make it clearer to you that Glassco is using these words ironically?

14. Look up *curiously* (12). Note carefully the quite different meanings of this word. Is Glassco employing the word in more than one sense? Explain your answer.

POINTS TO LEARN

1. Objective and subjective criticism can be effectively combined.

2. Carefully chosen diction and restrained irony enable a writer to pass judgments, without stating them directly, on a character he is describing.

3. Focusing on one particular aspect of a character's behavior can be an economical way of suggesting what his complete personality may be.

SUGGESTIONS FOR WRITING

Observe the clientele in the next restaurant you visit (but do not stare impolitely). Find two people whose manners suggest that they have contrasting personalities, and describe them in two separate paragraphs. Do not state your responses to these people directly; imply your judgments and feelings in your diction, your sentence structures, and, if possible, through the use of such devices as understatement, overstatement, and irony.

IMPROVING YOUR STYLE

In your composition:

1. Begin by describing the general atmosphere of the restaurant in two or three straightforward sentences.

2. Then make a careful transition from the general scene to a particular individual.

3. Use a series of participial phrases that both describe and implicitly judge one of the persons observed.

4. Make your choice of descriptive adjectives and adverbs as precise as possible.

William Joyce

Rebecca West is an English novelist, journalist, and critic. Her novels include *Harriet Hume* (1929), *The Thinking Reed* (1936), and *The Birds Fall Down* (1966). She is best known for *Black Lamb and Grey Falcon* (1942), a two-volume work about the Balkans, part travelogue and part social and political history, and for *The Meaning of Treason* (1945), from which the following passage comes. *The Meaning of Treason* is an account of the trial of William Joyce—known derisively as Lord Haw-Haw—a renegade Englishman who broadcast propaganda for Germany during World War II. After the war Joyce was tried as a traitor, convicted and hanged. West's book is much more than a report of the trial; it expands into a thoughtful examination of what constitutes treason in our time and of how the responsibilities of scientists and intellectuals have changed in the modern world.

The strong electrical light was merciless to William Joyce, whose appearance was a surprise to all of us who had not seen him before. His voice had suggested a large and flashy handsomeness. But he was a tiny little creature and, though not very ugly, was exhaustively so. His hair was mouse-coloured and grew thinly, particularly above his ears. His nose was joined to his face 5 at an odd angle, and its bridge and its point and its nostrils were all separately misshapen. Above his small dark-blue eyes, which were hard and shiny, like pebbles, his eyebrows were thick and pale and irregular. His neck was long and his shoulders were narrow and sloping. His arms were very short and very thick, so that his sleeves were like little bolsters. His 10 body looked flimsy yet coarse. There was nothing individual about him except a deep scar running across his right cheek from his ear to the corner of his mouth. But this did not create the savage and marred distinction that it

From *The Meaning of Treason* by Rebecca West. Copyright 1947, © renewed 1975 by Rebecca West. Reprinted by permission of Viking Penguin Inc., and A. D. Peters & Co. Ltd.

might suggest, for it gave a mincing immobility to his mouth, which was extremely small. His smile was pinched and governessy. He was dressed 15 with an intent and ambitious spruceness which did not succeed in giving any impression of well-being, but rather recalled some Eastern European peasant, newly driven off the land by poverty into a factory town and wearing his first suit of Western clothes. He moved with a jerky formality which would have been thought strange in any society. When he bowed to the 20 Judge, his bow seemed sincerely respectful but entirely inappropriate to the occasion, and it was difficult to think of any occasion to which it would have been appropriate.

QUESTIONS

READER AND PURPOSE

1. West's purpose is to make her reader see William Joyce as he stands in the dock. Does she succeed?

2. Of course, she might simply have printed a photograph of him. Would that have been better? Or does she do with words things that a photograph could not do, or not do as effectively?

3. Do you think West is writing for her contemporaries—that is, for people who lived through the war—or for a younger generation, for whom the war and those connected with it are history rather than personal experience?

ORGANIZATION

4. Which sentence (or sentences) may be said to act as the topic statement?

5. West's paragraph is organized in a loosely analytical manner. Thus from lines 3 to 11 she describes Joyce's general physical appearance. Is there any order to how she does it? Which phrase in the third sentence sets up and controls the details West describes in lines 3-11?

6. In line 11 she makes a slight change in her focus. Explain. Where else does she shift to different aspects of her subject?

7. Study sentences 2, 3, and 4. How does West unify these sentences, preventing her reader from feeling any sense of discontinuity in the paragraph? Where else does she employ essentially the same sentence pattern? Beginning too many sentences in the same way can be dangerous. Does she vary the pattern enough to avoid monotony?

8. Find places where West uses pointers * to help the reader follow her flow of thought. Does she depend chiefly upon pointers or upon sentence structure to maintain flow *?

9. Suppose the first sentence had read like this: "To William Joyce, whose appearance was a surprise to all of us who had not seen him before, the electrical light was merciless." Would it sound more "literary" (that is, more like books, less like speech) than West's sentence? Generally does she prefer the loose * type of sentence (typical of speech) or the periodic * (which is more formal and literary)?

10. How does this revision change the emphasis of West's sentence?

> *Revision:* Except for a deep scar running across his right cheek from his ear to the corner of his mouth, there was nothing individual about him.
>
> *West:* "There was nothing individual about him except a deep scar running across his right cheek from his ear to the corner of his mouth."
> (11-13)

11. Point out the chiasmus * in the last sentence of West's paragraph.

DICTION

12. Look up: *bolsters* (10), *flimsy* (11), *coarse* (11), *inappropriate* (21).

13. Much of the effectiveness of West's description comes from striking phrases which are rich in implications. Explain as fully as you can all that is implied by the following: *a large and flashy handsomeness* (3), *savage and marred distinction* (13), *mincing immobility* (14), *pinched and governessy* (15), *an intent and ambitious spruceness* (16), *jerky formality* (19).

14. What exactly does West mean by her remark that Joyce "though not very ugly, was exhaustively so" (4)?

15. What impression is conveyed by the description of his eyes as being "hard and shiny, like pebbles" (7-8)?

POINTS TO LEARN

1. In characterization, as in all description, impressions are more effectively communicated by being "rendered" in objective details than by being stated directly.

2. The loose sentence suggests informality.

SUGGESTIONS FOR WRITING

1. Write a one-paragraph character sketch of some public figure familiar to us from television. Your purpose is to convey an impression, but an impression rendered in physical details of appearance and mannerisms.

2. In a single paragraph discuss how West evaluates William Joyce, supporting your generalizations by citing from her text.

IMPROVING YOUR STYLE

In your composition include:

1. Two or three periodic sentences and two or three loose ones.
2. A simile * like the one West uses in lines 7-8, which conveys an impression in a sharp suggestive image *.

JAMES G. MacGREGOR

From Pack Saddles to Tête Jaune Cache

James G. MacGregor is an Edmonton businessman and historian who has written extensively on the discovery and settlement of the West. He has published histories of Alberta, of Edmonton, of the Klondike rush through Edmonton, of the Saskatchewan River, and of early railroad construction. He has also written books on such important figures as Father Lacombe, Peter Fidler, and Anthony Henday. The moving paragraph below is from his book on the first settlers and railroad builders who worked west from Edmonton to the Mt. Robson area.

1   The old-time land surveyors were a rare breed—quiet, thoughtful, accurate. Quiet, because for nearly a year at a time they worked perhaps hundreds of miles from the nearest settlement and with very few people to talk to. Thoughtful, for the star-studded skies, the great silences and the empty spaces induced profound thought, unhampered by the jabbering 5 crowds of civilization. Accurate, as with almanac, chronometer and transit they marked the times and the seasons of the stars, making intricate calculations in their carefully kept field books. Far out in the forest, two hundred miles from the nearest settlement or survey monument, they extracted information from the inscrutable stars. With Castor and Pollux, Sirius and 10 Polaris as guides they chopped a line through the forests or scratched it over rocky cliffs, and marked it with pits, cairns, mounds and pins, to testify to all men for all time that this meridian was exactly where they said it was. For all time, their fellows would judge them by the accuracy of this line. 15

From *Pack Saddles to Tête Jaune* by James G. MacGregor, reprinted by permission of The Canadian Publishers, McClelland and Stewart Limited, Toronto.

418

QUESTIONS

1. What sort of descriptive writing is this? Is MacGregor describing a combination of flat characters and round?

2. Could you object that this is an idealized description of the land surveyors?

3. How do you think MacGregor feels about his subject? Does he succeed in communicating his feelings to you? Or is something missing?

4. Like most description, the passage begins with a general impression, the key terms being "quiet, thoughtful, accurate." Which following details are specifications of the first of these impressions? Which of the third?

5. Is the last sentence a closing by return *? Is it only partially so?

6. What relationship is there between the first sentence and the rest of the selection? Is the first sentence an organizing sentence *? If it is not an organizing sentence, what type of sentence is it?

7. Discuss the flow * of the paragraph. Then relate your discussion to your answers to question 6.

8. Structuring consecutive sentences in the same way can be dangerous. How does MacGregor vary the pattern of sentences 2, 3, and 4 to avoid monotony? Is he successful?

9. How are the second, third, and fourth sentences parallel *?

10. Should there be an additional comma in l. 4 and l. 12? If so, precisely where and why? If not, why?

11. Would there be any difference of effect if the dash in l. 1 were replaced by a colon?

12. In ll. 12-13 do we find an example of asyndeton * or polysyndeton *? Or neither? Explain.

13. The opening sentence is grammatically simple *. Are any of the others? If not simple, are they compound *, complex *, or compound-complex?

14. The sixth sentence, much the longest in the paragraph, is a fine example of the cumulative * style. Analyze this sentence to show how the cumulation develops.

15. Look up: *induced* (5), *unhampered* (5), *almanac* (6), *chronometer* (6), *transit* (6), *inscrutable* (10), *cairns* (12), *meridian* (13).

16. Show how a precise knowledge of the following phrases helps your under-

standing of the passage: *rare breed* (1), *jabbering crowds* (5-6), *field books* (8), *inscrutable stars* (10).

17. Using an encyclopaedia or an astronomical handbook, discuss why Mac-Gregor refers to four specific stars (10-11) instead of simply to "the stars." How does this knowledge help you better appreciate the work of the surveyors?

18. When MacGregor says that the surveyors "extracted information" from the stars he is not, of course, speaking literally. Yet the expression is effective. Why?

POINTS TO LEARN

1. A type, or flat character, may be sympathetically described by a careful choice of details.

2. The cumulative sentence works by tacking on ideas, expanding a point by adding modifying clauses and phrases, appositives *, nominative absolutes *, and so on.

3. Consecutive sentences that are parallel should be varied slightly in order to avoid monotony.

SUGGESTIONS FOR WRITING

Write a brief description (10-12 lines) of a type of character: the typical school janitor, truck driver, drug-store clerk, campus politician, family physician, librarian, newspaper boy, hairdresser, etc. Your purpose is to convey a sympathetic impression, using details of appearance, attitudes, and mannerisms.

IMPROVING YOUR STYLE

In your description include:

1. An opening sentence that gives a general impression.

2. Three or four sentences that specify the impression of the first sentence.

3. At least two sentences that are parallel in structure.

Welcome to the Death Hilton

Paul Hemphill is a journalist whose methods, like those of John McPhee (page 263) and Tom Wolfe (page 309) exemplify what is loosely called the "new journalism." He has published articles in a number of magazines (*Cosmopolitan, Life, Sport, True*), and is the author of several books, among them *The Nashville Sound: Bright Lights and Country Music* and *The Good Old Boys* (1974). The latter, which is the source of the following essay, is a collection of pieces about interesting southerners (Hemphill is from Alabama), some famous, some once-famous, and some relatively obscure. But all are variants of a type known in the South as "the good old boy," a regionalism difficult to translate. Hemphill quotes a definition from Tom Wolfe's "The Last American Hero" which describes the qualities of the good old boy: "He has a good sense of humor and enjoys ironic jokes, is tolerant and easygoing enough to get along in long conversations at places like on the corner, and has a reasonable amount of physical courage . . ." On the whole, Hemphill admires the good old boy, but not uncritically. In this portrait of an enterprising funeral director named H. Raymond Ligon he shows both the type and its manifestation in one individual. And notice that he shows, he does not tell; he lets his subject speak and act for himself.

> Show me the manner in which a nation or a community cares for its dead, and I will measure with mathematical exactness the tender sympathies of its people, their respect for the laws of the land and their loyalty to high ideals.
>
> —*Gladstone*

1   "Wife found that quote somewhere, typed it up and gave it to me. Been carrying it around ever since. Believe in it. Ray Ligon's motto, don't you see." Reverently rereading it to himself, H. Raymond Ligon smiles at

From *The Good Old Boys*. Copyright © 1974 by Paul Hemphill. Reprinted by permission of Simon & Schuster, a Division of Gulf & Western Corporation, and The Sterling Lord Agency.

the card through black horn-rimmed glasses, stuffs the bulging billfold back
into his hip pocket, swings his dusty cowboy-booted feet onto the dishev- 5
eled desk and sways back deeply in a swivel chair. Everything is right on
this soft summer morning at the Woodlawn Cross Mausoleum and Funeral
Home, Inc., on the edge of downtown Nashville. Grieving families sit
quietly in several of the ten "repose rooms," waiting for services to begin.
Somber music drones through the carpeted hallways. Ligon's army of fu- 10
neral directors and embalmers and secretaries and janitors goes about its
business inside, while outside two dozen laborers preen the grassy undulating 192 acres representing the final resting place for some 100,000 souls.
But the true center of activity is behind the main building, where dozens
of hard-hatted construction workers swarm over a hulking square concrete- 15
and-steel edifice, now rising five stories out of the ground like one of the
Pyramids, soon to be the third tallest building in Nashville. Ray Ligon's
dream. A twenty-story mausoleum, cold storage for 129,500 bodies.

2   "Yes, sir," he is saying, "Ray Ligon is one of the most fortunate
people in the funeral business, and I'll tell you why." It is only nine o'clock, 20
but already he has been at work for nearly three hours, and the construction
on the mausoleum is going so well that he is in an ebullient mood, his
bright yellow shirt and gaudy boots and dyed black hair and leathery sunburned face belying his 70 years. "Hard work, and treating people right. I
remember one time this lady called and said she'd had a vision that her hus- 25
band was buried at my place with his head downhill. Said she couldn't
sleep for thinking about it. I told her to come on out, and I got two lawn
chairs and we sat there under a tree while the workers dug. When they put
a level on the coffin, the bubble was straight up. She appreciated what Ray
Ligon did for her, don't you see. Every human being is entitled to our love 30
and respect, and to a decent farewell."

3   Ligon's chief engineer on the mausoleum project opens the door to
the cluttered paneled office. He is wearing a bright yellow hardhat, and
holding a bill of lading in one hand. "Got a load we need you to sign for,
Mr. Ligon." 35

4   "What we got here?"

5   "One load of marble."

6   "Stuff from Italy?"

7   "Yes, sir."

8   "Fine. You know what to do with it." Ligon scrawls his signature
on the bill. "Keep 'em rolling." 40

9   That business done ("Sent my engineer all the way to Italy just to

find the right marble for the crypts"), Ligon sways back again and races off
on another monologue about himself and his plans. While he talks, a 76-
year-old retired newspaperman named Sewall B. Jackson—reedy, chain-   45
smoking, ruined voice, pencil-thin mustache, mod high-heeled shoes and
tacky checkered suit—takes shorthand notes for the book he will write on
Ligon's life. "If it's never been done before, I thrive," Ligon is saying.
"Night funerals. Funeral home and cemetery combined. Mausoleum. Ray
Ligon likes to do sensible things that've never been done before. I tell 'em   50
everything else in this world has changed, why not the funeral business.
Know what I'm thinking about doing next?" Sewall Jackson's pen poises.
He looks up at Ligon with an expectant conspiratorial grin. "Helicopters.
Here's a loved one at the airport. Died in Chicago, wanted to be buried
here. Put the remains on a helicopter, fly over here and land on top of the   55
mausoleum, bring him down on the elevator to the repose room. Save time,
save money. I can get a helicopter for $18,000, as cheap as a fancy hearse.
Got to keep thinking all the time, don't you see . . ."

10   For the time being, before he goes airborne, Raymond Ligon's
latest scheme will suffice in solidifying his claim as the most innovative,   60
if not controversial, funeral director in America. The largest mausoleum in
the country had been one of four floors at California's Forest Lawn, but
when Ligon announced his audacious design for the Woodlawn Cross
Mausoleum he left quite a target for any other entrepreneur who might
care to shoot for the record. At a cost of $12 million, the mausoleum will   65
provide, Ligon boasts, "a burial as fine as the Taj Mahal." The name Cross
Mausoleum comes from the shape of the building, its four wings con-
verging in the center, the foundation and immediate grounds consuming
only seven of the 300 acres held by Ligon. Each floor will have bright carpet, air conditioning, elevators, piped music, cushy sofas and seven tiers of   70
crypts beginning at floor level with the most expensive (the "Westminster"
for couples buried side by side) and ending at the ceiling with the least expensive vault (the "Heaven Level"). There will be nighttime funerals
("working folks can't make it in the daytime"), visiting at all hours, and
lounging downstairs in the Garden of Jesus: a natural underground spring   75
spilling water into a corner rock pile, a clear fiberglass roof allowing natural
sunlight to feed the flowers, and a "tomb of Jesus" made of rocks brought
over from Jerusalem.

11   The reaction to Ligon's plans ranged from utter disbelief to jollity.

"This is one time I'm sort of glad I can't see," said a blind Nashville singer   80
named Ronnie Milsap. Joked Johnny Carson on his television talk show:
"How would you like to be the elevator operator on duty about three in the
morning, and you're sitting on the sixth floor, and you hear somebody say,
'Down'?" One magazine referred to it as "the Death Hilton," and a Nashville newsman no longer surprised by anything Ligon does guessed that "as   85
soon as he finishes this one he'll go out and build a chain of the damned
things across the country." Buyers of space in the mausoleum were hard to
find at first, Southerners being more traditional about such matters as death
and religion than most, but an aggressive sales campaign ("Keeping up
with kings, queens and presidents costs less than you think," read one bro-   90
chure) soon brought into the coffers some $2 million in "Pre-need" sales—
the backbone of the burial business—so Ligon could begin construction.
When the first five floors were topped out and put into service this fall
(for the ribbon cutting, a state official landed atop the building in a helicopter), there remained some skeptics, one of them a disgruntled former   95
Ligon business associate: "I don't see any necessity for a 20-story mausoleum, except that it'll get Raymond a lot of publicity. He contends that
land in America is going to run out. I disagree. You can go three miles outside Nashville, on an old farm, and find plenty of land for plenty of
cemeteries."   100

12   To Ligon, though, the availability and price of land in America today make the argument for mausoleum burial overpowering. "We just can't
afford to keep on burying folks on these shady little hillsides," he says,
pointing out that he will bury the same number in a mausoleum covering
seven acres that he has buried on the 192 developed acres of his cemetery.   105
"I know what they say about the cemetery business, that you buy by the
acre and sell by the inch, but you can't even make any money that way
these days. Some of the land I paid $700 an acre for in the 1930s is worth
$35,000 today, and some adjoining property just brought $55,000 an acre.
We're sitting right next to the busiest intersection in Nashville now. I'm   110
just not going to develop another acre. It's mausoleums from now on.
Ground burial is going to go out." Armed with arguments, Ligon can
go on and on about the desirability—for himself and for the client family—
of mausoleum burial: it is dryer, less expensive (no need for a tombstone,
vault or elaborate coffin), offers lower maintenance costs (two people will   115
be able to take care of the mausoleum, while 28 are required for the cemetery grounds), and "if there was a strike, why me and the preacher could

get on the elevator and do the burying ourselves." Ligon does not mention
that 130,000 crypts sold at an average $2,000 would turn his $12 million
investment into $260 million, and that air space comes free.   120

13   "Let's go across the road for a minute and see the old place, Mr.
Jackson." Clapping his own personal yellow hardhat on his head, Ligon
strides through a maze of corridors until he bursts out into the bright
morning sun, quickly slipping behind the wheel of the luxury pickup truck
he prefers to drive. Gliding over the smooth paved lane leading to the main   125
entrance, he points straight ahead across busy Thompson Lane to a squat
two-story concrete building with the word MAUSOLEUM discreetly printed
on a green awning which shades the entrance. It was his first mausoleum—
and probably the first of any size in the South—and today, seven years later,
its 3,500 crypts are just about taken up. "I told 'em I wanted it soft and   130
beautiful like a living room, not harsh and cold," Ligon says as he steps into
the air conditioning and waves a hand over the bright carpeting and the
deep sofas. A woman is vacuuming, her machine drowning out the soft music, and Ligon asks her to stop when he sees that several people—most of
them old—are sitting around, apparently visiting family crypts.   135
14   "Mr. Ligon." Coming Ligon's way, his eyes red and bloated, is a
retired Army colonel who has lost his entire family during the past 18
months, the last a son killed in a skyjacking. The man says, "I just wanted
to thank you."
15   "What for, Colonel Giffe?"   140
16   "For this place you got here."
17   "Everything's all right, then."
18   "It's wonderful. Just wonderful. Well, you know what I mean. My
wife, she sat right there on that divan. She knew she was going. But she
wasn't horrified by this place. No, sir. Another thing, I can come visit with   145
her even if it's snowing."
19   Ligon nods to some of the others and makes a quick tour. "Here's
my first wife," he says, pointing to a crypt. The place is cool and quiet and
eerie, in spite of the flashy colors and deep carpet. Here and there against
the walls are small tables adorned with plastic flowers. On one of the tables   150
is a stack of index cards and a note inviting visitors to "leave word so we
can acknowledge your visit." One card has already been used. "Dear Lela,"
says a laborious scrawl. "Ethel and Norma came by to see you. We miss
you so much." Beside the note is a tiny framed picture of the dead woman.

20   The burial business has changed very little in the decade since the   155
publication of Jessica Mitford's scathing book *The American Way of
Death*, still regarded as the definitive work on the subject. (Who, for that
matter, can forget the grotesqueries in the movie made of Evelyn Waugh's
The Loved One?) Mitford gets to the point on the very second page of the
opening chapter: "Gradually, almost imperceptibly, over the years the fu-   160
neral men have constructed their own grotesque cloud-cuckooland where
the trappings of Gracious Living are transformed, as in a nightmare, into
the trappings of Gracious Dying." About 1 percent of America dies each
year, leaving the disposal of some 2 million bodies to 22,000 "funeral directors" (not "undertakers," please) who do a gross of $1.8 billion each   165
year. The competition is mean and often bitchy, the object of the hunt
usually a grieving widow suddenly forced to make her first major financial
decision within hours, and this fall the Federal Trade Commission announced an investigation into 76 District of Columbia funeral homes—
tantamount to a national study—following numerous complaints about in-   170
flated prices and the selling of unneeded services. In the burial business
today, as strongly as ever, "cremation" is a dirty word (35 percent of the
dead in England are cremated, only some 60,000 a year in the United
States). Indeed, semantics is important in the business: "grief therapy" and
"memory pictures" and "slumber room" are the ABCs of the burial sales-   175
man's language. Talk about everything but death. A hole in the ground is
a hole in the ground. *It's the last chance you will have to do something for
your loved one . . . Now here is a nice casket, fit for a man of his stature
. . . Oh, by all means, you'll want fresh flowers . . . For the memory picture, I would suggest a dark wool suit and a bowtie . . . It's going to be a*   180
nice funeral, I'm sure of that . . .
21   Sales, then, is the most important aspect of the business. "They say
Ray Ligon is a great salesman," says Ligon, "but he knows anybody can sell
a couple if they love each other." The head of Woodlawn's 15-man sales
force is Ligon's 34-year-old stepson, John Spivey, a handsome favorite at the   185
Tennessee statehouse, who recently received a six-year appointment to the
state's Youth Advisory Commission. When he dies, he says, somebody will
simply pull out a file in the business office at Woodlawn and it will all be
there: choice of casket, names of pallbearers, number of the crypt in the
mausoleum, and so forth. "I remember this young guy whose wife had   190
died," says Spivey. "Just before they closed the lid on her, he picked up his
four-year-old daughter and leaned her over and said, 'Kiss your mother

good-by.' A lot of people go hysterical at a funeral. You have all kinds. I
don't see any reason why that should happen; any reason why it should be
a hot, agonizing ordeal. It should be planned, together, in advance."   195
22   This "pre-need" selling is Spivey's responsibility, and he wraps his
arguments around the low-key, sensible, pragmatic trappings of, say, a life
insurance agent. "The funeral director doesn't have to put pressure on a
couple, the family does that," he says. "A funeral is the third largest investment you make in your life, behind a car and a house. You going to let   200
your brother-in-law do it? It's all a process of education, like my juvenile
job. I just tell them the straight true story and put it in an honest, be-
lievable, attractive package." At Woodlawn, one price covers all: coffin,
hearse, police escort, flowers, "open-and-close" grave charges, and so forth.
The price can vary greatly, depending on such choices as gravesite and cof-   205
fin, but Spivey says an average burial in the ground there runs around
$2,500. In the new mausoleum, however, he says he "can do one" for
$1,600. Woodlawn will also sell you the coffin, more than a dozen styles of
them being on display in a sales room at the funeral home, and for the
mausoleum there is a $495 Ligon-designed bier called the "cross repose,"   210
which is the cheapest way of all to go. "We don't back the hearse up to the
door," says Spivey, "we just tell them the facts. Pre-need is the way you
stop the high cost of dying." Ray Ligon, his stepson says with reverence, "is
the greatest teacher who ever lived."

23   The funeral business is all Herschel Raymond Ligon has known   215
since his birth in 1903 to the owner of the local funeral home in Lebanon,
one of those lovely little middle Tennessee towns about 30 miles east of
Nashville. When he graduated from high school ("All I've got is that di-
ploma and a Dale Carnegie course"), he became a partner in Ligon & Sons
Funeral Home, doing everything from embalming to directing services.   220
"The first service I ever held, I was 24 years old," he recalls. "A logger had
been killed on the job and he was so poor they were having to bury him out
back of the house in the garden, don't you see. We fixed him up nice and
took him over there, but there wasn't a preacher or any music. An old lady
pulled me aside and said, 'I'll sing a song if you'll read some scripture.' The   225
next day my father got a preacher to teach me how to lead a service, and I
was in business."
24   Ligon was too adventurous to stick around Lebanon forever, and
his chance at much bigger things came during the Depression when a large
holding company in Nashville went into bankruptcy. In addition to insur-   230

ance, real estate and a false-teeth factory, the group held a 40-acre cemetery in Nashville. One of the attorneys representing the creditors had been a high school classmate of Ligon's, so Ligon was hired as a trustee at $35 a week ("That's when folks felt lucky to make a dollar a day") and charged with disposing of the cemetery to pay off a $110,000 tax bill. He soon be-   235
came an expert on the cemetery business in America—visiting the major ones like Forest Lawn in Hollywood on fact-finding excursions—and when it came time to put the cemetery up on bids, Ligon decided *he* wanted it. His bid for $90,000 was the only one submitted, so he took over Memorial Park and prefixed Woodlawn to its name and began building an empire.   240
25   Accustomed to checking into the office at daylight, Ligon quickly became a national figure in the funeral industry and a financial power to be reckoned with in Nashville. Bit by bit he bought up surrounding land, some of it for as little as $700 an acre, ultimately acquiring a package of 300 acres. Stressing "pre-need" sales to a growing sales force, he was able to get his   245
hands on money and put it to his own use long before it was needed to service his clients. With the funds he began acquiring other cemeteries in the Nashville area and claiming endless "firsts" in the region: the first cre-matorium, the first funeral home-and-cemetery operation under one roof, the first night funeral services, the first weddings in the funeral home chapel,   250
the first previously all-white cemetery opened to blacks. That Ray Ligon knows how to come up with cash when necessary is never questioned around Nashville. "One time I needed some capital," he says, "so I an-nounced plans for a white 25-foot 'Tower of Memories' across the road. I got 450 people to put up $10 each in exchange for their name on a bronze   255
plaque. Me and two Negroes built it in no time." Finally, seven years ago, he raised his first mausoleum.

26   Today Ligon lives an active life. At one time or another in the past he has had his hands in many pies—a bronze works, a concrete vault factory, a half-dozen cemeteries, a finance company, a downtown office building—   260
but has divested himself of most of these so he can concentrate on his dream mausoleum. His two sons are well-set now—one operates the Mount Olivet cemetery in Nashville, the other a bank in Lebanon and a tourist at-traction in Gatlinburg called Christus Gardens—leaving Ligon and his sec-ond wife (a high-powered cemetery entrepreneur in her own right before   265
they married) alone in a roomy white brick ranch house, set on a wooded knoll across from the rising mausoleum, of a simplicity belying his esti-mated net worth of some $10 million. Except when he is on brief visits to

central Florida, overseeing a real estate development there, he starts his day
with a 6:30 A.M. meeting with construction engineers and spends the rest of   270
it swinging deals or hanging around the construction site. "He comes up
with the ideas," says the current Mrs. Ligon, "and we what you call 'implement' them." Says Ligon of his standing in the community: "You know
who criticizes me? Other funeral directors. You think there might be a little jealousy there?"   275

27   The man on the street in Nashville may hold little more than passing awe for a man audacious enough to build a skyscraper cemetery, but
there is a tight corps of others whose emotions toward Ligon run from be-
grudging respect to outright hostility. "He can easily differentiate between
the person who needs the services of a pious Bible-quoter and the one who   280
needs a drink," says Nat Caldwell, a veteran reporter for the *Nashville Ten-
nessean*. Says a young ex-banker who once wrote a 30-page report on Ligon's
financial empire: "It was so complex, if there was any hanky-panky going
on you couldn't find it." Says an embittered former associate who claims he
once lost $15,000 in a cemetery development scheme engineered by Ligon: 285
"Every time I get to thinking about the bastard, my angina starts acting up.
I wouldn't speak to him if I saw him on the street." Even his enemies, however, respect his drive. "If Raymond Ligon stayed straight," says one, "he'd
be the hottest thing in America."

28   The nearest Ligon has been to serious trouble was in the early   290
1960s when he became involved in the National Cemetery Development
Corporation, which eventually sued him and his sons for $240,000 in dam-
ages on the charge that "transactions . . . resulted in diversion of funds to
the Ligons." NCDC was organized in 1958 by a dozen or so Nashville businessmen, with plans to develop cemeteries and allied businesses all over the   295
nation. As soon as its formation was announced, Ligon offered his services
as an expert in the field and was promptly named president. More than
$1 million was raised in a public stock sale during the first four months, the
major partners kicking in as much as $30,000 each, and in the beginning all
was happiness and light. "People bought because of what they knew about   300
Woodlawn, because Ligon was obviously successful," says one of the original partners, Jim Bulleit, now a candy manufacturer in Nashville. "We
finally got around to going to Raymond Ligon to find out who he was."
Over the first three years the corporation lost some $300,000, bringing about
Ligon's "resignation" as president. Finally, in 1963, claiming that Ligon   305
and his sons were raking money off the top for themselves and doing little

else for the corporation, the NCDC filed suit. The NCDC lies dormant to-day, the suit still tabled somewhere in court, and the embittered partners seem to have little heart to continue fighting. "Hell," says one, "our attorney moved off to Florida and won't even return my calls." The publicity did 310 little good for Ligon, for when he tried to give a farm to his Church of Christ the church gave it right back on the grounds that it didn't want to get involved. "But the man has good lawyers," says reporter Caldwell, "and he always protects his flanks." Indeed, when the Securities Exchange Commission showed an interest in Ligon and the NCDC it was shut out of any 315 investigation because Ligon had seen to it that only Tennesseans bought stock in the group.

29   Late in the afternoon, curious to see what sort of progress the engineers have made during the day, Ligon invites a visitor to ride with him to the top of the mausoleum and check out the work. The dark elevator groans 320 and clangs as it rises from the wet and musty ground floor before finally bursting into the sparkling summer sunlight. Looking like one of the construction workers himself, hardhat and all, Ligon waves a hand at the two dozen men and asks the foreman to call the men together. Off in the distance can be seen Ligon's rambling house, sitting serenely in the cluster of 325 shade trees beyond the grassy acres of his cemetery. The spread is dotted with tiny oases Ligon calls his "Biblical Gardens," each featuring a statue of a character from the Bible standing amid a garden of flowers. "Boys," Ligon is saying, flopping his hardhat back and forth on his head, "this gentleman here is writing a story on us. *New York Times*. About the biggest 330 newspaper in the world. Wants to find out how excited you are about having a part in this, don't you see. Y'all talk to him, now." It was an awkward moment. The young ones suppressed giggles. The foreman babbled something he thought Ligon wanted to hear. "Let's go downstairs and relax," says Ligon, getting back onto the elevator and going down a couple of 335 floors.

30   He also has a conference room, which he hopes to entice various civic and business groups to use for their meetings. "Want to get 'em used to coming out to Woodlawn," he says. On the walls are pictures of Ligon with beasts he once shot on safari, and one of a group of middle-aged 340 women he once threw a party for on a whim. "Bought every one of 'em, 15 of 'em, a $165 dress," he is saying. "Silly. But they had fun."

31   "You hunt?" he is asked.

32   "Used to, all the time. Quit now. Got to where I didn't want to kill anything anymore."   345

33   For several minutes, he rambled on about life and death and his own machinations. You see one cremation, he says, you'll never believe in it ("Reminds you of Hitler and the Jews"). He may lease out the rest of his land, he says, and go mausoleum all the way ("Government's going to get 30 percent of the price if I sell the land, anyway"). On the first floor   350 of the mausoleum, he says, "we are already burying beautifully." People make jokes, he says, about funeral directors ("Call me the white Southern planter"), but you have to laugh with them and forget it. What would he be, he is asked, if he had it to do over?

34   "Evangelist," he says. "I never got to be what you'd call religious   355 until I was about 15 or 16. Just went to church and slept up until then. Now I give 10 percent a year to the church. Believe in it now. But I got to thinking about these evangelists, and me. Got the same things in common. Trying to console people, don't you see. *Help* people. And here I got this way with people, know how to talk 'em into things." He bends over in his   360 chair to knock some mud off his cowboy boots. "Yes, sir, an evangelist is what I'd want to be. Instead of working with their bodies, work with their souls, don't you see."

QUESTIONS

READER AND PURPOSE

1. In journalism a distinction is made between fact and comment. Facts are the province of the reporter, commentary of the editorial writer or columnist. Is Hemphill acting primarily as a reporter in this essay or as a commentator?

2. Because a reporter sticks to facts and offers no overt comments upon them, does not mean, of course, that he makes no judgments or offers no angle of vision from which the facts may be interpreted. But he effects such judgments tacitly by the careful selection and arrangement of details. For example, what details in the first paragraph influence our perceptions of and response to Ligon?

3. How do you think Hemphill feels about his subject? Does he succeed in communicating his feelings to you?

4. The essay begins with an epigraph from the liberal statesman William Gladstone, a prime minister of Great Britain in the late nineteenth century. It serves Ligon as a credo, justifying his life's work. Might it cast a different light upon Ligon's career?

ORGANIZATION

5. By extra spacing Hemphill divides his essay into seven sections. What shifts of subject do these involve? Give a brief title to each.

6. Like some short story writers Hemphill moves back and forth between present and past. On the one hand, we follow Ligon through a day's activities. Which of the seven sections are primarily concerned with this? Identify within them the word or words establishing the chronological structure.

7. On the other hand, some sections are primarily (though not exclusively) concerned with what in fiction is called "exposition," the background information which we need to know in order to understand what is happening in the present. Identify these sections. How do they enhance our understanding of Ligon and the funeral business?

8. What detail brought to our attention in the opening paragraph is repeated in the closing? What value has such repetition as a means of ending an essay? In this case, does the detail also provide an implicit authorial "comment"?

9. What is the topic sentence of paragraph 11? How is it supported? What is the topic of paragraph 20? How is paragraph 9 tied to the material that precedes it?

SENTENCES

10. Hemphill is fond of the intrusive sentence, an independent construction which is simply inserted into the middle of another statement without being syntactically connected to it. Here is an example: "That business done ('Sent my engineer all the way to Italy just to find the right marble for the crypts'), Ligon sways back again and races off on another monologue about himself and his plans" (42-44). Hemphill prevents confusion by using parentheses or dashes to signal that the enclosed construction is absolute (not connected to the main statement). Find other examples of such intrusive sentences. While such constructions are not syntactically integrated with the sentences that enclose them, they are, of course, related in idea. How does the parenthetical remark in lines 42-43 bear upon the writer's point? Be able to explain the relevancy of the other examples you find.

11. Does this technique of the intrusive sentence make Hemphill's style sound formal and literary, or relaxed and conversational? Do you think it would be appropriate for, say, a term paper in a history course?

12. Incidentally, in that sentence quoted in question 10, what is the grammatical term for the opening construction ("That business done")?

13. Point out the parallel * elements in the very first sentence of the essay and also in the sentence in lines 73-78.

DICTION

14. Look up: *somber* (10), *Taj Mahal* (66), *coffers* (91), *eerie* (149), *bitchy*

(166), *tantamount* (170), *low-key* (197), *pragmatic* (197), *bier* (210), *dormant* (307), *musty* (321), *entice* (337), *machinations* (347).

15. As fully as possible explain the meanings of the following phrases: *disheveled desk* (5-6), *scathing book* (156), *the definitive work* (157), *grotesque cloud-cuckooland* (161), *the trappings of Gracious Living* (162), *wooded knoll* (266-67).

16. What are the etymologies * of *mausoleum* (18), *crypts* (43), *brochure* (90), *divested* (261), *entrepreneur* (265), *audacious* (277), *evangelist* (361)?

17. Why are the following less effective than Hemphill's words? *Floats* for *drones* (10), *care for* for *preen* (12), *hums* for *groans and clangs* (320-21), *muttered* for *babbled* (333)?

18. Explain how these pointers * prepare us for the writer's turn of thought: *though* (101), *then* (182), *say* (197). Suppose that *though* were replaced by *however* or *nevertheless*: how would the tone * alter?

19. In what sense is the title of this essay ironic *?

POINTS TO LEARN
1. Reporters may "stick to the facts" yet subtly impose an interpretation upon the facts.
2. The intrusive sentence gives a colloquial * flavor to writing and is appropriate to a relaxed, conversational style.

SUGGESTIONS FOR WRITING
"Welcome to the Death Hilton" may be read as a criticism of the funeral business. Write a commentary upon Hemphill's essay from this point of view, discussing the more important failings that he tacitly suggests funeral directors are guilty of and supporting your points by evidence from Hemphill's text.

IMPROVING YOUR STYLE
In your essay include:

1. Two examples of intrusive sentences—that is, independent statements related in idea but not in syntax to the sentence which encloses them. Punctuate the intrusive sentences with dashes or parentheses.
2. Two cases of parallelism.
3. A nominative absolute *.
4. These connective * words to link sentences to what precedes them: *though, then, say.*

WAYNE GRADY

The Educated Imagination of Northrop Frye

Wayne Grady is a widely published essayist and book reviewer for such periodicals as *Saturday Night* and *Books in Canada*. He has translated French-Canadian short stories into English and has also edited the well-known *Penguin Book of Canadian Short Stories* (1980), as well as *The Penguin Book of Modern Canadian Short Stories* (1982). His essay on Northrop Frye describes one of the most influential literary critics in the English-speaking world.

1   When Northrop Frye was invited to London last spring to deliver the University of Western Ontario's Tamblyn Lectures, he and his wife, Helen, decided to go by train from Toronto. The Fryes haven't owned an automobile since they sold their old Studebaker in 1974, and Frye himself has never learned to drive. He likes to castigate all things mechanical, with 5 the possible exception of the typewriter: "I regard all machines as malignant demons," he has said. "The best thing they can do is come apart in my hands."

2   The train from Toronto to London travels for three hours through one of the most densely populated areas of Canada. Frye, sipping a gin-and- 10 tonic in the first-class carriage, gazes thoughtfully through the window at the apple orchards and the occasional town, and seems comfortably preoccupied with the lecture he is to give that evening. He doesn't actually succumb to a last-minute revision of his notes, but he speaks barely five words during the trip. It is possible that he has lost the knack of seeing 15 spring as something more than a literary symbol of the rebirth of nature in a cyclical universe: as an undergraduate in Toronto, he complained in his college magazine, *Acta Victoriana*, that the amount of work required to get an education in this country may account for the mediocrity of its literature, since it forces one to meet deadlines rather than to enjoy "the awaken- 20 ing enthusiasm of spring which those educated here have always missed—for

From *Saturday Night*, 96, 9 (October 1981). Reprinted by permission of the author.

the average man brought up on May examinations knows as little about spring as he does about a sunrise."

3   Perhaps, staring out on the countryside, he's recalling a passage from his book *Creation and Recreation*, in which he suggests that our cul- 25 tural insulation or "envelope"—which he elsewhere compares to the encir-cling wall of a garrison—"is rather like (to use a figure that has haunted me from childhood) the window of a lit-up railway carriage at night. Most of the time it is a mirror of our own concerns.... But occasionally the mirror turns into a real window, through which we can see only the vision of an indiffer- 30 ent nature . . ."

4   Whatever is passing through his mind, Frye has the appearance of someone resting between labors. He has just finished putting the final touches on his nineteenth book, unquestionably his masterpiece, *The Great Code*, the first volume of a projected two-volume study of the extent to which the Bible may be considered a work of literature, and the extent to 35 which that work has been the source of the rest of Western literature.

5   Until now, Frye's profound influence as a literary critic has been largely based on his *Anatomy of Criticism*, published in 1957; it has been read by almost everyone in the world involved in the advanced study or 40 teaching of English, and its publisher, Princeton University Press, still sells about 10,000 copies a year. Walter Jackson Bate of Harvard has called Frye "the most controversial, and probably the most influential critic writing in English since the 1950s," and Frye has lectured at universities and confer-ences in the United States, Japan, New Zealand, Guyana, Pakistan, Scandi- 45 navia, and Great Britain. His 1979 lecture tour to Milan, Venice, Florence, and Rome attracted front-page attention in every major newspaper in Italy—*La Republica* called him "uno dei massimi studiosi e critici litterari lingua inglese di questo secolo" (one of the great scholars and literary critics of the English language in this century)—and during the tour Frye was 50 interviewed for the lead-off program in a television series on the most influential personalities of the twentieth century. Although his highest academic degree is an Oxford BA, he has been awarded thirty honorary doctorates. *The Great Code*, when it is published next month, will increase his reputation by expanding it beyond literary criticism into a new realm of 55 discourse involving the relationship of language to thought and conscious-ness, and hence to society. As Frye's late colleague Marshall McLuhan said a few years ago, "Norrie is not struggling for his place in the sun. He *is* the sun."

6   Herman Northrop Frye was born on July 14, 1912, in Sherbrooke, 60 Québec. On his mother's side he is descended from a Catholic family that

settled in Virginia in the 1600s and came to Canada in the 1760s. "At some point or other," Frye recalled in his Victoria University office a few days before his London trip, "they turned from RC to Methodist; my mother's father was a Methodist circuit rider in Ontario in the nineteenth century." Frye's father was born in Windsor Mills, just outside Sherbrooke, "but *his* mother, Sarah Ann Northrop, after whom I was named, came from Lowell, Massachusetts. Partly under her influence my father went to Lowell to start into the hardware business—he'd been trained in a business college in Belleville, Ontario. I think he would have been content to stay in the United States, but my mother was determined to return to Canada. So my sister Vera was born in Lowell and I was born after they moved back to Sherbrooke."

7   Frye's father opened a hardware store. His mother, who had taught at Stanstead College before her marriage, taught her young son both to read and to play the piano at the age of three. She was a remarkable woman, Frye recalls, gazing through his office window at the Royal Ontario Museum. "If she hadn't grown up in a pauperized, Methodist, circuit-rider family with eight children, I think she could have had quite a career in either music or teaching." In 1918 the hardware store failed, and that year Frye's older brother was killed at Amiens, in France.

8   "I believe that my brother was one of the relatively few casualties caused by an airplane: one dropped a bomb over his trench. The psychological effect on my parents is what I chiefly remember: when you're six years old you go numb when something like that happens. You build a palisade around yourself. But I do remember that when my brother was killed it rather shot up the family, so that when we moved to Moncton we had psychologically almost retired. My father went on the road as a hardware salesman, taking up the Maritime agencies for various hardware companies. We settled in Moncton because, as the board of trade in that city will tell you, Moncton is the hub of the Maritimes."

9   Because of his father's peripatetic existence and his mother's excellence as a teacher, Frye was eight years old before he saw the inside of a school. He went directly into fourth grade. He was bored by school—he still regards it as "one of the milder forms of penal servitude"—and spent his time reading whatever was around the house: all of Scott's Waverley novels, all of Dickens. Many of the books came from the library of his grandfather, the circuit rider, but he also had a Methodist aunt in Alberta who was interested in literature. "Through her we acquired copies of Shaw and Ibsen and H. G. Wells, enough to get me started." Moncton finally got

around to opening a public library when Frye was fourteen; by fifteen he had, he says, "a fair grasp of nineteenth-century literature."

10   By then he was also becoming a very competent pianist. After his mother's deafness—which had come on shortly after her oldest son's death in France, but which Frye believes to have been "a hereditary factor" (Frye   105 himself is slightly hard of hearing)—Frye continued "splashing around on the piano" until he was thirteen, when his sister began paying for lessons "from a man I greatly admired and respected, George Ross," a graduate of the Royal College of Organists in London. What appealed most to Frye was Ross's "impersonal approach: the important thing was the music itself, not   110 his relation to me or to my performance." Ross was very likely the first real educator Frye had met (after his mother), and Ross's disinterested dedication to his art—his ability to exclude personality and emotion from his teaching—provided one basis for the theories and practice of education that Frye would follow for the rest of his life.   115

11   Unco-ordinated, myopic, hopeless at sports, Frye was unpopular at school, where the other students nicknamed him "the professor." At home, with a sister twelve years older than he was and parents who had effectively retired, he had "the feeling of being brought up by grandparents as an only child." He was haunted by a sense of isolation: cut off physically from the   120 rest of Canada, and by temperament from the rest of society, Frye turned to books and made them the real world. Or rather, he made them the cultural bricks in the garrison that protected him from the real world.

12   Frye came to two momentous conclusions: he would be a writer, and he would become a minister. "Ever since childhood I had thought of   125 myself as a writer. From about the age of six on." And he did not yet see any incompatibility between the two careers. "I had some hazy notion that a career as a minister might actually co-operate with writing," he says now. "To me, religion symbolized a cultivated life. I felt it would allow me to lead my own rather introverted lifestyle."   130

13   It did not. In 1934, while still a student preacher, Frye was sent by the United Church to southwestern Saskatchewan, where he ministered to three communities separated by twenty-six miles of prairie. "I got around on a mare named Katie who was a little older than I was. The services were held in school-houses." Frye found that, although he enjoyed delivering the   135 sermons and playing the organ, and the people were "cheerful and optimistic and breezy in spite of the Depression," he lacked the administrative and social abilities required for parish work. He found it an effort to meet people and impossible to make small talk over tea and biscuits, the clergy-

man's stock in trade. The story that he scared himself out of the ministry by   140
conjuring up a rainstorm in the dust-bowl is, he says, apocryphal. He simply
realized that "the academic life was the one I'd been suited for."

14   Frye prefers his office in Victoria University's New Academic
Building—an airless, modern temple of learning built as a series of tiny
rooms around a hollow core—to his equally modern but less private office   145
in Massey College. (His personal assistant, Jane Widdicombe, has her office
there, and Frye has had an office below hers since he became the U of T's
first University Professor in 1967.) At Vic, Frye is protected against the
intrusion of the outside world by tradition and privilege. He has the one
unlisted telephone number on campus—only his wife and Jane Widdicombe   150
can call him there—and he eats his lunch every day across the common in
the dining room of Burwash Hall, sitting at High Table: "one of the few
civilized traditions left," as he says.

15   He has been at Vic for fifty-two years. After high school, Frye, like
his father before him, took courses at a business college in Moncton on a   155
six-month scholarship, during which time he became fast enough on the
typewriter—a proficiency he attributes to his training on the piano—to be
chosen to represent New Brunswick in Underwood's 1929 national typing
competition in Toronto. Frye made the twenty-hour train trip, sat on the
stage of Massey Hall under the banner of New Brunswick, typed eighty   160
words a minute, and came in second. He can now type 150 wpm on his
IBM; his Vic colleagues say that when Frye is working it sounds as if he has
a Telex in his office.

16   It was during this Toronto trip that Frye visited Victoria for the
first time. His maternal grandfather, the circuit rider, had attended the   165
college back in its Cobourg days—Victoria continued to be a Methodist
stronghold long after it joined the U of T federation in 1892—and Frye's
visit was prompted as much by nostalgia as by curiosity. No one with
ambitions to be a writer can stay long in a business college, the glory and
excitement of typing championships notwithstanding. "I was offered vari-   170
ous secretarial jobs, but I was very anxious to get out of Moncton and the
Maritimes." He registered at Vic and came back for classes in September.
Underwood held its international competition at the end of September and
Frye took part, but didn't do well. "I had my mind on other things."

17   "I had been very introverted and thrown into myself for a very   175
large variety of reasons in Moncton," Frye says. "So as soon as I hit university I went into everything—dramatics, debating, editing the college

magazine. In fact I went into too much, undertaking jobs for which I had no qualifications whatever, such as being treasurer of the year." It's difficult to imagine Frye, with his shyness and his inability to make small talk, plunging grimly into residence executive meetings and attending Green Room parties. He seems forever to have been committing himself to tasks for which he was unsuited, almost as a kind of penance or balance for his talents in other areas. This may be the Methodist inheritance—John Wesley, Frye likes to point out, spent a great deal of his time editing the texts of novels for publication—or it may have been a form of self-prescribed therapy. Much as one may like to stay holed up in one's study, sooner or later the world on the other side of the window demands to be dealt with. This need was perhaps also behind his stint as editor of *The Canadian Forum* from 1948 to 1952: "I feel that one needs an activity," he says, "even if it's not a wholly congenial one—just to give a different pacing to what one is doing."

18   Morley Callaghan, in his 1948 book *The Varsity Story* (which deals with the University of Toronto in the 1920s and 1930s), describes Victoria College, as it was still called, as part of "the tradition of freedom, of independence of thought." The two great liberal lights on its faculty were the poet E. J. Pratt and the scholar Pelham Edgar, chairman of the English department from 1912 to 1938. Frye remembers Edgar as having "an extraordinarily sharp eye for people, but his lecturing was very erratic, spasmodic. Just to look at him, if you didn't know him, you would swear he had nothing on his mind except himself and his own comfort. But he was writing articles on 'Is There a Canadian Literature?' in *Saturday Night* as early as 1895." Edgar became for Frye a kind of extension of George Ross, Frye's old music teacher: an archetype of the ideal educator. "He wasn't a theorist at all," Frye says, perhaps a little regretfully, "and as a result of taking lectures from him you got very spasmodic information from your notes, but you realized that devoting your life to scholarship was somehow an honorable career. That was what he managed to put across." Edgar died in 1948. Frye dedicated his first book, *Fearful Symmetry*, to him, and Edgar's memoirs, *Across My Path*, which appeared in 1952, were edited by Frye.

19   Pratt, it seems, appealed less to Frye. "Pratt deliberately cultivated a reputation as an absent-minded duffer," Frye recalled a few years ago. "He loved parties and sitting at the head of the table and so on. And he loved conversation." Frye was becoming more interested in scholarship than in writing either novels or poetry, and so it was natural he should seek out for his role model a respected teacher and critic rather than the "muscular" (Callaghan's term) and garrulous Pratt. "I knew I was never a

poet," Frye says now. "A prose rhythm seems to have been built into my mind from the beginning. I had written sketches of novels. I wrote a number of—I wouldn't call them short stories. If someone like Borges had been known to me at the time, that is the kind of idiom that would have attracted   220 me." Five or six of these "little squibs" appeared in *The Canadian Forum* and in *Acta Victoriana* in the 1930s. "Some time around graduate school, I realized that I would have nothing to say as a fiction writer that others hadn't already said better, whereas as a critic I might have."

20   One further glimpse completes the picture of Frye as an under-   225 graduate. During his first year at Vic—in fact, a month after the second typing competition—the world outside the window intruded in the form of the Depression. Frye was able to survive the school year on scholarships, but summers required a different strategy. In the summer of 1930 he found a job pasting labels into books at the main branch of the Toronto Public   230 Library, which paid him the not inconsiderable sum of $15 a week (meals cost sixty-five cents a day). "One of the new books that came in," he recalls, "was Denis Saurat's book on William Blake, which I now know was half a nut book, but it fascinated me. I used to come to work an hour early to read it." Seventeen years later Frye's own book on Blake, *Fearful Symmetry*,   235 helped to change academe's image of Blake from that of a half-mad but occasionally brilliant poet/engraver—"Tyger tyger, burning bright,/In the forests of the night;/What immortal hand or eye,/Could frame thy fearful symmetry?"—to that of a major visionary and prophetic poet whose entire life's work (as Frye's was to be) was informed by a continuous and unifying   240 central myth: the Bible. *Fearful Symmetry* contained the seeds of all his subsequent writing. When asked recently how long he has been working on *The Great Code*, he replied, "All my life."

21   Because many of Frye's scholarships—he finished first at Victoria all four years—had been given to him as a future minister, Frye felt obliged,   245 after graduating in 1933, to enter Emmanuel College, the theological arm of Victoria. He knew, however, that his true vocation was literature, and although he was ordained in the United Church in 1936, he is now "on a sort of permanent leave of absence." He doesn't keep a register, so he can't perform marriages, but he has assisted in the marriages of a few colleagues   250 and friends. When Jane Widdicombe married five years ago, she asked Frye to give her away: "No," he replied gruffly; then he smiled, "I'll only lend you."

22   Frye went to Merton College, Oxford, on a Royal Society scholar-

ship in the fall of 1936, and it was there that his essential "Canadianness"   255
was driven home to him. It was manifested in a kind of intellectual and
apolitical conservatism: he had been sympathetic with the CCF in Canada,
ostensibly socialist but, as Robert Weaver points out, "probably the only
real conservative party in Canada at the time." And Morley Callaghan
refers in The Varsity Story to the "intellectual self-effacement proper to   260
Toronto"—his alter-ego, Arthur Tyndall, declares that "Victoria would represent that progressive liberal class. The powerful Canadian or Toronto
middle class . . ." Frye, as usual, states his own position more unequivocally:
"I've always been a sort of left-of-centre bourgeois liberal. To me, bourgeois
equals human being, and anything that isn't bourgeois is strictly in the   265
trees."

23   Oxford—and for that matter England—in the late 1930s seemed to
Frye to be caught in a kind of hypnotic trance, staring in fascinated stupor
into the basilisk eyes of Adolf Hitler. "I felt that England was in a horribly
demoralized state," Frye recalls. "I seemed to keep running into fascists all   270
the time. There was one little bugger who had come up to Oxford with a
personal scholarship from Sir Oswald Mosley!" Mosley, a former MP, had
resigned from the Labour Party in 1930 to head the British Union of Fascists.
"If you want to know what I felt about Oxford," says Frye, "read the first
chapter of Howard K. Smith's book, Last Train From Berlin."   275

24   Smith, an American journalist at Merton on a Rhodes Scholarship,
had spent a year in Germany reporting on Hitler's persecution of the Jews
and his incredible amassing of arms and men, to a generally disbelieving
and unalarmed America and England. When he left Germany to go to
Oxford in 1937, Smith found that "Oxford was bad medicine," and was   280
exasperated at "the stony calm with which that breed called 'Oxonians,'
both dons and students, heard my stormy predictions and awful warnings. I
acquired the reputation of a 'harmless but annoying zealot,' as one young
gentleman put it, my first night inside the grey walls of Merton College."

25   But for Frye there were compensations. Merton was, after all,   285
Oxford's oldest college and, at that time, the best college for English literature.
It was T. S. Eliot's old college, and even then Frye was very interested in
Eliot. The Sacred Wood (1920) had been a major influence on Frye's thought,
although Eliot's After Strange Gods (subtitled "A Primer on Modern Heresy"),
which came out in 1934, shocked the minister that lay hidden not far below   290
the surface of Frye: "I took it as an almost personal affront."

26   Frye's book on Eliot, written in 1963, is interesting for the parallels
it suggests between Eliot's life and Frye's: Eliot's father was in business in

St. Louis, Missouri, and his mother had been a writer. The Eliot family, like Frye's, had come from England in the seventeenth century and settled in   295 New England. Eliot journeyed to England with a sense of participating in a great tradition, and Eliot's literary criticism has had as deep an influence on critics as his poetry has had on poets: "So many critical theories claim to derive from Eliot," Frye wrote, "that he seems rather in the position of the country squire in Smollett to whom young women in the neighbourhood   300 ascribed their fatherless offspring, confident of his good-natured support." The same may now be said of Frye.

27   C. S. Lewis, the scholar and writer of fantasy, was also at Oxford ("He was the only lecturer worth going to"), and Frye's tutor was the poet Edmund Blunden. Blunden had served as an infantry lieutenant in France   305 during the First World War; his account of the experience, *Undertones of War*, was published in 1928. In it, Blunden describes his last day in France in 1918, standing a few miles from Amiens and listening to the distant booming of artillery and gunfire and feeling, like Robert Graves, a little guilty that he had survived while so many of his fellows had been killed. One of those   310 explosions Blunden heard may have been the bomb that killed Frye's brother.

28   In 1937 Frye returned to Victoria to teach English for a year as a lecturer. That year he married. He and Helen Kemp had met seven years earlier at a university performance of Gilbert and Sullivan—Frye had stood in one wing holding an arc light, Helen had been in another holding the   315 prompt book. The young couple was separated when Frye went back to Oxford for his final year; Helen stayed in Toronto, working at the Art Gallery of Toronto. Then Pelham Edgar invited Frye back to Victoria permanently. "I landed in Toronto," says Frye, "the day the Soviet-Nazi non-aggression pact was signed." That was August 24, 1939. Except for   320 lecture tours and the occasional visiting professorship, Frye has not left Victoria since.

29   The walls of the reading room in the modern E. J. Pratt Library at Victoria University are bare and grey, with only two pictures to relieve the impression of Methodist meeting-hall plainness. One is a huge landscape of   325 west coast mountains: bold blues and stark blue-whites; the cracked tongues of ageless glaciers pouring down between the cold granite teeth of the peaks. The other, smaller but no less awesome, is Douglas Martin's portrait of Frye. In the foreground is a fairly conventional representation of Frye sitting, knees together, hands folded on his right leg. The expression behind   330 the rimless glasses and below the shock of once-red hair (now salt and

cinnamon) is one of hard-earned confidence, stony imperturbability, and limitless impatience. But it is the background that attracts attention: Frye is suspended, without even a chair, in the overcast sky above a vast, treeless wasteland of barren cliffs and a wild, divided river, like a modern, rumple-   335
suited Christ transfiguring himself out of a Biblical wilderness.

30   Frye's expression in the painting suggests that he hated sitting for it; his comments suggest that he hates looking at it. "One doesn't like to be turned into an ikon before one is dead," he says drily. His antipathy goes deeper than an unwillingness to appear to be sitting halfway to heaven   340
waiting for his disciples to catch up with him. He doesn't want disciples at all. One very important element in Eliot's critical theory, contained in a chapter of *The Sacred Wood* entitled "Tradition and the Individual Talent," is the statement that a writer is being most individual when he is participating most thoroughly in his literary tradition; when he submerges himself in   345
it, perhaps paradoxically, until he all but disappears as a separate personality. Virtually every literary figure about whom Frye has written or lectured has been remembered solely for his work and not at all for his life: Shakespeare, Milton, Blake, and to a certain extent Eliot himself. The writers Frye definitely doesn't like are those who have intruded their personalities into their   350
books. After *Fearful Symmetry*, he contemplated writing a book about *Finnegans Wake*, but gave up the idea: "I would have gone much further with it except that it contains such a hell of a lot of information about that rather dreary little man, James Joyce."

31   For Eliot, the perfect critic "should have no emotions except those   355
immediately provoked by a work of art—and these are, when valid, perhaps not to be called emotions at all." What Eliot wanted was a rejection of "impressions" masquerading as criticism: that is, a critic should not write to produce a new work of art, but should try to elucidate an existing one. Eliot therefore believed that the perfect critic was one who, like himself, got rid   360
of his creative energy by writing poems or novels, and then was able to turn his more rational, scientific mind to the writing of literary criticism. "the two directions of sensibility," Eliot concluded, "are complementary, and as sensibility is rare, unpopular, and desirable, it is to be expected that the critic and the creative artist should frequently be the same person."   365

32   Frye's approach to literature is certainly scientific, in the sense that, like Aristotle and Carl Linnaeus, his first impulse is to identify and to categorize, to isolate the underlying "structure" of a work of art. "Structure is a term borrowed from architecture," he warns, "and is a tricky metaphor when applied to an art that moves in time, like literature." What Frye   370

means by a work's structure is the dominant, unifying concern, or idea, that makes it a pleasing and useful work of art rather than a jarring concatenation of words: what makes it, in fact, myth.

33   A myth, then, is any verbal structure. Many of Frye's theories have been influenced by his reading of *The Golden Bough* by Sir James Frazer, 375 the works of Carl Jung, and the Bible. What these disparate—and, ostensibly, unliterary—works have in common, Frye found, was that they all deal with myth. *The Golden Bough* started out as an examination of the priesthood of Diana and turned into a thirteen-volume compendium of the world's succession myths, which involve magic and religion. Jung's concept of the 380 collective unconscious grew out of an attempt to explain the effect of certain recurring, archetypal myths on actual human behaviour—this also, he found, involved magic and religion. And the Bible, as Frye sees it, is the fundamental source of all Western culture. All culture, in fact, is an imitation of religion and so all Western literature is an imitation of the Bible. 385

34   Culture, and therefore religion, is a protective wall that we construct around ourselves in order to prevent the fact of a cruel or indifferent nature from disturbing our sleep—this is the sense behind Frye's description of early Canadian literature as a product of a "garrison mentality." The verbal part of that garrison is myth; literature develops out of the story 390 patterns set up by a society's frequent repetition of its myths, since only those vital to its existence—its "survival myths"—get repeated often enough to pass into literature. The purpose of literary criticism on its highest level, then, is to identify the permutations that our cultural myths have undergone—most of which will not be consciously known by the artist—and to 395 trace them back to their true place in the cultural wall. Whether we call this process uniting ego and archetype or justifying God's ways to man, the purpose is to arrive at an understanding of our relationship to each other and to nature—to understand, in Frye's words, "how we are mythologically conditioned" or manipulated by cliché and propaganda. Through a better 400 understanding of literature we can achieve a better control over our own lives, rather than relinquish that control to a false or demonic prophet like Hitler (the second chapter of Howard K. Smith's *Last Train From Berlin* is called "Myth's Progress," an indication of how quickly literary criticism moves out of the ivory tower and into that problematic area of actuality we 405 call history).

35   In each of Frye's nineteen books his one organizing and recurring principle has been the relationship between the Bible and Western literature: "The Bible," he wrote in *Fearful Symmetry*, "is . . . the archetype of West-

ern culture, and the Bible, with its derivatives, provides the basis for most of   410
our major art: for Dante, Milton, Michelangelo, Raphael, Bach, the great
cathedrals, and so on." One can hardly be more inclusive than that, and so
Frye saw even then the course of his future writing. First he quotes the
aphorism from Blake that contains the title of a book he would not finish
for another thirty-four years: "The Old & New Testaments are the Great   415
Code of Art." Then he proceeds to establish the basis for what will be his
own life work: "We say that there is something universal in Quixote, Falstaff,
Hamlet, Milton's Satan. But 'something universal' is rather vague: just
what is universal about them? As soon as we attempt to answer this, we
begin in spite of ourselves to elaborate our own versions of the archetypal   420
myth." And in elaborating his versions of the archetypal myth, Frye turns
academic criticism into a creative act, and gives new meaning to Eliot's
concept of the perfect critic.

36   Because Frye's *Anatomy of Criticism*, published in 1957, is first of
all a monumental work of the imagination, its appeal to the reader's imagi-   425
nation is just as important as its appeal to the intellect. Its title and form are
taken from Robert Burton's *Anatomy of Melancholy* (1621), a huge tome
that started out as a treatise on a specific medical topic and expanded—like
Frazer's *Golden Bough*—into a multifaceted and complicated examination
of the life of man. Frye's *Anatomy* also has stylistic links with that other   430
great work of the critical imagination, Coleridge's unfinished *Biographia
Literaria*. In an article published in *The Hudson Review* in 1953, Frye remarks
that "Coleridge's thoughts obviously came to him much as the images of
Kubla Khan and *The Ancient Mariner* did, as a series of aphorisms crystalliz-
ing from his reading." The American writer Richard Kostelanetz, in an   435
article about Frye published in 1978, notes "the presence in his writing of
some splendid aphorisms," and quotes Frye himself explaining, "That's the
way my thinking comes to me. Most of my writings consist of an attempt to
translate aphorisms into continuous prose." More recently, Frye admits
having noticed that "my writing seems to be a string of metaphors, as a   440
poet's would be."

37   Frye's influence on Canadian literature has been subtle and per-
vasive, like a pebble dropped into a still pool. As the editor of *The Canadian
Forum* he not only wrote reviews of such varied works as *Don Quixote* and
Toynbee's *A Study of History*, he also recruited other young, ambitious   445
reviewers such as Robert Weaver, who remembers getting James T. Farrell's
Selected Essays in the mail with the cryptic note: "There's a lot of bullshit

here, but he's a good man in many ways." Frye also wrote the annual
Canadian poetry roundup for the *University of Toronto Quarterly* from 1950
to 1959—a crucial period in the development of Canadian poetry—and it is   450
a measure, albeit a negative one, of his influence on at least one poet that a
controversy stirred up in 1952 is still alive. Frye called Irving Layton's *The
Black Huntsman* "the work, not of the poet in him, but of a noisy hot-
gospeller who has no real respect for poetry." This sent Layton into a fit: his
next book contained a poem called "Archetypes" in which he refers to Frye   455
as "some crying fool from the sticks." Fifteen years later Layton was still
fuming—this time in the Toronto *Telegram*—against Frye's "perverse
brilliancy" by which "he seeks to construct a science of criticism which will
pigeonhole the wayward products of the creative mind and eschew all value
judgements."   460

38   There is a marked tendency on the part of Frye's students to become
converts, what some commentators have termed "small Frye" or "Frye-
dolators." Frye's students have included such poets as Margaret Atwood,
Jay Macpherson (to whom *The Well-Tempered Critic* [1963] is dedicated and
who now teaches at Victoria), James Reaney, Margaret Avison, Dennis Lee,   465
George Johnston, and Eli Mandel. "He doesn't tell you what to write,"
Atwood has said, which is not surprising—Frye's teaching method is not to
tell his students what to do or think, but to remove certain social repres-
sions or restraints from the mind, to expand his students' consciousness.
"His real influence on us," says Atwood, "was in the way he treats writing   470
as a very serious occupation." Almost exactly Frye's words about the influence of Pelham Edgar on *him*.

39   Many of the writers listed above have also produced books of literary criticism: Atwood's *Survival*, Lee's *Savage Fields*, Mandel's *Criticism:
The Silent-Speaking Words*. Add to these the book of another poet, though   475
not a Frye student—Doug Jones's *Butterfly on Rock*, whose introduction
sounds more like Frye than Frye does—and the cumulative effect of Frye's
example among Canada's writers can hardly be underestimated. "There is
no Frye school of mythopoeic poets," Frye wrote in 1965, but when Jay
Macpherson writes a poem called "The Garden of the Fall" we think of   480
Frye. When James Reaney writes, in a poem called "The Butterfly,"

> *From Time's cocoon*
> *And the caterpillar of prophecy*
> *Comes to Bethlehem*
> *A shining laughing baby butterfly.*   485

> *This butterfly is Christ whom we*
> *Since He is the Word made flesh*
> *Do fashion verbally.*

we are reminded directly of Blake and indirectly of *Fearful Symmetry*.

40   Frye's effect on Canada's and America's educational institutions— 490
under his guiding hand his American publishers, Harcourt Brace Jovanovich,
have issued a series of high school textbooks called *The Uses of the
Imagination*—is profound. His work has permeated the teaching and learning of literature, and, indeed, the very fabric of our culture. As John Robert
Colombo, another writer who took Frye's courses, has said, "McLuhan and 495
Frye are Canada's Aristotle and Plato. McLuhan is the scientist, Frye the
mystical theorist with the eternal paradigms and the everlasting forms."

41   Frye's influence on life outside the university has been so subtle
that writers like George Woodcock have doubted its existence altogether.
Frye did not, as Marshall McLuhan did, have whole university departments 500
set up in the wake of his public impact; we can hardly look at television now
without thinking of McLuhan. Frye, however, sat for "nine bloody years"
on the Canadian Radio-Television Commission (1968 to 1977), faithfully
attending public hearings and acting as the CRTC's "tame intellectual,"
and his work in the areas of culture and the imagination has influenced 505
the way we *think* about ourselves and our country.

42   Frye's simple statement, for example, that "historically a Canadian
is an American who has rejected the Revolution," implies a definitive
distinction between Canadian and American identities that has pervaded
not only our literature and painting, but also our television and magazine 510
policies. When, in a recent interview, Frye maintained that when a country
matures it becomes *more* regional, not less, he was articulating a change in
our whole view of history: suddenly those Canadians fighting for regional
independence no longer necessarily thought of themselves as fighting against
the larger pull of progress. A recent TV commercial for Newfoundland fish 515
shows a Newfoundlander in slicker and boots talking about his product in
an accent so thick that there are English subtitles on the screen. Ten years
ago that would never have happened. Frye's "legitimizing" of regionalism,
while perhaps not responsible for these changes, has helped us to view
them in perspective—as symbols of increasing maturity, rather than as 520
symptoms of cultural backwardness. It is at least partly due to Frye that we
are no longer ashamed of our differences.

43   I have often thought," says Northrop Frye, standing at the lectern before an audience of some 300 professors and students who have come to hear his first Tamblyn Lecture at Western, "that the University of Western   525 Ontario has the finest English department in the country—largely, I suppose, because almost everyone in it has been a student of mine at one time or another.

44   There is a titter of appreciation. The audience knows it is lucky to have Frye: the previous month he made a week-long lecture tour of New   530 Brunswick and two weeks hence he will be off to address the Academy of Arts and Sciences in Boston, and what he would really like to be doing tonight is resting and tinkering with the second volume of *The Great Code.* He is clearly tired and nervous, doing little one-handed push-ups against the lectern as he speaks (uncharacteristically, from notes) about Shakespeare's   535 *Measure for Measure,* which he sees as "a comedy about comedy." James Reaney, who teaches at Western and is an old friend, says that before the lecture Frye carried those notes about with him almost like a talisman; he was reluctant to put them down even during supper. Frye's lecturing style is proclamatory, like the Bible's—revelatory, and yet crystal clear, meta-   540 phorical. "As Marshall McLuhan said, 'Man's reach must exceed his grasp, or what's a metaphor?' " As with McLuhan, it may be a long time before anyone fully understands what Frye is saying, or where he fits into the various "isms" and schisms that modern critical writing has become. He is neither a New Critic nor a Structuralist. Chronologically his *Anatomy* falls   545 between those two schools, but *The Great Code* goes way beyond both of them in its emphasis on history and tradition, in its visionary overview of 2,000 years of literature.

45   His aim in *The Great Code* is to give "a presentation of a unified structure of narrative and imagery in the Bible." This alone would be a   550 Herculean task. But his original aim was soon overtaken by other, in some ways preparatory, aims: "Further study of [the Bible] could eventually lead us through literature into the broader question of the social function of words." And later, he says, "we may be entering a new phase altogether in our understanding of language. . . . God may have lost his function as the   555 subject or object of a predicate, but may not be so much dead as entombed in a dead language."

46   *The Great Code,* in fact, is a restatement of the *Anatomy* in a new context, which was a restatement of *Fearful Symmetry* on a more general scale, which in turn was an indirect result of his reading the Bible, which is   560 the subject of *The Great Code.* Frye's life work has been like one gigantic and all-inclusive epic poem—even his lectures, like this one in London, he calls "spin-offs." One is reminded of a passage in *Anatomy of Criticism*: "A narrative poet, a Southey or a Lydgate, may write any number of narratives, but an epic poet normally completes only one epic structure, the moment 565 when he decides on his theme being the crisis of his life."

47   "I had moments of mental enlightenment," Frye once said of his childhood, "when I glimpsed my own potential abilities. While walking to school one day, that claustrophobic, evangelical, Christian environment that I was brought up in just lifted from my shoulders. It just vanished, and 570 has never come back. Ever since then I have been interested in religion solely as a means of expanding the mind, not of contracting it."

48   After the lecture the chairman invites down anyone who may wish to ask Dr. Frye questions pertaining to his text, and a handful of Frye-dolators troop to the front of the theatre pretending to have a penetrating 575 question or two. There is a painfully obvious desire just to get close to Frye, to shake the great man's hand, to let him know that they understand how terrible it must be to have a message and to come so far to deliver it. Frye receives them politely and answers their questions with an earnestness that embarrasses both of them. This is how he discourages disciples: he treats 580 them all as equals. One of the handful, perhaps a little more familiar with Frye's crammed schedule than the others, asks him if he isn't exhausted after his long trip.

49   "Well," says Frye, passing a trembling hand over his wet brow, "this *is* a hell of a way to make a living." 585

QUESTIONS

READER AND PURPOSE
1. What kind of reader is Grady writing for? Read the first five paragraphs carefully before answering.
2. Grady makes several references in his essay to Frye's influence and importance. Does he make any other references or statements that qualify these assertions? Is he presenting Frye with unqualified approval, notwithstanding the generally favorable tone*?

ORGANIZATION
3. The first five paragraphs of the essay constitute Grady's introduction. Where, in these paragraphs, does he introduce the main argument of his essay?
4. What effect is produced in this introductory section by the use of the words "seems" (12), "possible" (15), "perhaps" (24), "appearance" (32)?

5. Why does Grady wait until paragraph 6 to provide biographical information about Frye? Would the essay have been improved if paragraph 6 had been the opening paragraph?

6. In what paragraph does Grady turn from Frye's biography to his more recent career? What connective* serves as a transition?

7. What aspects of Frye's biography does Grady stress as relevant for understanding his work as a literary scholar?

8. How do paragraphs 29 to 47 show *The Great Code* to be the culmination of Frye's career? Where has this been anticipated in the introductory section?

9. Do the two concluding paragraphs (48–49) encompass earlier points in the exposition of character, or are they merely a fading-out? Compare the last paragraph with the first two.

SENTENCES

10. Analyze the long fourth sentence of paragraph 2. Why is a colon used here, instead of a period? How well is the quotation integrated into the sentence? Is this an example of closing by return*? Would it be better to use "because" instead of "since" (20)?

11. Would the third sentence of paragraph 5 be improved if the material between the dashes had been presented as a separate sentence?

12. Where is the reference to "the garrison" (123) in paragraph 11 anticipated in paragraph 8? Where else in the essay are analogous words used?

13. How does Grady use tone* in paragraph 11 to suggest some possible criticisms of Frye's critical position? See also paragraphs 14 and 28.

14. What impression of Frye's personality is conveyed by the interrupted movement* of the second and third sentences in paragraph 44?

DICTION

15. Look up: *castigate* (5), *circuit rider* (65), *peripatetic* (92), *myopic* (116), *apocryphal* (141), *elucidate* (359), *archetypal* (382), *permeated* (493), *paradigms* (497), *titter* (529), *talisman* (538), *claustrophic* (569).

16. Consult a recent dictionary of literary terms and find the meanings of *New Critic* (544–45) and *Structuralist* (545).

17. Grady's essay uses few figures of speech.* Is this a defect, given his purpose?

18. How do Grady's allusions* contribute to the presentation of Frye? Consider *place in the sun* (58), *Scott's Waverley Novels, all of Dickens* (95–96), *Shaw, Ibsen and H. G. Wells* (99–100), *John Wesley* (184), *Borges* (219), *James Joyce* (354), *Aristotle* (367), *Carl Linnaeus* (367), *Herculean* (551).

19. Grady states that Frye's approach to literature is "scientific . . . like Aristotle" (366–67). Later he quotes John Robert Colombo, who says that "McLuhan and Frye are Canada's Aristotle and Plato" (495–96). Does this discrepancy weaken Grady's point?

20. Grady several times quotes Frye using colloquial* language. (See paragraphs 8, 10, 22, 23, 30, 37, 41, 49.) What does this contribute to his portrait of Frye?

POINTS TO LEARN

1. A generally favorable depiction of character need not omit unfavorable elements to be effective.
2. Presenting a character in several different situations and contexts can reveal different aspects of the personality.
3. Establishing the importance of a character usually takes precedence over the details of the biography. Biographical information should be relevant to the total effect intended, and not simply introduced for its own sake.

SUGGESTIONS FOR WRITING

Look up the entry for Frye in *The Oxford Companion to Canadian Literature* (1983). Compare this entry with Grady's essay, showing how differences in purpose in each case influence methods of organization, the selection of details, the diction, and the sentence structure.

IMPROVING YOUR STYLE

In your essay include:
1. Two sentences which incorporate quoted material.
2. Two sentences which use interrupted movement.
3. Both formal and colloquial diction.

Narration

At its simplest, narrative writing is much like descriptive. As description develops by analyzing a physical object or scene into its parts and arranging these in space, so narration develops by analyzing a story into the events that compose it and arranging these in time. In its more highly evolved forms, such as novels and short stories, narration obviously includes more than a mere reporting of events. The novelist will elaborate a finely drawn plot and pay quite as much attention to the psychology of his characters as to what they do. However, such literary refinements are beyond the usual needs of the composition student. Here we are concerned with a simpler type of narration which restricts itself to action and does not probe deeply into the motives of the actors. Such narrative writing is often adapted to the needs of exposition. The historian must frequently relate stories, and the essayist depends upon narration to develop illustrations and anecdotes.

For whatever it is used, the essence of good narration is organizing the story into beginning, middle, and end. Most often these parts are arranged in their natural order. On occasion they may be inverted, so that the story opens with the end and then turns back to the beginning and middle. A film that starts with its main character already on the gallows and then relates for ninety minutes the circumstances which brought him to so uncomfortable a position, is an example of such flashback technique. But the brief narrative employed in exposition is best organized in the usual chronological order.

In how much detail these parts are developed will depend, of course, upon the writer's intention and the space he has available. Long or short, however, all narration is highly selective. No reporter or historian can afford to tell us everything. He must choose only those details relevant to his purpose, and reject those which are not. His criteria of selection will be based upon his reason for telling the story—the meaning he sees in it.

This meaning is what the writer tries to communicate to his reader. It is here that beginners most often fail. The inexperienced writer is likely to step forth before he knows where he is going, before he has determined in his own mind exactly what meaning the story has. It is hardly surprising that his narrative turns out like a poorly mixed cake, lumpy with unrelated details and without the flavor of meaning. Even when he has understood its significance, the beginner is likely to commit another error. This is to be afraid to permit the story to stand on its own legs. We have all suffered the would-be comedian who is so concerned with pointing out why his story is funny that he kills its humor. The meaning of a narrative, like the point of a joke, is best left to the reader, for a well-written narrative clearly implies its meaning. The writer's task, especially in brief narration, is to concentrate upon the story itself. If he knows to begin with why the story is important and if he has selected and arranged its details accordingly, he will communicate its meaning.

The Loss of the Cospatrick

Robert Carse has combined two professions: those of seaman and writer. He has published more than thirty books about the sea, including *The Age of Piracy, Ports of Call,* and *The Twilight of Sailing Ships.* It is the last of these which supplies the following account of a fire at sea. Carse's narrative is well-constructed and well-paced. Much of its sense of realism and economy comes from the use of nautical terminology. Since some of these terms may not be familiar to you, we shall define them here. If you are a sailor you may skip on to Carse's narrative. But if you are not you will find the following brief discussion helpful.

On a ship *forward* (pronounced "for'ard") means "toward the bow" or front of the vessel; *aft* (adjective *after,* preposition *abaft*) means "toward the stern" or rear. *Aloft* refers to anyplace in the masts, yards, or rigging, and *below* to anyplace under the main deck. The *fore-peak* is a small hold or cargo space close behind the bow; the *quarter* is the side of the vessel from midships to stern, the starboard quarter being on the right (facing forward) and the port quarter on the left. *Quarter galleries* are small balconies on the after sides, extending to the stern. The *focsle* (a shortening of *forecastle*) is the crew's compartment and on sailing ships was usually forward of the first mast, and the *poop* is a small raised deck near the stern. *Bulkheads* are the internal walls of a ship, stiffening it and dividing it, in modern vessels, into watertight compartments. *Hatches* cover the openings in the deck through which cargo is loaded and unloaded; they were of wood in the nineteenth century and are of steel today. On three-masted vessels the mast nearest the bow is the *foremast,* the next is the *mainmast,* and the third is the *mizzenmast.*

Usually *frigate* refers to a naval vessel. Here, however, the word designates a merchant ship of a design somewhat old-fashioned in the mid-nineteenth century, having a forecastle and a quarterdeck raised above the main deck.

Rigging designates all the ropes, wires, and chains used to steady the masts and to work the sails. *Standing rigging,* which is relatively immobile once it has been set up, consists of the ropes and wires that support the masts:

From *The Twilight of Sailing Ships.* Copyright © 1965 by Robert Carse. Reprinted by permission of Grosset & Dunlap, Inc.

these are the *shrouds*, running to the sides of the vessel from the masts and strengthening them to withstand forces at right angles to the ship; and the *stays*, leading fore and aft and resisting forces from ahead or astern. *Ratlines* (pronounced "ratluns") are short lengths of tarred rope secured between adjacent shrouds and serving as ladder rungs for sailors to climb up and handle the sails. *Running rigging* includes all the ropes and chains that lead from the yards (heavy round lengths of wood at right angles to the masts from which the sails are hung) and sails to the deck. They enable seamen to raise and lower sails and to adjust them to the wind. *Sheets, braces, clewlines,* and *halyards* are various kinds of running rigging.

A ship is *standing* when it is sailing easily, maintaining a steady course and speed. It is *off the wind* when the wind is on the quarter or astern, the best point of sailing for the old square-riggers (that is, ships with square sails set on yards across the masts—the most common design of deepwater vessels in the eighteenth and nineteenth centuries). The *run* is the distance made good in a particular direction.

A ship's captain is known among seamen as her *master*; the officers under him, in order of importance, are the *first-, second-,* and *third-mates*. The *bosun* (from *boatswain*) is a petty officer responsible for keeping the ship seaworthy, particularly its boats, rigging, sails, paint, and so on. The crew in nineteenth-century ships were divided into two work gangs called *watches*, a *port watch* and a *starboard watch* (these terms had nothing to do in practice with the sides of the vessel the men worked or lived on). The watches alternated working the ship in four-hour stints. The group on duty was called *the watch on deck*; the group off, *the watch below*. (In emergencies all hands were called on deck.) The four-hour time units are also known as *watches*, and each of the six making up the twenty-four-hour day has a name: the *middle watch* is from midnight until 4:00 a.m. An *able-bodied seaman* (or *able seaman*) is an experienced deck hand, able, in the old-fashioned phrase to "hand, reef, and steer" (that is, to work the sails and steer the ship). An *ordinary seaman* is a hand of less experience and ability and receives less pay. Collectively, a ship's personnel are referred to as her *company* or her *people*.

1   Fire at sea aboard a wooden vessel that carried highly inflammable sails and tarred hemp rigging had always been one of the greatest concerns of any shipmaster. With crude and slow, hand-operated pumps, and no other fire-fighting equipment except axes and buckets, a ship might easily be consumed, and many were.   5

2   The loss of the splendidly built teakwood frigate *Cospatrick* stayed in the minds of shipowners on both sides of the Atlantic for a long time

after the event. Her tragic circumstances represented an extreme case, yet showed what could take place at any time aboard another vessel.

3   *Cospatrick* had been built in India in 1856, and was still in first class condition in 1874 when she sailed for Auckland, New Zealand from London with general cargo, 429 emigrants, and a crew of forty-four men. She was under the command of Captain John Elmslie, a veteran master, who had his wife aboard with him. *Cospatrick* had made a good run to the southward and was standing around Cape Horn in fair weather on November 17 when fire was reported.

4   This was at night, in the middle watch. The wind was light, Northwest, and on the quarter. "Fire!" had been cried from forward. The watch below came piling out of the focsle in their drawers and shirt tails. They were followed by the emigrants. Smoke plucked by the breeze billowed up from the fore-peak hatch. Captain Elmslie, quickly on deck, realized that the fire was in the fore-peak, and serious. The bosun kept the usual ship's stores there, which under the circumstances formed an almost explosive combination—shellack, varnish, turpentine, paint, oakum and rope.

5   The fire hose was connected at the main pump and led forward. *Cospatrick* was sailed off the wind. When pumping began and the fore part of the vessel was flooded, it seemed that she might be saved. But there was no fire-proof hatch that could be shut, no bulkheads that could contain the fire only to the fore-peak. Flame leaped high and streaked in the darkness along the sheets and running gear of the foremast. That finished the ship; she veered head-up into the wind.

6   The men handling the fire hose were driven aft by the thick, acrid masses of smoke. They were cut off from each other, and as the deck planks groaned and crackled under them with heat, the foresail caught fire. Emigrants panicked, the women screamed. Sailors could no longer hear the orders of their officers. Work was interrupted at the pump.

7   The fire gained furiously below. It sprang into the 'tween-decks, and then aloft through every hatchway, port-hole and ventilator shaft. Flame spiralled the rigging, raced swiftly along the tarred ratlines and shrouds. Then it widened out onto the yards. Sheets, braces, halyards and clewlines were next, and before they burned through and fell in charred tangles, they ignited the sails. The sails burned with wild, incandescent bursts of light; released from the gear, they dropped in great gouts of sparks upon the people crowding the main deck.

8   Discipline was gone. *Cospatrick's* people were seized by panic. Aflame fore and aft, there was no chance of saving her. It had taken a little

over an hour for the fire to make her condition hopeless. Captain Elmslie gave the order to abandon ship.

9   The starboard quarter boat was lowered away and put in the water. But then, frantic with fear, emigrants piled aboard her and she was cap- 50 sized. Flames licked forth at the longboat strakes when that craft was lowered from the ship, and she became useless. There were at last only two boats that got clear of the ship. They were the port and starboard lifeboats, one with forty-two persons, the other with thirty-nine aboard.

10   The starboard lifeboat was under the command of Henry Mac- 55 Donald, the second mate. He told both boats to lie off until the ship sank. It was a slow and terrible process. *Cospatrick* took thirty-six hours to go.

11   Flame spread steadily aft towards the remaining people, crowded together on the poop. The foremast fell blazing, and the main, and the mizzen. When the mizzen dropped, a number of passengers on the poop 60 were crushed to death. The rest never stopped shrieking. They gestured to Mr. MacDonald and the others in the boats—pleading for their lives.

12   But nothing could be done. Rescue was impossible with the boats overcrowded by weak, half-crazed men and women who sat in their night clothing, without food and water for a day and a night. Both boats lacked 65 masts and sails, and aboard Mr. MacDonald's boat there was only one oar. He kept the craft at a safe distance from *Cospatrick*.

13   Her quarter galleries gave during the second day, let go with a fierce gust of heat-compressed air, a belch of smoke and flame. The people left aboard her jumped. Captain Elmslie was the last. He tossed his wife down 70 into the sea, then leaped after her.

14   They drowned. The lifeboat people, unable to help them, could only sit and watch as the screaming victims begged for help. *Cospatrick* burned almost to the waterline before she sank. When she slipped beneath the waves, Mr. MacDonald gave the order, and slowly the boats moved away 75 on the course he had reckoned.

15   The boats stayed together until the night of November 21, when the weather became heavy. MacDonald's survived. The other boat was never again seen. MacDonald rigged a sea-anchor with the painter and the oar, but lost it. Then, two days later, with pieces of wood ripped from the thwarts 80 and floorboards, a second sea-anchor was made.

16   It held, eased the strain on the boat, and kept her up to the wind, although she was half-filled with water. During the night of November 26, just before daylight, a ship passed within fifty yards of them. They cried out with all their strength, but it was not enough, and they were not heard.   85

17   This was very hard for the survivors to take. Mr. MacDonald later testified at the inquiry that by November 27 "there were but five left—two able seamen, one ordinary, myself and one passenger. The passenger was out of his mind. All had drunk salt water. We were all dozing when the madman bit my foot and I woke up. We then saw a ship bearing down on us. She 90 proved to be the *British Sceptre*, from Calcutta to Dundee. We were then taken on board and treated very kindly. I got very bad on board of her. I was very nigh at death's door. We were not recovered when we got to St. Helena."

18   While aboard *British Sceptre*, both the ordinary seaman and the 95 passenger died. Mr. MacDonald and the two able-bodied sailors were the sole survivors out of the company of 473 persons which had left London in *Cospatrick*.

QUESTIONS

READER AND PURPOSE

1. In one or two sentences explain what you think Carse is attempting to do in this passage. Is he successful? Why or why not?
2. Does Carse assume that his readers are familiar with the sea and ships?

ORGANIZATIONS

3. In actuality an event such as a fire at sea does not divide neatly into acts and scenes like a play. The writer must impose an organization upon the continuous happening he describes and analyze it into parts. Paragraphs 1 and 2 compose the first part of Carse's narrative. What is their function?
4. The remaining sixteen paragraphs can be divided into three groups. At what points? Give a title to each section.
5. Events exist in time, and while the flow of time is more significant in some stories than in others, the writer of any narrative must establish temporal reference points. Does Carse? Can you make an outline fixing the dates and times of various events in his narrative?
6. Why does Carse make number 5 a separate paragraph? Numbers 6 and 7?
7. What word links paragraph 4 to 3? Paragraph 12 to 11? 14 to 13? 16 to 15? 17 to 16? These links are quick and light. Are they adequate for the writer's purpose?

SENTENCES

8. There is a change in sentence style after the third paragraph. Paragraph 1 has 51 words in two sentences, an average of 25.5 words per sentence. The

averages in paragraphs 2 and 3 are about the same: 23.5 and 27.3. In the fourth paragraph, however, the average drops to 11.5, even with the long final sentence; and in the eighth to 8.8. Why does Carse write shorter, simpler sentences in these places? What generalization might you make about the value of such a style in narrative?

9. What is the average number of words in the sentences of paragraph 6? Do these sentences sound too much the same, or are they varied enough to avoid monotony? If you think they are, explain generally how the variations are achieved.

10. Do these revisions improve Carse's sentences? Why or why not?

> (a) *Revision:* Flame spiralled all through the rigging, and then it raced swiftly along the tarred ratlines and the shrouds.
> *Carse:* "Flame spiralled the rigging, raced swiftly along the tarred ratlines and shrouds." (38-39)
> (b) *Revision:* Because the ship was aflame fore and aft, there was no chance of saving her.
> *Carse:* "Aflame fore and aft, there was no chance of saving her." (46)
> (c) *Revision:* Flame spread steadily aft towards the remaining people, who were crowded together on the poop.
> *Carse:* "Flame spread steadily aft towards the remaining people, crowded together on the poop." (58-59)

11. The sentence in lines 84-85 is an example of a tricolon *: one sentence composed of three independent clauses of roughly equal length and construction. Here the tricolon varies the simple style, linking three brief statements instead of expressing them separately. It also creates a pleasing rhythm by repeating the same pattern three times. On what word does the major emphasis come in each clause?

DICTION

12. Look up: *emigrants* (12), *oakum* (24), *acrid* (32), *incandescent* (42), *capsized* (50), *strakes* (51), *painter* (79), *thwarts* (80), *nigh* (93).

13. Why are these alternates less effective than Carse's words: *unfortunate* for *tragic* (8), *shouting* for *shrieking* (61), *burst* for *belch* (69)?

14. In paragraph 6 which words appeal to our sense of hearing?

15. In paragraph 7 *sprang, spiralled, raced, widened* all trace the progress of the fire. Are they good verbs for this purpose? Why or why not? What other words in this paragraph appeal to our vision?

POINTS TO LEARN

1. Narrative renders an event in words, showing what happened, when and where and how or why.
2. Vivid active verbs create a sense of movement, vital to good narrative.
3. Temporal reference points are important in narrative, enabling readers to trace the flow of events.
4. Short simple * sentences beginning with the subject and verb and without interruption express dramatic action.
5. Technical diction, while it makes demands upon the reader, is precise and economic.

SUGGESTIONS FOR WRITING

In three or four paragraphs (400-500 words) describe a dramatic event you have witnessed: a fire, an automobile accident, a fight, or a riot. Think carefully about the order of events and organize your narrative so that readers can grasp the pattern and time-flow. Try, however, to do this subtly; avoid such mechanical forumlae as "The first thing that happened was . . . The second thing was . . ."

IMPROVING YOUR STYLE

1. In your narrative use as many short strong sentences as you can to render the action. But vary this style occasionally so that it does not sound like a third-grade reader.
2. Include at least one tricolon.*
3. Experiment with verbs, choosing ones that convey a dramatic movement.

GEORGE SHEPHERD

The Dowser

After emigrating from England in 1908, at the age of eighteen, George Shepherd homesteaded in southern Saskatchewan. In 1913 he settled in Maple Creek, in the south-west corner of the province, to become a rancher. There he was able to indulge his life-long interests in local folklore and in native artifacts. In 1953 he was named curator of the Western Development Museum, whose collection of the relics of pioneer life has attracted visitors from around the world. In addition to his book on the homesteaders, of which "The Dowser" is an excerpt, Shepherd has written several articles on the development of the Canadian West.

1   The search for water was a continuous one on the endless prairies. Certainly a good water supply was of prime importance to the home-steader. Frequently the first settler, filing on land in a new locality, would select a quarter-section near a lake or a large slough. Slough water, for drinking purposes, was fine in the early spring. But with the advent of 5 warm weather, the bugs would have to be strained out of it. By summer, too, it would take on an amber colour. Many a homestead child arrived back with a pail of drinking water from a nearby slough to have his horrified mother discover a frog resting in the bottom of the pail. Occurrences such as these caused pioneer wives to agitate for the digging of a well. 10

2   Practically everyone believed in the witching of wells in the early days. A "dowser," to give him his technical title, prepared for his work by cutting a lithe willow branch, about half an inch thick, in the form of the letter "Y." Carrying the wand in his hands, with the bottom end of the dowsing stick, as it was called, in front of him, the diviner walked slowly 15 along, searching for an underground water supply. One of our local dowsers, Dad Sanderson, a typical tall Scot, used a more impressive method. He

From *West of Yesterday* by George Shepherd, edited by John H. Archer, reprinted by permission of The Canadian Publishers, McClelland and Stewart Limited, Toronto.

461

grasped the ends of the stick with thumbs toward the body, backs of the hands on top, and stick pointing out in front. In this rather awkward position, the divining rod swung up or down, as the circumstances indicated. I 20 have seen the bark twisted right off the stick, as the diviner engaged in his search. The stick was supposed to be drawn powerfully downward by some strong attraction as the holder walked over an underground stream of water. For the record, we found a tremendous and never-failing supply of water, at a depth of eighty feet, beneath the precise spot indicated by Mr. 25 Sanderson. Many agricultural-engineering authorities scoff at this practice, dismissing it as nothing more or less than a simple delusion. They back up their stand by quoting standard engineering principles. Unfortunately, such scientific knowledge was not available to us, untutored homesteaders that we were. Neither did we realize that there were twenty-five thousand water- 30 diviners engaged in this practice in North America. Nor were we aware of the fact that we were delving into the realms of spiritism.

QUESTIONS

READER AND PURPOSE

1. In the first paragraph Shepherd mentions *the first settler* (3), *many a homestead child* (7), and *pioneer wives* (10). In paragraph 2 he refers to *everyone* (11), *our* (16), *I* (20), and *we* (24). What is the purpose of this progressive change of point of view? What is he trying to establish?

2. What purpose does the expression *for the record* (24) serve? What does it tell us of Shepherd's attitude towards his subject?

3. How does the irony * of the last three sentences help Shepherd make his point?

ORGANIZATION

4. What two parallel expressions make the transition between Shepherd's paragraphs?

5. The topic sentence of an essay should be clearly relevant to every part of the essay. Is that true of this selection? After you have established what you think is the topic sentence, see how it is related (if at all) to the concluding sentence of each paragraph.

6. Using a diagram of your own invention, show how the first paragraph moves from the general to different levels, and kinds, of specific details.

7. Discuss the effectiveness (or lack of it) of the last sentence of paragraph 1 as the concluding sentence.

8. How does the sentence in ll. 16-17 act as a transition? What two points does it link together?

9. The transition referred to in the previous question marks a sub-division in this selection; that is, the two paragraphs are the major divisions, and paragraph 2 is further divided. What are these divisions of the second paragraph? How does Shepherd link these divisions to what precedes and/or to what follows?

10. Why is the second paragraph twice the length of the first?

SENTENCES

11. Two of Shepherd's first three sentences begin with adverbs. Does he begin many other sentences this way? Examine such sentences carefully. Do these beginning adverbs have any special effect?

12. The phrase "for drinking purposes" (4-5) is punctuated as a non-restrictive modifier (see p. 33, no. 9). Should it, however, be taken as a restrictive modifier—a modifier whose meaning is essential to the sentence and is thus not punctuated?

13. The sentence in l. 5 begins with *but,* a coordinating conjunction. Could this sentence be made part of the previous one, joining the two by a semi-colon between *spring* and *but?* What difference in effect would there be if they were joined?

DICTION

14. Look up: *prime* (2), *filing* (3), *slough* (4), *advent* (5), *amber* (7), *agitate* (10), *witching* (11), *diviner* (15), *scoff* (26), *delusion* (27), *untutored* (29), *homesteaders* (29), *spiritism* (32).

15. Is the expression *stream of water* (23-24) redundant? If so, can you justify its use?

16. Justify, or condemn, Shepherd's use of *tremendous* (24).

17. Why is the word *dowser* (12) placed within quotation marks? Why is the word not so enclosed in l. 16-17?

18. Why has Shepherd used the word *delving* (32) instead of, for example, "exploring," or "examining"? In order to answer this question, look carefully at the relationship between *delving* and the work of the diviner. Could the author have chosen a more appropriate word?

POINTS TO LEARN

1. The skilful use of irony can help an author make his point indirectly.

2. Transitions may be effectively used within a paragraph as well as between paragraphs.

3. A change in the author's point of view can bring about a corresponding change in the reader's attitude.

SUGGESTIONS FOR WRITING

Write a short (3 or 4 paragraphs) narrative essay in which you describe the work of someone who has an unusual occupation or hobby: magician, sword swallower, mime, restorer of antique autos, juggler, diamond cutter, glider pilot, deep-sea diver, weight lifter, bee keeper, trapper, bird watcher, chimney sweep, sheep shearer, dog catcher, etc.

IMPROVING YOUR STYLE

1. Concentrate on action, not on causes or effects.
2. Organize your essay into beginning, middle, and end.
3. Choose an overall objective for your narrative, and then include only those details which are relevant to this objective.

ABRAHAM ROTSTEIN

Through a Grid Darkly

Abraham Rotstein is a widely-published political economist at the University of Toronto. His writing displays a serious concern with the difficulties Canadian nationalism faces in a world increasingly dominated by technology, and in a country destined to face, because of its proximity, continued influence from the United States. Rotstein is no chauvinist, however; he is a nationalist who believes that the survival and development of an independent Canada will maintain the values of human diversity and humane living. In nis selection from his essay Rotstein narrates the events of the "great blackout" of 1965 in a manner intended to force the reader to consider the values inherent in the technological society.

1   Jonathan Swift was hardly the prophet of the new technology, yet he left unwittingly a graphic image of the electric society. Lemuel Gulliver, while asleep in Lilliput, has been tied to the ground with thousands of threads by the fearful and industrious Lilliputians. When he awakens, he discovers that he has been rendered immobile and the struggle to free himself is in vain.   5

2   A society dependent on the pervasive wires for virtually all vital tasks of daily life—light, heat, food, transport, production, communication and education—may also be tied down by its electric grid in a way not unlike that of Lemuel Gulliver. With this vital dependence on electricity, we   10 ourselves become, in an important sense, plugged into the grid.

3   The point was brought home in a dramatic fashion on November 9th, 1965, when at the height of the rush hour in the late afternoon, the lights flickered and went out in the eastern half of North America. It was the beginning of the most massive and puzzling blackout that had yet oc-   15 curred. In the industrial heartland of the United States and Canada, ex-

From *Nationalism in Canada*, edited by Peter Russell. Copyright © McGraw-Hill Company of Canada Limited. Reprinted by permission.

tending over some 80,000 square miles, the daily lives of thirty million people were temporarily disrupted—in some regions for as long as fourteen hours.

4   The blackout was only a brief moment in the twentieth century, yet it lit up the characteristic shape which existence had taken. We could suddenly "see" the all-encompassing electric grid. Some imagined that since the grid had become the central nervous system of our society, people might turn to panic and hysteria if it should cease to function. Others wondered whether the blackout was the result of sabotage, and still others wondered whether there would be violence and looting.

5   None of these fears were warranted. There were no indications of sabotage nor of violence or looting. Instead of panic, quiet camaraderie filled the air. Life suddenly ceased to be harried and frantic. Languid conversations took place in darkened offices. A light-hearted grace flowed everywhere, particularly in the normally rude and belligerent New York City. Those who managed to reach home had dinner by candlelight; many who did not whiled away the hours at a local lounge, not overly concerned with their fate. Businessmen stepped in with relish to direct traffic. Those who were stranded in subways, elevators and railway stations found the blackout less pleasant, but courtesy, calmness and an easy tolerance prevailed everywhere.

6   A political philosopher might even have been tempted to draw some conclusions about this facsimile "state of nature" of an industrial society. Notwithstanding Thomas Hobbes, people had turned out to be lambs rather than wolves.

7   We had a brief glimpse of a more benign world, but it was an artificial world and irretrievable. When the towering pylons and the ubiquitous wires sprang to life once more, and we had again donned the technological harness, peculiar questions still remained, not the least of which was the unsolved mystery of what had caused the blackout. There were also other questions: had we any assurances that it would not recur, and what, in any case, was this extensive Canadian-U.S. grid that bound the two countries together like a prolific vine? Thus, together with the questions about the interruption of the grid, there emerged questions about its normal operation. Perhaps in the blackout there lay a paradigm for the evolving technological society, some of whose features flickered briefly in high definition.

QUESTIONS

READER AND PURPOSE

1. As is often the case in effective narration, Rotstein does not make direct interpretive statements about the events he describes. Yet he does guide the reader in several ways toward an interpretation. It could be argued that the reader who recognizes the Biblical allusion * in Rotstein's title is already in a position to interpret the narrative that follows. (If the allusion is not familiar to you, locate it by using a concordance to the King James Bible and looking up the word "darkly.") Do you think this kind of allusion too obscure for most readers? Would you say the same of the allusion in the first paragraph to Book One of *Gulliver's Travels* by Swift? Of the reference to Thomas Hobbes in paragraph 6? (Information about Hobbes can be found in the *Dictionary of National Biography*.) On the basis of these allusions, describe the kind of audience you think Rotstein is writing for.

2. Rotstein offers further guidance to the reader in his final paragraph. Does he do this without making direct statements?

3. Can you now briefly state Rotstein's purpose for writing and the interpretation he puts on the events described?

4. Why does Rotstein address his audience in the first-person plural?

ORGANIZATION

5. Before beginning his narrative proper, Rotstein writes two paragraphs connecting the imprisoned Gulliver to modern man "tied down" by an electric grid. Is this an example of an analogy * or of an extended simile *? What purposes does it serve in the narrative? If properly-constructed narratives have beginnings, middles and ends, how do these two paragraphs constitute a beginning?

6. With what two separate words does the author qualify * his main point in sentence one of paragraph 2?

7. Paragraph 3 gives us a straightforward description of what happened when the lights went out. Does paragraph 4 do the same thing? Or something more? Before answering look carefully at the first two sentences of paragraph 4.

8. How would you describe the kinds of details Rotstein has selected for inclusion in paragraph 5? What signpost * does he use at the beginning of this paragraph, and how is it related to the details that follow? What implicit conclusion is Rotstein offering on the basis of these details?

9. Does the author make this conclusion explicit in paragraph 6? Does he need to? Could he have simply omitted the paragraph? Before answering reconsider what you know about Hobbes and Swift.

10. What repeated word in the concluding paragraph invites the reader to

interpret the narrative in a particular way? What qualifying word in the final sentence indicates that Rotstein does not, however, wish to force an interpretation on the reader?

11. Does the last sentence constitute a closing by return *? What word is repeated from the first sentence of paragraph 3? Does this word have the same connotations * in both sentences?

12. How often does Rotstein use transitions, signposts, and organizing sentences *? Try to find out what links each paragraph to the following one. If the links are not apparent, try rearranging the order of the paragraphs. If they cannot be rearranged, explain why the order Rotstein uses makes sense.

SENTENCES

13. If you have read Book Three of *Gulliver's Travels*, would you agree with Rotstein's opening sentence? If you disagree, would this weaken his argument for you?

14. Would you describe Rotstein's style as formal or informal?

15. How many simple * sentences can you find? How many examples of interrupted movement *? Of compound * sentences, complex * sentences, compound-complex * sentences, balanced * sentences?

16. Is the first sentence of paragraph 3 a periodic * sentence? Explain why, or why not.

17. Is Rotstein merely being careless or contradictory when he states, in the first sentence of paragraph 4, that "the blackout . . . lit up" our characteristic existence? If you think not, explain why.

18. Justify Rotstein's use of dashes in paragraph 2, sentence one, and in paragraph 3, sentence three.

DICTION

19. Look up: *unwittingly* (2), *graphic* (2), *pervasive* (7), *vital* (7), *camaraderie* (28), *frantic* (29), *languid* (29), *relish* (34), *benign* (42), *irretrievable* (43), *ubiquitous* (43-44), *paradigm* (51).

20. Look up the etymologies * of *sabotage* (25) and *facsimile* (39). Are these words used by Rotstein in their original meanings?

21. *The point was brought home* and *in a dramatic fashion* (12) are phrases that verge on being clichés (overworked expressions). Can you defend their use here as particularly appropriate to Rotstein's narrative?

22. To what image * earlier in the selection does the phrase *technological harness* (44-45) refer?

23. What effect does Rotstein achieve by using the simile *like a prolific vine* (49) to describe an apparently non-living entity such as a power grid?

POINTS TO LEARN

1. Effective narration uses carefully selected details to recreate experience.

2. The meaning of a narrative is better implied than stated.

3. Good narration usually possesses a clearly defined beginning, middle, and end.

4. Diction, sentence structures, and tone combine to create the narrative voice *.

SUGGESTIONS FOR WRITING

1. Compare and contrast, in three or four paragraphs, the narrative techniques used by Rotstein to analyze technology with the expository techniques used by Carl Becker (p. 101) to treat the same subject.

2. In several paragraphs, totalling about 600 words, narrate an episode in which you and other people found yourselves cut off from some important aspect of our society usually taken for granted. Use formal diction, complicated sentence structures, and a serious tone in your description. Have a clear sense of the audience you are addressing, one that will take your narrative seriously. Be clear in your mind about the meaning you wish to communicate to your audience, but do not state it directly.

IMPROVING YOUR STYLE

1. In your narrative use several varieties of complicated sentences, with a few simple sentences used for the sake of contrast or to emphasize a point.

2. Use two or three allusions as a way of suggesting but not stating your meaning.

3. Use, as Rotstein does, leading questions that direct your audience toward important matters of interpretation.

4. Qualify several of your statements, so as to encourage the reader to think about the events you are describing.

The Unicorn in the Garden

James Thurber (1894-1961) was one of the finest humorists and satirists of our time. Mostly he wrote loose personal essays and short stories, but he also collaborated with Elliot Nugent on a successful stage play, *The Male Animal* (1940) and was a notable cartoonist. He wrote too many books to list here; a good introduction to his work is *The Thurber Carnival*, an anthology published in 1945. The following piece is from *Fables for Our Time* (1940). A fable is, strictly speaking, a short tale in which birds or animals talk and act like human beings and which illustrates a simple moral truth, often literally stated in a closing tag or "moral." More loosely, the term *fable* applies to any short, illustrative tale even if the characters are human, as they are here. But even then the genre allows the use of fabulous elements, such as the unicorn. "The Unicorn in the Garden" is about one of Thurber's most constant themes: the struggle between men and women for dominance. It is funny, but below the humor—as so often in Thurber—the matter is serious.

1   Once upon a sunny morning a man who sat in a breakfast nook looked up from his scrambled eggs to see a white unicorn with a gold horn quietly cropping the roses in the garden. The man went up to the bedroom where his wife was still asleep and woke her. "There's a unicorn in the garden," he said. "Eating roses." She opened one unfriendly eye and looked 5 at him. "The unicorn is a mythical beast," she said, and turned her back on him. The man walked slowly downstairs and out into the garden. The unicorn was still there; he was now browsing among the tulips. "Here, unicorn," said the man, and he pulled up a lily and gave it to him. The unicorn ate it gravely. With a high heart, because there was a unicorn in his garden, 10 the man went upstairs and roused his wife again. "The unicorn," he said, "ate a lily." His wife sat up in bed and looked at him, coldly. "You are a

From *Fables for Our Time,* published by Harper & Row. Originally printed in *The New Yorker.* Copyright © 1940 by James Thurber; copyright © 1968 by Helen Thurber. Reprinted by permission of Mrs. James Thurber.

booby," she said, "and I am going to have you put in the booby-hatch." The
man, who had never liked the words "booby" and "booby-hatch," and who
liked them even less on a shining morning when there was a unicorn in the   15
garden, thought for a moment. "We'll see about that," he said. He walked
over to the door. "He has a golden horn in the middle of his forehead,"
he told her. Then he went back to the garden to watch the unicorn; but the
unicorn had gone away. The man sat down among the roses and went to
sleep.   20

2   As soon as the husband had gone out of the house, the wife got up
and dressed as fast as she could. She was very excited and there was a gloat
in her eye. She telephoned the police and she telephoned a psychiatrist; she
told them to hurry to her house and bring a strait-jacket. When the police
and the psychiatrist arrived they sat down in chairs and looked at her, with   25
great interest. "My husband," she said, "saw a unicorn this morning." The
police looked at the psychiatrist and the psychiatrist looked at the police.
"He told me it ate a lily," she said. The psychiatrist looked at the police and
the police looked at the psychiatrist. "He told me it had a golden horn
in the middle of its forehead," she said. At a solemn signal from the psy-   30
chiatrist, the police leaped from their chairs and seized the wife. They had
a hard time subduing her, for she put up a terrific struggle, but they finally
subdued her. Just as they got her into the strait-jacket, the husband came
back into the house.

3   "Did you tell your wife you saw a unicorn?" asked the police. "Of   35
course not," said the husband. "The unicorn is a mythical beast." "That's
all I wanted to know," said the psychiatrist. "Take her away. I'm sorry, sir,
but your wife is as crazy as a jay bird." So they took her away, cursing and
screaming, and shut her up in an institution. The husband lived happily
ever after.   40

4   *Moral: Don't count your boobies until they are hatched.*

QUESTIONS

READER AND PURPOSE
1. The essential elements of narrative are characters and action. Such things as
setting, symbols*, and imagery* may be made more, or less, important, but ultimately a story stands or falls on action and character. This important fact is
illustrated by Thurber's brief, but perhaps not-so-simple, fable. Consider first his
treatment of character. Deftly and quickly he creates the hero and the villain,
but he does not hang signs around their necks; he renders his characters dra-

matically, that is, in terms of what they say and do. We must infer what kind of people these are; the author does not tell us explicitly. The wife is plainly despicable. What does she do that makes her so? Although the husband is the hero in the sense of being the "good guy," he is no Achilles. Thurber's husbands are not cast in the mold of the Greek hero; they are mild little men—patient, gentle, long-suffering. Do you think that Thurber intends us to like this husband? Thurber's mild little men, however, often reveal another trait: they will be pushed just so far and then they turn upon their domineering wives and get even. At what point does this husband begin to turn?

2. Why do you suppose it is a unicorn that the man sees instead of, say, a pink elephant? Are we supposed to accept the unicorn of the story as real? It is clear that the wife, the police, and the psychiatrist do not. But has Thurber given us any reason to doubt that the unicorn the man sees is a real unicorn in a real garden, really browsing among the tulips and eating a lily? (Read the opening sentence carefully if you are unsure about how to answer this question.)

3. Assuming that he intends us to generalize from his couple, what is Thurber suggesting about marriage? He is poking fun at other things than lazy, vindictive wives. Do the psychiatrist and the police arouse our admiration? Are they any less literal-minded than the wife?

4. The "moral," with its pun upon *hatched*, suggests that sanity and insanity are less easy to distinguish than many people suppose. Has a rough sort of justice prevailed in this story—has the right booby been hatched?

5. There is more to the theme of "The Unicorn in the Garden," however, than is contained in its closing moral. In your own words discuss everything you think this story implies about men and women and the values by which they live.

ORGANIZATION

6. In the first paragraph the dramatic focus is upon which character? Does the focus shift in the second paragraph? If you think that it does, has Thurber provided an adequate transition?

7. A story is composed of bits of action called episodes, which are dramatically rendered in scenes. A scene is a unit of action defined by time, place, and characters; when any of these elements changes significantly a new scene begins. Thus in paragraph 1 the first scene depicts the man in the nook eating his breakfast and seeing the unicorn. When he goes upstairs to his wife's bedroom we have scene 2. This paragraph consists of five such scenes; identify the remaining three. Make a similar scenic analysis of paragraphs 2 and 3.

8. In a well-constructed story each scene must be informative; that is, it must relate something new about the characters, prepare for future action, clarify the theme in some way, or do all of these. What new bits of information are conveyed by each scene in paragraph 1?

9. In many stories the action is of the special kind called plot. Briefly, a plot

has these characteristics: (1) at least one character is working toward a specific goal; (2) this effort brings him into conflict with one or more of the other characters; (3) the conflict is ultimately resolved; (4) only episodes that bear upon either the goal or the conflict are included; and (5) all episodes are tied together in a tight chain of cause and effect. Show that the action of Thurber's story may properly be called a plot. In a well-made plot the action is brought to a logically satisfactory conclusion. Do you feel that such is the case here?

10. Plots begin with what we call a datum—an initial event, often implying a question or problem, out of which the goal and the conflict develop. What is the datum in Thurber's tale? Even more important is the climax. This is the scene in which the conflict is finally resolved; in a cowboy movie, for instance, the climax is the shoot-out between the white hat and the black. Which scene in Thurber's story constitutes the climax? For one character or another the climax of a plot usually involves a reversal—the black hat, for example, expects to win, not to be shot down in the dust. What is the reversal in "The Unicorn in the Garden"?

11. The plot generally carries an important part of the meaning of a story. Often in tragic drama, for instance, the plot demonstrates that the hero's destruction is the logically necessary consequence of a moral lapse; had Macbeth not murdered Duncan, he would not in turn have been killed by Macduff. What meaning is conveyed by Thurber's plot? There is an important difference, however, between a play like *Macbeth* and a fable. *Macbeth* presumably reflects the real world, however it may simplify that world; what happens to Macbeth is a sign of what will happen to similar men in real life. In fables and fairy tales, on the other hand, the point may be that the universe of the story does *not* reflect the world as we experience it. Do you think that such is the case in "The Unicorn in the Garden"?

12. The final element in a plot is often called the denouement. It logically follows the climax, wrapping up any loose threads and bringing the story to a close. What is the denouement of Thurber's fable?

SENTENCES

13. A narrative writer must solve the problem of fitting the bits and pieces of his action into appropriate compositional units. In a novel such units would include groups of paragraphs, chapters, and even whole books. Thurber's units, however, are paragraphs and sentences. Study the sentence plan of the first paragraph and be able to discuss whether or not Thurber has used his sentences effectively to analyze the action.

14. Comment upon these revisions of Thurber's sentences:

(a) *Revision:* His wife sat up in bed and coldly looked at him.
   Thurber: "His wife sat up in bed and looked at him, coldly." (12)

(b) *Revision:* The wife got up and dressed as fast as she could, as soon as the husband had gone out of the house.

Thurber: "As soon as the husband had gone out of the house, the wife got up and dressed as fast as she could." (21-22)

DICTION

15. Look up: *unicorn* (2), *cropping* (3), *mythical* (6).

16. In line 22 Thurber writes of the wife "that there was a gloat in her eye." *Gleam* would be more idiomatic here, but *gloat* is better. Why? And why is *shining* better in line 15 than *bright* would be?

17. What words in the first paragraph establish the wife's reaction to her husband? The husband's reaction to his wife? What words characterize the unicorn? Is it a nice unicorn? Is there any significance in the fact that the setting is a "*sunny* morning"?

POINTS TO LEARN

1. Character and action are the essence of narrative.

2. The action of a story must be organized and it must be presented as a series of scenes.

3. Plot is a common way of organizing action. A plot begins with a datum, develops a conflict, which it resolves in the climax, and concludes with a denouement.

4. Narrative action, whether or not it is plotted, must be fitted into compositional units appropriate to the length of the story; these units include clauses, sentences, sentence groups, paragraphs, paragraph groups, and chapters.

SUGGESTIONS FOR WRITING

It is far easier to analyze a fable than to write one. Indeed, because they must be stripped down to the essentials of narrative action, fables are much more difficult to write well than you may think. Listed below are several suggestions, but you should feel free to invent your own situation if none of these appeals. Before you begin to write decide in your own mind what your theme is, and as you write control your characters and action to demonstrate that theme. Do not, however, deliver the message in person. Simply tell the story and let your reader infer its point for himself.

The alligator in the phone booth
The horse in the bathtub
The yellow pussy cat who thought he was boss
The Great Dane who felt superior

IMPROVING YOUR STYLE

Before you begin to write, make:

1. A list of the characters and a synopsis of the plot.
2. A rough outline of the scenes through which the plot will develop. Indicate briefly what you want to accomplish in each scene.

Short Trip

Robert Lipsyte is a sports reporter and writer. His books include *The Masculine Mystique* (1966), *Assignment Sports* (1970), and *Sports World: An American Dreamland* (1975). The following piece appeared in *The New York Times* and is about the habitués of race tracks (in this case Aqueduct in New York). Unlike Thurber's fable in the preceding selection, this is not a story imagined to illustrate a moral, but rather a report about real people and events. Yet the difference is less important than it might seem. For while Lipsyte does not invent his characters, scenes, and action, he does select, arrange, and describe them. And like Thurber he does so for a purpose; he sees a meaning in what is going on. Thus whether they begin from the actual or from an imagined world, writers of narrative must look for and reveal the significance of the events they describe.

1   The fare to the Aqueduct Race Track is 75 cents on the special subway train from Times Square. This includes a send-off: the narrow escalator down to the platform ends beneath the words Good Luck printed on the grimy-gold arch of a huge wooden horseshoe. The subway car is as free of talk as the reading room of a library, and, in fact, all the travelers are reading: The Morning Telegraph, The Daily News, the latest bulletin from Clocker Lawton. They are very ordinary-looking men and a few women, a bit older than most people these days.

2   It hardly seems 30 minutes before the train bursts out of the black hole and onto an elevated track that winds above the two-family houses and cemetery fields of Queens. It is nearing mid-day, in the butt-end of another year, and the travelers blink briefly in the flat, hard sunlight. They are standing long before the train skids to a stop. They run down the ramp toward the $2 grandstand entrances, then on to daily-double windows five minutes away from closing.

© 1967 by the New York Times Company. Reprinted by permission.

3   Before the race of the day, at any track, anywhere, there is a sense
of happening, of a corner that might be turned, a door that might open.
There is almost a merry ring to the parimutuel machines punching out fresh
tickets to everywhere, and the players move out smartly, clapping down the
wooden seats of chairs, briskly stepping onto the pebbled concrete areas   20
that bear the remarkable signs, "No Chairs Permitted on Lawn." Seconds
after noon, the first race starts. It lasts little more than a minute, just long
enough to hold your breath, to scream, or fall to your knees against a metal
fence and pray, "Angel, Angel, Angel."

4   But on this day, Angel Cordero, the hot young jockey, finishes   25
fourth in the first race, and the praying man collapses on the fence like a
steer caught on barbed wire. Another man smiles coldly as he tears up tickets, and says: "Dropping down so fast like that, you mean to tell me he
couldn't stay in the money? Sure. Haw."

5   It is suddenly quiet again, and the day is no longer fresh and new,   30
the day is tired and old and familiar. An old, hooded man from Allied
Maintenance moves over the asphalt picking up torn tickets with a nail-
tipped stick, tapping like a blind man among the empty wastebaskets. Men
watch him to see if he is turning over the tickets looking for a winner
thrown away by mistake. He is not.   35

6   The race track settles into a predictable rhythm. In the half hour
or so between races, men study their charts, straddling green benches or
bent over stew and stale coffee in the drab cafeteria or hunkered down beneath the hot-air ceiling vent in a cavernous men's room, the warmest spot
at Aqueduct. As the minutes move toward post time, they gather beneath   40
the approximate odds board. They interpret the flickering numbers—smart
money moving, perhaps the making of a coup. At the last moment, they
bet, then rush out on the stone lawn for the race. A minute later they are
straggling back, chanting the old litany, "I woulda . . . . coulda . . . .
shoulda . . . ."   45

7   There are ebbs and flows throughout the day. People leave, others
come, the machines jangle on. There is a great deal of shuffling in the
grandstand area, and little loud talk. People move away from strangers.
When men speak of horses, they use numbers, not names, and when they
talk of jockeys, they frequently curse. It was, they whisper, an "election";   50
the jockeys decided last night who would win.

8   The day ends pale and chilly a few minutes before 4 P.M. and the
fans troop out to the subway station. There is no special train returning:
the city will get you out fast enough, but you can find your own way home.

9   Horseplayers are smart, and they all wait in the enclosed area near   55
the change booths, ready to bolt through the turnstiles onto the outdoor
platform when the train comes, and not a moment sooner. They stamp
their feet, muttering, "Woulda . . . . coulda . . . . shoulda." The losers
rail against crooked jocks, gutless horses, callous owners, the ugly track, the
greedy state that takes 10 cents of each dollar bet.   60

10   Then they bolt through the turnstiles, quick and practiced, tokens
in and spin out upon the platform. But there is no train yet, they all followed a fool, and now they curse him for five minutes in the cold until an
old shuddering train lumbers in to carry them away.

QUESTIONS

READER AND PURPOSE

1. The job of a reporter is to tell us "how it is." This requires him to do more
than simply chronicle facts; he must reveal their meaning. To be more exact,
he must give them meaning, for in themselves facts have no significance; they
acquire it only when they are observed and organized by a guiding intelligence.
What do you think is the meaning of "Short Trip"? "How is it" with Aqueduct Race Track and the people who patronize it?

2. Unlike that by James Thurber, Lipsyte's narrative is not focused upon
specific individuals. Instead of a single central character he has a number of
them who make up a composite type—"The Horseplayer." What are the characteristics of the Horseplayer? What is Lipsyte's attitude toward him? Who,
or what, constitutes the antagonist, the force opposing those who bet the
horses?

ORGANIZATION

3. This narrative has no plot in the usual sense. But the action is organized.
One might say that it is like a three-act play, with paragraphs 1-2 making up the
first act, paragraphs 3-7 the second, and 8-10 the third. Do you think this is a
reasonable analysis? Why or why not? Give each a title.

4. Each of the acts contains several scenes. Identify those in Act I. In Acts II
and III.

5. Lipsyte's organization is essentially chronological. Underline all the words
that indicate temporal progression. Paragraph 6 is an especially good example of
chronological structure. What words in the first sentence of this paragraph set
up the topic? Point out one or two other paragraphs in this selection in which
the opening sentences contain key words or phrases. Do they usually come toward the end of the sentence?

6. A good story conveys a feeling of completeness. It must have a beginning, a middle which evolves naturally from the beginning, and an ending which is the logical conclusion of all that has gone before. Does Lipsyte's story possess this sense of a completed form? He closes his narrative by the technique we call completing the circle, that is, by repeating in the ending something he mentioned in the beginning. How does Lipsyte complete his circle?

SENTENCES

7. Can you see a reason for the colon in line 2 instead of a semicolon?
8. The sentence in lines 7-8 concludes with the modifying construction "a bit older than most people these days." If you can, explain the syntax of this construction. The sentence might have read: "They are very ordinary-looking men and a few women, who are a bit older than most people these days." What is the advantage of handling it as Lipsyte has done? Does his sentence seem more, or less, formal than the one using *who are?* This kind of modifier is very useful; learn to employ it in your own sentences.
9. Identify the parallel * elements in the sentence in lines 16-17. Find one or two others of Lipsyte's sentences that effectively use parallelism.
10. Joining together the successive items in a series with *and* is called polysyndeton *, as in the clause in line 31: ". . . the day is tired and old and familiar." What advantages does polysyndeton have over the usual way of treating a series (e.g. ". . . the day is tired, old, and familiar")?
11. Locate two or three effective short sentences in these paragraphs and be prepared to discuss why you think them effective. Considering its context, why is this sentence especially well constructed: "People leave, others come, the machines jangled on" (46-47)? (This pattern is called tricolon *.)
12. The syntax of the first sentence in paragraph 10 is a bit obscure. How, for instance, would you construe the phrase *tokens in?* Yet the movement of this sentence is wonderfully appropriate to what the writer is describing. Why?

DICTION

13. Look up: *hunkered* (38), *coup* (42), *ebbs* (46), *flows* (46), *rail* (59).
14. Necessarily Lipsyte uses a number of expressions peculiar to horseracing. Try to define these as precisely as you can: *daily-double windows* (14), *parimutuel machines* (18), *a winner* (34), *post time* (40), *the approximate odds board* (41), *smart money* (41).
15. Setting is a more important element in Lipsyte's story than it was in Thurber's. For example, at the very beginning we are told that the wooden horseshoe is painted a *grimy-gold*. What is the significance of this detail? What images * in the second paragraph suggest the idea of sterility, even death? In paragraphs 3-7 what images describe the Race Track? Underline the words in the third paragraph that characterize the players before the first race.

16. Lipsyte's verbs are especially expressive. List half a dozen that strike you; explain why they are good.

17. *Litany* (44) is a metaphor *. What is being compared? Is the comparison apt—does it reveal something about horse-players? Identify the simile * in lines 26-27. Do you like it? Point out several other similes and metaphors in this selection.

18. In lines 18-19 Lipsyte speaks of the "parimutuel machines punching out fresh tickets to everywhere." What is he implying? He tells us in the final paragraph that in rushing out upon the platform too soon the crowd had "all followed a fool." Is there perhaps a double meaning in this phrase?

POINTS TO LEARN

1. A story should not simply stop. Rather it should be brought to a close, its action completed.

2. The images which describe setting often contribute significantly to the meaning of a story.

3. Tell the story well and its meaning will take care of itself.

SUGGESTIONS FOR WRITING

Imagine that you are a reporter and that you must write a narrative on one of the subjects listed below. First make up your own mind what you want to convey about the experience you describe, and then select details and organize action accordingly. Let the story imply its own theme.

> A bingo parlor on a crowded night
> A wrestling arena in a small city
> Evening visiting hours at the hospital
> A locker-room both before and after a game
> Backstage at a play or opera

IMPROVING YOUR STYLE

In your narrative include:

1. Several short, dramatic sentences.

2. A tricolon * like the one in lines 46-47 (see question 11).

3. A sentence containing an elliptical * clause similar to the construction in lines 7-8 (question 8).

4. An example of polysyndeton (question 10).

5. Several metaphors and several similes.

6. Some strong, expressive verbs.

Beginnings and Closings

Hilaire Belloc—who knew, if anyone did, how to begin and how to end an essay—once wrote that "to begin at the beginning is, next to ending at the end, the whole art of writing." If this be right, most essays have little claim to art, for it is sad but true that students pay little attention to the beginnings and the endings of their compositions. If they consider the opening and closing paragraphs at all, they treat them like luggage tags, hurriedly tied on to announce where they are going or where they have been. Beginnings and endings are more than this, and they are important. How a writer begins will determine whether her reader bothers to go on. And how she begins greatly affects what a writer will say. Starting an essay is like starting a journey: to turn left or to turn right will lead to very different destinations. Closings are equally important. It does little good to develop an idea through five pages only to lose the reader with an abrupt, inadequate final paragraph.

It is easy to assert the importance of the opening and closing paragraphs and to tell the student that she must begin well and end well. It is more difficult to explain how she goes about it. There is no simple answer; here as elsewhere learning is a slow and personal affair. Still, a few generalizations will help the inexperienced writer. First about beginnings. The purpose of an opening paragraph is to introduce the body of the essay. The introduction must include several things: the identification of the subject, indicating as well the limitations within which it will be treated; often a quick view of the organization of the essay to follow; and finally an effort to motivate the reader—to engage her interest.

The number of words required to do these things will vary according to the length and complexity of the essay they introduce. In a short, simple paper the beginning may be only a sentence; in a multi-volume historical study it may comprise fifty pages. For most student essays a single paragraph is enough, and if the essay is very short its beginning may be only a sentence or two.

As the length of the beginning is variable, so is the manner in which it is developed. In academic papers, designed for a narrow and professional audience, the writer often announces his subject explicitly. Thus Carl Berger begins *The Sense of Power*: "This book is a study in Canadian nationalist thought. It is an examination of the ideas and beliefs of a group of men in the late nineteenth and early twentieth centuries, who called their case imperial unity, their movement imperial federation, and themselves imperialists." Berger is concerned to be clear and precise, and is little interested in entertaining his reader; his formal, explicit beginning exactly suits his purpose. But such an opening is usually too stiff for freshman compositions, where it is better to work implicitly. The student should not begin, for instance, "The purpose of this essay is to discuss hockey"; this is much too wooden and weighty. He need only write "Hockey is the most popular of Canadian sports," leaving to the reader the obvious inference that the essay which follows is about hockey.

Generally the limitation of the subject goes hand in hand with its announcement and need never be pursued beyond what is absolutely necessary. If the next sentence of our imaginary baseball paper were "But few people realize the intricate business organization that supports a big league team," the broad topic of baseball would be sufficiently narrowed and the reader would know what to expect. It is sometimes desirable for the writer to tell what he is not going to do, but as a rule the subjects of student essays do not require extensive boundary fixing.

How closely the plan of the paper need be indicated in the beginning paragraphs depends upon subject, length, and purpose. In long, complicated essays a preview of the organization not only aids the reader but simplifies for the writer many future problems of transition. Here, too, the writer may work either explicitly or more subtly. Usually it is best to imply the plan of the essay, avoiding such heavy-handed obviousness as "This paper will be divided into four major sections." The typical English composition, however, is too simple and too brief to warrant laying out its organization in the beginning paragraph, whether by direct statement or by implication.

Equally variable is the effort a writer must make to engage her reader's interest. A physician reporting upon a new drug in a medical journal may safely assume that the professional audience for whom she writes is already interested, and she may concentrate upon being concise and informative. A journalist treating the same subject for a lay audience must make a greater effort to capture their attention. Generally the composition student, like the journalist, needs to think consciously of interesting her reader. This is simpler to say than to do; but there are ways.

The most common is to stress the importance of the subject. "Hockey is a popular game," for example, merely states a fact without attaching to it any special significance; as an opening sentence it would hardly awaken anyone not already a fan. But "Hockey is a uniquely Canadian game; he who would understand Canada must understand hockey," now gives the subject a particular importance which is more likely to attract the reader.

A more subtle way of catching the reader's interest is to puzzle him. Charles Lamb opens "A Chapter on Ears" with the cryptic remark, "I have no ear"; and his reader is intrigued. Rachel Carson's opening sentence— "There was once a town in the heart of America where all life seemed to live in harmony with its surroundings" (p. 495)—is intriguing because of its combination of the fairy tale ("There was once a town") and of the unusual meaning of her statement. This technique may take a stronger form and become a deliberate attempt to shock. To begin our theme on hockey with "Hockey is a game that appeals to fools," will probably stimulate the reader to go on, if only to learn more about the writer's eccentricities.

There are other devices useful in gaining the reader's attention. Cleverly employed, rhetorical questions, anecdotes, allusions, quotations, will all arouse interest. One of the finest beginnings in English is the first sentence of Bacon's essay "Of Truth": "What is truth? said jesting Pilate; and would not stay for an answer." Short as it is, the sentence contains a rhetorical question, an allusion, and even a brief anecdote. Another method is to begin with a brief common-place remark, which, to readers accustomed to openings of momentous significance, has the charm of surprise. "Everyone knows the traditional picture of Sir John Macdonald," is all Donald Creighton writes to begin one essay. Brand Blanshard begins his essay (p. 491) with a contrast between "pride in what our colleges have done" but, surprisingly, "a growing uneasiness about their product." And Dickens opens "A Christmas Carol" with the remarkably effective: "Marley was dead, to begin with. There is no doubt whatever about that."

Thus to interest the reader, to identify and limit the subject, and possibly to indicate the plan of the essay, are the purposes of the beginning. In attempting to fulfill them the inexperienced writer is liable to err in either one of two extremes. The first is to do too little, to bombard his readers with ideas before they have had a chance to settle down and learn what all this is about. The second is to do too much. A beginning introduces the subject—but it does not develop it; that is the job of what is to follow. Although learning to avoid both these extremes is not easy, it can be done. To be blunt, it must be; for no essay that begins badly can be successful.

The final paragraphs are no less important. A closing has one essential function: to say "the essay is finished." In the movie theatre we do not require the words "The End" to know that a well-directed film is over. We reach for our coats when the music swells and the heroine falls into the hero's arms. So in a well-written essay—the final paragraphs tell us that the writer has no more to say, and we do not need the white space at the bottom of the page to realize the fact. On occasion a writer may feel it necessary to do more in his last paragraph than merely signal the end. The subject may demand that he draw a final conclusion, and if his paper has been long and complex he may think a summary in order. When they are present, conclusions and summaries are in themselves signs of closing. But they are not always present, for not every essay requires them. Therefore the writer must learn to use other techniques of ending. Four are most common: signal words, changing the tempo of the last sentence, figurative closing, and returning to the beginning.

Most frequent is the signal word, of which there are a great many in English. Some—like *finally, in conclusion, at last*—can be obvious and rather mechanical. Carl Berger, however, makes his use of such a signal word, in the first sentence of his concluding paragraph, somewhat less obvious by not positioning it at the very beginning: "There is finally one further pattern that revealed itself in Morton's intellectual development." Other signal words—like *and so, then, thus*—are more subtle. Not all these terms are exact equivalents, of course, and a good writer will have ready to hand a number of them, selecting that which best fits his context.

Altering the speed of the final sentence requires a little more skill. Usually the change is a slowing down, and often a regularizing, of the rhythm. William Prescott ends the *History of the Conquest of Peru* with this long, slow, stately sentence: "With the benevolent mission of Gasca, then, the historian of the Conquest may be permitted to terminate his labors, —with feelings not unlike those of the traveller, who, having long journeyed among the dreary forests and dangerous defiles of the mountains, at length emerges on some pleasant landscape smiling in tranquillity and peace." The last sentence of George Woodcock's essay on Gabriel Dumont is a masterly example of a slow, majestic sentence which concludes an entire book. It is a long sentence (lines 32–42) built on a series of subordinate parallel constructions: "But when . . . where . . . where . . ." and finally, a "then . . . where" construction. Less often the final sentence may be quick, brief, matter-of-fact, especially if the preceding constructions have been long and complicated. Chesterton, for example, concludes "A Piece of Chalk" with this passage: "And I stood there in a trance of pleasure, realizing that this Southern England is not only a grand peninsula, and a tradition and a civilization; it is something even more admirable. It is a piece of chalk."

The third device, which we have called figurative closing, means simply the inclusion in the final paragraph of some sort of a comparison or a figure of speech—usually a simile or metaphor—which implies the idea of ending. There was a series of movie travelogues popular about twenty-five years ago which concluded invariably—or so it seemed—with our "leaving the beautiful isle of this or that and sailing into the sunset." The image of the sunset is comparable to a figure of closing. A less trite case is Prescott's traveller emerging on "some pleasant landscape smiling in tranquillity and peace." His travels are over, and so, the figure implies, is the book. The alert reader knows there is nothing more. But remember, if it is to do its job, the closing figure must seem natural to the context of the essay and not be a completely alien idea forced upon it from the outside. Thus Lin Green's "mulishly resisting the oncoming wave of anarchy regarding sex roles" (p. 24) briefly and colorfully summarizes the points she has been discussing. When they are natural, figures of closing are neat and effective ways of ending.

The final closing technique is the return to the beginning. Having set up a word or phrase in his opening, the writer swings back to it in the final paragraph, completing the circle. Chesterton, for instance, not only entitles his essay "A Piece of Chalk," but uses *chalks* in his first sentence; and on this word he ends. Of all ways of closing, the return to the beginning is perhaps the best. This is not simply because it is the least obvious. Even more importantly the cyclic return best completes the form of the essay; and such completeness is, as Belloc observes, the essence of art.

Art may seem a pretentious term in the workaday world of composition courses and term papers. Writing of this sort we do not usually dignify as art. Yet—no matter how practical and prosaic its subject—it is. A lawyer's brief, a piece of literary criticism, a freshman essay are all works of art; to say that they are well or poorly written is simply to say that they are good art or bad.

Nothing is so fatal to a work of art as failure to complete its form. A lopsided vase, a novel that fails to bring its plot to the demanded conclusion, annoy us. And so with an essay. It must be complete and whole within itself. This does not mean that the first and final paragraphs are the most important. A skillful introduction or a fine closing does not salvage an otherwise foolish or badly organized essay. It does mean that an essay must begin and must end—and not start and stop. Anyone can stop writing. Only writers can finish.

Beginnings

GEORGES ERASMUS

We the Dene

Georges Erasmus is the National Chief for the Assembly of First Nations. The opening paragraphs of his essay show how a controversial subject (the clash between the traditional Dene way of life and advancing technology) can be effectively introduced through explanation, repetition, and the careful control of tone.

1   The main issue facing the Dene is not the proposed Mackenzie Valley pipeline or some such other colonial development. The issue facing us today is the same issue that has confronted us since the first non-Dene arrived in our land. The issue is recognition of our national rights, recognition of our right to be a self-governing people.   5

2   Throughout the world, various peoples are asserting their right to be self-determining nations. Many Third World peoples are recognizing that their own "underdevelopment," their own political, economic, and social dependencies, are directly related to the "overdevelopment" of the industrialized world. The nationalism of the Third World is a sign of hope 10 for man's ability to build a more just and humanizing world order. People who were once confused and degraded by an experience of colonialism have declared their right to be regarded as self-determining peoples. They have declared their right to be more than just the objects of exploitation.

3   Within the industrialized nation-states, there exist nations of ab- 15 original peoples who do not share the wealth and power of the dominant society. These people have a history of exploitation by the developed countries similar to the Third World experience. The difference is that these people exist within the geographical boundaries of the "developed world." George Manuel, former president of the National Indian Brotherhood and 20 President of the World Council of Indigenous Peoples, has called such

From "We the Dene" by George Erasmus in *Dene Nation: The Colony Within*, ed. Mel Watkins. Reprinted by permission of George Erasmus.

486

domestic colonies the "Fourth World." We the Dene are acutely aware of our colonial relationship with North American society, and are struggling to achieve recognition of our right to be a self-determining people.

4   Long before Europeans decided to look for resources and riches 25 outside of their own boundaries, the Dene nation existed. We had our own way of life, we had our own laws by which we governed ourselves, by which we lived together—laws for educating young people, laws for respecting old people, laws respecting our land. We had our own ways of worship and our own economic system. We had a complete way of life. We ourselves de- 30 cided what was best for us and for our land.

5   The history of a people is the record of the choices they make over time. Before the coming of the Europeans, we the Dene made choices based on our experience. We made our own history. Our actions were based on our understanding of the world.   35

6   With the coming of the Europeans, our experience as a people changed. We experienced relationships in which we were made to feel inferior. We were treated as incompetent to make decisions for ourselves. Europeans would treat us in such a way as to make us feel that they knew, better than we ourselves, what was good for us. Those who presented them- 40 selves as "superior" began to define what was good for us. They began to define our world for us. They began to define us as well. Even physically, our communities and our landmarks were named in terms foreign to our understanding. We were no longer the actors—we were being acted upon. We were no longer naming the world—we were being named. We were 45 named "Indian," we were being called "non-status and status Indians" or "Métis."

7   All of these names were imposed on us. We have always called ourselves "Dene." Simply translated, we defined ourselves as "people," as different from the animals. With the coming of the Europeans, we developed 50 the term "Dene" to mean not only ourselves as a people separate from the animals, but ourselves as separate from the Europeans.

8   Traditionally, we acted; today, we are acted upon. Our history since contact is the record of our struggle to act on our own terms. It is the record of our struggle to decide for ourselves as a people in the face of all 55 the forces which have attempted to decide for us, define us, and act for us.

QUESTIONS

READER AND PURPOSE

1. In an effective beginning the writer clarifies his subject and defines its limitations. Does Erasmus succeed in achieving these ends? Explain your answer by briefly summarizing the main aspects of the author's subject and the limitations he has placed on it. Can you think of other aspects of his subject that he might have chosen to discuss?

2. How does Erasmus engage the reader's attention?

3. How would you describe the tone * he adopts: angry, objective, polemical (i.e. controversial), indignant? Support your answer by citing specific examples. Is his tone consistent throughout?

4. What point of view * does Erasmus employ? Look at the pronouns he uses. What do they tell us about the author's relationship to his material and his audience?

ORGANIZATION

5. Briefly summarize the main point Erasmus makes in each of his paragraphs. Can you explain why he presents his materials in this order? Is it the order of logical discourse? If you think that it is not, how would you describe it?

6. Identify the topic sentence of paragraph 1. How are the other sentences of the paragraph related to the topic? How does Erasmus use repetition to link these three sentences?

7. Does paragraph 2 continue to treat the topic of paragraph 1? Identify the topic sentence before answering. If this paragraph is treating a new topic, can you find a transitional sentence linking it to paragraph 1? Can you find repeated key words that link the two paragraphs? If you can, make a list of them.

8. Does paragraph 4 represent a significant change in the direction of the author's argument? If so, can you identify a signpost * that indicates the change? Are there any transitional devices that link paragraph 4 to the preceding paragraphs?

9. Explain why paragraphs 4-7 constitute a clearly-defined sub-section of Erasmus' opening. What main point is he making in these paragraphs? Can you detect a change in tone here?

10. Does Erasmus' brief concluding paragraph effectively summarize all that has preceded? Look closely at his choice of words before answering. How many of these words have used earlier in the selection? Could this be defined as an example of closing by return *?

11. Do you think that the concluding paragraph clarifies and stresses the importance of the author's subject? How does it combine with the rest of Erasmus' opening to arouse the reader's interest?

SENTENCES

12. Read this selection carefully and note the number of sentences that Erasmus begins with the subject-verb nucleus. Does he vary this pattern often enough to avoid monotony? Or is he choosing this sentence form deliberately? If so, how is it suited to his material? That is, how does it help to create a specific tone?

13. What elements are parallel * in sentences two and three of paragraph 4?

14. In lines 44 and 45 semi-colons could be used instead of dashes. What is the advantage of the dashes?

15. Is the first sentence of paragraph 6 a balanced * sentence?

16. Why does Erasmus use asyndeton * in the last line of paragraph 8? Is this also an example of ellipsis *?

DICTION

17. Look up: *colonial* (2), *rights* (4), *self-determining* (7), *humanizing* (11), *exploitation* (14), *aboriginal* (15-16), *Métis* (47).

18. If the phrase *non-status and status Indians* (46) is unfamiliar to you, look up the entries for "non-treaty" and "non-treaty Indian" in the *Dictionary of Canadianisms*. Erasmus' point might become even clearer if you were to look up, in the same dictionary, the entry for "treaty" and for each of the many compound words that follow this entry.

19. Do you think that Erasmus uses too many abstract * words and phrases—such as *rights, self-determining, colonial relationship, way of life, laws*? Does he attempt in any way to make these terms more concrete *?

20. Does the use of *nations* (15) strike you as odd? Do you ordinarily think of *nations* as existing within *nation-states* (15)? What do you think Erasmus means by this?

21. Erasmus insists on the right of a community to "name" the world it inhabits, and offers as one sinister example of colonialism the renaming of the Dene world in foreign terms. Look up the word *ethnocentrism*, which he might have used to describe this attitude on the part of Europeans. Has Erasmus made you see how language can be misused—can be an instrument of distortion rather than a means of discovery?

POINTS TO LEARN

1. Controversial subjects are best introduced by explaining the nature of the problem.

2. The author of a controversial essay should avoid an overly-emotional tone, even when he is confronting a potentially hostile audience and dealing with a subject that engages his feelings deeply.

3. Repetition of key words in straightforward sentences can be effective in clarifying the limits of a controversial subject.

4. Use of the first-person plural makes clear to the audience that the subject is being presented as something more than personal opinion.

SUGGESTIONS FOR WRITING

1. Imagine that you are writing an essay of about 1500 words on a controversial subject (such as "The Necessity for Censorship," "Why Western Canada Must Learn to Understand Quebec," "Students Need More Discipline," or something along these lines), and that your essay will be read by an audience not disposed to agree with you. Compose an opening of four or five paragraphs in which you state your topic in the first paragraph and indicate its limits. In the following paragraphs explain the importance of your topic and try to engage the attention of your audience. Remember that you are writing an introduction; do not try to cover the whole topic.

IMPROVING YOUR STYLE

In your composition:

1. Make most of your sentences straightforward statements.

2. Repeat the key words of your topic throughout to emphasize their importance.

3. Use parallel constructions and balanced sentences to conclude at least two of your paragraphs.

4. Write a short final paragraph in which, by reusing the key words, you sum up your introduction and indicate the importance of your topic as forcefully as you can.

5. Use the first-person plural throughout, and keep your tone from lapsing into one of excessive emotion.

From Education as Philosophy

Brand Blanshard is an English philosopher. He has taught at universities in both Great Britain and the United States and is the author of numerous books and articles on philosophical topics. He has also published a short but valuable book about writing, *On Philosophical Style* (1954), which will reward the attention of anyone who wishes to write with lucidity and grace, whether about philosophy or any other discipline.

The paragraph reprinted here is the opening of a talk Blanshard delivered to an audience of university educators (later published as an essay). It is worth studying both for the skill with which it achieves the functions of a beginning and for its masterly control of tone. Tone is especially important for the speaker. He stands in the physical presence of those he addresses, and if he is to succeed he has to attract and hold their attention and sympathy. He must not turn them off by awkwardness, arrogance, or a tactless disregard of their feelings. Thus for the speaker tone is all-important, and he has to pay close attention to establishing exactly the right attitudes toward his subject, himself, and his audience. But the speaker's concern with tone is only more immediate than the writer's; it is not essentially different. No more than a speaker can a writer afford to bore or irritate his readers. Observe, then, how Blanshard creates tone in his opening.

There is an immense and justified pride in what our colleges have done. At the same time there is a growing uneasiness about their product. The young men and women who carry away our degrees are a very attractive lot —in looks, in bodily fitness, in kindliness, energy, courage, and buoyancy. But what of their intellectual equipment? That too is in some ways ad- 5 mirable; for in spite of President Lowell's remark that the university should be a repository of great learning, since the freshmen always bring a stock with them and the seniors take little away, the fact is that our graduates

From "Education as Philosophy," *Swarthmore College Bulletin*, XLII, No. 4 (July, 1945). Reprinted by permission of the author.

have every chance to be well informed, and usually are so. Yet the uneasiness persists. When it becomes articulate, it takes the form of wishes that   10
these attractive young products of ours had more intellectual depth and
force, more at-homeness in the world of ideas, more of the firm, clear, quiet
thoughtfulness that is so potent and so needed a guard against besetting
humbug and quackery. The complaint commonly resolves itself into a bill
of three particulars. First, granting that our graduates know a good deal,   15
their knowledge lies about in fragments and never gets welded together into
the stuff of a tempered and mobile mind. Secondly, our university graduates
have been so busy boring holes for themselves, acquiring special knowledge
and skills, that in later life they have astonishingly little in common in the
way of ideas, standards, or principles. Thirdly, it is alleged that the past two   20
decades have revealed a singular want of clarity about the great ends of
living, attachment to which gives significance and direction to a life. Here
are three grave charges against American education, and I want to discuss
them briefly. My argument will be simple, perhaps too simple. What I shall
contend is that there is a great deal of truth in each of them, and that the   25
remedy for each is the same. It is larger infusion of the philosophic habit
of mind.

QUESTIONS

READER AND PURPOSE

1. Is Blanshard's point of view * personal or impersonal? Describe the kind
of reader for whom you think this essay is intended.

ORGANIZATION

2. Supposing that there were no title, how far would a reader have to go in this
opening paragraph before he learned the subject of the essay? How far before
he knew what particular aspects of that subject Blanshard would handle? If
he were alert, our reader could predict from this paragraph the major sections
in the remainder of the essay. How could he? What are these sections? How is
the *order* of these sections made clear? Blanshard does not literally say that
"first I shall discuss this, next that." How do you know, then, what the
organization will be?

3. Blanshard moves from the general to the particular, a common way of
opening, sometimes described as "focusing down." At what point in the paragraph does Blanshard adjust his focus from the general to the particular?

4. On either side of this point the paragraph falls into two roughly equal halves.

Suppose the first had been omitted, and the paragraph had begun: "There are three principal complaints against our colleges. First," continuing with what are now lines 15-27. This would have made a much briefer opening, yet one which told us all we really need to know about the subject and plan of the essay to follow. But this shorter version would not have been as good a beginning. What would it have sacrificed?

5. The idea developed in lines 6-8 ("in spite of . . . little away") is not important to the establishment of the subject or plan of Blanshard's paper. What is the purpose of the allusion to President Lowell's remark?

6. One of the most difficult tasks of the writer is to avoid oversimplification. It is easy to say that something is white or that it is black. Many things, however, are a little of both, and to indicate this complexity without confusing the reader is one hallmark of skilled writing. Blanshard is worth studying in this respect, for while he both praises and criticizes the American university, he does not confuse the reader about which is his chief purpose. He succeeds because he keeps returning to his main point in short, emphatic sentences. How many times in the first eleven lines does he restate the idea that people are growing uneasy about the American college graduate?

7. In the light of the preceding question, show why the following two beginnings are less effective than lines 1-9 of the text:

(a) There is an immense and justified pride in what our colleges have done, and at the same time there is a growing uneasiness about their product. Still the young men and women who carry away our degrees are very attractive, physically fit, kind, energetic, courageous, and buoyant; however their intellectual equipment is limited.

(b) Our colleges have failed.

How does "focusing down" make it easier for a writer to avoid oversimplification?

SENTENCES

8. Study the sentence in lines 17-20. Show that it analyzes a concept in terms of cause and effect, and indicate which part of the sentence defines the cause and which the effect.

9. Why is this rendering of the final three sentences less successful than what Blanshard wrote?

My argument will be simple, perhaps too simple, for I shall contend that there is a great deal of truth in each of them, and that the remedy for each is the same, being a larger infusion of the philosophic habit of mind.

DICTION

10. Look up: *buoyancy* (4), *repository* (7), *articulate* (10), *alleged* (20), *singular* (21), *contend* (25).

11. Explain in your own words what Blanshard means by these phrases: *besetting humbug and quackery* (14), *a tempered and mobile mind* (17), *the philosophic habit of mind* (26).

12. Look up *infusion* (26). What does this word suggest about the writer's attitude toward college education? What does it suggest about his tone *? Is he amused by the deficiencies of our graduates? Shocked and angered by the failure of higher education? Or is Blanshard's tone neither of these extremes?

POINTS TO LEARN

1. It is wise, especially in essays handling complicated, abstract * topics, to indicate something about the general plan in the very beginning.

2. "Focusing down" is a common, and advantageous, method of opening.

3. Unless the audience you are writing for is a very special one, you cannot take its interest for granted.

4. It requires constant attention to handle complex ideas honestly and clearly.

5. The proper tone is essential to effective writing, and it must be established in the beginning paragraphs.

SUGGESTIONS FOR WRITING

Write one paragraph, about as long as Blanchard's, designed to open a theme on a complex and controversial topic. Make your subject clear as quickly as possible, but begin broadly, suggesting its complexities. As you proceed, focus down, indicating the general plan and concluding with a sentence that places you in a position to step easily into the body of your essay.

IMPROVING YOUR STYLE

Before you begin your composition explain in several sentences the tone you want to achieve—that is, how you feel about your subject, how you want your readers to think of you, and how you regard them.

After you have finished, discuss in two or three sentences how you achieved the tone you aimed at, citing specific words and sentence patterns.

A Fable for Tomorrow

Rachel Carson (1907-64) was an American scientist and writer. She is best known for her popular books about oceanography, *Under the Sea Wind* (1941) and *The Sea Around Us* (1951), and for *Silent Spring* (1962), which fired one of the first shots in what has come to be called the environmental movement. The book discusses the pollution resulting from the massive and indiscriminate use of fertilizers and pesticides, a problem which most Americans were ignorant of until Carson's warning. The following paragraphs are the opening of *Silent Spring*.

1   There was once a town in the heart of America where all life seemed to live in harmony with its surroundings. The town lay in the midst of a checkerboard of prosperous farms, with fields of grain and hillsides of orchards where, in spring, white clouds of bloom drifted above the green fields. In autumn, oak and maple and birch set up a blaze of colour that 5 flamed and flickered across a backdrop of pines. Then foxes barked in the hills and deer silently crossed the fields, half hidden in the mists of the autumn mornings.

2   Along the roads, laurel, viburnum and alder, great ferns and wildflowers delighted the traveller's eye through much of the year. Even in winter 10 ter the roadsides were places of beauty, where countless birds came to feed on the berries and on the seed heads of the dried weeds rising above the snow. The countryside was, in fact, famous for the abundance and variety of its bird life, and when the flood of migrants was pouring through in spring and autumn people travelled from great distances to observe them. 15 Others came to fish the streams, which flowed clear and cold out of the hills and contained shady pools where trout lay. So it had been from the days many years ago when the first settlers raised their houses, sank their wells, and built their barns.

From *Silent Spring* by Rachel Carson. Copyright © 1962 by Rachel L. Carson. Reprinted by permission of the Houghton Mifflin Company.

3   Then a strange blight crept over the area and everything began to change. Some evil spell had settled on the community: mysterious maladies swept the flocks of chickens; the cattle and sheep sickened and died. Everywhere was a shadow of death. The farmers spoke of much illness among their families. In the town the doctors had become more and more puzzled by new kinds of sickness appearing among their patients. There had been several sudden and unexplained deaths, not only among adults but even among children, who would be stricken suddenly while at play and die within a few hours.

4   There was a strange stillness. The birds, for example—where had they gone? Many people spoke of them, puzzled and disturbed. The feeding stations in the backyards were deserted. The few birds seen anywhere were moribund; they trembled violently and could not fly. It was a spring without voices. On the mornings that had once throbbed with the dawn chorus of robins, catbirds, doves, jays, wrens, and scores of other bird voices there was now no sound; only silence lay over the fields and woods and marsh.

5   On the farms the hens brooded, but no chicks hatched. The farmers complained that they were unable to raise any pigs—the litters were small and the young survived only a few days. The apple trees were coming into bloom but no bees droned among the blossoms, so there was no pollination and there would be no fruit.

6   The roadsides, once so attractive, were now lined with browned and withered vegetation as though swept by fire. These, too, were silent, deserted by all living things. Even the streams were now lifeless. Anglers no longer visited them, for all the fish had died.

7   In the gutters under the eaves and between the shingles of the roofs, a white granular powder still showed a few patches; some weeks before it had fallen like snow upon the roofs and the lawns, the fields and streams.

8   No witchcraft, no enemy action had silenced the rebirth of new life in this stricken world. The people had done it themselves.

9   This town does not actually exist, but it might easily have a thousand counterparts in America or elsewhere in the world. I know of no community that has experienced all the misfortunes I describe. Yet every one of these disasters has actually happened somewhere, and many real communities have already suffered a substantial number of them. A grim spectre has crept upon us almost unnoticed, and this imagined tragedy may easily become a stark reality we all shall know.

10   What has already silenced the voices of spring in countless towns in America? This book is an attempt to explain.

QUESTIONS

1. Would you judge from this opening that Carson's purpose was simply to inform her readers of the problem, or to do more than inform? Do you think her beginning is adequate to her purpose? Why or why not?
2. Unlike the other beginnings we have studied, this one does not actually identify the subject. Is that a fault, or is it a deliberate and useful strategy?
3. Carson's book was criticized by spokesmen for the chemical industry as "alarmist." Could it be fairly argued that these opening paragraphs are misleading and trick the reader into taking an imaginary disaster for a real one?

4. Paragraphs 1-8 fall into two parts: at what point? What word marks the shift of focus?
5. Analyze the unity of paragraph 1, showing how each sentence after the first is linked to the preceding statement.
6. What is the topic sentence of the fourth paragraph? Indicate the key term in that sentence and the words which echo it later in the paragraph.
7. Paragraphs 4, 5, and 6 all begin in much the same manner. What is the virtue of such similarity?
8. What is the purpose of the extra spacing between paragraphs 8 and 9?

9. Point out the parallel * constructions in the sentence in lines 17-19.
10. What does the colon in line 21 signal to us about how the following construction will be related to what has just been said? Why does the writer use a semicolon in line 22 instead of a comma?
11. Explain how these revisions change the emphasis or meaning of Carson's sentences and whether you think them an improvement:

(a) *Revision*: In the heart of America a town once existed where all life seemed to live in harmony with its surroundings.
    Carson: "There was once a town in the heart of America where all life seemed to live in harmony with its surroundings." (1-2)
(b) *Revision*: On the farms no chicks hatched, but the hens brooded.
    Carson: "On the farms the hens brooded, but no chicks hatched."
    (36)

(c) *Revision:* This book is an attempt to explain what has already silenced the voices of spring in countless towns in America.
Carson: "What has already silenced the voices of spring in countless towns in America? This book is an attempt to explain." (58-59)

DICTION

12. Look up: *harmony* (2), *migrants* (14), *blight* (20), *maladies* (21), *moribund* (32), *litters* (37), *pollination* (39), *granular* (46), *spectre* (55), *stark* (57).
13. Why does Carson call her account a *fable?*
14. Which subsequent words in the third paragraph pick up the idea of *blight* (20)? Which echo the idea of *now* (41) in paragraph 6?
15. Study the diction of the first two paragraphs and indicate the words which reinforce the concept of a pure, undefiled nature.

POINTS TO LEARN

1. Occasionally it is good strategy not to identify the subject, but to create a mystery and thereby to arouse the reader's curiosity.
2. A focused and coherent paragraph will often echo in subsequent sentences the key idea expressed in its topic statement.

SUGGESTIONS FOR WRITING

1. Attempt a beginning of several paragraphs modeled on Carson's dealing with some such topic as "A Fable for Teachers" or "A Fable for Students" or "A Fable for Parents."
2. In a paragraph or two discuss more fully the point raised in question 3—whether Carson has deliberately attempted here to mislead her readers.

IMPROVING YOUR STYLE

1. In your composition include two or three sentences using parallel constructions.
2. Use a colon following a general assertion to introduce a series of specific instances.
3. In one passage repeat a key idea in different words as Carson repeats the concept of blight in her third paragraph.

From "George Brown, Sir John Macdonald, and the 'Workingman' "

Donald Creighton (1902-79) was, for much of his life, the premier historian of English-speaking Canada. He combined the talents of a scholar and researcher, a vigorous and formidable controversialist, and a writer of fluent and dramatic prose. His abilities won the respect even of his opponents. Among his books were the Governor General's Award-winning two-volume biography *Sir John A. Macdonald* (1952 and 1955), *Dominion of the North* (1944), *The Road to Confederation* (1964), and *Canada's First Century* (1970). *Towards the Discovery of Canada* (1972) is a selection of his essays and speeches. The opening paragraph below exhibits Creighton's mastery of style and purpose, his subtle wit, and his eye for telling detail.

1   On the north side of King Street, Toronto, a short distance east from Yonge, there stood in 1872 the offices of the Globe Printing Company. It was the sixth building which had been occupied by the *Globe* since its establishment back in 1844; and the solid opulence of its construction reflected the prosperity, the popularity, and the enormous influence 5 which the newspaper had gradually come to enjoy. Built of white brick, faced with imported stone, and lighted by the tall, narrow windows which were characteristic of the period, the building provided the ample accommodation of three spacious storeys.[1] The first floor was occupied by the counting house and the big printing presses; the third was taken up with 10 editorial offices and newsrooms; and in between, occupying the whole front of the second storey and overlooking the noisy activity of King Street, was the editorial sanctum of the proprietor and editor, George Brown. Here was the source and centre of Brown's authority and influence. Here, for the last fifteen years of his life, he did his best work as critic, promoter, and 15 crusader; and here also, at half past four on the afternoon of March 25,

[1] J. Timperlake, *Illustrated Toronto, Past and Present* (Toronto, 1877).

From *Towards the Discovery of Canada* by Donald Creighton, reprinted by permission of Macmillan of Canada, a Division of Gage Publishing Limited.

1880, George Bennett, the employee discharged for "intemperance", fired the shot that brought an end to the dynamic and assertive labours of the journalist's career.   20

QUESTIONS

READER AND PURPOSE

1. Creighton's argument in the essay as a whole is that Prime Minister Sir John A. Macdonald was much more the friend of the "workingman" than Brown was. How does this opening paragraph serve as an effective introduction to such an essay?
2. How has Creighton engaged the reader's interest? By stressing the importance of the subject? In any other ways?
3. Would you agree that Creighton's tone * is objective? How is his point of view * related to his tone?
4. What sort of audience do you think that Creighton is writing for?

ORGANIZATION

5. This introduction consists of a single paragraph. In what order are the details of the paragraph presented? Spatially? Temporally? In terms of cause and effect? In some combination of these?
6. What function does the first sentence serve? Where is the observer when he describes the *Globe* building in sentences two and three?
7. How has his vantage point shifted in sentence four? What links sentence four to sentence one?
8. What is Creighton leading up to in sentence four?
9. What purpose does sentence five have? Does it or any of the preceding sentences hint at what is described in sentence six?
10. How does the order of presentation in the first five sentences make the climactic event described in sentence six come as a shock and a surprise to the reader? How does Creighton's tone assist in achieving this effect?

SENTENCES

11. Identify the absolute * construction in sentence one. Is this a periodic * sentence? Is sentence three?
12. Point out the parallel * construction in sentence two. Why does Creighton use polysyndeton * in this sentence? And in sentence three?
13. What purpose is served by the interrupting phrases * in the third clause of sentence four?
14. Why is sentence four not an example of a tricolon *?
15. How does sentence five obviously differ from all the other sentences in the

paragraph? Why did Creighton not join it to the next sentence with a semi-colon, as he frequently does elsewhere in the paragraph?

16. Why does Creighton employ interrupting phrases in the second clause of sentence six? Would the sentence and its effect be weakened if the phrases were removed?

17. Is Creighton using understatement * in describing the death of Brown? Explain your answer.

18. The author makes considerable use of concrete * detail in several of his sentences. Make a list of these details and try to decide what purpose they serve in this introductory paragraph.

DICTION

19. Look up: *opulence* (4), *faced* (7), *counting house* (11), *sanctum* (14), *promoter* (16), *crusader* (17), *dynamic* (19).

20. Do the words *critic, promoter,* and *crusader* convey anything other than favorable connotations *?

21. Would you describe Creighton's diction as formal or informal? Make a list of words to support your answer.

POINTS TO LEARN

1. One way of capturing the reader's interest is to lead him, unobtrusively, up to a surprising or unexpected climax at the end of the opening paragraph.

2. A neutral or objective tone, formal diction, and understatement can make an unexpected climax even more effective.

3. Setting a shocking event in the concrete detail of a real world is one method of emphasizing its abnormal character.

4. Frequent use of commas, semi-colons, and interrupting or descriptive phrases slows the pace of a paragraph and stresses its conclusion.

SUGGESTIONS FOR WRITING

Compose an opening paragraph on a subject of your own choosing. Delay the climactic point of your paragraph until the final sentence (and as close to the end of the sentence as possible). Carefully control your tone throughout the paragraph, and—without hinting at it—lead your reader up to an unexpected event.

IMPROVING YOUR STYLE

In your paragraph include:

1. A consistent level of diction, appropriate to your subject.

2. Frequent internal punctuation; interrupting and descriptive phrases.

3. Specific concrete details.

ROBERT CHODOS and DRUMMOND BURGESS

Ma Bell Joins the Jet Set

Robert Chodos and Drummond Burgess are business writers. Their original
version of this article on the Bell Telephone Company appeared in the magazine *Last Post*. Chodos has also published an unflattering history of the Canadian Pacific Railroad, as well as a chronicle of four crucial years—1968 to 1972—
in the history of the province of Quebec. Their article on the Bell Company
is in the best tradition of "muckraking"; that is, it seeks the truth behind the
facade, even though the truth is often highly uncomplimentary.

1 The grey, nondescript, vaguely modern head office of Northern
Electric on Montreal's Dorchester Boulevard is a strange venue for American wheeler-dealer John Cunningham Lobb. Pushed off to the periphery of
the city's downtown business core, the building seems to symbolize a company that is staid, old-fashioned and far removed from the centre of action 5
in the skyscrapers a few blocks down the street. And the symbolism was
apt for the old, paternalistic Bell Canada subsidiary in the summer of 1971.
2 So when John Lobb was moved in to administer the company as
president in June of that year, everyone knew that Bell Canada wanted
something to happen. Northern's executives began to worry about their 10
jobs and nervously assured themselves they had done all they could; financial analysts began to speculate about a company whose existence had
scarcely seemed worthy of their time; the business pages of the newspapers
suddenly found space for interviews and thinkpieces.
3 For the new American boss had quite a record. As executive vice- 15
president of the multinational conglomerate International Telephone and
Telegraph, he had worked closely with ITT chief Harold Geneen, a man
not given to letting anyone, even governments foreign or domestic, stand in

From *Let Us Prey* edited by Robert Chodos and Rae Murphy (James Lorimer & Company Ltd., Publishers, 1974). Reprinted by permission.

the way of his takeovers. Lobb had also plied his trade with Chicago financier J. Patrick Lannan, with California's Norton Simon, who owns Hunt's 20 Foods and Canada Dry, with the Crucible Steel division of Colt Industries, and with the arcane world of Wall Street investment banking.

4   Northern's nervous managers did not have long to wait. Within days of moving in, Lobb ordered all Northern divisions to switch to the standing orders he had used at ITT and elsewhere. In booklet form, and 25 titled "Increase Profits by Cutting Sales", the orders were simple—but bad news for executives trained to think in terms of service, tradition and job protection down the line.

5   As Lobb explained in his covering letter, "at Crucible Steel we reduced the grades of tool steel from 108 to 34 over a two-year period. Sales 30 in that division dropped 18 per cent. But because we were so much more efficient, profits increased 15 per cent . . . After two years we were able to cut prices and get 20 per cent *more* of the total market at a larger profit—because of efficiency. Obviously Northern can do the same as ITT's telecommunications division—increase profits by eliminating unprofitable 35 sales."

6   The idea, Lobb explained, had worked for ITT in 32 nations and 183 divisions.

7   Much of this was to be accomplished by cutting out products, closing assembly lines, selling factories and getting rid of inventory. But the 40 booklet pointedly noted that this also meant getting rid of people. "Overhead is caused by people, who tend to multiply faster as profits drop. Production cutbacks must be accompanied by lay-offs at every level." It emphasized that "until management makes it emphatically clear that we are in business only to make a profit, no action will result." And it goes on to 45 say that "under the threat of closing plants down, or at least substantial layoffs, we get the drive needed for the future. And usually from within the division itself we can find people who can carry out the program. I believe adversity is healthy because it forces action not taken in good times."

8   The booklet is as near to being a bible of pure capitalism as one is 50 likely to find these days, and Lobb expresses amazement that over the past 20 years he has found so much fuzzy thinking on this subject in his travels through the industrialized world. But there had been no fuzzy thinking at ITT, there had been no fuzzy thinking at Crucible Steel, and there was going to be no more fuzzy thinking at Northern Electric or the axe was 55 going to swing, at manager and worker alike. (At least one top Northern executive would have no trouble adjusting to the ways of ITT, for Ewart

Orville Bridges, who had been executive vice-president for ITT Latin America Inc. and vice-president of ITT Telecommunications, had already signed on at Northern by the time Lobb moved into the executive suite.)   60

QUESTIONS

READER AND PURPOSE

1. After you read the first two paragraphs of this selection, did you want to go on? Why or why not?

2. These eight paragraphs introduce a 17-page essay. Are they effective as a beginning? Why or why not? In your discussion here, don't be afraid to take into account your own personal likes and dislikes.

3. How do the authors attempt to engage the reader's interest? Do they use any of the four techniques mentioned in the introduction to this section: stressing the importance of the subject; puzzling the reader; using such devices as rhetorical questions, anecdotes, allusions, and quotations; and beginning with a commonplace remark?

4. Do you think this selection would appeal more to an American audience than to a Canadian one? Do the authors make use of the reader's sympathy towards the underdog?

5. Would you say that the authors are critical of Lobb? How do you know?

6. Look closely at the last sentence of paragraph 4. The words *service* and *tradition* have good connotations, but the expression *job protection down the line* is a combination of jargon and cliché. Does such a combination in the same sentence indicate a somewhat ambivalent attitude on the part of the authors?

ORGANIZATION

7. The authors establish a contrast in paragraph 1: on the one hand we have the expressions *grey, nondescript, vaguely modern* (1), *staid, old-fashioned* (5), and *old, paternalistic* (7); on the other hand, *wheeler-dealer* (3) and *centre of action* (5). What is the effect of this contrast? To what extent (if at all) is it used in the rest of the selection?

8. *So* (8) and *for* (15) are obviously transitions, but how do they differ in joining paragraphs 1 and 2 and 2 and 3?

9. How does the expression "did not have long to wait" (23) serve as both transition and signpost *?

10. Why does paragraph 6 consist of only one short sentence? What effect (or effects) is achieved by such a paragraph that would not be achieved by a conventionally longer one?

11. The authors quote four times from John Lobb's booklet, "Increase Profits by Cutting Sales." How do they introduce these quotations? Does there appear to be a pattern in their manner of introducing them?

12. The authors use the phrase *fuzzy thinking* four times in paragraph 8. Is this irony *? Or do you think this repetition is too strong for irony?

SENTENCES

13. What effect is achieved by the dash in l. 26? Would this effect be increased, decreased, or lost by using a comma instead?

14. Why do the authors use asyndeton * in l. 1 but polysyndeton * in l. 5?

15. Comment on the structure of the sentence beginning in l. 10.

16. Do you think that the sentence beginning in l. 53 is an effective example of parallel * structure? Would the rhythm of this sentence be improved by the addition of a comma in l. 55?

DICTION

17. Look up: *nondescript* (1), *venue* (2), *periphery* (3), *staid* (5), *paternalistic* (7), *subsidiary* (7), *speculate* (12), *conglomerate* (16), *arcane* (22), *standing* (25), *inventory* (40), *overhead* (41-42), *adversity* (49).

18. Do you believe that the word *thinkpieces* (14) is appropriate to the tone * of paragraphs 1 and 2? To the tone of the entire selection? Of what relevance here is the title?

19. Do the authors use any colloquialisms *? List those words you think are colloquial and be prepared to explain the meaning of each one. Use a recent dictionary, such as the *Compact Dictionary of Canadian English*, or a specialized one, such as Eric Partridge's *Dictionary of Slang and Unconventional English*.

20. What does the pronoun *this* (39) refer to? Although even quite formal English uses pronouns to refer to general antecedents, the reference must be unmistakably clear. Is that the case here?

21. Why is *bible* (50) not capitalized? Should it be? Does its not being capitalized have anything to do with the tone of the selection?

22. Do you think the expressions *bad news* (26-27) and *the axe was going to swing* (55-56) are metaphors? Or are they the kinds of clichés (dead, overworked expressions) you might expect to hear from an unimaginative businessman?

POINTS TO LEARN

1. A word or phrase can serve effectively as both transition and signpost.

2. A short paragraph, even if it consists of only one brief sentence, can function well as either summary or contrast.

3. The tone of an essay can be deliberately changed by the careful use of colloquialisms.

SUGGESTIONS FOR WRITING

Choose as your subject a person who is unconventional, who does not always act or think in accepted ways, who does not mind upsetting the ordinary routine: a labour leader who sympathizes with strike breakers, a student-body president who revolts against the administration, a bank clerk who fights for nude bathing at the local beach, a minister who preaches against censorship, a politician who criticizes his own party, a waitress who writes a letter to the editor condemning the restaurant where she works—etc. Then, keeping in mind the four different ways of engaging the reader's interest, write the introductory paragraph to your essay twice, each time using one of these different ways.

IMPROVING YOUR STYLE

In your two introductions:
1. Use sufficient colloquial language to impart a definite tone.
2. Use polysyndeton and asyndeton at least once.

Closings

GEORGE WOODCOCK

From Gabriel Dumont

George Woodcock describes himself as a "man of letters" rather than a scholar or a journalist. However he is described, there is no question that Woodcock has been for the past thirty years one of Canada's most prolific writers. He is the author of more than forty books, books that reflect his cosmopolitan range of interests—biographies, histories, works of literary criticism, political commentaries, travel books, and his own poetry. In addition, he has been a frequent contributor to Canadian, American, and English periodicals. While teaching at the University of British Columbia, Woodcock founded *Canadian Literature* (the first literary journal in Canada devoted solely to the study of Canadian writing), which he edited from its inception in 1959 until 1977. Woodcock is especially interested in the art of biography, and his work in this genre has been much praised; in 1966 he received a Governor General's Award for *The Crystal Spirit: A Study of George Orwell*. Here, in the concluding paragraphs of *Gabriel Dumont*, Woodcock reveals his sympathetic insight into his subject as he describes the pathos and the irony of Dumont's last years, and at the same time draws together, in rhythmically effective prose, the main themes of the book as a whole.

1   The years passed, and now they were uneventful, for Gabriel was no longer a man to whom his fellows called for leadership, though sometimes they asked his advice, nor did he wish to lead them. He withdrew into the rhythms of the hunting years, doing a little trading, catching his own meat and fish, and always pleased when he had a few skins to sell at 5 one of the stores in Batoche or Duck Lake. On feast days he would put on a suit, and wear, as insignia of a heroic past, the gold watch from Massachusetts and the Silver medal from New York. He thought of that past without guilt and without rancour, glorying in his own deeds as Homer's

From George Woodcock, *Gabriel Dumont: The Métis Chief and His Lost World.* Reprinted by permission of Hurtig Publishers.

heroes must have done, yet sad always for that vanished primitive world to 10
which he had been so superbly adapted.

2   He never experienced sickness or felt the grip of decay. Just before
his death, he went on a hunting trip to Basin Lake, in the hills a few miles
east of Batoche. It was mid-May, the hunt was successful, and he enjoyed
the bright spring weather, the opening flowers, the flights of migrant birds. 15
When he came back, he complained to Alexis of pains in his chest and
arms, but as he seemed otherwise in perfect health they decided he had
merely strained his muscles. For the next few days he went about in his
usual way, doing a little fishing and a little walking, and talking to the
friends he met by the roadside. On Saturday, 19 May 1906, he went again 20
for a walk. When he returned, he went into Alexis's house and asked for
a bowl of soup. He sat down, ate a few mouthfuls, and then, without speaking, he walked across to a bed in the room and crumpled onto it. His
death was like the flash of his gun, sudden, accurate and—since one must
die—merciful.   25

3   When Gabriel Dumont died, the world did not think of him because the world did not know. He and the cause he fought for, and the
way of life he personified, had so faded out of memory that only the little
local newspapers in Battleford and Prince Albert noticed his death and his
funeral. The papers of Toronto and Winnipeg and Montreal, that once 30
had spoken of him with the kind of fearful admiration Milton reserved for
Satan, did not even remark his passing. But when he was buried in the
cemetery on the top of the hill at Batoche, where the dead men of the
rebellion were already lying under the great stark cross, the Métis from all
the settlements around came riding in, and the Cree tramped from Beardy's 35
and One Arrow's reserves to crowd into the little wooden church, scarred
with the bullet marks of Lieutenant Howard's Gatling, where Father
Moulin, his white beard hanging almost to his waist, conducted the service; then the young men of the Dumont clan carried Gabriel to his grave,
on the crest overlooking the point on the river where, twenty-one years ago 40
to within a few days, the *Northcote* came whistling round the bend to
open the battle of Batoche that marked the death of the Métis nation.

QUESTIONS

READER AND PURPOSE

1. Woodcock is clearly sympathetic to Dumont and his cause. How does the
tone * of these concluding paragraphs indicate this feeling?

2. Why do you think Woodcock has spent so little time on the actual circumstances of Dumont's death? Keep in mind that the book is largely concerned
with Dumont's role in the Métis rebellion of 1885 and his relationship with
Louis Riel, the Métis leader.

3. By pointing out, in the first paragraph, that Dumont sold his skins at stores
in Batoche and Duck Lake, Woodcock also recalls for the reader the important
battles that had occurred at these places. What is the irony * here? How is
this point related to the author's mention of the steamboat in the last sentence
of this selection?

ORGANIZATION

4. Is the first sentence a good introduction for this selection? Why or why not?

5. To what extent is the first sentence a brief summary of what follows?

6. The phrase *the years passed* (1)—akin to a pointer *—hints that Woodcock's
book is nearing the end. List the other phrases or words of this sort and explain
how these expressions indicate that these are the concluding paragraphs of the
book.

7. Which of the four closing techniques explained on pp. 403-07 does Woodcock use? Explain.

8. Summarize briefly the purpose of each paragraph, showing what part each
one plays in the development of Woodcock's conclusion.

9. Is the first sentence of paragraph 2 a completely logical topic sentence?
Examine the rest of the paragraph closely in relation to the first sentence.

10. The last paragraph has two parts, with the second part being introduced
by a contrasting word. Analyze the unity of this paragraph, showing how each
sentence after the first is related to the one preceding it as either development
or contrast.

SENTENCES

11. Compare the movement and rhythm of the last sentence with those of the
other three sentences in the final paragraph.

12. The author's mention of *rhythm* (4) is a hint that perhaps his sentences
try to reflect the rhythms he is referring to. Is this true of any of the sentences
in paragraph 1?

13. The elements of the first sentence are linked by the words *and* (1), *for*
(1), *though* (2), and *nor* (3). How are the elements of the final sentence of
this selection joined?

14. What type of sentence is the last one: parallel? cumulative? periodic?
some other type?

15. Why does the last sentence make an effective conclusion?

DICTION

16. Look up: *uneventful* (1), *insignia* (7), *rancour* (9), *primitive* (10), *personified* (28), *stark* (34), *Gatling* (37).

17. In an encyclopaedia or a handbook to literature, find out what is meant by the references to Homer (9) and Milton and Satan (31-32). How does this knowledge help further your understanding of this selection?

18. The small number of words you are asked to look up (question 16) from this selection, far fewer than from almost any other selection in this text, suggests that Woodcock's vocabulary is unusually plain. Do you think there is any relation between this point and the author's subject? To take the point one step further, does Woodcock use many figures of speech? Do the figures of speech (if there are any) reinforce this general impression of plainness?

POINTS TO LEARN

1. Tone indicates the writer's attitude towards his subject.
2. The rhythm of a sentence can reflect the idea being expressed.
3. The slow, rhythmic, balanced movement of a long concluding sentence can help emphasize the writer's tone.

SUGGESTIONS FOR WRITING

In the assignment concerning the selection by Robert Chodos and Drummond Burgess, "Ma Bell Joins the Jet Set" (p. 502), you were asked to write the introductory paragraph for an essay on one of the kinds of topics suggested. Now you will write the concluding paragraph for the same essay. Write the paragraph twice, each time using one of the four techniques for ending (see pp. 481-5). Do not, however, use the colloquial tone required in the previous assignment.

IMPROVING YOUR STYLE

In your paragraph include:
1. At least two sentences in which the rhythm is emphasized.
2. A dividing point marked by a word of contrast.

CARL BERGER

William Morton

Carl Berger is a professor of history at the University of Toronto. His innovative studies of the movement and influence of ideas in Canada have been received with widespread approval. Berger has written *The Sense of Power* (1970) and *The Writing of Canadian History* (1976), the latter winning the Governor General's Award for non-fiction. It is from this book that his concluding paragraph on William Morton is taken. The paragraph demonstrates how a complex exposition and analysis may be economically summed up by an effective closing.

1   There is finally one further pattern that revealed itself in Morton's intellectual development. He described restrospectively a dichotomy between the late-Victorian British milieu and the literary romanticism to which he was exposed and the landscape of the West that he struggled to come to terms with and express. In some respects his observations parallel 5 those of another western writer, Wallace Stegner, who diagnosed, perhaps in words too strong to apply with complete fidelity to Morton, a curious kind of intellectual schizophrenia that was produced by being brought up on a frontier—a place that had not been mentally assimilated and therefore had no history. "The lateness of my frontier," Stegner wrote, "and the fact 10 that it lay in Canada intensified the discrepancy between that part of me which reflects the folk culture and that part which reflects an education imported and often irrelevant. The dichotomy between American and European that exists to some extent in all of us exists most drastically in people reared on frontiers, for frontiers provide not only the rawest forms 15 of deculturation, but the most slavish respect for borrowed elegances." In his best work Morton managed to bring these twin poles of reference into creative equipoise. But Stegner's remark may explain the curious blending

From "William Morton: The Delicate Balance of Region and Nation", in *The Writing of Canadian History* by Carl Berger. Reprinted by permission of the publisher, Oxford University Press.

in Morton's outlook of an intense attachment to an agricultural region defined as pragmatic, experimental, and democratic on the one hand, and his   20
romanticism and his allegiances to the monarchical tradition and Anglo-
Canadian toryism on the other.

QUESTIONS

READER AND PURPOSE

1. In his essay Professor Berger has been examining the influences that formed
the mind, and the approach to his subject, of a distinguished Canadian historian. His concluding paragraph has two purposes: to sum up his argument,
and to do so by considering one additional—and very important—pattern of
Morton's thought. This combination of a summary, and a final comprehensive
point of the main argument, can make a concluding paragraph very effective.
Can you explain why? For example, does it clearly indicate to the reader that
the essay is finished? Is it more or less economical than other kinds of
conclusions?
2. How would you describe Berger's tone *? List some specific words and sentence structures in support of your answer.
3. On the basis of your answer to the previous question, describe the kind of
audience you think Berger is writing for. Would you include yourself as part
of it?

ORGANIZATION

4. What word in the first sentence signals to the reader that this is Professor
Berger's concluding paragraph? What phrase in this sentence also indicates
that he has a final point to make? In what sentence does he make the point?
5. Do you think that Berger explains satisfactorily, in sentence three, why he
chooses to quote Wallace Stegner as a way of clarifying Morton's thought?
Does he use any qualifying * phrases in introducing the quotation from Stegner?
6. Do Stegner's words in sentences four and five add anything to what Berger
has already said in sentence three? If you think not, can you justify the inclusion of the quotation? Look carefully at sentences six and seven before answering. Has the example taken from Stegner prepared us for these two sentences
in which Morton's creative achievement, and the "curious blending" of his
outlook, are asserted by Berger as the concluding points of his paragraph?
7. The final sentence of a conclusion is often short, as is Berger's sixth sentence. Why does Berger choose to end with sentence seven? Could the sentences be reversed in order? Can you find a connective * that the author uses
to make it clear that the existing order is deliberately chosen?

8. What words in sentence seven return us to the point made in sentence two? How does Berger's method of closing give the reader a sense of completeness appropriate to a conclusion? Can you now describe some of the advantages of combining the conclusion with the last major point of an essay?

SENTENCES

9. Does Berger make use of simple * sentences anywhere in this paragraph, including the quotation from Stegner? Can you explain why simple sentences would not have been appropriate in this paragraph? What would result if we rewrote sentence two as a series of simple sentences?

> He described retrospectively a dichotomy. On the one hand there was his exposure to a late-Victorian British milieu and literary romanticism. On the other there was the western landscape. He struggled to come to terms with this landscape.

Describe what has happened to the flow * and the rhythm * of Berger's sentence. What has been lost in terms of emphasis? Try rewriting the final sentence in the same way, and then answer the same questions. Also decide whether the rewritten sentences constitute a conclusion as effective as Berger's.

10. Is sentence two an example of parallel * construction? Why does Berger use no comma after "exposed"?

11. Is sentence three a periodic * sentence? List the interrupting phrases *. Is "place" an appositive? (Remember that appositives are efficient ways of expanding and clarifying ideas.) Why does Berger use a dash after "frontier"?

12. Berger and Stegner both say the frontiers have "no history." If we were to compare their attitudes with those of Georges Erasmus (p. 486) would Berger's argument be weakened?

13. Is sentence four an example of parallel construction?

14. How would you describe the structure of sentence six?

15. Is sentence seven a periodic sentence?

DICTION

16. Look up: *retrospectively* (2), *milieu* (3), *curious* (18), *deculturation* (16), *equipoise* (18), *pragmatic* (20), *romanticism* (3), *toryism* (22).

17. Look up the etymologies * of *dichotomy* (2) and *schizophrenia* (8).

18. Would you describe Berger's diction as abstract * or concrete *?

19. Does the diction of the quotation from Stegner clash in any way with Berger's characteristic diction?

POINTS TO LEARN

1. The final paragraph must make it clear to the reader that "this is the end."

2. Signal words such as "finally," "and so," and "thus" are one way of doing this.

3. Another is to slow down and emphasize the rhythms of the final sentence or sentences.

4. Combining the final point of an essay with the conclusion can be an economical way of ending, particularly in undergraduate essays that are too short to require concluding summaries.

5. An illustrative quotation can be effective in making a conclusion clearer.

6. A concluding paragraph that ends by expanding or restating a point made in its beginning produces a convincing effect of completeness.

7. The tone of a concluding paragraph should be consistent.

SUGGESTIONS FOR WRITING

1. Go back to the selection by Morton (p. 265) and find in it as many of the characteristics of his thought described by Berger as you can. Also note which ones are missing, if any. Now imagine that you are writing the concluding paragraph of a critique of Berger's view of Morton. Adopt a consistent tone and point of view, but do not attempt to imitate the styles of either Berger or Morton. Use as many devices as you can to signal to the reader that "this is the end." (Remember, in writing your paragraph, that the selection from Morton is only a small part of his work; beware of unwarranted generalizations.)

2. Choose a person about whom you know a great deal, someone you admire (a friend, family member, public figure, sports star, etc.). Write the concluding paragraph of an essay in which you have described this person's character and accomplishments. Do not write a summary of your essay, and bear in mind that even admirable people have some flaws, idiosyncrasies, and inconsistencies of behaviour.

IMPROVING YOUR STYLE

In both compositions:

1. Use a signal word or phrase of closing.

2. Pay special attention to the form of your final sentence (long and slow, or short and emphatic).

3. Make your concluding paragraph one that also treats the final point of your essay.

4. If you choose to adopt a formal style, write two periodic sentences and two that employ parallel constructions.

5. If you can find one, use a relevant quotation to clarify your point.

6. Try to end your paragraph by returning to a point you have made at the beginning.

The Feminist Revolution

Born in Halifax, Lin Green was a student at Sir George Williams University, and a part-time secretary, when she wrote the essay from which this selection comes. Her topic is one that often generates more heat than light, especially from writers (of either sex) who approach it with an inflexible thesis and a vocabulary better suited to altercation than argument. Green's concluding paragraphs show how persuasive techniques can be combined with those of argument, while at the same time signaling to the reader that the essay is drawing to a close.

1   "Vive la différence," say the French. Right. Without differences, life would be unbearable. We would exist in a vacuous no man's land of total equality. But there is a fine distinction to be made between differences of reason and differences of absurdity. Those of absurdity include many isms: racism, despotism, chauvinism, and sexism. What is valid and 5 important is individual difference; the knowledge that every human being is unique. Notwithstanding the fact that they have been for so long, human beings cannot be categorically labelled and shelved like so many jam preserves in society's cupboard.

2   Much has been written, to date, of the social restrictions placed 10 upon women, and of the effects of such restrictions. This, of course, is what Women's Liberation is all about. Not nearly as much has been said concerning the effects of society's restricting influences upon men. In any given society, male conditioning is the antithesis of whatever conditioning is inflicted upon the females of that society. Where females are not valued 15 as a useful and constructive social force, the entire onus is heaved upon the males to create and maintain their society. In other words, where the burden of repression is placed on the female, the burden of responsibility

is placed upon the male. Such responsibility cannot be undertaken in- definitely, and what is presently happening is the phenomenon of the re- 20 sponsible patriarchy teetering under the weight of its self-imposed obli- gations.

3   The only rational conclusion one can come to is that, rather than mulishly resisting the oncoming wave of anarchy regarding sex roles, men and women should yield to its influence and help in guiding it toward its 25 ultimate destiny, which is the establishment of human liberation.

QUESTIONS

READER AND PURPOSE

1. Judging from these concluding paragraphs, would you say that Green's essay was aimed mainly at men or at women? At both equally?
2. Is there any evidence that, although this is the conclusion of her essay, the author is trying to persuade as well as to conclude? You might refresh your memory by again reading the introduction to the section on persuasion, pp. 132-38.
3. Is the author's argument directed to the reader's mind? To the reader's emotions? To a combination of both? Is the subject of this selection more emotional than rational?

ORGANIZATION

4. This selection begins with a sweeping generalization. Identify this generali- zation, and then show how the author proceeds to narrow down her topic to more specific points.
5. Could it be logically argued that these paragraphs are *not* a conclusion, that the editors of this text have simply taken three paragraphs from an essay and told you that they are the conclusion?
6. Comment on the effectiveness of the first three sentences (ll. 1-2) as the introduction to this selection.
7. Is there a topic sentence for these three paragraphs? If so, identify it and show how it governs the selection. If not, explain how the paragraph is structured.
8. Is there a transition between paragraphs 1 and 2? If so, explain how it works. If not, justify the author's omission.

SENTENCES

9. How appropriate, or effective, is the one-word sentence in l. 1? Does the author use any other sentence fragments *?

10. What is the object of the verb *they have been* (7)? Comment on the clarity (or lack of it) of the first clause of this sentence.

11. Would it be better to replace the colon of l. 5 by the expression "such as"?

12. Is the group of words following the semi-colon in l. 6 a sentence fragment? Explain why or why not.

13. State in your own words the meaning of the sentence beginning in l. 13.

14. How is the logic of the last sentence affected by the word *mulishly* (24)?

15. What is the unargued assumption of the last sentence of paragraph 2?

DICTION

16. Look up: *vacuous* (2), *despotism* (5), *sexism* (5), *valid* (5), *unique* (7), *notwithstanding* (7), *categorically* (8), *restrictions* (10), *conditioning* (14), *antithesis* (14), *onus* (16), *repression* (18), *patriarchy* (21), *rational* (23), *anarchy* (24).

17. Two words in this selection, *chauvinism* (5) and *unique* (7), are often misused, as, for example, in the expressions "male chauvinism" and "most unique." Look these two words up in an unabridged dictionary, such as the *Oxford English Dictionary* or *Webster's Third International*. Then comment on whether Green is using these words correctly.

18. Since the author does not translate the French sentence in l. 1, is she expecting too much from her reader?

19. Identify and explain the figures of speech in the last sentence of paragraph 1.

20. Is the antecedent of the pronoun *this* (11) sufficiently clear?

21. Why is *Women's Liberation* (12) capitalized? Would it be correct not to capitalize this expression?

22. What does *where* (15) refer to? Would it be more precise to write "when"?

23. Explain the expression *onus is heaved upon* (16). Comment on the appropriateness of this expression.

24. Why does Green use the phrase *in other words* (17)? Does it tell you anything about the nature of her procedure?

POINTS TO LEARN

1. A sentence fragment can sometimes be an effective stylistic device.

2. Sweeping generalizations must be clarified or substantiated.

3. A one-sentence concluding paragraph can briefly summarize the main point of an argument and indicate what action needs to be taken.

SUGGESTIONS FOR WRITING

Compose the conclusion (two to four paragraphs) of your own essay on the liberation of women in sports, industry, or education. Begin with a generalization, support it, and finish with a brief paragraph which proposes a resolution to be taken or a course of action.

IMPROVING YOUR STYLE
In your conclusion include:
1. At least one sentence fragment.
2. A one-word sentence.
3. A final paragraph that consists of only one sentence.

EDITH HAMILTON

From Plato

An American classical scholar, Edith Hamilton (1867-1963) wrote a number of books about the culture and literature of ancient Greece, including *The Greek Way* (1930), *The Echo of Greece* (1957), and *The Ever-Present Past* (1964), a collection of essays from which these paragraphs come. They end a sympathetic account of Plato, the disciple of the philosopher Socrates. Plato develops his views in a series of *Dialogues*, philosophical discussions in the form of a dialectic, or progression of questions and answers, between Socrates and various of the older philosopher's friends. In one of his most famous *Dialogues*, the *Phaedo*, Plato describes the death of Socrates, who ran afoul of the authorities of Athens because of his searching and unconventional intellect. In 399 B.C. they convicted him of impiety and of misleading the young men of the city and condemned him to drink a cup of hemlock, a deadly poison. This Socrates does after a final talk with his friends. Hamilton closes her essay with an allusion to the *Phaedo*, which serves her as a way of suggesting the essential truth about Plato.

1   So the long talk ends. The poison is drunk. The last words Socrates speaks show better than all the arguments what he believed about immortality. As he felt the cold of the poison creeping up to his heart he said: "Remember, I owe a cock to Aesculapius." It was the Greek custom on recovering from an illness to make an offering to the Divine Healer. To himself Socrates was not dying. He was entering not into death, but into life, "life more abundantly."   5

2   Through the centuries Plato has received his rightful tribute of deep reverence but not often of deep understanding. Indeed, he has been misunderstood to such a degree that the word "Platonic" has come to have 10 an unreal meaning, a complete misstatement of that mighty mind. He had a great vision; he had nothing of the visionary in him. He was a very great artist; he had a supreme artist's knowledge of people, and he felt that to see

From *The Ever-Present Past*. © 1964 by W. W. Norton & Company, Inc. Reprinted by permission of the publisher.

them ever as finished, completed, was to stultify them. He saw them always in the presence of what he called the Beyond, never to be reached but a   15 perpetual summons to go forward. To him the proof of Socrates' truth was his life and death. The text of the Dialogues in general might well be Christ's saying, "He that willeth to do His will shall know the doctrine whether it be of God."

3   One of the young men with whom Socrates had been building the   20 Republic[1] says to him at the end, "I do not believe such a place ever has been or ever will be." "Perhaps," Socrates answers, "a pattern of it is laid up in heaven *for him who wants to see*. But whether it exists or ever will is no matter. A man can order his life by its laws."

QUESTIONS

READER AND PURPOSE

1. In a closing it is often necessary to draw a general conclusion about one's subject. What conclusion does Hamilton come to regarding Plato?
2. A quotation may prove effective in ending an essay as well as in beginning one. Does the quotation from the *Republic* suggest anything about the significance of Plato and Socrates for modern men and women?
3. Scholars have debated the significance of Socrates' very last words about owing an offering to Aesculapius. How does Hamilton interpret them?
4. Does Hamilton assume that her readers are familiar with Plato's *Dialogues*? Does she identify Aesculapius (4)? If so, how does she do it?

ORGANIZATION

5. What shift in topic justifies the second paragraph? The third?
6. Study paragraph 2 and indicate which words link each sentence to what precedes it.
7. Consider this revision of the final sentences:

> Socrates answers, "Perhaps a pattern of it is laid up in heaven *for him who wants to see,* but whether it exists or ever will is no matter since a man can order his life by its laws.

As a closing sentence is this more effective, or less? Why?
8. Identify the appositives * in the sentences in lines 6-7 and 9-11.
9. Contrast these revisions with Hamilton's sentences and decide if they are improvements:

[1] The *Republic* is one of Plato's longest and most important dialogues. In it Socrates defines justice and outlines the kind of state that would be ideally suited to achieve and maintain justice. [Editors' note]

(a) *Revision:* So the long talk ends and Socrates drinks the poison.
Hamilton: "So the long talk ends. The poison is drunk." (1)

(b) *Revision:* Socrates' life and death was the proof of his truth to him.
Hamilton: "To him the proof of Socrates' truth was his life and death." (16-17)

DICTION

10. Look up: *immortality* (2), *tribute* (8), *stultify* (14), *perpetual* (16), *doctrine* (18).

11. What is the difference between being a *visionary* and having *a great vision* (12)?

12. *Indeed* (8) is a signal word. What relationship of ideas does it indicate between the statement it introduces and the preceding one?

POINTS TO LEARN

1. An apt quotation is effective in closing an essay.

2. A closing may require a conclusion in the sense of a final assessment of value or meaning.

3. The end of an essay is generally better if the final passage is slowed and regulated by separating its syntactic units (within the conventions of modern punctuation) by stops—commas, semicolons, colons, dashes.

SUGGESTIONS FOR WRITING

Imagine that you are closing an essay about a relative, friend, or teacher whom you know well. In two or three paragraphs sum up what you consider the individual's essential quality. End the paragraph with a quotation (probably something you remember the person having said, or something you yourself make up) which by implication reinforces your conclusion. Whether it be one sentence or several, be sure that the quotation is slowed and regulated by appropriate stops.

IMPROVING YOUR STYLE

1. Include an appositive in one or two of your sentences.

2. Begin another sentence with *indeed.*

Personal Writing

All writing, in the broadest sense, is personal. Even a laundry list reveals something about the writer. Well aware of this fact, Napoleon, it is said, demanded to see a sample of an officer's writing before promoting him to one of the highest ranks. Exposition, argument, description, narration—all gradually, but surely, show us the writer by his choice of subject, the breadth and depth of his knowledge, the skill with which he shapes his material, and his ability to find what it means. Why, then, a collection of pieces labeled personal writing? The answer is that the personal element in essays, while always present, varies widely in its prominence.

As an essay approaches the almost pure exposition of a scientific treatise, the personality of the writer quite properly diminishes. The writer's purpose is utilitarian—the logical, efficient setting down of a body of fact. The language of such a treatise should be precise and unobtrusive, attention being diverted from the writer and his words to the subject at hand. The writer avoids the pronoun *I*, or uses it sparingly; his tone tends to be colorless. His writing is technical and usually of interest only to experts.

Very different is prose whose subject is chiefly, if not exclusively, the writer himself. Such writing is informal, familiar, and its aim, most often, to entertain more than to convey factual information. It may range from the profoundly serious to the satiric and humorous, but its distinguishing characteristic is its concern with personal feelings and personal values. Most often—though not always—the writer employs the pronoun *I*, and establishes himself simply as one individual talking to another. Informal, personal prose, then, is likely to be colloquial, more loosely organized than formal, and to have a distinctive tone. It is often a stylistic performance as well. We enjoy it. Indeed, it approaches imaginative literature in the pleasures it offers and may even be a kind of poetry.

The essays in this section have been chosen to illustrate prose in which the personal element is more prominent than usual. Within the section there is an instructive range of subject matter and strategy. In the first

522

two selections the Duc de La Rochefoucauld and Bertrand Russell are writing, quite literally, about themselves. Here subject and writer are the same, not absolutely identical, of course, for La Rochefoucauld and Russell, as writers, step back from themselves as subjects. Perhaps because they are so close to their subjects their tactic is to appear impersonal and distanced.

The other four essays have "subjects" in the more conventional sense—boxing, a visit to a lake, life on a Saskatchewan farm a generation ago, a contemporary teacher's apparently insoluble problems. Yet even here the subject is not really outside the writer. In each case the writer's consciousness so infuses what he or she is writing about that the "subject" becomes part of the self, or the self part of it.

Personal writing, then, is writing focused on the beliefs, feelings, responses of the writer, whatever the ostensible subject. It is one of the most interesting kinds of prose and one of the most revealing and surprising, both to a reader and to the writer himself. People often find when they attempt to compose a personal essay that their "selves" are more complicated than they had known. One way of discovering what you are is to try to explain to others what you believe and feel and value.

Portrait of Himself

François, Duc de La Rochefoucauld was born in Paris in 1613 and died there in 1680. He was an important member of the aristocracy—a *grand seigneur*, as the French say—but for political reasons fell out of favor and was forced to retire from court life. He is best remembered for his *Maxims*, a collection of brief, pointed observations about human beings—their virtues and vices, their follies and pretensions. The maxims are often cynical, often wise, but invariably witty and pithy. Here is a brief sampling:

> We all have enough strength to bear the misfortunes of others.
> We are easily consoled for the misfortunes of our friends, if they afford us an opportunity of displaying our affections.
> True love, like a ghost, is much talked of but seldom seen.
> Old people are fond of giving good advice to console themselves for being no longer able to give bad examples.
> Young people generally mistake rudeness and roughness for freedom from affectation.

The Self-Portrait, which is sometimes reprinted as a kind of Forward to the *Maxims*, was actually published earlier. The topic was a conventional one for writers of the period, and La Rochefoucauld's was intended to amuse his friends and not to be published. (It was printed without his authorization.) By all contemporary evidence it appears to be candid and accurate.

1   I am of medium height, supple, and well-made. My complexion is dark, and fairly uniform; I have a high and tolerably broad forehead; eyes dark, small, and deep-set, eyebrows dark and bushy, but well shaped. I find it difficult to describe my nose; for it is neither snub, aquiline, thick, nor pointed, at least to the best of my belief; all I can say is that it is big rather 5 than small, and somewhat too long. My mouth is large, the lips usually fairly

From *The Maxims of François, Duc de la Rochefoucauld*, translated by F. G. Stevens. Reprinted by permission of the publisher, Oxford University Press, Inc.

red, and neither well nor ill modeled. My teeth are white and tolerably regular. I have been told at times that I have rather too much chin; I have just been examining myself in the looking-glass to ascertain the truth, and I am not quite sure what to think of it. As for the shape of my face, it is either square or oval; which of the two, I should find it very hard to say. My hair is black and curls naturally, and is moreover of such length and thickness as enables me to lay claim to a handsome head.

2   My normal expression is somewhat bitter and haughty; which makes most people think me supercilious, though I am not the least so really. I have a very easy bearing, in fact rather too much so, as it leads me to gesticulate too freely when speaking. This frankly is what I think I look like and will, I believe, prove to be not far from the truth. I shall be equally faithful to fact in the rest of my portrait; for I have studied myself closely enough to know myself well, and I shall lack neither the courage to mention unreservedly any good points I may possess, nor the sincerity to acknowledge my faults with frankness.

3   In the first place I will speak of my temperament. I am inclined to melancholy, to such an extent that for the last three or four years there are scarcely three or four occasions on which I have been observed to laugh. But if my melancholy were the result of temperament alone, I think it would prove mild enough and easy to bear; it is due, however, to so many other causes, and so vexes my imagination and dominates my mind, that either I brood in silence, or else I give very little attention to what I am saying. I am very reserved with strangers, and not particularly open with most of my acquaintances. I am aware that this is a failing, and I would do my utmost to correct it; but as my somewhat gloomy expression tends to make me seem more reserved than I really am, and as it is not within our power to rid ourselves of faults of expression which are due to the natural cast of the features, I imagine that, though I should succeed in improving my inner disposition, I should still not fail to show the outward tokens of imperfection.

4   I am intellectual and am not afraid to say so; for what is the use of affectation? In my opinion too much circuity and delicacy in speaking of one's good points conceals a measure of vanity under a show of modesty, and is an adroit way of securing a reputation for more merit than one claims. Personally, I am content to be thought no more handsome than I claim to be, no more amiable than I depict myself, no more intellectual or sensible than I am. I repeat then that I am intellectual; but my wit is marred by my gloomy disposition: for though I possess a fair mastery of language, a good

memory, and a clear head, I am so much obsessed by melancholy that I often express myself indifferently.

5   One of the things which gives me most pleasure is the conversation of cultured people. I prefer that it should be serious, and principally devoted to moral subjects. Yet I can enjoy it when it is gay; and though I am 50 not much given to light jesting, that is not because I underrate witty trifles, or fail to derive much amusement from this kind of fooling, in which some ready and joyous wits achieve such marked success. I write good prose, and compose good verse; and if I desired the fame that these accomplishments bring, I believe that I could without much labour acquire a tolerable 55 reputation.

6   I am fond of reading in all shapes; but particularly such as tends to educate the mind and invigorate the spirit. Above all, I derive the keenest pleasure from reading in the company of a person of intelligence; for this conduces to continual reflection on the subject of the book, and from 60 such reflections arises the pleasantest possible conversation, and the most profitable.

7   I am a fair judge of composition both in prose and verse; but I am inclined to express my opinions too freely. Another of my failings is that my taste is sometimes too fastidious, and my criticism too severe. I do not 65 dislike hearing an argument, and sometimes I take part in it willingly enough: but I generally maintain my opinion with too much warmth; and when my opponent's contention is erroneous, sometimes, in the ardour of my passion for truth, I become unreasonable in my turn.

8   My sympathies are with virtue and I have a generous disposition, 70 and so keen a desire to be in all respects a man of honour that my friends can give me no greater pleasure than by frankly pointing at my faults. Those more intimate acquaintances, who have at times been kind enough to give me some hints in that direction, can bear witness that I have always accepted them with the greatest delight conceivable, and with as much hu- 75 mility as can be desired.

9   Not one of my passions is very ardent, and all are under control. I have scarcely even been seen to lose my temper, and I have never known hatred for anybody. At the same time I should not be incapable of revenge if I were insulted, and honour demanded that I should show my resentment 80 for the injury received. On the contrary, I am convinced that sense of duty would take the place of hatred in me so effectively that I should prosecute my vengeance even more vigorously than others.

10   I am not troubled by ambition in the least degree. I am not ap-

prehensive, and have absolutely no fear of death. I am little susceptible to 85
pity, and would prefer not to be so at all. Yet there is nothing I would not
do to alleviate another's suffering; and I am strongly of opinion that it is
our duty to do everything possible to that end, even to the extent of ex-
hibiting great sympathy; for unhappy people are so silly that that does them
all the good in the world: but I consider that we should be content to 90
exhibit sympathy, and take the greatest care not to entertain it. For it is a
feeling that is intrinsically valueless in a sound character; it tends to en-
feeble the spirit, and should be left to the common herd who, as they are
never guided by reason, need the stimulus of feeling to prompt them to
action of any kind. 95

11   I am fond of my friends, and that in such fashion that I would not
hesitate for a moment to sacrifice my own interests to theirs. I make allow-
ances for them; and I endure with patience their ill humour; but I am not
lavish with display of my affection, nor am I rendered uneasy by their
absence. 100

12   I am by nature little given to curiosity concerning most of the
matters which excite that passion in other people. I am very secretive and
no one has less difficulty in respecting the confidence of others. I am very
particular to keep my word: I never fail to do so, whatever be the consequences of my promise, and I have made this throughout my life a rule to 105
which I admit no exception. I observe towards women the strictest polite-
ness, and I believe I have never said anything in the presence of a woman
which could cause her pain. When women have wit, I prefer their conversation to that of men: they display a charm which is never found in our sex,
and besides, they seem to me to indicate their meaning with greater lucidity, 110
and give a more pleasing turn to their observations. As for light amours, I
have in the past indulged in these to some extent; but now I do so no
longer in spite of my youth. I have given up pretty compliments, and can
only wonder that there are still so many men of honour who spend their time
in peddling them. 115

13   I heartily sympathize with strong passion; it is an indication of
noble character; and though the restlessness it brings has in it something
which is repugnant to austere philosophy, it is otherwise so much in keeping with the strictest virtue that I do not think it can be fairly condemned.
Knowing as I do what a degree of strength and refinement can characterize 120
the emotions of true love, I shall assuredly love after that fashion, if I ever
fall in love at all; but, constituted as I am, I do not believe that that knowledge will ever again quit my head to find a dwelling in my heart.

QUESTIONS

1. There are a number of reasons why a man should try to draw a portrait of himself with words. List as many of these as you can. Which of them seems best to describe the purpose of La Rochefoucauld?

2. Compare and contrast La Rochefoucauld's character sketch of himself with the descriptions of character on pages 391 ff. What techniques of characterization has La Rochefoucauld failed to use? Could he have used any of these with profit? Explain.

3. Some writers, in characterizing themselves, write for the eyes of no one but themselves. Does La Rochefoucauld seem to be writing for himself or for an audience? What is the evidence for your answer? What words in paragraph 1 suggest that he is attempting to be objective in his self-appraisal? Would you say that he maintains this objectivity throughout the essay? Be able to support your answer. Nonetheless, does La Rochefoucauld unintentionally reveal any traits of personality? If so, how and where?

4. Make an outline of this essay, indicating its main sections and the major subdivisions within them. Give a brief title to each of these headings. Explain whether or not La Rochefoucauld followed any consistent plan in sketching his self-portrait. What suggestions can you give for improving the organization?

5. Study how La Rochefoucauld develops the physical description in paragraph 1. Is he following a plan here, or simply rambling on, jotting down his various features as they occur to him? Is he wise to begin with a physical description rather than, say, placing it last?

6. Why does he treat the material in paragraph 2 separately instead of including it as part of paragraph 1? Which sentences in paragraph 2 sum up the first section of the essay and prepare us for the next?

7. La Rochefoucauld does not bother with long summarizing transitions between his paragraphs, as, for instance: "Having finished describing my temperament, I will now discuss my taste in literature." Still, his paragraphs flow together. How does he unify them?

8. Discuss the beginning and the closing of this essay, explaining whether or not you think they do the jobs that a good beginning and closing should do. Try composing a final paragraph that will make a more graceful closing.

9. The final sentence of paragraph 3 is a good example of the complex style. It contains a number of clauses which carefully develop and explain and qualify

the rather complicated thought the writer is trying to express. Read the sentence several times and then in your own words explain what La Rochefoucauld is saying. Point out one or two other sentences similarly complicated.

DICTION

10. Look up: *supple* (1), *haughty* (14), *gesticulate* (17), *unreservedly* (21), *temperament* (23), *melancholy* (24), *vexes* (28), *reflection* (60), *fastidious* (65), *ardent* (77), *susceptible* (85), *alleviate* (87), *lavish* (99), *lucidity* (110).

11. Explain the meanings of the following phrases: *tolerably regular* (7-8), *outward tokens of imperfection* (36-37), *gloomy disposition* (45), *witty trifles* (51), *common herd* (93), *light amours* (111), *austere philosophy* (118).

12. Rewrite paragraph 4, substituting a Saxon vocabulary for the writer's Latinate diction wherever possible. How do these changes affect the tone * of the writing? Are the changes in each instance an improvement? What do you think of the advice that one should always prefer a simple Saxon word to one of Latin derivation?

13. Look up the etymologies * of the following: *aquiline, supercilious, adroit, intrinsically.* How does knowing the etymology of a word help the writer? What, by the way, is the etymology of *etymology*?

14. It is obvious near the end of paragraph 4 that La Rochefoucauld is repeating himself when he says that he is intellectual. Why, then, does he stress the obvious by writing "I repeat"? And why does he bother to repeat at all what he said clearly enough at the beginning of the paragraph?

15. What distinction is La Rochefoucauld making in paragraph 10 when he advises his reader to *exhibit* but not to *entertain* sympathy for unhappy people? La Rochefoucauld has often been accused of cynicism. Does this seem like cynical advice to you?

POINTS TO LEARN

1. Almost all writing, no matter how formal or informal, no matter how personal or impersonal, gains from a clear plan of organization.

2. To interest is to inform. The writer who is content with generalities in place of definite information will quickly lose his reader.

3. A writer reveals his personality not only by his choice of subject and by his beliefs openly stated, he also reveals himself by his sentence structure, his diction, and, what is closely related to both, his tone.

SUGGESTIONS FOR WRITING

Compose a self-portrait, imitating in a general way the procedure of La Rochefoucauld. Include, among other things, a section of physical description, of your likes and dislikes, of your virtues and your failings, of your talents and your weaknesses. Be as objective as you can and write with a purpose.

IMPROVING YOUR STYLE

1. Before you begin your sketch make a careful outline of what you intend to cover and in what order. If your teacher asks, turn the outline in along with the composition.

2. In your sketch include a long compound-complex sentence like the one that ends La Rochefoucauld's third paragraph.

Three Passions

Bertrand Russell (1872-1970) was a most unusual combination of mathematician, philosopher, and man of letters. One of the most important British mathematicians of this century, he wrote the very influential *Principia Mathematica* (with Alfred North Whitehead) in 1910 and *Introduction to Mathematical Philosophy* (1919). At the same time he was interested in social, ethical, and political issues, which he discussed in numerous essays. During the twenties he advocated feminism and a freer attitude toward sex, opinions which cost him his teaching position at the University of California, Los Angeles. In 1950 he was awarded the Nobel Prize for literature. In 1951, at the age of 79, he published his autobiography, from which the following selection is reprinted.

1   Three passions, simple but overwhelmingly strong, have governed my life: the longing for love, the search for knowledge, and unbearable pity for the suffering of mankind. These passions, like great winds, have blown me hither and thither, in a wayward course, over a deep ocean of anguish, reaching to the very verge of despair.   5

2   I have sought love, first, because it brings ecstasy—ecstasy so great that I would often have sacrificed all the rest of life for a few hours of this joy. I have sought it, next, because it relieves loneliness—that terrible loneliness in which one shivering consciousness looks over the rim of the world into the cold unfathomable lifeless abyss. I have sought it, finally, because in the 10 union of love I have seen, in a mystic miniature, the prefiguring vision of the heaven that saints and poets have imagined. This is what I sought, and though it might seem too good for human life, this is what—at last—I have found.

3   With equal passion I have sought knowledge. I have wished to 15

From *The Autobiography of Bertrand Russell* by Bertrand Russell. Reprinted by permission of Allen & Unwin.

understand the hearts of men. I have wished to know why the stars shine. And I have tried to apprehend the Pythagorean power by which number holds sway above the flux. A little of this, but not much, I have achieved.

4   Love and knowledge, so far as they were possible, led upward toward the heavens. But always pity brought me back to earth. Echoes of cries of   20 pain reverberate in my heart. Children in famine, victims tortured by oppressors, helpless old people a hated burden to their sons, and the whole world of loneliness, poverty, and pain make a mockery of what human life should be. I long to alleviate the evil, but I cannot, and I too suffer.

5   This has been my life. I have found it worth living, and would gladly   25 live it again if the chance were offered me.

QUESTIONS

READER AND PURPOSE

1. What do you think motivates famous men and women to write auto-biographies? Can you suggest two purposes shaping this excerpt from Russell's autobiography? What are the rewards of reading another person's life story?

2. Writing is personal when its subject is chiefly the writer's personality, values, and deeds, for then it reveals the writer, not only in terms of what he consciously tells us but what he "says" unconsciously. What can you infer about Bertrand Russell after reading his lines and whatever lies between them?

ORGANIZATION

3. Show that the first paragraph sets up the plan of the next three.

4. Does the order in which Russell discusses his "passions" suggest anything about his priorities of value? Suppose the sequence had been "pity for mankind," "search for knowledge," and "longing for love": would Russell's tone * and emphasis be changed?

5. Study the transitions between each paragraph. Are they smooth or abrupt? What words in the opening sentence of paragraph two link to what words in paragraph one? Which words link the third paragraph to the second? The fourth to the third?

6. Why do you suppose the last paragraph is so brief?

7. Show how the organization of paragraph two parallels the organization of the whole excerpt.

SENTENCES

8. Russell's prose, while its subject is formal and serious, is both forceful and emotional. These qualities result in part from his sentence structure. His most

frequent device of emphasis is interrupted movement *. How many examples can you find?

9. Repetition is another means of emphasis. Sometimes as in line 6 Russell immediately repeats a key term for emphasis, placing the second in apposition * to the first. The ancient Greeks called this rhetorical * technique *epizeuxis*; it has been common in English and other European languages for centuries. Find another example in this selection.

10. Identify examples of anaphora * in paragraphs 2 and 3. Does anaphora tend to heighten an emotional tone or to dampen it?

11. Explain why the following revisions are less emphatic than Russell's sentence:

> Revision (a): A little of this I have achieved, but not much.
> Revision (b): I have achieved a little of this, but not much.
> Russell: "A little of this, but not much, I have achieved." (18)

DICTION

12. Look up: *abyss* (10), *prefiguring* (11), *apprehend* (17), *Pythagorean* (17), *flux* (18), *alleviate* (24).

13. As important as sentence structure in creating the emotional force of Russell's prose in his diction. At least three devices are at work: figures (metaphors * and similes *), alliteration *, and adjectives with strong emotional coloring. Find examples of each.

14. Read this entire selection out loud and listen. Then read aloud the following revision of Russell's third paragraph:

> With the same interest I've looked for knowledge, since I've wanted to understand what people are thinking and how the universe is put together, so to speak. Also I've wanted to find some comprehension of what causes the eternalization of numbers when everything else is more or less in a state of deterioration. I've done something like this, but not so much as I had hoped for.

While the revision says approximately the same thing, there is a difference, the difference, to borrow a phrase from Mark Twain, between lightning and the lightning bug. Give as many reasons as you can why Russell's prose works and the revision fails.

POINTS TO LEARN

1. All writing is self-revelation. If in personal writing authors discuss themselves consciously, they reveal almost as much unconsciously by their words and sentence structure. Even the degree of clarity or of muddle in the organization

is a clue to their intelligence, their education, their willingness to work, and their consideration for others.

2. Personal writing is likely to succeed more easily than other kinds of exposition. Our own self is a subject most of us are thoroughly acquainted with and deeply care about.

3. The fact that the prose is serious does not mean that it is toneless. Russell's writing is an instructive combination of clarity, vigor, and emotion.

4. It is helpful to read good prose out loud; it is easy on the ear. You should routinely read aloud what you write, revising whatever strikes you as harsh or dull.

SUGGESTIONS FOR WRITING

1. Loosely organizing your essay on the model of the passage by Russell, list and briefly discuss the goals that shape your life.

2. Analyze and discuss briefly the values that form your personal code of ethics.

3. Write an essay in which you discuss what in your experience inclines you toward optimism (or pessimism).

IMPROVING YOUR STYLE

1. In your essay use one or two examples of *epizeuxis*. (See question 9.)

2. If your tone permits, use anaphora once or twice. (Question 10)

3. Experiment with interrupted movement in one or two sentences.

Toboganning

Harry J. Boyle has had an unconventional career. Born in Ontario in 1915, he became a journalist and broadcaster, and eventually a program supervisor for CBC radio. In 1968 he was appointed Vice-Chairman of the Canadian Radio-Television Commission, and later became its Chairman. Boyle has written extensively and in a variety of forms: numerous articles in periodicals as varied as *The Financial Post* and *Maclean's*; radio and stage plays; books of essays, one of which was awarded the Leacock Medal for humor; novels, of which the best known is *The Great Canadian Novel* (1972); and collections of short stories and reminiscences, such as *With a Pinch of Sin* (1966), from which the following selection is taken.

1   The year I made up my mind Santa Claus was only going to give me useful presents of mittens and scarves and a small treat like a book or a jackknife, he completely surprised me.

2   On Christmas morning, in place of the small wooden sleigh I had seen Grandfather working on, there was a toboggan.   5

3   Snow was lean that year and the Big Hill, being sandy and exposed to the sun had scarcely any sliding surface.

4   I went to bed each night after scanning the skies for any sign of snow and praying for a real blizzard. Perversely, the elements would sprinkle a little snow and then blow it into fence drifts or the hollows of the   10 fields.

5   It was beginning to look hopeless. I could sit in the kitchen and look out to where the toboggan leaned against the house in the lee of the veranda. It was varnished and new-looking. Pushing it around the yard was frustrating. This long, sleek affair was made for the big slopes and long   15 runs.

"Toboganning" from the book *With a Pinch of Sin* by Harry J. Boyle. Copyright © 1966 by Harry J. Boyle. Reprinted by permission of Doubleday & Company, Inc.

6   It looked as if I might have to go back to school after the New Year without having had a real outing on the toboggan. Then, on the Saturday before the New Year, the morning was overcast. The world seemed poised and waiting for something. Big snowflakes ruptured from the clouds and floated down to earth. They were melting as fast as they arrived, but the tempo increased and the bare spots soon had a thin coating of white. Mother had a time restraining me from pushing out to the hill.

7   The world was a creation of cotton batting by next morning. The teams on the sleigh made a convoy on the way to church. Everyone was sharing in that hearty friendliness that comes when nature has a transformation. Church was secondary in my thoughts to the anticipation of tobogganing, and when we got home I had to be almost forcibly restrained from going to the hill without anything to eat.

8   I was swallowing cake as I wallowed through the deep snow to the top of the hill. The toboggan was a delight. On the first run the snow flared out on each side with a great white spume effect. A touch of morning breeze had blown snow off the pond so that when we hit the ice the momentum carried the toboggan part way up the low hill opposite.

9   Snap, my old collie, was suspicious of getting on the toboggan at first, but he soon tired of romping through the deep snow and then having to wade back to the top. First time down he jumped halfway and landed head over heels in the snowbank. Next time he crouched and made the journey.

10   It had seemed all week that if the snow came my wildest dreams of play and happiness would come true. Yet, somehow I grew tired of being alone.

11   Grandfather was the first to wander over to the hill. He stamped around a bit and hedged about going down the hill for a ride. Sensing my mood, he got on, neglecting to take the pipe out of his mouth. He made a wild swipe for it about halfway down and left a foot dragging that sent both of us sprawling into the snow, while the conveyance went wildly to the bottom.

12   Father, at the stable door, yelled for us to stay where we were. He retrieved the toboggan and climbed the hill. "Takes some knack to handle one of these things," he suggested to Grandfather.

13   "You think you're so smart . . . then try it," retorted the older man.

14   "Well, I don't know what you're crowing about."

15   "Go on . . . just try it."

16   Father got on, adjusted his hands to the ropes, and nodded for a push. He sailed down gracefully, getting an extra boost where the hill bulged a bit, and flashed down to the pond. Lifting both hands in triumph as it came to the ice he flipped off as the toboggan went sideways and hit 60 a clump of grass frozen and protruding above the surface.

17   Grandfather laughed so hard Mother looked out from the kitchen. Soon, in fact before Father had trudged up the hill, she came out to investigate, wearing his overcoat and an old stocking cap. "Are you children having a good time?"   65

18   Father lurched to grab her. "Come on, see for yourself what it's like."

19   Grandfather gave them both a push, and they lost their balance and went sprawling on the toboggan. Down the hill they went but when they reached the bump, both rolled into the snow.   70

20   By the time Mother and Father came up, our neighbors Ed Higgins and his wife, driving along the concession in a horse and cutter, swung in the laneway.

21   "Do you see what you've done," exclaimed Mother in mock anger. "They thought you were killing me."   75

22   It developed they were just curious about the toboggan, and it took practically no coaxing to get both of them on the ride. I half expected to go along, but Mother shook her head. Then Father dared Ed to go down the hill standing up, and he did, keeping his balance almost to the pond.

23   After that Father tried it and flipped at the bump. Mother and 80 Mrs. Higgins got on and went down, taking ages to bring the toboggan back.

24   I finally got a chance to go down by myself, but when I looked up they had all gone. I trudged back up the hill, half hoping someone might come back to play with me. No one appeared, and when I went to the 85 house Grandfather was asleep on the sofa in the kitchen, Mother was on the couch in the front room, and Father had gone up to bed for a rest.

25   I kept looking at the models of toboggans in the catalogue until I fell asleep in the old chair. Mother woke me up with the noise as she started to get supper.   90

26   "Didn't you have a wonderful time with your toboggan?" she said.

27   I didn't answer her, and she was so busy she didn't notice. What was there to say?

QUESTIONS

READER AND PURPOSE

1. How old do you think the narrator (Harry Boyle) is on the occasion he describes here? What difference does it make to the reader whether the narrator is six or sixteen?

2. What do you think Boyle's purpose is in this essay: is he simply describing a part of his youth? Is he trying to make a moral point? Is he analyzing child-parent relationships? All of these? Something else?

3. There is in this essay a feeling of joy mingled with innocence which envelops all: the narrator, his dog, his parents and grandfather, the neighbors. How does Boyle achieve this sense of purity, of guiltlessness, of virtue? Is it realistic? How is it related (if at all) to the narrator as young boy?

4. For many readers a statement such as "church was secondary in my thoughts" (28) would be somewhat repellent, or at least a bit objectionable. Why is that not true here? What does this expression tell us about the kind of person the narrator is?

ORGANIZATION

5. Since there are some twenty-one paragraphs in this fairly short essay (each one averaging only about five lines), and since the first four paragraphs contain only five sentences in all, Boyle is clearly not developing his paragraphs in the normal way. Instead of being self-contained units, each with a topic sentence which is substantiated, or explained, Boyle's paragraphs are often no more than single thoughts or feelings, recorded as the narrator experiences them. How do you explain, or justify, this sort of structure?

6. In the first sentence the narrator mentions his complete surprise at the gift of the toboggan; in the last sentence he says that he had no reply to his mother's question. Is there any relation between these two comments? Does the last sentence constitute a form of closing by return *?

7. Is this essay organized as a narrative, i.e. with a beginning, middle, and end? Explain how it is, or isn't.

8. The ordering principle of this narrative is obviously chronological: events are recounted in the order in which they occurred. But what other methods are at work here? Why, for example, does the dog enter the story before the grandfather? Why does the father come after the grandfather and before the mother? Why does the mother's comment in l. 91 occur there instead of after l. 82?

9. There are a number of sentences that are both dividing points and transitions, such as that in ll. 42-43. Find the others, and then describe briefly what is contained in each part of this essay.

SENTENCES

10. Analyze the structure of the first four sentences. Are they simple *? Complex *? Compound *? Now do the same for the sentences in paragraph 8 and for the last five sentences of the essay. What pattern (if any) do you find?

11. Do you see any relation between the nature of Boyle's subject and his sentence structures? For example, can you say that Boyle's subject is an incident from simple, ordinary farm life which is expressed in simple sentences? Or that Boyle's subject is the complex child-parent relationship which is expressed in complex sentences? Can you see any other relationships between subject and style?

12. Is the last sentence a rhetorical question *? If so, why? If not, what sort of answer might the narrator provide?

13. Should there be a comma after *sun* (7)? Why or why not?

14. Explain how the first sentence is a periodic * sentence. Then rewrite this sentence to make it a loose * one, and explain the difference between the two.

DICTION

15. Look up: *perversely* (9), *elements* (9), *lee* (13), *tempo* (22), *spume* (33), *momentum* (35), *conveyance* (48), *knack* (51), *crowing* (55), *cutter* (72).

16. Boyle does not often use figures of speech, but he does use some, such as *snowflakes ruptured* (20) and *a creation of cotton batting* (25). Does he use any others? What effect is achieved by using figures of speech only occasionally?

17. How does one "push" a toboggan? Do you think Boyle meant the sentence in l. 14 to be taken literally or figuratively *?

18. How can a toboggan be called *sleek* (15)? To what specific word mentioned previously does *sleek* refer?

19. To what is the narrator referring when he says that "the tempo increased" (22)? Explain why *tempo* is or is not an appropriate word here, and, if it is not, supply a better one.

20. Explain whether the phrase "my old collie" (36) is an absolute construction * or an appositive *.

POINTS TO LEARN

1. In writing of a very personal nature, the normal development of paragraphs is sometimes neglected in favor of brief expressions of feelings or ideas.

2. There may be two methods of organization at work in a narrative at the same time.

3. A transitional sentence can also act as the indicator of a major division in a narrative.

SUGGESTIONS FOR WRITING

Writing in the first person, describe, in 500-700 words, a memorable experience from your youth. Organize your narrative chronologically, use figures of speech only occasionally, and ensure that your narrative has a beginning, middle, and end.

IMPROVING YOUR STYLE

In your narrative include:

1. A few subtle indications of your approximate age.
2. A number of brief paragraphs, of only one or two sentences, each containing only one idea or feeling.
3. A closing by return.
4. A number of sentences which act as both transitions and indicators of the major divisions of your narrative.

VICTORIA BRANDEN

Teaching the Unmotivated

As a freelance journalist, Vicki Branden has written articles on a wide variety of topics. In addition, she is the author of two novels and a non-fiction work, as well as numerous short stories and scripts for both radio and television drama. At the time she wrote the article below, she was teaching at Sheridan College in Oakville, Ontario. Her essay is a good example of highly personal writing.

1   It may be that the theories of Marshall McLuhan are now hopelessly out of style and one dates oneself by the mere mention of his name. Dreadful though such a fate may be, I have to accept it, because I see his ideas dramatically manifesting themselves every day in the classroom—just where he said it would happen.   5

2   Right now, community colleges—I teach in one—and the upper reaches of high schools contain a very large population of students who can barely read or write. This presents certain problems. The students I have encountered in these institutions fall neatly into two groups: those with a vocation, and those without. As long as an individual powerfully desires to 10 be a doctor, or a plumber, or a filmmaker, or a forester, the motivation to acquire the requisite skills and knowledge will keep him going. The motivated student will do the work, even those parts which don't particularly interest him, and his teachers will remember him nostalgically. He may not have been loveable, he may have been a perpetuator of the Protestant 15 work ethic and Calvinist morality; still, it was nice to be able to give him an A, with a clear conscience.

3   But the motivated students are in the minority and it is the great mass of The Unmotivated who present so many road-blocks for themselves

Vicki Branden "Teaching the Unmotivated", from *Saturday Night* (Sept. 1972), reprinted by permission of the author.

and their teachers and society at large. They don't know what they want to 20
do. They may be vaguely interested in a lot of things, but not strongly
drawn by anything. They have never learned, and are determined not to
learn, any habits of application and discipline.

4   They go into courses like journalism, general arts, advertising and
media studies, not because they wish to practise these mysteries but be- 25
cause they have drifted along the line of least resistance. They have an
idea (from movies and TV) that journalism and advertising are glamorous
and exciting and above all easy.

5   In one class of about forty advertising students that I taught, there
were perhaps half a dozen who were willing to work or who showed the 30
smallest aptitude for the field they were proposing to enter. One boy came
to a total of three classes, and at the end of term handed in a mishmash
of old high school themes; he was furious when I refused to give him a
credit. In general, this group was absolutely incapable of accepting or prof-
iting by criticism. One technique for dealing with a fault-finding teacher 35
was to keep repeating, with a winning disregard for truth or plausibility,
that they had been A-level students all through high school, and were now
getting A's in all their other subjects. That this story could be checked and
disproved did not deter them from using it.

6   "If you turned in a piece of work like this in any advertising 40
agency," I expostulated once, "they wouldn't bother correcting it. They'd
kick you right out the window, for wasting paper." The student laughed
cheerfully. He didn't plan to work in an advertising agency. He intended to
settle on a Caribbean island, supporting himself in unimaginable luxury by
writing poetry, an activity for which he showed no talent whatsoever. He 45
believed that, to write a poem, you slapped down whatever came into your
head, arranging it in uneven lines with no punctuation, and that was that.
He declined to read any poetry, to investigate the truth of his theory. "That
stuff bugs me."

7   In other periods of history, such students might never have stayed 50
in school beyond grade nine. But law requires that everyone stay in school
until age sixteen, and after sixteen jobs are scarce. Their parents' generation was brought up to regard education as, axiomatically, a good thing. So
here they are.

8   Their influence on the educational system has been destructive. 55
Throughout public and high school, students with little academic ability
are passed along from grade to grade by a process which has become dis-
mally familiar to everyone in the trade. I submit the case of Mary-Jane

who in grade twelve could not write "The cat sat on the mat" without making numerous errors in spelling, grammar, and punctuation. She failed, not because the teachers were mean but because she was unable to meet anything remotely like grade twelve requirements. At the promotion meetings, however, the teachers found themselves under pressure: couldn't they be at least human and give Mary-Jane a 50, so she could get her grade twelve certificate and go out and learn some useful trade? One by one, they fell.

9   I was staggered, a few years later, to discover that Mary-Jane had somehow contrived to get accepted at a university. How, heaven knows, when she wasn't working at a competent grade ten level. I don't think the poor girl really wanted to, but her parents were grimly determined that any child of theirs must attend university.

10   Far less pleasant than Mary-Jane, who is pathetic rather than obnoxious, is the potentially able student who has undertaken to buck the system and sees himself (it's usually a male) as a "rebel." He has no clear idea of what he's rebelling *against*, but generally it expresses itself in a refusal to do any work, and to resist bitterly all rules interfering with his freedom to smoke, drink, drug, fornicate, drive fast cars or attend porno films at the age of fourteen. He is a total disaster in the high schools, and he tends to drift in great numbers toward the community colleges.

11   There must be close to 200,000 students in the Canadian community colleges now (106,000 in 1969-70), and while it is essential to stress that many of them are brilliant and delightful people, a joy to be associated with in any capacity, we have a very large share of Mary-Janes and Rebel Males. The problems they present seem at times to defy solution. What can a teacher do, confronted by a roomful of people whose main concern is to avoid doing any work?

12   You can, of course, stick manfully to your guns, affirming that your subject is English or History or whatever, and you are by God going to teach that, and demand that they do assignments and achieve certain standards. Everyone will admire your integrity and no one will come to your classes. The word will get round that your course is tough, and nobody will sign up for it. And the administration, which at the beginning applauded your integrity, will discover that your classes are not "drawing," and advise you in threatening memoranda that you'd better find some way of making your courses more interesting and popular—or else.

13   Your next ploy is to do a crafty job of sugar-coating. You still attempt to teach literacy, but you conceal it under a seductive disguise. You

teach Propaganda or Parapsychology or Puppetry, or God knows what. Apropos of such desperate expedients, this conversation (overheard in the hall) has become a classic: 100

14   "What are you doing for English?"

15   "I'm making a quilt. What are you?"

16   "Me and my boy friend are doing telepathy."

17   Instructors try to smuggle literature into these courses, and con their darlings into writing something—anything—on paper, so that they 105 learn to express themselves, and you can help them with their spelling and grammar. But you find that your charges are expert at detecting the iron hand of effort under the velvet glove of entertainment, and they are particularly on guard against the poison of the word, read or written. Many of them, they've told me, would really have liked to take my course in Witch- 110 craft, Parapsychology or whatever it may be called in its current incarnation; but any mulish insistence on the indispensability of reading and writing has proved an insuperable obstacle. ("See, we don't write essays," they explain, ingenuously.)

18   A refinement of the above approach is to choose areas which are 115 the very stuff of the youth culture—comic books, astrology, science fiction, prime-time TV—and base a course on them. The subject may have sociological value, after all, and if you can just engage their interest, you can "reach them"—can't you? Last year I drew up an outline for what might have been the most popular course of all, the summit and peak of interest- 120 orientation: Dirty Lit and Porno Film. (Experiments, demonstrations, group projects.)

19   I don't know whether the administration would have let me teach it or not, because I decided against trying. I've always found pornography tedious, and it's difficult to teach a course where the students know the 125 subject better than the teacher. And here is the big snag in the youth-appeal ploy: the teacher, frequently an amateur and late-comer, is trying to move into a field in which the students are experts. Sure, you can try to approach it in depth, give it some contextual poles. But your students won't like *that*, you know.   130

20   Such course content omits consideration of another important factor. At first glance students may think they will enjoy a course in science fiction or horror stories or comic books. It shortly transpires that this is an error. These are the classic domains of the adolescent, and adult trespass is resented. The comic book was something to be hidden inside the history 135 text, a means by which the student escaped the tedium of the lesson and

showed his disrespect for authority. It was a symbol of rebellion against adult values. Now, when adults and authority try to muscle in, it loses all its symbolic value. It becomes just another school subject through which the sneaky establishment is trying to trick the adolescent into learning 140 something.

21   What else can a teacher try? Well, you can be very, very popular. You can give a course which requires no reading, no writing, and very little class attendance. The word will get round, and students will swarm to sign up. Your life will be easy, if your conscience is elastic enough. A few 145 old-fashioned students may get hostile—you always get the odd one who really thinks you ought to be teaching her something.

22   I said "her" at this point advisedly. Most such students are women. One of our colleges last year reached a point where there were exactly no classes in literature, as such, being offered in the English Department. A 150 group of students drew up a petition, actually asking for a literature course. The faculty swooned away as one: had the tide turned? The class was reported to be a delight. They read insatiably, and wrote brilliant papers. However, they turned out to be special cases: there was only one male among them, and several of the leading spirits were women who had raised 155 families and returned to school in their thirties and forties.

23   The role of gender and age in academic performance needs study. It is reckless to generalize on such a subject, but my own experience has been that while the top student in a class is often a brilliant and innovating male, girls are as a rule more conscientious and reliable than boys. Older 160 students are almost invariably better than those fresh from high school, regardless of IQ; some of the possessors of the highest IQ's are the most deeply sunken in lassitude. Girls are usually much more amenable to criticism, recognizing that your purpose is not simply to be horrid but to help them improve; a kind of prickly male vanity often makes boys reject it in- 165 dignantly and interpret it as a personal affront.

24   A class with a preponderance of The Unmotivated has a fearful effect on teacher morale. Elsewhere I have chronicled the case of the high school teacher in the four-year stream who, looking around at his rioting and blatting charges, fell into total despair. (It was a grade twelve class, 170 mostly male, and some of them were over twenty; this teacher was an imaginative, resourceful, thoroughly experienced, high qualified, male department head.) "What's the matter?" I said, struck by his look of gloom.

25   "They aren't interested in anything," he said. "Not *anything*."

26   I made commiserating noises.   175

27   "Tomorrow," he announced, "I'm going to play my last card. I'm going to tell them all to choose a partner and go into corners and copulate."

28   "I'm sure that will work," I said encouragingly. But he shook his head despondently.   180

29   "They'll probably all start bleating, 'Ahhhhh, why do we hafta? It's boring.' "

30   *Boring.*

31   That word has broken the spirit of more teachers than the outside world can possibly imagine. If you have prepared something exciting and 185 challenging, it is the death of the soul to present it to an apathetic mob who, slumped on their curvature-threatened spines, receive it with glazed lethargy. What you have to learn is that "boring" means in fact challenging, demanding, requiring some stretching of the mind.

32   By and large, they don't want to be challenged. They want to be 190 entertained and amused, passively, as they did when they were children in front of the TV screen. The teacher's job is to entertain them, they believe, TV-fashion; along the way, he may spoon some knowledge into their mouths. Some of them will deign to open their mouths to receive it, consciously doing the teacher a favour. Others will keep their mouths closed, 195 on the principle that the teacher is paid to make them open up to have the information pumped in.

QUESTIONS

READER AND PURPOSE

1. What kind of reader do you think Branden is writing for? Other teachers? The general public? Describe as fully as you can the kind of reader she seems to be appealing to, considering, for example, the points she expects her reader to agree with, to find amusing, to take seriously.

2. Would you agree that this essay is *not* intended for most students? Explain your answer, whether you agree or disagree.

3. Show how we can draw conclusions about Branden's personality as revealed in her diction, tone *, and point of view *.

4. Would you describe this selection as entertaining? As serious? As a combination of both? Explain your answer using specific examples.

ORGANIZATION

5. Often, especially in personal writing, the beginning identifies who, where, when, why, and how, thus providing a context for what follows. Can you answer these questions on the basis of Branden's first two paragraphs? Who is she? Where does her narrative take place? And when? Why is she offering it to the reader? How is she approaching her material?

6. Personal writing is often loosely organized, more like ordinary speech than carefully-written prose. Is this true of the selection by Branden? Answer the question by looking for the transitions, if any, between her paragraphs. In how many cases have transitions been omitted?

7. This selection has two main parts. What main point is Branden treating in each part?

8. From what source (or sources) does she draw examples to illustrate her points?

9. What paragraph in this selection serves as a transition between its two main parts? Does the point made in this paragraph contradict what Branden has said earlier in paragraph 3? Explain why, or why not.

10. Do you think that the final paragraph of this selection recalls for us the point of the opening paragraph? Explain the basis for your answer.

SENTENCES

11. In personal writing we often encounter sentence structures that can be termed colloquial *. (See question 10, following the selection by A. J. Liebling, p. 550.) Can you find examples of this kind of sentence structure in Branden's work? For example, how often does she use sentence fragments *? Does she avoid interrupted movement *? Are there relatively few complex * sentences? How often does she use short, simple * sentences? Does she make frequent use of the connectives * "and" and "but"? After answering these questions, would you describe most of Branden's sentences as colloquial?

12. Does sentence two of paragraph 9 employ alliteration? Explain why, or why not.

13. Why does Branden use dashes in sentence one of paragraph 2, sentence four of paragraph 11, sentence one of paragraph 13, sentences one and two of paragraph 14, and sentence six of paragraph 14? Be prepared to explain whether or not her purpose is the same in all six cases.

14. Branden italicizes *against* (75), *that* (130), *anything* (174), *boring* (183). Does she do so because these are key words? Because she wants to suggest one way words are emphasized in speech? For some other reason?

15. Read this selection carefully, and look at the pronouns Branden uses. Is there a consistent point of view or a shifting one? In either case, give the reasons for your answer and describe the effect Branden is seeking.

DICTION

16. Look up: *conscience* (17), *glamorous* (27), *axiomatically* (53), *pathetic* (72), *obnoxious* (72-73), *integrity* (90), *ploy* (127), *insuperable* (113), *ingenuously* (114), *insatiably* (153), *lassitude* (163), *apathetic* (186), *lethargy* (188). If you were judging only on the basis of these words, would you describe Branden's diction as formal or informal?

17. How would you revise your answer to the previous question after noting that she also uses words and phrases such as: *road-blocks* (19), *mishmash* (32), *buck the system* (73-74), *total disaster* (78), *your course is tough* (91), *con* (104), *big snag* (126), *muscle in* (138), *sneaky* (140)?

18. Point out several of the instances in which Branden uses understatement *, exaggeration, and sarcasm. What effect do you think she is attempting to achieve?

19. What kind of diction is used by the unmotivated students whose words Branden quotes? For what purposes do you think these quotations are included?

20. In how many places can you see Branden attempting to create comic effects through her own use of language? Is "stick manfully to your guns" (87) one such instance, in this case of a cliché brought back to life? Is "the big snag in the youth-appeal ploy" (126-127) a deliberately-mixed metaphor *? Do you think it is intended as a parody of "expertise"? Consider your other examples carefully and be prepared to describe some of the comic effects the author is trying to achieve and whether she is successful in achieving them.

21. Why is the phrase "reach them" (119) put in quotation marks, when other colloquial words and expressions are not?

POINTS TO LEARN

1. Personal writing can make a serious point without being consistently serious in tone.

2. The writer of a personal essay should quickly identify who, where, when, why, and how.

3. In a personal essay an informal relationship with the reader can be achieved through the use of humor (in language, and in supporting examples) as well as by the use of colloquial diction and sentence structures.

SUGGESTIONS FOR WRITING

1. Present your own view of unmotivated students. Give your essay a definite theme, and make it clear how you feel about the people you are describing.

2. Turn the tables on Branden, and describe "the unmotivated teacher." As with the preceding topic, establish a clear thematic focus and describe your own feelings about the subject.

IMPROVING YOUR STYLE

1. Remember to respect your reader. Humorous devices are effective; frivolity and name-calling are not.

2. Following Branden's use of the dash, use that mark three or four different ways in your essay.

3. Make use of colloquial language and sentence structures for effect, but do not weaken the effect by overdoing it.

Boxing with the Naked Eye

A. J. Liebling was primarily a journalist. He was a frequent contributor to *The New Yorker*, especially on the inadequacies of newspapers. Some of these pieces were collected in *The Wayward Pressman* (1947) and *The Press* (1961). But he wrote about other things: politics (*The Earl of Louisiana*, 1961); the World War (*The Road Back to Paris*, 1944); and boxing (*The Sweet Science*, 1956). The last is the source of the following essay, an account of a heavyweight championship fight between Joe Louis and Lee Savold in 1951. Liebling's title refers to the advantage of watching a bout at ringside rather than seeing it on television. (Twenty-five or thirty years ago boxing was telecast much more frequently than it is now.) As you will see, however, the essay involves more than boxing or television or even one particular fight. Most of all it involves Liebling.

1   Watching a fight on television has always seemed to me a poor substitute for being there. For one thing, you can't tell the fighters what to do. When I watch a fight, I like to study one boxer's problem, solve it, and then communicate my solution vocally. On occasion my advice is disregarded, as when I tell a man to stay away from the other fellow's left and he 5 doesn't, but in such cases I assume that he hasn't heard my counsel, or that his opponent has, and has acted on it. Some fighters hear better and are more suggestible than others—for example, the pre-television Joe Louis. "Let him have it, Joe!" I would yell whenever I saw him fight, and sooner or later he would let the other fellow have it. Another fighter like that was the 10 late Marcel Cerdan, whom I would coach in his own language, to prevent opposition seconds from picking up our signals. "*Vas-y, Marcel!*" I used to shout, and Marcel always *y allait*. I get a feeling of participation that way that I don't in front of a television screen. I could yell, of course, but I

From *The Sweet Science*. Copyright 1951 by A. J. Liebling. Originally published in *The New Yorker*. Reprinted by permission of Russell & Volkening, Inc., as agents for the author.

would know that if my suggestion was adopted, it would be by the merest 15
coincidence.

2   Besides, when you go to a fight, the boxers aren't the only ones you
want to be heard by. You are surrounded by people whose ignorance of the
ring is exceeded only by their unwillingness to face facts—the sharpness of
your boxer's punching, for instance. Such people may take it upon them- 20
selves to disparage the principal you are advising. This disparagement is less
generally addressed to the man himself (as "Gavilan, you're a bum!") than
to his opponent, whom they have wrong-headedly picked to win. ("He's a
cream puff, Miceli!" they may typically cry. "He can't hurt you. He can't
hurt nobody. Look—slaps! Ha, ha!") They thus get at your man—and, by 25
indirection, at you. To put them in their place, you address neither them
nor their man but your man. ("Get the other eye, Gavilan!" you cry.) This
throws them off balance, because they haven't noticed anything the matter
with either eye. Then, before they can think of anything to say, you thunder, "Look at that eye!" It doesn't much matter whether or not the man has 30
been hit in the eye; he will be. Addressing yourself to the fighter when you
want somebody else to hear you is a parliamentary device, like "Mr. Chairman . . ." Before television, a prize-fight was to a New Yorker the nearest
equivalent to the New England town meeting. It taught a man to think on
his seat. 35

3   Less malignant than rooters for the wrong man, but almost as dis-
quieting, are those who are on the right side but tactically unsound. At the
moment when you have steered your boxer to a safe lead on points but can
see the other fellow is still dangerous, one of these maniacs will encourage
recklessness. "Finish the jerk, Harry!" he will sing out. "Stop holding him 40
up! Don't lose him!" But you, knowing the enemy is a puncher, protect your
client's interests. "Move to your left, Harry!" you call. "Keep moving!
Keep moving! Don't let him set!" I sometimes finish a fight like that in a cold
sweat.

4   If you go to a fight with a friend, you can keep up unilateral con- 45
versations on two vocal levels—one at the top of your voice, directed at your
fighter, and the other a running *expertise* nominally aimed at your companion but loud enough to reach a modest fifteen feet in each direction.
"Reminds me of Panama Al Brown," you may say as a new fighter enters
the ring. "He was five feet eleven and weighed a hundred and eighteen 50
pounds. This fellow may be about forty pounds heavier and a couple of
inches shorter, but he's got the same kind of neck. I saw Brown box a fellow named Mascart in Paris in 1927. Guy stood up in the top gallery and

threw an apple and hit Brown right on the top of the head. The whole house started yelling, 'Finish him, Mascart! He's groggy!' " Then, as the bout be- 55 gins, "Boxes like Al, too, except this fellow's a southpaw." If he wins, you say, "I told you he reminded me of Al Brown," and if he loses, "Well, well, I guess he's no Al Brown. They don't make fighters like Al any more." This identifies you as a man who (a) has been in Paris, (b) has been going to fights for a long time, and (c) therefore enjoys what the fellows who write 60 for quarterlies call a frame of reference.

5   It may be argued that this doesn't get you anywhere, but it at least constitutes what a man I once met named Thomas S. Matthews called communication. Mr. Matthews, who was the editor of *Time*, said that the most important thing in journalism is not reporting but communication. "What 65 are you going to communicate?" I asked him. "The most important thing," he said, "is the man on one end of the circuit saying 'My God, I'm alive! You're alive!' and the fellow on the other end, receiving his message, saying 'My God, you're right! We're both alive!' " I still think it is a hell of a way to run a news magazine, but it is a good reason for going to fights in person. 70 Television, if unchecked, may carry us back to a pre-tribal state of social development, when the family was the largest conversational unit.

6   Fights are also a great place for adding to your repertory of witty sayings. I shall not forget my adolescent delight when I first heard a fight fan yell, "I hope youse bot' gets knocked out!" I thought he had made it up, al- 75 though I found out later it was a cliché. It is a formula adaptable to an endless variety of situations outside the ring. The only trouble with it is it never works out. The place where I first heard the line was Bill Brown's, a fight club in a big shed behind a trolley station in Far Rockaway.

7   On another night there, the time for the main bout arrived and one 80 of the principals hadn't. The other fighter sat in the ring, a bantamweight with a face like a well-worn coin, and the fans stamped in cadence and whistled and yelled for their money back. It was thirty years before television, but there were only a couple of hundred men on hand. The preliminary fights had been terrible. The little fighter kept looking at his hands, 85 which were resting on his knees in cracked boxing gloves, and every now and then he would spit on the mat and rub the spittle into the canvas with one of his scuffed ring shoes. The longer he waited, the more frequently he spat, and I presumed he was worrying about the money he was supposed to get; it wouldn't be more than fifty dollars with a house that size, even if the 90 other man turned up. He had come there from some remote place like West or East New York, and he may have been thinking about the last train

home on the Long Island Railroad, too. Finally, the other bantamweight got there, looking out of breath and flustered. He had lost his way on the railroad—changed to the wrong train at Jamaica and had to go back there   95 and start over. The crowd booed so loud that he looked embarrassed. When the fight began, the fellow who had been waiting walked right into the new boy and knocked him down. He acted impatient. The tardy fellow got up and fought back gamely, but the one who had been waiting nailed him again, and the latecomer just about pulled up to one knee at the count of   100 seven. He had been hit pretty hard, and you could see from his face that he was wondering whether to chuck it. Somebody in the crowd yelled out, "Hey, Hickey! You kept us all waiting! Why don't you stay around awhile?" So the fellow got up and caught for ten rounds and probably made the one who had come early miss his train. It's another formula with multiple ap-   105 plications, and I think the man who said it that night in Far Rockaway did make it up.

8   Because of the way I feel about watching fights on television, I was highly pleased when I read, back in June, 1951, that the fifteen-round match between Joe Louis and Lee Savold, scheduled for June thirteenth at the   110 Polo Grounds, was to be neither televised, except to eight theater audiences in places like Pittsburgh and Albany, nor broadcast over the radio. I hadn't seen Louis with the naked eye since we shook hands in a pub in London in 1944. He had fought often since then, and I had seen his two bouts with Jersey Joe Walcott on television, but there hadn't been any fun in it. Those   115 had been held in public places, naturally, and I could have gone, but television gives you so plausible an adumbration of a fight, for nothing, that you feel it would be extravagant to pay your way in. It is like the potato, which is only a succedaneum for something decent to eat but which, once intro-duced into Ireland, proved so cheap that the peasants gave up their grain-   120 and-meat diet in favor of it. After that, the landlords let them keep just enough money to buy potatoes. William Cobbett, a great Englishman, said that he would sack any workmen of his he caught eating one of the cursed things, because as soon as potatoes appeared anywhere they brought down the standard of eating. I sometimes think of Cobbett on my way home from   125 the races, looking at the television aerials on all the little houses between here and Belmont Park. As soon as I heard that the fight wouldn't be on the air, I determined to buy a ticket.

9   On the night of the thirteenth, a Wednesday, it rained, and on the next night it rained again, so on the evening of June fifteenth the promoters,   130

the International Boxing Club, confronted by a night game at the Polo Grounds, transferred the fight to Madison Square Garden. The postponements upset a plan I had had to go to the fight with a friend, who had another date for the third night. But alone is a good way to go to a fight or the races, because you have more time to look around you, and you always get 135 all the conversation you can use anyway. I went to the Garden box office early Friday afternoon and bought a ten-dollar seat in the side arena—the first tiers rising in back of the boxes, midway between Eighth and Ninth Avenues on the 49th Street side of the house. There was only a scattering of ticket buyers in the lobby, and the man at the ticket window was polite—a 140 bad omen for the gate. After buying the ticket, I got into a cab in front of the Garden, and the driver naturally asked me if I was going to see the fight. I said I was, and he said, "He's all through."

10   I knew he meant Louis, and I said, "I know, and that's why it may be a good fight. If he weren't through, he might kill this guy." 145

11   The driver said, "Savold is a hooker. He breaks noses."

12   I said, "He couldn't break his own nose, even," and then began to wonder how a man would go about trying to do that. "It's a shame he's so hard up he had to fight at all at his age," I said, knowing the driver would understand I meant Louis. I was surprised that the driver was against Louis, 150 and I was appealing to his better feelings.

13   "He must have plenty socked away," said the driver. "Playing golf for a hundred dollars a hole."

14   "Maybe that helped him go broke," I said. "And anyway, what does that prove? There's many a man with a small salary who bets more 155 than he can afford." I had seen a scratch sheet on the seat next to the hackie. I was glad I was riding only as far as Brentano's with him.

15   The driver I had on the long ride home was a better type. As soon as I told him I was going to the fight, which was at about the same time that he dropped the flag, he said, "I guess the old guy can still sock." 160

16   I said, "I saw him murder Max Baer sixteen years ago. He was a sweet fighter then."

17   The driver said, "Sixteen years is a long time for a fighter. I don't remember anybody lasted sixteen years in the big money. Still, Savold is almost as old as he is. When you're a bum, nobody notices how old you 165 get."

18   We had a pleasant time on the West Side Highway, talking about how Harry Greb had gone on fighting when he was blind in one eye, only nobody knew it but his manager, and how Pete Herman had been the best

infighter in the world, because he had been practically blind in both eyes, so   170
he couldn't afford to fool around outside. "What Herman did, you couldn't
learn a boy now," the driver said. "They got no patience."

19   The fellow who drove me from my house to the Garden after dinner was also a man of good will, but rather different. He knew I was going to
the fight as soon as I told him my destination, and once we had got under   175
way, he said, "It is a pity that a man like Louis should be exploited to such a
degree that he has to fight again." It was only nine-fifteen, and he agreed
with me that I had plenty of time to get to the Garden for the main bout,
which was scheduled to begin at ten, but when we got caught in unexpectedly heavy traffic on Eleventh Avenue he grew impatient. "Come on,   180
Jersey!" he said, giving a station wagon in front of us the horn. "In the last
analysis, we have got to get to the Garden sometime." But it didn't help
much, because most of the other cars were heading for the Garden, too. The
traffic was so slow going toward Eighth Avenue on Fiftieth Street that I
asked him to let me out near the Garden corner, and joined the people   185
hurrying from the Independent Subway exit toward the Garden marquee. A
high percentage of them were from Harlem, and they were dressed as if for
a levee, the men in shimmering gabardines and felt hats the color of freshly
unwrapped chewing gum, the women in spring suits and fur pieces—it was a
cool night—and what seemed to me the prettiest hats of the season. They   190
seemed to me the prettiest lot of women I had seen in a long time, too, and
I reflected that if the fight had been televised, I would have missed them.
"Step out," I heard one beau say as his group swept past me, "or we won't
maybe get in. It's just like I told you—he's still one hell of a draw." As I
made my way through the now crowded lobby, I could hear the special cop   195
next to the ticket window chanting, "Six-, eight-, ten-, and fifteen-dollar
tickets only," which meant that the two-and-a-halfdollar general-admission
and the twenty-dollar ringside seats were sold out. It made me feel good, because it showed there were still some gregarious people left in the world.

20   Inside the Garden there was the same old happy drone of voices   200
as when Jimmy McLarnin was fighting and Jimmy Walker was at the ringside. There was only one small patch of bare seats, in a particularly bad part
of the ringside section. I wondered what sort of occupant I would find in
my seat; I knew from experience that there would be somebody in it. It
turned out to be a small, frail colored man in wine-red livery. He sat up   205
straight and pressed his shoulder blades against the back of the chair, so I
couldn't see the number. When I showed him my ticket, he said, "I don't

know nothing about that. You better see the usher." He was offering this token resistance, I knew, only to protect his self-esteem—to maintain the shadowy fiction that he was in the seat by error. When an usher wandered within hailing distance of us, I called him, and the little man left, to drift to some other part of the Garden, where he had no reputation as a ten-dollar-seat holder to lose, and there to squat contentedly on a step.

21   My seat was midway between the east and west ends of the ring, and about fifteen feet above it. Two not very skillful colored boys were finishing a four-rounder that the man in the next seat told me was an emergency bout, put on because there had been several knockouts in the earlier preliminaries. It gave me a chance to settle down and look around. It was ten o'clock by the time the colored boys finished and the man with the microphone announced the decision, but there was no sign of Louis or Savold. The fight wasn't on the air, so there was no need of the punctuality required by the radio business. (Later I read in the newspapers that the bout had been delayed in deference to the hundreds of people who were still in line to buy tickets and who wanted to be sure of seeing the whole fight.) Nobody made any spiel about beer, as on the home screen, although a good volume of it was being drunk all around. Miss Gladys Gooding, an organist, played the national anthem and a tenor sang it, and we all applauded. After that, the announcer introduced a number of less than illustrious prizefighters from the ring, but nobody whistled or acted restless. It was a good-natured crowd.

22   Then Louis and his seconds—what the author of *Boxiana* would have called his faction—appeared from a runway under the north stands and headed toward the ring. The first thing I noticed, from where I sat, was that the top of Louis's head was bald. He looked taller than I had remembered him, although surely he couldn't have grown after the age of thirty, and his face was puffy and impassive. It has always been so. In the days of his greatness, the press read menace in it. He walked stiff-legged, as was natural for a heavy man of thirty-seven, but when his seconds pulled off his dressing robe, his body looked all right. He had never been a lean man; his muscles had always been well buried beneath his smooth beige skin. I recalled the first time I had seen him fight—against Baer. That was at the Yankee Stadium, in September, 1935, and not only the great ball park but the roofs of all the apartment houses around were crowded with spectators, and hundreds of people were getting out of trains at the elevated I.R.T. station, which overlooks the field, and trying to loiter long enough to catch a few moments of action. Louis had come East that summer, after a single year as a professional, and had knocked out Primo Carnera in a few rounds. Carnera had been the heavyweight champion of the world in 1934, when Baer knocked him out. Baer, when he fought Louis, was the most powerful and gifted heavyweight of the day, although he had already fumbled away his title. But this mature 250 Baer, who had fought everybody, was frightened stiff by the twenty-one-year old mulatto boy. Louis outclassed him. The whole thing went only four rounds. There hadn't been anybody remotely like Louis since Dempsey in the early twenties.

23   The week of the Louis-Baer fight, a man I know wrote in a maga- 255 zine: "With half an eye, one can observe that the town is more full of stir than it has been in many moons. It is hard to find a place to park, hard to get a table in a restaurant, hard to answer all the phone calls. . . . Economic seers can explain it, if you care to listen. We prefer to remember that a sudden inflation of the town's spirit can be just as much psychological or 260 accidental as economic." I figured it was Louis.

24   Savold had now come up into the other corner, a jutty-jawed man with a fair skin but a red back, probably sunburned at his training camp. He was twenty pounds lighter than Louis, but that isn't considered a crushing handicap among heavyweights; Ezzard Charles, who beat Louis the 265 previous year, was ten pounds lighter than Savold. Savold was thirty-five, and there didn't seem to be much bounce in him. I had seen him fight twice in the winter of 1946, and I knew he wasn't much. Both bouts had been against a young Negro heavyweight named Al Hoosman, a tall, skinny fellow just out of the Army. Hoosman had started well the first time, but 270 Savold had hurt him with body punches and won the decision. The second time, Hoosman had stayed away and jabbed him silly. An old third-rater like Savold, I knew, doesn't improve with five more years on him. But an old third-rater doesn't rattle easily, either, and I was sure he'd do his best. It made me more apprehensive, in one way, than if he'd been any good. I 275 wouldn't have liked to see Louis beaten by a good young fighter, but it would be awful to see him beaten by a clown. Not that I have anything against Savold; I just think it's immoral for a fellow without talent to get too far. A lot of others in the crowd must have felt the same way, because the house was quiet when the fight started—as if the Louis rooters didn't 280 want to ask too much of Joe. There weren't any audible rooters for Savold, though, of course, there would have been if he had landed one good punch.

25   I remembered reading in a newspaper that Savold had said he would walk right out and bang Louis in the temple with a right, which would

scramble his thinking. But all he did was come forward as he had against   285
Hoosman, with his left low. A fellow like that never changes. Louis walked
out straight and stiff-legged, and jabbed his left into Savold's face. He did
it again and again, and Savold didn't seem to know what to do about it. And
Louis jabs a lot harder than a fellow like Hoosman. Louis didn't have to
chase Savold, and he had no reason to run away from him, either, so the   290
stiff legs were all right. When the two men came close together, Louis jarred
Savold with short punches, and Savold couldn't push him around, so that
was all right, too. After the first round, the crowd knew Louis would win if
his legs would hold him.

26   In the second round Louis began hitting Savold with combinations—   295
quick sequences of punches, like a right under the heart and a left hook
to the right side of the head. A sports writer I know had told me that Louis
hadn't been putting combinations together for several fights back. Combinations demand a superior kind of coordination, but a fighter who has
once had that can partly regain it by hard work. A couple of times it looked   300
as if Louis was trying for a knockout, but when Savold didn't come apart,
Louis returned to jabbing. A man somewhere behind me kept saying to a
companion, "I read Savold was a tricky fighter. He's got to do something!"
But Savold didn't, until late in the fifth round, by which time his head must
have felt like a sick music box. Then he threw a right to Louis's head and it   305
landed. I thought I could see Louis shrink, as if he feared trouble. His response ten years ago would have been to tear right back into the man. Savold
threw another right, exactly the same kind, and that hit Louis, too. No good
fighter should have been hit twice in succession with that kind of foolish
punch. But the punches weren't hard enough to slow Louis down, and that   310
was the end of that. In the third minute of the sixth round, he hit Savold
with a couple of combinations no harder than those that had gone before,
but Savold was weak now. His legs were going limp, and Louis was pursuing
him as he backed toward my side of the ring. Then Louis swung like an axman with his right (he wasn't snapping it as he used to), and his left   315
dropped over Savold's guard and against his jaw, and the fellow was rolling
over and over on the mat, rolling the way football players do when they fall
on a fumbled ball. The referee was counting and Savold was rolling, and he
got up on either nine or ten, I couldn't tell which (later, I read that it was
ten, so he was out officially), but you could see he was knocked silly, and the   320
referee had his arms around him, and it was over.

27   The newspapermen, acres of them near the ring, were banging out
the leads for the running stories they had already telegraphed, and I felt sorry

for them, because they never have time to enjoy boxing matches. Since the
fight was not broadcast, there was no oily-voiced chap to drag Louis over to 325
a microphone and ask him stupid questions. He shook hands with Savold
twice, once right after the knockout and again a few minutes later, when
Savold was ready to leave the ring, as if he feared Savold wouldn't remember
the first handshake.

28   I drifted toward the lobby with the crowd. The chic Harlem people 330
were saying to one another, "It was terrific, darling! It was terrific!" I could
see that an element of continuity had been restored to their world. But there
wasn't any of the wild exultation that had followed those first Louis victories in 1935. These people had celebrated so many times—except, of
course, the younger ones, who were small children when Louis knocked out 335
Baer. I recognized one of the Garden promoters, usually a sour fellow, looking happy. The bout had brought in receipts of $94,684, including my ten
dollars, but, what was more important to the Garden, Louis was sure to
draw a lot more the next time, and at a higher scale of prices.

29   I walked downtown on Eighth Avenue to a point where the crowd 340
began to thin out, and climbed into a taxi that had been stopped by the
light on a cross street. This one had a Negro driver.

30   "The old fellow looked pretty good tonight," I said. "Had those
combinations going."

31   "Fight over?" the driver asked. If there had been television, or even 345
radio, he would have known about everything, and I wouldn't have had the
fun of telling him.

32   "Sure," I said. "He knocked the guy out in the sixth."

33   "I was afraid he wouldn't," said the driver. "You know, it's a funny
thing," he said, after we had gone on a way, "but I been twenty-five years in 350
New York now and never seen Joe Louis in the flesh."

34   "You've seen him on television, haven't you?"

35   "Yeah," he said. "But that don't count." After a while he said, "I
remember when he fought Carnera. The celebration in Harlem. They poisoned his mind before that fight, his managers and Jack Blackburn did. They 355
told him Carnera was Mussolini's man and Mussolini started the Ethiopian
War. He cut that man down like he was a tree."

QUESTIONS

READER AND PURPOSE

1. How does Liebling regard fight fans? Read carefully these two sentences: "Such people may take it upon themselves to disparage the principal you are advising"; and " 'Gavilan, you're a bum.' " The first is Liebling's description of what the fans say; the second is what they literally do say. The diction of the first sentence is inflated—that is, it is more serious and formal than the subject it describes—which is a time-honored device of satire. Consider again—what is Liebling's attitude toward his fellow spectators? How does he regard himself in the role of fight fan? Support your answer by evidence from the essay.

2. Compare to those quoted in question 1 this sentence from paragraph 26: "Then Louis swung like an axman with his right (he wasn't snapping it as he used to), and his left dropped over Savold's guard, and the fellow was rolling over and over on the mat, rolling the way football players do when they fall on a fumbled ball." Why does it suggest that Liebling takes fighting and fighters more seriously than he takes the fans?

You begin to realize that Liebling's tone * is complex rather than simple, not easily reduced to such a label as "serious" or "amused," "respectful" or "satiric." At times Liebling is serious, and at times he is pleasantly satiric; but these are not two separate attitudes which, like masks, he puts on and off as suits him. Rather they are two aspects of the same complex attitude. This complexity of tone is reflected in the diction, the sentence structure, and the organization of the essay.

ORGANIZATION

3. What constitutes the beginning of this essay—paragraph 1? paragraphs 1-3? paragraphs 1-7? Explain.

4. The section dealing with the Louis-Savold fight has four main parts. Identify and give a title to each.

5. The organization of this selection seems simpler and looser than it is. Before the essay is over we view the fight and its spectators from numerous angles. We see the action in the ring as a camera might record it; we see the fighters and the crowd through Liebling's eyes; we see Louis as other observers regard him; we see the fight and fighters projected against a background of other bouts and other boxers; and finally we see this match set in the general framework of prizefighting and its fans. To appreciate this complex organization, look again at the parts you identified in question 4. What does each contribute to our understanding of the Louis-Savold fight?

6. As much as the fight, the observer is here a part of the subject, and the essay moves us back and forth between the scene and the personality that watches it. Examine, for instance, paragraph 24. Although it begins with a sentence describing the scene ("Savold had now come up into the other corner . . ."), it soon slips away from the arena. In what sentence does the paragraph return to the fight? What does the writer do in between these points? Find two or three other paragraphs that illustrate this same movement between the scene and the man watching it. Do you think that a sports editor on a metropolitan morning paper would have accepted this account from a reporter assigned to cover a boxing match? Why or why not?

7. The complexity of Liebling's subject is perhaps best revealed in the attitudes he records of other fans: the "happy promoter" in lines 335-36, for example; the newsmen "banging out leads" (322); the "oily-voiced" announcer (325), happily absent on this night; the "chic Harlem people" (330); the four cabdrivers. To each of these the fight means something different. What does it mean to the promoter? to the announcer? to each of the others?

8. Of all these reactions, Liebling gives greatest weight to the comments of the fourth cabdriver. It is on his graphic description of Louis in his prime—" 'He cut that man down like he was a tree' "—that the essay stops. Is this a good closing? Why or why not? Why does Liebling end with this sudden flashback to the young, quick Louis?

9. Thus we see that the writer's purpose here is complex indeed. To describe a particular fight, the fans interested in it, their attitudes and comments, the people who profit from the fighters—and all these as they seem to a sensitive and experienced observer—this is Liebling's purpose. Yet there is one final complication; the closing suggests that Liebling is writing about more than one fight and one fighter, about more even than fighting—what?

SENTENCES

10. Liebling's sentence structure is relatively colloquial *, reflecting the rhythms of speech. This is achieved in three ways: by keeping the clauses brief; by avoiding interrupted movement *; and by multiple co-ordination *, that is, linking several clauses with *and* or *but*. All three techniques are illustrated in this sentence: "He [Louis] had fought often since then, and I had seen his two bouts with Jersey Joe Walcott on television, but there hadn't been any fun in it." Of course most of the sentences do not reveal all these devices so plainly; try, however, to find three or four others which do. Such a style appears simple, but the appearance is deceptive. Far from mechanically reproducing the actual patterns of speech, it rather suggests colloquial simplicity by careful selection and arrangement. Listen to the conversations of your friends and compare what you hear with what Liebling writes. What improvements has he made?

DICTION

11. Look up: *disparage* (21), *malignant* (36), *client* (42), *expertise* (47), *quarterlies* (61), *repertory* (73), *cliché* (76), *adumbration* (117), *hooker* (146), *beau* (193), *jabbing* (302), *leads* (323).

12. Liebling's diction is wide-ranging, sweeping from colloquialisms and even slang at one extreme (*hackies, spiel, third-rater*) to learned, Latinate terms at the other (*malignant, unilateral, succedaneum*). Point out four or five further examples of each extreme. Why is the diction of paragraphs 25 and 26 simpler than that of paragraphs 4 and 5?

13. Study paragraph 7. Economically but surely Liebling creates the scene in Brown's fight club. He does not bother to describe carefully the face of the "other fighter"; we are not told the color of his eyes, whether his cheekbones are prominent, his nose crooked, his ears large. Yet we receive a vivid impression of his face. In what words? What details of his equipment and of his actions as he waits make this fighter a real, living figure? Could an imaginative reader almost infer from these few details the life story of the "other fighter"? Try it.

14. With equal ease and brevity Liebling characterizes the four cabdrivers. What kind of man is each? Do the cabbies also serve to unify the various sections of the essay?

POINTS TO LEARN

1. Tone is not always simple. It may be exceedingly complicated.
2. The subject of an essay, like tone, may be complex and multiple.
3. Similes * are effective in description, particularly brief description.
4. Isolated, vivid details are sometimes better than a complete catalogue.

SUGGESTIONS FOR WRITING

Probably it will be better to imitate parts rather than the whole of this selection. Whichever topic you choose, write in the first person and make your own feelings and impressions a part of the subject. Work in also typical comments and attitudes of other observers. Since you are writing in the first person, remember that your sentence structure must be less formal than in a more impersonal, academic paper.

1. Modeling your treatment upon paragraphs 1-7, select one of these topics:

(a) football (or wrestling, basketball—any sport but boxing) with "the naked eye."

(b) why you prefer movies to television, or stage plays to films (reverse either topic if you wish).

2. Paragraphs 8-35:

(a) a particular baseball game (or any sport but boxing).

(b) a performance of the circus or a play, a political rally or other public event such as a parade or civic celebration.

3. Paragraphs 2-4:

(a) the types of baseball or wrestling fans.

(b) the women who attend bridge parties, the men who play poker.

4. Paragraphs 24-26:

the climactic moments of a sports event—a tennis match, say, or mile run. (Unless you have the technical knowledge required, however, leave this assignment alone.)

IMPROVING YOUR STYLE

In your composition include:

1. A colloquial freight-train * sentence like Liebling's in lines 114-15 (see Question 10).

2. Some experimentation with diction, trying especially for a wide range from colloquial even slangy words to learned, literary ones. (Remember, however, that the words, whether colloquial or literary, should be used because they convey exactly the right meaning and tone.)

Once More to the Lake

E. B. White (1899–1985) was a humorist and satirist, best known for his editorial comments in *The New Yorker*, collected in *The Wild Flag* (1946), and for his essays, which have been published in several collections, including *One Man's Meat* (1941) and *The Points of My Compass* (1962). But White also wrote short stories (*The Second Tree From the Corner*, 1952) and children's books (*Charlotte's Web*, 1952). "Once More to the Lake" is a classic of the personal essay, and it illustrates particularly well the pattern of that kind of essay, its progression from the outer world of things and other people to the inner world of the writer's responses. That inner world is the true subject of the kind of writing we call personal.

1   One summer, along about 1904, my father rented a camp on a lake in Maine and took us all there for the month of August. We all got ringworm from some kittens and had to rub Pond's Extract on our arms and legs night and morning, and my father rolled over in a canoe with all his clothes on; but outside of that the vacation was a success and from then 5 on none of us ever thought there was any place in the world like that lake in Maine. We returned summer after summer—always on August 1st for one month. I have since become a salt-water man, but sometimes in summer there are days when the restlessness of the tides and the fearful cold of the sea water and the incessant wind which blows across the afternoon and into 10 the evening make me wish for the placidity of a lake in the woods. A few weeks ago this feeling got so strong I bought myself a couple of bass hooks and a spinner and returned to the lake where we used to go, for a week's fishing and to revisit old haunts.

2   I took along my son, who had never had any fresh water up his 15 nose and who had seen lily pads only from train windows. On the journey over to the lake I began to wonder what it would be like. I wondered how

"Once More to the Lake" from *One Man's Meat* by E. B. White. Copyright 1941 by E. B. White. Reprinted by permission of Harper & Row, Publishers, Inc.

time would have marred this unique, this holy spot—the coves and streams, the hills that the sun set behind, the camps and the paths behind the camps. I was sure that the tarred road would have found it out and I won- 20 dered in what other ways it would be desolated. It is strange how much you can remember about places like that once you allow your mind to re- turn into the grooves which lead back. You remember one thing, and that suddenly reminds you of another thing. I guess I remembered clearest of all the early mornings, when the lake was cool and motionless, remembered 25 how the bedroom smelled of the lumber it was made of and of the wet woods whose scent entered through the screen. The partitions in the camp were thin and did not extend clear to the top of the rooms, and as I was always the first up I would dress softly so as not to wake the others, and sneak out into the sweet outdoors and start out in the canoe, keeping close 30 along the shore in the long shadows of the pines. I remembered being very careful never to rub my paddle against the gunwale for fear of disturbing the stillness of the cathedral.

3   The lake had never been what you would call a wild lake. There were cottages sprinkled around the shores, and it was in farming country 35 although the shores of the lake were quite heavily wooded. Some of the cottages were owned by nearby farmers, and you would live at the shore and eat your meals at the farmhouse. That's what our family did. But al- though it wasn't wild, it was a fairly large and undisturbed lake and there were places in it which, to a child at least, seemed infinitely remote and 40 primeval.

4   I was right about the tar: it led to within half a mile of the shore. But when I got back there, with my boy, and we settled into a camp near a farmhouse and into the kind of summertime I had known, I could tell that it was going to be pretty much the same as it had been before—I knew 45 it, lying in bed the first morning, smelling the bedroom, and hearing the boy sneak quietly out and go off along the shore in a boat. I began to sus- tain the illusion that he was I, and therefore, by simple transposition, that I was my father. This sensation persisted, kept cropping up all the time we were there. It was not an entirely new feeling, but in this setting it grew 50 much stronger. I seemed to be living a dual existence. I would be in the middle of some simple act, I would be picking up a bait box or laying down a table fork, or I would be saying something, and suddenly it would be not I but my father who was saying the words or making the gesture. It gave me a creepy sensation.   55

5   We went fishing the first morning. I felt the same damp moss cov-

ering the worms in the bait can, and saw the dragonfly alight on the tip of
my rod as it hovered a few inches from the surface of the water. It was the
arrival of this fly that convinced me beyond any doubt that everything was
as it always had been, that the years were a mirage and there had been no   60
years. The small waves were the same, chucking the rowboat under the chin
as we fished at anchor, and the boat was the same boat, the same color
green and the ribs broken in the same places, and under the floor-boards
the same fresh-water leavings and débris—the dead helgramite, the wisps of
moss, the rusty discarded fish-hook, the dried blood from yesterday's catch.   65
We stared silently at the tips of our rods, at the dragonflies that came and
went. I lowered the tip of mine into the water, tentatively, pensively dis-
lodging the fly, which darted two feet away, poised, darted two feet back,
and came to rest again a little farther up the rod. There had been no years
between the ducking of this dragonfly and the other one—the one that was   70
part of memory. I looked at the boy, who was silently watching his fly, and
it was my hands that held his rod, my eyes watching. I felt dizzy and didn't
know which rod I was at the end of.

6   We caught two bass, hauling them in briskly as though they were
mackerel, pulling them over the side of the boat in a businesslike manner   75
without any landing net, and stunning them with a blow on the back of
the head. When we got back for a swim before lunch, the lake was exactly
where we had left it, the same number of inches from the dock, and there
was only the merest suggestion of a breeze. This seemed an utterly enchanted sea, this lake you could leave to its own devices for a few hours and   80
come back to, and find that it had not stirred, this constant and trustworthy body of water. In the shallows, the dark, water-soaked sticks and
twigs, smooth and old, were undulating in clusters on the bottom against
the clean ribbed sand, and the track of the mussel was plain. A school of
minnows swam by, each minnow with its small individual shadow, dou-   85
bling the attendance, so clear and sharp in the sunlight. Some of the other
campers were in swimming, along the shore, one of them with a cake of
soap, and the water felt thin and clear and unsubstantial. Over the years
there had been this person with the cake of soap, this cultist, and here he
was. There had been no years.   90

7   Up to the farmhouse to dinner through the teeming, dusty field,
the road under our sneakers was only a two-track road. The middle track
was missing, the one with the marks of the hooves and the splotches of
dried, flaky manure. There had always been three tracks to choose from in

choosing which track to walk in; now the choice was narrowed down to   95
two. For a moment I missed terribly the middle alternative. But the way
led past the tennis court, and something about the way it lay there in the
sun reassured me; the tape had loosened along the backline, the alleys were
green with plantains and other weeds, and the net (installed in June and
removed in September) sagged in the dry noon, and the whole place   100
steamed with midday heat and hunger and emptiness. There was a choice
of pie for dessert, and one was blueberry and one was apple, and the waitresses were the same country girls, there having been no passage of time,
only the illusion of it as in a dropped curtain—the waitresses were still fifteen; their hair had been washed, that was the only difference—they had   105
been to the movies and seen the pretty girls with the clean hair.

8   Summertime, oh summertime, pattern of life indelible, the fade-
proof lake, the woods unshatterable, the pasture with the sweetfern and
the juniper forever and ever, summer without end; this was the background, and the life along the shore was the design, the cottages with their   110
innocent and tranquil design, their tiny docks with the flagpole and the
American flag floating against the white clouds in the blue sky, the little
paths over the roots of the trees leading from camp to camp and the paths
leading back to the outhouses and the can of lime for sprinkling, and at
the souvenir counters at the store the miniature birch-bark canoes and the   115
post cards that showed things looking a little better than they looked. This
was the American family at play, escaping the city heat, wondering whether
the newcomers in the camp at the head of the cove were "common" or
"nice," wondering whether it was true that the people who drove up for
Sunday dinner at the farmhouse were turned away because there wasn't   120
enough chicken.

9   It seemed to me, as I kept remembering all this, that those times
and those summers had been infinitely precious and worth saving. There
had been jollity and peace and goodness. The arriving (at the beginning
of August) had been so big a business in itself, at the railway station the   125
farm wagon drawn up, the first smell of the pine-laden air, the first glimpse
of the smiling farmer, and the great importance of the trunks and your father's enormous authority in such matters, and the feel of the wagon under
you for the long ten-mile haul, and at the top of the last long hill catching
the first view of the lake after eleven months of not seeing this cherished   130
body of water. The shouts and cries of the other campers when they saw
you, and the trunks to be unpacked, to give up their rich burden. (Arriving

was less exciting nowadays, when you sneaked up in your car and parked it under a tree near the camp and took out the bags and in five minutes it was all over, no fuss, no loud wonderful fuss about trunks.)   135

10   Peace and goodness and jollity. The only thing that was wrong now, really, was the sound of the place, an unfamiliar nervous sound of the outboard motors. This was the note that jarred, the one thing that would sometimes break the illusion and set the years moving. In those other summertimes all motors were inboard; and when they were at a little dis-   140 tance, the noise they made was a sedative, an ingredient of summer sleep. They were one-cylinder and two-cylinder engines, and some were make-and-break and some were jump-spark, but they all made a sleepy sound across the lake. The one-lungers throbbed and fluttered, and the twin-cylinder ones purred and purred, and that was a quiet sound too. But now the campers   145 all had outboards. In the daytime, in the hot mornings, these motors made a petulant, irritable sound; at night, in the still evening when the afterglow lit the water, they whined about one's ears like mosquitoes. My boy loved our rented outboard, and his great desire was to achieve singlehanded mastery over it, and authority, and he soon learned the trick of choking it a   150 little (but not too much), and the adjustment of the needle valve. Watching him I would remember the things you could do with the old one-cylinder engine with the heavy flywheel, how you could have it eating out of your hand if you got really close to it spiritually. Motor boats in those days didn't have clutches, and you would make a landing by shutting off the   155 motor at the proper time and coasting in with a dead rudder. But there was a way of reversing them, if you learned the trick, by cutting the switch and putting it on again exactly on the final dying revolution of the flywheel, so that it would kick back against compression and begin reversing. Approaching a dock in a strong following breeze, it was difficult to slow up sufficiently   160 by the ordinary coasting method, and if a boy felt he had complete mastery over his motor, he was tempted to keep it running beyond its time and then reverse it a few feet from the dock. It took a cool nerve, because if you threw the switch a twentieth of a second too soon you would catch the flywheel when it still had speed enough to go up past center, and the boat would   165 leap ahead, charging bull-fashion at the dock.

11   We had a good week at the camp. The bass were biting well and the sun shone endlessly, day after day. We would be tired at night and lie down in the accumulated heat of the little bed rooms after the long hot day and the breeze would stir almost imperceptibly outside and the smell of   170 the swamp drift in through the rusty screens. Sleep would come easily and

in the morning the red squirrel would be on the roof, tapping out his gay routine. I kept remembering everything, lying in bed in the mornings—the small steamboat that had a long rounded stern like the lip of a Ubangi, and how quietly she ran on the moonlight sails, when the older boys played 175 their mandolins and the girls sang and we ate doughnuts dipped in sugar, and how sweet the music was on the water in the shining night, and what it had felt like to think about girls then. After breakfast we would go up to the store and the things were in the same place—the minnows in a bottle, the plugs and spinners disarranged and pawed over by the youngsters from 180 the boys' camp, the fig newtons and the Beeman's gum. Outside, the road was tarred and cars stood in front of the store. Inside, all was just as it had always been, except there was more Coca Cola and not so much Moxie and root beer and birch beer and sarsaparilla. We would walk out with a bottle of pop apiece and sometimes the pop would backfire up our noses and hurt. 185 We explored the streams, quietly, where the turtles slid off the sunny logs and dug their way into the soft bottom; and we lay on the town wharf and fed worms to the tame bass. Everywhere we went I had trouble making out which was I, the one walking at my side, the one walking in my pants.

12   One afternoon while we were there at the lake a thunderstorm 190 came up. It was like the revival of an old melodrama that I had seen long ago with childish awe. The second-act climax of the drama of the electrical disturbance over a lake in America had not changed in any important respect. This was the big scene, still the big scene. The whole thing was so familiar, the first feeling of oppression and heat and a general air around 195 camp of not wanting to go very far away. In midafternoon (it was all the same) a curious darkening of the sky, and a lull in everything that had made life tick; and then the way the boats suddenly swung the other way at their moorings with the coming of a breeze out of the new quarter, and the premonitory rumble. Then the kettle drum, then the snare, then the 200 bass drum and cymbals, then crackling light against the dark, and the gods grinning and licking their chops in the hills. Afterward the calm, the rain steadily rustling in the calm lake, the return of light and hope and spirits, and the campers running out in joy and relief to go swimming in the rain, their bright cries perpetuating the deathless joke about how they were get- 205 ting simply drenched, and the children screaming with delight at the new sensation of bathing in the rain, and the joke about getting drenched linking the generations in a strong indestructible chain. And the comedian who waded in carrying an umbrella.

13   When the others went swimming my son said he was going in too. 210

He pulled his dripping trunks from the line where they had hung all through the shower, and wrung them out. Languidly, and with no thought of going in, I watched him, his hard little body, skinny and bare, saw him wince slightly as he pulled up around his vitals the small, soggy, icy garment. As he buckled the swollen belt suddenly my groin felt the chill of 215 death.

QUESTIONS

READER AND PURPOSE

1. "Once More to the Lake" appeals to almost everyone. Yet the degree of appeal probably varies. Describe the reader to whom it would appeal the most; the reader to whom it might appeal the least.

2. Which of the following do you think best expresses the theme of "Once More to the Lake"?

> (a) The first years of the twentieth century were more innocent, more idyllic than those of our violent, destructive, contaminated time.
> (b) Nothing ever really changes.
> (c) Summertime is the happiest season.
> (d) Expecting to find the lake changed and the past unrecapturable, the writer suddenly realizes that the real victim of time is not the lake, but himself.

ORGANIZATION

3. What does each of the first three paragraphs contribute to the beginning of the essay?

4. Among other things, a beginning often establishes the writer's tone *. What is E. B. White's feeling about the lake? About his son?

5. The middle portion of the essay (beginning with paragraph 4) is an analysis of the summer ritual. Paragraph 4 might be entitled "Settling In"; paragraphs 5 and 6, "Fishing the First Morning"; paragraph 7, "Returning to the Farmhouse for Dinner." Give a title to the remaining paragraphs of the middle section.

6. Each paragraph in the body of the essay deals with sameness, change, or a mixture of the two. Which predominates overall—change or sameness? Which appears to be the more unsettling to the writer? Underline those passages in which E. B. White expresses his deepest feelings about sameness and change.

7. What rather unusual method of development is used in paragraph 12?

8. The final paragraph is constructed so that it leads up to and ends on the

word *death*. Is this term (or rather the idea it denotes) central to White's essay? Do you think this paragraph makes an effective conclusion to the essay? Why or why not?

SENTENCES

9. The sentence in lines 61-5 ("The small waves . . .") is a detailed expansion of what key word near its beginning? Show how White similarly spins out the sentence in lines 107-16 by expanding a key term. Such expansion is not padding. What would have been lost had White simply written "The small boat was the same" and let it go at that? Too often people complain that they "can't think" of anything to write about, when all they have to do is to turn an abstract *, general statement into a series of particulars.

10. Point to places where White relieves long, complicated sentences like those referred to in the preceding question with short, direct ones.

DICTION

11. Look up: *incessant* (10), *placidity* (11), *spinner* (13), *gunwale* (32), *primeval* (41), *helgramite* (64), *undulating* (83), *mussel* (84), *cultist* (89), *teeming* (91), *plantains* (99), *indelible* (107), *juniper* (109), *petulant* (147), *Ubangi* (174), *Moxie* (183), *sarsaparilla* (184), *melodrama* (191), *premonitory* (200).

12. (For the mechanically-minded.) What do these expressions mean: *make-and-break* (142-43), *jump-spark* (143), *one-lungers* (144), *twin-cylinder ones* (144), *needle valve* (151), *flywheel* (153)?

13. This essay is remarkable for its concrete *, specific, and sensuous diction. Make a list of the various sounds, smells, tastes, and tactile sensations in "Once More to the Lake."

14. Compare the two revisions below with the sentence E. B. White wrote and explain why his diction is far better:

> *White:* "In the shallows, the dark, water-soaked sticks and twigs, smooth and old, were undulating in clusters on the bottom against the clean ribbed sand, and the track of the mussel was plain." (82-84)
>
> *Revision 1:* Where the water was shallow you saw the usual trash on the bottom.
>
> *Revision 2:* Smooth twigs and sticks bobbed near the bank, but the sand was clean. You could see the tracks made by some creature in the sand.

15. List four or five colloquial * words or phrases in this essay. The following words, on the other hand, are relatively formal: *placidity* (11), *primeval* (41), *imperceptibility* (170), *premonitory* (200). Which kind of diction is more common in this selection—formal or informal?

16. In paragraph 9 White says, "There had been jollity and peace and good-ness" (124). How would the emphasis and rhythm have changed had he written instead "jollity, peace and goodness"?

17. Point out all the similes * and metaphors * you can find in this selection. Which two or three did you like the most?

POINTS TO LEARN

1. Almost any kind of personal experience can be turned into enduring litera-ture if one has the eye, the ear, and the sensibility.

2. "Once More to the Lake" succeeds in part because the writer knows the names of things. His diction is concrete and specific. At the same time, E. B. White can use Latinate diction when precision of thought or feeling is re-quired. Colloquial diction gives the illusion of a speaking voice and reminds us that we are listening to an individual human being, to his longings, fears, joys, biases, and insights.

SUGGESTIONS FOR WRITING

1. Write your own version of "Once More to the Lake," describing a return to a place you once enjoyed. The setting, your reactions, and your interpretation will be different. But try to make your diction as wide-ranging, as specific, and therefore as interesting as E. B. White's.

2. Learning as much as you can from this essay, describe the texture of city life. Be specific and write with a definite tone so that your reader knows how you feel toward your subject.

IMPROVING YOUR STYLE

Include in your composition:

1. A long sentence like White's in lines 61-65 in which a general image * (in his case the boat) is expanded into a series of particulars.

2. Two or three short emphatic sentences.

3. Several metaphors and several similes.

Writing About Literature

Why write about Literature? Why not simply read it and enjoy it? Well, in part because a short story, play, poem, or film is a clear and ready-made subject; it has distinct boundaries and greatly simplifies the problem of invention, that is of finding something to write about. More importantly, writing about literature forces one to improve his reading and to sharpen his sensibilities. Just as we don't really look at something until we are forced to draw it, so we don't really perceive a literary work until we have to write about it.

Given a story or a poem to discuss, one may proceed in two rather different ways. On the one hand, he may work impressionistically, first describing or summarizing the work in general terms and then, in more detail, writing about how the work affected him, what emotions and ideas and associations it aroused. The danger in approaching literature in this way is that it is easy to slip away from the text altogether and to ramble on about one's "feelings" in a vague and sentimental way. To be done well, impression requires not only sensitivity and precise control of the language of feeling, but also the discipline to keep one's impressions within limits appropriate to the work. Without such discipline and sensitivity, impressionistic criticism is likely to become a kind of gush, which tells a reader little or nothing about the work and which does not even help the writer focus and define his responses.

For this reason, most writing about literature is not impressionism, but a more objective kind of analysis, critical analysis we may call it, though "critical" in this context does not have its usual sense of carping or fault-finding. Critical analysis is less concerned with the reader's feelings than with the work itself. It looks closely at each of the elements that go into the making of a story, play, or poem. It attempts to identify these elements, to understand the relationships among them, and hence to comprehend what meaning they imply, what complex reaction to man or society or the universe.

The value of such analysis lies in calling attention to what might otherwise go unnoticed. The inexperienced reader of literature is all too likely to suppose that a short story is no more than its plot, or that a poem has been understood when one is able to paraphrase it. In critical analysis, however, one does not generally rehash the plot (unless one has reason to suppose his readers are unfamiliar with it) or paraphrase the poem. Rather he works below such surfaces to reveal deeper patterns of meaning and structure, revelations which will enable other readers in turn to see more in the work. Critical analysis is organized around such topics as character relationships, conflicts, the significance of setting, how a writer uses symbols, manipulates his "point of view," or develops patterns in imagery, with the ultimate purpose of showing how such matters relate to, and reveal the meaning and overall structure of, the literary work. The analytical critic does not merely retell the story or the poem in his own words.

To convince his reader of the truth or reasonableness of his conclusions about characters, say, or setting, the literary analyst sticks closely to the "facts" of the work discussed, adding nothing that cannot objectively be shown to be present and omitting nothing of obvious prominence, a procedure that introduces at least some objectivity into literary discussion. Hence, it follows that the literary analyst will support his points by referring to these "facts," whether in his own words or by quoting from his text.

How to handle such quotations, how to divide the subject into its parts, and how to achieve the proper tone—all these and more can be learned from the close study of good models. Accordingly, this section reprints various ways of writing about literature. George Woodcock's essay is an example of literary impressionism, of writing that arouses our interest in a piece of literature without our having to analyze it closely. Guy Davenport, on the other hand, discusses a poem in relation to varying critical attitudes toward it, while John Ciardi shows through close and sensitive reading just how much can be seen and felt in a poem. Flannery O'Connor advises young writers about the craft of fiction, and along the way gives instructive advice about reading short stories. William Arthur Deacon shows how the critic may use humour to reveal the shortcomings of a literary work. X. J. Kennedy brings to the discussion of films the kind of close and revealing analysis applied to plays and novels. Finally, Maynard Mack's exploration of *Hamlet* reminds us that literary criticism can be not only exciting discovery, but also—sometimes—a work of art in itself.

Margaret Atwood: Poet as Novelist

George Woodcock's extensive writings (see pp. 507–10 and this essay) include a good deal of perceptive criticism and commentary on Canadian literature. In this selection he shows how a short poem can be analyzed with skill and precision in order to reveal its complexity. The critic's language is not simple, but it is appropriate for discovering and describing the subtleties of Atwood's poem.

1   The most recent of Margaret Atwood's six books of verse is a collection of poems of sexual communion—for it is a relationship too acrid to be called *love* in the ordinary sense that she describes—entitled with mordantly analogical appropriateness *Power Politics.* The opening poem is a terse and tense pair of couplets that not only set the acerbic tone of the 5 volume itself, but also present an image that takes one by an amazingly short cut to the very heart of Atwood's kind of poetry and—what is largely the same thing—her kind of perception:

> you fit into me
> like a hook into an eye   10
> a fish hook
> an open eye

2   It is as sharp and disillusioned an expression as one could expect of the cruel inevitabilities of love: that what is so appropriate (fitting) 15 should also be so painful. But look farther, Margaret Atwood is no mere black romantic, delighted only to uncover the horrors in what the polite world likes to dismiss as fortunate because it cannot be escaped. At least three essential characteristics of her poetic nature emerge from a closer look at this veritable caltrop of a poem—spiny in whatever direction you 20 turn it.

From "Margaret Atwood: Poet as Novelist" in *The Canadian Novel in the Twentieth Century* by George Woodcock. Reprinted by permission of The Canadian Publishers, McClelland and Stewart Limited, Toronto.

3   First there is her skill at the poetic booby trap—the sharp ironic inversion by which such an image of domestic bliss as the Victorian hook-and-eye—so secure a fastening until welcome hands undo it—is suddenly transformed by a shift to a related image which shuts out any thought of bliss, shuts it out like an eyelid, with its evocation of a pain one feels with 25 an almost physical twinge, in one's mind's eye.

4   But there is another, more intellectual kind of inversion involved: the poet proceeds from the metaphorical to the literal use of an image—that of the eye—and in this way reminds us of that world of resonant cor-respondences, of shading meanings and relationships in which our mental 30 patterns as well as our physical perceptions exist. And yet, in that complex of symbolic relationships, our attention is still held by that vital image, the eye itself which holds so much that is significant in Margaret Atwood's poetry. For the eye sees, and is hurt, and so perception and feeling merge into each other.   35

QUESTIONS

READER AND PURPOSE

1. As a critical reviewer Woodcock's purpose is to point out both the qualities and the faults in Atwood's book, *Power Politics*. Keeping in mind that this is only a brief part of Woodcock's essay, do you think that the job he does is suc-cessful? Adequate? Inadequate? Incompetent?

2. By reference only to Woodcock's diction and sentence structure, describe the sort of reader this selection is intended for.

3. Having read this selection carefully, would you now like to read Atwood's book? Or would you prefer to read the rest of Woodcock's essay? Neither? Explain your decision.

4. What sort of criticism is Woodcock using in the expression "a relationship too acrid to be called *love*" (2-3): impressionism or critical analysis? Explain. Does he use any other impressionistic expressions? Do you think they are effective?

ORGANIZATION

5. How effective as an introduction is Woodcock's first sentence? How (if at all) would you improve this sentence?

6. How are the first two sentences of paragraph 1 related?

7. Why does a new paragraph begin in l. 9? Is this paragraph not logically a part of paragraph 1?

8. After the signpost * in l. 18—*three essential characteristics*—Woodcock mentions *first* (21) and *there is another* (27). How does he introduce the third characteristic?

9. Discuss what relation—if any—there is between the first sentence and the last.

10. Show how the last sentence is, or is not, an effective concluding sentence.

SENTENCES

11. Woodcock uses dashes ten times in this selection: on three occasions (2-3, 7-8, and 28-29) he uses them in pairs, once (21-23) he uses three, and on another occasion he uses a single dash (19). Is his use of dashes consistently clear? Would the use of parentheses instead of dashes help or hinder clarity? Could the triple dash in the one sentence of paragraph 3 be better avoided by using separate sentences?

12. Justify, or condemn, Woodcock's use of the colon in ll. 8 and 14.

13. Why is there no comma after *intellectual* (27)? Should there be?

14. The overall effect of Woodcock's sentence structure is one of complexity. By analyzing any two sentences in this selection, indicate why this is so.

DICTION

15. Look up: *communion* (2), *acrid* (2), *mordantly* (3-4), *analogical* (4), *terse* (5), *acerbic* (5), *perception* (8), *disillusioned* (13), *inevitabilities* (14), *caltrop* (19), *inversion* (22), *evocation* (25), *resonant* (29), *perceptions* (31), *complex* (31), *merge* (34).

16. For the other work by Woodcock in this text—a selection from his book on Gabriel Dumont—you were asked to consider the relationship between his sentence structure and the plainness of his vocabulary (p. 431, #12). The same sort of question arises here, although now the vocabulary is quite unusual. Discuss this relationship.

17. What do you understand by the following expressions: *sexual communion* (2), *relationship too acrid* (2), *mordantly analogical appropriateness* (3-4), *a terse and tense pair* (4-5), *an amazingly short cut* (6-7), *the cruel inevitabilities of love* (14), *no mere black romantic* (15-16), *this veritable caltrop of a poem* (19), *until welcome hands undo it* (23), *that world of resonant correspondences* (29-30)?

18. What is the function of *fitting* (14)? Why is it placed inside parentheses?

19. What kind of figure of speech is found in ll. 16-17? How effective is it, and why?

20. Why is the verb *set* (5) in the plural instead of the singular?

21. Is the expression *in one's own mind's eye* (26) clumsy? Adequate? Graceful? Inappropriate?

22. Could (or should) the expression *and yet* (31) be replaced by "yet"?

POINTS TO LEARN

1. The expression of difficult and complex ideas sometimes requires complex sentences.

2. The analysis of a short poem can be a very complicated task, involving the use of an unusually large vocabulary.

3. Analyzing poems can involve making distinctions which are fine but precise.

SUGGESTIONS FOR WRITING

Choose for your analysis one short, self-contained stanza from a poem you like or admire. Analyze in detail the thought and/or feelings of this stanza and any figures of speech, pointing out all the subtleties that you can, without exaggerating, see.

IMPROVING YOUR STYLE

1. Establish a list of the characteristics of the poem, either as a main part of your essay or as conclusion.

2. Include two sentences that use dashes.

3. Include a one-sentence paragraph, of at least four lines, that deals with a complicated point.

Yes, "Trees" Is Popular With the Rotarians.
Yes, It's Vulnerable. But, Then . . .

Guy Davenport is a poet and teacher and critic. In this essay he takes a fresh and unorthodox look at a famous and popular poem, "Trees" by the American poet Joyce Kilmer (1886-1918). During the nineteen forties and fifties many academic critics convicted Kilmer's poem of being trite, sentimental, abstract, confused in its imagery, full of prosy statement, and transparent—the sort of thing, the critics felt, that passes for poetry in the popular mind but is not true poetry at all. (It is to this critical disdain that Davenport alludes in his title.) Today "Trees" appears in few anthologies prepared for college students; yet it continues to be read and admired. Here is the poem in its entirety. Read it before you read what Davenport has to say.

Trees

I think that I shall never see
A poem as lovely as a tree.
A tree whose hungry mouth is prest
Against the earth's sweet flowing breast;
A tree that looks at God all day,
And lifts her leafy arms to pray;
A tree that may in summer wear
A nest of robins in her hair;
Upon whose bosom snow has lain;
Who intimately lives with rain.
Poems are made by fools like me,
But only God can make a tree.

1   In June 1918, the Cincinnati poetess Eloise Robinson was in the wasteland of Picardy handing out chocolate and reciting poetry to the American Expeditionary Forces. Reciting poetry!

From *The New York Times* (January 28, 1978). © 1978 by the New York Times Company. Reprinted by permission. The poem "Trees" by Joyce Kilmer. Copyright 1913 and renewed 1941. Copyright assigned to Jerry Vogel Music Co., Inc., 58 West 45th Street, New York, N.Y. 10036. Used by permission of copyright owner. Reproduction prohibited.

579

2   It is all but unimaginable that in that hell of terror, gangrene, mustard gas, sleeplessness, lice, and fatigue, there were moments when bone-weary soldiers, for the most part mere boys, would sit in a circle around a poetess in an ankle-length khaki skirt and Boy Scout hat to hear poems. In the middle of one poem the poetess' memory flagged. She apologized profusely, for the poem, as she explained, was immensely popular back home. Whereupon a sergeant with a particularly boyish face held up his hand, as if in school, and volunteered to recite it. And did.

3   So that in the hideously ravaged orchards and strafed woods of the valley of the Ourcq, where the fields were cratered and strewn with coils of barbed wire, fields that reeked of cordite and carrion, a voice recited "Trees." How wonderful, said Eloise Robinson, that he should know it. "Well, ma'am," said the sergeant, "I guess I wrote it. I'm Joyce Kilmer."

4   He wrote it five years before, and sent it off to the newly founded magazine "Poetry," and Harriet Monroe, the editor, paid him $6 for it. Almost immediately it became one of the most famous poems in English, the staple of schoolteachers and the one poem known by practically everybody.

5   Sgt. Alfred Joyce Kilmer was killed by German gunfire on the heights above Seringes, 30 July 1918. The French gave him the Croix de Guerre for his gallantry. He was 32.

6   "Trees" is a poem that has various reputations. It is all right for tots and Middle-Western clubwomen, but you are supposed to outgrow it. It symbolizes the sentimentality and weakmindedness that characterizes middle-class muddle. It is Rotarian. Once, at a gathering of poets at the Library of Congress the poetess Babette Deutsch[1] was using it as an example of the taradiddle Congressmen recite at prayer breakfasts and other orgies, until Prof. Gordon Wayne coughed and reminded her that the poet's son Kenton was among those present. No one, however, rose to defend Rudyard Kipling and John Greenleaf Whittier, at whom La Deutsch was also having.

7   It is, Lord knows, a vulnerable poem. For one thing, it is a poem about poetry, and is thus turned in on itself, and smacks of propaganda for the art (but is therefore useful to teachers who find justifying poetry to barbarian students uphill work). For another, the opening sentiment is all too close to Gelett Burgess' "I never saw a Purple Cow," lines that had been flipping from the tongues of wits since 1895.

8   And if the tree is pressing its hungry mouth against the earth's sweet flowing breast, how can it then lift its leafy arms to pray? This is a position

---

[1] Babette Deutsch is known chiefly as a poet, but she is also a novelist, translator of German and Russian literature, and a distinguished teacher. [Editors' note]

worthy of Picasso but not of the Cosmopolitan Cover Art Nouveau[2] esthetic from which the poem derives. Ask any hard-nosed classicist, and she will tell you that the poem is a monster of mixed metaphors.

9   And yet there is a silvery, spare beauty about the thing that has not dated. Its six couplets have an inexplicable integrity and a pleasant, old- 45 fashioned music. It soothes, and seems to speak of verities.

10   The handbooks will tell you that William Butler Yeats and A. E. Housman influenced the poem, though one cannot suspect from it that Kilmer was one of the earliest admirers of Gerard Manley Hopkins. Poems of great energy are usually distillations of words and sentiments outside them- 50 selves. Poems are by nature a compression. Another chestnut, Henry Wadsworth Longfellow's "A Psalm of Life," was generated by the Scotch geologist Hugh Miller's "Footprints of the Creator" and "The Old Red Sandstone," books made popular in America by Longfellow's colleague at Harvard, the scientist Louis Agassiz.   55

11   It is an example of the miraculous (and of the transcendentally vague) how Longfellow, reading about fossils in Miller, latched onto the sandstone and the vestiges thereupon, to intone "Lives of great men all remind us / We can make our lives sublime / And in passing leave behind us / Footprints on the sands of time."   60

12   Poets work that way, condensing, rendering down to essence. Another poem, as popular in its day as "Trees," Edwin Markham's "The Man with the Hoe" lived in Ezra Pound's mind until it became the opening line of "The Pisan Cantos": "The enormous tragedy of the dream in the peasant's bent shoulders."   65

13   "Trees" is, if you look, very much of its time. Trees were favorite symbols for Yeats, Robert Frost, and even the young Pound. The nature of chlorophyll had just been discovered, and "Tarzan of the Apes"—set in a tree world—had just been published. Trees were everywhere in art of the period, and it was understood that they belonged to the region of ideas, to 70 George Santayana's Realm of Beauty.[3]

[2] Art Nouveau (New Art), popular in the 1890's, is a style of design based upon tree and other plant motifs arranged in flat, more or less naturalistic patterns. The style greatly influenced interior decoration and the illustration of books and magazines. Davenport suggests that "Trees" owes much to the rather prettified form of Art Nouveau and its celebration of vegetable beauty, and almost nothing—at least intentionally—to the radical and conscious distortions of nature sometimes seen in the work of Picasso. [Editors' note]

[3] George Santayana (1863-1952) taught philosophy at Harvard for some twenty-five years. His study of beauty is concerned less with trees or other objects as individual entities, but rather as ideal forms. [Editors' note]

14   But Kilmer had been reading about trees in another context that we have forgotten, one that accounts for the self-effacing closing lines ("Poems are made by fools like me, / But only God can make a tree"), lines that have elevated the poem into double duty as a religious homily.   75

15   Kilmer's young manhood was in step with the idealism of the century. One of the inventions in idealism that attracted much attention was the movement to stop child labor and to set up nursery schools in slums. One of the most diligent pioneers in this movement was the Englishwoman Margaret McMillan, who had the happy idea that a breath of fresh air and   80 an intimate acquaintance with grass and trees were worth all the pencils and desks in the whole school system. There was something about trees that she wanted her slum children to feel. She had them take naps under trees, roll on grass, dance around trees. Her word for pencils and desks was "apparatus."

16   And in her book "Labour and Childhood" (1907) you will find this   85 sentence: "Apparatus can be made by fools, but only God can make a tree."

QUESTIONS

READER AND PURPOSE

1. What should Davenport's reader ideally know? Can those who know less also enjoy his essay?

2. Which of these might be said fairly to describe Davenport's purpose?

    (a) To make a line-by-line analysis of "Trees"
    (b) To convict Kilmer of plagiarism
    (c) To acknowledge the enduring worth of "Trees" despite its obvious faults
    (d) To suggest, by example, how many good poems are made
    (e) To report a hitherto unknown source of "Trees"

ORGANIZATION

3. Study each of the following alternate beginnings and explain why each is less appropriate than Davenport's:

    (a) Poetry can, and does, speak powerfully to all kinds of people in all stations of life and in all periods of time. One good poem that has endured in spite of adverse criticism is Joyce Kilmer's "Trees." Kilmer wrote "Trees" in 1913 and sent it off to the newly founded magazine *Poetry*, and Harriet Monroe, the editor, paid him six dollars for it.
    (b) In Margaret McMillan's book *Labour and Childhood* (1907) you

will find this sentence: "Apparatus can be made by fools, but only God can make a tree." Is there something familiar about these words? There should be, because some of them appear in one of the best known couplets in American poetry, the conclusion of Joyce Kilmer's "Trees." Kilmer wrote "Trees" in 1913 and sent it off to the newly founded magazine *Poetry*.

4. Davenport does not simply stop; he closes. How does he signal that he is ending?

5. This essay was first published in *The New York Times*, and the short paragraphs reflect newspaper style. In revising it for a book the writer might prefer longer paragraphs. Which paragraphs might go together? Be able to explain why you think so.

6. How is the third paragraph linked to the second? The fourth to the third? Identify the links between paragraphs 8 and 9, 13 and 14, and 15 and 16.

7. Paragraphs 10, 11, and 12 concern the American poets Longfellow and Pound more than Kilmer. Has the writer sacrificed unity here? Why or why not?

SENTENCES

8. Note the difference in tone * and emphasis between "She was reciting poetry" and "Reciting poetry!" (line 3). What three means of emphasis are employed in Davenport's sentence? How does that sentence differ in tone from the more conventionally phrased revision? Find a similar construction in paragraph 2.

9. Identify the periodic sentence * in the third paragraph.

10. Locate several examples of interrupted movement *. Revise one or two of them to eliminate the interruption. Has the revision lost emphasis?

11. Why is the following revision less successful than the original?

> *Revision:* Tragically and wastefully Sgt. Alfred Joyce Kilmer was killed by German gunfire at age 32 on the heights above Seringes, 30 July 1918, but the French gave him, for his gallantry, the Croix de Guerre.
> *Davenport:* "Sgt. Alfred Joyce Kilmer was killed by German gunfire on the heights above Seringes, 30 July 1918. The French gave him the Croix de Guerre for gallantry. He was 32." (21-23)

12. Identify two sentences in paragraph 8 that vary the normal order of subject-verb-object. What is the purpose of the variation?

DICTION

13. Look up: *cordite* (14), *carrion* (14), *couplets* (45), *verities* (46), *transcendentally* (55), *homily* (75).

14. How do each of the following substitutions alter the basic meaning, the connotations *, or emotional force of Davenport's diction: *Poet* for *poetess* (7), *one is* for *you are* (25), *kind of thing* for *taradiddle* (29), *functions* for *orgies* (29), *Deutsch* for *La Deutsch* (32), *directing her criticism* for *having* (32), *he* for *she* (42), *silver, thin beauty* for *silvery spare beauty* (44), *it speaks of verities* for *it seems to speak of verities* (46), *poem* for *chestnut* (51), *sing* for *intone* (58)?

POINTS TO LEARN

1. An essay about a piece of literature may discuss the reputation of the work, its effect upon both sophisticated and unsophisticated readers, its sources, and its relation to other aspects of culture.

2. Essays, if at all complex, may have more than one purpose, but usually one aim is primary and shapes and controls the work.

3. Writing about literature is seldom detached, objective, "scientific." At its best, as in Davenport's essay, we are aware of another human being engaged with a poem or story—thinking, judging, feeling.

4. In conveying attitudes toward the work, himself, and his readers—all of which compose tone—the writer must do so through the careful attention to diction and sentence structure.

SUGGESTIONS FOR WRITING

1. What do you think of "Trees"—is it "a monster of mixed metaphors" or a poem of "silvery, spare beauty"? Compose an essay of about 600 words in response.

2. In an essay of similar length try to make your readers share your pleasure in a poem written during the last ten years or so. (The poem should be short and a copy included with your paper.)

IMPROVING YOUR STYLE

1. In your essay use several examples of interrupted movement to gain the kind of emphasis Davenport achieves with it.

2. Use *but* and *and* to begin one or two sentences each. But be careful not to overuse these, or any other, sentence openings.

JOHN CIARDI

Robert Frost: The Way to the Poem

John Ciardi (1916-1986) was a poet and teacher. Some of his published volumes are *Homeward to America* (1940), *In Fact* (1963), and *Person to Person* (1964). He also published a notable translation of Dante's *Divine Comedy* (1954-61). In this essay on a poem by Robert Frost, Ciardi shows what the ideal reader of poetry does. Reading, in the sense in which it applies here, is far from passively sitting back and letting words flow before you. It is cerebral activity of the most intense kind, an engagement of the mind on all levels with the language of the poem. Only such a total engagement will disclose something—though never everything— of what a complex poem means.

STOPPING BY WOODS ON A SNOWY EVENING
By Robert Frost

Whose woods these are I think I know.
His house is in the village, though;
He will not see me stopping here
To watch his woods fill up with snow.

My little horse must think it queer
To stop without a farmhouse near
Between the wood and frozen lake
The darkest evening of the year.

He gives his harness bells a shake
To ask if there is some mistake.
The only other sound's the sweep
Of easy wind and downy flake.

The woods are lovely, dark, and deep,
But I have promises to keep,

From *The Saturday Review*, April 12, 1958. Copyright 1958. Reprinted by permission of the Estate of John Ciardi. "Stopping By Woods on a Snowy Evening" is from *The Poetry of Robert Frost* edited by Edward Connery Lathem. Copyright 1923, © 1969 by Holt, Rinehart and Winston, Publishers.

And miles to go before I sleep,
And miles to go before I sleep.

1   The School System has much to say these days of the virtue of
reading widely, and not enough about the virtues of reading less but in
depth. There are any number of reading lists for poetry, but there is not
enough talk about individual poems. Poetry, finally, is one poem at a time.
To read any one poem carefully is the ideal preparation for reading an-   5
other. Only a poem can illustrate how poetry works.
2   Above, therefore, is a poem—one of the master lyrics of the English language, and almost certainly the best-known poem by an American
poet. What happens in it?—which is to say, not *what* does it mean, but *how*
does it mean? How does it go about being a human reenactment of a human   10
experience? The author—perhaps the thousandth reader would need to be
told—is Robert Frost.
3   Even the TV audience can see that this poem begins as a seemingly-
simple narration of a seemingly-simple incident but ends by suggesting
meanings far beyond anything specifically referred to in the narrative. And   15
even readers with only the most casual interest in poetry might be made to
note the additional fact that, though the poem suggests those larger meanings, it is very careful never to abandon its pretense to being simple narration. There is duplicity at work. The poet pretends to be talking about one
thing, and all the while he is talking about many others.   20
4   Many readers are forever unable to accept the poet's essential duplicity. It is almost safe to say that a poem is never about what it seems to
be about. As much could be said of the proverb. The bird in the hand, the
rolling stone, the stitch in time never (except by an artful double-decep-
tion) intend any sort of statement about birds, stones, or sewing. The inci-   25
dent of this poem, one must conclude, is at root a metaphor.
5   Duplicity aside, this poem's movement from the specific to the
general illustrates one of the basic formulas of all poetry. Such a grand
poem as Arnold's "Dover Beach" and such lesser, though unfortunately
better known, poems as Longfellow's "The Village Blacksmith" and   30
Holmes's "The Chambered Nautilus" are built on the same progression.
In these three poems, however, the generalization is markedly set apart
from the specific narration, and even seems additional to the telling rather
than intrinsic to it. It is this sense of division one has in mind in speaking
of "a tacked-on moral."   35

6   There is nothing wrong-in-itself with a tacked-on moral. Frost, in fact, makes excellent use of the device at times. In this poem, however, Frost is careful to let the whatever-the-moral-is grow out of the poem itself. When the action ends the poem ends. There is no epilogue and no explanation. Everything pretends to be about the narrated incident. And that 40 pretense sets the basic tone of the poem's performance of itself.

7   The dramatic force of that performance is best observable, I believe, as a progression in three scenes.

8   In scene one, which coincides with stanza one, a man—a New England man—is driving his sleigh somewhere at night. It is snowing, and as 45 the man passes a dark patch of woods he stops to watch the snow descend into the darkness. We know, moreover, that the man is familiar with these parts (he knows who owns the woods and where the owner lives), and we know that no one has seen him stop. As scene one forms itself in the theater of the mind's-eye, therefore, it serves to establish some as yet unspecified 50 relation between the man and the woods.

9   It is necessary, however, to stop here for a long parenthesis. Even so simple an opening statement raises any number of questions. It is impossible to address all the questions that rise from the poem stanza by stanza, but two that arise from stanza one illustrate the sort of thing one 55 might well ask of the poem detail by detail.

10   Why, for example, does the man not say what errand he is on? What is the force of leaving the errand generalized? He might just as well have told us that he was going to the general store, or returning from it with a jug of molasses he had promised to bring Aunt Harriet and two suits of 60 long underwear he had promised to bring the hired man. Frost, moreover, can handle homely detail to great effect. He preferred to leave his motive generalized. Why?

11   And why, on the other hand, does he say so much about knowing the absent owner of the woods and where he lives? Is it simply that one set 65 of details happened-in whereas another did not? To speak of things "happening-in" is to assault the integrity of a poem. Poetry cannot be discussed meaningfully unless one can assume that everything in the poem—every last comma and variant spelling—is in it by the poet's specific act of choice. Only bad poets allow into their poems what is haphazard or cheaply 70 chosen.

12   The errand, I will venture a bit brashly for lack of space, is left generalized in order the more aptly to suggest *any* errand in life, therefore, life itself. The owner is there because he is one of the forces of the poem.

Let it do to say that the force he represents is the village of mankind (that   75
village at the edge of winter) from which the poet finds himself separated
(has separated himself?) in his moment by the woods (and to which, he recalls finally, he has promises to keep). The owner is he-who-lives-in-his-
village-house, thereby locked away from the poet's awareness of the time-
the-snow-tells as it engulfs and obliterates the world the village man allows   80
himself to believe he "owns." Thus, the owner is a representative of an order of reality from which the poet has divided himself for the moment,
though to a certain extent he ends by reuniting with it. Scene one, therefore, establishes not only a relation between the man and the woods, but
the fact that the man's relation begins with his separation (though momen-   85
tarily) from mankind.

13   End parenthesis one, begin parenthesis two.

14   Still considering the first scene as a kind of dramatic performance
of forces, one must note that the poet has meticulously matched the simplicity of his language to the pretended simplicity of the narrative. Clearly,   90
the man stopped because the beauty of the scene moved him, but he neither
tells us that the scene is beautiful nor that he is moved. A bad writer, always ready to overdo, might have written: "The vastness gripped me, filling
my spirit with the slow steady sinking of the snow's crystalline perfection
into the glimmerless profundities of the hushed primeval wood." Frost's   95
avoidance of such a spate illustrates two principles of good writing. The
first, he has stated himself in "The Mowing": Anything *more* than the
truth would have seemed too weak" (italics mine). Understatement is one
of the basic sources of power in English poetry. The second principle is to
let the action speak for itself. A good novelist does not tell us that a given   100
character is good or bad (at least not since the passing of the Dickens
tradition): he shows us the character in action and then, watching him,
we know. Poetry, too, has fictional obligations: even when the characters
are ideas and metaphors rather than people, they must be *characterized
in action*. A poem does not *talk about* ideas; it *enacts* them. The force of   105
the poem's performance, in fact, is precisely to act out (and thereby to
make us act out empathically that is, to *feel out*, that is, *to identify with*
the speaker and why he stopped. The man is the principal actor in this
little "drama of why" and in scene one he is the only character, though as
noted, he is somehow related to the absent owner.   110

15   End second parenthesis.

16   In scene two (stanzas two and three) a *foil* is introduced. In fiction
and drama, a foil is a character who "plays against" a more important char-

acter. By presenting a different point of view or an opposed set of motives, the foil moves the more important character to react in ways that might not have found expression without such opposition. The more important character is thus more fully revealed—to the reader and to himself. The foil here is the horse.

17   The horse forces the question. Why did the man stop? Until it occurs to him that his "little horse must think it queer" he had not asked himself for reasons. He had simply stopped. But the man finds himself faced with the question he imagines the horse to be asking: what *is* there to stop for out there in the cold, away from bin and stall (house and village and mankind?) and all that any self-respecting beast could value on such a night? In sensing that other view, the man is forced to examine his own more deeply.

18   In stanza two the question arises only as a feeling within the man. In stanza three, however (still scene two), the horse acts. He gives his harness bells a shake. "What's wrong?" he seems to say. "What are we waiting for?"

19   By now, obviously, the horse—without losing its identity as horse—has also become a symbol. A symbol is something that stands for something else. Whatever that something else may be, it certainly begins as that order of life that does not understand why a man stops in the wintry middle of nowhere to watch the snow come down. (Can one fail to sense by now that the dark and the snowfall symbolize a death-wish, however momentary, *i.e.*, that hunger for final rest and surrender that a man may feel, but not a beast?)

20   So by the end of scene two the performance has given dramatic force to three elements that work upon the man. There is his relation to the world of the owner. There is his relation to the brute world of the horse. And there is that third presence of the unownable world, the movement of the all-engulfing snow across all the orders of life, the man's, the owner's, and the horse's—with the difference that the man knows of that second dark-within-the-dark of which the horse cannot, and the owner will not, know.

21   The man ends scene two with all these forces working upon him simultaneously. He feels himself moved to a decision. And he feels a last call from the darkness: "the sweep / Of easy wind and downy flake." It would be so easy and so downy to go into the woods and let himself be covered over.

22   But scene three (stanza four) produces a fourth force. This fourth

force can be given many names. It is certainly better, in fact, to give it many names than to attempt to limit it to one. It is social obligation, or personal commitment, or duty, or just the realization that a man cannot indulge a 155 mood forever. All of these and more. But, finally, he has a simple decision to make. He may go into the woods and let the darkness and the snow swallow him from the world of beast and man. Or he must move on. And unless he is going to stop here forever, it is time to remember that he has a long way to go and that he had best be getting there. (So there is something 160 to be said for the horse, too.)

23   Then and only then, his question driven more and more deeply into himself by these cross-forces, does the man venture a comment on what attracted him "The woods are lovely, dark and deep." His mood lingers over the thought of that lovely dark-and-deep (as do the very syllables in which 165 he phrases the thought), but the final decision is to put off the mood and move on. He has his man's way to go and his man's obligations to tend to before he can yield. He has miles to go before his sleep. He repeats that thought and the performance ends.

24   But why the repetition? The first time Frost says "And miles to go 170 before I sleep," there can be little doubt that the primary meaning is: "I have a long way to go before I get to bed tonight." The second time he says it, however, "miles to go" and "sleep" are suddenly transformed into symbols. What are those "something-elses" the symbols stand for? Hundreds of people have tried to ask Mr. Frost that question and he has always turned 175 it away. He has turned it away *because he cannot answer it*. He could answer some part of it. But some part is not enough.

25   For a symbol is like a rock dropped into a pool: it sends out ripples in all directions, and the ripples are in motion. Who can say where the last ripple disappears? One may have a sense that he knows the approximate 180 center point of the ripples, the point at which the stone struck the water. Yet even then he has trouble marking it surely. How does one make a mark on water? Oh very well—the center point of that second "miles to go" is probably approximately in the neighborhood of being close to meaning, perhaps, "the road of life"; and the second "before I sleep" is maybe that 185 close to meaning "before I take my final rest," the rest in darkness that seemed so temptingly dark-and-deep for the moment of the mood. But the ripples continue to move and the light to change on the water, and the longer one watches the more changes he sees. Such shifting-and-being-at-the-same-instant is of the very sparkle and life of poetry. One experiences 190 it as one experiences life, for everytime he looks at an experience he sees

something new, and he sees it change as he watches it. And that sense of
continuity in fluidity is one of the primary kinds of knowledge, one of man's
basic ways of knowing, and one that only the arts can teach, poetry foremost among them.   195

26   Frost himself certainly did not ask what that repeated last line
meant. It came to him and he received it. He "felt right" about it. And
what he "felt right" about was in no sense a "meaning" that, say, an essay
could apprehend, but an act of experience that could be fully presented
only by the dramatic enactment of forces which is the performance of the   200
poem.

27   Now look at the poem in another way. Did Frost know what he
was going to do when he began? Considering the poem simply as an act of
skill, as a piece of juggling, one cannot fail to respond to the magnificent
turn at the end where, with one flip, seven of the simplest words in the   205
language suddenly dazzle full of never-ending waves of thought and feeling.
Or, more precisely, of felt-thought. Certainly an equivalent stunt by a juggler—could there be an equivalent—would bring the house down. Was it to
cap his performance with that grand stunt that Frost wrote the poem?

28   Far from it. The obvious fact is that *Frost could not have known*   210
he was going to write those lines until he wrote them. Then a second fact
must be registered: *he wrote them because, for the fun of it, he had got*
himself into trouble.

29   Frost, like every good poet, began by playing a game with himself.
The most usual way of writing a four line stanza with four feet to the line   215
is to rhyme the third line with the first, and the fourth line with the second.
Even that much rhyme is so difficult in English that many poets and almost
all of the anonymous ballad makers do not bother to rhyme the first and
third lines at all, settling for two rhymes in four lines as good enough. For
English is a rhyme-poor language. In Italian and in French, for example, so   220
many words end with the same sounds that rhyming is relatively easy—so
easy that many modern French and Italian poets do not bother to rhyme at
all. English, being a more agglomerate language, has far more final sounds,
hence fewer of them rhyme. When an Italian poet writes a line ending with
"vita" (life) he has literally hundreds of rhyme choices available. When an   225
English poet writes "life" at the end of a line he can summon "strife, wife,
knife, fife, rife," and then he is in trouble. Now "life-strife" and "life-rife"
and "life-wife" seem to offer a combination of possible ideas that can be
related by more than just the rhyme. Inevitably, therefore, the poets have
had to work and rework these combinations until the sparkle has gone out   230

of them. The reader is normally tired of such rhyme-led associations. When he encounters "life-strife" he is certainly entitled to suspect that the poet did not really want to say "strife"—that had there been in English such a word as, say, "hife," meaning "infinite peace and harmony," the poet would as gladly have used that word instead of "strife." Thus, the reader 235 feels that the writing is haphazard, that the rhyme is making the poet say things he does not really feel, and which, therefore, the reader does not feel except as boredom. One likes to see the rhymes fall into place, but he must end with the belief that it is the poet who is deciding what is said and not the rhyme scheme that is forcing the saying. 240

30   So rhyme is a kind of game, and an especially difficult one in English. As in every game, the fun of the rhyme is to set one's difficulties high and then to meet them skilfully. As Frost himself once defined freedom, it consists of "moving easy in harness."

31   In "Stopping by Woods on a Snowy Evening" Frost took a long 245 chance. He decided to rhyme not two lines in each stanza, but three. Not even Frost could have sustained that much rhyme in a long poem (as Dante, for example, with the advantage of writing in Italian, sustained triple rhyme for thousands of lines in "The Divine Comedy"). Frost would have known instantly, therefore, when he took the original chance, 250 that he was going to write a short poem. He would have had that much foretaste of it.

32   So the first stanza emerged rhymed a-a-b-a. And with the sure sense that this was to be a short poem, Frost decided to take an additional chance and to redouble: in English three rhymes in four lines is more than 255 enough; there is no need to rhyme the fourth line. For the fun of it, however, Frost set himself to pick up that loose rhyme and to weave it into the pattern, thereby accepting the all but impossible burden of quadruple rhyme.

33   The miracle is that it worked. Despite the enormous freight of 260 rhyme, the poem not only came out as a neat pattern, but managed to do so with no sense of strain. Every word and every rhyme falls into place as naturally and as inevitably as if there were no rhyme restricting the poet's choices.

34   That ease-in-difficulty is certainly inseparable from the success of 265 the poem's performance. One watches the skill-man juggle three balls, then four, then five, and every addition makes the trick more wonderful. But unless he makes the hard trick seem as easy as an easy trick, then all is lost.

35   The real point, however, is not only that Frost took on a hard

rhyme-trick and made it seem easy. It is rather as if the juggler, carried 270
away, had tossed up one more ball than he could really handle, and then
amazed himself by actually handling it. So with the real triumph of this
poem. Frost could not have known what a stunning effect his repetition of
the last line was going to produce. He could not even know he was going to
repeat the line. He simply found himself up against a difficulty he almost 275
certainly had not foreseen and he had to improvise to meet it. For in picking up the rhyme from the third line of stanza one and carrying it over into
stanza two, he had created an endless chain-link form within which each
stanza left a hook sticking out for the next stanza to hang on. So by stanza
four, feeling the poem rounding to its end, Frost had to do something about 280
that extra rhyme.

36   He might have tucked it back into a third line rhyming with the
know-though-snow of stanza one. He could thus have rounded the poem
out to the mathematical symmetry of using each rhyme four times. But
though such a device might be defensible in theory, a rhyme repeated after 285
eleven lines is so far from its original rhyme sound that its feeling as rhyme
must certainly be lost. And what good is theory if the reader is not moved
by the writing?

37   It must have been in some such quandary that the final repetition
suggested itself—a suggestion born of the very difficulties the poet had let 290
himself in for. So there is that point beyond mere ease in handling a hard
thing, the point at which the very difficulty offers the poet the opportunity
to do better than he knew he could. What, aside from having that happen
to oneself, could be more self-delighting than to participate in its happening by one's reader-identification with the poem? 295

38   And by now a further point will have suggested itself: that the
human-insight of the poem and the technicalities of its poetic artifice are inseparable. Each feeds the other. That interplay is the poem's meaning, a
matter not of *what does it mean,* for no one can ever say entirely what a good
poem means, but of *how does it mean,* a process one can come much closer 300
to discussing.

39   There is a necessary epilogue. Mr. Frost has often discussed this
poem on the platform, or more usually in the course of a long-evening-
after a talk. Time and again I have heard him say that he just wrote it off,
that it just came to him, and that he set it down as it came. 305

40   Once at Bread Loaf, however, I heard him add one very essential
piece to the discussion of how it "just came." One night, he said, he had
sat down after supper to work at a long piece of blank verse. The piece

never worked out, but Mr. Frost found himself so absorbed in it that, when
next he looked up, dawn was at his window. He rose, crossed to the win-   310
dow, stood looking out for a few minutes, and *then* it was that "Stopping
by Woods" suddenly "just came," so that all he had to do was cross the
room and write it down.

41   Robert Frost is the sort of artist who hides his traces. I know of no
Frost worksheets anywhere. If someone has raided his wastebasket in secret,   315
it is possible that such worksheets exist somewhere, but Frost would not willingly allow anything but the finished product to leave him. Almost certainly, therefore, no one will ever know what was in that piece of unsuccessful blank verse he had been working at with such concentration, but I
for one would stake my life that could that worksheet be uncovered, it   320
would be found to contain the germinal stuff of "Stopping by Woods";
that what was a-simmer in him all night without finding its proper form,
suddenly, when he let his still-occupied mind look away, came at him from
a different direction, offered itself in a different form, and that finding that
form exactly right the impulse proceeded to marry itself to the new shape   325
in one of the most miraculous performances of English lyricism.

42   And that, too—whether or not one can accept so hypothetical a
discussion—is part of *how* the poem means. It means that marriage to the
perfect form, the poem's shapen declaration of itself, its moment's monument fixed beyond all possibility of change. And thus, finally, in every truly   330
good poem, "How does it mean?" must always be answered "Trium-
phantly." Whatever the poem "is about," *how* it means is always how
Genesis means: the word become a form, and the form become a thing,
and—when the becoming is true—the thing become a part of the knowledge
and experience of the race forever.   335

QUESTIONS

READER AND PURPOSE
1. Consider the following different attitudes toward poetry:

   (a) The poet has an idea (theme, content, meaning) to begin with,
       and he then finds a suitable vehicle or form in which to convey it.
       The form is the means of presenting the really important thing—
       the initial idea.
   (b) Any attention to the form of a poem is frivolous, even pointless.

(c) The poet always knows exactly what his poem does and does not mean.

(d) A poem means just what it literally says.

How many of these opinions did you agree with before reading Ciardi's essay? How many do you still accept? Do you think Ciardi agrees with any of them?

2. Is the writer's purpose chiefly to explain, or to persuade? Or is it some combination of the two?

ORGANIZATION

3. The organization of this essay is unusually clear. Probably most readers would agree that its main parts are as follows: I—paragraphs 1-6; II—paragraphs 7-23; III—paragraphs 24-28; IV—paragraphs 29-39; V—paragraphs 40-42. Give a title to each of these five sections.

4. The second part contains several subdivisions. Indicate what these are by paragraph numbers and give each a descriptive title. Do the same for part IV.

5. What is the organizational function of paragraphs 7, 13, 15, and 28?

6. What techniques of closing does the author use in his final paragraph?

7. Ciardi is exceedingly skillful in making transitions between paragraphs. Be able to explain how he links each paragraph with what precedes it.

8. Analyze the structure of paragraph 14. What is its topic sentence? Show how each successive sentence relates to the preceding one. What techniques of paragraph development are used here?

9. Point out a paragraph developed by analogy.

SENTENCES

10. Explain how in each of the following pairs of sentences the revision differs from Ciardi's statement:

(a) *Revision:* The thousandth reader would need to be told that the author is Robert Frost.
Ciardi: "The author—perhaps the thousandth reader would need to be told—is Robert Frost." (11-12)

(b) *Revision:* The more important character is thus more fully revealed to the reader and to himself.
Ciardi: "The more important character is thus more fully revealed—to the reader and to himself." (116-17)

(c) *Revision:* The truth is far from it.
Ciardi: "Far from it." (210)

(d) *Revision:* . . . rhyming is so easy that many modern French and Italian poets do not bother to rhyme at all.
Ciardi: ". . . rhyming is relatively easy—so easy that many mod-

ern French and Italian poets do not bother to rhyme at all."
(221-23)

11. Rhetorical questions * appear frequently in these paragraphs. Are they over-used—a mannerism? Or can one defend them as appropriate and effective?

DICTION

12. Look up: *lyrics* (7), *intrinsic* (34), *epilogue* (39), *integrity* (67), *brashly* (72), *obliterates* (80), *meticulously* (89), *spate* (96), *understatement* (98), *quandry* (289).
13. What does Ciardi mean by "TV audience" when he writes, "Even the TV audience can see that this poem begins as a seemingly-simple narration . . ." (13-14)?
14. What is meant in line 223 by the reference to English as a "more agglomerate language" than Italian or French?
15. Explain the allusion * to Genesis in the final paragraph of Ciardi's essay.
16. In paragraphs 28-31 of her essay "Writing Short Stories" (reprinted on pages 598 ff. of this text) Flannery O'Connor describes how she wrote a short story called "Good Country People." To what extent is her account similar or dissimilar to Robert Frost's experience as Ciardi reconstructs it? (Flannery O'Connor's closing paragraph is also pertinent to this question.)

POINTS TO LEARN

1. Exposition and persuasion are often blended in the same essay.
2. Persuasion rests, of course, upon the proper use of evidence and upon sound logic, but persuasion is greatly enhanced by skillful writing.
3. One way of achieving clarity in an essay is to use organizing sentences and to provide signposts * (as in Ciardi's paragraphs 13 and 28); these guide the reader from one major section of an essay to another. In well-organized writing the reader knows where he is, and where he has been, and where he is going.
4. Although the sentences in this selection are relatively short and uncomplicated, they are astonishingly emphatic. Ciardi varies the simple sentence by using rhetorical questions, fragments *, interrupted movement *, parallelism *, and by isolating important words by means of a dash. Italics indicate vocal stress on single words and call attention to important statements.

SUGGESTIONS FOR WRITING

Modeling your essay in a general way upon paragraphs 7-40 of John Ciardi's essay, write an interpretation of a short poem by Robert Frost, such as "Tree at My Window," "Acquainted with the Night," "Nothing Gold Can Stay." Do not merely paraphrase the poem, but organize your composition by sections on the speaker, listener (if any), and situation, symbols, patterns of analogy or contrast, the meaning of the poem as a whole, the relation of form to meaning.

IMPROVING YOUR STYLE

1. In your essay experiment with emphasis, using rhetorical questions, short simple * sentences, and fragments.

2. Use dashes to punctuate appositives * and interrupters and to isolate key phrases and words as Ciardi does in lines 11-12, 45, 117, and 327-28.

Writing Short Stories

Flannery O'Connor (1925-64) was one of the finest short story writers of her time. Her books include *The Artificial Nigger* (1957), *The Violent Bear It Away* (1960), and *Everything That Rises Must Converge* (1965). The principal conflict in her stories concerns the relationship of the individual to God, but her themes are "religious" in an unusual, highly personal sense, not in a conventional one. She is much interested in the grotesqueries of behavior both of those who seek God and of those who deny Him. The following piece, however, is not a story but an essay, and its topic is more mundane: the problems of writing short stories. It is from a collection of articles about literary topics: *Mystery and Manners* (1957).

1   I have heard people say that the short story was one of the most difficult literary forms, and I've always tried to decide why people feel this way about what seems to me to be one of the most natural and fundamental ways of human expression. After all, you begin to hear and tell stories when you're a child, and there doesn't seem to be anything very complicated 5 about it. I suspect that most of you have been telling stories all your lives, and yet here you sit—come to find out how to do it.

2   Then last week, after I had written down some of these serene thoughts to use here today, my calm was shattered when I was sent seven of your manuscripts to read. 10

3   After this experience, I found myself ready to admit, if not that the short story is one of the most difficult literary forms, at least that it is more difficult for some than for others.

4   I still suspect that most people start out with some kind of ability

"Writing Short Stories" from *Mystery and Manners* by Flannery O'Connor. Copyright © 1957, 1961, 1963, 1964, 1966, 1967, 1969 by the Estate of Mary Flannery O'Connor. Copyright © 1962 by Flannery O'Connor. Copyright © 1961 by Farrar, Straus and Cudahy, Inc. Reprinted by permission of Farrar, Straus and Giroux, Inc.

to tell a story but that it gets lost along the way. Of course, the ability to   15
create life with words is essentially a gift. If you have it in the first place, you
can develop it; if you don't have it, you might as well forget it.

5   But I have found that people who don't have it are frequently the
ones hell-bent on writing stories. I'm sure anyway that they are the ones
who write the books and the magazine articles on how-to-write-short-stories.   20
I have a friend who is taking a correspondence course in this subject, and
she has passed a few of the chapter headings on to me—such as "The
Story Formula for Writers," "How to Create Characters," "Let's Plot!"
This form of corruption is costing her twenty-seven dollars.

6   I feel that discussing story-writing in terms of plot, character, and   25
theme is like trying to describe the expression on a face by saying where the
eyes, nose, and mouth are. I've heard students say, "I'm very good with plot,
but I can't do a thing with character," or "I have this theme but I don't
have a plot for it," and once I heard one say, "I've got the story but I don't
have any technique."   30

7   Technique is a word they all trot out. I talked to a writers' club
once, and during the question time, one good soul said, "Will you give me
the technique for the frame-within-a-frame short story?" I had to admit I
was so ignorant I didn't even know what that was, but she assured me there
was such a thing because she had entered a contest to write one and the   35
prize was fifty dollars.

8   But setting aside the people who have no talent for it, there are
others who do have the talent but who flounder around because they don't
really know what a story is.

9   I suppose that obvious things are the hardest to define. Everybody   40
thinks he knows what a story is. But if you ask a beginning student to write
a story, you're liable to get almost anything—a reminiscence, an episode, an
opinion, an anecdote, anything under the sun but a story. A story is a complete dramatic action—and in good stories, the characters are shown through
the action and the action is controlled through the characters, and the re-   45
sult of this is meaning that derives from the whole presented experience. I
myself prefer to say that a story is a dramatic event that involves a person
because he is a person, and a particular person—that is, because he shares
in the general human condition and in some specific human situation. A
story always involves, in a dramatic way, the mystery of personality. I lent   50
some stories to a country lady who lives down the road from me, and when
she returned them, she said, "Well, them stories just gone and shown you
how some folks *would* do," and I thought to myself that that was right; when

you write stories, you have to be content to start exactly there—showing how some specific folks *will* do, *will* do in spite of everything.   55

10   Now this is a very humble level to have to begin on, and most people who think they want to write stories are not willing to start there. They
want to write about problems, not people; or about abstract issues, not concrete situations. They have an idea, or a feeling, or an overflowing ego, or
they want to Be A Writer, or they want to give their wisdom to the world   60
in a simple-enough way for the world to be able to absorb it. In any case,
they don't have a story and they wouldn't be willing to write it if they did;
and in the absence of a story, they set out to find a theory or a formula or a
technique.

11   Now none of this is to say that when you write a story, you are sup-   65
posed to forget or give up any moral position that you hold. Your beliefs
will be the light by which you see, but they will not be what you see and
they will not be a substitute for seeing. For the writer of fiction, everything
has its testing point in the eye, and the eye is an organ that eventually involves the whole personality, and as much of the world as can be got into   70
it. It involves judgment. Judgment is something that begins in the act of vision, and when it does not, or when it becomes separated from vision, then
a confusion exists in the mind which transfers itself to the story.

12   Fiction operates through the senses, and I think one reason that
people find it so difficult to write stories is that they forget how much time   75
and patience is required to convince through the senses. No reader who
doesn't actually experience, who isn't made to feel, the story is going to believe anything the fiction writer merely tells him. The first and most obvious characteristic of fiction is that it deals with reality through what can
be seen, heard, smelt, tasted, and touched.   80

13   Now this is something that can't be learned only in the head; it has
to be learned in the habits. It has to become a way that you habitually look
at things. The fiction writer has to realize that he can't create compassion
with compassion, or emotion with emotion, or thought with thought. He
has to provide all these things with a body; he has to create a world with   85
weight and extension.

14   I have found that the stories of beginning writers usually bristle
with emotion, but *whose* emotion is often very hard to determine. Dialogue
frequently proceeds without the assistance of any characters that you can
actually see, and uncontained thought leaks out of every corner of the   90
story. The reason is usually that the student is wholly interested in his
thoughts and his emotions and not in his dramatic action, and that he is

too lazy or highfalutin to descend to the concrete where fiction operates. He thinks that judgment exists in one place and sense-impression in another. But for the fiction writer, judgment begins in the details he sees and how he sees them. 95

15   Fiction writers who are not concerned with these concrete details are guilty of what Henry James called "weak specification." The eye will glide over their words while the attention goes to sleep. Ford Madox Ford taught that you couldn't have a man appear long enough to sell a newspa- 100 per in a story unless you put him there with enough detail to make the reader see him.

16   I have a friend who is taking acting classes in New York from a Russian lady who is supposed to be very good at teaching actors. My friend wrote me that the first month they didn't speak a line, they only learned to 105 see. Now learning to see is the basis for learning all the arts except music. I know a good many fiction writers who paint, not because they're any good at painting, but because it helps their writing. It forces them to look at things. Fiction writing is very seldom a matter of saying things; it is a matter of showing things. 110

17   However, to say that fiction proceeds by the use of detail does not mean the simple, mechanical piling-up of detail. Detail has to be controlled by some overall purpose, and every detail has to be put to work for you. Art is selective. What is there is essential and creates movement.

18   Now all this requires time. A good short story should not have less 115 meaning than a novel, nor should its action be less complete. Nothing essential to the main experience can be left out of a short story. All the action has to be satisfactorily accounted for in terms of motivation, and there has to be a beginning, a middle, and an end, though not necessarily in that order. I think many people decide that they want to write short stories be- 120 cause they're short, and by short, they mean short in every way. They think that a short story is an incomplete action in which a very little is shown and a great deal suggested, and they think you suggest something by leaving it out. It's very hard to disabuse a student of this notion, because he thinks that when he leaves something out, he's being subtle; and when you tell 125 him that he has to put something in before anything can be there, he thinks you're an insensitive idiot.

19   Perhaps the central question to be considered in any discussion of the short story is what do we mean by short. Being short does not mean being slight. A short story should be long in depth and should give us an ex- 130 perience of meaning. I have an aunt who thinks that nothing happens in a

story unless somebody gets married or shot at the end of it. I wrote a story about a tramp who marries an old woman's idiot daughter in order to acquire the old woman's automobile. After the marriage, he takes the daughter off on a wedding trip in the automobile and abandons her in an eating 135
place and drives on by himself. Now that is a complete story. There is nothing more relating to the mystery of that man's personality that could be shown through that particular dramatization. But I've never been able to convince my aunt that it's a complete story. She wants to know what happened to the idiot daughter after that. 140

20   Not long ago that story was adapted for a television play, and the adapter, knowing his business, had the tramp have a change of heart and go back and pick up the idiot daughter and the two of them ride away, grinning madly. My aunt believes that the story is complete at last, but I have other sentiments about it—which are not suitable for public utter- 145
ance. When you write a story, you only have to write one story, but there will always be people who will refuse to read the story you have written.

21   And this naturally brings up the awful question of what kind of a reader you are writing for when you write fiction. Perhaps we each think we have a personal solution for this problem. For my own part, I have a 150
very high opinion of the art of fiction and a very low opinion of what is called the "average" reader. I tell myself that I can't escape him, that this is the personality I am supposed to keep awake, but that at the same time, I am also supposed to provide the intelligent reader with the deeper experience that he looks for in fiction. Now actually, both of these readers are 155
just aspects of the writer's own personality, and in the last analysis, the only reader he can know anything about is himself. We all write at our own level of understanding, but it is the peculiar characteristic of fiction that its literal surface can be made to yield entertainment on an obvious physical plane to one sort of reader while the selfsame surface can be made to yield 160
meaning to the person equipped to experience it there.

22   Meaning is what keeps the short story from being short. I prefer to talk about the meaning in a story rather than the theme of a story. People talk about the theme of a story as if the theme were like the string that a sack of chicken feed is tied with. They think that if you can pick out the 165
theme, the way you pick the right thread in the chicken-feed sack, you can rip the story open and feed the chickens. But this is not the way meaning works in fiction.

23   When you can state the theme of a story, when you can separate it from the story itself, then you can be sure the story is not a very good one. 170

The meaning of a story has to be embodied in it, has to be made concrete in it. A story is a way to say something that can't be said any other way, and it takes every word in the story to say what the meaning is. You tell a story because a statement would be inadequate. When anybody asks what a story is about, the only proper thing is to tell him to read the story. The meaning of fiction is not abstract meaning but experienced meaning, and the purpose of making statements about the meaning of a story is only to help you to experience that meaning more fully.

24 Fiction is an art that calls for the strictest attention to the real—whether the writer is writing a naturalistic story or a fantasy. I mean that we always begin with what is or with what has an eminent possibility of truth about it. Even when one writes a fantasy, reality is the proper basis of it. A thing is fantastic because it is so real, so real that it is fantastic. Graham Greene has said that he can't write, "I stood over a bottomless pit," because that couldn't be true, or "Running down the stairs I jumped into a taxi," because that couldn't be true either. But Elizabeth Bowen can write about one of her characters that "she snatched at her hair as if she heard something in it," because that is eminently possible.

25 I would even go so far as to say that the person writing a fantasy has to be even more strictly attentive to the concrete detail than someone writing in a naturalistic vein—because the greater the story's strain on the credulity, the more convincing the properties in it have to be.

26 A good example of this is a story called "The Metamorphosis" by Franz Kafka. This is a story about a man who wakes up one morning to find that he has turned into a cockroach overnight, while not discarding his human nature. The rest of the story concerns his life and feelings and eventual death as an insect with human nature, and this situation is accepted by the reader because the concrete detail of the story is absolutely convincing. The fact is that this story describes the dual nature of man in such a realistic fashion that it is almost unbearable. The truth is not distorted here, but rather, a certain distortion is used to get at the truth. If we admit, as we must, that appearance is not the same thing as reality, then we must give the artist the liberty to make certain rearrangements of nature if these will lead to greater depths of vision. The artist himself always has to remember that what he is rearranging *is* nature, and that he has to know it and be able to describe it accurately in order to have the authority to rearrange it at all.

27 The peculiar problem of the short-story writer is how to make the action he describes reveal as much of the mystery of existence as possible. He has only a short space to do it in and he can't do it by statement. He

has to do it by showing, not by saying, and by showing the concrete—so that   210
his problem is really how to make the concrete work double time for him.

28   In good fiction, certain of the details will tend to accumulate meaning from the action of the story itself, and when this happens they become
symbolic in the way they work. I once wrote a story called "Good Country
People" in which a lady Ph.D. has her wooden leg stolen by a Bible sales-   215
man whom she has tried to seduce. Now I'll admit that, paraphrased in this
way, the situation is simply a low joke. The average reader is pleased to observe anybody's wooden leg being stolen. But without ceasing to appeal to
him and without making any statements of high intention, this story does
manage to operate at another level of experience, by letting the wooden leg   220
accumulate meaning. Early in the story, we're presented with the fact that
the Ph.D. is spiritually as well as physically crippled. She believes in nothing but her own belief in nothing, and we perceive that there is a wooden
part of her soul that corresponds to her wooden leg. Now of course this is
never stated. The fiction writer states as little as possible. The reader makes   225
this connection from things he is shown. He may not even know that he
makes the connection, but the connection is there nevertheless and it has
its effect on him. As the story goes on, the wooden leg continues to accumulate meaning. The reader learns how the girl feels about her leg, how
her mother feels about it, and how the country woman on the place feels   230
about it; and finally, by the time the Bible salesman comes along, the leg
has accumulated so much meaning that it is, as the saying goes, loaded.
And when the Bible salesman steals it, the reader realizes that he has taken
away part of the girl's personality and has revealed her deeper affliction to
her for the first time.   235

29   If you want to say that the wooden leg is a symbol, you can say
that. But it is a wooden leg first, and as a wooden leg it is absolutely necessary to the story. It has its place on the literal level of the story, but it operates in depth as well as on the surface. It increases the story in every direction, and this is essentially the way a story escapes being short.   240

30   Now a little might be said about the way in which this happens. I
wouldn't want you to think that in that story I sat down and said, "I am
now going to write a story about a Ph.D. with a wooden leg, using the
wooden leg as a symbol for another kind of affliction." I doubt myself if
many writers know what they are going to do when they start out. When I   245
started writing that story, I didn't know there was going to be a Ph.D. with
a wooden leg in it. I merely found myself one morning writing a description
of two women that I knew something about, and before I realized it, I had

equipped one of them with a daughter with a wooden leg. As the story pro- 250
gressed, I brought in the Bible salesman, but I had no idea what I was going to do with him. I didn't know he was going to steal that wooden leg until ten or twelve lines before he did it, but when I found out that this was
what was going to happen, I realized that it was inevitable. This is a story
that produces a shock for the reader, and I think one reason for this is that
it produced a shock for the writer. 255

31 Now despite the fact that this story came about in this seemingly
mindless fashion, it is a story that almost no rewriting was done on. It is a
story that was under control throughout the writing of it, and it might be
asked how this kind of control comes about, since it is not entirely conscious.

32 I think the answer to this is what Maritain calls "the habit of art." 260
It is a fact that fiction writing is something in which the whole personality
takes part—the conscious as well as the unconscious mind. Art is the habit
of the artist; and habits have to be rooted deep in the whole personality.
They have to be cultivated like any other habit, over a long period of time,
by experience; and teaching any kind of writing is largely a matter of help- 265
ing the student develop the habit of art. I think this is more than just a discipline, although it is that; I think it is a way of looking at the created
world and of using the senses so as to make them find as much meaning as
possible in things.

33 Now I am not so naïve as to suppose that most people come to 270
writers' conferences in order to hear what kind of vision is necessary to
write stories that will become a permanent part of our literature. Even if
you do wish to hear this, your greatest concerns are immediately practical.
You want to know how you can actually write a good story, and further,
how you can tell when you've done it; and so you want to know what the 275
form of a short story is, as if the form were something that existed outside
of each story and could be applied or imposed on the material. Of course,
the more you write, the more you will realize that the form is organic, that
it is something that grows out of the material, that the form of each story
is unique. A story that is any good can't be reduced, it can only be ex- 280
panded. A story is good when you continue to see more and more in it, and
when it continues to escape you. In fiction two and two is always more than
four.

34 The only way, I think, to learn to write short stories is to write
them, and then to try to discover what you have done. The time to think of 285
technique is when you've actually got the story in front of you. The teacher

can help the student by looking at his individual work and trying to help him decide if he has written a complete story, one in which the action fully illuminates the meaning.

35   Perhaps the most profitable thing I can do is to tell you about   290
some of the general observations I made about these seven stories I read of yours. All of these observations will not fit any one of the stories exactly, but they are points nevertheless that won't hurt anyone interested in writing to think about.

36   The first thing that any professional writer is conscious of in read-   295
ing anything is, naturally, the use of language. Now the use of language in these stories was such that, with one exception, it would be difficult to distinguish one story from another. While I can recall running into several clichés, I can't remember one image or one metaphor from the seven stories. I don't mean there weren't images in them; I just mean that there weren't   300
any that were effective enough to take away with you.

37   In connection with this, I made another observation that startled me considerably. With the exception of one story, there was practically no use made of the local idiom. Now this is a Southern Writers' Conference. All the addresses on these stories were from Georgia or Tennessee, yet there   305
was no distinctive sense of Southern life in them. A few place-names were dropped, Savannah or Atlanta or Jacksonville, but these could just as easily have been changed to Pittsburgh or Passaic without calling for any other alteration in the story. The characters spoke as if they had never heard any kind of language except what came out of a television set. This indicates   310
that something is way out of focus.

38   There are two qualities that make fiction. One is the sense of mystery and the other is the sense of manners. You get the manners from the texture of existence that surrounds you. The great advantage of being a Southern writer is that we don't have to go anywhere to look for manners;   315
bad or good, we've got them in abundance. We in the South live in a society that is rich in contradiction, rich in irony, rich in contrast, and particularly rich in its speech. And yet here are six stories by Southerners in which almost no use is made of the gifts of the region.

39   Of course the reason for this may be that you have seen these gifts   320
abused so often that you have become self-conscious about using them. There is nothing worse than the writer who doesn't *use* the gifts of the region, but wallows in them. Everything becomes so Southern that it's sickening, so local that it is unintelligible, so literally reproduced that it con-

veys nothing. The general gets lost in the particular instead of being shown   325
through it.

40   However, when the life that actually surrounds us is totally ig-
nored, when our patterns of speech are absolutely overlooked, then something is out of kilter. The writer should then ask himself if he is not reaching out for a kind of life that is artificial to him.   330

41   An idiom characterizes a society, and when you ignore the idiom,
you are very likely ignoring the whole social fabric that could make a
meaningful character. You can't cut characters off from their society and
say much about them as individuals. You can't say anything meaningful
about the mystery of a personality unless you put that personality in a be-   335
lievable and significant social context. And the best way to do this is through
the character's own language. When the old lady in one of Andrew Lytle's
stories says contemptuously that she has a mule that is older than Birming-
ham, we get in that one sentence a sense of a society and its history. A great
deal of the Southern writer's work is done for him before he begins, because   340
our history lives in our talk. In one of Eudora Welty's stories a character
says, "Where I come from, we use fox for yard dogs and owls for chickens,
but we sing true." Now there is a whole book in that one sentence; and
when the people of your section can talk like that, and you ignore it, you're
just not taking advantage of what's yours. The sound of our talk is too def-   345
inite to be discarded with impunity, and if the writer tries to get rid of it,
he is liable to destroy the better part of his creative power.

42   Another thing I observed about these stories is that most of them
don't go very far inside a character, don't reveal very much of the character. I don't mean that they don't enter the character's mind, but they sim-   350
ply don't show that he has a personality. Again this goes back partly to
speech. These characters have no distinctive speech to reveal themselves
with; and sometimes they have no really distinctive features. You feel in
the end that no personality is revealed because no personality is there. In
most good stories it is the character's personality that creates the action of   355
the story. In most of these stories, I feel that the writer has thought of some
action and then scrounged up a character to perform it. You will usually be
more successful if you start the other way around. If you start with a real
personality, a real character, then something is bound to happen; and you
don't have to know what before you begin. In fact it may be better if you   360
don't know what before you begin. You ought to be able to discover something from your stories. If you don't, probably nobody else will.

QUESTIONS

1. What specific group was Flannery O'Connor addressing on the occasion of her lecture? Of course she was speaking, at least potentially, to a wider audience. Describe the type of reader for whom this essay would be appropriate.

2. Of special interest here is the author's tone *. What has she assumed about the interests of those in her original audience, about their knowledge of short stories, their abilities, their mistaken notions? Does she appear to take her listeners and their ambitions seriously, or does she talk down to them? Use specific passages to illustrate your answers.

3. What does Flannery O'Connor think of her aunt's literary judgment in paragraph 19? Of correspondence courses in writing short stories in paragraph 5? Of the television version of her short story in paragraph 20? Of the "average reader" in paragraph 21?

4. How does the author conceive of her own role: as a high priestess of fiction, a hard-working professional impatient with amateurs, an honest craftsman exasperated by ignorance and humbug? Or as something else?

5. If Flannery O'Connor insists upon her own superior knowledge of fiction, how does she win the approval of her audience?

6. Which paragraphs constitute the introduction? Where does the writer indicate her subject in a broad, general sense? Where does she narrow down the subject? What else does her introduction accomplish? Suppose she had begun like this: "My subject this evening is how, and how not, to write short stories. My purpose is to give you a number of do's and don't's, with special reference to the stories you have given me to read. But first, let us attempt to define what is meant by the term *short story*." Why would such an opening be much poorer?

7. Following the introduction, Flannery O'Connor defines a short story. Which paragraphs make up this definition? What methods of defining does she use? Show that her definition is also advice about writing short stories.

8. Identify and entitle the remaining part (or parts) of this essay.

9. Which paragraphs constitute the conclusion? Does the ending seem prepared for, or abrupt and unexpected? What means of signaling conclusion has the writer employed? Can you think of any other ways of closing this essay?

10. Paragraphs 2, 3, and 8—among others—consist of a single sentence. Would the force or clarity of the essay be improved if paragraphs 2 and 3 were combined with 4? If paragraphs 5, 6, 7, and 8 were brought together? Most of

Flannery O'Connor's paragraphs consist of three or more sentences. Is it possible to justify these one-sentence paragraphs?

11. Analyze how the writer develops her topic in paragraphs 12, 24, and 28.

SENTENCES

12. The overall effect of Flannery O'Connor's sentence style is one of simplicity. Yet she skillfully varies her sentence patterns. Find examples of parallelism *, interrupted movement *, balanced construction *, and antithesis *.

13. Explain why the following sentence is an example of chiasmus *: "A thing is fantastic because it is so real; so real that it is fantastic." Find a similar sentence in paragraph 26.

14. Study these two sentences and explain why the revision is inferior to what Flannery O'Connor wrote:

> *Revision:* We in the South live in a society that is rich in contradiction, replete with irony, heavily endowed with contrasts, and blessed in its speech.
> *O'Connor:* "We in the South live in a society that is rich in contradiction, rich in irony, rich in contrast, and particularly rich in its speech." (316-18)

DICTION

15. Look up: *highfalutin* (93), *concrete* (93), *motivation* (118), *disabuse* (124), *awful* (148), *naturalistic* (180), *fantasy* (180), *eminent* (181), *properties* (192), *peculiar* (207), *paraphrased* (216), *organic* (278), *impunity* (346).

16. Carefully differentiate the meanings of these related terms in lines 42-43: *reminiscence, episode, opinion, anecdote, story.*

17. Point to words and expressions that are informal, even colloquial *, suggesting the rhythms of spoken English. Find examples of more formal, literary diction.

18. Why does the writer employ capitals in "they want to Be A Writer" in line 60? What does she imply by her use of hyphens in "books and magazine articles on how-to-write-short-stories" (20)?

19. The word *now* appears often in this essay, especially as the first word of a paragraph. What exactly does it mean? Explain how it affects the tone of the essay. If you think it has been overused, suggest one or two monosyllabic equivalents of *now*.

POINTS TO LEARN

1. A formal style seldom sounds effective in a lecture or a speech; on the other hand, writing designed for an audience to listen to often works very well as an informal essay.

2. Informal writing reveals a writer's personality more clearly than does a formal, literary style. Informal essays have a distinct tone, which results from a combination of diction and sentence structure and which expresses the writer's attitude toward readers (or audience), toward subject, and toward himself. Tone, skillfully managed, helps the writer to entertain his readers as well as to inform them, and may enhance any effort he makes to persuade them of something.

3. The informal essayist uses both literary and more commonplace diction. At times he is deliberately casual or colloquial; he may tell anecdotes and report bits of conversation. At other times he employs more formal words, with precision and clarity his foremost consideration.

4. And similarly the informal essayist makes use of a wide range of sentence structure, from short, simple sentences to more complex patterns such as parallelism, balance, antithesis, and an occasional chiasmus.

SUGGESTIONS FOR WRITING

1. Analyze a short story by Flannery O'Connor, Eudora Welty, Margaret Laurence, or Alice Munro in the light of Flannery O'Connor's advice to short-story writers. Pay particular attention to such matters as the principal characters' share in the "general human condition" and their relation to "the mysteries of personality." Use short quotations from the essay if you can work them in neatly.

2. Read Flannery O'Connor's story "The Life You Save May Be Your Own," which she refers to on page 602 of this essay. Analyze the story as an "experience of meaning." Show that it is complete in the sense in which Flannery O'Connor uses that term and that it deals with "the mystery of personality." Along the way you might allude to the author's exasperation with the television script of her story.

3. Imagining that you will be reading it aloud to your classmates, compose an essay in which you show how manners and speech define characters and overall meaning in a short story by Henry James, Graham Greene, Hugh Hood, or Flannery O'Connor.

4. Flannery O'Connor suggests that the personalities of fictional characters are shaped, at least in part, by the personalities of their creators. Study several of her short stories and discuss what they (along with this essay) reveal about Flannery O'Connor's personality.

IMPROVING YOUR STYLE

1. In your essay include examples of the balanced sentence, of parallelism, and of antithesis.

2. Include also a sentence using chiasmus (see Question 13).

3. Experiment with *now* in two or three places as a transitional word, using it as O'Connor does in lines 81, 115, 241, and 256. The exact value of *now* in such passages is difficult to define. Partly it is a weak intensive asking for the reader's attention. Partly it signals movement to another topic, too loosely related to what has just been said to warrant a more precise logical connective * such as *consequently* or *for* or *hence*. And partly it is an informal, colloquial word, important in establishing a relaxed, conversational tone.

What a Canadian Has Done for Canada

William Arthur Deacon (1890-1977) was born in Pembroke, Ontario, and after studying at the Universities of Toronto and Manitoba began a career as a lawyer in Winnipeg in 1918. In 1922 he became the literary editor of *Saturday Night* and soon displayed those qualities of wit, vigorous humor, and outspokenness that combined to make him a widely-read reviewer and a figure of influence on the Canadian literary scene. He moved from *Saturday Night* to the *Mail and Empire* (now the *Globe and Mail*) in 1928 and continued there as a reviewer and columnist until his retirement in 1959. In addition to *Poteen* (1926)—the word is Irish in origin, and refers to illegally distilled whisky— Deacon's books include *Pens and Pirates* (1923), *The Four Jameses* (1927), a straight-faced, pseudo-academic (and highly comic) study of four very bad Canadian poets, and *My Vision of Canada* (1933). In the selection below Deacon's gifts are much in evidence, as he launches a hilarious and devastating attack on a novel of very dubious merits.

1   In the timber-lands at the fringe of the Barrens, then, is a mining camp; and it is the purpose of the author to turn naked into the wilds a young Canadian engineer of 30 and a wealthy and useless, though somewhat ornamental, New York society girl of 19, as hero and heroine who shall create civilization with its many inventions out of the raw material 5 afforded by Nature. The launching is accomplished by the girl getting caught in the rapids leading out of Barrier Lake while she is fishing in her canoe before breakfast. Grimshaw, the camp-boss, still in his pyjamas, sees her go and rushes to her aid by rowing a York-boat. Now a small York-boat is 30 feet long, carries four tons of freight and a crew of eight to twelve 10 men. Why he did not take one of the other canoes is one of the myriad entrancing mysteries in the book. But single-handed he propels the York-

From "What a Canadian Has Done for Canada" in *Poteen* (Ottawa: Graphic Publishers, 1926), reprinted by permission of Lloyd Haines.

boat down the lake at break-neck speed, and the two of them shoot the seven miles of rapids. The hero is evidently an acrobat too, for his boat springing a leak, he, standing, tossed by the furious waves, removes both 15 parts of his pyjamas to mend the leak. He also "steers" the drifting boat by means of a sweep, though this is physically impossible. The girl's bathing suit rips and comes off, though such garments usually stand contact with water. Both craft are lost, so the people reach shore at the lower end of the rapids naked and without baggage.   20

2   Though they started shortly after dawn, and were hurled down at lightning speed, they reach the bottom of the rapids late in the afternoon. I, having shot a seven-mile rapid in about half an hour, deplore this dilatoriness; but am forced to admire the efficiency and speed of the hero once he is on land. Between, say, 4.30 P.M. and dark he manages to cut and 25 weave clothes for them both out of willow branches, erects a substantial log house and puts a roof on; makes beds out of "armful after armful of cat-tails"; makes a barricade for the door; catches two fish with his hands— one a five pound maskalonge, not native to that section of the country; makes a bone knife, bark platter and drinking cup; cleans the fish; goes out 30 and inspects timber, climbing uplands to do so; notes bear and moose indications; digs cedar roots, though no cedars grow that far north; collects punk and bird feathers.

3   The author is careful to tell us that the seven miles of land separating the twain from the camp (where Mr. Endicott, Claire's father and 35 Grimshaw's employer, is at the moment) is impassable on account of rock faces and muskeg. As a matter of fact, a long, precipitous rapid could not flow through a muskeg. The walls of the river were high and rocky, and any rock can be scaled or walked around. But the story must go on; hence this mythical screen cutting the castaways off from their kind. And in the 40 book it is three months before an aeroplane can reach them.

4   Miracles now happen thick and fast. The accomplishment of the first evening is a mere nothing to this superwoodsman, who makes errors in woodlore discreditable to a boy scout. After supper on the first full day in camp, Grimshaw attacks a bull moose of 1,000 pounds weight and actually 45 succeeds in drawing blood by striking it on the neck with his deer-rib knife. The bull is infuriated, as it has every right to be, strikes the man with its "fore-paws", knocks him down and jumps on him. An ordinary moose with hard, sharp hoofs would certainly have killed him; but this one, doubtless because equipped by the author with "paws", only succeeds in giving him 50 "a bruise or two" which cause him no trouble. Claire, witnessing the first

part of this unequal combat, leaps on the animal's back and "paralyzes" it by thrusting her wooden, stone-tipped spear through its spine, a moose's spine being about as soft as reinforced concrete sewer-pipe. The beast was possibly paralyzed with astonishment, went into hysteria and suffered a 55 nervous breakdown. Anyway, Grimshaw kills it—with the deer-rib. There were two bull moose when Grimshaw came up, but the author makes a concession to realism by telling us that "the other one got away". Hardly less wonderful is the episode of a later day when Grimshaw kills a caribou by sticking a spear into her rump.   60

5   Of all the necessities, conveniences and sheer luxuries manufactured by the marvellous Grimshaw, it must be remembered that most of them were the products of the first six days' toil. He worked very hard. On the second full day in camp, for instance, he got breakfast of berries and bannocks made of parched bulrush bulbs pounded between stones into 65 flour, and broiled moose meat; rewashed the heavy-haired skin, and laid it out for scraping; split the moosehead and saved the brains; washed and stretched the intestines for fish lines; dug out the precious white sinew along the spine; found the prow of his boat with some iron on it; made wooden, stone-tipped tongs to handle hot metal; made a stone hammer; 70 made a kiln; made charcoal in the kiln; made a forge of stone, chinked with clay; made a bellows for the forge out of moose-hide; made a leg-bone into a draft conductor; got two slabs of tamarack; charred the slabs; resmoked the moose-hide over the fire, dressing it with a mixture of fish-fat and brains; drilled holes through the slabs; fixed leg-bone to slat; fitted and 75 sewed discs of moose-hide; finished bellows and forge; made another kiln of charcoal; from the iron he made a chisel, a knife, an axehead, two sewing-awls and a spearhead. Then he called it a day, and laid off!

6   About two weeks after landing they had plenty of time to build a fine, large log-house, whitewashed and decorated, divided into rooms, having 80 windows, a planed floor, furniture, a brick chimney and bake-oven, and a fireplace of glazed tiles. They possessed two iron table knives, forks and spoons of bone, a razor made from a single "medium-sized" nail (presumably a wire nail), cups, saucers and plates of glazed earthenware ornamented with colored designs, storage crocks, pails and tubs, wash basins, 85 candles, curtains and rugs, willow chairs, tooth brushes, scented toilet soap, scissors, and the following articles all of solid gold: a comb, hair pins, buttons, a ring and a frying pan—the last of which is made out to be a *useful* cooking implement. In the third month preparations for winter were so complete that time hung heavily upon their hands, and one wonders why 90

they did not make a Mah Jongg set, or construct a radio and get the news
from home, or even send a message to Dad, seven miles away, telling him
where they were.

7   "In all this world I don't suppose a man and a woman have ever
been thrown together as we've been thrown together in this wilderness",   95
remarks Claire, and I cannot help agreeing with her that the author did
throw his characters together somewhat heedlessly. He calls their life "a
splendid crudity", and spoke more truly than he knew. For within nine
days the girl, who had probably never even dressed herself, had become an
expert cook, dressmaker, archer, hunter and woodsman. Her first attempt   100
at sewing resulted in the satisfactory cutting-out and making of garments.
She eats birch-buds in the fall, though they grow only in spring. She put
a fish in a jack-pine to protect it from mink, marten and wolverine, whereas
all of them can climb and the marten *lives* in trees. But she was a green-
horn and can be excused for her author's faults.   105

QUESTIONS

READER AND PURPOSE

1. The subject of Deacon's essay is a novel written by Arthur Stringer, *Empty
Hands* (1924), and Deacon has—he says—chosen to write about it "because
Stringer, being a Canadian by birth, may be mistaken for a realist by readers
in other countries." After reading this selection from his essay, what other
purposes do you think Deacon had for writing?
2. Plot summaries are usually not part of serious literary criticism, yet Deacon
does little more than summarize the plot and make comments on it. Explain
why, in this case, his critical method is effective.
3. Deacon obviously does not take *Empty Hands* seriously as a work of literature, and, equally obviously, he expects his readers to agree with him. What
attitudes to literature does Deacon assume the reader shares with him? What
range of information about the Canadian North?
4. What is Deacon's point of view *? How is it used to reinforce his criticism?
5. This selection shows us one way of dealing with a novel of poor quality—
simply to expose its absurdity, instead of subjecting it to detailed analysis
(which Deacon implies would not be worth our time). Give as many reasons
as you can in support of the view that Deacon's method would be inappropriate
if applied to a good novel.

ORGANIZATION

6. What sort of tone * does Deacon establish in the first paragraph of this

selection? Describe his attitude to the novel he is discussing and his attitude to his readers. What impression does he convey of himself?

7. One of Deacon's problems here is to keep his combination of plot summary and commentary from becoming monotonous. How does he avoid monotony? For example, can you point to instances where he varies the position of his own comments within a paragraph? Does he comment in the same detail on all the absurdities of the plot? Does he let some of them speak for themselves?

8. The organization of this selection is quite straightforward; Deacon merely follows the order of events in Stringer's plot. Can you think of any other way in which the material could have been effectively arranged?

9. Can you defend Deacon's paragraphing of his material? Is there an overlapping of topics from one paragraph to another? Be sure to look closely at Deacon's references to chronology before answering.

SENTENCES

10. Describe the form of sentence seven in paragraph 1. Why does it produce a comic effect?

11. Is sentence two of paragraph 2 an example of ellipsis *?

12. Would you describe sentence three of paragraph 2 as a cumulative * sentence? As a freight-train * sentence? Where else does Deacon use this kind of sentence? Is the reader intended to see this rapid accumulation of detail as comic? Explain why, or why not.

13. Many of Deacon's sentences are quite long. Locate some instances where he uses short sentences for emphasis and contrast.

14. Explain why Deacon uses dashes in lines 28, 56, 88.

DICTION

15. Look up: *myriad* (11), *entrancing* (12), *sweep* (17), *dilatoriness* (23-24), *maskalonge* (29), *muskeg* (38), *mythical* (40), *hysteria* (55), *bannocks* (65), *Mah Jongg* (91).

16. Look up the etymology * of *punk* (33). In what sense is Deacon using the word? How has it developed into a colloquial * term for describing a certain kind of person?

17. Describe some of the comic effects Deacon creates through understatement *, exaggeration, and irony *.

18. Is Deacon employing irony in sentences one and two of paragraph 7? If you think so, explain at whom he is directing his irony.

19. Deacon is fond of alliteration *, as in *myriad entrancing mysteries* (11-12). Point out other instances. Is this device also used for comic purposes? If so, how?

20. Why does the author put quotation marks around *steers* (16), *fore-paws* (48), *paws* (50), *paralyzes* (52), *medium-sized* (83)? Why does he italicize *useful* (88) and *lives* (104)?

POINTS TO LEARN

1. One of the most efficient ways of dealing with bad literature is to make the reader laugh at its absurdity.

2. Absurdity or improbability need not always be pointed out directly; sometimes it should merely be quoted and left to speak for itself.

3. An author can make his audience recognize improbability by referring to common knowledge or to his own specialized experience.

4. Comedy and irony can be effective means of satire, provided they are not exaggerated or overworked.

SUGGESTIONS FOR WRITING

Write a review of a recent film, novel, or television production that you consider so poor you cannot take it seriously. In a general way, model your approach and organization on Deacon's—but do not merely imitate him.

IMPROVING YOUR STYLE

In your essay include:

1. Sentences in which you employ understatement, exaggeration, and irony.

2. Long cataloguing sentences which in themselves produce comic effects.

3. Attempts at alliteration in one or two places.

Who Killed King Kong?

X. J. Kennedy is a critic, teacher, and poet. His published poems include the volumes *Nude Descending a Staircase* (1961) and *Growing into Love* (1969). Here he examines the phenomenon of *King Kong*, a perennial film classic produced in 1933. While Kennedy is not primarily a film critic, he is fully sensitive to the nature of motion pictures. His focus, however, is not simply upon the movie itself but includes its relationship to our culture, the reason for *King Kong's* enduring popularity. Kennedy's forceful prose in this essay exploits almost all the resources of diction and is noteworthy also for its skillful control of tone.

1   The ordeal and spectacular death of King Kong, the giant ape, undoubtedly have been witnessed by more Americans than have ever seen a performance of *Hamlet, Iphigenia at Aulis*, or even *Tobacco Road*. Since RKO-Radio Pictures first released *King Kong*, a quarter-century has gone by; yet year after year, from prints that grow more rain-beaten, from sound tracks that grow more tinny, ticket-buyers by thousands still pursue Kong's luckless fight against the forces of technology, tabloid journalism, and the DAR. They see him chloroformed to sleep, see him whisked from his jungle isle to New York and placed on show, see him burst his chains to roam the city (lugging a frightened blonde), at last to plunge from the spire of the Empire State Building, machine-gunned by model airplanes.

2   Though Kong may die, one begins to think his legend unkillable. No clearer proof of his hold upon the popular imagination may be seen than what emerged one catastrophic week in March 1955, when New York WOR-TV programmed *Kong* for seven evenings in a row (a total of sixteen showings). Many a rival network vice-president must have scowled when surveys showed that *Kong*—the 1933 B-picture—had lured away fat segments

From *Dissent* (Spring 1960). Reprinted by permission of the publisher.

of the viewing populace from such powerful competitors as Ed Sullivan, Groucho Marx and Bishop Sheen.

3   But even television has failed to run *King Kong* into oblivion. Coffee-   20
in-the-lobby cinemas still show the old hunk of hokum, with the apology that in its use of composite shots and animated models the film remains technically interesting. And no other monster in movie history has won so devoted a popular audience. None of the plodding mummies, the stultified draculas, the white-coated Lugosis[1] with their shiny pinball-machine labora-   25
tories, none of the invisible stranglers, berserk robots, or menaces from Mars has ever enjoyed so many resurrections.

4   Why does the American public refuse to let King Kong rest in peace? It is true, I'll admit, that Kong outdid every monster movie before or since in sheer carnage. Producers Cooper and Schoedsack crammed into it dinosaurs,   30
headhunters, riots, aerial battles, bullets, bombs, bloodletting. Heroine Fay Wray, whose function is mainly to scream, shuts her mouth for hardly one uninterrupted minute from first reel to last. It is also true that *Kong* is larded with good healthy sadism, for those whose joy it is to see the frantic girl dangled from cliffs and harried by pterodactyls. But it seems to me that the   35
abiding appeal of the giant ape rests on other foundations.

5   Kong has, first of all, the attraction of being manlike. His simian nature gives him one huge advantage over giant ants and walking vegetables in that an audience may conceivably identify with him. Kong's appeal has the quality that established the Tarzan series as American myth—for what   40
man doesn't secretly image himself a huge hairy howler against whom no other monster has a chance? If Tarzan recalls the ape in us, then Kong may well appeal to that great-granddaddy primordial brute from whose tribe we have all deteriorated.

6   Intentionally or not, the producers of *King Kong* encourage this   45
identification by etching the character of Kong with keen sympathy. For the ape is a figure in a tradition familiar to moviegoers: the tradition of the pitiable monster. We think of Lon Chaney in the role of Quasimodo, of Karloff in the original *Frankenstein*. As we watch the Frankenstein monster's fumbling and disastrous attempts to befriend a flower-picking child, our sym-   50
pathies are enlisted with the monster in his impenetrable loneliness. And so with Kong. As he roars in his chains, while barkers sell tickets to boobs who gape at him, we perhaps feel something more deep than pathos. We begin to sense something of the problem that engaged Eugene O'Neill in *The Hairy*

---

[1] An actor in many horror movies. [Editors' note]

Ape: the dilemma of a displaced animal spirit forced to live in a jungle built   55
by machines.

7   *King Kong,* it is true, had special relevance in 1933. Landscapes of
the depression are glimpsed early in the film when an impresario, seeking
some desperate pretty girl to play the lead in a jungle movie, visits souplines
and a Woman's Home Mission. In Fay Wray—who's been caught snitching   60
an apple from a fruitstand—his search is ended. When he gives her a big feed
and a movie contract, the girl is magic-carpeted out of the world of the National Recovery Act. And when, in the film's climax, Kong smashes that very
Third Avenue landscape in which Fay had wandered hungry, audiences of
1933 may well have felt a personal satisfaction.   65

8   What is curious is that audiences of 1960 remain hooked. For in the
heart of urban man, one suspects, lurks the impulse to fling a bomb. Though
machines speed him to the scene of his daily grind, though IBM comptome-
ters ("freeing the human mind from drudgery") enable him to drudge more
efficiently once he arrives, there comes a moment when he wishes to turn   70
upon his machines and kick hell out of them. He wants to hurl his combination radio-alarmclock out the bedroom window and listen to its smash. What
subway commuter wouldn't love—just for once—to see the downtown express smack head-on into the uptown local? Such a wish is gratified in that
memorable scene in *Kong* that opens with a wide-angle shot: interior of a   75
railway car on the Third Avenue El. Straphangers are nodding, the literate
refold their newspapers. Unknown to them, Kong has torn away a section of
trestle toward which the train now speeds. The motorman spies Kong up
ahead, jams on the brakes. Passengers hurtle together like so many peas in a
pail. In a window of the car appear Kong's bloodshot eyes. Women shriek.   80
Kong picks up the railway car as if it were a rat, flips it to the street and ties
knots in it, or something. To any commuter the scene must appear one of the
most satisfactory pieces of celluloid ever exposed.

9   Yet however violent his acts, Kong remains a gentleman. Remarkable
in his sense of chivalry. Whenever a fresh boa constrictor threatens Fay,   85
Kong first sees that the lady is safely parked, then manfully thrashes her at-
tacker. (And she, the ingrate, runs away every time his back is turned.) Atop
the Empire State Building, ignoring his pursuers, Kong places Fay on a
ledge as tenderly as if she were a dozen eggs. He fondles her, then turns to
face the Army Air Force. And Kong is perhaps the most disinterested lover   90
since Cyrano: his attentions to the lady are utterly without hope of reward.
After all, between a five-foot blonde and a fifty-foot ape, love can hardly be
more than an intellectual flirtation. In his simian way King Kong is the

hopelessly yearning lover of Petrarchan convention. His forced exit from his jungle, in chains, results directly from his single-minded pursuit of Fay. He 95 smashes a Broadway theater when the notion enters his dull brain that the flashbulbs of photographers somehow endanger the lady. His perilous shinny-ing up a skyscraper to pluck Fay from her boudoir is an act of the kindliest of hearts. He's impossible to discourage even though the love of his life can't lay eyes on him without shrieking murder.   100

10   The tragedy of King Kong then, is to be the beast who at the end of the fable fails to turn into the handsome prince. This is the conviction that the scriptwriters would leave with us in the film's closing line. As Kong's corpse lies blocking traffic in the street, the entrepreneur who brought Kong to New York turns to the assembled reporters and proclaims: "That's your 105 story, boys—it was Beauty killed the Beast!" But greater forces than those of the screaming Lady have combined to lay Kong low, if you ask me. Kong lives for a time as one of those persecuted near-animal souls bewildered in the middle of an industrial order, whose simple desires are thwarted at every turn. He climbs the Empire State Building because in all New York it's the 110 closest thing he can find to the clifftop of his jungle isle. He dies, a pitiful dolt, and the army brass and publicity-men cackle over him. His death is the only possible outcome to as neat a tragic dilemma as you can ask for. The machine-guns do him in, while the manicured human hero (a nice clean Dartmouth boy) carries away Kong's sweetheart to the altar. O, the misery 115 of it all. There's far more truth about upper-middle-class American life in *King Kong* than in the last seven dozen novels of John P. Marquand.

11   A Negro friend from Atlanta tells me that in movie houses in colored neighborhoods throughout the South, *Kong* does a constant business. They show the thing in Atlanta at least every year, presumably to the same audi- 120 ences. Perhaps this popularity may simply be due to the fact that Kong is one of the most watchable movies ever constructed, but I wonder whether Negro audiences may not find some archetypical appeal in this serio-comic tale of a huge black powerful free spirit whom all the hardworking white policemen are out to kill.   125

12   Every day in the week on a screen somewhere in the world, King Kong relives his agony. Again and again he expires on the Empire State Building, as audiences of the devout assist his sacrifice. We watch him die, and by extension kill the ape within our bones, but these little deaths of ours occur in prosaic surroundings. We do not die on a tower, New York before 130 our feet, nor do we give our lives to smash a few flying machines. It is not for us to bring to a momentary standstill the civilization in which we move.

King Kong does this for us. And so we kill him again and again, in much-spliced celluloid, while the ape in us expires from day to day, obscure, in desperation.

135

QUESTIONS

READER AND PURPOSE

1. Which sentence in the first four paragraphs gives the clearest clue to Kennedy's purpose? Is that purpose most adequately described as: (a) to explain the enduring appeal of *King Kong*, or (b) to write a critical appreciation of the film as great art?

2. What can you infer about the sort of readers Kennedy is writing for? Are they over or under thirty? Have they gone to college? Are they city-dwellers or do they live in small towns? Politically liberal or conservative? Does he assume that they have seen *King Kong*?

ORGANIZATION

3. Which paragraphs constitute the beginning? What does each contribute?

4. A closing may employ one or more of several techniques: summation, drawing a logical conclusion, returning to the beginning, signal words and phrases (*in conclusion, finally,* and so on), referring to some natural image * of ending, varying the rhythm and pace of the final sentence. How many of these does Kennedy employ in his last paragraph?

5. Which of the following techniques of development primarily shapes the middle of the essay: illustration, cause and effect, definition, comparison and contrast, analogy, classification and division?

SENTENCES

6. Why are Kennedy's sentences more effective than the revisions?

    (a) *Revision:* Even television has failed to run *King Kong* into oblivion, however.
    Kennedy: "But even television has failed to run *King Kong* into oblivion." (20)

    (b) *Revision:* None of the usual movie monsters has ever enjoyed so many resurrections.
    Kennedy: "None of the plodding mummies, the stultified draculas, the white-coated Lugosis with their shiny pinball-machine laboratories, none of the invisible stranglers, berserk robots, or menaces from Mars has ever enjoyed so many resurrections." (24-27)

(c) *Revision:* Any subway commuter just for once would love to see the downtown express smack head-on into the uptown local.
Kennedy: "What subway commuter wouldn't love—just for once—to see the downtown express smack head-on into the uptown local?" (72-74)

(d) *Revision:* His sense of chivalry is remarkable.
Kennedy: "Remarkable is his sense of chivalry." (84-85)

(e) *Revision:* We kill him again and again in much-spliced celluloid. The obscure ape in us expires in desperation from day to day.
Kennedy: "And so we kill him again and again, in much-spliced celluloid, while the ape in us expires from day to day, obscure, in desperation." (133-35)

DICTION

7. Look up: *tabloid* (7), *stultified* (24), *carnage* (30), *harried* (35), *pterodactyls* (35), *simian* (37), *impresario* (58), *Cyrano* (91), *entrepreneur* (104), *archetypical* (123).

8. What do these phrases signify: *National Recovery Act* (63), *Petrarchan convention* (94), *much-spliced celluloid* (133-34)?

9. The following expressions attract attention because they are unusual. Explain, if you can, exactly how each is unusual: *coffee-in-the-lobby cinemas* (20-21), *draculas* (25), *good healthy sadism* (34), *great-granddaddy primordial brute* (43), *magic-carpeted* (62), *a fresh boa-constrictor* (85), *watchable* (122).

10. What is the difference between *disinterested* (90) and *uninterested?*

11. *Huge hairy howler* (41) is an example of a rhetorical * device some teachers frown on. What is that device called? Does it work here? Why or why not? Locate other examples in this essay.

12. Kennedy draws words from several levels of usage. Find examples of slang; colloquialisms *; formal, literary words; technical terms. Would the effect have been better, or worse, if he had kept his diction more uniform—all formal, say, or all colloquial? When should a writer consistently use formal diction?

13. How much can you infer from his diction about Kennedy's interests, personality, and values?

POINTS TO LEARN

1. Among the common purposes of writing about literature are these:

(a) To describe a personal, and often emotional, response to a particular work—the kind of writing we have called impressionistic.

(b) To analyze objectively the formal elements of a work to show how their relationships produce a unity of meaning and feeling.

(c) To evaluate a literary work according to some artistic standard.

(d) To help would-be authors to write.

(e) To assign a work its proper place in the history of literature.

(f) To study how the work came to be—its sources in other literary and sub-literary pieces, its roots in the author's life and sensibility.

(g) To discuss the literary work in relation to some system of psychology, philosophy, theology, politics, sociology, or myth—as Kennedy does in "Who Killed King Kong?"

2. More than one of these purposes may be at work in any critical essay, but generally one primarily controls and shapes the piece.

3. At its best writing about literature is a work of art in itself, a combination of explanation and entertainment. In such cases the personality of the writer is an important element in the total effect. Without being obtrusive, the writer must understand what his readers need to be told and what they already know, and the writer must strive to make himself or herself pleasing. Success requires careful control of diction.

SUGGESTIONS FOR WRITING

1. Loosely using Kennedy's essay as a model, explain the popularity of a well-known film other than *King Kong*.

2. Account for the popularity of a type of film or television show generally regarded as an inferior kind of art—the cowboy movie, for example, or the cops-and-robbers melodrama, science fiction films, and so on. While you probably will want to generalize, cite examples from specific TV shows or movies.

IMPROVING YOUR STYLE

1. In your essay pay close attention to diction. Avoid clichés and seek vigorous concrete * words—especially verbs—to enliven your prose. Attempt also to widen the range of your diction, as Kennedy has, by using a judicious combination of slang, colloquialisms, technical terms, and formal words. In every case, however, take care that your diction is accurate and appropriate, working with your tone *, not against it.

2. Include a rhetorical question and sentences with interrupted movement * and inversion *.

3. Model your final sentence on Kennedy's, interrupting it and slowing it as a way of signaling closing.

The World of *Hamlet*

Maynard Mack is a foremost Renaissance scholar and taught, before his retirement, at Yale University. His essay on *Hamlet* is an example of interpretative criticism, that is, of the kind of literary analysis that seeks to get at the essential meaning which informs a poem or play or story. This meaning is often referred to as the "theme," but theme should not be thought of as a more or less clear-cut and brief statement of significance which can be inferred from the work, cut loose, and tied on like a name tag. The theme of a complex drama like *Hamlet* is, in a sense, co-extensive with the work itself and not really detachable. The task of the interpretative critic is to approach as full a statement of meaning as he can see, but always with the tacit understanding that he will not see everything and that his statement will be incomplete. *Hamlet*, because of its central ambiguities, has always resisted interpretation while at the same time demanding it. Maynard Mack's remarkable effort to get to the heart of the play is interpretative criticism at its finest.

1 My subject is the world of *Hamlet*. I do not of course mean Denmark, except as Denmark is given a body by the play; and I do not mean Elizabethan England, though this is necessarily close behind the scenes. I mean simply the imaginative environment that the play asks us to enter when we read it or go to see it. 5

2 Great plays, as we know, do present us with something that can be called a world, a microcosm—a world like our own in being made of people, actions, situations, thoughts, feelings and much more, but unlike our own in being perfectly, or almost perfectly, significant and coherent. In a play's world, each part implies the other parts, and each lives, each means, with the 10 life and meaning of the rest.

3 This is the reason, as we also know, that the worlds of great plays greatly differ. Othello in Hamlet's position, we sometimes say, would have

From *The Yale Review*, Vol. XLI, No. 4 (Summer 1952), pp. 502–23. Copyright Yale University. Reprinted by permission of the author.

no problem; but what we are really saying is that Othello in Hamlet's position would not exist. The conception we have of Othello is a function of the characters who help define him, Desdemona, honest Iago, Cassio, and the rest; of his history of travel and war; of a great storm that divides his ships from Cassio's, and a handkerchief; of a quiet night in Venice broken by cries about an old black ram; of a quiet night in Cyprus broken by sword-play; of a quiet bedroom where a woman goes to bed in her wedding sheets and a man comes in with a light to put out the light; and above all, of a language, a language with many voices in it, gentle, rasping, querulous, or foul, but all counterpointing the one great voice: [15] [20]

Put up your bright swords, for the dew will rust them.   [25]

O thou weed
Who art so lovely fair and smell'st so sweet
That the sense aches at thee. . . .
Yet I'll not shed her blood
Nor scar that whiter skin of hers than snow,   [30]
And smooth as monumental alabaster.

I pray you in your letters,
When you shall these unlucky deeds relate,
Speak of me as I am; nothing extenuate,
Nor set down aught in malice; then must you speak   [35]
Of one that loved not wisely but too well;
Of one not easily jealous, but being wrought,
Perplex'd in th' extreme; of one whose hand,
Like the base Indian, threw a pearl away
Richer than all his tribe. . . .

4   Without his particular world of voices, persons, events, the world [40] that both expresses and contains him, Othello is unimaginable. And so, I think, are Antony, King Lear, Macbeth—and Hamlet. We come back then to Hamlet's world, of all the tragic worlds that Shakespeare made, easily the most various and brilliant, the most elusive. It is with no thought of doing justice to it that I have singled out three of its attributes for comment. [45] I know too well, if I may echo a sentiment of Mr. E. M. W. Tillyard's, that no one is likely to accept another man's reading of *Hamlet*, that anyone who tries to throw light on one part of the play usually throws the rest into deeper shadow, and that what I have to say leaves out many problems—to mention only one, the knotty problem of the text. All I would say in defense [50]

of the materials I have chosen is that they seem to me interesting, close to
the root of the matter even if we continue to differ about what the root of
the matter is, and explanatory, in a modest way, of this play's peculiar hold
on everyone's imagination, its almost mythic status, one might say, as a
paradigm of the life of man.   55

5   The first attribute that impresses us, I think, is mysteriousness. We
often hear it said, perhaps with truth, that every great work of art has a mystery at the heart; but the mystery of *Hamlet* is something else. We feel its
presence in the numberless explanations that have been brought forward for
Hamlet's delay, his madness, his ghost, his treatment of Polonius, or Ophe- 60
lia, or his mother; and in the controversies that still go on about whether the
play is "undoubtedly a failure" (Eliot's phrase) or one of the greatest artistic triumphs; whether, if it is a triumph, it belongs to the highest order of
tragedy; whether, if it is such a tragedy, its hero is to be taken as a man of
exquisite moral sensibility (Bradley's view) or an egomaniac (Madariaga's 65
view).

6   Doubtless there have been more of these controversies and explanations than the play requires; for in Hamlet, to paraphrase a remark of Falstaff's, we have a character who is not only mad in himself but a cause that
madness is in the rest of us. Still, the very existence of so many theories and 70
counter-theories, many of them formulated by sober heads, gives food for
thought. *Hamlet* seems to lie closer to the illogical logic of life than Shakespeare's other tragedies. And while the causes of this situation may be
sought by saying that Shakespeare revised the play so often that eventually
the motivations were smudged over, or that the original old play has been 75
here or there imperfectly digested, or that the problems of Hamlet lay so
close to Shakespeare's heart that he could not quite distance them in the
formal terms of art, we have still as critics to deal with effects, not causes. If
I may quote again from Mr. Tillyard, the play's very lack of a rigorous type
of causal logic seems to be a part of its point.   80

7   Moreover, the matter goes deeper than this. Hamlet's world is pre-
ëminently in the interrogative mood. It reverberates with questions, an-
guished, meditative, alarmed. There are questions that in this play, to an
extent I think unparalleled in any other, mark the phases and even the
nuances of the action, helping to establish its peculiar baffled tone. There 85
are other questions whose interrogations, innocent at first glance, are subsequently seen to have reached beyond their contexts and to point towards
some pervasive inscrutability in Hamlet's world as a whole. Such is that
tense series of challenges with which the tragedy begins: Bernardo's of Fran-

cisco, "Who's there?" Francisco's of Horatio and Marcellus, "Who is   90
there?" Horatio's of the ghost, "What art thou . . . ?" And then there are
the famous questions. In them the interrogations seem to point not only beyond the context but beyond the play, out of Hamlet's predicaments into
everyone's: "What a piece of work is a man! . . . And yet to me what is
this quintessence of dust?" "To be, or not to be, that is the question." "Get   95
thee to a nunnery. Why wouldst thou be a breeder of sinners?" "I am very
proud, revengeful, ambitious, with more offences at my beck than I have
thoughts to put them in, imagination to give them shape, or time to act
them in. What should such fellows as I do crawling between earth and
heaven?" "Dost thou think Alexander look'd o' this fashion i' th' earth?   100
. . . And smelt so?"

8   Further, Hamlet's world is a world of riddles. The hero's own language is often riddling, as the critics have pointed out. When he puns, his
puns have receding depths in them, like the one which constitutes his first
speech: "A little more than kin, and less than kind." His utterances in mad-   105
ness, even if wild and whirling, are simultaneously, as Polonius discovers,
pregnant: "Do you know me, my lord?" "Excellent well. You are a fish-
monger." Even the madness itself is riddling: How much is real? How much
is feigned? What does it mean? Sane or mad, Hamlet's mind plays restlessly
about his world, turning up one riddle upon another. The riddle of char-   110
acter, for example, and how it is that in a man whose virtues else are "pure
as grace," some vicious mole of nature, some "dram of eale," can "all the
noble substance oft adulter." Or the riddle of the player's art, and how a
man can so project himself into a fiction, a dream of passion, that he can
weep for Hecuba. Or the riddle of action: how we may think too little—   115
"What to ourselves in passion we propose," says the player-king, "The passion ending, doth the purpose lose"; and again, how we may think too
much: "Thus conscience does make cowards of us all, And thus the native
hue of resolution Is sicklied o'er with the pale cast of thought."

9   There are also more immediate riddles. His mother—how could she   120
"on this fair mountain leave to feed, And batten on this moor?" The ghost
—which may be a devil, for "The de'il hath power T' assume a pleasing
shape." Ophelia—what does her behavior to him mean? Surprising her in
her closet, he falls to such perusal of her face as he would draw it. Even the
king at his prayers is a riddle. Will a revenge that takes him in the purging   125
of his soul be vengeance, or hire and salary? As for himself, Hamlet realizes,
he is the greatest riddle of all—a mystery, he warns Rosencrantz and Guildenstern, from which he will not have the heart plucked out. He cannot

tell why he has of late lost all his mirth, forgone all custom of exercises. Still
less can he tell why he delays: "I do not know Why yet I live to say, 'This   130
thing's to do,' Sith I have cause and will and strength and means To do't."
10   Thus the mysteriousness of Hamlet's world is of a piece. It is not
simply a matter of missing motivations, to be expunged if only we could find
the perfect clue. It is built in. It is evidently an important part of what the
play wishes to say to us. And it is certainly an element that the play thrusts   135
upon us from the opening word. Everyone, I think, recalls the mysteriousness of that first scene. The cold middle of the night on the castle platform,
the muffled sentries, the uneasy atmosphere of apprehension, the challenges
leaping out of the dark, the questions that follow the challenges, feeling out
the darkness, searching for identities, for relations, for assurance. "Ber-   140
nardo?" "Have you had quiet guard?" "Who hath reliev'd you?" "What, is
Horatio there?" "What, has this thing appear'd again tonight?" "Looks 'a
not like the king?" "How now, Horatio! . . . Is not this something more
than fantasy? What think you on 't?" "Is it not like the king?" "Why this
same strict and most observant watch . . . ?" "Shall I strike at it with my   145
partisan?" "Do you consent we shall acquaint [young Hamlet] with it?"
11   We need not be surprised that critics and playgoers alike have been
tempted to see in this an evocation not simply of Hamlet's world but of
their own. Man in his aspect of bafflement, moving in darkness on a rampart
between two worlds, unable to reject, or quite accept, the one that, when he   150
faces it, "to-shakes" his disposition with thoughts beyond the reaches of his
soul—comforting himself with hints and guesses. We hear these hints and
guesses whispering through the darkness as the several watchers speak. "At
least, the whisper goes so," says one. "I think it be no other but e'en so,"
says another. "I have heard" that on the crowing of the cock "Th' extrava-   155
gant and erring spirit hies To his confine," says a third. "Some say" at
Christmas time "this bird of dawning" sings all night, "And then, they say,
no spirit dare stir abroad." "So have I heard," says the first, "and do in part
believe it." However we choose to take the scene, it is clear that it creates a
world where uncertainties are of the essence.   160
12   Meantime, such is Shakespeare's economy, a second attribute of
Hamlet's world has been put before us. This is the problematic nature of
reality and the relation of reality to appearance. The play begins with an appearance, an "apparition," to use Marcellus's term—the ghost. And the
ghost is somehow real, indeed the vehicle of realities. Through its revelation,   165
the glittering surface of Claudius's court is pierced, and Hamlet comes to
know, and we do, that the king is not only hateful to him but the murderer

of his father, that his mother is guilty of adultery as well as incest. Yet there is a dilemma in the revelation. For possibly the apparition *is* an apparition, a devil who has assumed his father's shape.   170

13   This dilemma, once established, recurs on every hand. From the court's point of view, there is Hamlet's madness. Polonius investigates and gets some strange advice about his daughter: "Conception is a blessing, but as your daughter may conceive, friend, look to 't." Rosencrantz and Guildenstern investigate and get the strange confidence that "Man delights not   175 me; no, nor woman neither." Ophelia is "loosed" to Hamlet (Polonius's vulgar word), while Polonius and the king hide behind the arras; and what they hear is a strange indictment of human nature, and a riddling threat: "Those that are married already, all but one, shall live."

14   On the other hand, from Hamlet's point of view, there is Ophelia.   180 Kneeling here at her prayers, she seems the image of innocence and devotion. Yet she is of the sex for whom he has already found the name Frailty, and she is also, as he seems either madly or sanely to divine, a decoy in a trick. The famous cry—"Get thee to a nunnery"—shows the anguish of his uncertainty. If Ophelia is what she seems, this dirty-minded world of   185 murder, incest, lust, adultery, is no place for her. Were she "as chaste as ice, as pure as snow," she could not escape its calumny. And if she is not what she seems, then a nunnery in its other sense of brothel is relevant to her. In the scene that follows he treats her as if she were indeed an inmate of a brothel.   190

15   Likewise, from Hamlet's point of view, there is the enigma of the king. If the ghost is *only* an appearance, then possibly the king's appearance is reality. He must try it further. By means of a second and different kind of "apparition," the play within the play, he does so. But then, immediately after, he stumbles on the king at prayer. This appearance has a relish of   195 salvation in it. If the king dies now, his soul may yet be saved. Yet actually, as we know, the king's efforts to come to terms with heaven have been unavailing; his words fly up, his thoughts remain below. If Hamlet means the conventional revenger's reasons that he gives for sparing Claudius, it was the perfect moment not to spare him—when the sinner was acknowledging his   200 guilt, yet unrepentant. The perfect moment, but it was hidden, like so much else in the play, behind an arras.

16   There are two arrases in his mother's room. Hamlet thrusts his sword through one of them. Now at last he has got to the heart of the evil, or so he thinks. But now it is the wrong man; now he himself is a murderer.   205 The other arras he stabs through with his words—like daggers, says the

queen. He makes her shrink under the contrast he points between her present husband and his father. But as the play now stands (matters are somewhat clearer in the bad Quarto), it is hard to be sure how far the queen grasps the fact that her second husband is the murderer of her first. And it is   210
hard to say what may be signified by her inability to see the ghost, who now for the last time appears. In one sense at least, the ghost is the supreme reality, representative of the hidden ultimate power, in Bradley's terms—witnessing from beyond the grave against this hollow world. Yet the man who is capable of seeing through to this reality, the queen thinks is mad. "To   215
whom do you speak this?" she cries to her son. "Do you see nothing there?" he asks, incredulous. And she replies: "Nothing at all; yet all that is I see." Here certainly we have the imperturbable self-confidence of the worldly world, its layers on layers of habituation, so that when the reality is before its very eyes it cannot detect its presence.   220

17   Like mystery, this problem of reality is central to the play and written deep into its idiom. Shakespeare's favorite terms in *Hamlet* are words of ordinary usage that pose the question of appearances in a fundamental form. "Apparition" I have already mentioned. Another term is "seems." When we say, as Ophelia says of Hamlet leaving her closet, "He seem'd to   225
find his way without his eyes," we mean one thing. When we say, as Hamlet says to his mother in the first court-scene, "Seems, Madam! . . . I know not 'seems,' " we mean another. And when we say, as Hamlet says to Horatio before the play within the play, "And after, we will both our judgments join In censure of his seeming," we mean both at once. The ambiguities of   230
"seem" coil and uncoil throughout this play, and over against them is set the idea of "seeing." So Hamlet challenges the king in his triumphant letter announcing his return to Denmark: "Tomorrow shall I beg leave to see your kingly eyes." Yet "seeing" itself can be ambiguous, as we recognize from Hamlet's uncertainty about the ghost; or from that statement of his   235
mother's already quoted: "Nothing at all; yet all that is I see."

18   Another term of like importance is "assume." What we assume may be what we are not: "The de'il hath power T' assume a pleasing shape." But it may be what we are: "If it assume my noble father's person, I'll speak to it." And it may be what we are not yet, but would become; thus Hamlet ad-   240
vises his mother, "Assume a virtue, if you have it not." The perplexity in the word points to a real perplexity in Hamlet's and our own experience. We assume our habits—and habits are like costumes, as the word implies: "My father in his habit as he liv'd!" Yet these habits become ourselves in time: "That monster, custom, who all sense doth eat Of habits evil, is angel   245

yet in this, That to the use of actions fair and good He likewise gives a frock of livery That aptly is put on."

19   Two other terms I wish to instance are "put on" and "shape." The shape of something is the form under which we are accustomed to apprehend it: "Do you see yonder cloud that's almost in shape of a camel?" But a shape may also be a disguise—even, in Shakespeare's time, an actor's costume or an actor's role. This is the meaning when the king says to Laertes as they lay the plot against Hamlet's life: "Weigh what convenience both of time and means May fit us to our shape." "Put on" supplies an analogous ambiguity. Shakespeare's mind seems to worry this phrase in the play much as Hamlet's mind worries the problem of acting in a world of surfaces, or the king's mind worries the meaning of Hamlet's transformation. Hamlet has put an antic disposition on, that the king knows. But what does "put on" mean? A mask, or a frock or livery—our "habit"? The king is left guessing, and so are we.

20   What is found in the play's key terms is also found in its imagery. Miss Spurgeon has called attention to a pattern of disease images in *Hamlet*, to which I shall return. But the play has other patterns equally striking. One of these, as my earlier quotations hint, is based on clothes. In the world of surfaces to which Shakespeare exposes us in *Hamlet*, clothes are naturally a factor of importance. "The apparel oft proclaims the man," Polonius assures Laertes, cataloguing maxims in the young man's ear as he is about to leave for Paris. Oft, but not always. And so he sends his man Reynaldo to look into Laertes' life there—even, if need be, to put a false dress of accusation upon his son ("What forgeries you please"), the better by indirections to find directions out. On the same grounds, he takes Hamlet's vows to Ophelia as false apparel. They are bawds, he tells her—or if we do not like Theobald's emendation, they are bonds—in masquerade, "Not of that dye which their investments show, But mere implorators of unholy suits."

21   This breach between the outer and the inner stirs no special emotion in Polonius, because he is always either behind an arras or prying into one, but it shakes Hamlet to the core. Here so recently was his mother in her widow's weeds, the tears still flushing in her galled eyes; yet now within a month, a little month, before even her funeral shoes are old, she has married with his uncle. Her mourning was all clothes. Not so his own, he bitterly replies, when she asks him to cast his "nighted color off." "Tis not alone my inky cloak, good mother"—and not alone, he adds, the sighs, the tears, the dejected havior of the visage—"that can denote me truly."

250

255

260

265

270

275

280

> These indeed seem,
> For they are actions that a man might play;   285
> But I have that within which passes show;
> These but the trappings and the suits of woe.

22   What we must not overlook here is Hamlet's visible attire, giving the verbal imagery a theatrical extension. Hamlet's apparel now is his inky cloak, mark of his grief for his father, mark also of his character as a man   290 of melancholy, mark possibly too of his being one in whom appearance and reality are attuned. Later, in his madness, with his mind disordered, he will wear his costume in a corresponding disarray, the disarray that Ophelia describes so vividly to Polonius and that producers of the play rarely give sufficient heed to: "Lord Hamlet with his doublet all unbrac'd, No hat upon his   295 head; his stockings foul'd, Ungarter'd, and downgyved to his ankle." Here the only question will be, as with the madness itself, how much is studied, how much is real. Still later, by a third costume, the simple traveler's garb in which we find him new come from shipboard, Shakespeare will show us that we have a third aspect of the man.   300

23   A second pattern of imagery springs from terms of painting: the paints, the colorings, the varnishes that may either conceal, or, as in the painter's art, reveal. Art in Claudius conceals. "The harlot's cheek," he tells us in his one aside, "beautied with plastering art, Is not more ugly to the thing that helps it Than is my deed to my most painted word." Art in Ophe-   305 lia, loosed to Hamlet in the episode already noticed to which this speech of the king's is prelude, is more complex. She looks so beautiful—"the celestial, and my soul's idol, the most beautified Ophelia," Hamlet has called her in his love letter. But now, what does beautified mean? Perfected with all the innocent beauties of a lovely woman? Or "beautied" like the harlot's cheek?   310 "I have heard of your paintings too, well enough. God hath given you one face, and you make yourselves another."

24   Yet art, differently used, may serve the truth. By using an "image" (his own word) of a murder done in Vienna, Hamlet cuts through to the king's guilt; holds "as 'twere, the mirror up to nature," shows "virtue her   315 own feature, scorn her own image, and the very age and body of the time" —which is out of joint—"his form and pressure." Something similar he does again in his mother's bedroom, painting for her in words "the rank sweat of an enseamed bed," making her recoil in horror from his "counterfeit presentment of two brothers," and holding, if we may trust a stage tradition,   320 his father's picture beside his uncle's. Here again the verbal imagery is realized visually on the stage.

25   The most pervasive of Shakespeare's image patterns in this play, however, is the pattern evolved around the three words, show, act, play. "Show" seems to be Shakespeare's unifying image in *Hamlet*. Through it 325 he pulls together and exhibits in a single focus much of the diverse material in his play. The ideas of seeming, assuming, and putting on; the images of clothing, painting, mirroring; the episode of the dumb show and the play within the play; the characters of Polonius, Laertes, Ophelia, Claudius, Gertrude, Rosencrantz and Guildenstern, Hamlet himself—all these at one 330 time or another, and usually more than once, are drawn into the range of implications flung round the play by "show."

26   "Act," on the other hand, I take to be the play's radical metaphor. It distills the various perplexities about the character of reality into a residual perplexity about the character of an act. What, this play asks again and 335 again, is an act? What is its relation to the inner act, the intent? "If I drown myself wittingly," says the clown in the graveyard, "it argues an act, and an act hath three branches; it is to act, to do, to perform." Or again, the play asks, how does action relate to passion, that "laps'd in time and passion" I can let "go by Th' important acting of your dread command"; and to 340 thought, which can so sickly o'er the native hue of resolution that "enterprises of great pitch and moment With this regard their currents turn awry, And lose the name of action"; and to words, which are not acts, and so we dare not be content to unpack our hearts with them, and yet are acts of a sort, for we may speak daggers though we use none. Or still again, how does 345 an act (a deed) relate to an act (a pretense)? For an action may be nothing but pretense. So Polonius readying Ophelia for the interview with Hamlet, with "pious action," as he phrases it, "sugar [s] o'er The devil himself." Or it may not be a pretense, yet not what it appears. So Hamlet spares the king, finding him in an act that has some "relish of salvation in 't." Or it may be 350 a pretense that is also the first foothold of a new reality, as when we assume a virtue though we have it not. Or it may be a pretense that is actually a mirroring of reality, like the play within the play, or the tragedy of *Hamlet*.

27   To this network of implications, the third term, play, adds an additional dimension. "Play" is a more precise word, in Elizabethan parlance at 355 least, for all the elements in *Hamlet* that pertain to the art of the theatre; and it extends their field of reference till we see that every major personage in the tragedy is a player in some sense, and every major episode a play. The court plays, Hamlet plays, the players play, Rosencrantz and Guildenstern

try to play on Hamlet, though they cannot play on his recorders—here we   360
have an extension to a musical sense. And the final duel, by a further extension, becomes itself a play, in which everyone but Claudius and Laertes
plays his role in ignorance: "The queen desires you to show some gentle
entertainment to Laertes before you fall to play." "I . . . will this brother's
wager frankly play." "Give him the cup."—"I'll play this bout first."   365
28   The full extension of this theme is best evidenced in the play within
the play itself. Here, in the bodily presence of these traveling players, bringing with them the latest playhouse gossip out of London, we have suddenly
a situation that tends to dissolve the normal barriers between the fictive and
the real. For here on the stage before us is a play of false appearances in   370
which an actor called the player-king is playing. But there is also on the
stage, Claudius, another player-king, who is a spectator of this player. And
there is on the stage, besides, a prince who is a spectator of both these
player-kings and who plays with great intensity a player's role himself. And
around these kings and that prince is a group of courtly spectators—Ger-   375
trude, Rosencrantz, Guildenstern, Polonius, and the rest—and they, as we
have come to know, are players too. And lastly there are ourselves, an audience watching all these audiences who are also players. Where, it may
suddenly occur to us to ask, does the playing end? Which *are* the guilty
creatures sitting at a play? When is an act not an "act"?   380
29   The mysteriousness of Hamlet's world, while it pervades the tragedy, finds its point of greatest dramatic concentration in the first act, and
its symbol in the first scene. The problems of appearance and reality also
pervade the play as a whole, but come to a climax in Acts II and III, and
possibly their best symbol is the play within the play. Our third attribute,   385
though again it is one that crops out everywhere, reaches its full development in Acts IV and V. It is not easy to find an appropriate name for this
attribute, but perhaps "mortality" will serve, if we remember to mean by
mortality the heartache and the thousand natural shocks that flesh is heir
to, not simply death.   390
30   The powerful sense of mortality in *Hamlet* is conveyed to us, I
think, in three ways. First, there is the play's emphasis on human weakness,
the instability of human purpose, the subjection of humanity to fortune—
all that we might call the aspect of failure in man. Hamlet opens this theme
in Act I, when he describes how from that single blemish, perhaps not even   395
the victim's fault, a man's whole character may take corruption. Claudius
dwells on it again, to an extent that goes far beyond the needs of the occasion, while engaged in seducing Laertes to step behind the arras of a

seemer's world and dispose of Hamlet by a trick. Time qualifies everything, Claudius says, including love, including purpose. As for love—it has a "plurisy" in it and dies of its own too much. As for purpose—"That we would do, We should do when we would, for this 'would' changes, And hath abatements and delays as many As there are tongues, are hands, are accidents; And then this 'should' is like a spendthrift's sigh, That hurts by easing." The player-king, in his long speeches to his queen in the play within the play, sets the matter in a still darker light. She means these protestations of undying love, he knows, but our purposes depend on our memory, and our memory fades fast. Or else, he suggests, we propose something to ourselves in a condition of strong feeling, but then the feeling goes, and with it the resolve. Or else our fortunes change, he adds, and with these our loves: "The great man down, you mark his favorite flies." The subjection of human aims to fortune is a reiterated theme in *Hamlet*, as subsequently in *Lear*. Fortune is the harlot goddess in whose secret parts men like Rosencrantz and Guildenstern live and thrive; the strumpet who threw down Troy and Hecuba and Priam; the outrageous foe whose slings and arrows a man of principle must suffer or seek release in suicide. Horatio suffers them with composure: he is one of the blessed few "Whose blood and judgment are so well co-mingled That they are not a pipe for fortune's finger To sound what stop she please." For Hamlet the task is of a greater difficulty.

31   Next, and intimately related to this matter of infirmity, is the emphasis on infection—the ulcer, the hidden abscess, "th' imposthume of much wealth and peace That inward breaks and shows no cause without Why the man dies." Miss Spurgeon, who was the first to call attention to this aspect of the play, has well remarked that so far as Shakespeare's pictorial imagination is concerned, the problem in *Hamlet* is not a problem of the will and reason, "of a mind too philosophical or a nature temperamentally unfitted to act quickly," nor even a problem of an individual at all. Rather, it is a condition—"a condition for which the individual himself is apparently not responsible, any more than the sick man is to blame for the infection which strikes and devours him, but which, nevertheless, in its course and development, impartially and relentlessly, annihilates him and others, innocent and guilty alike." "That," she adds, "is the tragedy of *Hamlet*, as it is perhaps the chief tragic mystery of life." This is a perceptive comment, for it reminds us that Hamlet's situation is mainly not of his own manufacture, as are the situations of Shakespeare's other tragic heroes. He has inherited it; he is "born to set it right."

32   We must not, however, neglect to add to this what another student
of Shakespeare's imagery has noticed—that the infection in Denmark is
presented alternatively as poison. Here, of course, responsibility is implied,   440
for the poisoner of the play is Claudius. The juice he pours into the ear of
the elder Hamlet is a combined poison and disease, a "leperous distilment"
that curds "the thin and wholesome blood." From this fatal center, un-
wholesomeness spreads out till there is something rotten in all Denmark.
Hamlet tells us that his "wit's diseased," the queen speaks of her "sick soul,"   445
the king is troubled by "the hectic" in his blood, Laertes meditates revenge
to warm "the sickness in my heart," the people of the kingdom grow "mud-
died, Thick and unwholesome in their thoughts"; and even Ophelia's madness is said to be "the poison of deep grief." In the end, all save Ophelia
die of that poison in a literal as well as figurative sense.   450

33   But the chief form in which the theme of mortality reaches us, it
seems to me, is a profound consciousness of loss. Hamlet's father expresses something of the kind when he tells Hamlet how his "[most] seem-
ing-virtuous queen," betraying a love which "was of that dignity That it
went hand in hand even with the vow I made to her in marriage," had   455
chosen to "decline Upon a wretch whose natural gifts were poor To those
of mine." "O Hamlet, what a falling off was there!" Ophelia expresses it
again, on hearing Hamlet's denunciation of love and woman in the nunnery
scene, which she takes to be the product of a disordered brain:

> O what a noble mind is here o'erthrown!   460
> The courtier's, soldier's, scholar's, eye, tongue, sword;
> Th' expectancy and rose of the fair state,
> The glass of fashion and the mould of form,
> Th' observ'd of all observers, quite, quite down!

The passage invites us to remember that we have never actually seen such a   465
Hamlet—that his mother's marriage has brought a falling off in him before
we meet him. And then there is that further falling off, if I may call it so,
when Ophelia too goes mad—"Divided from herself and her fair judgment,
Without the which we are pictures, or mere beasts."

34   Time was, the play keeps reminding us, when Denmark was a differ-   470
ent place. That was before Hamlet's mother took off "the rose From the
fair forehead of an innocent love" and set a blister there. Hamlet then was
still "Th' expectancy and rose of the fair state"; Ophelia, the "rose of May."
For Denmark was a garden then, when his father ruled. There had been
something heroic about his father—a king who met the threats to Denmark   475

in open battle, fought with Norway, smote the sledded Polacks on the ice, slew the elder Fortinbras in an honorable trial of strength. There had been something godlike about his father too: "Hyperion's curls, the front of Jove himself, An eye like Mars . . . , A station like the herald Mercury." But, the ghost reveals, a serpent was in the garden, and "the serpent that did sting 480 thy father's life Now wears his crown." The martial virtues are put by now. The threats to Denmark are attended to by policy, by agents working deviously for and through an uncle. The moral virtues are put by too. Hyperion's throne is occupied by "a vice of kings," "A king of shreds and patches": Hyperion's bed, by a satyr, a paddock, a bat, a gib, a bloat king 485 with reechy kisses. The garden is unweeded now, and "grows to seed; things rank and gross in nature Possess it merely." Even in himself he feels the taint, the taint of being his mother's son; and that other taint, from an earlier garden, of which he admonishes Ophelia: "Our virtue cannot so inoculate our old stock but we shall relish of it." "Why wouldst thou be a 490 breeder of sinners?" "What should such fellows as I do crawling between earth and heaven?"

35   "Hamlet is painfully aware," says Professor Tillyard, "of the baffling human predicament between the angels and the beasts, between the glory of having been made in God's image and the incrimination of being de- 495 scended from fallen Adam." To this we may add, I think, that Hamlet is more than aware of it; he exemplifies it; and it is for this reason that his problem appeals to us so powerfully as an image of our own.

36   Hamlet's problem, in its crudest form, is simply the problem of the avenger: he must carry out the injunction of the ghost and kill the king. But 500 this problem, as I ventured to suggest at the outset, is presented in terms of a certain kind of world. The ghost's injunction to act becomes so inextricably bound up for Hamlet with the character of the world in which the action must be taken—its mysteriousness, its baffling appearances, its deep consciousness of infection, frailty, and loss—that he cannot come to terms 505 with either without coming to terms with both.

37   When we first see him in the play, he is clearly a very young man, sensitive and idealistic, suffering the first shock of growing up. He has taken the garden at face value, we might say, supposing mankind to be only a little lower than the angels. Now in his mother's hasty and incestuous marriage, 510 he discovers evidence of something else, something bestial—though even a beast, he thinks, would have mourned longer. Then comes the revelation of the ghost, bringing a second shock. Not so much because he now knows that his serpent-uncle killed his father; his prophetic soul had almost sus-

pected this. Not entirely, even, because he knows now how far below the 515
angels humanity has fallen in his mother, and how lust—these were the
ghost's words—"though to a radiant angel link'd Will sate itself in a celestial bed, And prey on garbage." Rather, because he now sees everywhere,
but especially in his own nature, the general taint, taking from life its meaning, from woman her integrity, from the will its strength, turning reason 520
into madness. "Why wouldst thou be a breeder of sinners?" "What should
such fellows as I do crawling between earth and heaven?" Hamlet is not the
first young man to have felt the heavy and the weary weight of all this unintelligible world; and, like the others, he must come to terms with it.

38   The ghost's injunction to revenge unfolds a different facet of his 525
problem. The young man growing up is not to be allowed simply to endure
a rotten world, he must also act in it. Yet how to begin, among so many
enigmatic surfaces? Even Claudius, whom he now knows to be the core of
the ulcer, has a plausible exterior. And around Claudius, swathing the evil
out of sight, he encounters all those other exteriors, as we have seen. Some 530
of them already deeply infected beneath, like his mother. Some noble, but
marked for infection, like Laertes. Some not particularly corrupt but infinitely corruptible, like Rosencrantz and Guildenstern; some mostly weak
and foolish like Polonius and Osric. Some, like Ophelia, innocent, yet in
their innocence still serving to "skin and film the ulcerous place." 535

39   And this is not all. The act required of him, though retributive
justice, is one that necessarily involves the doer in the general guilt. Not only
because it involves a killing; but because to get at the world of seeming one
sometimes has to use its weapons. He himself, before he finishes, has become a player, has put an antic disposition on, has killed a man—the wrong 540
man—has helped drive Ophelia mad, and has sent two friends of his youth
to death, mining below their mines, and hoisting the engineer with his own
petard. He had never meant to dirty himself with these things, but from the
moment of the ghost's challenge to act, this dirtying was inevitable. It is the
condition of living at all in such a world. To quote Polonius, who knew 545
that world so well, men become "a little soil'd i' th' working." Here is another matter with which Hamlet has to come to terms.

40   Human infirmity—all that I have discussed with reference to instability, infection, loss—supplies the problem with its third phase. Hamlet
has not only to accept the mystery of man's condition between the angels 550
and the brutes, and not only to act in a perplexing and soiling world. He
has also to act within the human limits—"with shabby equipment always de-
teriorating," if I may adapt some phrases from Eliot's *East Coker*, "In the

general mess of imprecision of feeling, Undisciplined squads of emotion."
Hamlet is aware of that fine poise of body and mind, feeling and thought,   555
that suits the action to the word, the word to the action; that acquires and
begets a temperance in the very torrent, tempest, and whirlwind of passion;
but he cannot at first achieve it in himself. He vacillates between undisciplined squads of emotion and thinking too precisely on the event. He learns
to his cost how easily action can be lost in "acting," and loses it there for a   560
time himself. But these again are only the terms of every man's life. As Anatole France reminds us in a now famous apostrophe to Hamlet: "What one
of us thinks without contradiction and acts without incoherence? What
one of us is not mad? What one of us does not say with a mixture of pity,
comradeship, admiration, and horror, Goodnight, sweet Prince!"   565

41   In the last act of the play (or so it seems to me, for I know there
can be differences on this point), Hamlet accepts his world and we discover
a different man. Shakespeare does not outline for us the process of acceptance any more than he had done with Romeo or was to do with Othello.
But he leads us strongly to expect an altered Hamlet, and then, in my   570
opinion, provides him. We must recall that at this point Hamlet has been
absent from the stage during several scenes, and that such absences in
Shakespearean tragedy usually warn us to be on the watch for a new phase
in the development of the character. It is so when we leave King Lear in
Gloucester's farmhouse and find him again in Dover fields. It is so when we   575
leave Macbeth at the witches' cave and rejoin him at Dunsinane, hearing of
the armies that beset it. Furthermore, and this is an important matter in the
theatre—especially important in a play in which the symbolism of clothing
has figured largely—Hamlet now looks different. He is wearing a different
dress—probably, as Granville-Barker thinks, his "seagown scarf'd" about   580
him, but in any case no longer the disordered costume of his antic disposition. The effect is not entirely dissimilar to that in *Lear*, when the old king
wakes out of his madness to find fresh garments on him.

42   Still more important, Hamlet displays a considerable change of
mood. This is not a matter of the way we take the passage about defying   585
augury, as Mr. Tillyard among others seems to think. It is a matter of Hamlet's whole deportment, in which I feel we may legitimately see the deportment of a man who has been "illuminated" in the tragic sense. Bradley's
term for it is fatalism, but if this is what we wish to call it, we must at least
acknowledge that it is fatalism of a very distinctive kind—a kind that Shake-   590
speare has been willing to touch with the associations of the saying in St.
Matthew about the fall of a sparrow, and with Hamlet's recognition that a

divinity shapes our ends. The point is not that Hamlet has suddenly become religious; he has been religious all through the play. The point is that he has now learned, and accepted, the boundaries in which human action, human 595 judgment, are enclosed.

43   Till his return from the voyage he had been trying to act beyond these, had been encroaching on the role of providence, if I may exaggerate to make a vital point. He had been too quick to take the burden of the whole world and its condition upon his limited and finite self. Faced with a task of 600 sufficient difficulty in its own right, he had dilated it into a cosmic problem—as indeed every task is, but if we think about this too precisely we cannot act at all. The whole time is out of joint, he feels, and in his young man's egocentricity, he will set it right. Hence he misjudges Ophelia, seeing in her only a breeder of sinners. Hence he misjudges himself, seeing himself 605 a vermin crawling between earth and heaven. Hence he takes it upon himself to be his mother's conscience, though the ghost has warned that this is no fit task for him, and returns to repeat the warning: "Leave her to heaven, And to those thorns that in her bosom lodge." Even with the king, Hamlet has sought to play at God. *He* it must be who decides the issue of Claudius's 610 salvation, saving him for a more damnable occasion. Now, he has learned that there are limits to the before and after that human reason can comprehend. Rashness, even, is sometimes good. Through rashness he has saved his life from the commission for his death, "and prais'd be rashness for it." This happy circumstance and the unexpected arrival of the pirate ship make it 615 plain that the roles of life are not entirely self-assigned. "There is a divinity that shapes our ends, Roughhew them how we will." Hamlet is ready now for what may happen, seeking neither to foreknow it nor avoid it. "If it be now, 'tis not to come; if it be not to come, it will be now; if it be not now, yet it will come: the readiness is all." 620

44   The crucial evidence of Hamlet's new frame of mind, as I understand it, is the graveyard scene. Here, in its ultimate symbol, he confronts, recognizes, and accepts the condition of being man. It is not simply that he now accepts death, though Shakespeare shows him accepting it in ever more poignant forms: first, in the imagined persons of the politician, the courtier, 625 and the lawyer, who laid their little schemes "to circumvent God," as Hamlet puts it, but now lie here; then in Yorick, whom he knew and played with as a child; and then in Ophelia. This last death tears from him a final cry of passion, but the striking contrast between his behavior and Laertes's reveals how deeply he has changed. 630

45   Still, it is not the fact of death that invests this scene with its

peculiar power. It is instead the haunting mystery of life itself that Hamlet's speeches point to, holding in its inscrutable folds those other mysteries that he has wrestled with so long. These he now knows for what they are, and lays them by. The mystery of evil is present here—for this is after all the universal graveyard, where, as the clown says humorously, he holds up Adam's profession; where the scheming politician, the hollow courtier, the tricky lawyer, the emperor and the clown and the beautiful young maiden, all come together in an emblem of the world; where even, Hamlet murmurs, one might expect to stumble on "Cain's jawbone, that did the first mur- ther." The mystery of reality is here too—for death puts the question, "What is real?" in its irreducible form, and in the end uncovers all ap- pearances: "Is this the fine of his fines and the recovery of his recoveries, to have his fine pate full of fine dirt?" "Now get you to my lady's chamber, and tell her, let her paint an inch thick, to this favor she must come." Or if we need more evidence of this mystery, there is the anger of Laertes at the lack of ceremonial trappings, and the ambiguous character of Ophelia's own death. "Is she to be buried in Christian burial when she wilfully seeks her own salvation?" asks the gravedigger. And last of all, but most pervasive of all, there is the mystery of human limitation. The grotesque nature of man's little joys, his big ambitions. The fact that the man who used to bear us on his back is now a skull that smells; that the noble dust of Alexander somewhere plugs a bunghole; that "Imperious Caesar, dead and turn'd to clay, Might stop a hole to keep the wind away." Above all, the fact that a pit of clay is "meet" for such a guest as man, as the gravedigger tells us in his song, and yet that, despite all frailties and limitations, "That skull had a tongue in it and could sing once."

46   After the graveyard and what it indicates has come to pass in him, we know that Hamlet is ready for the final contest of mighty opposites. He accepts the world as it is, the world as a duel, in which, whether we know it or not, evil holds the poisoned rapier and the poisoned chalice waits; and in which, if we win at all, it costs not less than everything. I think we under- stand by the close of Shakespeare's *Hamlet* why it is that unlike the other tragic heroes he is given a soldier's rites upon the stage. For as William Butler Yeats once said, "Why should we honor those who die on the field of battle? A man may show as reckless a courage in entering into the abyss of himself."

QUESTIONS

1. Describe at length the author's ideal reader, and, as fully as you can, the author's tone * and purpose.

2. Good writing is an expression of good manners. Obviously, it is good manners for the writer to be as clear, as forceful, and as graceful as he can; but courtesy toward the reader may be expressed more directly, as it is, for example, in paragraph 4. Find and mark other phrases, sentences, and passages that reflect a similar tone.

ORGANIZATION

3. What paragraphs form the introduction of the essay? Imagine "The World of *Hamlet*" without the first paragraph, beginning instead with paragraph 2: "Great plays, as we know, do present us with something that can be called a world . . ." Why would this opening be less effective?

4. What is the point of discussing *Othello* in an essay about *Hamlet*? What does paragraph 3 contribute to the introduction?

5. Make a detailed outline of this essay under six or seven major headings. Explain why "The World of *Hamlet*" is easy to outline; mark words, phrases, and sentences that help the reader to follow the plan of the essay.

6. In paragraph 20 the author anticipates his order of presentation by referring in the second sentence to Spurgeon's observations about disease imagery * in *Hamlet*. Why? Where does he discuss Spurgeon's view? It may help the writer to organize clearly by occasionally pointing forward; it is also helpful to tell the reader what has been covered already. As an example of this summarizing, see the first sentence of paragraph 40. How does paragraph 29 contribute to the organization of the writer's material?

7. In paragraph 36 the author begins an interpretation of Hamlet's problem. Would placing this material first in the essay (1) improve the organization, (2) weaken it, or (3) make little difference? Explain.

8. Identify the techniques of closing in the last section of "The World of *Hamlet*." Which of these do you consider most important? Which are accessory?

9. The simple, clear, and forceful exposition of this essay owes much to the writer's skill in constructing paragraphs. His topic sentences, especially, repay study. Write down one below the other, the topic sentences of paragraphs 18 through 28. What qualities do they have in common?

10. The author often develops his paragraphs with several quotations from *Hamlet*. What is the advantage of doing so? Observe that Professor Mack is careful to introduce each group of quotations, telling us what they illustrate;

and to follow them, usually, with some perceptive comment, thus making doubly sure that we know what each cluster of quotations has exemplified. Study paragraph 26 as a model of development by quotation.

11. Why does the writer handle some quotations by setting them off from the text, as he does in paragraph 3 and paragraph 21, and handle others by working them into the sentences of the text? Should he have identified the act and scene of each quotation? Why or why not?

12. Paragraph 6 is developed, in part, by making important qualifications * and concessions. Indicate each one. What words introduce these qualifications? What words signal a return to the main point?

SENTENCES

13. Are the following revisions acceptable substitutes for Professor Mack's sentences?

  (a) *Revision:* But the ghost reveals that a serpent was in the garden. . . .
      Mack: "But, the ghost reveals, a serpent was in the garden. . . ."
      (479-80)
  (b) *Revision:* Having decided the issue of Claudius's salvation, Hamlet saves him for a more damnable occasion.
      Mack: "*He* it must be who decides the issue of Claudius's salvation, saving him for a more damnable occasion." (610-11)

14. Interrupted movement * is often characteristic of formal exposition. It allows the writer to emphasize particular words or phrases within a sentence, and it is one rather graceful form of subordination *. Study the interrupted movement of the sentences in paragraph 30, observing how it establishes subtle shadings of emphasis.

15. Why the repetitions of *hence* at the beginnings of successive sentences in paragraph 43? Are there instances of similar repetition elsewhere?

16. The third sentence of paragraph 5 ("We feel its presence . . .") is long and elaborate. Is it effective? Would the substitution of two or three shorter sentences improve the writing? How would you describe the structure of this sentence?

DICTION

17. Look up: *attributes* (45), *egomaniac* (65), *evocation* (148), *rampart* (149), *dilemma* (169), *quarto* (209), *habituation* (219), *disarray* (293), *pervasive* (323), *perplexities* (334), *annihilates* (432), *denunciation* (458), *injunction* (500), *encroaching* (598), *abyss* (666).

18. Explain the meanings of the following phrases: *imaginative environment* (4), *world of surfaces* (264-65), *the dejected havior of the visage* (283), *dumb*

show (328), *network of implications* (354), *field of reference* (357), *leperous distilment* (442), *martial virtues* (481), *retributive justice* (536-37).

19. Good diction has range and richness; for example a writer may achieve a pleasing sort of emphasis by choosing from time to time words that are both precise and unusual. *Microcosm* (7) is such a word; *fictive* (369) is another. Make a list of ten or twelve such words in this essay. At the other end of the spectrum the writer may employ, for variety, words that suggest conversational expressions of the educated speaker. Hamlet's world, we are told, is "of a piece" (132). Find similar locutions.

20. Which of the following is the most effective in its diction? Which is the least effective?

    (a) *Hamlet* is a true-to-life play.
    (b) *Hamlet* is "a paradigm of the life of man." (55)
    (c) *Hamlet* is a realistic picture of life.

21. Find several examples of figurative * language in this essay. Substituting a literal, non-figurative expression for the metaphor * or simile *, rewrite the sentences, keeping as close as possible to the sense of the original. What, if anything, has been lost? Are such figures mere decoration, or do they help a writer to communicate his meaning more precisely? Explain.

22. In the first sentence of paragraph 26 we find the phrase *radical metaphor*. The careless, inexperienced reader will assume that *radical* means *extreme* or *extravagant*. But the more careful reader will see that this meaning does not harmonize with the meaning of the second sentence of the paragraph. What does *radical* mean in this context?

POINTS TO LEARN

1. Good writing is good manners. Often a writer can be more convincing if he avoids a dogmatic tone, if he acknowledges the possibility of other views than his own.

2. Well-organized writing is easy to outline.

3. Development by quotation is an important technique in the discussion of a literary text, one that most college students ought to master. Ideally, the writer should steer a middle course between using so many quotations that his work seems like a pointless job of copying out passages and using so few quotations that the reader remains unconvinced that the writer's interpretation is grounded firmly in the text. Long quotations must be used sparingly; the use of many short quotations is usually more effective. Observe, too, the possibility of paraphrasing quotations and of combining paraphrase with the quotation of a key phrase or key word.

4. To avoid "flat" diction a writer may use, if he does not overuse, rare words,

allusions *, figures of speech—especially metaphor and simile—and words that suggest educated conversation. Within the limits, always, of appropriateness, one secret of good diction is its variety.

SUGGESTIONS FOR WRITING

1. Write an essay in which you describe the "world" of *Macbeth* or *King Lear* as it is revealed in one or more scenes. Use short quotations as one means of illustrating and supporting your interpretation.

2. Study again paragraphs 20-32. Then, modelling your writing in a general way upon the presentation of Professor Mack, write a theme about one of the major images in *Macbeth*. You might want to choose as your subject one of these: clothing, sleep, feasting, seeds and growing things, darkness, storm, blood.

3. Describe the "world" of a novel or short story you have read recently. As possibilities you might consider *Wuthering Heights, The Return of the Native, Heart of Darkness, Settlers of the Marsh, Lord of the Flies, The Apprenticeship of Duddy Kravitz, Lady Oracle.*

IMPROVING YOUR STYLE

1. Be sure to cite specific passages from the work you are discussing, and experiment with how you incorporate them into your text. Sometimes introduce a quotation with a colon as Mack does in line 89. Sometimes fit it to your words without any mark of introduction (lines 436 and 445 ff.). And sometimes let the quotation stand against your sentence as an implicit example, that is, without any such label as "for example" or "for instance" (lines 140 ff.).

2. In your essay compose several sentences with interrupted movement.

3. Use *hence* to introduce a sentence. You might even try to employ it repetitively as Mack does in paragraph 43.

Style: A Closer Look

The ultimate, and in many ways the most interesting, problem of writing prose is style. Yet to the student—quite understandably—his first question about style is likely to be, "Why bother about style at all?" And he is likely to add that it's hard enough to be clear, concise, and emphatic, without trying to be fancy as well. This feeling about style, which unfortunately is all too common, reflects some of the misconceptions that surround and obscure this important subject. One of the most important points to realize at the outset is this: style is not a surface decoration the writer can apply to his meaning or leave off, depending upon whether he likes things fancy or plain. Every writer, no matter how humble his task, is inescapably concerned with style—whether or not he is aware of it. His problem is to choose the best way of treating his subject as he sees it. Whatever his subject (argument, narration, exposition, description) he must choose a style that will work *for* his purpose and not *against* it. Style, for example, is behind the forcefulness of a hard-hitting argument like "The Third Knight's Speech" by T. S. Eliot (p. 162).

The writer's style, then, is inseparable from his thought and his expression of that thought. Consequently, it follows that all writing—indeed all utterances of any kind—have style. Every essay the student of composition has written thus far has style—even if the style is at times defective or deplorable. Although obviously some styles are more appropriate and more effective than others and although every writer's aim is to improve his style, style is not something only great writers achieve. Nor is the ability to manage a good prose style something one is born with; it must be learned. And while no amount of study and diligence and practice will produce great writing, it is equally true that there can be no great writing without study and diligence and practice. The study of writing, in one way or another, must consider the principles of style. Therefore the study of style is important to the beginning writer—as it is to every other kind of writer—for three reasons at least: First, by understanding some of the basic problems and principles connected with style, he can improve the vigor and effectiveness of his own writing. Second, the study of style should greatly improve his ability to *read* good prose. And, third, his increased verbal skill and his increased sensitivity to language should become a source of constant pleasure.

At this point we can pose three fundamental questions. What precisely do we mean by style? How does a writer create his style? And how can the beginning writer apply to his own writing what he learns from the study of style? These questions themselves are more important than any answers we suggest in this brief introduction, answers which are only tentative and, hopefully, provocative. To begin with, we had better essay a working definition of style.

The first point to notice is that style is a pattern of linguistic features distinguishing one piece of writing from another, or one category of writings from another. Margaret Laurence's *The Stone Angel* possesses unique combinations of linguistic characteristics different from the unique traits of Callaghan's *Strange Fugitive:* the styles of the two novels, we say, are different. And although a writer's style often varies from work to work there is usually enough uniformity in his prose to let us observe that his over-all style differs from another writer's style. Laurence's style differs from Callaghan's. Similarly we may say that the style of twentieth-century American writers differs from that of eighteenth-century writers. In this sense, style does not necessarily imply excellence—only a pattern of distinctive linguistic traits. Nor is style confined to what we commonly call literature. It is just as important in exposition, argument, and description as it is in fiction. But if all utterances have style, it is obvious that in some, style is more effective than in others. Our assumption, then, is that there are various kinds of style and that they vary in their effective range. We must allow, too, for the possibility of inappropriateness or the misuse of style.

Merely to point out, however, that style is a distinguishing combination of linguistic traits and that style appears in both literary and non-literary texts is not of much help to the student of composition. A really useful answer to the question, "What is style?" requires a closer look at a writer as he prepares to write and at what happens as he begins to compose sentences. We observe, for one thing, that a writer is not an entirely free agent. Provided he is to write effectively, a significant part of what he says and how he says it is more or less determined in advance by two things. One we may call the broad context of his writing: his subject and his purpose and his reader. If his purpose, for instance, is to write an objective, factual report about the ability of a new material to withstand stress, then words conveying personal feelings and evaluations should be filtered out, so that expressions like *beautiful, charming, revolting,* and *disgusting* will appear infrequently or not at all. The second thing that determines a writer's prose concerns "rules" of language so basic that ignoring them produces a total loss of communication. Among these, for example, are the rules of English word order. No one who intends to be understood is free to write "Powers he that the is of shows do everything he can thought man that human what do sphere could valuable enlarges he." English syntax, however *does* permit Samuel Johnson to say, "Everything that enlarges the sphere of human powers, that shows man he can do what he thought he could do, is valuable."

But although a part of writing is predetermined by the writer's subject, purpose, and reader as well as by certain basic conventions of his language, much of what he produces is the result of free choices he is making constantly as he writes. These choices implicitly and explicitly convey not only the writer's message, ideas, directions, descriptions, and so on, but also often the writer's cast of mind, his temperament, his taste, his values— in short, himself as he wishes us to believe he is, at least at the instant of his writing. His free choices, broadly speaking are of two types: (1) what details of the subject to include or emphasize; and (2) what linguistic forms to select in order to achieve his purpose. Since "reality" is not a simple, constant entity that each of us grasps in exactly the same way, the writer is free to select those details from the flux of experience that seem to him most significant. And just as important, of course, is the way in which the writer forms his details into meaningful patterns, the way in which he conceives his subject. Thus, two historians witnessing the same battle will perhaps agree broadly in their descriptions of it. But no doubt each will interpret it, and perhaps evaluate it, differently.

Secondly, a writer makes choices concerning matters of diction, organization, sentence structure, punctuation, and so on. Sometimes these are binary choices: shall the writer choose the active or the passive voice? shall he repeat a noun or employ a pronoun? shall he use a colon or a dash? Other choices may involve three or four alternatives as is often the case in matters of sentence structure or word order, and still others may allow an even wider range of choices, as is sometimes true of diction. Of course, some of these choices are unconscious—so much a part of a writer's training, habit, adherence to fashion, and way of thinking that they seem not to be choices at all. Still, many, perhaps most, *are* conscious, as the untidy appearance of any rough draft will show. In this area of free choice, then, the writer creates his style. As an illustration we offer three examples. The third is a passage from James Joyce's story "Two Gallants"; the first two are versions of the same passage as less gifted writers might have handled it.

> 1. It was Sunday night. The streets were full of people in their Sunday clothes. The street lights were on, and all sorts of people were on the sidewalks. They were walking up and down and talking.
>
> 2. In the streets the Sunday evening crowds in their awkward Sunday clothes milled about under the street lamps, their voices swelling to a monotonous din.
>
> 3. The streets, shuttered for the repose of Sunday, swarmed with a gaily-coloured crowd. Like illumined pearls the lamps shone from the summits of their tall poles upon the living texture below, which, changing shape and hue unceasingly, sent up into the warm grey evening air an unchanging, unceasing murmur.

Each of these examples conveys approximately, though by no means entirely, the same *referential* meaning: in each the time and place are the same, and each points to, or designates, the same crowd of people talking under street lights. Yet the passages produce different effects upon the reader. Each one is different, for instance, in its *expressive* meanings, that is, in the feelings it arouses in the reader about the street lamps and the people in the streets.

The first revision of Joyce's sentences communicates little expressive meaning. Its diction and sentence structure are comparatively bland and noncommittal, as if the writer neither liked nor disliked his subject, or as if he were bored by it. He chooses merely to point to the scene rather than to react to it. In place of active verbs he uses only linking verbs. He is content with the vague diction of "all sorts of people." In short, his writing reveals little awareness of the range of effects that style can produce. In order to pass a final judgment upon the success or the failure of this passage, however, we should have to see it in a much wider linguistic context. It might indeed be merely flat writing such as the inexperienced writer is likely to produce. But in another context this simple flat writing might be just what the writer wants for his particular purpose. The first example bears some faint resemblance to the kind of effect often achieved by Hemingway, who sometimes creates expressiveness by removing all overt emotional coloring from his sentences.

The hypothetical writer of the second passage exhibits a more decided emotional response. We suspect from his diction that he dislikes the people he is describing and probably feels superior to them. He is more aware, seemingly, of words as imagery and of words as sounds, although the clustering of unstressed syllables in the phrase "swelling to a monotonous din" sounds awkward. Yet this second passage seems colorless and inexpressive when placed side by side with the two sentences by James Joyce.

Joyce feels deeply about this city and its people. Phrases like "gaily-coloured," "illumined pearls," "living texture," and "warm grey evening" both designate and evaluate. But perhaps it is Joyce's sensitivity to the sound of words, as much as anything, which surrounds his subject with an aura of approval. While this short extract is ordinary enough in the context of Joyce's entire work, it is a striking example in comparison with the first two versions. One of its sound effects is the frequent use of consonance, or internal alliteration, such as the repetition of *l* sounds in "Like *ill*umined pear*l*s the *l*amps shone . . ." or the repetition of *s* and *d* sounds in the first sentence or the repetition of -*ing* toward the end of the second sentence. Emphasis and retarded movement result from the clustering of stressed syllables in the phrase "warm grey evening air." Further emphasis stems from the repetition of sounds and rhythms at the end of the second sentence in "an unchanging, unceasing murmur." In addition to using consonance, various repetitions, and unusual rhythms, Joyce creates his stylistic effects by means of active verbs, unusual words, a simile, imagery, and interrupted movement. Thus his expressive style not only gives his description force and grace, it is an important part of his meaning. It is not mere ornament.

Skillful handling of expressive meaning, such as Joyce employs in his two sentences, usually results in winning the reader's assent—at least momentarily—to the writer's feelings and viewpoint. Style, then, is also a means of persuasion. Or put another way, effective style, as opposed to awkward or inappropriate style is in part the result of taking pains to convince the reader.

But if style is a choice that persuades, style is also, in an important sense, discovery. In creating his style the writer is trying to force language to conform to all the subtleties of his thought and feeling. In *striving* to say exactly what he wants to say, the writer *discovers* a more accurate expression of what he wants to say. As he considers which of his various stylistic choices to make, a writer often recognizes the possibility of a more precise, more emphatic, more graceful manifestation of his thought and emotion than he had imagined in merely contemplating the subject in his mind. Furthermore, it may well be that style is discovery for the reader too, giving him a sharper pair of eyes or making him aware of new and fresh and possibly startling ways of thinking about the writer's subject.

By now it should be apparent that style is not merely a fancy way of expressing content. Even content, as we have seen, involves stylistic choices. And style, far from being ornamentation, is an important component of meaning. Since style is the result of many choices, it often reveals to us a portrait of the writer, or at any rate of the person the writer wishes to seem. Even if this portrait is not identical with the "real" writer, it is nevertheless a significant part of the total impression, for it does matter what kind of writer seems to be standing behind a piece of prose. From a writer's style we can often infer much about his conception of himself, his intellectual and emotional attitude toward his subject, and the way in which he regards his reader—about all, in short, that we call tone. And while it goes without saying that factual and referential information may often be more important than any other kind of meaning—especially in expository prose—style, no matter what the purpose of a piece of writing, is more than fancy dress. Style is meaning, judgment, and often the writer's moral conception—whether in argument, description, general exposition, or narration.

To summarize our tentative definition of style we might do well to repeat the following points:

1. Style includes the writer's way of thinking about his subject and his characteristic way of presenting it for a particular reader and purpose.

2. Style results from linguistic choices; the more frequently these choices are exercised and the more wide-ranging they are, the higher the probability they will effectively express the writer's unique thought and feeling.

3. Style, therefore, is, or may be, a means of discovery, for both writer and reader.

4. Style sharpens expressive meaning as well as referential meaning. Style intensifies the tone of writing, and, all else being equal, prose with a definite tone is likely to be more persuasive than writing with little tone.

5. Style is not mere ornament; rather it conveys important subtleties of meaning and evaluation, especially as they define the nature of the writer, his basic attitudes, his presuppositions, his moral stance, and his relation to his subject and his reader.

6. These points only begin to suggest the vast implications of style. They are offered only as a tentative working definition for students of composition, not as a confident solution to the enormous problems raised by the study of style.

Turning from our attempt to define style, we come to the question, What produces style? The answer involves, of course, all possible methods and techniques of expression known to rhetoric. To study the creation of style is to study the organization of the whole composition, paragraph development, sentence structure, sentence rhythm, diction, punctuation, and whatever else contributes to the process of communication. Style, however, results most frequently from those rhetorical devices of diction and sentence structure that produce emphasis and emotion.

Diction is especially useful because of the tremendous range of choice available to the writer, a fact that will become abundantly clear in the selections that follow this introduction. An author, of course, may prefer for some special purpose to keep his diction simple and fairly limited, using a large proportion of monosyllables as Hemingway sometimes does. Or he may prefer a diction of extraordinary variety as do Shakespeare, Milton, and Joyce. A writer is always free to choose (within the limits of his subject, purpose, and reader) from monosyllables, polysyllables, rare words, technical and scientific words, highly connotative words, slang, colloquialisms, vivid imagery, abstractions, dialect words, figurative expressions, archaic words, obsolete words, allusions, onomatopoeic words, and other words with appropriate sounds. He will manage different effects depending upon his vocabulary of active verbs or his handling of participles or the frequency and kind of his adjectives and adverbs.

Sentence structure is no less important than diction, for here a writer is also capable of choosing among forms that can produce surprise, emotion, variation, and emphasis. And once again variety is usually desirable. A writer uses short sentences, rhetorical questions, long sentences, parallelism, balance, antithesis, interrupted movement, periodic sentences, inversion, various kinds of repetition, and different kinds of subordinate constructions, each with a different effect.

In the study of style it is not sufficient, of course, merely to identify techniques of diction, sentence structure, and so on. Adequately to describe a writer's style, or even some feature of it, one must do a certain amount of statistical analysis, noting, say, the frequency of balanced clauses in proportion to simple, straightforward sentences. Sometimes a writer uses balance no oftener than the majority of writers. Or sometimes a writer uses balance with such significant frequency that it becomes one identifying characteristic of his work. Or again a given device may appear so often that it becomes an irritating mannerism and so loses its effectiveness. The point is that a description of style must proceed partly by making qualitative observations and judgments and partly by quantitative analysis. The purpose of such a description should be to demonstrate how a writer uniquely combines linguistic features so as to communicate his individual thought and feeling and judgment.

In the selections that follow, the comments and questions are designed to encourage the reader to identify and describe the styles of very different writers, some of whom write upon similar subjects with very different voices and with very different interpretations owing to the differences in the personalities behind each piece of prose. Not all these passages are equally effective, nor are all the styles, in our judgment, equally appropriate to their subjects. But all, we trust, have something to teach the student of composition. As exercises, we believe imitations and parodies are useful ways of expressing one's understanding of a writer's style and the principles—positive or negative—to be learned from it. Students may wish to try their hands at describing the styles of writers like Joan Didion, Margaret Atwood, Pierre Berton, Brand Blanshard, and A. J. Liebling, using selections appearing earlier in this textbook.

Even this brief and simple introduction suggests that the close description and study of style can be extremely useful to a student of composition. It reveals something of the virtually infinite number of choices available to a writer. Learning what some of these are and what kinds of meaning and emotion and effect they produce is an important step toward acquiring a style of one's own. Perhaps equally important is that recognizing the subtleties of style is a source of great pleasure. Like poetry, prose has its special rewards and delights.

Young Joan

Pierre Champion was a noted historian and authority on Joan of Arc. In 1920-21 he edited the record of her trial for witchcraft (held in 1431). There was considerable interest at the time in the French heroine, who had only recently been canonized in 1920, an interest reflected not only in Champion's publication but in a famous play presented in 1924, George Bernard Shaw's *Saint Joan* (an excerpt from the Preface to the play is the next selection). The following passage is from Champion's article on Joan written for *The Encyclopaedia Britannica* (fourteenth edition, 1937). As you read Champion's prose, and later Shaw's, contrast their styles. The differences are due in part to the personalities and values of the two men, but in part also to the fact that their interests in Joan were directed to different purposes and readers.

1   . . . Hardly anything is known of Joan's childhood; from her mother she learnt her prayers and the lives of the Saints, and she played till she was 12 or 13 with the other village children. The boys of Domrémy, who were French in their sympathies, were at frequent odds with the boys of the Burgundian village, on the other side of the Meuse. Saint Remy, 5 patron saint of the cathedral of Reims, was also that of the church at Domrémy. Joan, who was baptized by the *curé* Minet, was a pious child, and often went with her companions to bear wreaths of flowers to Notre Dame de Bermont. She had heard, without believing, the story of the fairies who haunted the spring among the bushes. She was almost certainly ignorant of 10 Merlin's prophecy that a maid should come from the Bois Chenu to do great deeds.

2   Joan helped her parents in tillage, tended the animals, and was skilled with her needle and in other feminine arts. She was pious, and often went to church when the other girls were dancing. She was in her 13th year 15 when, in her father's garden, she heard for the first time a voice from God.

From "Joan of Arc," *Encyclopaedia Britannica*, 14th edition (1937), XIII, 72-73. Reprinted by permission of the *Encyclopaedia Britannica*, Inc., Chicago, Illinois.

Thereupon she vowed to remain a virgin and to lead a godly life. During the next five years she heard the voices two or three times a week. Among them she distinguished those of Saint Catherine and Saint Margaret, who appeared to her, in the guise of queens, wearing rich and precious crowns.   20
Sometimes their coming was heralded by Saint Michael. With these visions Joan became still more serious, and more given to prayer. The troubles of Domrémy between 1419 and 1428 made her early acquainted with the horrors of war. Her voices commanded her to go to France, and to raise the siege of Orleans, which had been begun in October 1428.   25

3   We do not know the exact moment at which Joan decided to obey her voices, and to go to France. The captain of the fortified town nearest to Domrémy on the French side was Robert de Baudricourt, commandant at Vaucouleurs, four leagues away. Joan approached him for the first time in May 1428, accompanied by a relative on her mother's side, one Durand   30
Laxart ou Lassois. She was in her 16th year. At this time an army was being raised in England for the conquest of the Dauphin's territory south of the Loire. The journey was made without the knowledge of her family, for when Joan had spoken of going into France, her father had said that he would rather drown her with his own hands. She told the Dauphin's com-   35
mandant that she was sent by Our Lord, and asked him to write to the Dauphin saying that, by the will of God, she was to lead him to his crowning. Baudricourt attached no importance to the visit, and set her back to her parents. At home Joan talked more and more of her great mission. In July 1428, the governor of Champagne, Antoine de Vergy, undertook to   40
subdue the country around Vaucouleurs for the English. The people of Domrémy retreated with their cattle to Neufchâteau where Joan spent a fortnight with a woman called La Rousse, who kept an inn. This is the origin of the false Burgundian legend that she was a light woman, liking the company of men-at-arms and horses. Some time after, she was summoned   45
for breach of promise of marriage, before the magistrates of Toul, by a young man who had sought her hand. On the return of the family to Domrémy, they found the village burned to the ground, and Joan had to attend the church of Greux. Towards the end of October, she learned that Orleans was besieged by the English, who had garrisoned the towns along the Loire.   50

QUESTIONS

1. What is the purpose of most encyclopedia articles? In what way does an encyclopedia article differ from a personal essay? From an argument?

2. What kind of reader does Pierre Champion seem to be writing for? Describe the "assumed" reader of "Young Joan" as fully as you can.

3. Describe the man Pierre Champion seems to be. Granted that "Young Joan" shows us only one side of the "true" man, what personal characteristics does the writer choose to reveal in this historical sketch? Support your conclusions by pointing to specific words, phrases, and sentences.

4. How does he regard Joan of Arc? With utter detachment? With strong bias in her favor? With strong bias against her? If you think his attitude is mainly, but not entirely, objective, can you detect any subtle feeling for or against her? In answering all the questions in this section be sure to support your answers by referring to the language the writer uses.

5. In short, what is the tone * of the writing? Although style includes more than the means by which a writer creates his tone—embracing his characteristic way of planning and executing every aspect of his writing—the description of a writer's style should always include a detailed description of the writer's tone.

6. Since your answers at first will be largely intuitive, you may wish to test their validity by looking more closely into the means by which Pierre Champion creates his tone and his individual manner of presenting his subject. Are the sentences in this selection for the most part varied in length? How many words appear in the longest sentence? In the shortest? Do most of the sentences vary between the very short and the very long, or do most of them have a moderate length? You may, if you wish, count the number of sentences and the number of words in each sentence. After such a count note how many sentences fall between 6-15 words; how many fall between 16-25 words; how many between 26-35 words.

7. What is the pattern of the majority of Pierre Champion's sentences—simple *, compound *, complex *, compound-complex? Is their total effect one of simplicity or complexity?

8. To what extent does the writer vary sentence beginnings? How many begin with the subject of the sentence? How many begin with something else? What is the writer's most common variation? In what way might the handling of sentence openers affect a writer's style?

9. To what extent does the writer employ rhetorical questions *, inversions *, isolation of words and phrases, parallelism *, anaphora *, polysyndeton *, repetition, figures of speech *? What different effects result from employing these devices sparingly? From employing them frequently?

10. Is interrupted movement * frequent or infrequent? Are appositives * frequent or infrequent? Why?

11. Does the writer use dashes, parentheses, exclamation marks, and italics? Why or why not?

12. How many periodic sentences occur in this selection?

13. Sometimes even good sentences require careful, close reading because of the

inherent subtlety and complexity of the writer's thought. Generally, however, such complicated syntax is inappropriate to an encyclopedia, the readers of which want readily available information. Are Champion's sentences good or bad examples of the "encyclopedia style"? You might at this point wish to summarize how this writer's sentence structure helps to create his tone and style.

14. Is the diction of "Young Joan" largely abstract and general or concrete and particular? Are the majority of the words monosyllabic and disyllabic, or polysyllabic? Is the diction mostly Latinate or Saxon? Are the qualities of his diction referred to in this question appropriate or inappropriate to his subject, purpose, and reader? Why or why not?

15. Does the writer have a fondness for unusual or rare words? Have any words been used largely for their sound? Does Champion use slang, colloquialisms *, or contractions? Are there any archaic, obsolete, or dialect words? If any such words occur, point to examples. How does the presence or absence of any of these classes of words help to create the writer's tone?

16. Do any words or expressions characterize this writing as belonging to the twentieth century rather than to earlier centuries?

17. Are allusions * and proper nouns rare or frequent? If frequent of what sort are they? Do they come from mythology, literature, history, geography, the Bible, or from some other source? Are they appropriate? Do they make the writing more or less readable? Why or why not?

18. Would you describe the writer's language as largely emotive or referential? What are the connotations of the following phrases and clauses:

> from her mother she learnt her prayers (1-2)
> a pious child (7)
> She had heard, without believing, the story of the fairies . . . (9)
> Joan . . . was skilled with her needle and in other feminine arts. (13-14)

19. In telling his story does the writer ever apply to Joan words with unfavorable connotations *?

20. Consider this revision of the passage in lines 15-21:

> She was thirteen years old when, in her father's garden, she said she heard for the first time a voice from God. Thereupon she vowed, according to her own account, to remain a virgin and lead a godly life. During the next five years she affirmed that she heard the voices two or three times a week. Among them she claimed to distinguish those of Saint Catherine and Saint Margaret, who she said appeared to her in the guise of queens, wearing rich and precious crowns. Sometimes their coming she declared to be heralded by Saint Michael.

In what way has the style changed?

SUGGESTIONS FOR WRITING

1. Revise one paragraph of this selection to show some emotion on the writer's part and subtle disapproval of Joan of Arc.

2. In one or two paragraphs attempt a parody of this writer's style, using some such subject as Hercules or Paul Bunyan. (Before attempting this subject you might wish to read or reread Dwight Macdonald's "Parody" (p. 151).

3. Using some historical figure, the facts of whose life you have gathered, write a one- or two-paragraph imitation of Pierre Champion's style.

4. After studying Shaw's style in the next selection, rewrite paragraph 3 as Shaw might have written it. In asking for parodies and stylistic imitations we are not urging you to model your future writing as closely as possible upon Shaw or upon the style of some other writer. Nor does parody necessarily imply an adverse criticism of a writer's style. But parody and imitation are useful methods of identifying a writer's distinguishing characteristics and require an understanding of the interplay between a writer's thought and his expression of that thought. Improving one's own style results from the close study of many different writers.

The Evolutionary Appetite

George Bernard Shaw (1856-1958)—playwright, critic, Fabian socialist, wit, and brilliant platform speaker—was one of the major figures of twentieth-century British literature. His devotion to liberal reforms and his constant goading of the Establishment is seen in his plays and in the long prefaces he composed for each of them. The dramas themselves range from a serious problem play like *Mrs. Warren's Profession* (1898), concerning prostitution, to the sparkling comedy *Pygmalion* (1913), the source of the Broadway musical, *My Fair Lady* (1955). Perhaps Shaw's finest play is *Saint Joan* (1924). He sees Joan as an example of the great individual whose destiny is to move humanity forward at the cost of intense personal suffering. The following excerpt from the "Preface" to *Saint Joan* passionately defends her character and analyzes the forces impelling her to greatness and to tragedy.

1   What then is the modern view of Joan's voices and visions and messages from God? The nineteenth century said that they were delusions, but that as she was a pretty girl, and had been abominably ill-treated and finally done to death by a superstitious rabble of medieval priests hounded on by a corrupt political bishop, it must be assumed that she was the in-   5
nocent dupe of these delusions. The twentieth century finds this explanation too vapidly commonplace, and demands something more mystic. I think the twentieth century is right, because an explanation which amounts to Joan being mentally defective instead of, as she obviously was, mentally excessive, will not wash. I cannot believe, nor, if I could, could I expect all   10
my readers to believe, as Joan did, that three ocularly visible well dressed persons, named respectively Saint Catherine, Saint Margaret, and Saint Michael, came down from heaven and gave her certain instructions with which they were charged by God for her. Not that such a belief would be

Reprinted from the "Preface" to *Saint Joan* in *Nine Great Plays* by Bernard Shaw, New York, Dodd, Mead and Company, 1947. Reprinted by permission of The Society of Authors on behalf of the Bernard Shaw Estate.

more improbable or fantastic than some modern beliefs which we all 15
swallow; but there are fashions and family habits in belief, and it happens
that, my fashion being Victorian and my family habit Protestant, I find
myself unable to attach any such objective validity to the form of Joan's
visions.

2   But that there are forces at work which use individuals for purposes 20
far transcending the purpose of keeping these individuals alive and prosperous and respectable and safe and happy in the middle station in life, which
is all any good bourgeois can reasonably require, is established by the fact
that men will, in the pursuit of knowledge and of social readjustments for
which they will not be a penny the better, and are indeed often many 25
pence the worse, face poverty, infamy, exile, imprisonment, dreadful hardship, and death. Even the selfish pursuit of personal power does not nerve
men to the efforts and sacrifices which are eagerly made in pursuit of extensions of our power over nature, though these extensions may not touch
the personal life of the seeker at any point. There is no more mystery about 30
this appetite for knowledge and power than about the appetite for food:
both are known as facts and as facts only, the difference between them
being that the appetite for food is necessary to the life of the hungry man
and is therefore a personal appetite, whereas the other is an appetite for
evolution, and therefore a superpersonal need.   35

3   The diverse manners in which our imaginations dramatize the approach of the superpersonal forces is a problem for the psychologist, not
for the historian. Only, the historian must understand that visionaries are
neither impostors nor lunatics. It is one thing to say that the figure Joan
recognized as St Catherine was not really St Catherine, but the dramatiza- 40
tion by Joan's imagination of that pressure upon her of the driving force
that is behind evolution which I have just called the evolutionary appetite.
It is quite another to class her visions with the vision of two moons seen by
a drunken person, or with Brocken spectres, echoes and the like. Saint
Catherine's instructions were far too cogent for that; and the simplest 45
French peasant who believes in apparitions of celestial personages to
favored mortals is nearer to the scientific truth about Joan than the Ration-
alist and Materialist historians and essayists who feel obliged to set down
a girl who saw saints and heard them talking to her as either crazy or men-
dacious. If Joan was mad, all Christendom was mad too; for people who 50
believe devoutly in the existence of celestial personages are every whit as
mad in that sense as the people who think they see them. Luther, when he
threw his inkhorn at the devil, was no more mad than any other Augus-

tinian monk: he had a more vivid imagination, and had perhaps eaten and slept less: that was all.   55

QUESTIONS

1. In "The Evolutionary Appetite" Shaw argues that Joan is one of those superior individuals who form the advance guard of the evolutionary process. Because they belong more to the future than to the present, they are likely to be accused, as Joan was and still is, of neurosis or lunacy. Unlike Pierre Champion's "Young Joan," therefore, "The Evolutionary Appetite" is more argument than narration. What is Shaw's attitude toward himself? Does he, for example, regard himself seriously? Does he ever laugh at himself? Does he allow for the possibility that his view is merely one of a number of legitimate interpretations of Joan? Does he think of himself as less than infallible? Support your answer by specific references to Shaw's language. What kind of reader does he assume? What does Shaw suppose are his readers' probable assumptions about Joan of Arc?

2. Shaw's sentences are longer than those in Pierre Champion's "Young Joan." Count the number of sentences and the number of words in each sentence. How long is Shaw's average sentence? What is the length of his shortest sentence? His longest? What kinds of subordination * does Shaw use? What is his most common method of subordination? Why do you think Shaw writes longer sentences than those of Pierre Champion?

3. Classify each sentence as simple *, compound *, complex *, compound-complex. Which of these types appears most often? Which is the second most common?

4. Shaw's sentences are much more vigorous than those of Pierre Champion. How many examples of the following variations for emphasis can you identify in this selection: rhetorical questions *, interrupted movement *, emphasis by isolation of words or phrases, fragmentary * sentences or clauses, nominative absolutes * as interrupters, parallelism *, antithesis *, short sentences or clauses, polysyndeton *, repetition, periodic * structure? Which of these does Shaw use most often? Why? Is Shaw over-emphatic? Is it possible to be over-emphatic? Would Pierre Champion's prose have been improved if he had used more frequently such techniques of emphasis as those listed above?

5. Often in Shaw's prose there is a feeling that a debate is taking place. Shaw is fond of stating his opponent's position and then demolishing it by several smashing blows. Point to two or three examples. How does Shaw's sentence structure help to convey this conflict of ideas?

6. Does Shaw use more or fewer emotive words than Pierre Champion? Illustrate your answer by examples.

7. Since Shaw is arguing, he naturally uses logical connectives * in the construc-

tion of his argument. What are some of the most common of these in "The Evolutionary Appetite"?

8. Shaw's argument often involves comparisons and disjunctions. Correlative conjunctions and pairs of words framing * comparisons appear often and create an effect on dignified symmetry. Examples are:

> more . . . than
> no more . . . than
> either . . . or.

Can you find similar constructions?

9. Is Shaw's diction primarily formal and Latinate or simple and informal? Make a list of polysyllabic words of Latin origin beginning with, say, *abominably*. Make a parallel list of one- or two-syllable Saxon words like *whit*. Which is the longer list? Should Shaw have used only the kind of words appearing on the longer list? Why or why not?

10. Does Shaw ever use slang or colloquial * expressions along with formal diction? Is he wise to mix the two kinds of diction? Explain.

11. Does Shaw use adjectives and adverbs more, or less, frequently than does Pierre Champion? How do Shaw's adjectives and adverbs affect his tone? Might any be omitted?

12. Most readers would probably conclude that Pierre Champion's style is appropriate to his reader and purpose. Is Shaw's very different style appropriate to *his* reader and purpose? Why or why not?

13. Which of these styles do you prefer to read? Why? Are there any criteria by which we could judge the style of one of these writer's prose to be superior to the other?

SUGGESTIONS FOR WRITING

1. Write an argument of about the same length as "The Evolutionary Appetite" in which you imitate Shaw's style as closely as you can, without slipping into parody.

2. Rewrite "The Evolutionary Appetite," making Shaw's argument as unemotional and as dispassionate as possible. Simplify his diction wherever possible.

3. Using Shaw's style as much as possible, write an unsympathetic treatment of Joan of Arc.

4. Either in class discussion or in an essay identify several characteristics of Shaw's style not mentioned in the questions.

A, B, and C

Stephen Leacock (1869-1944), Canada's most famous humorist, was born in England and emigrated to this country with his family in 1876. He was educated at Upper Canada College and the University of Toronto, and did post-graduate work at the University of Chicago. Leacock spent most of his professional life teaching political economy, and serving as chairman of his department, at McGill University. Although he published a number of volumes on economics, politics, history, and literature, he is best known today for his humorous books, of which he wrote more than twenty, and through them gained an international reputation as the best comic writer in English of the time. Leacock's most successful works of humor include *Literary Lapses* (1910), *Nonsense Novels* (1911), *Sunshine Sketches of a Little Town* (1912), *Arcadian Adventures with the Idle Rich* (1914), *Moonbeams from the Larger Lunacy* (1915), and *My Discovery of England* (1922). The story that follows, one of his most popular, is from *Literary Lapses*.

1   The student of arithmetic who has mastered the first four rules of his art, and successfully striven with money sums and fractions, finds himself confronted by an unbroken expanse of questions known as problems. These are short stories of adventure and industry with the end omitted, and though betraying a strong family resemblance, are not without a cer-   5
tain element of romance.

2   The characters in the plot of a problem are three people called A, B, and C. The form of the question is generally of this sort:

"A, B, and C do a certain piece of work. A can do as much work in one hour as B in two, or C in four. Find how long they work at it."   10

3   Or thus:

"A, B, and C are employed to dig a ditch. A can dig as much in

From *Literary Lapses* by Stephen Leacock, reprinted by permission of The Canadian Publishers, McClelland and Stewart Limited, Toronto.

one hour as B can dig in two, and B can dig twice as fast as C. Find how long, etc. etc."

4   Or after this wise: 15
        "A lays a wager that he can walk faster than B or C. A can walk half as fast again as B, and C is only an indifferent walker. Find how far, and so forth."

5   The occupations of A, B, and C are many and varied. In the older arithmetics they contented themselves with doing "a certain piece of 20 work." This statement of the case, however, was found too sly and mysterious, or possibly lacking in romantic charm. It became the fashion to define the job more clearly and to set them at walking matches, ditch-digging, regattas, and piling cord wood. At times, they became commercial and entered into partnership, having with their old mystery a "certain" 25 capital. Above all they revel in motion. When they tire of walking-matches— A rides on horseback, or borrows a bicycle and competes with his weaker-minded associates on foot. Now they race on locomotives; now they row; or again they become historical and engage stage-coaches; or at times they are aquatic and swim. If their occupation is actual work they prefer to 30 pump water into cisterns, two of which leak through holes in the bottom and one of which is watertight. A, of course, has the good one; he also takes the bicycle, and the best locomotive, and the right of swimming with the current. Whatever they do they put money on it, being all three sports. A always wins.   35

6   In the early chapters of the arithmetic, their identity is concealed under the names John, William, and Henry, and they wrangle over the division of marbles. In algebra they are often called X, Y, Z. But these are only their Christian names, and they are really the same people.

7   Now to one who has followed the history of these men through 40 countless pages of problems, watched them in their leisure hours dallying with cord wood, and seen their panting sides heave in the full frenzy of filling a cistern with a leak in it, they become something more than mere symbols. They appear as creatures of flesh and blood, living men with their own passions, ambitions, and aspirations like the rest of us. Let us view 45 them in turn. A is a full-blooded blustering fellow, of energetic temperament, hot-headed and strong-willed. It is he who proposes everything, challenges B to work, makes the bets, and bends the others to his will. He is a man of great physical strength and phenomenal endurance. He has been known to walk forty-eight hours at a stretch, and to pump ninety-six. His 50 life is arduous and full of peril. A mistake in the working of a sum may

keep him digging a fortnight without sleep. A repeating decimal in the answer might kill him.

8   B is a quiet, easy-going fellow, afraid of A and bullied by him, but very gentle and brotherly to little C, the weakling. He is quite in A's power, 55 having lost all his money in bets.

9   Poor C is an undersized, frail man, with a plaintive face. Constant walking, digging, and pumping has broken his health and ruined his nervous system. His joyless life has driven him to drink and smoke more than is good for him, and his hand often shakes as he digs ditches. He has not 60 the strength to work as the others can, in fact, as Hamlin Smith has said, "A can do more work in one hour than C in four."

10   The first time that ever I saw these men was one evening after a regatta. They had all been rowing in it, and it had transpired that A could row as much in one hour as B in two, or C in four. B and C had come in 65 dead fagged and C was coughing badly. "Never mind, old fellow," I heard B say, "I'll fix you up on the sofa and get you some hot tea." Just then A came blustering in and shouted, "I say, you fellows, Hamlin Smith has shown me three cisterns in his garden and he says we can pump them until to-morrow night. I bet I can beat you both. Come on. You can pump in 70 your rowing things, you know. Your cistern leaks a little, I think, C." I heard B growl that it was a dirty shame and that C was used up now, but they went, and presently I could tell from the sound of the water that A was pumping four times as fast as C.

11   For years after that I used to see them constantly about town and 75 always busy. I never heard of any of them eating or sleeping. Then owing to a long absence from home, I lost sight of them. On my return I was surprised to no longer find A, B, and C at their accustomed tasks; on inquiry I heard that work in this line was now done by N, M, and O, and that some people were employing for algebraical jobs four foreigners called 80 Alpha, Beta, Gamma, and Delta.

12   Now it chanced one day that I stumbled upon old D, in the little garden in front of his cottage, hoeing in the sun. D is an aged labouring man who used occasionally to be called in to help A, B, and C. "Did I know 'em, sir?" he answered, "why, I knowed 'em ever since they was lit- 85 tle fellows in brackets. Master A, he were a fine lad, sir, though I always said, give me Master B for kind-heartedness-like. Many's the job as we've been on together, sir, though I never did no racing nor aught of that, but just the plain labour, as you might say. I'm getting a bit too old and stiff for it nowadays, sir—just scratch about in the garden here and grow a bit 90

of a logarithm, or raise a common denominator or two. But Mr. Euclid he use me still for them propositions, he do."

13   From the garrulous old man I learned the melancholy end of my former acquaintances. Soon after I left town, he told me, C had been taken ill. It seems that A and B had been rowing on the river for a wager, 95 and C had been running on the bank and then sat in a draught. Of course the bank had refused the draught and C was taken ill. A and B came home and found C lying helpless in bed. A shook him roughly and said, "Get up, C, we're going to pile wood." C looked so worn and pitiful that B said, "Look here, A, I won't stand this, he isn't fit to pile wood to-night." C 100 smiled feebly and said, "Perhaps I might pile a little if I sat up in bed." Then B, thoroughly alarmed, said, "See here, A, I'm going to fetch a doctor; he's dying." A flared up and answered, "You've no money to fetch a doctor." "I'll reduce him to his lowest terms," B said firmly, "that'll fetch him." C's life might even then have been saved but they made a mistake 105 about the medicine. It stood at the head of the bed on a bracket, and the nurse accidentally removed it from the bracket without changing the sign. After the fatal blunder C seems to have sunk rapidly. On the evening of the next day, as the shadows deepened in the little room, it was clear to all that the end was near. I think that even A was affected at the last as he 110 stood with bowed head, aimlessly offering to bet with the doctor on C's laboured breathing. "A," whispered C, "I think I'm going fast." "How fast do you think you'll go, old man?" murmured A. "I don't know," said C, "but I'm going at any rate."—The end came soon after that. C rallied for a moment and asked for a certain piece of work that he had left down- 115 stairs. A put it in his arms and he expired. As his soul sped heavenward A watched its flight with melancholy admiration. B burst into a passionate flood of tears and sobbed, "Put away his little cistern and the rowing clothes he used to wear, I feel as if I could hardly ever dig again."—The funeral was plain and unostentatious. It differed in nothing from the ordi- 120 nary, except that out of deference to sporting men and mathematicians, A engaged two hearses. Both vehicles started at the same time, B driving the one which bore the sable parallelopiped containing the last remains of his ill-fated friend. A on the box of the empty hearse generously consented to a handicap of a hundred yards, but arrived first at the cemetery by driving 125 four times as fast as B. (Find the distance to the cemetery.) As the sarcophagus was lowered, the grave was surrounded by the broken figures of the first book of Euclid.—It was noticed that after the death of C, A became a changed man. He lost interest in racing with B, and dug but lan-

guidly. He finally gave up his work and settled down to live on the interest 130
of his bets.—B never recovered from the shock of C's death; his grief
preyed upon his intellect and it became deranged. He grew moody and
spoke only in monosyllables. His disease became rapidly aggravated, and
he presently spoke only in words whose spelling was regular and which
presented no difficulty to the beginner. Realizing his precarious condition 135
he voluntarily submitted to be incarcerated in an asylum, where he abjured
mathematics and devoted himself to writing the History of the Swiss Family
Robinson in words of one syllable.

QUESTIONS

1. What does the sub-title tell you about this essay, not just with regard to
subject matter but, especially, about the author's attitude? Is the title of the
book—*Literary Lapses*—from which this selection is taken also relevant here?
2. The phrase "the student of" is usually applied to the advanced study of a
difficult topic; thus one reads of "the student of physics," "the student of
Aristotle," "the student of Renaissance literature." How, then, does Leacock's
"the student of arithmetic" strike you? Note that he does not use the words
"mathematics" or "algebra." What connotations * is Leacock working with
that he expects his readers to grasp fully?
3. The tone * of Leacock's essay is established at the beginning, when we find
out, in paragraph 1, that, although his topic is the very ordinary (even dull)
one of problems in arithmetic, yet these problems are really "short stories of
adventure and industry" (4) which contain "a certain element of romance"
(5-6). What other means of establishing tone does Leacock use in the first
seven paragraphs? In attempting to answer this important question, look closely
at, among other things, the implications of the two quotations above.
4. In paragraph 8 (54-56) we see Leacock not only dealing with the elements
of a mathematical problem as living characters, but exaggerating the characterization to the point of the ridiculous. How does this affect the tone of the
essay? Is he being consistent?
5. What is the function of paragraph 12? Do you think that it accomplishes
its purpose effectively, or not?
6. The last two paragraphs are introduced by the familiar expression "now it
chanced one day" (82). Comment on the effectiveness of this introduction,
in view of what is dealt with in these final paragraphs.
7. Is the last sentence of this essay an effective conclusion? Why, or why not?
Would you have omitted the last two lines of this sentence?
8. On a number of occasions Leacock uses plays on words and puns, as for
example, in ll. 85-86, 90-91, 96-97, 106-107, and 114. Do you think such

word games detract from the overall effect of the essay? Or are they consistent with the tone?

9. Paragraph 6 begins with two periodic * sentences. Do these appear normal, or do they strike you as slightly artificial? Find the other periodic sentences (if there are any) in the first five paragraphs, and comment on their effectiveness, or lack of it.

10. Comment on the sentence in l. 45 as an organizing * sentence.

11. Why is there no comma after *full-blooded* (46) and after *hot-headed* (47)? How would these sentences be affected by inserting commas after these words?

12. Analyze the sentence structure of paragraphs 1, 8, and 13 (from l. 119). Deal with such questions as these: are the sentences simple *, compound *, complex *, or compound-complex? Do they begin with the subject-verb nucleus, with a subordinate clause *, or with a phrase? Are they loose *, balanced *, cumulative *, freight-train *, parallel, or periodic? Does the writer use dashes and parentheses? Does he use interrupted movement *, antithesis *, appositives *, or emphasis by isolation of words or phrases? Finally, compare the sentence structures of these paragraphs, and draw what conclusions seem to you both justified and appropriate.

SUGGESTIONS FOR WRITING

1. Rewrite the first six paragraphs of this essay in as straightforward and factual a manner as possible, removing all traces of humor. Then comment on the differences between your version and the original, and try to show how Leacock achieves his comic effects.

2. In four or five paragraphs, try to write an imitation of Leacock. Use a different subject, however, such as one of these: the geography of the western provinces; the economics of the supermarket; the differences among the forms of the sonnet; the importance of the various Canadian political parties; the difficulties of learning the irregular verbs in French; the apparatus of the apprentice chemist; etc.

Courtesy to Readers—Clarity

F. L. Lucas (1894-1967)—British essayist and critic—was a Fellow of King's College, Cambridge, and a university Reader in English. His critical works reflect his interest in the personalities of writers and their moral values. Typical of his best criticism is *The Search for Good Sense; Four Eighteenth-Century Characters: Johnson, Chesterfield, Boswell, Goldsmith* (1958), a model of lively, urbane prose. Lucas was thoroughly grounded in the classics and widely acquainted with European literature. His familiarity with the finest prose in several languages accounts for the success of his book *Style* (1955), from which the following selection comes.

> One should not aim at being possible to understand, but at being impossible to misunderstand.   QUINTILIAN
>
> Obscurité . . . vicieuse affectation.   MONTAIGNE

1   Character, I have suggested, is the first thing to think about in style. The next step is to consider what characteristics can win a hearer's or a reader's sympathy. For example, it is bad manners to give them needless trouble. Therefore clarity. It is bad manners to waste their time. Therefore brevity.   5

2   There clings in my memory a story once told me by Professor Sisson. A Frenchman said to him: "In France it is the writer that takes the trouble; in Germany, the reader; in England it is betwixt and between." The generalization is over-simple; perhaps even libellous; but not without truth. It gives, I think, another reason why the level of French prose has 10 remained so high. And this may in its turn be partly because French culture has been based more than ours on conversation and the salon. In most conversation, if he is muddled, wordy, or tedious, a man is soon made,

From *Style* by F. L. Lucas. Reprinted by permission of the publisher Cassell Ltd.

unless he is a hippopotamus, to feel it. Further, the salon has been particularly influenced by women; who, as a rule, are less tolerant of tedium and   15
clumsiness than men.

3   First, then, clarity. The social purpose of language is communication—to inform, misinform, or otherwise influence our fellows. True, we
also use words in solitude to think our own thoughts, and to express our
feelings to ourselves. But writing is concerned rather with communication   20
than with self-communing; though some writers, especially poets, may talk
to themselves in public. Yet, as I have said, even these, though in a sense
overheard rather than heard, have generally tried to reach an audience. No
doubt in some modern literature there has appeared a tendency to replace
communication by a private maundering to oneself which shall inspire   25
one's audience to maunder privately to *themselves*—rather as if the author
handed round a box of drugged cigarettes of his concoction to stimulate
each guest to his own solitary dreams. But I have yet to be convinced that
such activities are very valuable; or that one's own dreams and meditations
are much heightened by the stimulus of some other voice soliloquizing in   30
Chinese. The irrational, now in politics, now in poetics, has been the sinister opium of our tormented and demented century.

4   For most prose, at all events, there is a good deal in Defoe's view
of what style should be: "I would answer, that in which a man speaking to
five hundred people, of all common and various capacities, idiots or lunatics   35
excepted, should be understood by them all." This is, indeed, very like the
verdict of Anatole France on the three most important qualities of French
style: "d'abord la clarté, puis encore la clarté, et enfin la clarté." Poetry, and
poetic prose, may sometimes gain by a looming mystery like that of a
mountain-cloud or thunderstorm; but ordinary prose, I think, is happiest   40
when it is clear as the air of a spring day in Attica.

5   True, obscurity cannot always be avoided. It is impossible to make
easy the ideas of an Einstein, or the psychology of a Proust. But even abstruse subjects are often made needlessly difficult; for instance, by the type
of philosopher who, sometimes from a sound instinct of self-preservation,   45
consistently refuses to illustrate his meaning by *examples*; or by the type of
scientific writer who goes decked out with technical jargon as an Indian
brave with feathers. Most obscurity is an unmixed, and unnecessary, evil.

6   It may be caused by incoherence; by inconsiderateness; by over-
crowding of ideas; by pomp and circumstance; by sheer charlatanism; and   50
doubtless by other things I have not thought of.

. . .

7   And how is clarity to be acquired? Mainly by taking trouble; and by writing to serve people rather than to impress them. Most obscurity, I suspect, comes not so much from incompetence as from ambition—the ambition to be admired for depth of sense, or pomp of sound, or wealth of ornament. It is for the writer to think and rethink his ideas till they are clear; to put them in a clear order; to prefer (other things equal, and subject to the law of variety) short words, sentences, and paragraphs to long; not to try to say too many things at once; to eschew irrelevances; and, above all, to put himself with imaginative sympathy in his reader's place. Everyone knows of Molière reading his plays to his cook; eight centuries before him, in distant China, Po Chu-i had done the like; and Swift's Dublin publisher, Faulkner, would similarly read Swift's proofs aloud to him and two of his men-servants—"which, if they did not comprehend, he would alter and amend, until they understood it perfectly well." In short, it is usually the pretentious and the egotistic who are obscure, especially in prose; those who write with wider sympathy, to serve some purpose beyond themselves, must usually be muddy-minded creatures if they cannot, or will not, be clear.

QUESTIONS

1. Contrast F. L. Lucas's sentences with those of Ralph Heintzman, especially with reference to length, the number of ideas expressed per sentence, and variety of sentence structure. How would you describe Lucas's most common type of sentence in this selection? What means does he employ to achieve emphasis in his sentences?

2. Identify the number and kind of sentence openers in this selection. Are they more or less varied than those in Ralph Heintzman's prose?

3. Most of Lucas's words are simple, and polysyllabic words do not occur as often as words of one and two syllables. Yet he sometimes uses rare or unusual words that help to give his prose interest, variety, and emphasis—*maundering*, for example (25). How many others can you identify?

4. Frequent allusions * and quotations are characteristic of Lucas's style. Point out several. Do these contribute to, or detract from, the clarity of his writing? Explain.

5. Several times Lucas uses metaphors * and similes *. Identify each one and explain its purpose. Rewrite each sentence containing one of these figures in order to express the same idea in nonfigurative language. Describe the difference in effect in each instance.

6. Does Lucas win his reader's sympathy in this selection? If so, how? If not, why not?

7. Describe as fully as you can the personality behind this prose. What are Lucas's assumptions about writing, about literature, about what we vaguely call a philosophy of life? What does he like and dislike? How does he regard his reader? What kind of reader might be hostile to this writer?

SUGGESTIONS FOR WRITING

1. Imitating this style generally, but not slavishly, write an essay on the virtue of either economy or simplicity in prose.

2. Rewrite one or two of Lucas' paragraphs in the style of Heintzman.

3. Choosing your best theme, compare and contrast your own prose with that of F. L. Lucas. Try also to improve the clarity and grace of one of your less successful themes by applying Lucas's advice.

D. G. JONES

From "Eve in Dejection"

D. G. Jones is a professor of English at Sherbrooke University and a respected Canadian poet. Among his publications on Canadian literature is the very influential *Butterfly on Rock* (1970), which extends the theories of Northrop Frye as the basis for an examination of a wide range of Canadian poetry and fiction. The following selection, taken from Jones' book, is an example of his critical approach, as applied in this case to characters in Margaret Laurence's *The Stone Angel*.

1   Early in life Hagar had married Bram Shipley, despite the opposition of her father and of the community as a whole, only to reject him later on. In doing so she rejects the land and the spontaneous joy and creative fulfilment which she might have known in her own life. She embraces instead the barren security and respectability of the garrison culture, be- 5 coming the living embodiment of the stone angel which her father has placed over her mother's grave.

2   Hagar Shipley's father is a man of property, an energetic and successful merchant. He teaches his children the Scottish traditions of the family: clan, pipe-tune, and motto, "Gainsay who dare." He is a god-fearing 10 man who fears no one, not even God. "God might have created heaven and earth and the majority of people, but," says Hagar, "Father was a self-made man, as he himself had told us often enough." Still, he owns a pew in the church and never misses a Sunday service. He puts his real faith, however, in maxims such as, "God helps those who help themselves." One 15 of the first things he teaches his daughters is the system of weights and measures. It is he who brings the stone angel, carved in marble, all the way from Europe as a proper memorial to place on his wife's grave. It is the petrified symbol of his cultural ideal.

From *Butterfly on Rock* by D. G. Jones. Copyright © University of Toronto Press 1970. Reprinted by permission.

3   Bram Shipley is his opposite, a bearded, ungrammatical, rudely 20
virile ne'er-do-well, who swears better than he farms, keeps horses for the
horses' sake and not for profit, likes to ride, drink, make love, and have
children. He is a man who doesn't give a damn about property or proper
appearances, though he loves the land as it is.

4   Hagar meets Bram at a dance. She discovers in him a passion and 25
gaiety her own world lacks and marries him. But despite her marriage to
Bram against her father's wishes, Hagar is made in her father's image. She
cannot accept her husband as he is and tries to change him: to polish his
grammar, correct his dress, furnish his house, and turn him into a successful farmer. She would refashion him in a style that the community respects. 30
But Bram remains unfashionable, and when Hagar realizes she cannot remake him she rejects him. She leaves and goes to Vancouver, where she
continues to serve the world of appearances working as housekeeper for a
wealthy old man with a great houseful of furniture. Only towards the end
of her life does she again reject the ideals embodied in the stone angel and 35
welcome the world she had known in Bram. An old woman, ill, but utterly
fed up at last with the neat, respectable, and yet perfectly barren life which
her one surviving son continues to serve, she walks out of his house and
goes down to the sea. It is one of her great and last adventures. Struggling
down a steep bank, labouring through the underbrush and finally collaps- 40
ing in what is, for her, a wilderness, she is yet intent upon rediscovering her
identification with the land and the minute, teeming life of nature. Self-
exiled from the streets and houses of the town, she spends the night in an
abandoned fish cannery. Here she unbends, accepting the company of an
unknown man, sharing his wine and his warmth, until she becomes so ill 45
she must be taken to the hospital. Hagar Shipley has, in effect, returned to
Bram and accepted what the masculine figure stands for.

QUESTIONS

1. How would you, on the basis of Professor Jones' selection, describe the personality behind the prose? (See p. 674.) For example, in discussing Margaret
Laurence's characters does he reveal some of his own values? Obviously he
does, insofar as he makes judgments about them. But what standards of "right"
and "wrong" is Jones applying? Define them as clearly as you can in your own
words, and state how they are applied to each of the characters referred to in
this selection. Now what would you say about Jones' personality? How do you,
as a reader, respond to it?

2. Do the author's sentence structures and diction work to reinforce the judgments he is making? Consider paragraph 2, in which Hagar's father is described. What effect is produced by beginning most of the sentences in this paragraph with the subject-verb nucleus? By repeating the pronoun "he" instead of naming Hagar's father? By the irony * of sentence three (ll. 10-11)? By the references to "real faith" (l. 14), "the system of weights and measures" (ll. 16-17), and "the petrified symbol of his cultural ideal" (ll. 18-19)? All these devices are intended to evoke a specific response from the reader. Do you agree that the response is a negative one? Could you have responded in any other way?

3. Paragraph 4 describes Bram Shipley in terms that have favorable connotations * according to Jones' standards of judgment. Point out the words and phrases that make us see Bram as "the opposite" of Hagar's father. Does the loose * structure of the first sentence (ll. 20-24) also contribute to the desired effect? Compare it to the sentence structures of the previous paragraph and explain how it differs. Why is it an appropriate kind of sentence in which to describe Bram Shipley? Note as well the use of colloquialism * (l. 23). Is this also appropriate?

4. In his first three paragraphs Professor Jones has set up an opposition between, on the one hand, the land, spontaneity, creativity and love, and, on the other, property, respectability, communal repression and the absence of love. These latter characteristics are subsumed in the phrase "garrison culture" (l. 5), which Jones has taken from Northrop Frye. (See Frye's "Conclusion" to the *Literary History of Canada*, 1st edition, pp. 830-31.) Would a reader not familiar with Frye's work be able to understand the term, given the context in which Jones uses it? If not, then Jones could be accused of writing for an audience of specialists. Can you defend him against this charge? Bear in mind that this is a different matter from his use of an allusion * to John Galsworthy's novel, *The Man of Property* (l. 8). This brief allusion is given no context, and seems intended for specialists; but nothing essential is lost from Jones' argument if other readers fail to pick up the allusion.

5. How does Jones use the opposition referred to in the previous question as a way of focusing his materials in paragraph 4? Can you point to words and phrases in this paragraph that are repeated directly, or echoed by synonymous terms, from earlier paragraphs?

6. Jones treats Laurence's characters as symbols *, as persons who not merely stand for but actually embody specific values. The problem facing a writer who sees characters in this way is to avoid excessive abstraction *. Does paragraph 4 in fact avoid this problem? Can you point to images * and concrete * details that Jones uses to make the reader see Hagar not only as a symbol but also as a vivid and distinct personality? Is the structure of sentence eleven (ll. 39-42) intended to achieve the same effect? How?

7. Jones' phrasing might be questioned at a few points. For example, is "living

embodiment" (l. 6) redundant? Is "utterly fed up" (ll. 36-37) an unsuccessful mixture of formal and colloquial diction? Is "great and last adventure" (ll. 39) an awkward way of avoiding the more conventional "last and greatest"? Look carefully at these phrases, and try to defend them as appropriate to the total effect of the selection. Whether you decide that each phrase can or cannot be defended, explain the reasoning behind your answers.

8. An effective style ought to make the reader approve of the person the writer seems to be. The style ought to persuade the reader or at least win the reader's respect. Of the writers whom we have so far analyzed in this section, which do you think has the most persuasive style? Which one has the least? Explain your decision in each case, using specific examples from the two writers to support the judgments you make.

SUGGESTIONS FOR WRITING

1. Choose, from a novel or short story you know well, two contrasting characters who symbolize different values. Describe these characters in two contrasting paragraphs, as Jones does, deliberately using appropriate elements of style to convey your disapproval of one character and your admiration for the other.

2. Write a short essay in which you explain why Jones has, through his style, succeeded (or not succeeded) in persuading you and winning your respect. Use short quotations to support your argument.

3. Choosing any subject you like, write a short essay—from the third-person point of view *—in which you try to convey through your style (not by direct statements about yourself) the kind of person you are. Be as objective as you can in analyzing your personality and values before you start to write.

From "Life and Time: Laurence's *The Stone Angel*"

W. H. New is a professor of English at the University of British Columbia and the present editor of *Canadian Literature*. He has published extensively on Canadian and Commonwealth literature. His critical method, unlike that of Jones, emphasizes analysis, argument, and evaluation; his style and tone also differ. Taken together, this selection and the previous one provide the student with a useful opportunity to compare and contrast the approaches to literature of two highly-regarded Canadian critics.

1   Even Mrs. Laurence's most recent book, then, takes us back into *The Stone Angel*, into the memories and the viewpoint of its central character, Hagar Shipley, who "often wondered why one discovers so many things too late. The jokes of God." Any mention of raging also takes us to Hagar, for her rages are one of the most vividly memorable things about 5 her. Some of these are roaring reactions against meekness; some grow from impatience with her own physical frailty; but all are connected with pride, and typified by the clan motto her father has dinned into her "Gainsay who dare." Who does dare when Hagar rages? Her husband, Bram, and her second son, John, dare certainly, and in another way, Time itself. In 10 the memories of her men and in reminders of her mortality, Hagar's character is unfolded.

2   In fact, the novel, told from Hagar's point of view, develops very much as an unfolding. Layer on layer of irony, character and meaning are revealed in the succession of events that the present brings back to the old 15 lady's mind. The way in which present and past are brought together actually contributes to the irony of the characterization. Early in the novel, Hagar momentarily but consciously recognizes and refutes the idea that in aging she sometimes regrets her life: "Oh, my lost men. No, I will not

W. H. New "Life and Times: Laurence's *The Stone Angel*" from *Articulating West*. Reprinted by permission of Press Porcepic Ltd.

think of that." But she does think, does lament, does remember, and her 20
consciousness ceases to be always in control. The fact that she also rages
and, in a special way, comes to love as well, makes her more complex still.
3   There are several key phrases that help us to comprehend Hagar's
exploration of her struggle with life. When she contemplates the difference
between an event and its continued existence in the mind, she muses "how 25
small the town was, and how short a time it took to leave it, as we measure
time." How else can it be measured? we ask. And the novel considers this
question. Again, Hagar has dreamed of the perfect future: "To move to a
new place—that's the greatest excitement. For a while you believe you carry
nothing with you—." But when you come right down to it, Hagar doesn't 30
really want perfection. Or if she does, she wants it on her own terms: thus,
as when Troy, the young minister, comes to pay a duty call on her, she will
mentally or verbally lacerate a person who does not accept her reality:

> Even if heaven were real, and measured as Revelation says, so many
> cubits this way and that, how gimcrack a place it would be, crammed 35
> with its pavements of gold, its gates of pearl and topaz, like a gigantic
> chunk of costume jewelry. Saint John of Patmos can keep his sequined
> heaven, or share it with Mr. Troy, for all I care, and spend eternity in
> fingering the gems and telling each other gleefully they're worth a
> fortune.   40

However, even when she says this, she is concerned about her years—about
whether or not they were good ones, about what one should get for their
being "good," about their being "unfair," and about who or what is to
blame for the injustices of an often bitter and always mortal life. They are 45
the questions disturbing the old lady and us, if we think about them, for
they focus ultimately on the problem of human responsibility. How much
individuality and how much choice do we have in a world that is influenced
by "jests of God"? Hagar's answer lies again in raging against the night, and
in coming by this raging to an assertion of self and to a recognition of the 50
self she has asserted.

QUESTIONS

1. This selection from Professor New's essay is part of a larger argument—that
Laurence's *The Stone Angel* was, at the time New was writing (in 1967), her
best novel and a major contribution to Canadian literature. He is, in other
words, evaluating the novel's importance to the reader. At what point in this

selection does New state directly his evaluation of the novel? What sign-post *
does he use to indicate it?

2. Trace the argument by which New leads up to his evaluation and explain—
by analyzing its logic and organization—why you find the argument persuasive
or not persuasive.

3. In the previous selection Professor Jones treated the characters of *The Stone
Angel* for the most part as symbolic *. Does New do the same in discussing
Hagar Shipley here? If not, describe what he does do. Is she more vividly and
concretely presented here than she is by Jones? Do you think that you know
more about her by reading New's discussion?

4. Point out as many concrete * details and effective images * in this selection
as you can. Explain how these function in creating the view of Hagar that New
wants us to have. What do they reveal as well about the writer himself? Describe as precisely as you can how New's personality appears to differ from
Jones'. Which writer makes the stronger appeal to the reader? And why?

5. Explain how New's repeated references (direct and indirect) to *time* are
used to focus his discussion. Show how they are also related to his evaluation.

6. What point of view * is New employing? Does he use it consistently? Is it
the same as Jones'? Is it more or less effective in engaging the reader's interest?
Explain why.

7. The phrase "roaring reactions" (1. 6) is an example of alliteration *. How
many other examples can you find? Do they serve a useful purpose in New's
argument?

8. Is the question in line 9 rhetorical * or real? Is it the same kind of question
as is asked in line 27? Is the idea of "questioning" itself a theme in this selection? If so, how is it related to the final evaluation?

9. New states that there are "several key phrases" (1. 23) that help us understand the novel. Is it clear to the reader whether he means phrases from the
novel or phrases of his own?

10. Both New and Jones quote from the novel to support their respective
arguments. Can you say that one uses quotations more effectively than the
other? Or do they both use quotations in a manner suited to the style and
structure of their analyses?

11. New's sentences range in length from six to fifty-two words. Can you
argue, with examples, that this variation is intended to produce emphasis on
major points? Can you explain why the longest sentence (ll. 41-44) is effectively
positioned where it is?

12. Look at the sentence beginning in line 6 and note the repeated word
"some". In what other sentences does New repeat words in this way? Is there
anything significant about the location of these sentences in the selection?

13. Earlier in his essay, New has made a brief analogy * between Hagar's "rage"
and Dylan Thomas' use of the word in "Do Not Go Gentle into that Good

Night." Read Thomas' poem, and try to decide how much of the effectiveness of New's argument depends upon the reader's familiarity with that poem. If you were not familiar with it, did you find New persuasive nevertheless?

SUGGESTIONS FOR WRITING

1. If you have not read *The Stone Angel* explain, in a brief essay, which selection—Jones' or New's—most succeeded in making you want to read the book. If you found both writers about equally persuasive, then explain how both selections achieved their purpose despite their differences of style and approach.

2. If you have read *The Stone Angel*, write a brief essay in which you show, with examples from the novel and from the two critics, that one style is better suited to deal with the novel than is the other.

3. Choose the central character from a novel you know well, and describe and analyze this person in three or four paragraphs. Use effective repetition, concrete details, vivid images, and varied sentence lengths, and write your essay from the first-person plural point of view. Make your conclusion one in which, on the basis of your discussion of the character, you point to the value of the novel for its readers (including yourself).

From In Our Time

Ernest Hemingway (1898-1961) wrote short stories and novels whose style has influenced hundreds of writers. Much of his finest work was done in the twenties—novels such as *The Sun Also Rises* (1926), *A Farewell to Arms* (1929), and collections of short stories like *Men Without Women* (1927). The following selection is taken from another collection of stories, *In Our Time* (1925), most of which have to do with a young man's encounters with the suffering, evil, and emptiness of life shortly before and after World War I. Between each pair of stories is a brief, untitled narrative vignette or "snapshot" unrelated to the stories themselves, except in so far as each depicts a scene of violence or horror typical of our time. The following piece is one of those vignettes. Keep in mind that it is a total composition, complete within itself.

They shot the six cabinet ministers at half-past six in the morning against the wall of a hospital. There were pools of water in the courtyard. There were wet dead leaves on the paving of the courtyard. It rained hard. All the shutters of the hospital were nailed shut. One of the ministers was sick with typhoid. Two soldiers carried him down stairs and out into the rain. They tried to   5 hold him up against the wall but he sat down in a puddle of water. The other five stood very quietly against the wall. Finally the officer told the soldiers it was no good trying to make him stand up. When they fired the first volley he was sitting down in the water with his head on his knees.

QUESTIONS

1. This selection is about as simple as a style can be without appearing childish or child-like. At the same time this prose is highly sophisticated, and its impact upon the reader is powerful. What is its emotional effect?

Used by permission of Charles Scribner's Sons from *In Our Time* by Ernest Hemingway. Copyright 1925 Charles Scribner's Sons; renewal copyright 1953 Ernest Hemingway.

2. Count the number of sentences and the number of words in each sentence. What is the number of words in the shortest sentence? In the longest? What is the average number of words in Hemingway's sentences? How does this average compare with the average length of sentences in Champion, Shaw, Leacock, Lucas, Jones, and New?

3. What is Hemingway's most common sentence opener? How many of these does he use? What variations does he employ and how often?

4. Sentences 1, 2, and 3 have about the same construction and the same rhythm. Demonstrate this fact by analyzing the structure of each sentence. What is the effect upon the reader of treating an execution and the description of a court-yard in exactly the same tone, or seeming lack of tone?

5. The fourth sentence—three words of one syllable—is a variation in sentence length and paragraph rhythm. Ordinarily such a variation underscores an important point. Here, it laconically describes the weather rather than the execution. Why?

6. Observe how many sentences end with a prepositional phrase or a series of prepositional phrases. How do these constructions affect the rhythm of the paragraph? Do they tend to make the sentences emphatic or unemphatic? Do they help to make the whole paragraph strongly rhythmic? Why or why not? Is a strong sentence rhythm an advantage or a disadvantage in this selection? Explain.

7. Hemingway's last sentence might have been written: "When he was sitting down in the water with his head on his knees they fired the first volley." Why does this revision detract from Hemingway's stylistic strategy and purpose?

8. Hemingway uses no punctuation within his sentences. Where might he have used semicolons, commas, or dashes? Why is this prose better without such internal punctuation?

9. Note the number of repetitions in this selection. For example, the second sentence ends "in the courtyard"; the third sentence ends "of the courtyard." Identify seven or eight similar repetitions or echoes. In this passage at least, they seem to be an important feature of Hemingway's style. What do you think is their purpose or their effect on the reader?

10. Hemingway uses very few adjectives in this prose. Most of these are merely denotative: there are *six* cabinet ministers; "*Two* soldiers carried him down stairs . . ." and so on. In each sentence Hemingway seems merely to be telling us tonelessly and precisely who did what, where, and when. The one exception is the reference to "wet dead leaves" in line 3. *Wet* and *dead* are, of course, concrete and denotative, but they have connotations too. Why doesn't Hemingway apply connotative adjectives to the ministers about to be executed?

SUGGESTIONS FOR WRITING

1. Revise Hemingway's sketch using an aggregating style. Supply details, sentence patterns, and diction that will more directly and obviously elicit the horror of the scene.

2. Imitating the principles of style employed by Hemingway, describe a combat operation, a painful event, a disaster or catastrophe that you have witnessed or taken part in.

ARTHUR R. M. LOWER

That Humble Fellow, The Historian—
Some Reflections on Writing History

Arthur Lower, who was born in 1899, is widely regarded as one of the most
eminent social historians Canada has produced. He is the author of such important books as *Canadians in the Making* (1958), the first comprehensive
social history of Canada, and *Colony to Nation: A History of Canada* (1946),
one of the best one-volume histories of this country. Lower's *This Most Famous
Stream*, a study of liberalism, won the Governor General's Award for non-
fiction in 1954. His style has been termed conversational, yet the attentive
reader will see that, in spite of their lack of formality, Lower's sentences are
very carefully structured.

1   Can any good historical writing, in fact, be done which does not
have a considerable imaginative faculty behind it? Evidence must not be
imagined, that is, manufactured, but how far will one get in reconstructing
a past situation if he cannot put himself to some degree in other men's
shoes, see through other men's eyes, look into motives, discern the logic of 5
events and circumstances? It is dull history that merely proceeds rigorously
from footnote to footnote, useful history, no doubt, in a pedestrian way,
but "missing so much and so much."
2   That is another way of saying that between the writer and his
material a creative act must take place. I may illustrate what I have in 10
mind from one of the other arts, music. A piano stands in a room. When a
small child goes to it, he bangs at the keys and makes a noise. When a
pianist sits before the piano, he looks at the strange script of black dots
and other marks before him, puts his fingers on the keys and there comes
forth something ordered and measured. If it is a simple song, persons pre- 15
sent may easily learn to hum it, whistle it, sing it. More complex music

From *Journal of Canadian Studies*, Vol. 7, No. 1. Reprinted by permission of the
Journal of Canadian Studies and Arthur R. M. Lower.

takes more reproduction, but what has come forth seems to have an independent existence of its own. Something has occurred between the mechanical contraption, the piano, and the player. Something hanging there 20 between them in the air, as it were, independent of both of them once it has been made—a new "fact" (*factum*: something made, created). It will be said that something came out of the musician's mind or brain. Something did. Something also came out of his fingers, out of the notes of the music and out of the piano. Between this complex whole, whose com- 25 plexities I have only suggested, something has been *made* or, if you like, *created*. I will not push the figure back farther to the original composer of the music, for that is not necessary, though the composer might perhaps come into the analogy as God, the Creator, whose original act is being perceived and fulfilled by the secondary figures of musician and piano. The 30 figure I present, the player and the piano is adequate: it gives a good illustration of the situation of the historian and his material. Out of the complex, in this case historian and documents, as with the music, there comes a creative act, a new thing under the sun, the historical work. It is no doubt the same in all creative acts.
                                                                 35

3   Then there is constantly presenting itself to the historian that topic which of all topics fires the imagination, time. The historian is bound up with time, life is bound up with time. The years inexorably roll on: the historian must be able to feel their motion. He can draw on his own life-span, and note how its perspectives change as the years pass by. He can measure 40 his own life time against the passage of the generations. Through family memories he may reach back a century or two. And then he has to walk without a stick. How measure the centuries against one's own life, however long, or one's person-to-person memories, however far they stretch? How recapture the "atmosphere" of the long ago? Whatever the external 45 aids—documents, pictures, monuments—one finds himself trying to dream into it, that is, to imagine it. For the ordinary person the past is past, what's over is over and that's that. Of this the historian finds it hard to convince himself. Must all that busy, pulsing life be gone? May it not go on somehow as does the life of a city he has left? Silly, of course, but is the 50 dead past dead? Never quite to one whose business it is to bring it to life.

4   One day a few years ago, I sat looking out over the Straits of Dover, out over the course that Roman ships followed in the long-ago. It is supposed that a few triremes may have been maintained against the Saxon pirates in a near-by harbour long since destroyed by the sea. I closed my 55 eyes and tried to imagine what I might have seen eighteen hundred years ago. Opening them, far out at sea, I saw the sun glance on a patch of white. Roman trireme? Of course not: just the upper works of a tanker. So triremes and all that they imply had to be imagined. But what would one give for a "snatch" of incidental conversation among those Roman sailors, a "snatch" such as the novelist can hear on every street corner? No 60 tape-recorders in those days, alas! It may be that such mechanical devices will make historians-to-come less imaginative, not more. Will they be better historians?

5   The relentless march of time forces on one more than imaginative day-dreaming. Historian, archaeologist, anthropologist, geologist, physicist, 65 astronomer, all stand in a great chain, all exploring the unexplorable, so to speak, all pushing back the bounds of knowledge—of life! So the scholar or scientist who is not also a philosopher, whether formally so called or not, can never be in the front rank. Historian and philosopher, dealing with humanity and life, can not be far apart. And does not contemplation of 70 time lead into contemplation of time's nature, to the eternal verities, indeed? Is there not a direct chain between the here and the now and the origins of it all long ago (if it had origins!)?

QUESTIONS

1. Does Lower's argument convince you? Is it biased or one-sided? Does he dispel any of the objections that could be made, as, for example, to his generalization that "it is no doubt the same in all creative acts" (33-34)? How does he use some of the persuasive modes mentioned in an earlier section of this text, such as argument, satire, and eloquence?

2. One quite obvious fact about Lower's style is the mixture of long, fairly complex sentences and quite short ones. Choose two or three representative samples of each, analyze their structure, explain how they are logically a part of their context, and, finally, justify or condemn them as either long or short sentences.

3. One of the marks of a good stylist is that, even when he is dealing with a difficult topic (such as the writing of history), he does so in such a way that the reader is always aware of where he is in the essay. How does Lower do this? In trying to answer this question, consider especially the positioning of topic sentences, the nature and positioning of signposts *, the use of transitional words and phrases between and within paragraphs, the use of pointers *, and the repetition (of the same words or different ones) of the main topic or of paragraph topics.

4. Analyze Lower's sentence structures in paragraphs 1 and 5 with regard to the

following: average number of sentences in each paragraph, average number of words in each sentence, structure of each sentence (whether simple *, complex *, compound *, or compound-complex). Then do the same for paragraphs 1 and 3 of the essay by Pierre Champion, the other historian represented in this section on style. Finally, compare the sentence structures of these two historians, on the basis of your analyses.

5. Choose any three sentences from Lower's essay (each from a different paragraph) and analyze the use Lower makes of descriptive words and phrases, such as adjectives, adverbs, and modifying phrases. Do the same for the selection by Dylan Thomas (pp. 689–92). Your comparison of the two will then attempt to show what similarities and differences there are in the ways in which language is used by a historian and by a poet.

6. To what extent does Lower use examples to prove his argument that the historian needs imagination? What kinds of examples does he use? Do they seem to follow logically from his discussion, or do they appear somewhat far-fetched? Do they really illuminate the points he is trying to make?

7. Comment on Lower's use of questions by dealing with such points as these: How often does he use questions? Does he use rhetorical questions *? If so, what dramatic effects is he trying to achieve? Do his questions help to advance his argument? Does he ask questions which a university student can answer, or are they much too difficult?

8. Study Lower's use of interrupted movement *—for example, the expressions *in fact* (1), *that is* (3), *no doubt* (7), etc. Does he use such expressions often? In what ways? With what effects (if any)? Are all such expressions necessary, or could some of them be omitted without seriously affecting either the sentence or the argument?

9. What is Lower getting at in the parenthetical remark in the last line? Does this not seem to be a last-minute thought—an unfortunate one?

SUGGESTIONS FOR WRITING

1. Lower's main point is that the historian must have imagination. Your essay (600-800 words) will argue the obverse: i.e., that the imaginative artist (poet, novelist, painter, musician, etc.) must have a strong sense of the historical. You should not try to imitate Lower's style, but you should use some of his stylistic devices: the justifiable alternation of long and short sentences, rhetorical questions, and well-chosen examples.

2. Using the results you obtained in answering questions 2, 3, and 4, write two paragraphs (about 200 words each) in which you imitate Lower's style as closely as you can. Choose any topic you wish, provided that it has nothing to do with Lower's topic.

From Holiday Memory

Dylan Thomas (1914-53), one of the finest of modern British poets, also wrote stories, essays, and autobiographical sketches, which appeared in *Portrait of the Artist as a Young Dog* (1946) and *Quite Early One Morning* (1954), pieces collected by his publisher after Thomas's death. While some of these essays concern poets and writing poetry, others describe Thomas's childhood and adolescence in Swansea, Wales, where he was born and where he lived until 1934. The following excerpt from "Holiday Memory" reveals a poet's mastery of words and rhythm. It deserves to be read aloud more than once.

1   I remember the smell of sea and seaweed, wet flesh, wet hair, wet bathing-dresses, the warm smell as of a rabbity field after rain, the smell of pop and splashed sunshades and toffee, the stable-and-straw smell of hot, tossed, tumbled, dug and trodden sand, the swill-and-gaslamp smell of Saturday night, though the sun shone strong, from the bellying beer-tents, the 5 smell of the vinegar on shelled cockles, winkle-smell, shrimp-smell, the dripping-oily back-street winter-smell of chips in newspapers, the smell of ships from the sundazed docks around the corner of the sandhills, the smell of the known and paddled-in sea moving, full of the drowned and herrings, out and away and beyond and further still towards the antipodes that hung 10 their koala-bears and Maoris, kangaroos and boomerangs, upside down over the backs of the stars.

2   And the noise of pummelling Punch and Judy falling, and a clock tolling or telling no time in the tenantless town; now and again a bell from a lost tower or a train on the lines behind us clearing its throat, and always 15 the hopeless, ravenous swearing and pleading of the gulls, donkey-bray and hawker-cry, harmonicas and toy trumpets, shouting and laughing and singing, hooting of tugs and tramps, the clip of the chair-attendant's puncher, the

From Dylan Thomas, *Quite Early One Morning*. Reprinted by permission of David Higham Associates Limited, The Trustees for the Copyrights of the late Dylan Thomas.

motor-boat coughing in the bay, and the same hymn and washing of
the sea that was heard in the Bible.   20

3   "If it could only just, if it could only just," your lips said again and
again as you scooped, in the hob-hot sand, dungeons, garages, torture-cham-
bers, train tunnels, arsenals (hangars for zeppelins, witches' kitchens, vam-
pires' parlours, smugglers' cellars, trolls' grog-shops, sewers, under the ponderous and cracking castle, "If it could only just be like this for ever and   25
ever amen." August Monday all over the earth, from Mumbles where the
aunties grew like ladies on a seaside tree to brown, bear-hugging Henty-land
and the turtled Ballantyne Islands.

4   "Could donkeys go on the ice?"
       "Only if they got snowshoes."   30
       We snowshoed a meek, complaining donkey and galloped him off in
the wake of the ten-foot-tall and Atlas-muscled Mounties, rifled and pem-
micanned, who always, in the white Gold Rush wastes, got their black-
oathed-and-bearded Man.
       "Are there donkeys on desert islands?"   35
       "Only sort-of-donkeys."
       "What d'you mean, sort of donkeys?"
       "Native donkeys. They hunt things on them!"
       "Sort-of walruses and seals and things?"
       "Donkeys can't swim!"   40
       "These donkeys can. They swim like whales, they swim like any-
            thing, they swim like—"
       "Liar."
       "Liar yourself."

5   And two small boys fought fiercely and silently in the sand, rolling   45
together in a ball of legs and bottoms. Then they went and saw the pier-
rots, or bought vanilla ices.

6   Lolling or larriking that unsoiled, boiling beauty of a common day,
great gods with their braces over their vests sang, spat pips, puffed smoke
at wasps, gulped and ogled, forgot the rent, embraced, posed for the dicky   50
bird, were coarse, had rainbow-coloured arm-pits, winked, belched, blamed
the radishes, looked at Ilfracombe, played hymns on paper and comb,
peeled bananas, scratched, found seaweed in their panamas, blew up paper-
bags and banged them, wished for nothing. But over all the beautiful
beach I remember most the children playing, boys and girls tumbling, mov-   55
ing jewels, who might never be happy again. And "happy as a sandboy" is
true as the heat of the sun.

QUESTIONS

1. This sample of Dylan Thomas's prose is taken from the essay "Holiday Memory," a composite, no doubt, of many August holidays by the seaside near the author's native town of Swansea, Wales. As often happens, a sophisticated adult is writing of childhood and sees it partly through the eyes of a child and partly from the more mature point of view * of an adult. This double vision gives to Thomas's essay a specific tone *. Point out passages which suggest the child's view; others that reveal the adult's.

2. The first paragraph is a single sentence of about 130 words. Should it have been divided into two or three shorter sentences? Explain why you think it is, or is not, overloaded.

3. In the first paragraph what is the ratio of verbs to adjectives? Which carries most of the description?

4. How many adjectives in the first paragraph are single words; how many are compounds; and how many are participles *, either past or present?

5. Thomas's compound adjectives are especially striking. What are some of their advantages? Can you easily find one-word equivalents for those Thomas uses in the first paragraph? Do they have any disadvantages?

6. If for emphasis a writer repeats a single word in several sentences or throughout an entire paragraph, he is using a rhetorical figure called *tautotes*. Identify the tautotes in paragraph 1.

7. Find two examples of polysyndeton * in the first sentence of this selection.

8. Why does Thomas include the details in line 11? What do they tell us about the child?

9. How are the diction and sentence structure of paragraph 2 like those of paragraph 1? How do the two paragraphs differ?

10. What is unusual about the structure of the first sentence of paragraph 3?

11. How does this revision alter the emphasis and movement of Thomas's sentence?

> *Revision:* I remember the noise as Punch pummelled Judy and both fell. A clock struck and told no time in the empty town; now and then a bell from a lost tower or a train on the lines cleared its throat. Hopeless, ravenous gulls pleaded and swore. Donkeys brayed and hawkers cried.
>
> *Thomas:* "And the noise of pummelling Punch and Judy falling, and a clock tolling or telling no time in the tenantless town; now and again a bell from a lost tower or a train on the lines behind us clearing its throat, and always the hopeless, ravenous swearing and pleading of the gulls, donkey-bray and hawker-cry. . . ." (13-17)

12. How many abstract * words can you find in this selection? How many rare words and technical terms? Are many of Thomas's words derived from Latin? Do many of his words, or only a few of them, refer to things intrinsically beautiful?

13. Dylan Thomas was a famous poet, and he has a poet's ear for language, exploiting such qualities of sound as onomatopoeia, alliteration *, assonance *, and consonance *. Point out examples of each of these.

14. Thomas is also fond of metaphor *, simile *, personification *, and puns, all of which are devices more common in poetry, though certainly found also in prose. Find instances of these.

15. Finally, he uses an occasional adjective in the post position * (that is, placed after the noun instead of before it) and employs grammatical shift now and then (the use of a word which is normally one part of speech to function as another, as a verb acting as a noun). Find some examples.

SUGGESTIONS FOR WRITING

1. Compare the prose styles of Harry Boyle's "Tobogganing" and the passage from "Holiday Memory," discussing both their similarities and their differences.

2. It has been claimed that "style is the man"; that is, that style is a manifestation of the writer's essential personality. Describe the personality of Dylan Thomas as it is reflected through his prose.

3. Write about some group activity that you have enjoyed. Try to be as concrete in your imagery as Thomas and to use a wide range of verbal effects (but don't fall into the bad habit of repeating any of these so much that it becomes a mannerism).

From "City of the End of Things"

Northrop Frye was born in Sherbrooke, Quebec in 1912. After completing his education at the Universities of Toronto and Oxford, Frye joined the department of English at the University of Toronto, where he taught for many years. As a result of such books as *Fearful Symmetry: A Study of William Blake* (1947), *Anatomy of Criticism* (1957), *The Well-Tempered Critic* (1963), *The Secular Scripture: A Study of the Structure of Romance* (1976), *Creation and Recreation* (1980), and *The Great Code* (1982), as well as several other works on English, Canadian, and American literature and on the nature and function of literary criticism, Frye has established a reputation as one of the principal literary critics of the twentieth century in the Western world (see p. 434). He is also a frequent and perceptive commentator on the social and cultural issues of our time, as the following selection shows.

1   Culturally, the primary fact about the modern world, or at least about our "Western" and "democratic" part of it, is that it is probably the first civilization in history that has attempted to study itself objectively, to become aware of the presuppositions underlying its behaviour, to understand its relation to previous history and to see whether its future could in 5 some measure be controlled by its own will. This self-consciousness has created a sharp cultural dialectic in society, an intellectual antagonism between two mental attitudes. On one side are those who struggle for an active and conscious relation to their time, who study what is happening in the world, survey the conditions of life that seem most likely to occur, and 10 try to acquire some sense of what can be done to build up from those conditions a way of life that is at least self-respecting. On the other side are those who adopt a passive and negative attitude, responding to the daily news and similar stimuli, aware of what is going on but making no effort to understand either the underlying causes or the future possibilities. The 15 theatre of this conflict in attitudes is formed by the creative and the com-

From "City of the End of Things" in *The Modern Century* by Northrop Frye. Reprinted by permission of the publisher, Oxford University Press.

693

municating arts. The creative arts are almost entirely on the active side: they mean nothing, or infinitely less, to a passive response. The subject-matter of contemporary literature being its own time, the passive and un-critical attitude is seen as its most dangerous enemy. Many aspects of con- 20 temporary literature—its ironic tone, its emphasis on anxiety and absurdity, its queasy apocalyptic forebodings—derive from this situation.

2   The communicating arts, including the so-called mass media, are a mixture of things. Some of them are arts in their own right, like the film. Some are or include different techniques of presenting the arts we already 25 have, like television. Some are not arts, but present analogies to techniques in the arts which the arts may enrich themselves by employing, as the newspaper may influence collage in painting or the field theory of com-position in poetry. Some are applied arts, where the appeal is no longer disinterested, as it normally is in the creative arts proper. Thus propaganda 30 is an interested use of the literary techniques of rhetoric. As usual, there are deficiencies in vocabulary: there are no words that really convey the in-tellectual and moral contrast of the active and passive attitudes to culture. The phrase "mass culture" conveys emotional overtones of passivity: it sug-gests someone eating peanuts at a baseball game, and thereby contrasting 35 himself to someone eating canapés at the opening of a sculpture exhibition. The trouble with this picture is that the former is probably part of a better educated audience, in the sense that he is likely to know more about base-ball than his counterpart knows about sculpture. Hence his attitude to his chosen area of culture may well be the more active of the two. And just as 40 there can be an active response to mass culture, so there can be passive responses to the highbrow arts. These range from "Why can't the artist make his work mean something to the ordinary man?" to the significant syntax of the student's question: "Why is this considered a good poem?" The words advertising and propaganda come closest to suggesting a com- 45 munication deliberately imposed and passively received. They represent respectively the communicating interests of the two major areas of society, the economic and the political. Recently these two conceptions have begun to merge into the single category of "public relations."

3   One very obvious feature of our age is the speeding up of process: 50 it is an age of revolution and metamorphosis, where one lives through changes that formerly took centuries in a matter of a few years. In a world where dynasties rise and fall at much the same rate as women's hemlines, the dynasty and the hemline look much alike in importance, and get much the same amount of featuring in the news. Thus the progression of events 55

is two-dimensional, a child's drawing reflecting an eye that observes without seeing depth, and even the effort to see depth has still to deal with the whole surface. Some new groupings result: for example, what used to be called the trivial or ephemeral takes on a function of *symbolizing* the significant. A new art of divination or augury has developed, in which the 60 underlying trends of the contemporary world are interpreted by vogues and fashions in dress, speech or entertainment. Thus if there appears a vogue for white lipstick among certain groups of young women, that may represent a new impersonality in sexual relationship, a parody of white supremacy, the dramatization of a death-wish, or the social projection of the clown 65 archetype. Any number may play, but the game is a somewhat self-defeating one, without much power of sustaining its own interest. For even the effort to identify something in the passing show has the effect of dating it, as whatever is sufficiently formed to be recognized has already receded into the past.   70

4   It is not surprising if some people should be frustrated by the effort to keep riding up and down the manic-depressive roller-coaster of fashion, of what's in and what's out, what is u and what non-u, what is hip and what is square, what is corny and what is camp. There are perhaps not as many of these unhappy people as our newspapers and magazines suggest 75 there are: in any case, what is important is not this group, if it exists, but the general sense, in our society, of the panic of change. The variety of things that occur in the world, combined with the relentless continuity of their appearance day after day, impress us with the sense of a process going by a little too fast for our minds to focus on anything in it.   80

QUESTIONS

1. Any reader of this selection is likely to be impressed by the way in which Frye writes with authority about the problems of culture and community in our time. What aspects of his style produce this authoritative tone *? Is it authoritative without being consistently formal and unbending? Does Frye also seem to possess a sense of humor? After answering these questions, describe the effect that the author's tone has on you. Is it persuasive, or not?

2. The first part of Frye's first sentence begins with a sweeping generalization about "the modern world," a generalization which Frye promptly modifies twice. First, show how Frye restricts his generalization, and then describe how you react to such a generalized introduction. Do you refuse to accept it unless it is proven? Does Frye prove it, or does he expect you to grant him his main

assumption at the outset? Remember, all arguments necessarily rest upon assumptions.

3. Professor Frye is here discussing, in a few pages, important contemporary cultural issues. Is his discussion presented largely in terms of abstractions *, or does he also use concrete * details that bring home to us the relevance of what he is saying? Examine the selection closely, in order to get some sense of the ratio of abstract words to concrete details.

4. How successfully does Frye guide his reader by means of the organization of his argument? Can you point to examples of organizing phrases, repeated key words, and logical pointers *?

5. Justify, or condemn, Frye's metaphor "the theatre of this conflict in attitudes" (15-16). Does he explain what he means, or does he leave this up to the reader? If your answer is the former, explain his meaning. If the latter, comment on whether Frye is expecting too much from his reader.

6. Explain in your own words the meaning of "its queasy apocalyptic forebodings" (22), "an interested use" (31), and "what is corny and what is camp" (74).

7. Comment on Frye's diction, considering such questions as these: does he use many difficult words, or words you have never seen before? Does he use slang, or colloquialisms *? If so, is his use of such words appropriate, or does it seem exaggerated, striving for effect? Does he use mainly Anglo-Saxon words or Latinate ones? Are his figures of speech clear? Are they appropriate to his meaning, or do they seem somewhat far-fetched?

8. What does Frye mean by "the significant syntax of the student's question" (43-44)? How could the student's question be rephrased so that its syntax would not be "significant"?

9. Point out the instances where Frye uses irony *, comic similes, and exaggeration. What effect do these have on the way we respond to his argument? Do you think Frye's humor is sometimes too subtle for most readers? Did you have to look up *divination* and *augury* to see that Frye's tongue was in his cheek in the fifth sentence of paragraph 3?

10. Of the thirty-four sentences in this selection, only ten have fewer than twenty words, and none of the shorter sentences occur in the last two paragraphs. After you have identified these shorter sentences, examine what part they play in Frye's argument, and then draw what conclusions you can. For example, does the fact that the sentence in ll. 15-17 is a form of organizing sentence * account for its brevity? Is the first sentence in paragraph 2 relatively short because it is a topic sentence?

11. Although the sentences are for the most part relatively long, are they varied in their structure? For example, compare the structure of the first sentence of paragraph 1 with the structures of sentences 2-5 of paragraph 2. Compare the structure of sentence three of paragraph 1 with that of sentence four

in the same paragraph. Compare the structures of the first two sentences of paragraph 3.

SUGGESTIONS FOR WRITING

1. In an essay of four or five paragraphs closely compare Frye's style with that of a newspaper editorial or popular magazine article on the subject of culture (or a specific aspect of it, such as film, literature, painting, theatre). Analyze the differences in style; describe the kind of audience each style assumes; and explain which style is more capable of dealing with such a complex subject.

2. Compare the style used by Frye to discuss modern culture in a comprehensive way with the style used by George F. Will (pp. 235-9) to describe one specific feature of modern culture.

Glossary

This glossary offers brief definitions of those grammatical and rhetorical terms that are used in the questions. The first time such a term appears in any group of questions, it is marked with an asterisk, a signal that it appears in the Glossary.

ABSOLUTE CONSTRUCTION: A word or phrase grammatically unrelated to any one part of a sentence is absolute. "The candle stood on the counter, *its flame solemnly wagging in a draught;* and by that inconsiderable movement the whole room was filled with noiseless bustle and kept heaving like a sea; *the tall shadows nodding, the gross blots of darkness swelling and dwindling as with respiration, the faces of the portraits and the china gods changing and wavering like images in water.*" The italicized constructions are neither subjects, verbs, objects, nor modifiers of any one word in the main clauses. Independent of the grammatical structure of these clauses, each loosely modifies the whole statement.

The most common kind of absolute is the one illustrated above: the NOMINATIVE ABSOLUTE (a noun plus a participial phrase). It is used to show cause and effect: *"The search having failed,* the men returned to camp" and also attendant circumstances: "She fled down the stairs, *her hair streaming behind her."*

ABSTRACT, ABSTRACTION: A word or phrase that refers to ideas, relationships, generalities is abstract: e.g. *truth, justice, democracy, realism, interdependent.* Unlike concrete words, which name specific things, abstractions make little or no appeal to the senses; they are qualities, characteristics, or essences shared by a large class of things. Not all abstractions, however, are equally general in meaning. The word *man,* for example, is more specific than *organism.* But *man* seems quite abstract when set beside "a sturdy, corpulent old man, with a three-cornered hat, red waistcoat, leather breeches, and a stout oaken cudgel." The more general the meaning of any given word the more abstract it tends to be.

Abstractions must be used with caution. They tempt the writer to speak in hazy generalities, to forget that good writing is specific. The writer

698

cannot avoid abstract words, especially in exposition, but he should anchor his thoughts as firmly as possible in concrete reality. The number of abstract words in any composition of course will depend upon the writer's subject and purpose: the philosopher discussing the nature of being will use more abstract words than a traveler describing the ruins of Rome. Wherever possible abstract words should be avoided. When the key words in any essay are abstractions, they should be defined and illustrated at the beginning. See CONCRETE.

ADJECTIVES IN POST POSITION: Adjectives placed after their nouns instead of before: "The blue noonday sky, *cloudless*, has lost its old look of immensity." (Lewis Thomas) "The national states are not physical groups; they are social symbols, *profound* and *terrible*." (Susan K. Langer) Such adjectives draw our attention and hence are emphatic.

ALLITERATION: The repetition in successive words of the same initial consonant sound or of any vowel sound is alliteration. Most often the sound in the first syllable is repeated: "The majestic, the magnificent Mississippi." Alliteration should be used only when the writer makes a strong emotional response to his subject; it is usually out of place in matter-of-fact exposition. But even in emotive writing alliteration must be used rarely and with extreme caution. Excessive alliteration is offensive. The effect of successful alliteration is beauty of sound and emphasis.

ALLUSION: An allusion is a reference to a generally familiar person, place, or thing, whether real or legendary: Queen Elizabeth, Cleopatra, Apollo, Adam, Gabriel Dumont, Tom Sawyer, Montreal, the Garden of Eden, the C.N. Tower, the Great Pyramid, the shield of Achilles. Most allusions are drawn from history, geography, the Bible, mythology, and literature. One value of allusions is their economy; they allow the writer to evoke in one or two words an atmosphere, a whole story, a whole period of history.

AMBIGUITY, AMBIGUOUS: When a word or passage can be understood in either of two ways, it is ambiguous. (More loosely, the term applies even when three or more interpretations are possible.) Unintentional ambiguity is usually a fault, as in: "*He forgot his book on the piano*" where it is not clear whether the book was about the piano or was left lying on top of a piano. Sometimes, however, ambiguity is a deliberate strategy, either as a kind of humor or irony or as a way of suggesting the complexities and uncertainties of experience.

ANAPHORA: The repetition of a word, or group of words, at the beginning of successive clauses, sentences, or lines of poetry. Like most forms of deliberate repetition it is emphatic; it has the secondary effect of aiding the writer's coherence or flow. In the following passage Loren Eiseley is scolding modern man for his resistance to fact in his political and social thinking: "*We are always more willing* to accept mechanical changes in an automobile than to revise, or even to examine our racial prejudices, to use one painful example. *We are more willing* to swallow a pill that we hope will relax our tensions than to make the sustained conscious effort necessary to alter our daily living habits." [Italics ours.—Eds.]

ANTITHESIS, ANTITHETICAL: A balancing of two opposite or contrasting words, phrases, clauses, paragraphs, or even larger units of writing. Antithesis refers most often, however, to the balancing of opposites in independent clauses within a sentence or in two adjacent sentences. Sir William Osler, for example, writes: "The quest for righteousness is Oriental, the quest for knowledge, Occidental." Frequently, as here, the second clause is elliptical, the verb being represented by a comma. Mark Twain makes dependent clauses antithetical: "Good breeding consists in concealing how much we think of ourselves and how little we think of the other person." Samuel Butler creates antithesis in two short sentences: "God is Love, I dare say. But what a mischievous devil Love is." Antitheses are emphatic, often witty, and usually memorable. If not overused, they are effective in development by contrast.

APPOSITIVE: A noun that stands after another noun and repeats the meaning of the first is an appositive: "Francis Bacon, the youngest *son* of Sir Nicholas, was born at York House, his father's *residence* in the Strand, on the twenty-second of January 1561." Here *son* repeats and further identifies *Francis Bacon* just as *residence* repeats and further identifies *York House*. In each instance the second noun is said to be in apposition with the first. The appositive is in effect an abbreviated clause in place of "who was the youngest son of Sir Nicholas" and "which was his father's residence in the Strand."

ASSONANCE: The repetition of internal vowel sounds in closely following words is called assonance: "a d*ee*p gr*ee*n str*ea*m." The same warnings that apply to alliteration also apply to assonance. See ALLITERATION.

ASYNDETON: The use of commas to separate members of a compound construction, most often a series of words. Rather than A, B, and C asyndeton employs A, B, C, which gives equal emphasis to each member of the series instead of placing slightly more stress on the last member, as in A, B, and C. Asyndeton speeds up the sentence: "Drays, carts, men, boys, all go hurrying to a common center, the wharf." (Mark Twain) See POLYSYNDETON.

BALANCE, BALANCED CONSTRUCTION, BALANCED SENTENCE: A balanced construction or sentence contains two distinct halves or parts, each of about the same length and importance. Similar constructions appear in the same place in each half and balance one another: "Our heritage of Greek literature and art is priceless, the example of Greek life possesses for us not the slightest value"; "There's never time to do it right, but there's always time to do it over."

CHIASMUS: A repetition and arrangement of two key terms in a sentence, forming the pattern A B B A: "We should eat to live, not live to eat." Chiasmus appears in proverbs and aphorisms, being unusual, emphatic, and easily remembered. G. K. Chesterton uses chiasmus as a kind of summary and punch line: "If the Superman may possibly be a thief, you can bet your boots that the next thief will be a Superman."

CLAUSE: A clause is a grammatically related group of words containing a subject and a predicate. The two principal kinds are *main* (or *independent*) and *dependent*. A main clause (if taken out of the sentence in which it is found) can stand by itself as a complete sentence: "From the beginnings of civilization until very recently, *women in most societies were literally the property of their husbands and fathers.*" (Ellen Willis) The italicized main clause here could be used by itself as a whole sentence.

A dependent clause (if taken out of the sentence in which it is found) cannot stand alone as a complete sentence: "*When the Liberal government of Premier Ross Thatcher cut off all welfare for 'employables,'* the economy of the town collapsed." (Charles K. Long) The italicized dependent clause here cannot act by itself as a whole sentence; it needs a main clause to complete its meaning. Note that dependent clauses (also called subordinate clauses) are introduced by words that make them subordinate. Thus, omitting "when" (the subordinating word) from the example would leave "The Liberal government of Premier Ross Thatcher cut off all welfare for 'employables' "—now a main (or independent) clause.

Dependent clauses are of three kinds: noun clauses, which have the same functions in a sentence as nouns (subjects, objects, complements); adjective clauses, which modify nouns, pronouns, or groups of words acting as nouns or pronouns; and adverb clauses, which modify verbs, adjectives, adverbs, clauses, or even entire sentences.

For more detailed information, students should consult a standard writing handbook.

CLOSING BY RETURN: To end a long paragraph or one section of an essay or an entire composition, the writer sometimes returns to an image, an idea, or a statement that occurs in the beginning. This completed cycle, or closing by return, signals to the reader that the unit of writing is done. See, for instance, the first and last sentences in the introductory paragraph of Lester Pearson's "The Implications of a Free Society."

COLLOCATION: Generally "collocation" means the arrangement of words in a sentence. In linguistics it is a technical term signifying the probability of a word appearing in the context of other specific words. Thus since "oink" is often found in the same context as "pig," we say that "oink" collocates with "pig"; but it does not collocate with, say, "elephant." A good writer acquires a feel for collocation and is careful about violating the probabilities of word occurrence. As a feature of style unusual collocations may be a fault or a virtue. They are faulty when they are the result of ignorance or carelessness and violate our expectancies to no purpose. Probably, for instance, it would be awkward to write "the duchess grinned" because a duchess "smiles"; she does not "grin." On the other hand, an unusual word may be very effective. "Apoplectic," for example, collocates with "man" but not with "flower"; yet when the Scottish poet Hugh MacDiarmid writes of "apoplectic peonies," it is, while an unusual collocation, a singularly apt one, evoking a sharp visual image of the bright and bursting red of the flower.

COLLOQUIALISM, COLLOQUIAL: A colloquial expression (or colloquialism) is language which occurs more often in speech than in writing: "He revered the dignity of her face and the quiet beauty of her smile; in sum, he thought that she was pretty cute." The last clause here is colloquial; it is obviously inappropriate in this context. The same sort of error occurs here: "After having committed a succession of grisly murders, he was thrown into the slammer for life."

Colloquialisms can give writing something of the flavor of talk, making it more informal and more entertaining. They must, however, be appropriate to the context.

COMPLEX SENTENCE: A sentence containing one independent clause and at least one dependent clause: "Fifty years ago, when all type was set by hand, the labor of several men was required to print, fold, and arrange in piles the signatures of a book." (Carl Becker)

COMPOUND SENTENCE: Two or more independent clauses joined by one or more co-ordinate conjunctions: "General Custer could fight all right, but there was a great deal of question about his competence as a commander." (Ralph K. Andrist)

CONCRETE: Words or phrases that name specific things as opposed to generalities are concrete: e.g. *coarse sandpaper, a rotten orange, a blue silk gown with four flounces, dirty snow, the buzzing of yellow bees.* It is not quite accurate to say that concrete words make a direct appeal to one or more of the five senses and abstractions do not. Some words, like *chair,* are at once both concrete and abstract. The word *chair* is a general term that names a large class of objects; yet *chair* brings to mind a clearer mental image than *furniture,* and it is more specific. However, *chair* is not as concrete as "the battered old Windsor chair in my grandmother's attic," which identifies a single object that really exists. Words move toward the concrete as they re-create actual, specific things. For most purposes, we can define concrete words as those that make us touch, smell, taste, hear, and see. Since, like good writing, concrete words are definite and specific, they are usually preferable to abstractions. See ABSTRACT.

CONJUNCTIVE ADVERB: A conjunctive adverb functions as both adverb and as conjunction. As adverb, it answers the questions in what manner, under what conditions; it signifies the logical relationships like addition, contrast or contradiction, cause and effect. As conjunction, it co-ordinates two independent clauses. It is almost always preceded by a semicolon. English is particularly rich in conjunctive adverbs, among the most common being *therefore, while, however, nevertheless, moreover, consequently*: "There is a standing order for fifty luncheons at the inn; while they eat the Leader lectures them through a megaphone." (Nancy Mitford)

CONNECTIVES: Any word or phrase that signifies a relationship between two words, phrases, clauses, sentences, or paragraphs can be called a connective. Thus, the term encompasses parts of speech like prepositions, pronouns, conjunctions, and conjunctive adverbs in addition to connective phrases like *of course, for example, in fine, to be sure*. Most beginning writers need to build their active vocabulary of connective words and phrases, for although it is possible to overuse them, the student writer seldom uses them enough. Connectives express, among others, such ideas as (1) addition (*and, moreover, furthermore, in addition*); (2) contrast or contradiction (*but, yet, in contrast, however*); (3) cause and effect (*so, therefore, for this reason*); (4) disjunction and division (*some . . . others, either . . . or*); (5) conclusion (*finally, at last, ultimately*). These are only a few of the great number of connectives and only a few of the logical notions they can express. Connectives deserve the student's closest attention.

CONNOTATION: The connotation of a word is not the thing or idea the word stands for, but the attitudes, feelings, and emotions aroused by the word. Connotations tend to be favorable or unfavorable. Thus *village* and *hick town* both refer to a small settlement. *Village* is favorable, or at least neutral, in its connotations, but *hick town* suggests the writer's scorn or contempt. The denotation of a word refers only to the thing the word represents, stripped of any emotional associations the word might carry. The denotation of both *village* and *hick town* is the same; both identify a small community.

CONSONANCE: In verse, consonance is a kind of rhyme in which the same consonant follows different vowel sounds: for example, the rhyme of *late* and *light*. In prose, the term generally refers to a harmonious repetition of internal consonant sounds as in the phrase "a pa*l*e go*l*d c*l*oud."

CO-ORDINATE CLAUSES: Two independent clauses of grammatically equal importance joined together are said to be co-ordinate. They are linked either by a semicolon or by one of the co-ordinate conjunctions—*and, but, or, nor, for*. See SUBORDINATE CLAUSES.

CUMULATIVE SENTENCE: A cumulative sentence is an extended variety of the LOOSE sentence. Often used in description, the cumulative sentence begins with a general statement which it then expands in a series of particulars, as in this description of a ward in a state mental hospital: "The geriatric section is always the most unattractive, poorly lighted, no brightness, no pictures, no laughter. Just long green corridors, lined by doors; white-gowned nurses moving silently, expressionless; large wards with beds filling the room, allowing no space for anything." (Sharon R. Curtin) See LOOSE SENTENCE, PERIODIC SENTENCE.

DEPENDENT CLAUSE: See CLAUSE.

ELLIPSIS: This is the omission of words necessary to the syntax of a sentence but not to its sense, as in "He is taller than I," where the words "am tall" are understood but not expressed. Ellipses often contribute concision and emphasis to one's style.

ENTHYMEME: An enthymeme is an abbreviated syllogism in which one of the premises is less than fully stated or else only implied. Consider, for example, the following syllogism:

> All men are mortal.
> Socrates is a man.
> Therefore Socrates is mortal.

As an enthymeme this syllogism might appear in some such form as this: "Being human Socrates is mortal." Needless to say, one seldom encounters a full-blown syllogism in most argument. Yet enthymemes can be expanded into syllogisms in order to test their validity.

ETYMOLOGY: The derivation or origin of a word, whatever its source—a person, a place, a thing, a word from another language—is called its etymology: *telescope* . . .[NL. *telescopium* fr. Gr. *tēleskopos*, viewing afar, farseeing, fr. *tēle*, far, far off + *skopos*, a watcher.] Some dictionaries list etymologies in brackets just before the definition. Etymologies often help the writer to understand the first or root meaning of a word, from which any further meanings have been derived. Knowing an etymology helps the writer to remember a word and to use it accurately.

FIGURE OF SPEECH, FIGURATIVE, FIGURATIVELY: Any use of language for stylistic effect other than the plain, normal, straightforward manner of writing or speaking is called figurative. Some of the common figures (see this glossary) are metaphor, simile, personification, alliteration, assonance, irony, metonymy.

FLOW: The continuity, or coherence, among the sentences of a paragraph. Flow is created (1) by repeating a key word or its synonym in successive sentences; (2) by using logical connectives; (3) by using a pronoun whose antecedent is in the preceding sentence; (4) by using identical or similar grammatical constructions at the beginning of successive sentences. The following illustrates all of these techniques: "One never forgets Masefield's face. It is not the face of a young man, for it is lined and grave. And yet it is not the face of an old man, for youth is still in the bright eyes. Its dominant quality is humility." (Beverley Nichols)

FRAGMENT: Conventionally defined, a sentence is a grammatically independent statement containing a subject and a finite verb. Any construction punctuated as a sentence but not conforming to this definition is a fragment: e.g. *Men who live in Vancouver. Men living in Vancouver. When we visited Vancouver.* Generally fragments are a serious fault; wisely employed, they may prove more emphatic or realistic than grammatically complete sentences: e.g., "I have another Sicilian memory that will not soon fade. *The waiter."* It is worth noting, however, that a fragment such as this is deliberate effect of style, not, as is so often the case in student essays, the accident of carelessness or ignorance. Even such successful fragments quickly become an awkward mannerism if used very often. Students are well advised to leave fragments alone, or if they wish to use one now and again to ask their instructor's advice.

FRAMING WORDS: To separate clearly and to introduce the several divisions of a subject or thought, the writer often uses framing words: *First, Second, Third; First, Next, Last; The most significant effect, A less important effect,* and so on. These usually occur in a paragraph introduced by an organizing sentence. See ORGANIZING SENTENCE.

FREIGHT-TRAIN SENTENCE: A freight-train sentence consists of three or more independent clauses, usually relatively short and joined either by coordinating conjunctions (commonly *and*) or by semicolons without conjunctions: "It was a hot day and the sky was very bright and blue and the road was white and dusty." (Ernest Hemingway)

GERUND: See PARTICIPLE.

IMAGE, IMAGERY: At its simplest an image is a picture made with words, although images also may appeal to touch, smell, hearing, and taste. In this sense, "imagery" refers to an author's use of specific images. But "imagery" is also often used in a much broader sense to refer to the use an author makes of figures of speech of any kind. Description and narration make frequent use of images, but imagery appears in exposition as well. See CONCRETE.

INDEPENDENT CLAUSE: See CLAUSE.

INTERRUPTED MOVEMENT: The normal word order of the English sentence is subject, verb, object (or complement). Normally, short modifiers like adjectives, adverbs, or prepositional phrases may stand between subject and verb or between a verb and its object. Such normal word order may be called straightforward movement. But to introduce a clause or an absolute word or phrase between subject and verb or between a verb (or verbal) and its object creates interrupted movement: "The Renaissance, as we have seen, has not yet reached Northern Europe." Here the clause *as we have seen* interrupts the normal order. Interrupted movement is an important variation of normal sentence structure, but it is more at home in a relatively formal style than in very informal writing.

INVERSION, INVERTED WORD ORDER: Any variation of the normal order of subject, verb, object (complement) is inversion. In some sentences the object stands first: "That story I did not believe." Occasionally a verb appears before the subject: "In the far corner of the room sat a very old man." Such inversions are emphatic, but like all variations of the normal their emphasis depends upon their rarity.

IRONY, IRONIC, IRONICALLY: When the writer uses words to mean something different from what they seem to say on the surface, he is ironic. The simplest form of irony means the reverse of what it says. Thus a terrible stench may be called a perfume; a stupid man a genius. Yet irony may range from a complete reversal of meaning to a subtle qualification of the surface meaning. Irony surprises and makes its point with the greatest emphasis because it forces us to contemplate two incongruous things. Most often a device of satire and persuasion, irony appears in all kinds of prose except the driest kind of exposition.

LOOSE SENTENCE: The loose sentence begins with the main idea, which is then followed by explanation, details, and modifiers: "The mountain climber must use his head first, and only then his rope, ice-axe, and pitons." The word "loose" has no bad connotations here but simply refers to a more or less "natural" sentence order, as opposed to the periodic sentence, in which elements are reversed. See CUMULATIVE SENTENCE, PERIODIC SENTENCE.

METAPHOR: A metaphor is an implied comparison between two things seemingly quite different: "All the world's a stage, / And all the men and women merely players." Or to take an example from prose: "Man's imagination is limited by the horizon of his experience." Since one term of the metaphor is usually commonplace and concrete, the metaphor not only makes writing more vivid, it may help the writer to make his point clearly. Metaphors make the abstract, concrete; the elusive, definite; the unfamiliar, familiar.

METONYMY: The figure of speech called metonymy substitutes something closely associated with a thing for the thing itself. We may speak of Shakespeare to mean his works; we speak of seeing three sails on the horizon to mean three ships, of the Crown to mean the British monarch.

NEGATIVE-POSITIVE RESTATEMENT: A type of emphasis in which a statement of what is not the case is followed by an assertion of what is: "They did not leave because they were tired; they left because they were frustrated and angry."

NOMINATIVE ABSOLUTE: See ABSOLUTE.

ORGANIZING SENTENCE: Standing at the beginning of a paragraph or of a major section of an essay or at the beginning of the composition, an organizing sentence indicates the subject to be treated, how it is to be divided, and into how many parts the division falls: "There were four underlying causes of the recession of 1984."

PARALLEL, PARALLELISM, PARALLEL CONSTRUCTION: Constructions are parallel when two or more words, phrases, or clauses of the same grammatical rank are related in the same way to the same word or words. Thus two or more subjects of the same verb are parallel; two or more verbs with the same subject are parallel; two or more adverbial clauses modifying the same verb are parallel; and so on. In the following sentence Rachel Carson is describing the face of the sea:

```
Crossed                            by   colors,
                                        lights,
                                   and  moving shadows,

sparkling
mysterious                    in the sun,
                              in the twilight,
                              its aspects
                    and       its moods
                              vary hour by hour.
```

Here the writer uses three parallel adjectives (two are participles) to modify the same parallel subjects *aspects* and *moods*. Each adjective is modified by a prepositional phrase, the first with three parallel objects.

In the eighteenth century many writers often strove for a more involved parallelism combined with balance. In the following example, Samuel Johnson balances a series of parallel independent clauses in the first half of the sentence against parallel dependent clauses in the second half. This already complex pattern he further complicates by parallel constructions within the dependent clauses:

```
. . . much of my life      has been lost under the pressures of disease;
        much               has been trifled away;
and     much               has always been spent in provision for the day
                               that was passing over me;
                                               useless
        but I shall not think my employment useless
                                      or    ignoble

        if by my assistance       foreign nations,
                          and      distant ages,
              gain access to the propagators of knowledge,
```

and   understand the teachers of truth;

if my labours   afford light to the repositories of science,

      and   add celebrity

                to Bacon,

                to Hooker,

                to Milton,

     and   to Boyle.

This elaborate architecture has all but disappeared from even the most formal writing. Yet parallelism of a much simpler kind appears often in both formal and informal writing. In skillful hands it is an interesting variation of the normal sentence pattern, allowing the writer to compress many ideas into a small space. Parallelism may be used to sustain a mood or to suggest rapid action, as it does in this description of a boxing match by A. J. Liebling:

Instead of   flicking,

            moving around,

 and so   piling up enough unhurting points to goad Johnson into

            some possible late activity,

he was reconnoitering in close, looking the challenger over as if he had never seen him before.

PARTICIPLE, PARTICIPIAL: A participle is a form of the verb. There are several types, but the most frequently used are the present active participle (for example, *exciting*) and the past active (*excited*). Participles function in verb phrases: "The people *were excited* by the news"; and also as modifiers: "An *exciting* trip to Paris," "The *excited* crowd rushed to the scene," or "*Excited*, the crowd rushed to the scene."

Participial phrases are word groups built around participles; as modifiers they are an efficient way of working additional information into a sentence.

The GERUND is the participle used as a noun. Usually it is the present participle which is used in this way: "*Jogging* is good exercise."

PERIODIC SENTENCE: A sentence which delays the expression of a complete thought until the end, or until near the end, is called periodic. The following is an example from an essay by Virginia Woolf: "If behind the erratic gunfire of the press the author felt that there was another kind of criticism, the opinion of people reading for the love of reading, slowly and unprofessionally, and judging with great sympathy and yet with great severity, might not this improve the quality of his work?" One must read this entire sentence before a complete thought emerges. In contrast, most sentences exhibit what is called *loose structure*, as does this sentence from the same essay by Virginia Woolf: "Thus the desire grows upon us to have done with half-statements and approximations;

to cease from searching out the minute shades of human character, to enjoy the greater abstractness, the purer truth of fiction." This sentence can be terminated at several points before the end and still make complete sense. The periodic sentence, because it is rare and because it demands closer attention from the reader than does the loose sentence, is one means of achieving emphasis through sentence structure. Although it appears in all kinds of writing, the periodic sentence, especially when long, is more suited to the formal than to the informal level of usage. If overused, the periodic sentence becomes an irritating mannerism, but it is extremely useful for variation and emphasis.

PERSONIFICATION: In the figure of speech called personification, ideas, animals, or things are given human attributes. Justice, for example, is often personified as a blindfolded woman of heroic proportions holding a pair of scales.

POINTER: A word or phrase (more conventionally called a conjunctive, or transitional, adverb) which stands at or near the beginning of a sentence or of an independent clause and prepares the reader for a turn of thought. Thus the word *however* points to an approaching contradiction; *for instance* to an oncoming illustration; *therefore* to a logical conclusion. It is possible to overuse pointers, but more often students tend to use too few of them. See CONJUNCTIVE ADVERB, CONNECTIVE.

POINT OF VIEW: In the study of prose, point of view can mean two things. It can, first, refer to the writer's attitudes or values, his way of looking at things in general, his viewpoint. The range of possibilities here is almost endless. It can perhaps be exemplified by a house fire: the wife, who knows that her husband is trapped in the burning attic, is intensely involved in the situation; the fireman, who has faced this sort of thing before, is more dispassionate.

More precisely, however, point of view refers to the grammatical person of the writer's composition. He may use *I*, (the first-person point of view) explaining what happened to him, what he thought, or what he saw happen to others. This is the point of view of autobiography, much narrative, and often of the familiar essay. The third-person point of view detaches the writer from any personal relationship with his material. In place of *I*, the writer uses a noun or third-person pronoun; not "I like to travel," but "Traveling is the best of educations."

POLYSYNDETON: The use of *and* to separate each member of a compound construction, especially the members of a series. Instead of A, B, and C, polysyndeton uses A and B and C. Mark Twain, describing a steamboat, writes: "And the boat *is* rather a handsome sight, too. She is long and sharp and trim and pretty." Polysyndeton stresses equally each member of the series, but is slower and more emphatic than asyndeton. See ASYNDETON.

POST POSITION: See ADJECTIVES IN POST POSITION.

QUALIFICATION: Usually a sweeping statement must be slightly altered or modified in the interest of truth. This modification or adjustment we call qualification. Thus George Orwell writing of Dickens might have said, "One cannot point to a single one of his central characters who is primarily interested in his job." But what he does say in order to be accurate is this: "With the doubtful exception of David Copperfield (merely Dickens himself), one cannot point to a single one of his central characters who is primarily interested in his job." Qualifications are often necessary, but they must not overshadow the statements they qualify.

RHETORICAL QUESTION: A rhetorical question is a question asked for dramatic effect: "What student of politics has not heard of Karl Marx or Thomas Jefferson?" It does not normally demand an answer. In prose, rhetorical questions often serve an organizing purpose, setting up the point the writer wishes to develop.

SCAN, SCANSION: Scansion is a method of analyzing the rhythm of prose or poetry by marking the stressed and unstressed syllables. In poetry the line is divided into feet, indicating the units of the rhythmic pattern. Stresses are usually indicated by ('), unstressed syllables by (◡), and the foot division by (/). Thus, a line from a poem by Marvell scans:

$$\overset{\smile}{\text{The}} \overset{\prime}{\text{grave's}} / \overset{\smile}{\text{a}} \overset{\prime}{\text{fine}} / \overset{\smile}{\text{and}} \overset{\prime}{\text{pri}} / \overset{\smile}{\text{vate}} \overset{\prime}{\text{place.}}$$

In prose a rhythm is always present, but usually it does not, and should not, have the regularity of poetic rhythm.

SENTENCE: See COMPLEX SENTENCE, COMPOUND SENTENCE, SIMPLE SENTENCE.

SIGNPOST: Any word, phrase, clause, or sentence that tells us what the writer plans to do next, is currently doing, has already done, or will not do at all. Examples of signposts are: "Next we must consider . . ."; "This is a point we shall treat more fully in the following chapter; here we must concentrate upon . . ."; "As was noted in the preceding section . . ."; "This is a matter, which, interesting though it is, cannot be discussed in this essay." Like pointers (q.v.), signposts can be overused as well as used too little.

SIMILE: Using *like* or *as*, a simile makes a brief comparison between things seemingly unlike: "The air seemed blindingly clear and cold, like arctic summer" (Orwell, p. 322). "When all is done," writes Sir William Temple, "human life is, at the greatest and best, but like a froward child that must be played with and humored a little to keep it quiet till it falls asleep, and then the care is done." At times the simile can be rather extended: "Anybody, like a schoolmaster, a stage director or an orchestral conductor, whose business it is to teach others to do something, knows that, on occasions, the quickest—perhaps

the only—way to get those under him to do their best is to make them angry"
(W. H. Auden, p. 123). The purpose of simile is the same as that of metaphor.
See METAPHOR.

SIMPLE SENTENCE: A simple sentence contains one subject-verb nucleus: "The
boys rowed across the lake." It is possible for a sentence to have multiple subjects and verbs, yet to remain simple so long as these form only one nucleus:
"The *boys* and *girls rowed* across the lake and *had* a picnic on the other side."

STRAIGHTFORWARD MOVEMENT: See INTERRUPTED MOVEMENT.

SUBORDINATE CLAUSE: A clause functioning within a sentence as an adjective,
adverb, or noun is said to be subordinate. Since it is grammatically less important than the main clause, a subordinate clause should express ideas of lesser
importance. See CLAUSE.

SYMBOL: A symbol is a person, place, or thing that exists both in its own right
as something real and tangible and also as something greater than itself—an attitude, a belief, a quality, a value. The word *symbol* is sometimes loosely applied to an object, the only function of which is to stand for something other
than itself. Thus, the Canadian flag can be called a symbol of Canada.

TONE: A writer's tone results from (1) his attitude toward his subject and (2)
his attitude toward his reader. A writer may love his subject, despise it, revere
it, laugh at it, or seem detached from it. He may wish to shock his reader, outrage him, charm him, play upon his prejudices, amuse him, or merely inform
him in the briefest and most efficient way possible. A writer conveys his tone
largely through his diction, through the connotations of the words he uses. But
tone may be carried by sentence structure as well.

TRICOLON: A tricolon is a sentence consisting of three clearly defined parts of
roughly equal length and weight. Usually the three parts are independent
clauses: "Her showmanship was superb; her timing matchless; her dramatic instinct uncanny." (Carey McWilliams)

UNDERSTATEMENT: To understate is to play down or soften something that is
startling, horrifying, shocking, painful, or otherwise deserving of more emotion
and attention than the writer gives it. The striking contrast between what the
subject calls for and the restrained treatment with which it is dealt, effectively
calls attention to the subject. Understatement, or litotes, as it is sometimes
called, is therefore a device of emphasis. It has the additional advantage of relieving the writer of any charge of exaggeration or emotionalism. One possible
disadvantage of understatement is that an uneducated audience may not respond
to it, but may instead regard the writer as callous. Readers of any experience or
sophistication, however, often prefer understatement to exaggeration—a more
obvious form of emphasis.

VOICE: Generally in composition courses voice means whether the action designated by the verb originates in the subject or is received by the subject. Here, however, voice means the illusion—common in good prose—of a unique personality speaking to the reader.

AUTHOR-TITLE INDEX

713